Special Edition

Using
Visual
InterDev™ 6

que®

Special Edition

Using

Using
Visual
InterDev™ 6

Steve Banick and
Michael Morrison

Special Edition Using Visual InterDev™ 6

International Standard Book Number: 0-7897-1549-X

Library of Congress Catalog Card Number: 98-84677

Printed in the United States of America

First Printing: September 1998

00 99 98   4 3 2 1

Trademarks

All terms mentioned in this book that are known to be trademarks or service marks have been appropriately capitalized. Que Corporation cannot attest to the accuracy of this information. Use of a term in this book should not be regarded as affecting the validity of any trademark or service mark.

Visual InterDev is a trademark of Microsoft Corporation.

Warning and Disclaimer

Every effort has been made to make this book as complete and as accurate as possible, but no warranty or fitness is implied. The information provided is on an "as is" basis. The authors and the publisher shall have neither liability nor responsibility to any person or entity with respect to any loss or damages arising from the information contained in this book.

Contents at a Glance

Introduction   1

I | Creating Web Sites with Visual InterDev 6

1   Getting Started with Visual InterDev 6   13
2   Organizing a Web Site with Visual InterDev 6   35
3   Using the Source, Design, and Script Editors   59
4   Using the Site Designer and Link View   83

II | Active Scripting for Web Sites

5   Active Scripting Overview   99
6   Client-Side Scripting   127
7   Server-Side Scripting   145
8   Script Debugging with Visual InterDev 6   167
9   Creating Pages with Dynamic HTML   189

III | Creating and Using ActiveX Controls

10   Using ActiveX Controls   211
11   Designing with Design-Time Controls   235
12   Building ActiveX Controls with Visual Basic   261
13   Building and Deploying Server Components   283

IV | Database Programming Basics

14   Database Programming Basics   311
15   Setting Up a Database   327
16   Using the Visual InterDev 6 Data Environment   345
17   Working with ADO and RDS   359

V | Visual InterDev 6 Creativity Tool

18   The Image Composer and GIF Animator   389

VI | **Administrating Visual InterDev 6**

    19   Windows NT Server Basics   403

    20   Using the Internet Information Server (IIS)   433

    21   Working with Site Server, Enterprise Edition   455

    22   SQL Server Basics   465

    23   Understanding Visual InterDev 6 Security   481

    24   Using Developer Isolation and Visual SourceSafe   497

VII | **Advanced Site Development**

    25   Designing and Organizing Web Sites   517

    26   Team Development with FrontPage 98 and InterDev 6   539

    27   Increasing Site Performance   549

VIII | **Appendixes**

    A   Resources   581

    B   Quick Reference   587

    C   Glossary   613

    Index   631

Table of Contents

Introduction   1

A First-Generation Development
Environment   2

Visual InterDev 6: Best of the Breed   3

Building Using Open Standards   3

About This Book   4

How This Book Is Organized   5
Part I. Creating Web Sites with Visual
InterDev 6   6
Part II. Active Scripting for Web
Sites   7
Part III. Creating and Using ActiveX
Controls   7
Part IV. Database Programming
Basics   7
Part V. Visual InterDev 6 Creativity
Tool   8
Part VI. Administrating Visual
InterDev 6   8
Part VII. Advanced Site
Development   9
Part VIII. Appendixes   9

Our Thanks to You, the Reader   9

**I Creating Web Sites with Visual
InterDev 6   11**

**1 Getting Started with Visual
InterDev 6   13**

Introducing Visual InterDev 6   14

Key Features of Visual InterDev 6   14
Rapid Application Development   14
Powerful Server-Side Development   17
Standards-Based Team
Development   17
Support for the Latest Web
Standards   18
Powerful Integrated Database
Tools   18
A Smart Work Environment   19

Quick Start: Getting Down to Business   20
Creating a Workspace and a Project   20
Using Site Designer to Create a
Prototype for a Project   22
Working with the Source Editor   26
Connecting to a Database   27

From Here...   33

**2 Organizing a Web Site with Visual
InterDev 6   35**

Organizing a Web Site   36

Understanding the Visual InterDev 6
Development Process   36
Organization of a Web Site   37
Projects   37
Solutions/Workspaces   37
Editing Content   38
The Development Process   38
Advantages of the Visual InterDev
Architecture   39

Using the MSDN Library   39
Organization of the MSDN Library   39
Using the MSDN Library   40

Creating Solutions   44

Managing Solutions   45
Using Visual InterDev's Project
Wizards   45
Managing Projects   50
Adding Existing Documents and
Projects   50
Local Working Copies   52
Deploying to Another Site   52

Working with Multiple Sites on One
Server   53
Root Webs and Child Webs   54
Shared Components   55

Customizing Developer Studio 6   55
   Customizing the Environment   56
   Text Editor Preferences   57
   Debugger Options   58
   Data Tools Preferences   58
   HTML Options   58
   Project Preferences   58

From Here...   58

3 Using the Source, Design, and Script Editors   59

Introduction to the Visual InterDev 6 Editors   60

Design Editor: WYSIWYG Editing with InterDev   60
   Creating and Editing a New Page   61
   Working with the HTML Toolbar   63
   Inserting Images   65
   Creating Links   66
   Adding Tables   68

Using the Source Editor for Ongoing Source Entry   69
   The HTML Document Outline   70
   Script Pop-Up Statement Completion   71
   Scripting Using the Script Outline   71
   Using Find and Replace   72

Working with the InterDev Toolbox   75
   HTML Tab   76
   ActiveX Controls Tab   76
   Design-Time Controls Tab   76
   Server Objects Tab   77
   Customizing the Toolbox   77

Property Pages and the Properties Browser   78
   Using the Properties Browser   78
   Working with Property Pages   79

Applying Themes and Layouts   80
   Choosing a Theme   80
   Adding a Layout   82

4 Using the Site Designer and Link View   83

Prototyping with the Site Designer   84
   Creating a Site Diagram   85
   Adding and Removing Pages in the Diagram   85
   Establishing Relationships   89
   Working with the Global Navigational Bar   90

Managing a Site Diagram   91
   Controlling the View   91
   Using the Site Designer as a Launch Pad   91

Maintaining Site Integrity with Link View   92
   Viewing Links for an Item   92
   Filtering Links   94
   Verifying External Links   94
   Repairing Links   95

From Here...   96

II Active Scripting for Web Sites   97

5 Active Scripting Overview   99

Introduction to Active Scripting for Web Sites   100

Scripting Languages Versus Programming Languages   100

Client- and Server-Side Scripting   101

Data Types and Variables   102
   Data Types and Scripting   103
   Declaring and Naming Variables   104

VBScript Functions and JScript Objects   106
   VBScript Functions   107
   JScript's Built-In Functions   110
   JScript Objects   110
   Creating Your Own Functions   113

The Browser Object Model   114
A High-Level Overview   114
document Properties, Collections, and
Methods   116
document Events   118

Adding Script to Pages   119
Specifying the Default Language   120
Manual Versus Script Block   120

Using the Script Outline and Script
Builder   121
Building Script with the Script
Builder   121
Navigating with the Outline   123
Synchronizing the Outline and the
Page   123

Differences Between Client- and Server-
Side Scripting   124
Advantages and Disadvantages of Client-
Side Scripting   124
Advantages and Disadvantages of
Server-Side Scripting   125

Which Should I Use: Client- or Server-Side
Scripting?   125

From Here...   125

6   Client-Side Scripting   127

What Is Client-Side Scripting?   128
Benefits of VBScript   129
How Client-Side VBScripts Work   129
What VBScript Cannot Do   129

Client-Side Form Validation   130
The HTML Document Form   130
Validating Forms Entries with
VBScript   132
Validating Complete Forms with
VBScript   135

Extending Functionality with ActiveX
Controls   138
What Are ActiveX Controls?   138
Controlling ActiveX Controls with
VBScript   138

Scripting Browser Events   139
Document Events   139
Window Events   141
Scripting the Event   141

From Here...   143

7   Server-Side Scripting   145

Introduction to Server-Side Scripting   146

Active Server Pages (ASP)   146
Creating an Active Server Page   146
Setting ASP Page Properties   148

Active Server Pages: Built-in Objects   149
Application Object   149
Request Object   150
Response Object   151
Server Object   151
Session Object   151

Server-Side Components   152
AdRotator   153
BrowserType   155
Database Access   156
NextLink   156
FileSystemObject   157
Collaboration Data Objects (CDO) for
NTS Component   157
Tools   158
Status   160
MyInfo   160
Counters   161
ContentRotator   162
PageCounter   162
PermissionChecker   163

From Here...   165

8   Script Debugging with Visual
InterDev 6   167

In the Beginning, There Was No
Debugger...   168

Categories of Errors   168

Similarities to VB's Debugger   169

Let's Get Debugging! 170
  Enabling the Debugging Features 170
  The Nuances of Debugging
  Scripts 172
  Oh, What the Debugger Can Do! 172
  Ready to Launch 172
  Stepping Through Your Script 176
  Changing the Value of a Variable 178
  The Debugging Windows 180

Client Script Debugging with Visual
InterDev 6 181

Server-Side Script Debugging 183
  Processing Server-Side Script 183
  Server-Side Script Debugging 184

Debugging Mixed Client and Server
Script 185
  Keeping Track of Breakpoints 185
  Debugging Mixed Scripts 185

Exception to the Rule: Global.asa 187

From Here... 188

**9 Creating Pages with Dynamic
HTML 189**

Introducing the Power of Dynamic
HTML 190

The Internet Explorer Object Model 192
  Window 193
  Document 193

Understanding Events and Event
Bubbling 195

Using Style and Positioning for Better
Layouts 196

Adding Multimedia Effects to Pages 199

Building Channels and Desktop
Items 203

Creating Scriptlets 205

From Here... 207

**III Creating and Using ActiveX
Controls 209**

10 Using ActiveX Controls 211

Quick Refresher on ActiveX Controls 212

Easy Multimedia—The Animated
GIF 212

Using the Toolbox and Script Builder 215
  Inserting a Control 216
  Customizing the Toolbox 218
  Using the Script Builder 219

Multimedia ActiveX Controls 220

Scrolling Text and Marquees 221
  The *<MARQUEE>* Tag 221
  The Marquee ActiveX Control 223

The ActiveMovie Control 224
  Properties 225
  Methods 227
  Events 228
  Building a Simple Movie Player 228

Other Multimedia Options 232
  The Path Control 232
  The Sprite Control 232
  The Structured Graphic Control 233

From Here... 233

**11 Designing with Design-Time
Controls 235**

Introducing Design-Time Controls
(DTCs) 236
  Design-Time Controls Versus Other
  Components 236
  The Advantage of Design-Time
  Controls 237

Controls Available in Visual
InterDev 6 237

Inserting DTCs into Your Web Pages 238
  Manipulating Control Properties 240
  The Scripting Object Model 240
  Runtime Text 241

The Form Controls   244
    Example 1: Server-Side Forms   244
    Example 2: Client-Side Script   247

Data-Bound Controls   248
    The Data Connection   249
    The Grid Control   249
    The Recordset NavBar   255

The Multimedia Controls   256
    The Page Transitions Control   256
    The Timelines Control   257

From Here...   260

12 Building ActiveX Controls with Visual Basic   261

Introducing ActiveX Controls   262

Using Visual Basic for ActiveX   263
    COM Development with VB   263
    The ActiveX Control Interface
    Wizard   264

Using the VB Development
Environment   264
    Getting Around in VB   265
    Fiddling with the Options   265
    Activating an Add-In   266

Building Your First ActiveX Control   267
    Mapping Out the Control   267
    Starting the Project   267
    Laying Out the Constituent
    Controls   268
    Using the ActiveX Control Interface
    Wizard   269
    Adding Property-Handling Code   272
    Coding Around User Errors   274
    Creating a Tester Application   275
    Compiling the Control   276

Deploying ActiveX Controls   277
    Using the Application Setup
    Wizard   277
    Using the Control with Visual
    InterDev   279

From Here...   281

13 Building and Deploying Server Components   283

Life Before the Web   284
    Beyond Client/Server   285
    Advantages and Disadvantages of
    N-Tier   286

Brief History of ActiveX   287
    Client/Server ActiveX   288
    The Different Flavors of ActiveX   289
    The Advantages and Disadvantages of
    ActiveX   291

Creating Components with Visual
Basic   292
    Creating the Project   292
    Reviewing the Component's
    Properties   293
    Reviewing the Code   294
    Making the Cut   296

Using the Component   296
    Using Components in Visual Basic   296
    Using Components on the Server   298
    Using the Component in ASP   300

Components and Microsoft Transaction
Server   301
    Installing Transaction Server   302
    Registering Components with
    MTS   303
    Component Context   305

From Here...   308

IV Database Programming Basics   309

14 Database Programming Basics   311

What Is a Relational Database?   312
    Introducing Tables   312

Creating Database Indexes   316
    Clustered Indexes   316
    Nonclustered Indexes   317

Normalized Database Development   317
  Normalizing Data   318
  Denormalized Database
  Development   322
  Overnormalization in Database
  Development   323

Referential Integrity   325

From Here...   326

15 Setting Up a Database   327

Introducing Visual InterDev 6 and
Databases   328

Connecting to Databases with ODBC   328
  The User DSN   329
  The System DSN   329
  The File DSN   330
  Drivers   330
  The Tracing Tab   330
  The Connection Pooling Tab   330
  The About Tab   330

Using SQL Server Databases   330
  Setting Up an Existing SQL Server
  Database   330

Creating a Data Connection to Use Access
Databases   340
  Authentication   340
  Miscellaneous   341
  Using the Data Connection   342

Using FoxPro Databases   342

From Here...   343

16 Using the Visual InterDev 6 Data Environment   345

The Data Environment   346
  Data Environment Contents   346
  Creating a Data Command   348
  Creating a Data Command Using SQL
  Statements   349
  Dragging and Dropping from the Data
  Environment   351

Controlling Database Views   352

Using Stored Procedures   354
  Debugging Stored Procedures   357

From Here...   357

17 Working with ADO and RDS   359

What Is ADO (ActiveX Database
Objects)?   360

ADO Features   360

Methods, Objects, and Properties of
ADO   361
  Objects in ADO   362
  Errors Collection   380
  Fields and *Properties* Collections   381

Tuning ADO for Performance   382
  Indexes   383
  Recordset Types   383

Debugging ADO-Based Applications   383

ADO Error Codes   383

From Here...   385

V Visual InterDev 6 Creativity Tool   387

18 The Image Composer and GIF Animator   389

The Image Composer   390

Key Features of Image Composer 1.5   390

Using Image Composer with Visual
InterDev   391

Getting Started with the Image Composer
Interface   391

Creating and Editing Your First
Sprites   393

Changing and Copying Sprites   395

Using Composition Guides   396

Using Clip Art and Buttons   397

Using the GIF Animator 398

From Here... 400

VI Administrating Visual InterDev 6 401

19 Windows NT Server Basics 403

NT Server Configuration for Visual InterDev 6 404

The NT Server 4.0 Advantages 404
Integration 404
Scalability 405
Fault Tolerance 405

Setting Up User Accounts and Security 407
Creating a User 408
Groups: Adding and Removing Users 409
Setting Access Rights 410

Administering Windows NT 412

Windows NT Performance Tuning 412
Performance Monitor: Your Window to Your Server's Health 413
Event Viewer: Your Server's Own News Service 423
Task Manager: Real-Time Server Monitoring 428
Resource Management 431

From Here... 432

20 Using the Internet Information Server (IIS) 433

IIS 434

What's New with IIS 4.0 434

Using the Management Console to Build Web Sites for VID 436
Introducing the Management Console 436

Introducing Index Server 2.0 for Visual InterDev 444
Getting Started with Index Server 444
Creating the Search Form 446

Incorporating Microsoft Transaction Server 447
Transacted Active Server Pages 448
Application Services 448

Using the SMTP Server 449
Key Components to the Microsoft SMTP Service 449
Creating an SMTP Mail Domain 450

Using the NNTP Server 451
Creating an NNTP Newsgroup 451
Controlling Access in Your Newsgroup 453

From Here... 454

21 Working with Site Server Enterprise Edition 455

What Is Site Server? 456

Working with the Publishing Features of Site Server 457
Customizable Starter Sites 457
Content Management 458
Content Deployment 459

Site Indexing with Site Server Search 459

Delivering Content with Site Server 460
Site Server Knowledge Manager 460
Push Publishing 461
Personalization and Membership Services 461
Site Server Analysis 462

Site Server Commerce Edition 463
Engaging Customers 463
Transacting with Customers 464
Analyzing the Results 464

From Here... 464

22 SQL Server Basics   465

Introducing SQL Server   466

Setting Up User Accounts and Security   466
  Adding SQL Server Logins   467
  Using Windows NT Accounts in SQL Server   468
  Removing Logins from SQL Server   473

SQL Server Administration   473
  Creating a New Database   473
  Removing a Database   474
  Adding a New Database Device   474
  Creating a Backup Device   475
  Backing Up a Database   476
  Restoring from a Backup   477

SQL Server Performance Tuning   478
  Resizing Databases   478
  Using the Database Maintenance Plan Wizard   479

From Here...   480

23 Understanding Visual InterDev 6 Security   481

An Introduction to Web Security   482

Planning Ahead   482

Windows NT Security   484
  NT Security Features   484
  Setting Up Accounts   485

About NTFS   486

Security with Internet Information Server   488
  Using the Anonymous Account   488
  Additional Security in IIS   490
  Using Secure Sockets Layer   491

Other Security Considerations   492
  Correct Services   492
  Further Understanding NTFS   492
  IIS Logging   493
  Account Security   493
  Timeout Period/Maximum Connections   493

Firewalls   493
Disable Directory Browsing   494

Tying It All Back to Visual InterDev   495

Further Security References   495

From Here...   495

24 Using Developer Isolation and Visual SourceSafe   497

Understanding Developer Isolation   498
  Choosing the Mode   498
  Working with Local Mode   499
  Updating the Master Web   500

Overview of Visual SourceSafe   500

Installing Visual SourceSafe   500

Understanding SourceSafe   501
  Visual SourceSafe Concepts   501
  Visual SourceSafe Functions   502
  Visual SourceSafe Version and Tracking Control   503

Using SourceSafe in Visual InterDev   504
  Working with Source Control   505

Administering Visual SourceSafe   508
  Adding Users to VSS   509
  Limiting Access to Projects   509
  Locking the SourceSafe Database   511
  Managing File Types in VSS Administrator   512

From Here...   513

VII Advanced Site Development   515

25 Designing and Organizing Web Sites   517

Designing the Site   518
  Defining the Scope of the Project   518
  Design Considerations   525
  Production Considerations   534

Organizing Your Site 535
Setting Up Workspaces and Projects 536
Create Cascading Style Sheets 536
Dealing with Content 537

From Here... 537

26 Team Development with FrontPage 98 and Visual InterDev 6 539

Introducing FrontPage 98 540
Similarities and Differences 540
When FrontPage 98 Is Not Enough 543

Designing Visual InterDev 6 Sites for FrontPage 98 544
Use ASP Elements Only When Needed 545
Modularize Your Web Application 545
Test Pages with the FrontPage Editor 545

FrontPage Security Issues 545

Training End Users to Maintain Sites with FrontPage 98 546

From Here... 547

27 Increasing Site Performance 549

Guidelines for Web Site Performance 550

Testing Client Performance 550
Downloading from Different Sources 551
Testing with Different Browsers 552

Testing Server Performance 553
Introducing the Performance Monitor 553
Using the Performance Monitor Counters 554
Placing Limits on Resources 556

Tracking Internet Routes 557
Using *tracert* to Follow Internet Routes 557
Putting *tracert* Knowledge to Work 558

Increasing Client-Side Performance in Visual InterDev 560
Defining Your Space 560
Working with HTTP (Not Against It) 563
Leveraging Your Client-Side Cache 565
Using Your Tags Effectively 568
Multimedia Data Compression 571

Increasing Server-Side Performance with Visual InterDev 575
Know Your Scripting Language 575
Know Your Bottlenecks 576
Use the Application Object Over the Session Object 577
Consider ISAPI Over CGI 577

Planning for Quicker Service 577

From Here... 578

VIII Appendixes 579

A Resources 581

Books 582

Magazines 582

Online Resources 582
Web Sites 582
Newsgroups 584
Listservers 584

User Groups 585

Training 585
Microsoft Online Institute 585
Microsoft Certified Professional Program 586
32X, Inc. 586

Beta Testing 586

B Quick Reference 587

HTML 588
Tags for the Document Head 588
Tags for the Document Body 589

VBScript   592
  Array Handling   593
  Assignments   593
  Comments   593
  Constants and Literals   593
  Control Flow   593
  Conversions   594
  Dates and Times   595
  Declarations   595
  Error Handling   595
  Input/Output   595
  Math   596
  Operators   596
  Objects   597
  Options   597
  Procedures   597
  Strings   597
  Variants   598

JavaScript/JScript   598
  Statements   599
  Operators   600
  Objects   602
  Functions   603
  Reserved Words   603

Active Server Page Scripting   604
  The GLOBAL.ASA File   604
  Built-in Objects   604
  Events   605

Cascading Style Sheets (CSS)   605
  CSS Elements   605
  In-Line CSS   609
  Embedding a Style Block   610
  Linking to External CSS   611

C Glossary   613

Index   631

Credits

EXECUTIVE EDITOR
Bradley L. Jones

ACQUISITIONS EDITOR
Kelly Marshall

DEVELOPMENT EDITOR
Greg Guntle

MANAGING EDITOR
Jodi Jensen

SENIOR EDITOR
Susan Ross Moore

COPY EDITORS
Kelli M. Brooks
Chuck Hutchinson

INDEXER
Greg Pearson

TECHNICAL EDITOR
Robert Neimela

TEAM COORDINATOR
Carol Ackerman

SOFTWARE DEVELOPMENT SPECIALIST
John Warriner

COVER DESIGNER
Maureen McCarty

INTERIOR DESIGNER
Ruth Lewis

PRODUCTION
Michael Henry
Linda Knose
Tim Osborn
Staci Somers
Mark Walchle

Composed in *Century Old Style* and *ITC Franklin Gothic* by Que Corporation.

About the Authors

Steve Banick: Life is nothing like a box of chocolates; however, it can offer you rich rewards in the form of Juicy Fruit. Steve Banick is a network administrator and graphic designer (what a duo!) who is currently the client software developer for TELUS PLAnet Internet Services in Alberta, Canada. He has settled into a peaceful coexistence with his wife Christina and two dogs. He pursues with vehemence the cure to the plague that ails all of modern man: cable television. Steve can be reached on the Web at **http://www.banick.com**, and via email at **steve@banick.com.**

His published works as a contributing and lead author include: *Special Edition Using Microsoft Commercial Internet System, Special Edition Using Visual InterDev, Web Management with Microsoft Visual SourceSafe 5.0, Special Edition Using Microsoft Internet Information Server 4.0, Platinum Edition Using Windows NT Server 4.0, Platinum Edition Using HTML 4, Java 1.1, and JavaScript 1.2, Using FrontPage 98, FrontPage Unleashed 98*, and *Special Edition Using Photoshop 5.0.*

Steve still remembers fondly the days of "Mule" and "Miner 2049er."

Chris Denschikoff leads a busy little life in the busy little town of Calgary, Alberta. When not attempting to write he's usually designing Web sites for the benefit of his local telephone company. He usually can be found slumming anyplace where people of questionable taste gather, and enjoys nothing more than a good breakfast.

He is a Leo, and can be reached at **chris.denschikoff@telus.com** if you have any flaming compliments.

Craig Eddy works for Pipestream Technologies, Inc. where he is Program Manager for Pipestream's thin-client version of its popular customer information management software, Sales Continuum 98. Craig resides in Richmond, VA and can often be found surfing the Web or the sands of the Outer Banks in North Carolina. Craig can be reached via email at **craig.eddy@cyberdude.com.**

John J. Kottler has been programming for 15 years and has spent the past seven years developing applications for the Windows platform; he has also been programming multimedia applications and developing for the Web for the past three years. His knowledge includes C/C++, Visual Basic, multimedia and digital video production, and Internet development. In the past he has published computer articles and has recently been published in numerous Sams.net's books including *DHTML Unleashed, Visual InterDev Unleashed, Web Page Wizardry, Web Publishing Unleashed, Netscape Unleashed, Presenting ActiveX*, as well as Sams Publishing's *Programming Windows 95 Unleashed*. A graduate of Rutgers University with a degree in computer science, he enjoys inline skating, cycling, or playing digital music in his spare time. John can be reached at **jkottler@erols.com.**

Duncan Mackenzie is a Microsoft Certified Solution Developer and independent consultant (**www.dmconsulting.mb.ca**) in Winnipeg, Canada, where he specializes in custom application development and Web site design. He has contributed to several books for New Riders, Sams, and Que Publishing and can be reached at **duncanm@dmconsulting.mb.ca**.

John Papa is a Technical Lead and a Trainer at DBBasics, a software development company, in Raleigh, North Carolina. At DBBasics, he develops, writes courseware, and instructs technical classes on such technologies as Visual InterDev, Visual Basic, IIS, MTS, SQL Server, ASP, and ADO. John graduated from Siena College near his hometown of Albany, New York and has been developing intranet/Internet applications with Visual InterDev since before version 1 first hit the market. He has become an MS Certified Solutions Developer (MCSD) in the areas of SQL Server, Visual Basic, and the Windows Architecture as well as contributing to several other books. Some of John's books include *SQL Server 6.5 Programming Unleashed* and the upcoming *SQL Server 7.0 Programming Unleashed*, both by Sams publishing. He is also a Microsoft Certified Trainer.

John prides himself on his closely knit Italian family and attributes all that he has (and will) achieve to God, his parents John and Peggy, and his loving wife, Colleen. You can reach John at **johnp@dbbasics.com** or at **papajc@ix.netcom.com**.

Suniel Sahi is a Microsoft "guru." He has spent the last 12 years growing with Microsoft development and networking tools. He is an MCSD and should be an MCSE by the time this book is published. He started off his career at CAE Electronics in Montreal and has been a consultant for companies such as FEDEX. He is currently working for MEDCAN Health Management Inc. in Toronto.

On the lighter side, his ideal dream would be golfing in Hawaii, playing poker on the beach, and enjoying a cruise with the wife. Until these dreams come true, he will continue to enjoy mastering Microsoft software.

Dedication

This book is dedicated to the power of positive thinking while being all consumed with the great sugar and caffeine rush. Oh, and God bless those little twisted mints you get at restaurants...

Acknowledgments

Thanks and acknowledgements to: Errol Barrie, Chris Denschikoff, Jay Reid, Dale Winarski, Sean Lassu, Dale Dallinger, Chris Fulsom, and Julie May. Notable hellos and thanks to the TPS Crew, specifically Kevin Stickel, Perry Petrushko, Bob Sample, Will Downs, Eddie Mah, Kent Embleton, Janna Rausch Ferguson, Michelle Stoetzel, and Bill Lillie. Love and thanks to my wife Christina who still thinks that the keyboard is attached to my fingers.

Tell Us What You Think!

As the reader of this book, *you* are our most important critic and commentator. We value your opinion and want to know what we're doing right, what we could do better, what areas you'd like to see us publish in, and any other words of wisdom you're willing to pass our way.

As the Executive Editor for the Advanced Programming team at Macmillan Computer Publishing, I welcome your comments. You can fax, email, or write me directly to let me know what you did or didn't like about this book—as well as what we can do to make our books stronger.

Please note that I cannot help you with technical problems related to the topic of this book, and that due to the high volume of mail I receive, I might not be able to reply to every message.

When you write, please be sure to include this book's title and author as well as your name and phone or fax number. I will carefully review your comments and share them with the author and editors who worked on the book.

Fax: 317-817-7070

Email: **adv_prog@mcp.com**

Mail: Bradley L. Jones
          Executive Editor
          Advanced Programming Team
          Macmillan Computer Publishing
          201 West 103rd Street
          Indianapolis, IN 46290 USA

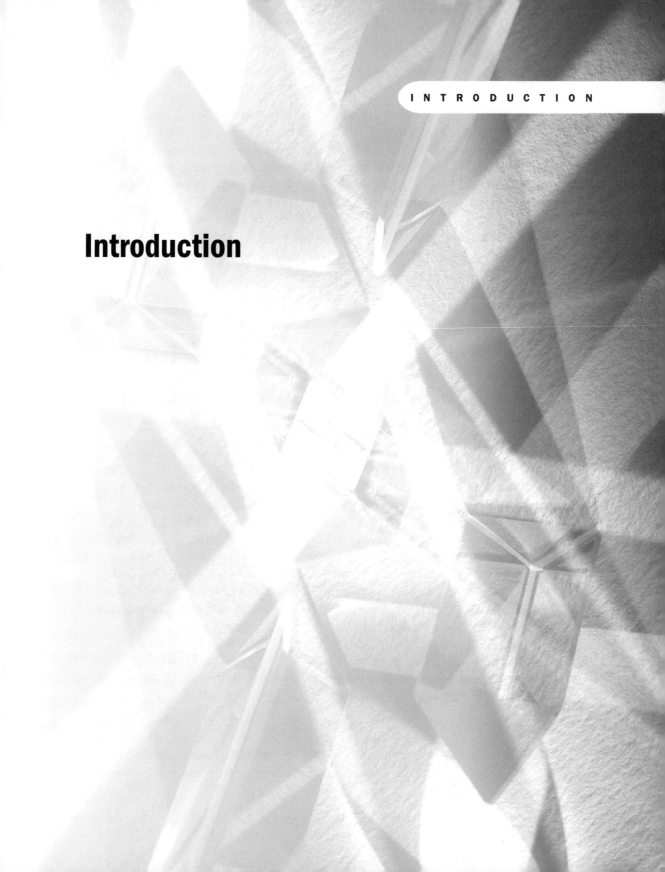

Introduction

When Microsoft introduced the early betas of Visual InterDev in 1996, it was easy to see that the Web had come along way. The concepts of "Web applications" and "activated Web sites" have begun to permeate the consciousness of developers around the globe, as a wave of interest in interactive Web sites, intranets, and low-cost administration crept into the minds of middle managers and Webmasters everywhere. The concept of an activated Web site was simple: Take a traditional Web site that delivered static and manually updated pages, and bring it to life programmatically by creating a site that could dynamically deliver information based on need or situation. Pulling information from a database or other resources, an activated Web site could be fresh and innovative at each visit. Web applications took the concept a step further: Take a traditional client/server program and migrate the applications for easy deployment over the Web, using the standards of the Internet. The benefits were also easy to see: no more messy deployment of custom clients to thousands of desktops, no messy upgrades required each time a change occurred, and most important, accessibility from nearly any desktop equipped with a Web browser. These applications were very different from the traditional application that was specifically written for an individual platform and required care and attention when deploying it to the masses.

A First-Generation Development Environment

The first release of InterDev was one of the first products on the market that focused specifically on creating powerful applications on the Web platform. Other tools hinted at possibilities but tended to rely more on Web site creation and management rather than the underlying task of creating a functional application. For all its inroads into application development, InterDev also had its weaknesses. InterDev recognized the need for the raw access and programmability that every developer needs and focused on the seedy underbelly of Web applications—the engine and the architecture. Database connectivity and management took precedence over fancy GUI Web design. Although InterDev included a specialized version of the FrontPage editor, the obvious focus of this product was to develop hardcore applications. Many InterDev users opted to use an external Web editor to create the pieces that made up the site and use the InterDev environment to assemble the pieces into a complete application.

The power of InterDev's Developer Studio interface was obvious; however, it also suffered from some of the environment's own weaknesses. The environment was clearly geared around other Microsoft development tools, such as Visual C++ and Visual J++. The applicability of many of the interface features with Web development was questionable. Even with interface and environment quibbles aside, the choice of a mature development environment made tremendous sense: Microsoft had an existing product that was tried and true for developers, including direct links into important tools such as version control with Visual SourceSafe.

Visual InterDev 6: Best of the Breed

Since the release of Visual InterDev 97, Microsoft has reexamined its development approach and Web applications in particular. This rethinking and retooling are evident when you first open Visual InterDev 6. The interface springs to life as a much more sensible and useful extension to a developer's mindset. The focus on usability resulted in a cleaner tool that empowers developers to create smarter and better Web applications without compromising their productivity. The need for reliance on outside tools has diminished; however, the support for them has continued. Developers now have a tool that works around them rather than the other way around.

Microsoft's continued emphasis on new technologies and developing new standards is also unmistakable in this new release. Support for the newest Web-based technologies, such as Dynamic HTML, is smoothly integrated into the development environment. InterDev also makes you work more efficiently with improved deployment, testing, and management features as well as rapid application facilities. Simply put, Visual InterDev 6 is the culmination of many developers' wish lists into one mature product.

Building Using Open Standards

The Internet has brought a level of connectivity to the computers of the world that has never been seen before. More than that, though, this connectivity has forced the development of standards that span virtually every type of microprocessor, operating system, and communication device. These standards have filtered across corporate borders and national borders, and have even moved into the homes of millions of users. This development is, without a doubt, significant.

The incompatibilities of software and hardware that have held back the computer industry for so many years are finally starting to dissipate. Intranet technology is an application of this phenomenon. This grand unification is making possible today software and hardware applications that people never dreamed of just a few years ago. Even most science fiction has not envisioned the type of inexpensive, global communication that is available today thanks to the Internet.

If there is one important message to convey about this topic, it is this: Center your application development around Internet standards and protocols.

Why? There are a number of reasons. First, developing applications based on Internet standards and protocols means that you have access to the latest technology today. You won't find any major software developer today that does not gear toward Internet standards. For example, say you're a database developer, and you have a client who needs a simple database application. The application must run on the client's in-house network, which has a variety of PCs running various versions of Windows. Develop the application with a Web-based front end, and you won't have to worry what type of machine or operating system the client has. In addition, as updates are made to the application, you won't need to run around and reinstall it on every client, because every time the application is run, any new controls or code will be downloaded to the user transparently.

Second, you leave your options open for the future. If the company ever decides to go online with a direct Internet connection, the same application will be available from anywhere on the planet. Although it may be true today that not all applications are best developed using Internet standards and protocols, with the current growth of the Internet and its capabilities, that may not be the case in the near future.

About This Book

In many ways, this book is a continuation of the previous edition, picking up where it left off, and introducing the new features and technologies offered in Visual InterDev 6. This book has been designed around one primary goal: to educate you quickly in using Microsoft Visual InterDev 6 to the maximum of its capabilities, rather than the maximum of your own. Each chapter in this book has been clearly mapped to step you through the various features and offerings within this new tool without compromising your productivity. This book is meant to complement your development and production rather than hinder it. You should not need to immerse yourself into this book from start to finish, unless you specifically want to. The goal here is for you to refer to this book when you need it and then set it neatly to the side.

If you read the first edition of Que's *Special Edition Using Visual InterDev,* you will likely find much of the material within this volume familiar. Applicable information from the previous edition has been incorporated into this book without neglecting to document the changes in this release. This way, previous readers should be able to pace their discoveries and experimentation. New users will also benefit from this maturation of subject matter, as it has been refined and updated from a well-regarded previous edition. Essentially, you are getting two books in one: the best of the old and the best of the new.

How This Book Is Organized

This book has been divided into eight distinct sections. Each section is a logical grouping of similar topics so that you can quickly locate the information of interest to you. You can use these groupings for your own benefit. Familiarize yourself with these sections, as listed here, so that you can find what you need when you want it:

- Part I. Creating Web Sites with Visual InterDev 6

  The most familiar aspect of Web applications is the Web front end. Creating a successful and activated Web site relies on your knowledge and skill. This section, coupled with Visual InterDev 6, introduces and explores the design and implementation of Web sites from the ground up.

- Part II. Active Scripting for Web Sites

  The difference between a Web application and a Web site is the engine behind it. Using Microsoft Active Server Pages, your Web site can become a powerful and useful tool with client- and server-side scripting. Whether you are an experienced scripter or new to the game, this part of the book covers this important and powerful aspect of development.

- Part III. Creating and Using ActiveX Controls

  Extending the power of both the client and the server is the goal behind ActiveX controls. For interactivity and functions that are beyond scripting, ActiveX components are the ideal selection. Part III of this book focuses on the creation and integration of server- and client-side ActiveX controls.

- Part IV. Database Programming Basics

  The power of databases is apparent in activated Web sites and Web applications. Using a database backend and the information in this section, you can empower your Web site with dynamic information.

■ Part V. Visual InterDev 6 Creativity Tool

Regardless of how powerful your site may be, it still relies on functionality and appearance to be appealing for people to use. Visual InterDev 6 includes a tool for creative design and site enhancement. This section explores this tool and how to complement your site.

■ Part VI. Administrating Visual InterDev 6

After your site or application is complete, the work is not yet done. On-going administration and maintenance are required for any successful site or application. This section explores the administration of Visual InterDev 6, your project, and the server backend.

■ Part VII. Advanced Site Development

Creating a successful application or site takes considerable time and expertise. Part VII of this book delves into focused design and planning, performance of your site, and team development.

■ Part VIII. Appendixes

Where would any book be without a useful series of appendixes? Handy resources are located in this section of the book. You will find references outside this book, a quick reference for the software, and a glossary.

Part I. Creating Web Sites with Visual InterDev 6

Visual InterDev 6 is a massive tool that offers you a great deal of flexibility and power in your development. As you become more comfortable with InterDev, you can begin the real work of creating a Web site. The four chapters in this section emphasize the actual Web site design and creation. You will learn how to use the Visual InterDev interface, the different editors located inside Visual InterDev, the Multimedia Editor, and the Site Designer. Familiarity with these tools is essential if you plan to work on large projects with intricate behavior.

■ Chapter 1, "Getting Started with Visual InterDev 6"

■ Chapter 2, "Organizing a Web Site with Visual InterDev 6"

■ Chapter 3, "Using the Source, Design, and Script Editors"

■ Chapter 4, "Using the Site Designer and Link View"

Part II. Active Scripting for Web Sites

When you are looking beyond a traditional Web site, you are likely looking to add life to the interactivity of the site itself. The process, often called "activating the site," is very much the heart of "Web applications." This section's six chapters clearly detail how active scripting works and how it can enliven your Web site. You will find client- and server-side scripting information, as well as information on debugging your new interactive site. This section would be incomplete if it did not have a chapter dedicated exclusively to Dynamic HTML and how to empower your pages with this new technology.

- Chapter 5, "Active Scripting Overview"

- Chapter 6, "Client-Side Scripting"

- Chapter 7, "Server-Side Scripting"

- Chapter 8, "Script Debugging with Visual InterDev 6"

- Chapter 9, "Creating Pages with Dynamic HTML"

Part III. Creating and Using ActiveX Controls

ActiveX technology offers great potential for enhancing Web sites and applications. This section, which includes four chapters, provides you with practical examples and tutorials on how to create your own controls and how to integrate them for programmatic manipulation. Additionally, you can learn how to enhance the server with Active Server Controls that tie into Microsoft Transaction Server.

- Chapter 10, "Using ActiveX Controls"

- Chapter 11, "Designing with Design-Time Controls"

- Chapter 12, "Building ActiveX Controls with Visual Basic"

- Chapter 13, "Building and Deploying Server Components"

Part IV. Database Programming Basics

The four chapters that make up Part IV, "Database Programming Basics," are primers on using the power of databases in your Web sites. Databases allow you to conveniently store vast amounts of information for programmatic retrieval at any time. You can also use databases to create exciting, dynamic sites that are tailored to the visitors' needs and desires. If you are new to database development, this section will get your feet wet so that you can confidently work with data sources.

- Chapter 14, "Database Programming Basics"
- Chapter 15, "Setting Up a Database"
- Chapter 16, "Using the Visual InterDev 6 Data Environment"
- Chapter 17, "Working with ADO and RDS"

Part V. Visual InterDev 6 Creativity Tool

This junior section of the book contains a chapter that focuses on the tool included with Visual InterDev 6 used to create imaginative sites: the Microsoft Image Composer with the GIF Animator. This tool can help you create a visually attractive and functional Web site and easily add images to your Visual InterDev projects.

- Chapter 18, "The Image Composer and GIF Animator"

Part VI. Administrating Visual InterDev 6

Powerful sites incorporate a powerful backend. The Microsoft BackOffice suite provides you with an incredibly powerful system that you can take advantage of in your Web site. The six chapters in this section focus on the server and enhancements to Visual InterDev that can make your development easier and your site better. Introductory information on setting up and administrating Windows NT Server, Internet Information Server, and SQL Server is what you need to create your backend. Details on using Site Server for enhancements to your Web site, including site and usage analysis, are also important for good management. Finally, you will find documentation on securing your sites and applications with the security features of Windows NT and version control with Visual SourceSafe in this section.

- Chapter 19, "Windows NT Server Basics"
- Chapter 20, "Using the Internet Information Server (IIS)"
- Chapter 21, "Working with Site Server Enterprise Edition"
- Chapter 22, "SQL Server Basics"

- Chapter 23, "Understanding Visual InterDev 6 Security"
- Chapter 24, "Using Developer Isolation and Visual SourceSafe"

Part VII. Advanced Site Development

Planning and creating a successful Web site requires considerable skill and effort. The three chapters in this section have been written to help you to make the tough choices in the work ahead of you. You will find important information on proper organization and design and information on optimizing your site for the best performance possible. This section also includes a chapter dedicated to team development using both Visual InterDev 6 and FrontPage 98.

- Chapter 25, "Designing and Organizing Web Sites"
- Chapter 26, "Team Development with FrontPage 98 and Visual InterDev 6"
- Chapter 27, "Increasing Site Performance"

Part VIII. Appendixes

The appendixes provide as much reference material as possible to make your development with Visual InterDev 6 a breeze. Appendix A, "Resources," covers many topics, such as the Visual InterDev FAQ, related books and magazines, as well as Visual InterDev newsgroups and Web sites. Appendix B, "Quick Reference," provides you with a convenient quick reference to Web technologies and Visual InterDev. Appendix C, "Glossary," is a useful tool for deciphering those ever-increasing acronyms so common on the Web.

- Appendix A, "Resources"
- Appendix B, "Quick Reference"
- Appendix C, "Glossary"

Our Thanks to You, the Reader

We thank you for purchasing this edition and your ongoing support of Macmillan Computer Publishing. We are endeavoring to provide you with the most comprehensive and timely references to help you get to work. The authors of this book have all been proud to contribute to this volume, and would like to remind you that we are regular users of this tool, day in and day out. Our practical experience with this tool has helped us prepare a reference that documents the software from a user's perspective. We hope that you find this book of use in your day-to-day work and wish you the best of success with this new release of Visual InterDev 6.

The authors welcome your comments or suggestions. Please do not hesitate to contact us at the following addresses:

Steven Banick (**steve@banick.com**)

with material from

Chris Denschikoff (**chris.denschikoff@telus.com**)

Craig Eddy (**craige@pipestream.com**)

Jay Kottler (**JKottle@CORUS.JNJ.com**)

Mike Morrison (**mikem@netst.com**)

John Papa (**johnP@DBBasics.com**)

Suniel Sahi (**sunielsahi@medcan.com**)

Creating Web Sites with Visual InterDev 6

1   Getting Started with Visual InterDev 6   13

2   Organizing a Web Site with Visual InterDev 6   35

3   Using the Source, Design, and Script Editors   59

4   Using the Site Designer and Link View   83

Getting Started with Visual InterDev 6

In this chapter

Introducing Visual InterDev 6   **14**

Key Features of Visual InterDev 6   **14**

Quick Start: Getting Down to Business   **20**

Introducing Visual InterDev 6

Visual InterDev 6 is a radical overhaul of the successful first iteration of Microsoft's Web application development tool. InterDev 6 refines many of the key features that were present in the previous version, in addition to introducing many powerful new features that make you more productive and your development easier. This chapter acts as an introduction to Visual InterDev 6, for both users of the previous version and those who are new to the InterDev product line.

Key Features of Visual InterDev 6

Visual InterDev's features have been dramatically enhanced with the release of InterDev 6. The integration and support for new Web technologies and software, such as Microsoft Internet Explorer 4.0 and Microsoft Internet Information Server 4.0, have been key to the enhancements in Visual InterDev 6. The new features introduced in this release enable developers to build data-driven Web applications much faster than before. Recent enhancements in Web browser technologies and HTML have also been incorporated into InterDev 6 to allow developers to create dynamic applications that can talk to any Web browser and any database, regardless of operating environment. The new features added to InterDev 6, combined with the refined features from the previous version, create a powerful team-based development environment for designing, building, and debugging Web applications.

You can think of InterDev 6 as an evolutionary upgrade over the previous release. Previous users will see strong similarities between the two versions; however, more obvious are the changes and improvements in the new release. These improvements include a reworked interface (the Visual Studio 98 interface that is present in the newest generation of Microsoft development tools) and a much stronger focus on rapid application development and bug-free deployment. The following are several key features of InterDev 6:

- Rapid application development
- Powerful server-side development
- Standards-based team development
- Support for the latest Web standards
- Powerful integrated database tools
- Evolutionary enhancements to create a smart work environment

Rapid Application Development

Visual InterDev 6 focuses on improving the rapid application development, or RAD, aspect of Web application development. *Rapid application development* is a familiar term for many developers working with tools outside Web development (such as Visual Basic and Borland Delphi, among others). The emphasis of RAD is on efficient and timely design and building of applications using visual construction metaphors. Instead of relying on code written by hand to create a user interface, developers can use a RAD interface to construct sophisticated interfaces visually and then create the code that is driven behind these interfaces, through "events." Microsoft promotes Visual InterDev 6 as a tool that emphasizes "rapid end-to-end application development." End to end development provides you with the ability to use Visual InterDev from the first steps of page creation all the way through to the publication of the page on a live Web server. This translates into a goal-oriented environment that lets developers rapidly design, build, and debug Web applications with minimal effort.

Integrated Editors: Design, Source, and Quick View   The previous release of InterDev relied on an integrated Source Editor (essentially the Visual Studio 97 Editor) and a specialized version of FrontPage 97 that could be called upon to edit pages. InterDev 6 takes a significant step forward in its use of editors by providing three distinct editor modes: Design, Source, and Quick View. Each mode represents a powerful way of interacting with your pages.

The new WYSIWYG page designer, shown in Figure 1.1, provides a Toolbox palette of reusable objects that you can drag and drop to assemble pages quickly. This editor fully supports the newest Web specifications, such as HTML 4.0, the Document Object Model (DOM), and Dynamic HTML (DHTML). The Source Editor, on the other hand, provides you with a powerful editing environment for manipulating raw HTML code. This editor offers powerful code coloring while preserving source code formatting. Finally, Quick View lets you take a quick look at what your page will look like from the Web. This lets you quickly spot potential problems that may not be as obvious in either the Design or Source editors.

FIG. 1.1

The new integrated Design (WYSIWYG) page editor lets you visually create sophisticated Web pages.

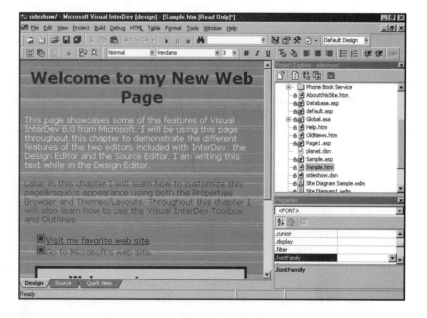

Powerful Debugging   One of the most requested features for inclusion in InterDev 6 was complete support for debugging. InterDev 6 now enables you to make your Web application development more efficient. You can debug your code with step-through debugging of both client- and server-side scripting, using either VBScript or Jscript/JavaScript, and HTML. This also includes support for ECMAScript. You can debug at any time in the development cycle. The debugger offers an Immediate window, line-by-line stepping, a call stack, a watch window, and more features that help you find and fix bugs quickly (see Figure 1.2).

FIG. 1.2
Visual InterDev 6 provides you with a full-featured debugger for both your HTML and scripted code.

Remote Deployment   Using InterDev 6, you can now develop and deploy enterprise-ready, scalable Web applications using reusable components. Direct support for Microsoft Transaction Server and COM-based components is included; deployment is easy if you use Microsoft FrontPage Server Extensions and powerful rapid application development deployment extensions. These extensions make it easier for you to create server-side extensions for your Web application and deliver them to the server. Centralized deployment and management are easy when you use InterDev and Web applications.

Site Designer   Taking a cue from Microsoft FrontPage 98, InterDev 6 includes a new Site Designer, as shown in Figure 1.3. Using the Site Designer, you can easily visualize your site layout and establish consistent navigation. As with FrontPage 98, you can use this mode to apply global themes and layouts for all aspects of your Web site and application. You can also manage your content files while inspecting for dependencies and broken links. Broken links and hyperlinks can automatically be repaired without requiring tedious code editing. Using this tool, you can design the look, structure, and flow of your Web site visually while InterDev automatically creates the file structure and interface elements for navigation.

FIG. 1.3
The InterDev 6 Site Designer is similar to the one provided in FrontPage 98 but provides considerably more power for developers.

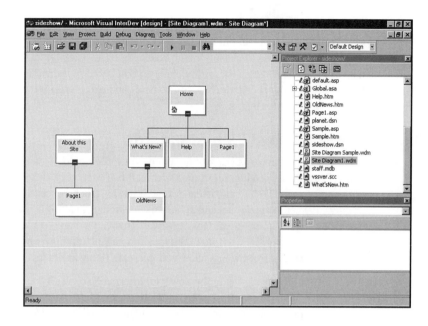

Powerful Server-Side Development

With the introduction of Internet Information Server (IIS) 4.0, the power of server-side development blossomed. InterDev 6 directly interfaces with IIS 4.0 to empower developers with comprehensive server-side development tools. Direct integration with Microsoft Transaction Server and COM-based components lets developers create rich and powerful Web applications. Coupled with the debugging and database features of InterDev 6, server-side development has become considerably easier.

▶ For more information about Internet Information Server 4.0, **see** Chapter 20, "Using the Internet Information Server (IIS)," on **p. 433**

Standards-Based Team Development

Today's Web applications are being developed by tight-knit groups of developers, each bringing to the table his own skills and abilities. Team development, in the past, was always a frustrating aspect of creating Web applications. The risk of losing information, introducing new bugs, and other complexities prevented many teams from taking full advantage of distributed development. InterDev 6 refines the previous versions' powers for team development and introduces powerful new features to make team development easier.

Local Mode   New to InterDev 6 is *Local mode*. Local mode allows individual developers to work and develop parts of a project against a local Web server without interrupting other members of the team. After the development is complete, the developers can synchronize and deploy their changes to the shared master project. This capability allows you, as a developer, to work safely in an isolated environment and then share your changes with the entire team—after you are satisfied that your development is ready to be integrated.

Enhanced Team Support   With InterDev 6, developers, content creators, and designers can work on a single project without conflict. Web source and content files can safely be locked and version-controlled using Microsoft Visual SourceSafe (see Chapter 24, "Using Developer Isolation and Visual SourceSafe," for more details on SourceSafe). Individual files to version-control can be added, or project-oriented version control can be implemented to provide check-in/check-out capability for teams.

Support for the Latest Web Standards

It is no secret that Microsoft has been making every attempt to be one of the leaders on the Internet. Through its product offerings, Microsoft has been very clear that it is serious about the Internet, and the Web in particular. Visual InterDev 6 is no exception; it has support for emerging Internet technologies and standards, including HTML 4.0, Extensible Markup Language (XML), HTML Document Object Model (DOM), Dynamic HTML (DHTML), and Design Time Controls (DTC). Two of the most important additions are for Dynamic HTML and Design Time Controls, which allow you to create richly interactive Web applications.

Dynamic HTML Support   Using the powerful Internet Explorer 4.0 (and higher) Dynamic HTML features, you can develop more interactive client experiences. Dynamic HTML offers you the power of complex data manipulation and interactivity using VBScript or JScript to tie together events and similar code. By using this power, you can create pages that change dynamically (hence the name) based on what the user is doing, as opposed to delivering static pages that do not change or adapt to events. InterDev 6 offers tight integration of Dynamic HTML into its environment through a powerful script wizard.

Data Bound Design Time Controls   Using visual Design Time Controls (DTCs), you can build complex pages including data-bound forms and reports. Using DTCs, you can automatically generate server-side or client-side scripting and database logic for applications. You can accomplish all this work using prebuilt components that you can drag and drop into place.

Powerful Integrated Database Tools

The RAD approach also extends to interaction with data sources. Regardless of what kind of database you may be integrating into your Web application, InterDev enables you to visually design and modify database schemas and create stored procedures. You can attach to and browse the data in tables and views while visually creating SQL queries. You can build and reuse database queries without any programming. You can even drag and drop information from a data source into your pages to create sophisticated database-driven pages (see Figure 1.4). The chapters in Part IV, "Database Programming Basics," describe database programming in more detail.

Ultimately, this RAD approach extends throughout the entire tool, providing you with a powerful and intuitive work environment. Using InterDev 6, you can connect to any ODBC-compliant database; you can even access host and mainframe data using integration with Microsoft SNA Server. You also can construct complex SQL statements and test them in the live test pane before adding them to your Web application.

FIG. 1.4

In the new drag-and-drop environment, you can easily add data-bound components to your pages. This capability makes database interaction all the easier in InterDev 6.

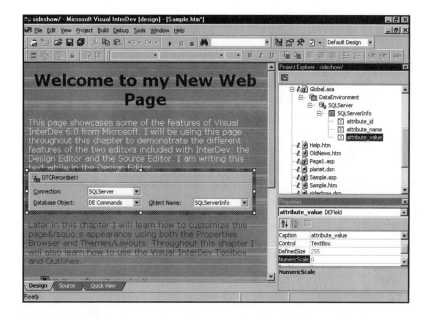

A Smart Work Environment

InterDev 6 makes incredible leaps forward in usability and functionality. The new Visual Studio interface gives you a flexible work tool that you can customize to suit your own needs. Microsoft IntelliSense technology increases coding speed with script development support. IntelliSense helps you work more efficiently by offering statement completion and quick tips for both VBScript and JScript. InterDev 6 also provides new and improved wizards that simplify your workflow. Creating new sites, developing data-bound pages, and creating reports are all the easier in this new version. To add to the mix, a new Task List, shown in Figure 1.5, has been added to InterDev 6 to help you manage your project better. Finally, the Visual Studio environment is extensible and customizable. You can create your own custom menus and actions to suit your personal needs. With all these factors and features combined, you can easily see that InterDev 6 is indeed a useful and powerful new product to help you develop more efficiently.

FIG. 1.5

The Task List enables you to keep an eye on what you've accomplished with your project and what you have ahead of you.

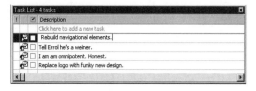

Quick Start: Getting Down to Business

With the new and improved features of InterDev 6 in mind, you can begin exploring the program and how it can help you create better sites and applications. This section is intended as a "getting up and running quickly" overview of the InterDev 6 interface. If you are already familiar with InterDev 6, you can skip this section and move on to Chapter 2, "Organizing a Web Site with Visual InterDev 6." If you are new to InterDev 6, read on to begin working with this tool.

N O T E This chapter assumes that you have previously installed Visual InterDev 6 and its related components. For information on installation, refer to the documentation provided with the software. ▨

Creating a Workspace and a Project

For your first Visual InterDev project, you'll create a simple corporate Web site. The fictitious company is called Pubs Publishing, and the site will feature four main areas: a home page, an online data-driven catalog, an About Our Company page, and a Links to Our Partners page.

The home page will simply introduce visitors to the site and provide links to the other pages. The online catalog will have a live connection to an ODBC data source, enabling visitors to look up current titles, perform searches, and even alter information in the database (although that is not typically an option you would provide the general public). The About Our Company page will offer a brief corporate background, and the Links to Our Partners page will include a few links to external Web sites.

All Visual InterDev Web sites have a standard hierarchy. First, you create a *solution*. A solution is also known as a *workspace*, which should be familiar to Developer Studio users. This process is sometimes done automatically; for example, when you use a wizard to create a project and you don't have a workspace loaded, one is created for you. A workspace can hold a number of different projects, perhaps related to one client. When you insert a database or Web site into your workspace, it becomes a project.

N O T E Workspace files are saved with the extension .DSW (Developer Studio workspace). Project files are saved with the extension .DSP (Developer Studio project). ▨

Visual InterDev has a variety of different project types, depending on what you are aiming to create. For this example, you will create a Web project. To create your first workspace and Web project, follow these instructions:

1. Choose File, New Project to open the New Project dialog box, as shown in Figure 1.6.
2. In the New Project dialog box, select the New tab if it is not selected already. This tab displays the different types of projects that you can create.
3. Select Visual InterDev Projects from the list of project types on the left side of the dialog box. This selection displays the types of Web projects that can be created on the right side of the dialog box.

FIG. 1.6

In the New Project dialog box, you can select the type of project you want to create. Typically, you will choose a new Web project.

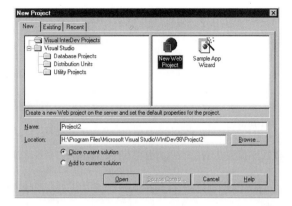

4. Select the New Web Project icon. This action activates the Name and Location text boxes.

5. Enter a name for your new project in the Name text box. For example, type `PubsPublishing`. Your project name cannot contain any spaces.

6. Enter the local directory path for your new project in the Location text box. Optionally, you can click the Browse button to select a path using the GUI Browse for Folder dialog box.

7. Click the Open button to create your new project. The Open or Create Web Project dialog box appears, as shown in Figure 1.7.

FIG. 1.7

You use the Open or Create Web Project dialog box to specify the Web server that hosts your Web application project, as well as the Web name itself.

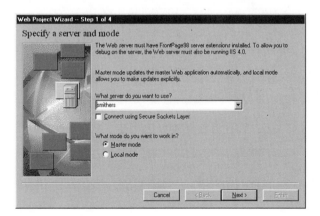

8. Enter the URL to your Web server, not including the name of the Web site itself, in the Web Server URL text box. For example, type `http://www.banick.com`.

9. Enter the Web name for your project in the Web Name text box. The Web name is the name that is used to represent your project on the Web server. This name cannot contain spaces. For example, type `PubsPublishing`.

10. Select the Create New Web radio button to indicate that this Web project should be created from scratch.

11. Click OK to create the project on the Web server.

Visual InterDev opens a connection to the specified Web server, using the FrontPage Server Extensions, to create the new Web project on the server. It populates the project with the basic files to begin. After this process is complete, Visual InterDev is ready to begin with an empty project, as shown in Figure 1.8.

FIG. 1.8
Visual InterDev 6 lists all project contents in the Project Explorer on the side of the Visual InterDev window.

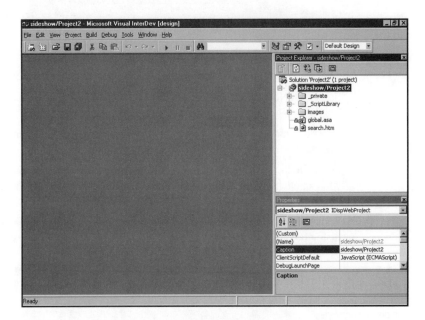

Using Site Designer to Create a Prototype for a Project

The Visual InterDev Site Designer is a powerful tool that you can use to create a prototype for and plan your Web site or application. Using the Site Designer, you can establish a flow for your Web site and determine its structure. You can also apply a site-wide theme and layout that are automatically updated by Visual InterDev. The Site Designer is ideal for mapping out new projects and projects that have not yet been fully developed. To begin with the Site Designer, you need to create a *site map* by following these instructions:

1. Select the Project Explorer. This window, typically located on the right side of the InterDev workspace, displays all the files associated with the projects in your solution.

2. Right-click the name of your Web project in the Project Explorer. From the context menu, select New Site Diagram. You also can choose Project, Add Item.

3. When the Add Item dialog box appears, as shown in Figure 1.9, select the Site Diagram icon from the list of file types on the right side of the dialog box.

FIG. 1.9

You use the Add Item dialog box to add new items to your site. In this case, you are adding a new site diagram for the Site Designer.

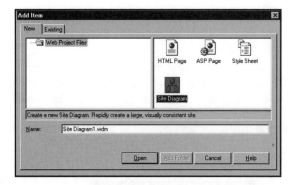

4. Enter a name for your site diagram in the Name text box with .WDM for the extension. For example, type `PubsPublishing.wdm`.

5. Click Open to create the new site diagram.

At this point, an empty Web Diagram window appears. This window, which is the core of the Site Designer, is used to create a prototype for your site structure and layout. Each page or item within your site can appear within this window. Linked items are represented by connecting lines between the boxes. Each item displayed in the window is titled and may have one or more icons below its title. These icons represent the following:

■ *House.* This icon represents the starting "home" page of the site.

■ *Web Document (Globe).* This icon indicates that the item is part of the global navigation bar.

■ *Pencil.* This icon indicates that the item and/or the site diagram has been modified and has not yet been saved.

To work with the Web diagram, follow these steps:

1. In the Site Diagram toolbar, shown in Figure 1.10, click the Add Home Page button. This button adds an icon to the diagram to represent your starting page.

2. The title of the new home page is selected. Enter the title for your starting page, such as `Welcome to Pubs Publishing`.

3. To add a new page to your site, click the New Page button on the Site Diagram toolbar. A new icon is added to represent your page, using a generic title, as shown in Figure 1.11.

4. Rename your new page to `What's New`.

5. To link your new page to your site's home page, drag the new page's box over the top of the home page until you see a linking box that appears. A solid line appears, representing the link between the pages (see Figure 1.12).

6. To add a new page that will be part of the common navigation bar for your site, click the New Page button in the Site Designer toolbar once again.

7. Select the new page, and title it `About Our Company`.

8. Select the new page, and click the Add to Global NavBar button on the Site Designer toolbar. A new icon appears below the page's title, representing its inclusion in the global navigation bar.

9. To modify the view of the Web diagram, click the Rotate button on the Site Designer toolbar. Clicking this button rotates the diagram to a different perspective. You can also control the level of magnification in the diagram from the Zoom drop-down list box.

FIG. 1.10

The Site Diagram toolbar is present when the Web Diagram window is open. Use this toolbar to create a prototype for your site layout.

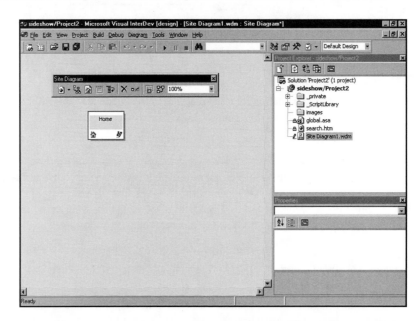

FIG. 1.11

As you add new pages to your Web site, the Web diagram displays each page as a box with an icon.

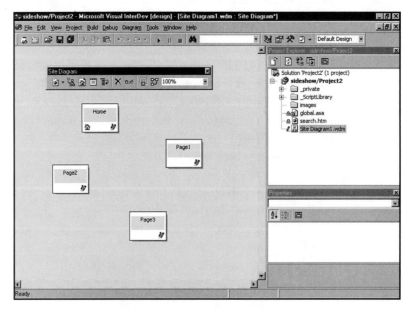

Part

I

Ch

1

FIG. 1.12
Linking pages in the Site Designer is simply a matter of dragging one page over the top of another. A solid line represents an existing link.

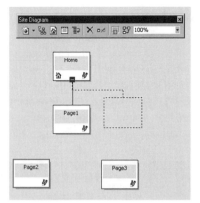

Congratulations! You have now created a basic Web site layout with three distinct pages, and it is ready to view on the Web using a Web browser. This layout will be the foundation for the sample project that you create in this chapter. From these few steps, you can probably see how the Site Designer is a powerful tool for creating prototypes for your site. When you're creating prototypes, you are creating the initial structure and layout for the site's foundation. Here are a few tips when you are working with the Site Designer and Web diagrams:

■ You can drag and drop items from the Project Explorer into the Web diagram window. This way, you can add a new item to the diagram.

■ If you have a page selected when you click the New Page button on the Site Designer toolbar, the new page is created with a link to the previously selected item.

■ To view the properties of any page, select it from the Web diagram, and click the Property Pages button in the Site Designer toolbar. You also can right-click a page and select Property Pages from the context menu. The Property Pages dialog box then appears, as shown in Figure 1.13.

■ When deleting items from the diagram, you can also have them removed from the Web site. However, this does not always have to be the case.

FIG. 1.13
In the Property Pages dialog box, you can modify and view the properties of a page in the Web diagram.

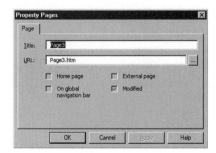

Working with the Source Editor

Visual InterDev 6's Source Editor is a powerful tool when you want to work with the raw HTML code for your pages. Visual editing of pages is a convenient and quick way of creating sites; however, many expert developers prefer to work with their code on their own. Visual InterDev's Source Editor provides you with a comfortable and streamlined text editor for developing your pages. It also includes several niceties to make source code development easier. The Source Editor, shown in Figure 1.14, is more than a simple editor, though. In fact, it is a powerful mix between a traditional source code editor and a rapid application development GUI.

FIG. 1.14

The Visual InterDev 6 Source Editor is more than a text editor. In fact, it combines many elements of RAD into traditional source code editing.

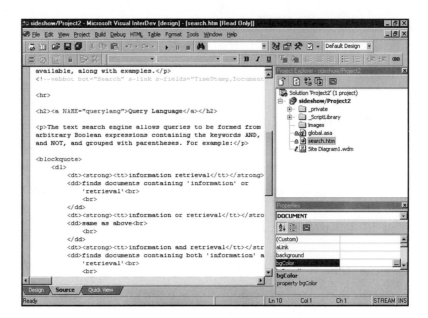

The source code editor offers many convenient enhancements over a traditional editor. First, it offers code highlighting. This feature automatically colorizes segments of your code based on specific criteria. For example, all server-side scripting code can be highlighted in a different color than client-side scripting code. With this color coding, you can visually isolate areas of your code for efficient editing. In addition to formatting, the Source Editor can also represent objects, such as ActiveX controls, in your Web pages as a graphical representation. You have the option of viewing all the source code associated with the object, or a graphical representation of the object that you can manipulate and control through the Properties window, as shown in Figure 1.15.

To experiment with the Source Editor, follow these instructions:

1. From the Project Explorer, open the Default.htm file by double-clicking the filename. This action opens the page into the default editor view, Design.

2. Switch to the Source Editor mode by clicking the Source tab at the bottom of the editor window. This window displays the source code for the Default.htm file.

FIG. 1.15

In the Properties window, you can specify the property values of selected items—for example, a page, a graphic, or even the entire site. This capability may be familiar to Visual Basic programmers.

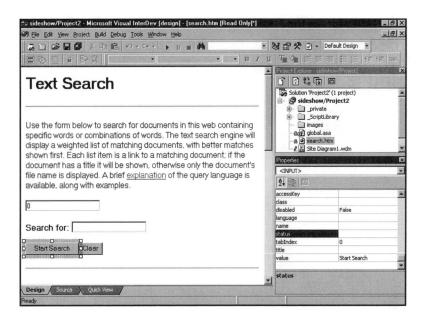

3. Locate the <BODY> tag in the document. On a new line, enter the following text into the editor:

```
<p align=center><font face="arial" size=6>
<strong><em>Welcome to Pubs Publishing</em></strong>
</p>
<hr>
```

The source code is automatically highlighted as you type it, depending on the HTML tags you enter. See Figure 1.16.

4. Save the file by choosing File, Save default.htm.

5. Switch back to Design mode by clicking the Design tab at the bottom of the editor. Your newly modified page then appears, as shown in Figure 1.17.

Connecting to a Database

Using a database source within your Web site is an easy task in InterDev 6. Visual InterDev provides you with a visual means of creating a connection to a database, querying the data, and displaying it on your Web page. Before you can use the database within your Web site, you must create a connection to the database called a *data connection*.

N O T E For the sake of example, the data source illustrated here is a sample Access database provided by Microsoft. You can use any database to experiment with, preferably one with data present inside it.

The sample database has one table, named `categories`, that contains a list of items. I will use this table as a sample for these instructions. If you are using your own database with different tables, feel free to replace `categories` with the name of your own table. ■

FIG. 1.16
The newly entered source code is automatically high-lighted according to the HTML tags used. This feature allows you to isolate broken anchors and incorrect syntax quickly.

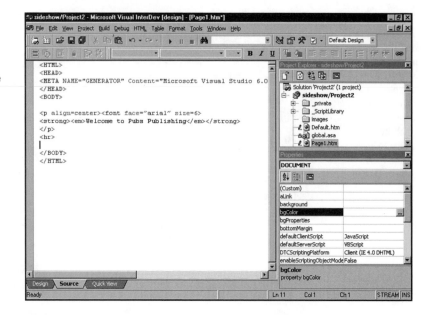

FIG. 1.17
The changes you make in the Source Editor instantly translate into the WYSIWYG Design Editor.

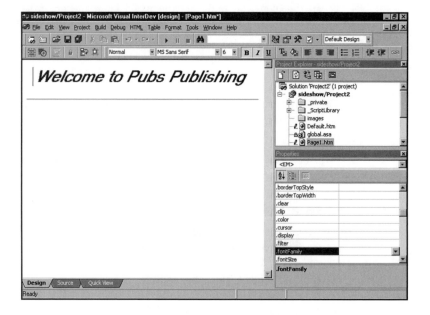

To create a data connection, follow these steps:

1. With your Web project still open, choose File, Add Project to open the Add Project dialog box.

2. From the list of projects available on the left side of the dialog box, select Visual InterDev Database Projects.

3. On the right side of the dialog box, select New Database Project.

4. In the Name text box, enter a name for your new database project. For example, type PubsData, or even accept the default name.

5. Enter the local project path in the Location text box, or use the Browse button to locate a local directory.

6. Select the Add to Current Solution radio button, if it is not already selected.

7. Click the Open button to create your new database project.

8. When the Select Data Source dialog box appears, as shown in Figure 1.18, click the Machine Data Source tab.

FIG. 1.18
The Select Data Source dialog box is the standard Windows ODBC selection tool. You should use a Machine Data Source so that it is available to all users.

9. Select the existing data source from the list. If you do not have an existing source, you must create one. (See the preceding note.)

10. Click OK to link to the data source. The new database project then is added to your solution in the Project Explorer, as shown in Figure 1.19.

After you establish the database connection, you must create queries for pulling data from the database itself. Creating queries within Visual InterDev is remarkably easy, thanks to a RAD approach: Just drag and drop and visually select tables and fields. Additionally, you can enter the raw SQL statements to retrieve information from the database, if you prefer to do things the old-fashioned way. All your queries can be tested from a database test window that displays the results of your queries. If you are new to SQL, you will appreciate InterDev's capability to test the SQL syntax before the queries are added to your Web site.

FIG. 1.19
The newly added database project is visible with your Web project in the Project Explorer. As with all projects, it represents its components within an expandable tree.

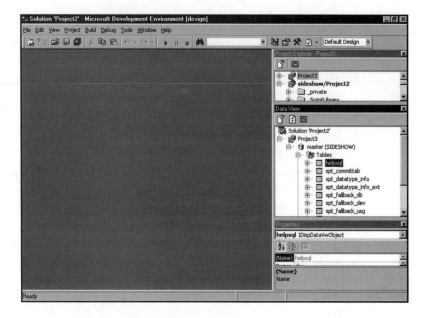

To begin creating your query, follow these steps:

1. In the Project Explorer, right-click the first data source. It should be named for the path to your database. From the context menu, choose New Query.

   When the Query Builder appears, as shown in Figure 1.20, it offers four panels: Diagram, Grid, SQL, and Results.

2. In the SQL panel, enter the SQL statement to retrieve data from the database. For example, to pull all data from the `categories` table, enter the following:

   ```
   SELECT *
   FROM categories
   ```

3. After entering the SQL statement, click the Verify SQL Syntax button to confirm that your SQL command is correct. If the syntax is correct, Visual InterDev returns an acknowledgment, as shown in Figure 1.21. If the syntax is incorrect, Visual InterDev returns an error.

   After your syntax has been verified, the diagram pane is updated to reflect your table and query.

4. Select specific columns to be queried from the table, as shown in Figure 1.22. (In the example, attribute_id and attribute_name are selected.)

   As you select columns in the diagram panel, the SQL statement modifies itself accordingly.

FIG. 1.20
The Query Designer presents you with four panels to design your queries. You can use them in combination or independently.

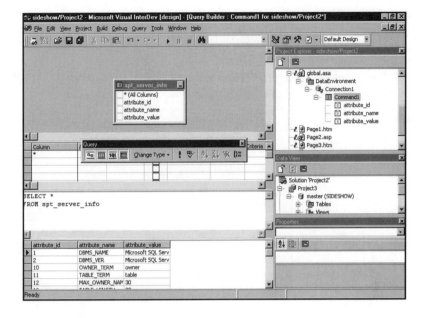

FIG. 1.21
Visual InterDev 6 verifies that the SQL statement you entered is correct in syntax. It does not confirm the existence of the correct table, though.

5. Use the grid pane to adjust the query by deselecting the original query, querying all (*) from the database, and leaving only the new query for the specific column (attribute_name in the example). Again, the SQL statement updates to reflect the changes.

6. Click the Run Query button on the SQL toolbar to execute the query and see the output in the Results pane, as shown in Figure 1.23.

7. Save your query by choosing File, Save Query1. The Save File As dialog box then appears, as shown in Figure 1.24.

8. Enter the query name into the File Name text box, and click the Save button.

FIG. 1.22

Using the diagram panel, you can select certain columns from tables. This way, you can dynamically and quickly change your queries as the need arises.

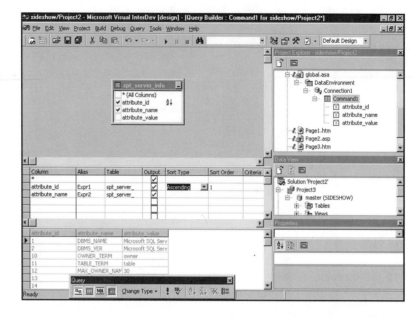

FIG. 1.23

The output from the SQL query is shown in the results pane. This output tells you precisely what your query will return within your site.

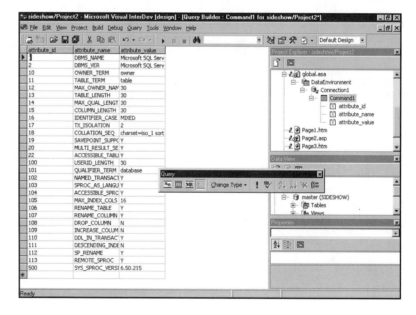

FIG. 1.24

In the Save File As dialog box, you can save your query as a .DTQ file. You can then reuse these queries as often as you need.

Your newly created query is now visible in the Project Explorer, below your data source. After you create the query, you can then implement it in your Web site using scripts and components.

▶ To learn more about using the database features of Visual InterDev, **see** Part IV, "Database Programming Basics," on **p. 309**. You can begin with Chapter 14, "Database Programming Basics," on **p. 311**.

From Here...

Now that you've gotten your feet wet with Visual InterDev, you can leap into the fray by learning the intricate details. The following chapters explore Visual InterDev in more detail, including using the editors and beginning in activating your site.

- Chapter 2, "Organizing a Web Site with Visual InterDev 6," takes you into the details of using Visual InterDev as an organizational and architectural tool when building your sites.

- Chapter 3, "Using the Source, Design, and Script Editors," is the place to learn the details on using the two fundamental editors of Visual InterDev.

- Chapter 5, "Active Scripting Overview," introduces the concepts of server-side and client-side scripting and how to make your Web site an interactive experience.

CHAPTER 2

Organizing a Web Site with Visual InterDev 6

In this chapter

Organizing a Web Site   **36**

Understanding the Visual InterDev 6 Development Process   **36**

Using the MSDN Library   **39**

Creating Solutions   **44**

Managing Solutions   **45**

Working with Multiple Sites on One Server   **53**

Customizing Developer Studio 6   **55**

Organizing a Web Site

One of the things that can make the difference between a good Web site and a great one is how it is organized. A great site invites the casual visitor to wander through it, without being difficult to navigate for the person who knows exactly what he or she is looking for. The best way to make your site meet this ideal is to have its structure and development path well laid out on the design side. This way, you don't lose track of what you've done, what you still need to accomplish, and when you need to accomplish it.

As your site becomes larger and more complex, you begin to realize that it's composed of many separate Web sites below the main one. For example, different groups within your organization might want to add their own sections to the site, or you might need to include a database-driven feedback feature. All these changes mean that you must orchestrate style sheets, updates, internal hyperlinks, and more.

Visual InterDev is particularly good at helping you keep all aspects of your site in synch and under control. It gives you the tools to organize the different components of your site, as well as what you need to tie it all together. By using the methods outlined in this chapter, you get a good start toward building a site that people want to visit again and again.

Understanding the Visual InterDev 6 Development Process

Web site development with Visual InterDev requires software on both client and server. On the client side, you have the Visual InterDev development environment, and on the server side, you have a Web server with the Visual InterDev server extensions, including FrontPage Web extensions and remote debugging services. Both the client and server sides of Visual InterDev work together to help organize your Web sites. The server side of Visual InterDev is transparent to the developer and requires no maintenance, so from here on, when you see the name *InterDev*, it refers to the Visual InterDev client-side development environment, unless otherwise noted.

InterDev 6 itself runs on the Microsoft Developer Studio 6.0 environment. This development environment is also used with other Microsoft Visual tools, including Visual Basic, Visual C++, Visual J++, and Visual FoxPro.

Other tools that ship with InterDev are the Visual Database Tools. The Visual Database Tools are seamlessly integrated into InterDev, so you have a single solution for building complex Web sites as well as database applications. More important, you can easily integrate these two technologies together, thus building either data-driven, dynamically changing Web sites or database applications using standard Internet protocols that replace existing client/server solutions.

Organization of a Web Site

InterDev organizes your Web sites and databases by means of *projects* and *solutions*. A project is simply an individual database or Web site. A solution is InterDev's method of storing multiple projects together to comprise the Web application. For example, a solution can contain a Web site project and a database project that are interrelated. A solution is also known as a *workspace*.

When you create a new Web site project in InterDev, you have the option of adding to an existing solution or creating a new one. If you choose to create a new one, InterDev creates a directory on both the server and your local InterDev workstation with the same name as your project. On the local workstation, this directory is typically a subdirectory of \DevStudio\MyProjects. On the server, this directory is a subdirectory of your \inetpub\wwwroot directory. On the server, InterDev also creates a virtual directory using the name of the project and points that directory to the new \inetsvr\wwwroot*myprojectname* subdirectory (where *myprojectname* is the name of your project). Within this directory on the server, it also creates an \images subdirectory as a default to store the site's images, in addition to other subdirectories that contain information specific to your Web site (such as scripts, themes, and so forth). On the client workstation, it duplicates the server directory structure and uses this structure when bringing local copies of the files down for editing.

Projects

Project information is stored in a DSP (Developer Studio Project) file within the project's directory. You can create both Web site and database projects. Just as a Web site project points to a single Web site, a database project points to a single database. If you need to work on more than one Web site or database concurrently, you can add multiple projects to a solution. You can add database projects to your solution by using the New Database Project Wizard or by simply adding a data connection to your Web site using the Data Connection Wizard.

Solutions/Workspaces

Solution information is stored in an SLN (Developer Studio Solution) file within a project directory on the client side. The project directory used is the one that was created at the time the solution was created. If you create an empty solution with no projects in it, you still are asked for a name; this name is then used to create a subdirectory in the \DevStudio\MyProjects subdirectory.

Within a solution, you can create multiple projects. This capability does present a slight dilemma in that you also can delete projects from a solution. If you delete a solution's original project, the project directory remains in place because it still has a solution (SLN) file in it.

> **CAUTION**
>
> Be aware that if you delete a solution's original project, that project's directory is not deleted from the \DevStudio\MyProjects directory.

Editing Content

As you load a Web page into the Visual InterDev developer environment for editing, a copy of the page is made locally. Then, as you make changes to this page, you work with a local copy. Whenever you save any changes, InterDev detects this fact and updates the server's copy.

The advantage of this process is that because the page is copied locally, you can then edit it with the editor of your choice. For example, you may want to use Adobe Photoshop instead of Microsoft Composer to edit images. After setting up Photoshop as a content editor for images, you can then double-click the image to open it; InterDev copies it locally, and then Photoshop can work with the image. As you save the image from Photoshop, InterDev detects the save and updates the copy of the image on the server.

The Development Process

The development process falls into the following three steps:

1. Create a solution and projects.
2. Author the content.
3. Program scripts and components.

After you complete the last two steps, your Web site is finished, because you're working directly with your live Web site.

Create a Solution with Projects   First, you need to set up your Visual InterDev solution. Normally, you do so simply by creating a Web site or database project, because InterDev automatically creates a solution if you don't assign the new project to an existing one. You can also import existing projects into a solution.

If you run the Insert Data Connection Wizard to create a database project, it creates a GLOBAL.ASA file specifying the database connection for the site.

Author the Content   Next, you are ready to start authoring your content. For static sites that don't change very often, you can usually accomplish this feat by using straight HTML pages and perhaps a few ActiveX controls such as the HTML Layout Control (ALX files). Content authoring can run concurrently with any programming requirements. More complex sites, however, can take considerably more effort and more content to complete.

Program Scripts and Components   At the same time that the content authoring is taking place, you can also develop any scripting or programming for dynamic/data-driven content. For scripting, you can use client- or server-side scripting with VBScript or JavaScript/JScript. You can also get more advanced by programming your own ActiveX components, which can likewise run either on the server or the client. You can program these controls in virtually any programming language that supports COM (Component Object Model) development. The most common languages for programming are C++, Visual Basic, and Java.

Advantages of the Visual InterDev Architecture

The Visual InterDev architecture provides the following advantages:

- Several developers can work on files in the same Web site without source control, simply by creating their own local project files that point to the same Web site. However, if you do need extensive source control, InterDev supports Visual SourceSafe.

- Both Visual InterDev and FrontPage developers can work on the same Web site at the same time because both development tools use the FrontPage server extensions.

- Because the master files are updated automatically on the Web server when saved, you can test scripts and view HTML files immediately.

- Visual InterDev automatically configures the Web server for the changes in your application, such as database connections and global variables.

- Because all access to the server occurs through HTTP, you don't need physical access to the Web server machine to create, modify, and even remove Web application files. Because proxy servers allow HTTP to pass through, you can even author content on a server on the other side of a firewall.

Part

I

Ch

2

Using the MSDN Library

The Microsoft Developer Network (MSDN) provides developers of all kinds with tremendous resources and information. The MSDN Library, which is the main forum for this information, contains the documentation for Visual Studio products, including Visual InterDev. The MSDN Library is an optional component during the installation process for Visual InterDev and should be installed on your development workstation.

Organization of the MSDN Library

The MSDN Library organizes information into logical units and groupings, as defined here:

- *Visual Studio Documentation.* This documentation applies to all Visual Studio family members and specifically to the Visual Studio development environment.

- *Product Documentation.* Each Visual Studio family member has its own section of documentation, including Visual InterDev. The product documentation is for all intents and purposes the reference manual for the software and tools.

- *Tools and Technologies.* Microsoft uses this important and relevant documentation on assorted tools and technologies with Visual Studio. This documentation includes information on Active Server Pages (ASPs), FrontPage, and other products/technologies.

- *SDK/DDK Documentation.* This documentation on the assorted Software Development Kits and Device Driver Kits is also present in the MSDN Library. It provides you with comprehensive information on developing for a particular technology introduced by Microsoft.

■ *Resource Kits*. Microsoft releases valuable Resource Kits for each of its platforms, including Microsoft Windows 95, Windows NT, and BackOffice. You can find the complete contents of these Resource Kits in the MSDN Library.

■ *Specifications*. Initiatives and technologies that Microsoft created (such as DHTML) or had a hand in (such as Cascading Style Sheets) are detailed in the Specifications section of the MSDN Library. It includes documentation on existing and upcoming technologies.

■ *Knowledge Base*. This timely snapshot of Microsoft's online knowledge base (**http://www.microsoft.com/support**) is included for most of Microsoft's development, server, or platform products.

■ *Technical Articles and Backgrounders*. Articles of interest to developers are located in this section. Articles may include information on developing for a particular project or technology or may reflect important information with certain tools.

■ *Books*. Relevant Microsoft Press books are included as part of the MSDN Library. These books include system design guides, interface design guidelines, and information on the development of internationally localized software.

■ *Periodicals*. Conveniently, Microsoft has also included excerpts from several different publications for inclusion in the MSDN Library. Articles of note from different magazines (print and electronic) are contained here.

■ *Conference Papers*. Finally, the MSDN Library contains relevant conference papers from the key development events, such as the Professional Developers Conference (PDC) and Tech*Ed.

Using the MSDN Library

The MSDN Library interface, called the MSDN Library Browser, is a working example of Microsoft's HTML-help interface. The MSDN Library uses a familiar "explorer" hierarchical tree to represent groupings of information and a large "browser" panel that displays the selected information. The MSDN Library is shown in Figure 2.1. Along the top toolbar of the program are Internet Explorer–like navigational buttons that can be used to move around the content.

To navigate through the wealth of information, select the appropriate category from the Contents tab. If the side panel becomes intrusive or is taking up too much space, you can hide it by clicking the Hide button in the toolbar. Clicking this button enlarges the display panel to the full size of the MSDN Library window. You can reenable the panel by clicking the Show button in the toolbar.

 TIP You can print topics for reference away from the library by selecting any topic for display and clicking the Print button in the toolbar.

Using the Index and Searching for Information   With the mass of information present in the library, familiarizing yourself with the Index and Search facilities is important. The tabbed panel to the left of the display window is called the Navigation Tabs panel. These tabs can be used to move quickly around the library's contents. The second tab, the Index tab, contains a complete index to the contents of the library. You can quickly locate information in this index by following these steps:

1. Click the Index tab to switch your display to one similar to the one shown in Figure 2.2.

FIG. 2.1

The MSDN Library is built from Microsoft's HTML-help interface. It is, in fact, a series of Web pages using a customized Web browser interface.

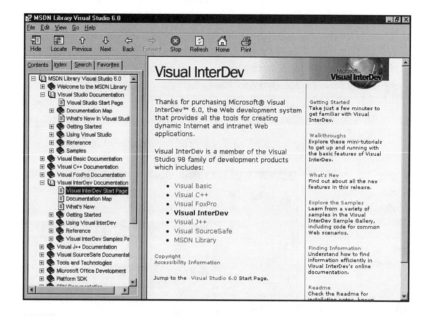

FIG. 2.2

Using the Index tab is a convenient way of locating a topic in the library.

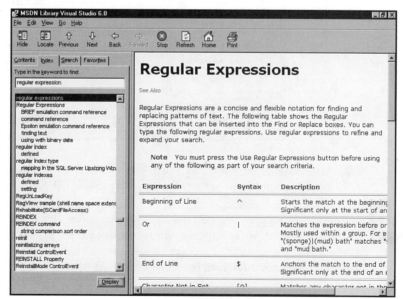

Part

I

Ch

2

2. In the Type in the <u>K</u>eyword to Find text box, enter a keyword to search. For example, if you need information on GIF files, you can enter gif. The keywords are not case sensitive.

3. The index synchronizes with any matching keywords to represent the closest match. To view a topic, select a matching item and click the <u>D</u>isplay button.

4. The display panel refreshes to display the content for the selected item. When you are finished, repeat the process to locate further information.

 T I P Pages in the MSDN Library itself also contain hyperlinks to other material. Remember that the MSDN Library Browser is actually a Web browser and follows the same usage conventions.

To search for information from the Search tab, follow these instructions:

1. Click the <u>S</u>earch tab to display the screen shown in Figure 2.3.

FIG. 2.3
You can search the MSDN contents using complex queries. You can also search from the previous results to create finely tuned lists of topics.

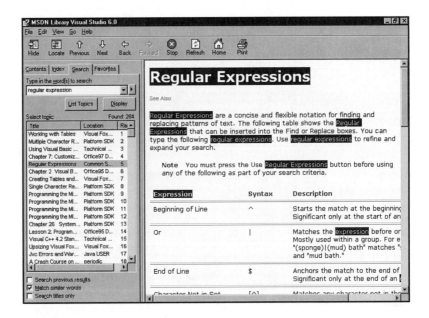

2. In the Type in the <u>W</u>ord(s) to Search text box, enter the keywords you want to search for. For example, type gif for all topics that mention GIF files.

 T I P The Search tab conveniently remembers previous queries. You can use a previous query by selecting it from the drop-down list. You can also qualify your queries more precisely by using Boolean logic statements: AND, OR, NEAR, and NOT. For example, if you want to search for all topics that mention GIF files but do not mention JPG files, you can enter this query: gif AND NOT jpg.

3. Click the List Topics button to search the contents of the library. Any matches are returned and listed with the title, location, and rank in the search.

4. Select the topic you want to read, and click the Display button to show the content in the display panel.

Bookmarking Material with Favorites   With as much information as the MSDN Library has, you can easily lose track of information. To avoid having to hunt for something again in the future, you can "dog-ear" or "bookmark" topics that you want to visit again by using Favorites. Favorites in the MSDN Library are identical to those found in Internet Explorer. To bookmark a topic, follow these instructions:

1. After reading the article you want to bookmark, click the Favorites tab to display the screen shown in Figure 2.4.

FIG. 2.4

Favorites in the MSDN Library Browser let you quickly revisit topics when you need to.

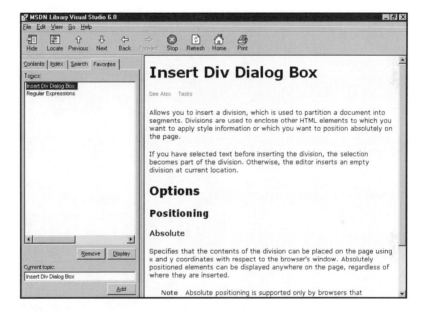

2. Click the Add button to bookmark the currently displayed topic into the Topics list. With it bookmarked, you can safely view other topics or exit the program.

3. When you want to revisit the topic, reenter the MSDN Library Browser and click the Favorites tab.

4. Select the bookmark from the Topics list.

5. Click the Display button to show the selected favorite.

6. After you finish rereading the article, you can remove the favorite by clicking the Remove button.

Part

I

Ch

2

Creating Solutions

A Web-based application is like a complex, interwoven tapestry. It has hundreds of smaller components in it, each one dedicated to telling some part of the story. Each has specific properties and is tied to the whole work in carefully planned places. If any one of the components fails to work correctly or is not correctly connected to the rest, the entire thing starts to unravel.

The Visual InterDev concept of the *solution* is something like the loom on which you weave your well-planned web of HTML documents, Active Server Pages, database connections, images, and more. Your solution encompasses everything that you need to work with related to the overall project. It provides a convenient place to access everything that you need to manage your site, and it also helps you understand and manage the relationships between all the parts. Figure 2.5 shows an example of a solution that contains a Web project and a database project.

FIG. 2.5

This typical Web site solution in the Visual InterDev environment shows the tree expansion of the Web content.

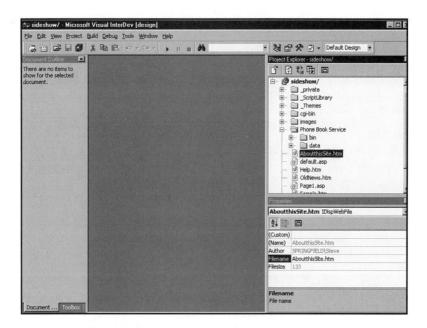

Fortunately, the creators of Visual InterDev designed it to be much easier to learn and use than the weaver's tools of yore. Creating a new solution is a simple process: To start, choose File, New Project. Visual InterDev displays the New Project dialog box, as shown in Figure 2.6. From the New tab, select New Web Project in the Visual InterDev Projects folder.

Fill in the project Name text box and the Location text box, if needed. Click Open, and Visual InterDev launches a wizard to help you create a new solution with a new project.

FIG. 2.6

The New Project dialog box lets you start a new project, which in turn creates a new solution.

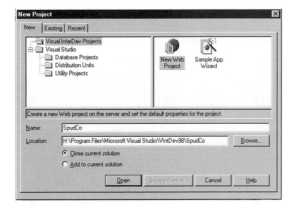

Managing Solutions

Visual InterDev derives the concept of a solution from the model of a large programming project, with many interdependent parts. Different people can work on the parts, but you need to be able to see the whole thing in one place. Putting all the components of your Visual InterDev Web application into a single, unified solution lets you better manage their interrelationships and dependencies.

You can treat this solution as if it's a sort of virtual directory of your entire Web application. Different components might actually reside in separate directories—even on separate servers—but the solution lets you see them together so that you can see how they fit together.

After you establish your solution, you can save a lot of time and effort if you configure it in such a way that it helps you do your job. The tool should never be in the way; it should not be something to work around. Instead, with Visual InterDev's solution configuration options, you can set it up to work the way you prefer.

Using Visual InterDev's Project Wizards

If the solution is the cabinet for your Web application, then the project is an individual drawer in it. You can have practically any number of projects within a solution, and they can be any mix of supported Visual InterDev project types. The primary project types that you create in Visual InterDev are the Web project and the database project. This section also describes other sorts of projects you might want to work with in your Web application and how to use the Visual InterDev Project Wizards with them.

The starting point for nearly any new project in Visual InterDev is one of the Project Wizards Microsoft includes with the package. One of the best ways to learn a new technology is to work with a functioning example of it. The Project Wizards give you these examples and so make terrific learning tools. Of course, they also give you a great framework on which to build your Web application, and you can use them as examples with which to extend an existing project.

You will use two basic Project Wizards included with Visual InterDev to do the following:

- Create a Web application or Web site
- Create a database project for inclusion in a Web site

To start any of the wizards, simply choose File, New Project and click the New tab (see Figure 2.6). To create a Web project, select New Web Project from the Visual InterDev Projects folder. To create a database project, select New Database Project from the Database Projects folder. If you already have a solution open, and you prefer to add the project to it, click the Add to Current Solution option button. The wizard then adds a new project to your solution, with the name you've specified.

After you fill in the name and select your solution options, click Open to proceed with whichever wizard you're using. For each wizard, two or more steps follow, with Visual InterDev walking you through its options. The following sections give overviews of the steps in each.

Web Project Wizard   The Web Project Wizard steps you through the initial creation process of your Web site. This wizard establishes a connection with your development Web server and creates the required files on both the server and your workstation. A new Web project may actually be a new Web site being created for the first time or even an existing Web site that is being imported into Visual InterDev for subsequent development. To create a new Web project, follow these instructions:

1. From the New Project dialog box, select New Web Project.
2. Enter a name for your project in the Name text box. Project names cannot have spaces in them.
3. Provide a location for your project in the Location text box if you are not satisfied with the default. Optionally, you can click the Browse button to select a location to store the project.
4. Click the Open button. If an open solution already exists, you can select Add to Current Solution before clicking Open.
5. The Web Project Wizard appears, as shown in Figure 2.7. Enter the name of the Web server running FrontPage Server Extensions to which you want to connect. For example, type www.banick.com.

FIG. 2.7

The Web Project Wizard handles the chore of establishing a connection to the Web server and creating the required files for your project.

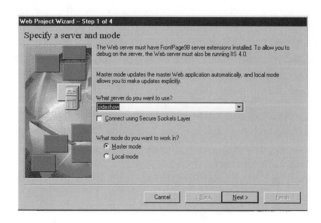

6. If your Web server supports secure connections through the Secure Sockets Layer (SSL) protocol, select the Connect Using Secure Sockets Layer check box.

7. Select the mode in which you want to develop: Master Mode or Local Mode.

Master Mode Versus Local Mode

One of the important enhancements in Visual InterDev 6 has been the differentiation between Master mode and Local mode for Web projects. Traditionally, Visual InterDev (1.0) projects were always in Master mode. This meant that any changes that a developer made to a Web project were immediately carried out on the Web server and on the local workstation files. Local mode, however, changes this situation.

Local mode carries out the changes only on the local workstation. Changes have to be committed to the master Web server to force an explicit update of the Web server's files. This releases the working copy and synchronizes the local and master Web sites.

When combined with Version Control (such as Visual SourceSafe, detailed in Chapter 24, "Using Developer Isolation and Visual SourceSafe"), Local mode lets a team of developers work together without fear of overwriting or significantly affecting another developer's work.

In the name of performance and security, it is recommended that you always work in Local mode and then update the master Web site after you finish your changes.

8. Click the Next button to proceed to the next page of the wizard, shown in Figure 2.8. Visual InterDev contacts and communicates with the Web server before proceeding.

FIG. 2.8

Step two of the Web Project Wizard lets you specify your Web application's name or open an existing Web site on the server.

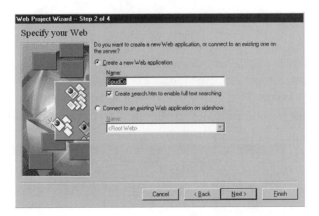

9. You have the option of creating a new Web site on the Web server or opening an existing Web site. To create a new site, click the Create a New Web Application radio button. You optionally can select the Create Search.htm to Enable Full Text Searching radio button to enable searching on this site.

10. To open an existing Web site on the server as your project, select the Connect to an Existing Web Application on *<Your Server>* radio button. Select the Web site name from the Name drop-down list box.

N O T E   The terms *Web site* and *Web* on the remote server refer to FrontPage Webs. A FrontPage Web is a logical grouping of Web content into one "site." This site can be accessed from a URL such as **http://www.mysite.dom**, or even **http://www.myserver.dom/mysite**. In FrontPage parlance, a *Web* is a distinctly individual Web site that runs atop a Web server.

11. If you selected to open an existing Web application, click the Finish button to open this site into your project and solution. Otherwise, click the Next button to proceed to the next step of the wizard, as shown in Figure 2.9.

FIG. 2.9

The third step of the wizard lets you apply a layout for your new Web site project. Layouts place navigational elements throughout your site for consistency.

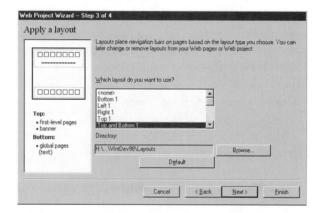

12. Select the layout you want to use for your Web application. A variety of layouts are provided, but you also have the option of opening one of your own making by using the Browse button. If you do not want to use a layout, select <None>.

13. Click the Next button to view the final page of the wizard, as shown in Figure 2.10.

FIG. 2.10

Finally, you can apply a theme to your new site. Themes are useful for creating an easy and attractive site that maintains visual consistency.

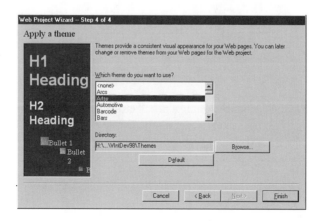

14. Select a theme to apply to your new Web application. Each theme represents a distinctly different look for your Web site. You also have the option of locating a different theme by clicking the Browse button. If you do not want to use a theme, select <None>.

15. Click the Finish button to complete the wizard. The wizard then creates the project files on both your local workstation and your Web server. Depending on what options you selected and the connection speed to your server, this process may take some time. When it is complete, Visual InterDev automatically opens your new solution and project.

Database Project Wizard   One of the most important capabilities of Visual InterDev's target environment, Internet Information Server, is easily connecting a Web application with Open Database Connectivity (ODBC) compliant databases.

ODBC is a database connection standard promulgated by Microsoft with the introduction of Access 1.0. Since then, it has grown to be the accepted standard for connecting to all varieties of databases in all flavors of Microsoft Windows. Almost every major database vendor has supplied ODBC drivers, and many database management systems have competing third-party developers providing different flavors of ODBC drivers for their systems.

The Database Project Wizard helps you connect your Web application to an existing database that uses ODBC 3.0. Visual InterDev includes compliant drivers for most of the leading database systems, including Access, dBASE, Paradox, SQL Server, and Oracle. (If you are not sure that a database you're using has ODBC 3.0-compliant drivers, check with Microsoft or the vendor.) After you start the wizard, it displays the Select Data Source dialog box (see Figure 2.11).

FIG. 2.11

The Select Data Source dialog box displays all your installed data sources. Here, you can see an example of a typical selection of data sources.

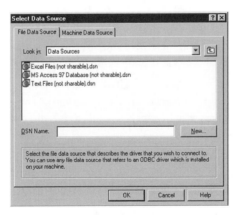

Here, you can choose from the displayed data sources, locate another one, or create a new data source. The default listing includes any file data source that you have set up on your system. You can select one of the displayed sources or browse through your system to another source by selecting a new directory in the pull-down list or clicking the button with a folder icon on it.

For file data sources, their ODBC connection information is saved in a file, which makes them easier to maintain for most Web-based applications. The second tab of this dialog box, Machine

Data Sources, includes data sources whose ODBC connection information you have saved in your Windows Registry.

If you need to create a new data source, click the New button on the File Data Source tab, and follow the prompts through selecting an appropriate ODBC driver, naming your data source, and selecting a location for it.

▶ **See** Part IV, "Database Programming Basics," **p. 309**

If your Web application will ultimately reside on an Internet Information Server by the IUSR_*machinename* account, you should ensure that the data source you select is available to the anonymous user account. If you're planning to use the Personal Web Server, you need to be sure that the visitor account has access to the data source, too.

Managing Projects

One of Visual InterDev's great strengths is that it enables you to see many parts of your Web application in one unified solution. You can better visualize the parts of one Web project that are dependent upon the data sources in another project. You get a clear idea of what documents you have completed and which ones need some attention.

To get the most out of these capabilities, you need to have a thorough understanding of the tools Visual InterDev includes. Its creators designed the entire product to make your job as a Webmaster or Web application developer easier and more enjoyable. After you understand how Visual InterDev is supposed to accomplish that job, you can start to make the most of it.

Adding Existing Documents and Projects

When you have content that you've produced outside Visual InterDev, you can easily import it so that you can manage it along with the rest of your Web application. You also can use these tools when components of your Web application come from other resources.

For example, if your organization is like most, an external agency produces logos and other corporate artwork. Press releases, policy notices, and the like all come from different parts of the organization. Having an easy way to import such materials directly into your Web application is handy.

First, be sure that you have a Web project in your solution, and that it is the active project. Select the project in the Project Explorer to make it the active project. Next, choose Project, Add Item to open the Add Item dialog box, as shown in Figure 2.12.

With the Add Item dialog box open, select the type of file you want to create or add. This file can be an HTML page, an ASP (Active Server Page) file, a style sheet, or a site diagram (explained in Chapter 4, "Using the Site Designer and Link View"). You can also add existing files by clicking the Existing tab at the top of the dialog box. This action switches the view to the one shown in Figure 2.13.

Use this dialog box to navigate through your file system to find the file(s) that you want to add. To add a file, select it from the explorer panel and click the Open button. To add multiple files, hold down the Ctrl key while selecting the files, and click the Open button. If you want to add an entire folder's contents to your Web project, select the folder and click the Add Folder button. This action adds the folder and its contents to the selected project.

FIG. 2.12
The Add Item dialog box lets you create a new item to add to the selected project or open an existing file to add.

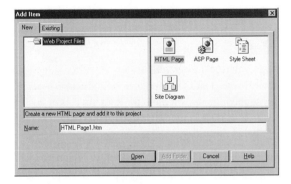

FIG. 2.13
The Existing tab lets you add existing files to your Web project. You can also add complete folders to your project using the Add Folder button.

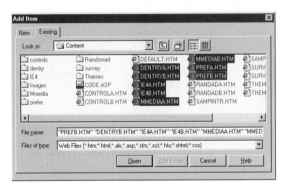

 T I P To quickly add files or folders (with their contents) directly to your projects, just drag them from your Windows Explorer window into the Project Explorer. Drop them right into the project where you want them to appear, and Visual InterDev takes care of the rest.

Being able to load projects from other Web applications is often very convenient—whether to copy parts between them, compare structure, or just because you're a multitasking sort of person. When you need to add an existing project to your solution, just choose File, Add Project, browse to your project's location in the file dialog box, and select it. Select the Add to Current Solution radio button if it is not already selected, and click the Open button.

You can also use this procedure when you have established a library of images, code, or other components that you need to standardize across all parts of your Web application. Using this procedure is the easiest way to make sure that you can make changes in one place and ensure that the changes are reflected globally.

Because Visual InterDev shares Visual Studio (the environment that it works under) with Visual C++ 6.0, Visual Basic 6.0, Visual FoxPro 6.0, and Visual J++ 6.0, you can also include projects from these programming languages right along with your HTML, ASP, and other Web-based projects. Start as if you were going to insert another Web project, but browse to the location of the desired "foreign-language" project instead. After you select it, you can use all the normal compilers and debuggers with it that you would be able to use in its native environment.

Local Working Copies

When the Web servers you're working with are on the other side of a narrow-bandwidth pipe, working with documents that reside on them can be tedious. Visual InterDev helps you deal with this problem by supplying a mechanism for keeping a *local working copy* of the contents of your Web projects. It just stores a copy of the documents in a temporary area in your local Visual InterDev installation directory.

To create a copy, right-click the project or document for which you want a local copy. Select Get Working Copy from the pop-up menu, and you're ready to start editing. You can also choose to Get Latest Version from the Web server. When you finish editing the document, Visual InterDev automatically updates it on the server if you are in Master mode. To update your site on the Web server when in Local mode, right-click the Web project name in the Project Explorer and select Working Mode, Master from the context menu. You then are asked to confirm your selection.

▶ **See** "Updating the Master Web," **p. 500**

N O T E Visual InterDev displays documents that you have copied locally with a full-color icon; it dims the icons of those documents that exist only on the server. ■

Deploying to Another Site

A common Web application development model is to work with a local Web server (such as the Personal Web Server) for speed and safety during the actual development and then "publish" to the live Web server. Visual InterDev supports this model nicely using *deployment*. Deployment is the catchword used by Visual InterDev to represent the physical duplication of your Web site content to another Web server, typically the production server. In version 1.0 of Visual InterDev, deployment was referred to as "Copy Web."

With a Web project active, choose Project, New Deployment Target. In the New Deployment Target dialog box that appears (see Figure 2.14), you can specify where the Web project should go. Fill in the Deploy to URL text box with the complete URL for the new target site. Then click OK to close the dialog box. The Project Explorer switches to the Deployment Explorer shown in Figure 2.15.

To deploy your site to the alternate target, right-click the deployment target name in the Deployment Explorer, and select Deploy from the context menu. If the destination server requires authentication, a dialog box prompts you for the information. Again, depending on the speed of your connection and the quantity of material to be copied, this might be a good time to practice some yoga. It might even be a good time to start learning yoga. (Computers free our minds to pursue higher tasks...while we wait for them.)

FIG. 2.14
You can specify multiple deployment targets for future use.

FIG. 2.15
The Deployment Explorer lists each deployment target for your Web application. You can view the output of deployments as well.

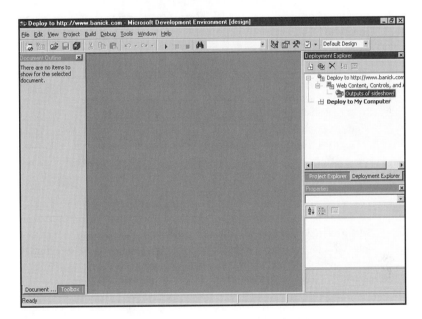

Working with Multiple Sites on One Server

Because of the economic realities of building a Web server and establishing access to it on the Internet, the owners of many servers opt to configure them for use by multiple sites. The Microsoft suite of Internet tools supports this model completely. The designers of Visual InterDev kept this fact in mind, so you can use the tools they included to manage many separate sites on the same server easily.

One common variation on this practice is to enable a single physical system to appear to the Internet as if it were several machines. Each of these "virtual servers" has its own IP address (and corresponding URL listings). In this instance, your browser sees each IP address exactly as if it were a distinct physical machine; Visual InterDev sees it the exact same way. In other words, when you configure your Web server this way, you don't need to take any special steps to account for it; just enter the appropriate IP address or URL when you are attaching to or publishing to each "virtual server," and the Web server automatically places your documents where you intended.

Another approach to the problem of needing to get more work out of one server than just a single Web site requires is to use the child Web concept. The following sections concentrate on how to make the most of this method and manage several sites that all have the same root address.

Root Webs and Child Webs

A Web server's *root Web* is the Web whose default document the server retrieves when a visitor just enters its base URL. It's analogous to the root directory on your hard drive. For example, pointing your browser to the URL **http://www.microsoft.com** connects you to Microsoft's root Web.

Each *child Web* is a folder that is subordinate to your Web server's root Web. You also manage each with its own Web project files. A child Web often has all the components of a complete Web project but requires more than just the Web server's name to access it.

Note that the child Webs are not visible from within the root Web project. However, the root Web can contain folders. They are not child Webs because Visual InterDev stores their configuration data together with that of the root Web. Folders within the root Web also cannot have the same names as child Webs; this restriction helps you to avoid document-name collisions at publish time. After you publish the folders in the root Web and the child Webs, the visitor normally sees no difference between them.

An example of a child Web is **http://www.microsoft.com/vinterdev/**. The Visual InterDev site is a child Web within Microsoft's Web site. You can set it up as a complete Web project, although, like many child Webs, it has links to standard outside library components, such as logos and menu images. You would not want to copy these elements to every Web project. The process of managing them centrally and simply linking out to them is much more efficient.

Of course, many child Webs are completely independent of each other and their root Web. The personal Web space that many Internet service providers provide for their customers' use is a good example of this kind of child Web. Each Web carries the individual stamp of its owner, and the various child Webs probably have little in common.

N O T E   Understanding the distinction between a child Web and a Web project is important. A child
Web refers to a specific subdirectory off a root Web, with its own configuration data, stored
in its own Web project. The root Web is analogous to the root directory of a hard drive. A Web project
can (and many do) contain documents that exist in several directories. ▪

Because Visual InterDev makes managing completely separate Web projects within the same solution easy, it's a great vehicle for managing either sort of child Web. You can see and maintain the links within a set of related child Webs, yet manage them separately when you don't need to see the big picture.

Shared Components

Providing a library of standard graphics, help documents, or server-side tools, and so on, is often handy when several sites are hosted on one server. The fact that you can easily import an existing Web project into any solution makes doing so all the more convenient.

You can use this concept when you want to retain a similar look and feel over a large and complex site, even when many different departments, individuals, and teams provide the content. As the manager of the overall site, you can easily maintain and alter the common elements, without needing to micromanage every child Web.

For example, you can set up a Web project that contains just the standard images you want everyone in the organization to use. To maintain a consistent look and feel, you can include elements such as a standard background image, organizational logo, and so on. Then, when ACME Consolidated buys out your company, you are ready with the new logo, the site changes globally with no fuss, and the post-merger downsizing spares your position. Chalk up another win for Visual InterDev.

Similarly, after you've developed a set of tools for accepting customer orders in one part of a Web site, you can reuse them simply by importing the appropriate project(s) into another Web application solution.

Customizing Developer Studio 6

Visual Studio, the heart of Visual InterDev, is a flexible and adaptable environment used by millions of developers worldwide. The Visual Studio interface has evolved through the many revisions of the Visual Studio tool suite, leading to the enhancements found in Visual Studio 6.0. The Visual Studio interface, regardless of which Visual Studio product you are using, shares a consistent approach and set of features that can be tweaked to suit your needs. Each individual Visual Studio product, in turn, offers further options for customizability as appropriate for its feature set. To customize Visual Studio, choose Tools, Options to open the Options dialog box, as shown in Figure 2.16.

FIG. 2.16

The Options dialog box divides the different aspects of Visual Studio that you can customize. Keep in mind that not every section necessarily relates to Visual InterDev or your installation.

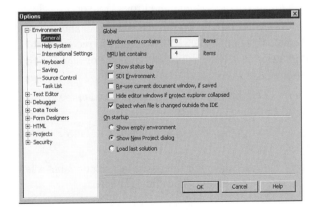

Each of the following sections documents the options available to you in the key areas of the Options dialog box. Each area can be selected from the menu tree on the left side of the dialog box.

Customizing the Environment

The Visual Studio environment itself can be customized to suit your personal needs and tastes. The Environment customization options for Visual Studio relate to the overall look and feel of Visual Studio as a tool. In this section, you can select overall appearance and behavior controls. The following options are available to you:

- General
- Help System
- International Settings
- Keyboard
- Saving
- Source Control
- Task List

General   The General options relate to global appearance and behavior controls. You have to customize these options:

- *Window Menu Contains*. This option establishes how many entries can appear in the Window menu. If more windows are open in the Visual Studio environment than entries available, they must be selected using the Windows option from the Window menu.

- *MRU List Contains*. You can limit the Most Recently Used list in the File menu to how many entries it displays by using this option.

- *Show Status Bar*. This option toggles the display of the status bar at the bottom of the Visual Studio window.

- *SDI Environment*. By default, Visual Studio is a Multiple Document Interface (MDI) environment, with one large window containing several sub-windows. It can be switched to a Single Document Interface environment with no containing window.

- *Re-use Current Document Window, If Saved*. If this option is enabled, an open document window is recycled and used for another document if the existing document is saved.

- *Hide Editor Windows If Project Explorer Is Collapsed*. This option removes the different editor windows from the screen if the Project Explorer has been collapsed from view.

- *Detect When File Is Changed Outside the IDE*. If a change has been made to a file with an outside editor, this option allows Visual Studio to recognize the change and refresh the file within the project. Refreshing can cause performance problems with large files and busy systems.

- *Show Empty Environment*. This option displays an empty Visual Studio environment on application startup.

- *Show New Project Dialog*. This option displays the New Project dialog box when the application is opened.

- *Load Last Solution*. This option opens the last solution that was worked on in the preceding session when the application is opened.

Help System   The Help System options let you specify the Preferred Language for your help files (assuming other languages are present in your installation) as well as the Preferred Collection of help files if more than one collection is present on your system.

International Settings   The International Settings area lets you specify the language and font for the development environment.

Keyboard   Visual Studio lets you creatively control your keyboard while working in the environment. Using the Keyboard options, you can create your own keyboard mapping schemes. These keyboard mapping schemes let you create shortcut keys for commands and features for use during your work. Different schemes can be used for different requirements or users.

Saving   Visual Studio lets you choose how files will be saved in your projects. By default, when you run or preview a file or application, Visual Studio saves the file first. You can have Visual Studio prompt to save changes or not to save the files at all (Don't Save). You can also choose to have Visual Studio prompt you for a location of all files being saved in your solution.

Source Control   When you are working with source control and Web projects, Visual Studio gives you a great deal of flexibility in how it is managed. The Source Control options area lets you determine file check-outs/check-ins when opening and closing solutions and whether status updates should be made in the background of your work. Additionally, you can have Visual Studio prompt you for information on key source control events, such as updates or retrievals.

Finally, this area lets you choose the method of source control that you want to use. The methods available to you depend on your development environment and the options you have installed, such as Visual SourceSafe. You can specify a login for your source control system at this point.

Task List   The Visual Studio Task List takes a strong cue from the Task List in Microsoft FrontPage. You can use this Task List to get an idea of your progress and organize your project management. It is ideal when working in multiple-developer environments. The Task List can be customized through the addition of custom comment tokens. These tokens can be used to establish your own priority groups and actions. You can also determine how the Task List behaves when a task is completed and removed.

Text Editor Preferences

The Text Editor in Visual Studio 6 took tremendous strides past the one provided in previous Visual Studio versions. This text editor lets you customize its behavior through several different display and behavior options. You can also establish preferences based on the type of text you are editing:

- HTML (Hypertext Markup Language)
- PL/SQL (Oracle Pascal Language/Structured Query Language)
- Plain Text
- SQL (Structured Query Language)
- T-SQL (Microsoft Transact Structured Query Language)

Part

I

Ch

2

Finally, you can also customize the fonts and colors for your text editor to suit your personal preferences.

Debugger Options

The Visual InterDev Debugger is perhaps one of the most powerful and useful enhancements in Visual InterDev 6. Using these options, you can customize the behavior of the debugger:

- *Hexadecimal Display.* This option displays numerical values (parameters, return values, and expressions) in hexadecimal format.
- *Attach to Running Programs.* With this option enabled, you can attach the debugger to a running script or Java program and debug the program without having the Visual Studio development environment open.
- *Just In-Time Debugging.* This option allows you to catch faults that occur while a program (script or Java) is running outside the debugging environment. It also allows you to start the debugging process.

Data Tools Preferences

The Visual InterDev Data Environment lets you quickly and easily interact with data sources in your Web applications. To accommodate efficient interaction, Visual Studio gives you several options to suit the Data Tools to your personal needs. These options customize how the Data Tools react and display their results to you. Additionally, you can limit data output and time-out lengths.

HTML Options

With the different editors provided for you in Visual InterDev, you may want to have some element of control over how they work and when they appear. You can use the HTML options to customize how the editors display information, what is the initial view, and how to use InterDev's new auto-completion features.

Project Preferences

Finally, you can establish project settings on a global scale. Visual Studio lets you decide how you want it to treat projects. Should a GLOBAL.ASA file be created for new projects? Do you want to remove the local copies of files when checking them into the Web site or source control? Do you want to enable link-repair for broken hyperlinks within your Web site? You can also control the proxy settings used by Visual InterDev if you are working from behind a proxy server or firewall.

From Here...

This chapter walked you through the basics of using Visual InterDev. In the next chapters, you will begin to work in more detail with its many features. This includes

- Chapter 3, "Using the Source, Design, and Script Editors."

Using the Source, Design, and Script Editors

In this chapter

Introduction to the Visual InterDev 6 Editors   **60**

Design Editor: WYSIWYG Editing with InterDev   **60**

Using the Source Editor for Ongoing Source Entry   **69**

Working with the InterDev Toolbox   **75**

Property Pages and the Properties Browser   **78**

Applying Themes and Layouts   **80**

Introduction to the Visual InterDev 6 Editors

The heart and soul of Visual InterDev are the Design and Source Editors. Within these two editors, all the action happens. Your work in designing and developing Web applications takes place in these two editors. Each editor represents a particular "mode" of working. Thankfully, you can rapidly switch between editors to suit your needs for the moment. The editors in Visual InterDev 6 have taken an incredible leap forward over those included with Visual InterDev 1.0. This chapter describes these evolved tools.

People who use Visual InterDev tend to have two distinct frames of mind when working with Web pages and Web applications. Visual InterDev neatly divides these two mindsets into the two predominant editors in version 6.0: the Design Editor and the Source Editor. These editors are your default tools when working with InterDev. You will most likely be using these two editors in conjunction with one another on an ongoing basis, every time you sit down to do development. Taking its cue from competing products, InterDev 6.0 provides you with a powerful work environment for raw Web and script coding as well as visually oriented Web design.

Understanding the motivation behind the use of each editor is important. Consider these points:

- *Designers want a tool that gives them What-You-See-Is-What-You-Get (WYSIWYG) graphical Web design.* The Design Editor gives you the means of visualizing and authoring your pages without requiring a great deal of tedious manual code entry. The Design Editor has facilities for integrating media and file types, as well as implementing components on both the server and client side.

- *Programmers want a flexible environment that lets them quickly code what is needed.* The InterDev 6 Source Editor is actually an enhanced version of the very same editor found in Visual C++ 6.0, Visual J++ 6.0, and Visual Basic 6.0. It has been powered up with clever HTML and Web-oriented features that make source editing easier and more fluid. The Source Editor also is used to program the client- and server-side script that is present in even the most basic of Web applications. This editor has been suited ideally for the task of developing complex Web application pages.

- *Most Web developers need to rely on a combination of both methods.* To be a truly effective Web developer, you must have not only an eye for aesthetics, but also the nature of a programmer to slog through raw code and develop the underlying engine required for your pages. InterDev 6's two editors are twins separated at birth; they have formed a symbiotic relationship that lets you rapidly switch between the two modes for the same page, without losing functionality.

Design Editor: WYSIWYG Editing with InterDev

Although early Web editors were exclusively source-level text editors, the next generation of Web development tools focuses on the visual nature of the medium. Most designers are more comfortable working in a graphical environment, similar to their other tools (image manipulation software, desktop publishing or layout software, and so forth). What-You-See-Is-What-You-

Get (WYSIWYG) editors have evolved greatly since they first started to appear in the marketplace. Today, most WYSIWYG editors can closely (if not precisely) duplicate the presentation in a browser much like contemporary layout software or word processors do paper. Visual InterDev's Design Editor, shown in Figure 3.1, is more than a simple WYSIWYG editor; in fact, it is a powerful product in its own right.

FIG. 3.1

The Visual InterDev 6 Design Editor has grown from being a customized version of FrontPage to its own mature product suited for rapid application development on the Web.

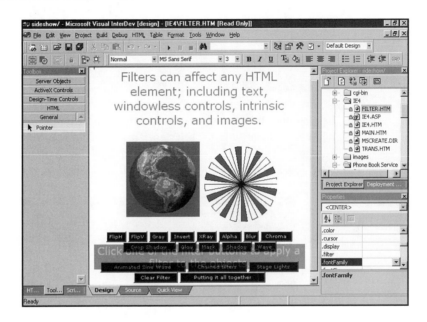

Part

I

Ch

3

Creating and Editing a New Page

The Design Editor relies on the supporting interface elements of InterDev for its features. You will explore several of the related interface elements in this chapter (specifically the Toolbox in "Working with the InterDev Toolbox" and the Properties Browser in "Property Pages and the Properties Browser"). The Design Editor itself is straightforward in its usage, much like most word processors or other WYSIWYG editors. The editor translates the entries you make (such as typing or incorporating an image) into the raw code required to display the page to a Web browser. Consciously, you are not required to consider the code or the browser viewing the page; that is the role of InterDev. Realistically, however, you will be working in both the Design Editor and the Source Editor.

To begin using the Design Editor, create a new blank page in your Web project by following these steps:

1. Choose Project, Add Item to open the Add Item dialog box, shown in Figure 3.2.
2. Select HTML Page from the Web Project Files folder in the dialog box.
3. Enter a name for your new page in the Name text box, such as sample.htm. Remember to include the .HTM or .HTML extension.

FIG. 3.2

You use the Add Item dialog box to add both new and existing items to your project.

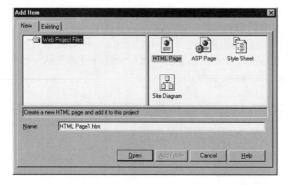

4. Click the Open button to create your new page and add it to the Project Explorer. If your project has a theme or layout selected, it is automatically applied to your page. (See "Applying Themes and Layouts" later in this chapter.) The page is automatically opened in the Design Editor, as shown in Figure 3.3.

FIG. 3.3

Your new page is added to the Project Explorer and opened in the Design Editor for changes.

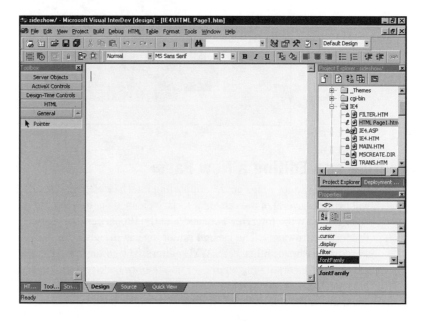

With your page newly created, you can now begin to customize it to suit your needs. Start by editing the new page to include some basic text:

1. Click in the Design Editor, and type this headline for your page: Welcome to my New Web Page. Then press Enter twice.

2. Type the following text:

```
This page showcases some of the features of Visual InterDev 6.0 from
Microsoft. I will be using this page throughout this chapter to
```

demonstrate the different features of the two editors included with InterDev: the Design Editor and the Source Editor. I am writing this text while in the Design Editor.

Later in this chapter I will learn how to customize this page's appearance using both the Properties Browser and Themes/Layouts. Throughout this chapter I will also learn how to use the Visual InterDev Toolbox and Outlines.

N O T E You're welcome to enter your own text in place of this sample text. Use this example as an opportunity to begin work on your own pages. ▪

3. Save your page by choosing File, Save *<filename>*.

With a WYSIWYG editor, you can safely assume that however you enter your content into the Design Editor is how end users will view it in their Web browsers. Thankfully, you can quickly make changes to your pages using the same operations found in a word processor: using the mouse and the cursor to move around the document to make changes. Following this entry, your page should resemble the one shown in Figure 3.4.

Part

I

Ch

3

FIG. 3.4
Your new page is screaming out for attention: Customize me!

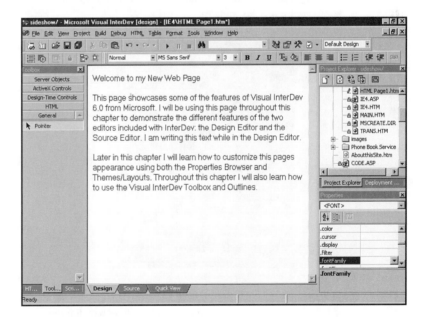

Working with the HTML Toolbar

With the basics of your page in place, you can now begin to customize it to suit your personal tastes. The HTML toolbar, shown in Figure 3.5, is used much like the formatting toolbar found in most word processors. This toolbar lets you select the format, font, size, and style for text in your page. You can also use this toolbar to change colors and paragraph alignment and to create bulleted or numbered lists and indented items.

FIG. 3.5

The HTML toolbar closely resembles its cousins in Microsoft FrontPage and Microsoft Word.

To begin using this toolbar, follow these simple steps with your existing sample page:

1. Select the headline for the page you have just created (`Welcome to my New Web Page`) by using the mouse.

2. From the Paragraph Format drop-down list box in the HTML toolbar, select Heading 1. This format changes your headline to a much more distinct and stately style of text.

3. With your headline still selected, click the Center button in the toolbar. With this button pressed, your headline appears centered in the middle of the page.

4. Select the last paragraph of your page's contents so that the full block is highlighted.

5. Click the Foreground Color button in the HTML toolbar. The Color Picker dialog box, shown in Figure 3.6, appears.

FIG. 3.6

The Color Picker lets you quickly choose a color swatch.

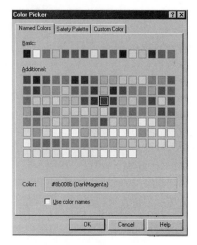

6. Select a new color for your paragraph from the color swatches, and click OK. The Design Editor refreshes your paragraph to select its newly defined color.

7. Click the end of the last paragraph so that the cursor appears. Press Enter once.

8. Click the Bulleted List button on the toolbar. A new bullet appears, awaiting your typing.

9. Enter the following lines. At the end of each line, press Enter once.

   `Visit my favorite web site.`

   `Send me email.`

10. Click the Bulleted List button once again to turn off the bulleted list.

11. Save the changes to your page by choosing File, Save *<filename>*.

Your page should look similar to the one shown in Figure 3.7.

FIG. 3.7
Your sample page is starting to take shape with some basic formatting elements.

Part

I

Ch

3

Inserting Images

Slowly but surely your page is starting to take a step toward maturity. The next step in customizing your page is incorporating an image. Adding images to pages is a simple process, lending the editor well to complex graphical layouts. To begin, make sure that you have an image present in your project. If you do not already have an image in your project, skip ahead to "Creating Links" to add an image quickly. To insert your image, follow these steps:

1. Locate your graphic in the Project Explorer, and drag it into the Design Editor window.

2. Reposition your graphic to the bottom of your page by dragging it with the left mouse button.

3. Resize your image by using the handles on the edges of the bounding box. Size the image so that it fits clearly at the bottom of your page, similar to the image shown in Figure 3.8.

4. Save the changes to your page by choosing File, Save *<filename>*.

FIG. 3.8
You can easily manipulate images in the Design Editor. You will also experiment with properties of images in this chapter.

Creating Links

You can incorporate hyperlinks in the Design Editor by using the HTML toolbar and the Link button. The Link button lets you create a hyperlink tied to text or an image for any URL, be it a reference to another Web page, to an email address, or even to an FTP site. The URL is then interpreted by the browser, so InterDev itself cares little about the URL. InterDev has facilities for tracking and verifying links to internal pages and external sites as well, and is covered in Chapter 4, "Using the Site Designer and Link View."

To create a hyperlink in your sample page, follow these steps:

1. Select the first bulleted item in your page, `Visit my favorite web site`.

2. Click the Link button in the HTML toolbar. The Hyperlink dialog box, shown in Figure 3.9, appears.

FIG. 3.9
The Hyperlink dialog box lets you specify the URL for your link.

3. Select the type of hyperlink from the Type drop-down list box. Typically, it is an **http://** URL that refers to another Web page or Web site, but it could just as easily be an **ftp://** or **mailto:** URL.

InterDev Hyperlink Types

The Visual InterDev editors provide the following nine different URL link types:

- *file*. A direct file reference on the client's computer.
- *ftp*. A File Transfer Protocol (FTP) connection to an FTP server.
- *gopher*. A connection to a Gopher server resource.
- *http*. A standard Web Hypertext Transfer Protocol (HTTP) connection.
- *https*. Secure HTTP Web connection.
- *mailto*. An electronic mail address to send a message.
- *news*. A reference to a specific NNTP news server and/or newsgroup.
- *telnet*. A terminal connection to a network host.
- *wais*. A connection to a Wide Area Information System resource.

In addition to these basic types, you can enter your own URL moniker, as required.

Part

I

Ch

3

4. Enter the link's URL in the URL text box. In this case, enter the URL to your favorite Web site, such as **http://www.banick.com**.

5. You can optionally click the Browse button to search for the link's destination. When you click the Browse button, the Create URL dialog box, shown in Figure 3.10, appears.

FIG. 3.10

The Create URL dialog box is a more advanced version of the Hyperlink dialog box.

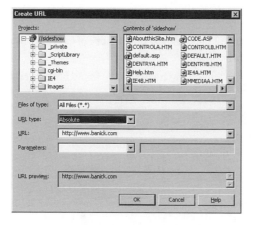

6. To link to a local Web page within your project, you can select the project from the Projects tree. Click your project title, and select the root folder for your Web site.

7. When the Contents of '*<folder name>*' box refreshes to reflect the items available in the selected folder, select one of the pages present in the box, such as default.asp. You can use the Files of Type drop-down list box to choose the type of item to display.

8. Select the method for the link from the URL type drop-down list box. This list box determines how the URL is presented to the browser. For example, should this be a relative reference based on the current directory? Or should it be an absolute reference including the complete hostname?

9. When the selected filename appears in the URL text box, replace the value in this box once again with the URL for your favorite Web site.

10. Click OK to close this dialog box and create your hyperlink.

 T I P You can pass information to destination Web pages that understand it by using the Parameters drop-down list box and text box. These boxes are ideal for passing information to ASP pages within your Web site.

With your link created for the bulleted item, the text changes in the Design Editor to represent a hyperlink. Now you can create a mailto: link for the second bulleted item (Send me email) that points to your email address, following the preceding instructions but using a mailto: URL type.

Adding Tables

A complex aspect of Web authoring is tables. Tables provide a powerful means of controlling layout and organizing information in a Web page. However, tables are easily messed up due to their rigid reliance on accurate code. If a table is not coded correctly, elements of the table may render incorrectly in the user's browser, if at all. The Design Editor has fluid support for tables, making the chore of table creation and management much easier. In fact, InterDev's table support owes a lot to both Microsoft FrontPage and Microsoft Word.

To create a table in your sample page, follow these steps:

1. Click the last line of the page so that the cursor appears after your image. Press Enter twice to add extra whitespace.

2. Choose Table, Insert Table. The Insert Table dialog box, shown in Figure 3.11, appears.

FIG. 3.11
The Insert Table dialog box lets you quickly create a table with the required number of rows and columns.

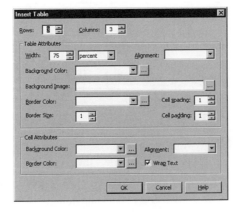

3. Select the number of rows for the table from the Rows spin box. For this example, choose 2.

4. Select the number of columns for the table from the Columns spin box. For this example, choose 2 as well.

5. From the Border Color drop-down list box, select the color to outline this table. In this example, choose Red.

6. Use the Border Size spin box to set the width of the border for the table. A value of 0 means that no border will be displayed. In this example, set the border to 2.

7. Click OK to create the table with these values and the remaining defaults. The dialog box closes, and you are returned to your page, shown in Figure 3.12.

FIG. 3.12
Tables can contain images, text, controls— basically anything that can appear in a page.

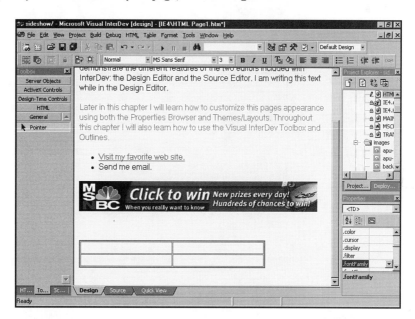

After having worked briefly with the Design Editor, it is easy to see that creating attractive Web sites with minimal effort is a distinct possibility. As you work more with the Design Editor, you will see how it interacts with other aspects of Visual InterDev.

Using the Source Editor for Ongoing Source Entry

The Source Editor lights a fire in the eyes of programmers and those who love raw HTML code. Visual InterDev's Source Editor is a powerful text editor that is integrated with the rest of the InterDev environment. It also has clever and unique features that have been added to make the job of Web application development easier. Using the Source Editor, shown in Figure 3.13, you can work on the fundamental HTML level of Web pages and server- and client-side scripting. In the Source Editor, the core engine of all Web applications is developed. In this section, you use the Source Editor to continue working with your sample Web page, this time from the backend.

N O T E   Using the Source Editor requires a firm understanding of HTML, and in the case of Web applications, programming scripting languages. This section assumes that you have a good understanding of HTML and the concepts of scripting. Client- and server-side scripting are detailed in Part II, "Active Scripting for Web Sites." ▧

FIG. 3.13
The Source Editor is more than a glorified version of Notepad.

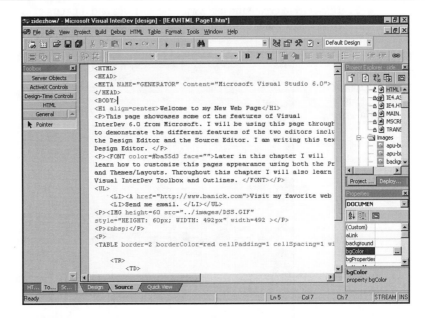

Using the Source Editor is much like using most text editors. The most obvious difference between the Source Editor and other editors is the formatting of code. The Source Editor color-codes your pages based on the types of tags and content in the file. With this color coding, you can quickly spot broken anchors and mistakes in your code. You can customize the color coding itself using the Visual Studio Options dialog box, which you open by choosing Tools, Options. In addition to colorization of your code, the Source Editor also offers several key useful features to differentiate it from a common text editor.

The HTML Document Outline

The HTML Outline panel, opened on the left of the Visual Studio window by default, is used to visualize the structure of your Web page. Shown in Figure 3.14, the HTML Outline (also known as the document outline) is also opened from the View menu; you open it by choosing View, Other Windows, Document Outline. The document outline appears in the form of a hierarchical list with the root being the document <BODY> tag. As an item is selected in the outline, the Source Editor updates the cursor to the selected item's location in the page. The Properties Browser is also updated to reflect the current properties for the selected item.

You can use the HTML Outline for several tasks:

▧ Spotting missing tags in your code at a glance

▧ Identifying the structure of your Web page

- Diagnosing formatting problems
- Quickly moving between elements in your Web page
- Taking an "overview" look at the page itself

FIG. 3.14
The HTML Outline is useful for troubleshooting your Web page code.

N O T E You also can use the HTML Outline view in the Design Editor; however, it is not as closely knit with the Design Editor's features. ■

Script Pop-Up Statement Completion

When you are working with client- and server-side scripting, the Source Editor offers a powerful feature called *Intellisense*, or *pop-up statement completion*. This feature, illustrated in Figure 3.15, assists you in coding your scripts by popping up information relevant to your code. The pop-ups offer you information on available arguments and statements in your code syntax. Server- and client-side scripts, in addition to the Visual InterDev Editor's features to assist with these scripts, are covered in Part II, "Active Scripting for Web Sites."

Scripting Using the Script Outline

Much like the HTML Outline view, the Script Outline view enables you to look at your page from a high level. Unlike the HTML Outline, however, the Script Outline concentrates on the programming and scripting aspects of your page. This view, shown in Figure 3.16, provides you with quick and easy access for defining scripts based on events or elements in your Web page. This capability is convenient for quickly isolating the specific object and event you want to work on at any one time. As mentioned previously, scripting in Visual InterDev is detailed in Part II.

FIG. 3.15
Auto pop-up statement completion takes much of the drudgery of programming away from your work.

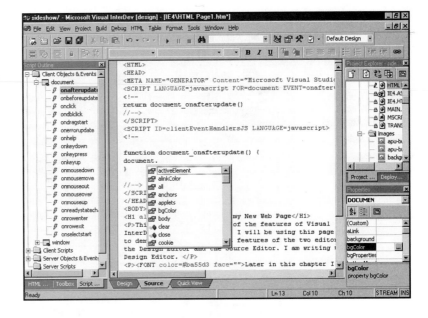

FIG. 3.16
Script Outline view displays both client and server objects and events.

Using Find and Replace

One of the more common features that you will use in the Source Editor (and the Design Editor) is Visual InterDev's comprehensive Find and Replace feature. The Find dialog box, shown in Figure 3.17, can be used not only to locate a string of text and replace it with an alternative string in the current document, it also can be used to replace all instances of a string throughout a selection of files or a series of folders. This capability is ideal when you are making changes that affect more than one page (such as changing a title that appears on all pages inside your site).

To search for a specific string, follow these instructions:

1. Choose Edit, Find to open the Find dialog box, shown in Figure 3.17.

2. Enter the string to search for in the Find text box. Your string can also be a *regular expression*.

FIG. 3.17

You can use the Find dialog box to search and replace a string of text.

Regular Expressions

A regular expression is a notation used for finding or replacing patterns of text. Regular expressions are also known as wildcards. You can use regular expressions to refine and expand your search, as long as you have the Use Regular Expression button selected in the Find dialog box. See Table 3.1, at the end of these steps, for a few of the regular expressions that are available to you.

3. If you want to replace the specified string with a different string, enter the new string in the Replace text box.

4. From the Look In drop-down list box, select where you want to search for this string. You can choose the current document, the current selection of text in your document, all open documents in Visual Studio, or all files in a specified directory.

5. If you are searching through files, you can choose to search directories below the specified directory by selecting the Subfolders check box.

6. If you are searching through files, click the Browse button to open the Look In Folders dialog box, shown in Figure 3.18.

FIG. 3.18

The Look In Folders dialog box lets you choose the file system folders (either local or network) to search.

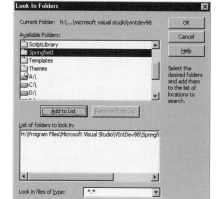

7. From the Available Folders list box, navigate to the folder that you want to search, and select the folder.

8. Click the Add to List button to add the folder to the List of Folders to Look In box. If you accidentally choose the wrong folder, you can select the same folder and click Remove from List, or continue to add additional folders.

9. Constrain the types of files to look into by choosing file types from the Look in Files of Type drop-down list box. By default, Visual InterDev searches in all files (*.*).

10. Click OK to close this dialog box and return to the Find dialog box.

 TIP If you select the Subfolders check box, Visual InterDev searches the selected folders and all folders below them.

11. Click the Find button to find a matching string. Clicking the Find button again takes you to the next match.

12. To replace the matching string with your new string, click the Replace button. Clicking the Replace button again takes you to the next match and replaces it as well. If you want to replace all matching strings, click the Replace All button.

CAUTION

Use extreme care when using Replace All. If you click it, you will replace all incidents of matching text.

13. After you finish your activities, close the Find dialog box.

Table 3.1 Regular Expressions for Find/Replace

Expression	Syntax	Description
Beginning of line	^	Starts the match at the beginning of the line. This syntax must be used at the start of an expression.
Or	|	Matches the expression before or after the |—for example, (sponge)¦(mud) bath.
End of Line	$	Anchors the match to the end of a line. This syntax must be used at the end of an expression.
Character not in set	[^]	Matches any character not in the set of characters following the ^.
Tagged Expression	{}	Tags the text match by the enclosed expression.
Grouping	()	Groups a subexpression.
Nth Tagged Text	\N	Matches or replaces the text match by the Nth expression, where N is a number from 1 to 9.
Any Character	.	Matches any one character.

Expression	Syntax	Description
One or More	+	Matches at least one occurrence of the expression preceding the +.
Maximum of One or More	#	Matches at least one occurrence of the expression, matching as many characters as possible.
Escape	\	Matches the character following the backslash.
Prevent Match	~X	Prevents a match when X appears at this point in the expression.
Repeat N Times	^N	Matches N occurrences of the preceding expression.

Working with the InterDev Toolbox

The Toolbox is an advantageous addition to Visual InterDev in version 6.0. The Toolbox, which can be used in both the Design and Source Editors, is used for quick and easy access to elements and components for Web application development. The Toolbox, shown in Figure 3.19, has several different tabs that slide into view when clicked. These tabs each represent a grouping of similar items. By default, these tabs are split into five groups: General, HTML, Design-Time Controls, ActiveX Controls, and Server Objects. To suit your needs, you can customize these tabs or add your own as required. The Toolbox is identical in purpose between Visual InterDev and Visual Basic—a means of selecting the "tool" to add to a project.

FIG. 3.19

The Toolbox can be customized to suit your needs.

Use of the Toolbox is straightforward and simple. To incorporate an item from the Toolbox, select the item and drag it onto your Web page to the position where you want it. You can incorporate an element in either Design or Source Editor view. Attributes for the incorporated object or element differ from item to item; however, you can customize them from the Property

Browser (see "Property Pages and the Properties Browser"). Items that you add to your page can be dragged, resized, repositioned, and manipulated in both the Design Editor and the Source Editor.

HTML Tab

The HTML tab contains frequently used HTML elements that can be easily added to your Web page. You can also add your own items to the list (see "Customizing the Toolbox"). The following items are present in the default HTML tab:

- Form
- Textbox
- Password
- File Field
- Text Area
- Checkbox
- Radio Button
- Dropdown
- Space

- Listbox
- Submit Button
- Submit Button
- Reset Button
- Button
- Horizontal Rule
- Line Break
- Paragraph Break

ActiveX Controls Tab

Client-side ActiveX components are easily integrated with your Web page using the ActiveX Controls tab. This tab houses several convenient and useful components that can be used in your Web page by ActiveX-compatible browsers (for example, Microsoft Internet Explorer 3.0+). The default ActiveX Controls tab includes the following components:

- Animation
- Calendar
- Date Picker
- WalletAddress
- WalletPayment
- List View
- Month View
- Progress Bar
- Slider

- Status Bar
- Tab Strip
- Toolbar
- Treeview
- UpDown
- Path
- Sprite
- Structured Graphics

▶ **See** Part III, "Creating and Using ActiveX Controls," **p. 209**

Design-Time Controls Tab

Design-time controls provide a convenient means of customizing a page with information that is replaced when a user views your page. InterDev includes several design-time controls that allow you to present a graphical user interface for changing settings for a Web application, creating runtime scripts for both the client and server, and data binding to a remote database. The Design-Time Controls tab contains the following controls by default:

▪ Recordset	▪ Grid
▪ Label	▪ RecordSetNavBar
▪ Textbox	▪ FormManager
▪ Listbox	▪ PageNavBar
▪ Checkbox	▪ Timelines
▪ OptionGroup	▪ PageTransitions
▪ Button	▪ PageObject

▶ **See** Chapter 11, "Designing with Design-Time Controls," **p. 235**

Server Objects Tab

When working with server-side scripting, you are interacting with objects that perform functions and actions on the server side. The Server Objects tab provides you with a means of easily incorporating links to these objects within the editors of Visual InterDev. These objects may communicate with databases or the server file system, or perhaps determine the capabilities of the user's Web browser. The default Server Objects tab contains the following objects:

▪ ADO Command	▪ CDONTS NewMail
▪ ADO Connection	▪ CDONTS Session
▪ ADO Recordset	▪ Index Server Query
▪ Ad Rotator	▪ Index Server Utility
▪ Browser Capabilities	▪ MSMQ Query
▪ Content Linking	▪ MSMQ QueueInfo
▪ My Info	▪ MSMQ Message
▪ Dictionary	▪ MSMQ MailEmail
▪ Filesystem Object	

▶ **See** Part II, "Active Scripting for Web Sites," **p. 97**

Customizing the Toolbox

The Toolbox can be customized to suit your personal needs through the addition of new tabs and items. You can also remove existing items or elements and tabs that you do not use. You also can add the following:

- ▪ Selections of text from the Clipboard
- ▪ ActiveX controls or design-time controls
- ▪ File system items, such as folders and documents

To customize the Toolbox, drag elements between tabs by holding the Ctrl key, drag items from the Windows Explorer onto a tab, paste an item from the Clipboard, or use the Customize Toolbox dialog box (see Figure 3.20). To open this dialog box, right-click the Toolbox and choose Customize Toolbox from the context menu.

FIG. 3.20

The Customize Toolbox dialog box lets you add or remove controls from your system.

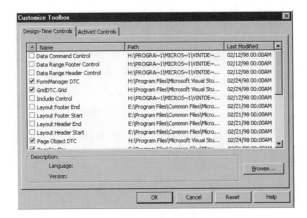

Property Pages and the Properties Browser

The Properties window, also known as the Properties Browser, is used to view and modify the attributes of elements in your Web page. All aspects of a Web page, ranging from the page itself to an image gracing the top of it, have properties that can be customized to suit your needs. The Properties window in Visual InterDev behaves identically to the one found in Visual Basic and other programming languages. When an item is selected in either the Design or Source Editor, the Properties window refreshes to display the properties for the selected item, as shown in Figure 3.21.

Using the Properties Browser

When an element is selected in either editor, the Properties window refreshes to display the properties appropriate for the selected item. Not all elements share the same properties, so Element A may have a different list of properties in the window than Element B. You modify a property by selecting it from the Properties window and entering a value in the text box to the right. Some properties provide drop-down boxes of different predefined options. To experiment with properties, follow these steps:

1. Open your sample page, and switch to the Design Editor.

2. Select the image at the bottom of your page. The Properties window refreshes to display the properties applicable to an image file.

3. In the Properties window, scroll down until you find border. Enter a value of 5 into the text box to the right to place a thick border around your image in the default color.

4. Locate the alignment property. From the drop-down list box to the right of the property, choose left to align your image to the left side of the page.

FIG. 3.21

The Properties window lets you control the attributes for elements in your Web application.

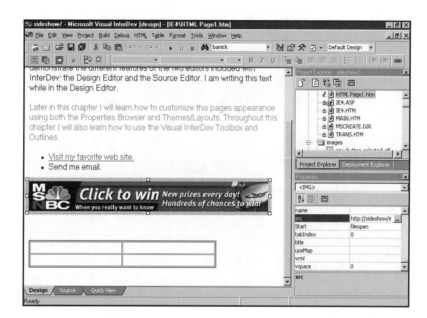

Properties in the Properties window can be sorted either alphabetically or categorically. To switch the sorting method, click the appropriate button at the top of the Properties window. You can also switch between elements to modify by selecting the element you want from the drop-down list at the top of the window.

Working with Property Pages

Using the Properties window is a quick and easy way of customizing your item's properties; however, using this window can become confusing when a large number of attributes can be customized. Many elements have another means of property management, called a *property page*. A sample property page for an image file is shown in Figure 3.22. The property page condenses most of the available attributes for an element into a convenient dialog box that lets you easily modify an element's property settings. Each different element has a different style of property page, depending on the properties available to the item.

FIG. 3.22
The Property Pages dialog box gives you more convenient access for customizing an element in your Web page.

Applying Themes and Layouts

Visual InterDev provides a convenient means of maintaining visual consistency throughout your Web site. You can apply a visual *theme* to your Web site to control the appearance throughout your site's pages. Themes enable you to select a striking appearance for your site without requiring considerable manual effort in designing a page.

On the other hand, Visual InterDev uses *layouts* to organize navigational and design consistency throughout your pages. You use layouts to define standard locations for navigational elements and headlines throughout your site. The big advantage to using themes and layouts is that you are not required to enforce these appearance and layout choices manually: the chore is handled by Visual InterDev itself. InterDev includes several sample themes and layouts that may suit your needs, but you can also use themes or layouts developed by others or on your own.

Choosing a Theme

A theme can be applied either to your entire Web site or to select pages. You can choose to have your entire site abide by a single theme, or you can use several different themes in different areas of your Web site. You can easily choose and implement a theme by using Visual InterDev's Project Explorer. Follow these instructions to apply a theme:

1. Right-click either a Web page, folder, or the project root of your Web site in the Project Explorer. In this example, click the sample page you have been using throughout this chapter. Choose Apply Theme and Layout from the context menu.

2. When the Apply Theme and Layout dialog box, shown in Figure 3.23, appears, select the Apply Theme radio button.

FIG. 3.23

Select one of the themes to apply to a page or to your entire Web site.

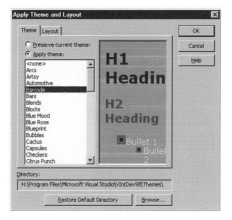

Part

I

Ch

3

3. From the list box of themes, select the theme you want to use. A preview of the selected theme is then displayed to the right. If you want to open a theme located outside the default directory, click the Browse button to search for it. For this example, choose Barcode from the list.

4. Click OK to apply the theme.

After you apply a theme, the theme files are uploaded from your workstation to the Web server. These files must be present on the Web server so that visitors can see the graphics and files referenced by the theme. With a theme applied, your page should look similar to the one shown in Figure 3.24.

FIG. 3.24

This sample page has the barcode theme.

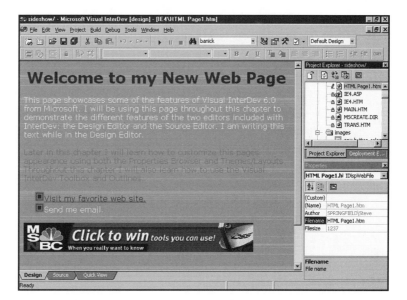

Adding a Layout

Adding a layout to your site or page is just as easy as applying a theme. In fact, it is partially the same process. Keep in mind that a layout creates new navigational elements for your affected pages that may interfere with any you may have created already. Follow these steps to add a layout to your page:

1. Right-click either a Web page, folder, or the project root of your Web site in the Project Explorer. In this example, click the sample page you have been using throughout this chapter. Choose Apply Theme and Layout from the context menu.

2. When the Apply Theme and Layout dialog box appears, click the Layout tab to switch to the page shown in Figure 3.25.

3. Several different layouts offer advanced features such as DHTML roll-overs. Select the Apply Layout and Theme radio button.

FIG. 3.25

The Layouts tab lists several sample designs that you can use.

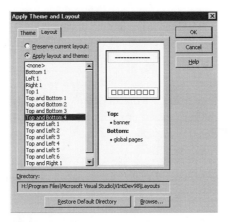

4. From the list box of layouts, select the layout you want to use. A preview of the selected layout is then displayed to the right. If you want to open a layout located outside the default directory, click the Browse button to search for it. For this example, choose Top 1 from the list.

5. Click OK to apply the layout.

N O T E   Layout's navigational references rely on the Site Designer to create references to parent pages and child pages. The Site Designer is documented in Chapter 4, "Using the Site Designer and Link View."

Using the Site Designer and Link View

In this chapter

Prototyping with the Site Designer   **84**

Managing a Site Diagram   **91**

Maintaining Site Integrity with Link View   **92**

Prototyping with the Site Designer

The chore of creating a solid and consistent site is a large one. Ensuring the quality of your site's structure and navigation as well as the integrity of the site's links is an ongoing duty of Web developers and Web administrators. Visual InterDev 6 provides you with two key features for managing your Web application's organization: *Site Designer* and *Link View*. These two features of Visual InterDev give you the means to create a consistent and manageable site structure and ensure that all links within your site are functional. This chapter outlines the use of these two features that can make a good Web site great.

The creation of a good Web site requires considerable effort and research. Careful planning and testing of your Web application are necessary to ensure that you organize your information in a manner that users will anticipate. Navigation through Web sites can be a frustrating task for users if the site's plan is not carefully considered. Visual InterDev's Site Designer uses *site diagrams* for creating the layout and flow of your Web site. These diagrams have no bearing on the content itself; the content is typically already present for it to be incorporated into the site diagram. You can also use the site diagram to create new pages for content to be added. Armed with your content, you can begin to establish a hierarchical relationship between your pages and map out the navigational flow of your site.

The Site Designer, or Site Diagram mode as it is also known, provides a simple diagram approach to organizing your Web site. Each page in your Web application is represented by a box in the diagram. The relationship between pages in your site is illustrated through connecting lines and icons. A sample site diagram is shown in Figure 4.1.

FIG. 4.1
Site diagrams use boxes to indicate individual pages. The lines linking the pages represent their relationship. Each box can also contain several icons representing other features.

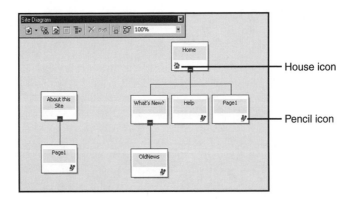

The site diagram contains several icons that may appear on pages within the boxes representing pages. These icons are as follows:

- *House.* This page represents your site's home page, or start page. You can change it by right-clicking a page in the Project Explorer and choosing Set as Start Page from the context menu.

- *Menu box.* This page is part of the global navigational bar, available from all pages in your site.

- *Globe.* This page is an external page or URL.
- *Pencil.* This page has been modified or added to the site diagram and has not yet been saved.

Creating a Site Diagram

The first step in prototyping your site is creating a site diagram. Remember that site diagrams are the visual "map" to your site's structure and organization. Visual InterDev considers the site diagram as another content file that comprises your site. To create a new site diagram, follow these steps:

1. Choose <u>P</u>roject, Add <u>I</u>tem to open the Add Item dialog box, shown in Figure 4.2.

FIG. 4.2
By using the Add Item dialog box, you can add site diagrams, Web pages, Active Server Pages, and style sheets.

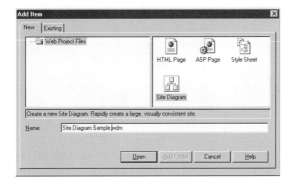

2. From the Web Project Files folder, select Site Diagram.
3. Enter a name for your new site diagram in the <u>N</u>ame text box. Site diagrams have the extension .WDM.
4. Click the <u>O</u>pen button. The new site diagram is created and opened, leaving you with a starting diagram like the one shown in Figure 4.3.

Adding and Removing Pages in the Diagram

Without pages, your site diagram is nothing but an empty sheet. To begin prototyping your site, you must begin to add pages to your diagram. Alternatively, you may want to remove some pages that were previously added to the diagram. Incorporating pages into the diagram is an effortless task. You can add both existing content plus create new files to be incorporated into your site. You can use the following three features to add pages to your diagram:

- The Site Diagram toolbar
- The Project Explorer
- The Context menu

FIG. 4.3

Your new site diagram is like an empty slate ready for you to begin prototyping.

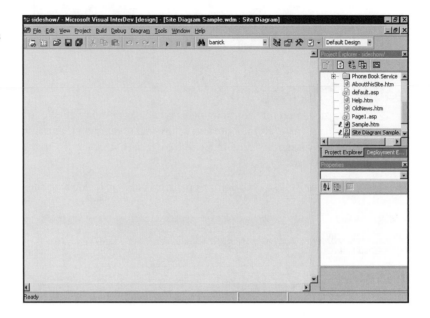

 Throughout this section, you will see references to adding "pages" to or removing them from your site diagram. Other content files can just as easily be incorporated, even graphics. You can add any type of file or URL that you want linked to your navigational bars in place of a traditional page.

Adding Pages with the Site Diagram Toolbar   Using the Site Diagram toolbar, shown in Figure 4.4, is the most common method for adding new pages to the site diagram. The toolbar is also one of the two features that you can use to incorporate an external URL into your site diagram.

FIG. 4.4

You can use the Site Diagram toolbar to add, remove, and organize pages in your site diagram.

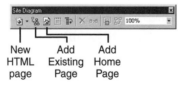

New HTML page   Add Existing Page   Add Home Page

The toolbar itself has three buttons that you can use to add to your diagram:

- *New HTML Page*. This drop-down button lets you create a new HTML Page or ASP Page to be added to your site diagram. Clicking this button creates a new addition to your site diagram for a page that will have to be edited later.

- *Add Existing Page*. If you already have content files that you want to add to the diagram, this button lets you select them. This button is also used to add an external URL to your site diagram.

■ *Add Home Page*. Clicking this button adds the start page for your Web application to the site diagram.

To add a new page to the site diagram, follow these steps:

1. Click the arrow to the right of the New HTML Page button. From the drop-down list, select the type of page you want to add: HTML or ASP.

2. Click the selected type of page. A new box is added to the diagram to represent your new page, as shown in Figure 4.5.

FIG. 4.5

A new page added to the diagram has a default title. You can rename the page immediately after it is added to the diagram.

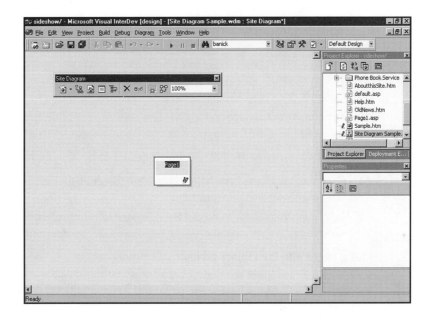

3. The title of your new page is selected. Enter a title for your new page, and press Enter.

4. To commit your change and add the new page to your project, save your diagram by choosing File, Save *<filename>*. The pencil icon disappears from your page's box.

To add an existing page or URL to the diagram, follow these steps:

1. Click the Add Existing Page button on the Site Diagram toolbar. The Choose URL dialog box, shown in Figure 4.6, appears.

2. From the Projects tree, select the folder that contains the files in your project. If you are adding an external URL, skip to step 5.

3. From the Contents of Folder list, select the page you want to add to your diagram, and skip to step 5.

4. If you are referencing a URL outside your project, enter the complete URL in the URL text box.

Part

I

Ch

4

FIG. 4.6

By using the Choose URL dialog box, you can add both existing pages in your project and URLs outside it to the site diagram.

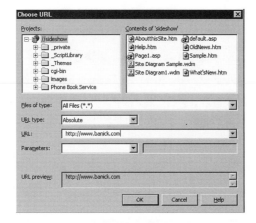

5. Click OK. Your new addition to the site diagram then appears.

6. To commit your change and add the new page to your project, save your diagram by choosing File, Save <filename>. The pencil icon disappears from your page's box.

To add your start page to the diagram, follow these steps:

1. Click the Add Home Page button on the Site Diagram toolbar. Your Web application's start page is added to the diagram.

2. To commit your change and add the new page to your project, save your diagram by choosing File, Save <filename>. The pencil icon disappears from your page's box.

Adding Pages with the Project Explorer   Incorporating existing pages into the site diagram is easily accomplished using the Project Explorer. You can add pages to the site diagram simply by dragging and dropping them from the Project Explorer into the site diagram itself. This procedure can be done with any page in your project; however, you cannot add external URLs through this method.

Adding Pages with the Context Menu or Menu Bar   Right-clicking the site diagram opens the predictable Windows context menu. From the context menu, you can choose to add new or existing files to your site diagram. The methodology is identical to that of the Site Diagram toolbar, except that you are using the context menu as a shortcut. You can also incorporate new or existing pages by using the Diagram menu on the menu bar. Both menus provide you with the same options:

■ Create New HTML or ASP Page

■ Add Existing Page

■ Add Home Page

Removing Pages   Sometimes you may want to remove a page from your global navigation bars. To do so, you may want to remove the page from your site diagram. To remove a page, follow these steps:

1. Select the offending page from the site diagram.

2. Either click the Delete button on the Site Diagram toolbar, or right-click the page and choose Delete from the context menu. The Delete Pages dialog box appears, as shown in Figure 4.7.

FIG. 4.7

You should use the Delete Pages dialog box with caution. Don't delete pages unless you really want to.

3. To remove the page(s) only from the navigation elements of your site but still leave the files in the project, choose the Remove These Pages from All Navigation Bars radio button. Alternatively, to remove the page(s) from the Web project entirely, choose the Delete These Pages from the Web Project radio button.

4. Click OK to close the dialog box.

5. To commit your change and add the new page to your project, save your diagram by choosing File, Save <filename>. The pencil icon disappears from your page's box.

Establishing Relationships

The hierarchical relationship between items in your site diagram is based on links. These links may not be hyperlinks beyond those present in the global navigation bar. The best way to visualize the relationship between items in your site diagram is to picture the site diagram itself as a tree. At its root level are your core pages, which likely represent sections of your site. Those core sections are related to one another only through the global navigation bar, and are not necessarily directly linked. Content pages below each sectional page, however, are clearly linked by being branches in the tree. This tree analogy continues throughout the diagram: Pages branch off sections established by the pages before them. Pages that are visibly linked are part of the same branch, although they may be children rather than parents in the tree. Figure 4.8 demonstrates this relationship.

FIG. 4.8

All elements in the site diagram are typically interrelated through a "tree." This structure establishes relations of "parent items" and "child items" throughout your site.

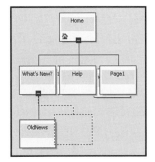

Relationships between pages are established by dragging the pages near to the bottom of another. When they are close to one another, a visible line appears to indicate the relationship to the other page. A line from one page to another denotes the first page as the "parent" to the child that is being dragged near it. To remove the relationship, drag the "child" page away from the parent to remove the linking line. In this fashion, pages can be removed as children of one parent and easily moved to another parent in the diagram.

N O T E   Remember that not all pages need to be children of another page. Pages can be left isolated and linked into the site through the global navigation bar. These pages themselves are "core" pages at the root level. ▪

Working with the Global Navigational Bar

The global navigation bar contains pages that are available throughout your site. Regardless of how "deep" into your site a visitor travels, he or she can always access the pages linked in the global navigation bar. This capability is useful for creating "core" pages or sections at the root level of your site. The following are sample pages that would be useful to have in the global navigation bar:

- A What's New page for your site's changes and updates
- A search page for locating information in your site
- Help references
- Sectional headings, such as Products, Services, and so on, as appropriate

Adding a page to the global navigation bar severs its links with other pages if it is a child page. To add a page to the global navigation bar, follow these steps:

1. Select the page you want to add to the global navigation bar from the site diagram.
2. Click the Add to Global Navigation Bar button in the Site Diagram toolbar. The Global Navigation Bar icon appears in the page's box.
3. To commit your change and add the new page to your project, save your diagram by choosing File, Save *<filename>*. The pencil icon disappears from your page's box.

To remove a page from the global navigation bar yet still keep it as part of your site diagram, follow these steps:

1. Select the page you want to remove from the global navigation bar from the site diagram.
2. Click the Remove from Global Navigation Bar button in the Site Diagram toolbar. The Global Navigation Bar icon disappears from the page's box.
3. To commit your change and add the new page to your project, save your diagram by choosing File, Save *<filename>*. The pencil icon disappears from your page's box.

▶ **See** "The Recordset NavBar," **p. 255**

Managing a Site Diagram

With your site diagram created, you are now free to pursue other interests and forget about your Web site's structure, right? Wrong. The process of maintaining and managing your Web site's structure is an ongoing effort that requires close monitoring of how your site is performing and how it is being used by your visitors. Use the regular feedback you receive from your visitors as a framework for future enhancements and improvements, and plan on implementing them. The site diagram is a tool that you can use on an ongoing basis for fine-tuning your site's structure and navigation. This tool is not limited to the inception of your site: You should probably be using the site diagram on a regular basis, as long as your Web site is operating.

Controlling the View

You can control how the site diagram appears when you are working on it, to suit your needs. The Site Diagram toolbar provides you with useful features that make working with site diagrams easier, particularly in a large site environment. The toolbar enables you to resize, rotate, and expand or collapse the site diagram as you need. You can control your view in the site diagram by using the following methods:

- From the Zoom drop-down list box on the Site Diagram toolbar, select the level of zoom that you want to use during your work. You have the option of a zoom from 50 percent of actual size to 200 percent of actual size, or choosing "to fit," which automatically sizes your entire diagram to fit in the current window.

- Rotate your site diagram by clicking the Rotate button on the Site Diagram toolbar. Clicking this button rotates your entire diagram 90 degrees to give you a better angle.

- Expand or collapse trees in your site diagram by selecting the parent page and clicking the Collapse/Expand button in the Site Diagram toolbar. This action lets you reduce trees out of view when you don't need them and to expand them into view when you do.

Part

I

Ch

4

Using the Site Designer as a Launch Pad

You can use the site diagram as a starting point for all your ongoing work and development. The site diagram provides a convenient means of creating new pages and quickly opening them for editing. You learned earlier how to create new HTML and ASP pages to add to your diagram. To edit any page in your site diagram, follow these steps:

1. Right-click the selected page in the site diagram.

2. To open a page for editing, choose Open. This action opens the selected page in the Source Editor for changes.

3. To view the selected page in your Web browser, choose View in Browser from the context menu. This action opens the selected page so that you can view it as your users would, in a Web browser.

Maintaining Site Integrity with Link View

The chore of maintaining links within a Web site can cause enough strain to make even the most experienced Web developer wish to become a shut-in. Visual InterDev thankfully provides a useful facility for maintaining the integrity of your site's links. This feature, called Link View, is used to display all links within your site to internal or external resources. Broken links can easily be identified and repaired. Figure 4.9 shows the Visual InterDev Link View in action.

FIG. 4.9
Viewing links for a resource gives you a clear indication of the place where your resource is linked to and linked from.

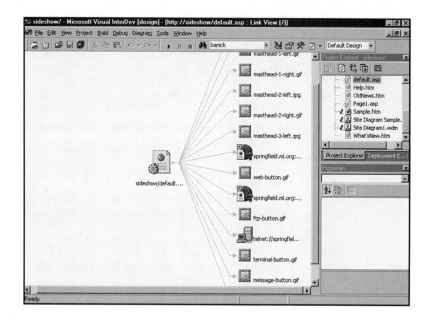

Viewing Links for an Item

To view the links for an item, locate it in the Project Explorer. Right-click the item, and choose View Links from the context menu. A Link View diagram appears, such as the one shown in Figure 4.9. This diagram represents the links from your resource. You can tailor this view using the Link View toolbar, shown in Figure 4.10.

This toolbar lets you control the Link View diagram. The options available to you in this toolbar, from left to right, are as follows:

- *Expand Links.* Much like the site diagram, links in the Link View diagram can be expanded or collapsed to constrain the space they occupy.

- *Verify.* External links can be verified to ensure that they are current and operational. Broken links are identified in the diagram by being "broken" and in red.

- *Change Diagram Layout.* The traditional Link View diagram displays links in an orderly "tree." You can choose to view the diagram in a different view, representing a circle with all links radiating out of the original page. The alternate view is shown in Figure 4.11.

FIG. 4.10

The Link View toolbar lets you establish filters for your view, the layout of the diagram, and the display of incoming or outgoing links.

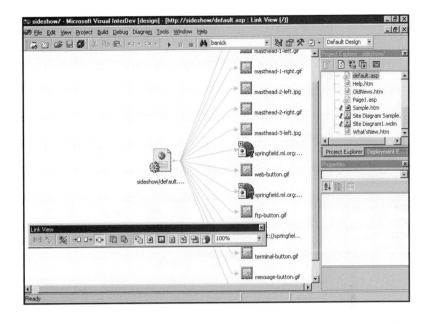

FIG. 4.11

The alternate Link View diagram layout offers a different perspective. This layout may be more convenient with densely packed diagrams.

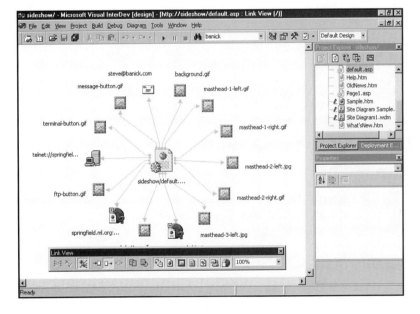

- *Show In Links*. This option displays the links *to* the selected resource from within your project.
- *Show Out Links*. This option displays the links *from* the selected resource. It is the default.
- *Show In and Out Links*. This option displays both the links *to* the selected resource from within your project and the links *from* the selected resource.

As with the Site Diagram toolbar, the Link View toolbar provides you with the means to control the zoom level of the diagram. You may need to minimize the zoom or select To Fit so that your entire diagram occupies the visible workspace.

Filtering Links

In addition to the buttons listed in the preceding section, the Link View toolbar also contains several buttons that are used to "filter" the links to or from your resource. Link View offers you several different types of links to view:

- *Repeated Links*. Links that are used more than once in the selected resource.
- *Links Inside Pages*. Many pages that refer to the same resource and can be viewed or filtered from view.
- *HTML Pages*. Links to other HTML/ASP pages within your project.
- *Multimedia Files*. Links to multimedia (images, sound, video) files within your project.
- *Documents*. Documents, other than HTML pages, that are referenced within your project.
- *Executable Files*. Links to CGI or server-side programs.
- *Other Protocols*. Links to other network protocols, such as mailto:, telnet, news, and so forth.
- *External Links*. Links to resources outside your project.

You can use the Link View toolbar to select what types of links you want to display. The Show All button selects all links to be displayed. If you want to selectively display only certain types of links, click the Show All button to deselect it and then select the appropriate link types from the toolbar. The Link View diagram instantly refreshes to display the types of links you have selected, if any are present.

Verifying External Links

Links to external resources from your Web application are at the mercy of those sites. If a change occurs on those sites to make the referenced URL unusable, you are left with a dead link that will confuse or frustrate your users. You can use Visual InterDev's Link View to verify the status of an external link by following these steps:

1. Right-click the external link in the Link View diagram.
2. Choose Verify from the context menu to force Visual InterDev to check the status of the hyperlink.

If the link is invalid and broken, the link is marked in red and noted with a "broken" icon. However, if the link is valid and functional, Visual InterDev happily leaves the diagram as it was.

N O T E You can use the Verify Link feature to check on the status of **http://** and **ftp://** URL references only. You must have an active network connection to verify links outside your Web site and to other sites on the Internet or your intranet. ■

Repairing Links

As mentioned earlier, broken links in the Link View are displayed with a red line and a "broken" icon, as shown in Figure 4.12. Using this visual clue, you can quickly determine which pages and links you need to repair using the Source or Design Editor. If you locate a broken link in your diagram, double-click the page that contains the link. This action opens the page in the Design Editor with the offending link highlighted so that you can quickly correct the broken link.

FIG. 4.12
A broken link in the Link View diagram is distinctly red and easily identified by its "broken" icon.

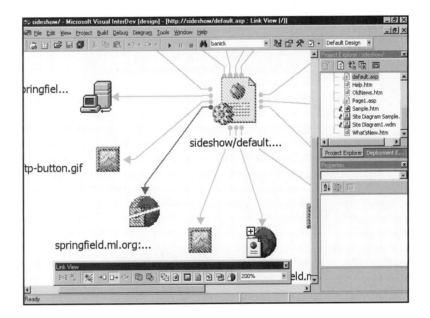

Part

I

Ch

4

T I P   Before you repair any broken links, you should always rebuild the links index for your Web site on the Web server itself. To do so, right-click your Web application project in the Project Explorer, and choose Recalculate Links from the context menu. Choosing this option forces the Web server to reexamine all links within your site. After you recalculate the links, refresh the Link View diagram by right-clicking it and choosing Refresh.

Using this quick shortcut, you can easily repair any broken links within your Web project. Make sure that you regularly check your Web site's links to ensure that no changes either internal to your Web site or external to the site have resulted in a broken link.

From Here...

The Site Designer and Link View features are powerful tools for creating a coherent and well organized Web site. For more information on organizing your Web site, look at these chapters:

- Chapter 25, "Designing and Organizing Web Sites."
- Chapter 27, "Increasing Site Performance."

Active Scripting for Web Sites

5 Active Scripting Overview   99

6 Client-Side Scripting   127

7 Server-Side Scripting   145

8 Script Debugging with Visual InterDev 6   167

9 Creating Pages with Dynamic HTML   189

CHAPTER 5

Active Scripting Overview

In this chapter

Introduction to Active Scripting for Web Sites   **100**

Scripting Languages Versus Programming Languages   **100**

Client- and Server-Side Scripting   **101**

Data Types and Variables   **102**

VBScript Functions and JScript Objects   **106**

The Browser Object Model   **114**

Adding Script to Pages   **119**

Using the Script Outline and Script Builder   **121**

Differences Between Client- and Server-Side Scripting   **124**

Which Should I Use: Client- or Server-Side Scripting?   **125**

Introduction to Active Scripting for Web Sites

In this chapter, the first in Part II, "Active Scripting for Web Sites," you learn the concepts and techniques behind the whole reason Microsoft built Visual InterDev in the first place: scripting. Visual InterDev 1.0 had very few visual components. It was intended primarily as a tool for Web site programmers to program server-side script using the Active Server Pages (ASP) engines. In the Editor window of version 1.0, there was only the equivalent of the InterDev 6.0's Source tab. There was no Design tab and certainly no Quick View tab.

Still, InterDev 1.0 was the best tool available for programming server-side script code. There was nothing to stop a Web designer from programming client-side script, but this wasn't the focus of InterDev 1.0. With the latest release, though, InterDev has become the best tool on the market for coding BOTH client- and server-side script (not to mention the other page design capabilities).

N O T E There are several names for JavaScript. Microsoft calls its version "JScript" to highlight that it is indeed different from Netscape's proprietary JavaScript language. Because this book is about a Microsoft tool and InterDev focuses on JScript, this chapter is all about JScript as opposed to JavaScript. The code listings show the <SCRIPT> tags as JavaScript, but Internet Explorer knows to use its JScript engine.

There's also what's called "ECMAScript," which is the Web's only official "standard" scripting language specification. Microsoft's JScript version 3.0 (and higher) fully supports this language specification. ▦

So, just what is script code and how can you utilize it? That's the topic of this chapter. You'll learn about the differences between client- and server-side script, get introduced to VBScript and JScript (the two primary scripting languages Microsoft supports), and learn a bit about what Dynamic HTML browsers make available to the client-side script code you write. Hopefully, by the time you finish this chapter, your appetite will be whetted enough that you'll pursue further information about Dynamic HTML and Active Server Page programming and check out *Dynamic HTML Unleashed* and *Active Server Pages Unleashed*, both published by Sams.

N O T E You can also check out Microsoft's Scripting site at **http://www.microsoft.com/scripting** for detailed documentation and samples of both VBScript and JScript. ▦

Scripting Languages Versus Programming Languages

What's the difference between a scripting language and a programming language? That's the question most people ask when they're first exposed to Active Scripting. We attempt to answer that question in this section.

First off, we need to determine if there indeed *is* a difference between scripting languages and programming languages. The answer to this question, as we'll demonstrate here, is Yes. And No.

First, the Yes answer. The biggest difference between scripting languages and programming languages comes in the application that *hosts*, or executes, the code you write. With scripting languages, the host is typically a Web browser or the Active Server Pages engine. With a programming language, the host is the operating system itself. This leads us to the second major difference between the two. Programming languages, because they are hosted by the operating system, typically produce a compiled executable. Scripting languages, on the other hand, are interpreted by their host and do not require a compile operation.

Another difference between programming and scripting languages is the depth of system resources that each has access to. Because programming languages are hosted by the operating system, they have access to all the resources provided by that operating system. Any Windows operating system (3.1, 95, 98, or NT) is what's known as an open system. This means that it has an application programming interface (API) that provides access to all of its internal functions. Such an API allows programs written for the Windows platform to have complete access to the entire operating system. Scripting languages, however, only have access to those resources provided by the host application. In the case where Internet Explorer 4.0 is the host, the scripting language has access to the object model provided by the browser (see the section "The Browser Object Model" later in this chapter). When you're writing script for Active Server Pages, the ASP engine provides a different object model which exposes pieces of the ASP environment to your script. Both of these hosts also provide you with the ability to invoke ActiveX components on the host system, but these are typically written using a programming language.

Having read the preceding paragraphs, you are probably wondering how programming languages and scripting languages are alike. They're alike in the fact that they share common syntax and constructs. Take the case of VBScript. This is a broad subset of the more common Visual Basic programming language. Any code that you write in VBScript can easily be ported to a Visual Basic project. The converse is not always true, but it is possible (and I've done it many times) to start with a Visual Basic project and move the code to a script host such as an Internet Explorer Web page.

Part
II

Ch
5

Client- and Server-Side Scripting

Now that you've seen a few of the similarities and differences between scripting and programming languages, it's time to look at a more important subject for the Web developer: the client-side versus server-side scripting. We'll hold off on a full-blown discussion until the end of the chapter; the basic difference is discussed now, as it's germane to the contents of the remainder of this chapter. In the two chapters following this one (Chapters 6, "Client-Side Scripting" and 7, "Server-Side Scripting") you'll learn in-depth how each "side" works and what each is capable of providing.

As you've probably guessed, the biggest difference between the two is their locations. Client-side script runs within the Web page that's delivered to the browser. The browser is the host for this code. Server-side script runs on the Web server itself and is hosted by the ASP engine. The Web browser never sees the contents of the server-side script, only its output.

The similarity between these two is that they can be the exact same script language. In other words, you can use VBScript or JScript (or any other Active Script engine) on both the client and the server. The code itself is vastly different, however, as the two hosts provide a different set of resources to the script.

When developing a Web site geared for ASP and a script-enabled browser such as IE4, most of the pages you create will probably contain a combination of client-side and server-side script, as demonstrated by the Source tab view shown in Figure 5.1.

FIG. 5.1
Your Web pages will probably contain both client-side and server-side script, as this page does.

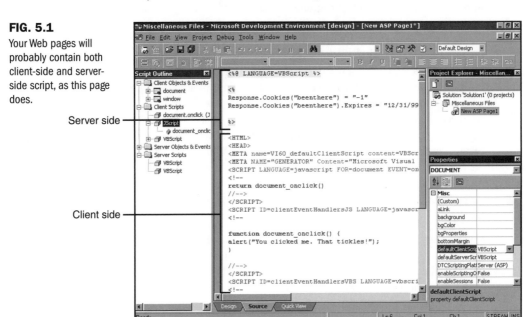

The following sections detail the basics of scripting and how to implement scripting, both client-side and server-side, with Visual InterDev.

Data Types and Variables

Just like programming languages, scripting languages provide the capability to use *variables*, which are slots in memory that are used to hold information for use at a later time. Every variable has a *data type* that identifies what kind of information it stores: strings, numbers, dates, objects, and so on.

VBScript and JScript for the most part treat variables identically, but there are a few differences. In this section, you learn the basics of creating and working with variables.

N O T E In the remainder of this chapter, we concentrate on VBScript and JScript, and our discussion will apply only to these two languages. Other scripting languages may, and probably do, introduce other considerations. ■

Data Types and Scripting

VBScript and JScript differ slightly in the handling of variable data types. In VBScript there is only one data type: variant. JScript, on the other hand, is what's known as a *loosely typed* language. You do not have to explicitly specify the data type for a variable but there are several supported data types.

First, let's look at the variant data type provided by VBScript. A variable in VBScript can hold any type of data you throw its way. The actual storage requirements of a variable, therefore, cannot be determined until data is actually assigned to the variable. The variant type has many *subtypes*, which more explicitly specify the type of data stored within the variable. The current subtype of a variable is not available until data has been assigned to the variable. The various subtypes are defined in Table 5.1.

Table 5.1   The VBScript Variant Subtypes

Subtype	Description
Boolean	Takes a value of either `true` or `false`. Uses very little storage space. Commonly used for conditional expressions.
Byte	A number that is in the range 0 to 255. Like `Boolean`, takes up very little space in memory.
Integer	A number in the range –32,768 to 32,768. Takes up the equivalent of 2 `Byte` variables in memory, but obviously stores much larger numbers.
Long	Taking up 4 bytes of memory, this subtype stores numbers in the range –2,147,483,648 to 2,147,483,648.
Single	Stores a single-precision, floating point number. Single precision refers to the number of bytes (and therefore digits) that are used to store the fractional portion of the number. `Single` variables can store negative numbers in the range –3.402823E38 to –1.401298E-45 and positive numbers in the range 1.401298E-45 to 3.402823E38.
Double	The `Double` subtype is useful for storing very precise numbers. It has a range of –1.79769313486232E308 to –4.94065645841247E-324 for negative numbers to 4.94065645841247E-324 to 1.79769313486232E308 for positive numbers.
Currency	Contains a number in the range of –922,337,203,685,477.5808 to 922,337,203,685,477.5807.
String	This subtype stores characters, up to approximately 2 billion of them in a single string.
Date	The `Date` subtype holds date values in the range of January 1, 100 to December 31, 9999.
Empty	This is the subtype assigned to variables that haven't been initialized to a value yet. If the variable is converted to a number, it will return `0`. If converted to a string, `""`.

continues

Part

II

Ch

5

Table 5.1 Continued	
Subtype	**Description**
Object	This subtype is for storing instances of an ActiveX component or an OLE Automation object.
Error	A special subtype used with error handling.

VBScript provides several functions for converting data of one subtype to another subtype, and for determining exactly what subtype a variable's data belongs to. These are described in the section "VBScript Functions and JScript Objects."

Now let's look at JScript's handling of data types. JScript provides three built-in data types but does not require that you specify a data type for a variable; nor are you required to use one of these types. The data types are

- string—A group of characters.
- number—Unlike VBScript's subtypes, JScript does not distinguish among the various kinds of numbers (integer, long, double, and so on).
- boolean—Just like VBScript: true or false.

Although these are the only data types supported by JScript, the language does support a number of built-in objects that provide additional capabilities. We cover those in the upcoming "VBScript Functions and JScript Objects" section.

Declaring and Naming Variables

The act of declaring a variable simply instructs the script host that you're going to use a variable. You are not required to declare variables before you use them, but it's generally a good idea. Likewise, there are some rules you must follow when naming your variables.

In VBScript, variables are declared using the keyword Dim, as in

```
Dim myVariable, AnotherVariable
```

Because VBScript has only a single data type, you cannot specify one when declaring variables (this is one major difference between VBScript and Visual Basic, where you can and, in most cases, should specify the data type for a variable). You can place as many variable declarations on a single line as you want, but it's generally best to use one line per variable. This makes your script code easier to read and allows you to document the usage of each variable on the same line as its declaration:

```
Dim sPassword        'string for the entered password
```

In JScript, variables are declared using the keyword var, as in

```
var sPassword = "";
```

Like VBScript, you do not specify a data type for the variable. But, unlike VBScript, you can assign an initial value to the variable. The initial value does not have to be a constant expression as shown above. You could use something akin to

```
function addemup(initialValue, addition) {
var x = initialValue;
var y = x + addition;
return y;
}
```

Both JScript and VBScript have similar rules for naming variables. You must start your variables with either a letter or (in JScript) an underscore. You can then use any combination of letters, digits, and underscores throughout the remainder of the name. Variable names are limited to 255 characters in length, but you should have no reason to test this limit! You can only declare a variable once in each routine.

Global Variables Both VBScript and JScript support *global variables* (also known simply as *globals*), which are variables that are visible at all times to all of the script code in the page. A variable that is declared outside of any subroutine is considered to be a global variable. For example, the variable iMaxRows in the following snippet is global to all of the routines:

```
<SCRIPT LANGUAGE="JavaScript">
var iMaxRows = 7;
function AddRow(sDefinition) {
    if (table1.rows.length < iMaxRows)
        table1.rows.add(sDefinition);
}
function InitTable() {
    var j;
    for (j = 1; j <= iMaxRows; j++)
        table1.rows.add("");
}
</SCRIPT>
```

As you can see, the variable iMaxRows is referenced by two different functions. Global variables are also visible beyond the <SCRIPT> section in which it is declared. Likewise, if you use a mixture of VBScript and JScript in your pages (and there are many good reasons to do so), the globals declared in one language are visible to routines coded in the other language. This comes in handy when you want to predefine the values for variables you want to use in VBScript. Simply declare them with the predefined value in a JScript <SCRIPT> section and then use them in your VBScript code.

Requiring Declaration As stated earlier, neither language requires you to declare your variables before using them. However, it is a generally accepted practice to do so. In VBScript, there's a statement that, when placed in your code, requires you to declare variables before they're used. This prevents many spelling mistakes that seem to be common among programmers. My particular handicap is dyslexic fingers; I'm always reversing characters in my coding. By requiring variable declaration, your code produces a runtime error whenever an undeclared variable is encountered.

Part

II

Ch

5

You use the `Option Explicit` statement to require variable declaration. The following snippet from a Web page produces a runtime error when loaded:

```
<HTML><HEAD><TITLE>Hello World!</TITLE>
<SCRIPT language="VBScript">
Option Explicit
Sub window_onload
    sTitle = document.title
    window.status = "You just came from " & sTilte
end sub
</SCRIPT></HEAD>
```

Not only does this produce a runtime error, but if you remove the `Option Explicit` and reload the page, your results resemble Figure 5.2. Notice that the status panel and the title don't match. Now look closely at the line of code where we assign to `window.status`. Had we used `Option Explicit` and declared the variable `sTitle`, we would have received a runtime error on this line informing us that we used an undeclared variable. We would have discovered our spelling mistake after a few moments of hard staring at the line of code.

FIG. 5.2
Bugs in code that are caused by spelling mistakes are masked by not requiring variable declaration!

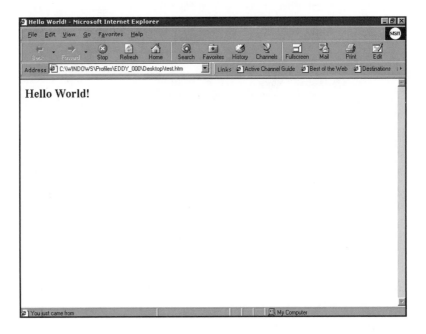

VBScript Functions and JScript Objects

Now that you've seen how VBScript and JScript handle variables, let's take a look at the real heart of the two languages. VBScript is a subset of Visual Basic and, as such, provides you with a vast array of Visual Basic's built-in functions. JScript, on the other hand, has only a few functions that are truly built-in functions. Instead, JScript provides several built-in objects, each having its own set of properties and methods that replace the built-in functions most programmers are used to using.

In fact, the number of functions available in VBScript makes it prohibitive to list them all here. You can download the complete documentation for both VBScript and JScript from Microsoft's Scripting site (**http://www.microsoft.com/scripting**). Instead, we'll focus our attention on the various categories of functions available and highlight a few of the more useful functions in each category. After we've looked at the VBScript functions, we'll go through the various JScript objects.

VBScript Functions

The functions provided by VBScript can be lumped into six general categories:

- Data type identification and conversion functions
- Date/time functions
- Math functions
- Object management functions
- String functions
- Script engine functions

Data Type and Conversion Functions   These functions are used to convert values from one data type to another. There are also functions for identifying the subtype of a variable or constant expression. Table 5.2 lists some of the more useful functions.

Table 5.2   VBScript Data Type and Conversion Functions

Function	Description
CBool, CByte, CDate, CDbl, CInt, CLng, CSng, CStr, CCur	These functions convert the value to the specified subtype.
VarType	Returns a number indicating the subtype of the variable. The values for each subtype are provided in Table 5.3.
IsArray, IsDate, IsEmpty, IsNull, IsNumeric	Returns a Boolean value indicating whether or not a variable meets the specified condition.
Asc	Returns the ANSI code for the first character in a string.
Chr	Returns the string whose ANSI code matches the number supplied as the parameter to the function.

Table 5.3   Values Returned by the VBScript *VarType* Function

Constant	Value	Description
VbEmpty	0	Empty (uninitialized)
vbNull	1	Null (no valid data)
vbInteger	2	Integer
vbLong	3	Long
vbSingle	4	Single
vbDouble	5	Double
vbCurrency	6	Currency
vbDate	7	Date
vbString	8	String
vbObject	9	Automation object
vbError	10	Error
vbBoolean	11	Boolean
vbVariant	12	Variant (used only with arrays of Variants)
vbDataObject	13	A data-access object
vbByte	17	Byte
vbArray	8192	Array

Date/Time Functions   These functions either return date/time values based on the system clock, or they manipulate date/time values. There are a plethora of these functions, enabling you to manipulate date/time data three ways to Sunday (no pun intended).

The Date function, for example, returns the current system date. The Now function returns the current date and time. A really handy function is the MonthName function, which returns a string containing the name of the specified month.

To manipulate date values, you can use the DateAdd function, which returns the date/time value computed by adding a specified interval to a specified date/time value. Similarly, the DateDiff function returns the number of intervals (such as day, month, year) that occur between the two provided dates.

Math Functions   There are a few mathematical functions provided by VBScript. These all correspond to the mathematical function of the same name. Table 5.4 lists the various mathematical functions.

Table 5.4   The VBScript Mathematical Functions

Function	Description
Atn	Returns the arctangent of a number
Cos	Returns the cosine of an angle
Exp	Returns e raised to a power
Log	Returns the natural logarithm of a number
Randomize	Initializes the random-number engine
Rnd	Returns a random number
Sin	Returns the sine of an angle
Sqr	Returns the square root of a number
Tan	Returns the tangent of an angle

Object Management Functions   VBScript provides two functions that are used to create and retrieve references to ActiveX components: CreateObject and GetObject. The CreateObject function creates a new instance of a new ActiveX component and returns a reference to it. GetObject returns a reference to an existing ActiveX component or OLE Automation object.

String Functions   There are many, many string functions that provide the means of manipulating character data. There are formatting functions such as FormatDateTime that return a character representation of a value using a specified format. There are functions such as Left and Right that allow you to retrieve specific pieces of a string. There are functions such as LCase and StrReverse that allow you to change the characters stored in a string. And finally, there are functions such as InStr that search a string for the occurrence of another string. For a complete listing of the string functions and their usage, see the VBScript documentation provided by Microsoft (you can download this from **http://www.microsoft.com/scripting**).

Part
II

Ch
5

Script Engine Functions   Finally, VBScript provides a few functions that tell you about the actual script engine executing your code. Many features have been added to VBScript since its first rendition but that doesn't mean that there aren't still machines out there that are running older versions of the script engine. Therefore, if you do not have control over the user's environment and want to be really nice to him, you should use the script engine functions listed in Table 5.5 to determine if the code you'd like to run is compatible with the script engine the user has available.

Table 5.5 The VBScript Script Engine Functions

Function	Description
ScriptEngine	Returns a string containing the major, minor, and build version numbers of the script engine.
ScriptEngineMajorVersion	Returns a number representing the major version of the engine.
ScriptEngineMinorVersion	Returns a number representing the minor version of the engine.
ScriptEngineBuildVersion	Returns a number representing the build version of the engine.

JScript's Built-In Functions

Compared to VBScript, JScript's list of built-in functions is pretty sparse. However, there are a few worth mentioning here.

The escape(*charstring*) function returns a new String object that is encoded to be read on all computers. For example, the space character is returned as %20. This function is useful when you need to display special HTML characters, such as the angle brackets < and > in your pages. There is a corresponding unescape(*charstring*) that takes an encoded string and returns the original characters based on the ASCII character set.

The eval(*codestring*) function evaluates the expression passed to it and returns the result. The *codestring* argument is a String object that contains valid JScript code. Using this function, you can dynamically generate code to execute. For example,

```
eval("var TodaysDate = new Date();");
```

returns a Date object containing today's date.

JScript also has two data type functions, isNaN and typeOf. The isNaN function takes a value parameter and returns a Boolean indicating whether or not it is a legal number. The typeOf function returns a string representing the data type of the object passed to it.

JScript Objects

JScript provides a suite of built-in objects that can be used as typed variables (that is, variables that have a data type). Each object has its own set of properties and methods that your script code can access and utilize. This section describes the major objects and provides brief examples of each of them.

The *ActiveXObject* Object This object is used to enable and return a reference to an Automation object. There are no properties or methods for this object, just a way to initialize a new instance of one:

```
var objMyObject = new ActiveXObject(class);
```

where *class* is a string in the form *server.class*. The *server* portion is the application providing the object and the *class* portion is the type or class to create. For example, to create a new Excel spreadsheet object you would use

```
var NewSheet = new ActiveXObject("Excel.Sheet");
```

After you have a reference to an Automation object, you simply invoke its methods or manipulate its properties using syntax such as

```
NewSheet.ActiveSheet.Cells(1,3).Value = "Hello Excel!";
NewSheet.Application.Visible = true;
```

The *Array* Object   The Array object is the mechanism for creating and working with arrays in JScript. There are a few methods that make working with arrays a breeze.

To create a new array, you can use any of the following:

```
arrEmpty = new Array();          //create an empty array
arrStuff = new Array(99);        //create an array with 99 elements
//create an array and fill it with data:
arrFilled = new Array("foo", "bar", "WWW", "FTP");
```

To access the elements of an array, you use

```
arrFilled[2] = "www";
```

Arrays in JScript are zero-based, meaning that the first element in an array is indexed with 0. Arrays have a length property that returns the number of elements in the array. You can also change the size of the array by setting this property to the new size. For example, to add an element to the array, use

```
arrFilled.length = arrFilled.length + 1;
```

Finally, there are five methods provided by the Array object:

- concat(*array2*) returns a concatenation of the original Array object with the *array2* parameter, which is another Array object. The elements in *array2* are added to the end of the original array.

- join([*separator*]) returns a String containing each element of the array. If the optional *separator* parameter is provided, the elements are separated by the character provided.

- reverse() reverses the order of the elements in the array. In other words, if an array has five elements, after the reverse() method is invoked, the value in element 0 will be found in element 4, and vice versa.

- slice(*start*, [*end*]) returns an Array object that contains the elements of the original array that are between *start* and the optional *end* parameter. If *end* is not provided, the last element of the array is used.

- sort([*functionname*]) sorts an array's elements. If *functionname* is provided, it must be the name of a valid JScript function. This function is provided two elements from the array to compare. It should return a negative number if its first argument is less than the second, zero if the two arguments are equal, and a positive number if the first argument

Part

II

Ch

5

is greater than the second. If *functionname* is not provided, the array is sorted ascending based on the ASCI character order.

The *Boolean* Object The `Boolean` object is a simple object that stores Boolean data. To create a new `Boolean`, use

```
var bValue = new Boolean([value]);
```

If *value* is `0`, `null`, an empty string, or is not provided, `bValue` evaluates to `false`. Any other value provided (including the string `"false"`) causes `bValue` to evaluate to `True`.

This object provides two methods. The `toString()` method returns a string representation of the current value (`"true"` or `"false"`). To use the `Boolean` object in calculations, use the `valueOf()` method, which returns a numeric value representing the current value of the object.

The *Date* Object The `Date` object is the equivalent of VBScript's `Date` subtype, but has methods to replace the date/time functions provided by VBScript. We won't list all of these methods here. You should refer to the JScript reference available at Microsoft's Scripting site or in the Internet Client SDK.

To create a new `Date` object, use any of the following:

```
var newDate = new Date();
var newDate = new Date([dateVal]);
var newDate = new Date(year,month,date[,hours[,minutes[,seconds[,ms]]]])
```

The first example returns the current date/time into `newDate`.

In the second example, the *dateval* parameter, if numeric, is used as the number of milliseconds that have elapsed since January 1, 1970. The date/time that represents the date and time that you'd calculate if you added this value to midnight on January 1, 1970 is the value that is returned. If the parameter is a string, it is parsed to retrieve the date/time it represents.

In the third example, the date/time represented by the various parameters is returned.

One of the big differences between the `Date` object and the VBScript built-in date/time functions is that the `Date` object provides methods for dealing with date/time values in GMT (Greenwich Mean Time) format. There is `toGMTString()`, which converts the value in the `Date` object from local time to GMT and `toLocaleString()`, which performs the opposite conversion (from GMT to local time).

The *Math* Object The `Math` object provides basic mathematical functions and constants. Most are replacements of the VBScript built-in mathematical functions, but again there are a few additions. For a complete listing of the available properties (which are the constants) and methods of this object, refer to the JScript Language Reference.

The *Number* Object The `Number` object provides a way to work with numeric values. There are several properties which, like the `Math` object, are constants. Like the `Boolean` object, this object has only two methods: `toString` and `valueOf`. The `toString` function takes an optional parameter that allows you to specify the base to use when returning the string. If not provided, base-10 is used.

The *String* Object   The `String` object is used for manipulating string values. It has a single property, length, which, surprisingly enough, returns the number of characters contained in the string. The methods provided by the `String` object are used to manipulate the string or search for characters within the string.

There is a series of methods that returns the string enclosed in HTML tags. The `bold()` method, for example, returns the original string enclosed in `<B>` and `</B>` tags. These methods come in handy when building HTML on-the-fly.

To search a string for the first occurrence of another string, use the `indexOf` method. This method takes the string to find as a required parameter and returns the index of the first occurrence of this string. An optional second numeric parameter specifies the place to start looking in the string. For example, when the following code is executed

```
var myString = String("Hello World!");
var x = myString.indexOf("o");
var y = myString.indexOf("o", x + 1);
```

the variable x evaluates to 4 and the value y to 7. The first character of the string is at index 0.

Again, the list of methods is long. See the JScript Language Reference for the complete details.

Creating Your Own Functions

Now that we've looked at the built-in features of both scripting languages, let's investigate ways to add our own functions. Like standard programming languages, VBScript and JScript provide a means for you to add your own subroutines to the code. You can then call these routines at will.

In VBScript, you can create either functions, which return a value, or subroutines, which execute code without returning a value. In JScript, everything is considered a function, but you aren't required to return a value nor are you required to use the return value when you call a function.

To create a subroutine in VBScript, use

```
Sub MySubroutine(param1, param2)
...
End Sub
```

And call this subroutine using something like

```
MySubroutine 12, 24
```

To create a function in VBScript:

```
Function AddEmUp(param1, param2)
   AddEmUp = param1 + param2
End Function
```

Notice that the return value is set by assigning to the function name. To call the function, use

```
xyz = AddEmUp(1,2)
```

Part

II

Ch

5

When executed, the value of xyz will be set to 3.

In JScript, functions are defined by using

```
Function AddEmUp(param1 + param2) {
    return param1 + param2;
}
```

Notice the use of the return statement to specify the return value for the function. This function is used in a way almost identical to the VBScript method:

```
xyz = AddEmUp(1,2);
```

The Browser Object Model

Now that you've learned the basics of scripting, let's take a look at the resources provided by Internet Explorer 4.0 when it is the host for your script code. Note that Netscape's 4.0 browser differs significantly in its object model from Internet Explorer. In general, this section will apply only to Internet Explorer 4.0.

Recall that a scripting language uses some other program as its host and has access only to the resources that are provided by the host. There are many available hosts for your script code, including the Windows Shell Host, Web browsers, and even third-party applications that have nothing to do with the Internet or the Web. My company, Pipestream Technologies, provides a host for script code in many areas of our sales-force automation software. For example, the end user can write a VBScript or JScript function that executes when a sale opportunity record is modified. In this case, our application is the script host and we provide the script code access to specific resources within our application.

Internet Explorer 4.0 works in a similar manner, providing your script code with access to the various pieces that make up the Web page currently being displayed to and manipulated by the user. This is done using the browser object model, which is the subject of this section. Complete coverage of the browser object model is beyond the scope of this chapter, so I refer you once again to the Internet Client SDK which contains the complete reference for the object model. At the time of this writing, the SDK can be downloaded from Microsoft's Web site at **http://www.microsoft.com/msdn/sdk/inetsdk/asetup/default.htm** or viewed online at **http://www.microsoft.com/workshop/default.htm**.

A High-Level Overview

The browser object model serves as the interface between script code and the Web browser. This includes not only the Web browser application but also the contents of the current page. Using the browser object model, you can retrieve and manipulate the properties of every element contained in an HTML page. This section provides an overview of the pieces of the object model. In the sections that follow, you get a glimpse of some of the properties, methods, and events these objects expose to your script code. In Chapter 9, "Creating Pages with Dynamic HTML," you learn even more about the browser object model and how it can be used.

Figure 5.3 provides a graphical view of the browser object model. As you can see, the `window` object is at the top of the hierarchy. It is also the default object in scripting code. This means that any properties or methods of the `window` object can be references without specifying `window.` explicitly. For example, instead of

```
window.alert( "Hello World!" );
```

you can simply use

```
alert( "Hello World!" );
```

FIG. 5.3

The browser object model exposed by Internet Explorer 4.

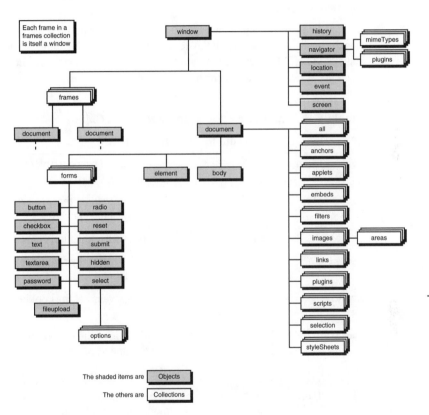

Of particular importance to scripting is the `document` object. This is the object that provides access to all of the elements on the page. You use the `all` collection (a property of the `document` object) to gain access to the elements.

Another important object in using scripting to modify a page's elements is the `style` object. This object, which is a property of nearly every HTML element you'll encounter on a page, provides access to an element's individual style properties. These include such properties as `backgroundColor`, `fontSize`, and positioning properties such as `left` and `top`.

Part
II

Ch
5

document Properties, Collections, and Methods

Because the document object is the real workhorse in the browser object model, let's take a look at some of the properties, collections, and methods it provides.

To access a property of the document object using script, you simply use either

```
window.document.property
```

or (because window is the default object),

```
document.property
```

Replace *property* with the name of the property you want to access, and you've got it! Table 5.6 lists the available properties of the document object. The Attribute Name column provides the name of the HTML attribute that corresponds to the property. You use this value in the <BODY> tag of the HTML page to specify a starting value for the corresponding property.

Table 5.6   The Properties of the *document* Object

Property	Attribute Name	Description
activeElement		Returns a reference to the element that currently has the focus on the page
alinkColor	ALINK	The color for links that are active (that is, are currently being clicked)
bgColor	BGCOLOR	The page's background color
body		Returns a read-only reference to the document's body object (defined by the <BODY> tag)
cookie		The string value of the cookie stored for this document
domain		The domain of the current document, used for cookies and security
fgColor	TEXT	The foreground color of the text in the document
lastModified		The date that the document's physical file was last modified (if available)
linkColor	LINK	The foreground color for unvisited links in the page
location		The URL of the document
parentWindow		Returns a reference to the window object that houses the document
readyState		Returns the current state of the document's download process
referrer		Returns the URL of the page that caused this document to be loaded

Property	Attribute Name	Description
selection		Returns a read-only reference to the document's `selection` object (which contains any text or elements that are selected, or highlighted, on the page)
title	TITLE	The document's title
url	URL	The URL for the current document
vLinkColor	VLINK	The color for links on the page that have already been visited

Table 5.7 describes the collections available to the `document` object.

Table 5.7 The Collections of the *document* Object

Collection	Description
all	Returns all the tags and elements within the document's `<BODY>` tag
anchors	All the anchors (links) in the document
applets	All the objects in the document, including intrinsic controls, images, applets, embeds, and other objects
embeds	All the `<EMBED>` elements
forms	All the `<FORM>` elements
frames	Returns all the frames within a `<FRAMESET>` tag
images	All the `<IMG>` tags
links	Collection of all the links and `<AREA>` tags
plugins	Another name for the `embeds` collection
scripts	Collection of all the `<SCRIPT>` elements defined in the page
styleSheets	Collection of all the style sheets corresponding to each `<LINK>` or `<STYLE>` element

Finally, the methods provided by the `document` object are listed in Table 5.8.

Table 5.8 The *document* Object's Methods

Method	Description
clear	Clears the contents of the document
close	Closes a document that has been opened using the `open` method and causes the browser to write out its contents

continues

Part
II

Ch
5

Table 5.8   Continued

Method	Description
createElement(*tag*)	Creates a new instance of an image or a new <OPTION> tag for an existing <SELECT> element
createStyleSheet	Creates a new style sheet
elementFromPoint(*x*,*y*)	Returns the element at the specified *x* and *y* coordinates
execCommand	Executes a command over the current document selection or range
open	Opens the document for writing
queryCommandEnabled	Returns Boolean based on whether or not the specified command is available
queryCommandIndeterm	Returns true if the specified command is in an indeterminate state
queryCommandState	Returns the current state of the command
queryCommandSupported	Indicates whether or not the specified command is supported
querCommandValue	Returns the value of the specified command
write	Writes text and HTML to the document
writeln	Writes the specified text or HTML to the document and then writes a carriage return

document Events

The document object supports a myriad of events that your script code can trap. To trap an event using VBScript, the following will do:

```
<SCRIPT LANGUAGE="VBScript">
sub document_onclick
    msgbox "You clicked me! That tickles..."
end sub
</SCRIPT>
```

To write your event handling code in JScript, you could use any of the following:

```
<SCRIPT LANGUAGE="JavaScript" FOR=document EVENT=onclick>
    alert("You clicked me! That tickles...");
</SCRIPT>
```

or:

```
<SCRIPT LANGUAGE="JavaScript">
function document.onclick() {
    alert("You clicked me! That tickles...");
}
</SCRIPT>
```

or:

```
<SCRIPT LANGUAGE="JavaScript">
function MyOnClick() {
    alert("You clicked me! That tickles...");
}
</SCRIPT>
<BODY onclick="MyOnClick()">
```

Table 5.9 lists the various events raised by the document object.

Table 5.9   The *document* Object's Events

Event	Description
onclick	Occurs when the mouse is clicked
ondblclick	Occurs when the mouse is double-clicked
ondragstart	Occurs when the user starts to drag an element
onerror	Fires when an error loading the document occurs
onhelp	Occurs when the user presses the F1 or Help key
onkeydown	Fires when any key is pressed
onkeypress	Occurs when a key is pressed and the character is available
onkeyup	Occurs when the pressed key has been released
onload	Fires when the document has completely loaded
onmousedown	Occurs when a mouse button is pressed
onmousemove	Occurs when the mouse moves
onmouseout	Occurs when the mouse leaves the area occupied by the document
onmouseover	Fires when the mouse moves into the area occupied by the element
onmouseup	Occurs when a mouse button is released
onreadstatechange	Fires when the readyState property changes

Part

II

Ch

5

Adding Script to Pages

We've covered a lot of ground in this chapter so far. And we haven't even touched InterDev this whole time. That's about to change drastically, however. You've learned the basics of Active Scripting, learned about the functions and objects provided by VBScript and JScript, and seen the resources to which the browser object model provides you access.

In this and the following section, you learn about the tools that InterDev provides for use in adding script code to your Web pages. There are tools for adding both client-side and server-side script.

If you want to follow along, fire up InterDev and open an existing or a new project. If you don't want to work in a project, these tools are just as applicable to individual ASP or HTML files.

Specifying the Default Language

Visual InterDev provides every page with a default scripting language property for both client-side and server-side script. The value of this property tells InterDev which scripting language to use when it inserts script code into the page.

You can change the value of these properties using either the Properties window or the document's Property Pages dialog box. Figure 5.4 shows the Property Pages dialog box for the document. To get to this dialog box, go to the Source tab, click inside the <HTML> tag (you can click elsewhere too, but this is the quickest way to make sure you get the correct property pages), right-click, and select Properties.

FIG. 5.4

The Property Pages dialog box for the document, showing the Default Scripting Language properties.

The Default Scripting Language properties are in the middle of the General tab. You can select VBScript or JScript from the drop-down lists, or you can enter any valid Active Script language for which you have an engine installed. You can set the properties separately for client and server script.

Manual Versus Script Block

Now that we know how to specify which language InterDev should use when we activate its script tools, let's learn about the available tools. The simplest and most generic of these tools is the Script Block.

While on the Source tab, you can easily insert a script block at any place in the current file. Simply put the cursor at the spot where you want to insert the script block and use the HTML, Script Block, Client or the HTML, Script Block, Server menu items. Figure 5.5 shows the results of using each of these menu items on a new ASP file. Notice that the server-side script specifies the RUNAT element of the <SCRIPT> tag. Also, the blocks have used the default scripting languages we specified (or left alone) on the document's property page.

FIG. 5.5
Script blocks inserted with the Script Block menu items.

Using the Script Outline and Script Builder

Script Block provides a quick way to insert generic script sections into the current file. However, InterDev's tools go way beyond this simple capability. The Script Outline is one of the secondary windows available in Visual InterDev's design environment. If you don't see a Script Outline tab like the one in Figure 5.5, use the View, Other Windows, Script Outline menu item or press Ctrl+Alt+S.

The Script Outline is only available when you're on the editor window's Source tab. If you're not on the Source tab, the Script Outline simply shows a label informing you that it only operates when you're on the Source tab.

This section covers some of the details and features of the Script Outline, so if you want to follow along you should have InterDev running and a new ASP file open.

Building Script with the Script Builder

One of the most useful features of the Script Outline is the Script Builder. You won't find a Script Builder menu item anywhere, but it's there nonetheless. The Script Builder allows you to easily build script code for the events that are supported by the objects contained in the current page.

Part
II

Ch
5

To see how to use the Script Builder, move to the Source tab of any ASP or HTML file, activate the Script Outline, and expand the Client Objects & Events branch. You'll see an entry for the document object, the window object, and any other elements for which you have provided values for the id property (you won't be able to capture the events of a specific element if you haven't given it an id).

Expand the branch for the document object and you'll see entries in the tree for each of the events supported by the document object. To create a script section for a particular event, simply double-click the event name in the tree. InterDev inserts a stub of the procedure for handling the event. You simply enter the specific script code within the bounds of this stub.

Figure 5.6 shows what happens when you double-click the onclick event for the document object. Notice that the script language chosen conforms to the value of the default client-side scripting language property.

FIG. 5.6

The results of using the Script Builder for the document object's onclick event.

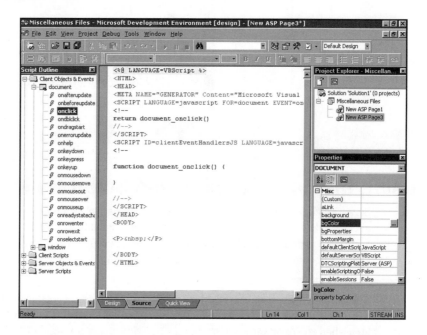

Now, use the Properties window to change the defaultClientScript property to VBScript. Notice that the entry in the Script Outline for the document object's onclick event changes to show you that it's a piece of JScript.

Crack open the window object's branch in the Script Outline and double-click the onload event. InterDev adds VBScript code to serve as the stub for the onload event handler. Figure 5.7 shows the results of this action.

FIG. 5.7
The results of using the Script Builder when VBScript is the default client script language.

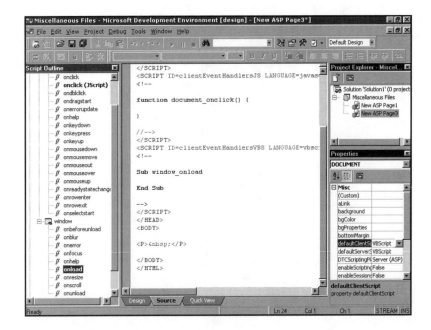

Navigating with the Outline

Now that you know how to use the Script Outline to add code to your page, let's look at another useful feature provided by the Script Outline. If you're following along, close the Client Objects & Events branch of the Script Outline. Now open the Client Scripts branch.

If you've followed all the steps from the previous section, you should see an entry labeled `document.onclick (JScript)`, an entry labeled `JScript`, and one labeled `VBScript`. Expand the branches for the JScript and VBScript entries. You'll see the entries for the `window_onload` and `document_onclick` routines.

The Script Outline keeps your script routines neatly organized and makes it easy to locate the script code on your pages. To view the code for a particular routine, simply double-click its entry in the outline and InterDev places the cursor into that routine. For example, double-click the `document_onclick (JScript)` entry and your screen should resemble Figure 5.8.

Synchronizing the Outline and the Page

Now let's go in the opposite direction. Close the branch that contains the Client Scripts. Click in the editor window and move the cursor to the line that reads

```
function document_onload() {
```

Right-click over the current cursor position and select the Sync Script Outline item (or use the View, Sync Script Outline menu item). InterDev responds by expanding the Client Scripts branch and highlighting the `document_onclick` entry in the Script Outline.

Part
II

Ch
5

FIG. 5.8

Using the Script Outline to locate the actual code for a scripted event.

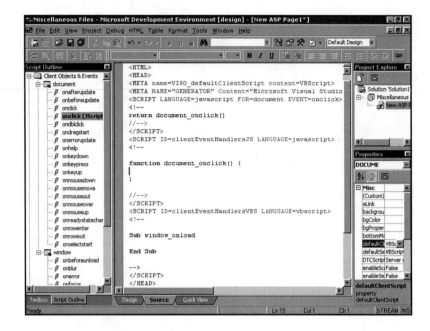

> **NOTE** The same techniques described in the preceding apply to any server-side script you might have in your files as well. ■

Differences Between Client- and Server-Side Scripting

Now that you've seen a lot of what can be accomplished using script code, let's return to the debate over whether you should use client-side or server-side scripting. This section details some of the advantages and disadvantages of both "sides" of the argument. The final section of this chapter answers, once and for all, this age-old question.

Advantages and Disadvantages of Client-Side Scripting

Let's take a quick look at the advantages and disadvantages of client-side script.

Advantages:

- Less load on your server. Data validation can be performed on the client side.
- Allows for greater interactivity with the Web page in-place.
- Does not require additional download time required round-trip to the server.
- You can do things that are pretty much impossible with server-side script, such as show and hide sections of the page without reloading the entire page.

Disadvantages:

- Code is exposed to the user (using the View Source menu item of the Web browser).
- Relies on the browser's support of both the script engine and the browser object model.

Advantages and Disadvantages of Server-Side Scripting

Now let's take a look at the advantages and disadvantages of server-side script.

Advantages:

- You can leverage the robust resources of a central, high-powered machine.
- You can create a browser-independent site because all script code is executed on the Web server machine.
- You can do things that just aren't possible with client-side script, such as maintain and display the way multiple users are currently utilizing the Web site.

Disadvantages:

- Relies on a Web server that supports server-side scripting.
- Poorly written script code can cause the server to lock up, requiring the server to be stopped and restarted.
- Requires resources on the server to be available for multiple users simultaneously.

Which Should I Use: Client- or Server-Side Scripting?

Now that you've worked with script code and seen some of the advantages and disadvantages of both client and server-side script, which should you use?

The answer is probably obvious to you by this time, especially if you've paid attention to the InterDev user interface. Just as the InterDev UI combines client- and server-side script as if they were inseparable, the answer to this great debate is that you should plan on using *both* client- and server-side script in your Web applications. Using a judicious balance of client- and server-side script allows you to use the advantages of each to your benefit and to cancel out their inherent disadvantages.

Sorry if this isn't the climactic answer you were expecting, but in my humble opinion, that's the simple answer to a complex question.

From Here...

In this chapter, you learned the concepts and techniques behind scripting languages, how to apply them to an object model such as the one provided by Internet Explorer 4.0, and how Visual InterDev makes working with scripting code a breeze.

For further information on scripting Internet Explorer and Dynamic HTML, check out *Dynamic HTML Unleashed* published by Sams. And, of course, don't forget to check out Microsoft's Scripting site at **http://www.microsoft.com/scripting**.

In the next chapter you'll learn about client-side scripting and how you can apply the material you've learned here to some real-world situations such as form validation.

CHAPTER 6

Client-Side Scripting

In this chapter

What Is Client-Side Scripting?   **128**

Client-Side Form Validation   **130**

Extending Functionality with ActiveX Controls   **138**

Scripting Browser Events   **139**

What Is Client-Side Scripting?

Microsoft's Visual Basic Scripting Edition (VBScript) is a powerful language and can be one of the most important tools for you to use to, as Microsoft puts it, "activate your Web site." It can be the glue that ties everything together within an HTML document—HTML forms, ActiveX controls, Java applets, and the Web browser itself. If you are an experienced VB developer, you'll feel right a home with VBScript. If you are new to programming, you'll find VBScript an excellent place to start. Client-side scripting with VBScript allows you to add intelligence to your Web pages with just a few lines of code.

Chapter 5, "Active Scripting Overview," provided an excellent overview of the differences between client-side and server-side scripting. In this chapter, you get more detail and a chance to build some scripts of your own. Before you roll up your sleeves and start coding, let's take a minute for a quick review. Client-side scripts are small programs that you embed in your HTML text. The small programs are sent to your client's Web browser, where they are compiled and executed. Because these scripts run entirely in the client's browser, they are called client-side scripts. As a Web developer, you can also create server-side scripts, which are executed on your Web server.

Microsoft Internet Explorer can execute client-side scripts that are written in JScript, Microsoft's open implementation of Netscape's JavaScript language, or VBScript. This chapter concentrates on building scripts using VBScript. Client-side scripts are included directly into HTML documents by being embedded in the HTML <SCRIPT>...</SCRIPT> container tags with a reference to the scripting language. For example:

```
<SCRIPT LANGUAGE="VBSCRIPT">
Your Code Here
</SCRIPT>
```

JavaScript can be referenced by the version of JavaScript:

```
<SCRIPT LANGUAGE="JavaScript 1.2">
Your Code Here
</SCRIPT>
```

And you can reference Microsoft JScript specifically (meaning that the script will not work in Netscape) by using:

```
<SCRIPT LANGUAGE="Jscript">
Your Code Here
</SCRIPT>
```

VBScript and JavaScript are both powerful scripting languages. VBScript is very similar in syntax to Visual Basic and Visual Basic for Applications, while JavaScript looks a lot like Java and C/C++. Neither is particularly hard to learn, however.

This chapter focuses on client-side scripting with VBScript. As you'll see, VBScript can be used to add a lot of interactivity and intelligence to your HTML documents. In combination with ActiveX controls, the possibilities for creating interactive, dynamic, and exciting Web pages are quite literally endless.

Benefits of VBScript

Chapter 5, "Active Scripting Overview," includes an extensive list of the advantages and disadvantages of VBScript. For you to determine where VBScript fits into your Web plans, it is necessary that you have a good understanding of VBScript's many advantages. So here is a quick review of some of the key benefits of VBScript:

- Move processing tasks from the server to the client
- Control ActiveX controls
- Control the browser's user interface
- Create dynamic Web forms
- Update your Web programming easily

▶ For more information about VBScript, **see** Chapter 5, "Active Scripting Overview," on **p. 99**

How Client-Side VBScripts Work

When a user visits your site, she does so by requesting an HTML document using her Web browser. This request is sent to your Web server, where an HTTP server loads the requested file and transmits it to the user.

It does not matter what HTTP software you have running on your Web server when you are serving pages that contain VBScript. This is because the VBScript source code contained in your document is interpreted and executed in the user's browser and looks like nothing more than a standard HTML file to your HTTP server.

N O T E If you want to program server-side scripting in VBScript, you must be using a Web server that is supports server-side VBScript, such as Internet Information Server 4.0's Active Server Pages. ■

As the HTML document containing a VBScript is received in a compatible browser, it begins translating and displaying the HTML code. When the browser encounters a `<SCRIPT>` tag, first it looks for the language parameter to determine the scripting language used. If the browser supports VBScript, it reads the ensuing text as a script until it encounters the `</SCRIPT>` tag. The VBScript code is either executed or, in the case of a function or subroutine, saved until it is called.

What VBScript Cannot Do

You can do a lot of processing tasks and Web automation with just a few lines of VBScript code. However, because of safety considerations, there are many things that VBScripts cannot do. Microsoft has not included in VBScript any commands that could be used to harm (or reconfigure) a user's machine. This means that all file I/O has been removed. You cannot read or write from any files, especially the user's Registry. This makes client-side scripting a good choice for data validation and simple programming tasks, but a poor choice for full-blown Web applications.

Part

II

Ch

6

Even though this is a nuisance, you don't need to worry too much about the limitations of VBScript, because you can easily use ActiveX controls to do any of the tasks that VBScript cannot do. Implementing ActiveX controls does require a few more steps (downloading, code signing, and so on) than plain VBScript, but you will find that the VBScript/ActiveX control combination provides you with the power and flexibility you need as a developer, while at the same time keeping your end users out of harm's way.

▶ **See** Part III, "Creating and Using ActiveX Controls," to get an idea of what it takes to create your own ActiveX controls, **p. 209**

Client-Side Form Validation

Your first task in implementing client-side scripting in your site is probably form validation. Many Web applications need to gather input from users. Traditionally, this data is entered in the browser and then transmitted to the server. The server checks the validity of the data and either stores the data on the server or sends back a message to the user requesting additional information or asking him to enter valid data.

Not only does this slow down your Web sever, but it creates unnecessary Web traffic as well. With just a few lines of code, you can validate much of this data on the client's machine and send it to the server only when it is complete.

To demonstrate how this works, first you'll design an HTML document using a traditional form using standard HTML, and then you'll enhance it with client-side scripting.

The HTML Document Form

Listing 6.1 is an example of a traditional HTML page used to gather input from a user. Let's take a closer look at a few of the elements of this page.

Listing 6.1   FORM.HTM   Form.htm—An HTML Document Using a Standard HTML Form

```
<HTML>
<HEAD>
<TITLE>Forms Verification</TITLE>
</HEAD>
<BODY BGCOLOR="#FFFFFF">
<FONT FACE="Verdana">
<H1>Credit Card Payment Information</H1>
<HR>
<B>All information must be entered before the form can be submitted...</B>
<HR>
<FORM NAME="MyForm">
<TABLE>
<TR><TD>First Name:</TD>
    <TD> </TD>
    <TD><INPUT TYPE=TEXT NAME="FirstName" SIZE=20 Value=""></TD></TR>
<TR><TD>Last Name:</TD>
```

```
    <TD> </TD>
    <TD><INPUT TYPE=TEXT NAME="LastName"   SIZE=20 Value=""></TD></TR>
<TR><TD COLSPAN=3><HR></TD></TR>
<TR><TD>Payment Date:</TD>
    <TD> </TD>
    <TD><INPUT TYPE=TEXT NAME="PayDate"   SIZE=10 Value=""></TD></TR>
<TR><TD>Payment Amount:</TD>
    <TD><B>$</B></TD>
    <TD><INPUT TYPE=TEXT NAME="Amount"   SIZE=10 Value=""></TD></TR>
<TR><TD>Credit Card Number:</TD>
    <TD> </TD>
    <TD><INPUT TYPE=TEXT NAME="CCNumber"   SIZE=20 Value=""></TD></TR>
<TR><TD>Expiration Date:</TD>
    <TD> </TD>
    <TD><INPUT TYPE=TEXT NAME="ExpDate"   SIZE=10 Value=""></TD></TR>
</TABLE>
<HR>
<INPUT TYPE=SUBMIT NAME="MySubmit" SIZE=20 Value="SUBMIT PAYMENT INFORMATION">
</FORM>
</FONT>
</BODY>
</HTML>
```

This HTML document, when viewed in Internet Explorer, appears as in Figure 6.1. The different elements of the HTML document, as shown in Listing 6.1, are as follows:

FIG. 6.1
Standard HTML Forms elements can be used to set up a document for receiving user input.

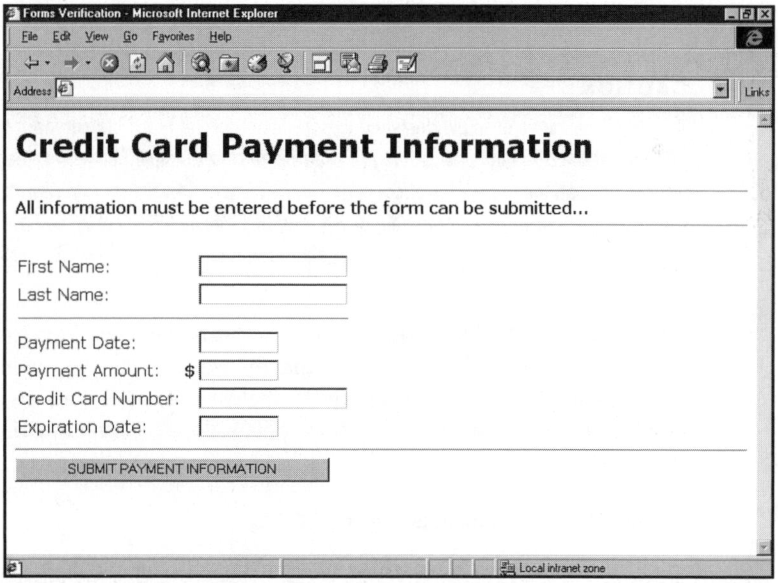

Credit Card Payment Information

All information must be entered before the form can be submitted...

First Name:
Last Name:

Payment Date:
Payment Amount: $
Credit Card Number:
Expiration Date:

SUBMIT PAYMENT INFORMATION

Part

II

Ch

6

■ `<FORM>...</FORM>` tags

These are the container tags that must surround the HTML Forms input elements. The `NAME="MyForm"` attribute is used to help identify the form from which that data came when it is being processed. You might notice that neither the `METHOD` nor `ACTION` attribute for the `<FORM>` tag has been sent. This is because this form is being used as an example. Normally, you would set `METHOD=POST` and set the `ACTION` to the appropriate URL of where on your Web server you want the data to be sent.

■ `<INPUT TYPE=TEXT>` tags

Each of these tags is used to receive one piece of information from the user. Each is named, using the `NAME` attribute, to allow the resulting data to be identified.

■ `<INPUT TYPE=SUBMIT>` tag

This tag puts the button on the form that is used to submit it. Like the other elements, it is named using the `NAME` attribute, and the `VALUE` attribute is used to customize the text appearing on the button.

Validating Forms Entries with VBScript

A form powered by VBScript looks pretty much the same as a form that isn't. However, in the background the page could include VBScript to perform a variety of client-side scripting functions to validate elements of the form before it is submitted to the Web server. Note that not all of the form validation can be done at the client—for this example, you would definitely need to validate the payment information at the server—but some of the simpler things definitely can be.

CAUTION

This is an illustrative example designed to show some of the types of user input that can be validated using VBScript at the client. It is not a realistic example of how to implement a Web-based payment system. If you want to do that, there are a lot of concerns with security and validation of payment information that are not addressed here. If you are interested, and depending on what Web server you are using, you can find this information in Que's *Special Edition Using Microsoft Internet Information Server 4*.

Using VBScript to Prefill Entries   The only apparent change from the unscripted to scripted version of this example in Figure 6.2 is that the payment date has been prefilled. Because an obvious default entry exists for this field—the current date—it makes sense to let VBScript do this and save the user a little bit of effort. This is done by executing the VBScript statement

```
Document.MyForm.PayDate.Value = Date()
```

when the HTML document is loaded.

Note that the user can change this entry, picking a payment date that is after the current date. You might not want to allow the user to select a payment date prior to the current date, however—if his payment is late, for instance, you don't want him to be able to predate his check. You can easily prevent this with VBScript, as shown in the following section.

Validating and Formatting Currency Entries   Listing 6.2 shows Check_Amount, a VBScript subroutine for validating and formatting an entry that is meant to be an amount of money. Primarily, this entry needs to be a numerical value, but it is a little more forgiving than that, as it will remove a leading dollar sign if the user has put one in. Then, after making sure that the value is numerical, the subroutine formats it as dollars and cents and writes it back out to the form field from which it came.

This subroutine is called by attaching the attribute onChange="Check_Amount(MyForm.Amount)" to the <INPUT> element for the appropriate entry. Recall from Listing 6.1 that the form was named MyForm and the payment amount entry named Amount. Check_Amount is then called whenever the entry is changed and the cursor is moved to another entry. (This method is used to call the validation functions for the other fields, as well.)

Listing 6.2   FORMSCR.HTM—VBScript Subroutine to Validate and Format Currency (excerpt)

```
Sub Check_Amount(Obj)
   Dim Temp
'
'  Get object value and remove leading $, if present
'
   Temp = Mid(Obj.VALUE,InStr(Obj.Value,"$")+1)
   If Not IsNumeric(Temp) Then
'
'     If not numeric (not a valid currency), blank out value
'
      Temp = ""
   Else
'
'     Format current as dollars and cents
'
      Temp = CStr(Fix(100*CDbl(Temp)))
      Temp = Left(Temp,Len(Temp)-2) & "." & Right(Temp,2)
   End If
'
'  Write value back into object
'
   Obj.Value = Temp
End Sub
```

If you are not familiar with VBScript, you might be confused a little by the Check_Amount subroutine, as it seems to treat the same value alternatively as a number or as a string. VBScript has only one type of data, known as Variant, which can be used to store any kind of data that VBScript recognizes. VBScript generally treats data as the subtype—such as integer, floating point, or string—appropriate to the operation. You can explicitly tell VBScript to treat the data as a specific subtype by using one of its conversion functions, such as the CStr and CDbl functions used in the Check_Amount subroutine.

As a final note, you can see that, for an entry that is incorrectly formatted, `Check_Amount` blanks the entry. How your VBScripts respond to incorrect entries is up to you: you can remove the incorrect entry, as is done in this example, leave it but set an error flag that prevents the form from being submitted until it is corrected, bring up an Alert box, or anything else you want.

Validating and Formatting Date Entries   Check_Date, shown in Listing 6.3, is very similar to Check_Amount, except that it validates a correct date entry rather than amount. Note that by explicitly calling the CDate function, even after the entry has been verified to be a valid date, Check_Date gets VBScript to complete the date. If just the month and day are entered, the current year is appended. If just the month and year are entered, a day (the first of the month) is added.

Listing 6.3   FORMSCR.HTM—VBScript Subroutine to Validate and Format Date (excerpt)

```
'
' This subroutine checks to see if the value of the object that is
' passed to it is a valid date, and then formats it.
'
Sub Check_Date(Obj)
   Dim Temp
   '
   ' Get object value
   '
   Temp = Obj.Value
   If Not IsDate(Temp) Then
   '
   '    If not a valid date, blank out value
   '
      Temp = ""
   Else
   '
   '    Format date according to local settings
   '
      Temp = CDate(Temp)
   End If
   '
   ' Write value back into object
   '
   Obj.Value = Temp
End Sub
```

Validating Numerical Entries   Even if it was possible, you probably would not want to verify a credit card number on the client, for reasons of account security. However, we can perform a little bit of validation on the numerical credit card number entry before the form data is sent along for final validation at the Web server. Check_Number, shown in Listing 6.4, makes sure that this entry is numerical and is a proper length for a credit card number (defined here as between 13 and 16 digits, though this can be adjusted, if necessary).

Listing 6.4 FORMSCR.HTM—VBScript Subroutine to Validate Numerical Entry (excerpt)

```
' This subroutine checks to see if the value of the object that is
' passed to it is a valid credit card number.

Sub Check_CCNumber(Obj)
    Dim Temp,minLength,maxLength

    ' Specify minimum and maximum length of valid credit card numbers

    minLength = 13
    maxLength = 16

    ' Get object value

    Temp = Obj.Value
    If Not IsNumeric(Temp) Then

        ' If not a valid number, blank out value

        Temp = ""
    Else
        TempLength = Len(CStr(Temp))
        If TempLength < minLength Or TempLength > maxLength Then

            ' If too short or too long, blank out value

            Temp = ""
        End If
    End If

    ' If value has changed, write back new value to object

    If Temp <> Obj.Value Then
        Obj.Value = Temp
    End If
End Sub
```

Validating Complete Forms with VBScript

After all the information has been entered into the form and each individual entry has been validated, there are still some form-level checks that you might want to do before the form is submitted. This can be done by attaching a VBScript function to the onSubmit event of the Submit button with onSubmit="Check_Form(MyForm)". If the function returns True, the form is submitted; if it returns False, it is not. Check_Form is shown in Listing 6.5.

**Listing 6.5   FORMSCR.HTM—VBScript Function to Validate Form
Prior to Submission (excerpt)**

```
'
' This function will verify that the current form is ready to
' be submitted before allowing it to be submitted.
'
Function Check_Form(Obj)
'
'  Verify that all fields have information in them
'
    If (Len(Obj.FirstName.Value) = 0) Or _
       (Len(Obj.LastName.Value)  = 0) Or _
       (Len(Obj.PayDate.Value)   = 0) Or _
       (Len(Obj.Amount.Value)    = 0) Or _
       (Len(Obj.CCNumber.Value)  = 0) Or _
       (Len(Obj.ExpDate.Value)   = 0) Then
       Alert "All fields must be filled with valid information!"
       Check_Form = False
       Exit Function
    End If
'
'  Verify that the payment date is on or after the current date
'
    If DateDiff("d",Obj.PayDate.Value,Date()) > 0 Then
       Alert "Payment date must be on or after current date!"
       Check_Form = False
       Exit Function
    End If
'
'  Verify that the payment date is on or before the card expiration date
'
    If DateDiff("d",Obj.PayDate.Value,Obj.ExpDate.Value) < 0 Then
       Alert "Payment date must be on or before card expiration date!"
       Check_Form = False
       Exit Function
    End If
'
'  Allow form to be submitted
'
    Alert "Submitting payment information..."
    Check_Form = True
End Function
```

Check_Form does three things. First, it verifies that information has been entered into each field
on the form. If not, an Alert box is given (see Figure 6.2) and the form is not submitted.

Even if the form is completely filled out and each of the entries has the correct type of data in
it, there might still be problems that you can catch at the client with VBScript. Check_Form also
checks for two types of invalid entries that can occur with either the payment or credit card
expiration date. It is incorrect if either the payment date is after the expiration date of the card
(see Figure 6.3), or the payment date is before the current date. In either of these cases, an
appropriate Alert box is displayed, as shown in Figure 6.3, and the form is not submitted.

FIG. 6.2

Client-side processing is ideal for catching incorrect entries, such as this incomplete form, prior to submission.

FIG. 6.3

Although this form looks properly filled out, note that the credit card has apparently expired.

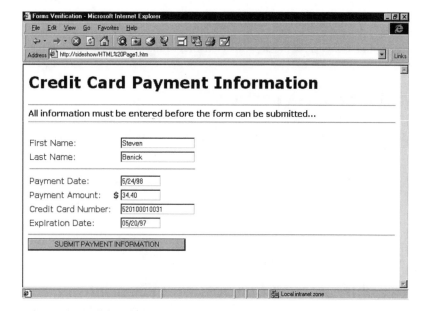

FIG. 6.4

You can save effort on your Web server by using scripting to catch simple errors, such as this one, at the client.

When all the entries in the form have been verified, it is then ready to be submitted to the Web server for further verification of the payment information. VBScript can also be used to put up an Alert box to let you know that your information is on its way (see Figure 6.5).

FIG. 6.5

When all of the entries are validated at the client as much as possible, they can be submitted to processing at the server.

Extending Functionality with ActiveX Controls

In addition to controlling and interacting with HTML Forms, VBScript is a great way to work with ActiveX controls within an HTML document. By themselves, each ActiveX control is an island of functionality. Some of them, such as Microsoft's Stock Ticker Control, are complete enough to be used effectively by themselves.

To be able truly to interact with the users and one another, as well as interact with other elements in the HTML document and Web browser environments, ActiveX controls need VBScript or another scripting language, such as JScript. These scripting languages are the glue that brings all of the separate elements within the Web browser together and allows them all to work together.

What Are ActiveX Controls?

ActiveX controls are typically small applications (though they can be any size, and some are huge) that can operate only within a compatible container application. Internet Explorer is one such application. Unlike VBScript or JavaScript (and Microsoft's JScript), which was designed with a limited capability to interact with the client machine (thus making it more secure for transmission over the Web), ActiveX controls, when installed, can do literally anything. Internet Explorer includes a variety of security settings that allow you to determine how much risk you are willing to live with when installing ActiveX controls on your machine.

ActiveX controls, their authoring, and use are covered in other parts of this book, particularly in Part III, "Creating and Using ActiveX Controls."

Controlling ActiveX Controls with VBScript

Just as HTML Forms expose properties and events that can be used by VBScript—such as the Value property and onChange event of the text boxes used in the FORMSCR.HTML example—ActiveX controls do the same. Each control has a list of properties, events, and methods that can be used by VBScript to customize how each control behaves within the Web browser (or other compatible application) environment.

Troubleshooting

I can't find any documentation on my ActiveX controls.

Although many people and companies are producing tons of ActiveX controls—some freeware, some commercial—these controls are not always well documented. This is particularly true of the ones that are freely available. The best way to find out the properties, events, and methods that are contained in just about any ActiveX control meant to be included in an HTML document is to load a document containing such a control into FrontPage 98 or Visual InterDev 6. When you open such a page, the scripting events associated with the control can be examined completely.

Scripting Browser Events

One of the more powerful aspects of client-side scripting is the managing of events within the browser. Visual InterDev 6 makes it very easy to create scripts that are executed when a certain condition or actions take place in the browser. In fact, this is one of the fundamental advantages of scripting inside of Visual InterDev using the Script Outline. As shown in Figure 6.6, the Script Outline displays all client-side objects and events as a node in the Script Outline tree. By default, two key objects are listed: document and window. These are the root level objects of the Web browser (Microsoft Internet Explorer). Each object has different methods or events tied to them that can be scripted. This allows you to create custom scripted code that takes place when an event or action takes place within the document or the window. As other objects (such as an ActiveX control) are added to the page, more objects become available for scripting with different events and methods.

FIG. 6.6
The Script Outline displays all the events tied to objects within the page.

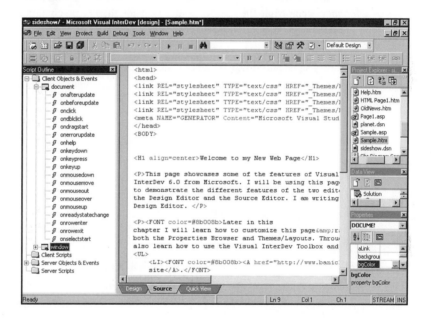

Document Events

In Internet Explorer, a Web page is a root-level object called document. The document has a number of different properties and methods attached to it that can be programmatically controlled. The Script Outline displays the standard events that are related to the document object. Each event can be scripted to provide actions to take place in that event.

NOTE Both Microsoft Internet Explorer and Netscape Navigator have their own Document Object Model. In some cases, these models overlap and provide you with similar (if not the same) events in both browsers. This section discusses Microsoft Internet Explorer; however, you may feel free to experiment with Netscape Navigator as well. ■

Part
II

Ch
6

The standard events for the document object are

- onafterupdate—Fires after a successful transfer of data from the object to the data provider (such as a form element). This takes place after the onbeforeupdate event. This event is dependent on a databound object that has had an onbeforeupdate event fired.

- onbeforeupdate—Fired before the transfer of data from the object to the data provider (such as a form element). This event fires when the object loses focus or the page attempts to unload when the value of the object has changed.

- onclick—Fires when the user presses and releases the left mouse button or when the user presses keys, such as Enter and Esc, in a form. If the user clicks the left mouse button, the onclick event for an object only occurs if the mouse pointer is over the object and both an onmousedown and an onmouseup event occur in order.

- ondblclick—Fired when the left mouse button is depressed and released twice in quick succession while the mouse pointer is inside the region contained by the object's boundaries.

- ondragstart—Fires when the user first starts to drag a selection or selected object.

- onerrorupdate—Fired when the onbeforeupdate event specified for the object has canceled the data transfer. This event is fired instead of the onafterupdate event. This event only fires when an onbeforeupdate event has fired.

- onhelp—Fires when the user presses F1 or the help key in the browser.

- onkeydown—Fires when the user presses a key. This event returns the keycode of the key that was pressed.

- onkeyup—Fires when the user releases a key. This event returns the keycode of the key that was pressed.

- onmousedown—Fires when the user presses a button on the mouse (or other pointing device). Mouse related events execute in the following order: onmousedown, onmouseup, onclick, ondblclick, and onmouseup.

- onmousemove—Fires when the user moves the mouse.

- onmouseup—Fires when the user releases the mouse button. Mouse related events execute in the following order: onmousedown, onmouseup, onclick, ondblclick, and onmouseup.

- onreadystatechange—Fired whenever the readyState for the object has changed. When the object changes to the loaded state, this event is fired before the firing of the loaded event.

- onrowenter—Fires in data-bound objects to indicate that the current row has changed and new data is available.

- onrowexit—Fires prior to a data source changing the current row. The object must be data bound and identifies itself as a data provider.

- onselectstart—Fired at the beginning of an object selection.

N O T E   Additional events for both the document and window objects (see below) might be defined in the Document Object Model (DOM). For more information on the Document Object Model that makes up Internet Explorer, you should refer to the DOM and Internet Client SDK located in the MSDN Library disc with Visual InterDev. Information on this model can also be found in Microsoft's Developer Network Online on the World Wide Web at **http://www.microsoft.com/msdn**.

Window Events

The browser window itself is also an object. This object, called window, has a number of standard events that can be scripted. These events occur regardless of what is happening within the document itself.

N O T E   As mentioned earlier, both Microsoft Internet Explorer and Netscape Navigator have their own Document Object Model. Some of the following Window events may work similarly in Netscape Navigator, however the information here is provided for use with Microsoft Internet Explorer.

The standard events in the Script Outline are

- onbeforeunload—Fires prior to the current document (page) being unloaded from the browser. By returning a string to this event, a dialog box is displayed and gives the user the option to stay on the current page. The returned string is displayed in a predefined area to provide the user with the reason. This event also fires on the document.open event and when a frameset is created.
- onblur—Fired when an object, such as a button or check box, loses the input focus. This event is also fired even when clicking another control or the background of the page, switching applications, or opening another window within the browser.
- onerror—Fires when a scripting error occurs in the document. This event is typically used for error handling.
- onfocus—Fires when an object or control receives focus from the mouse.
- onhelp—Fires when the user presses F1 or the help key in the browser.
- onload—Fires when the browser loads the given object. This event might be fired before the rest of a document is loaded, due the order in which the elements/objects are loaded. Scripts referencing this event should be defined before the element/object is loaded.
- onresize—Fires at the beginning of a resize operation.
- onscroll—Fires when the scroll box is repositioned.
- onunload—Fires immediately before the page is unloaded from the browser.

Scripting the Event

Creating the script for the event is straightforward, assuming you understand the scripting language. All script is developed in the Source Editor, using the Script Outline as a reference.

Part

II

Ch

6

Using the Script Outline, you can quickly create the shell of the script inside your Web page, ready for your development. In the following example, we will add a simple time stamp to the footer of an existing Web page. This time stamp will accurately display the time and date that the Web browser displayed the page.

To begin scripting the event, first we want to switch the default scripting language for the client to VBScript. Follow these steps:

1. Open an existing Web page and switch to the Source Editor.
2. In the Properties Browser, select Document from the drop-down list. This displays the properties for the current Web page document.
3. Locate the `defaultClientScript` property.
4. From the drop-down list, choose VBScript. A new <META> tag is added to your document to indicate your scripting preference change. This line appears as:

```
<META name=VI60_defaultClientScript content=VBScript>
```

5. Save your changes.

With the default scripting language changed for the Web browser, you are ready to create your scripted event. When you want to create a script for an event, the first thing you do is locate the client-side event by double-clicking on it from the Client Objects & Events node in the Script Outline. This creates the shell of the script in your document. To create your sample script, follow these steps:

1. While still in your open Web page, move to the bottom of your document before the <BODY> tag in the Source Editor.
2. Double-click on the `onload` event from the window object. The handler for client-side events is added to your Web page, including a subroutine for the `onload` event. The code should resemble this:

```
<SCRIPT ID=clientEventHandlersVBS LANGUAGE=vbscript>
<!--
Sub window_onload
End Sub
-->
</SCRIPT>
```

3. The `window_onload` subroutine is recognized by the Web browser as instructions to be carried out each time the document is loaded and refreshed. Enter the scripted code for our time stamp as follows:

```
document.write "<HR>"
document.write "<CENTER><H5>This document was displayed
➥ at: " & now & "</H5></CENTER>"
```

4. Save your changes by choosing File, Save <filename>....
5. Preview your page in a Web browser. A sample result is shown in Figure 6.7.

FIG. 6.7
The newly created time stamp is added to the bottom of the page. Each time this page is reloaded, the time stamp is updated on the client side.

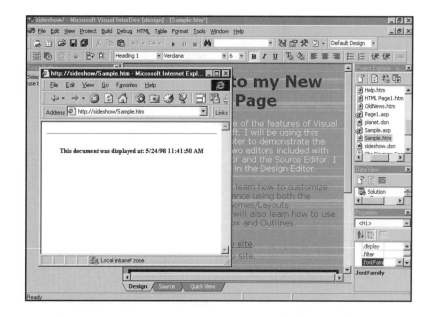

N O T E Client-side scripting becomes exponentially more powerful when using Dynamic HTML (DHTML) and Design Time Controls (DTCs). Refer to Chapters 9, "Creating Pages with Dynamic HTML" and 11, "Designing with Design-Time Controls" for more information. ■

From Here...

Adding client-side scripting to your Web applications is very much a necessity in creating truly interactive experiences for your users. Client-side scripting also is invaluable for adding logic to your Web site without falling back on your Web server and overburdening its resources. Closely tied to client-side scripting, however, is solid server-side scripting and careful use of client-side objects. These chapters offer more information and insight to activating your Web pages:

- Chapter 7, "Server-Side Scripting."
- Chapter 9, "Creating Pages with Dynamic HTML."
- Chapter 10, "Using ActiveX Controls."

Part
II

Ch
6

Server-Side Scripting

In this chapter

Introduction to Server-Side Scripting   **146**

Active Server Pages (ASP)   **146**

Active Server Pages: Built-in Objects   **149**

Server-Side Components   **152**

Introduction to Server-Side Scripting

In this new era of Web development, developers can use the benefit of server-side scripting such as the code, DLLs, and scripts that reside at the server which are consistent while browsers on the client are inconsistent. This means that the developer can be sure of what is on the server while the browser maybe a variety of Internet Explorer, Netscape Navigator, and so forth. Server-side scripting can consist of the following:

- Active Server Pages
- Active Server Built-in Objects
- Server Side Components

For the developer, server-side scripting allows the developer to use tools that reside on the server.

Active Server Pages (ASP)

Active Server Pages allow you, as the developer, to use server-side objects to deliver an enhanced Web experience. Server-side scripting allows you to unleash the power of components that reside on the server. Advertisements, database access, counters, file access, and browser capabilities are examples of server-side components that are accessible through Active Server Pages. You can access methods and properties to determine client browser properties to decide what type of page to deliver to the Web client. Say you want to have a corporate Web site that will reach as many types of browsers as possible and still give a rich experience to the Web client. Historically, you would have either created two or more Web sites for the different types of browsers or used straight HTML. Now, with Active Server Pages, you can have one page that determines the browser's capabilities.

Active Server Pages are Web pages that are preprocessed by the Web server before being sent to the client Web browser. Because these pages are preprocessed, the Web server has to support Active Server Pages. Internet Information Server (IIS) 3.0 and 4.0 as well as Personal WebServer 98 for Windows 95 or 98 support Active Server Pages. IIS 4.0 allows client- and server-side debugging in Visual InterDev 6.

Creating an Active Server Page

With Visual InterDev 6, creating ASP pages is a snap. Just follow these steps:

1. Create a new Web project.
2. Choose File, New File, as shown in Figure 7.1.
3. In the New File dialog box, shown in Figure 7.2, click the New tab, and then select Visual InterDev Folder on the left side. Next, click the ASP Page icon on the right.

FIG. 7.1
Creating an ASP page
using VI 6.

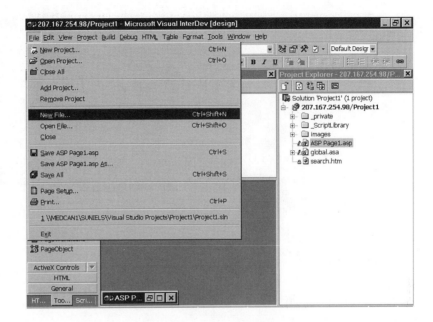

FIG. 7.2
Adding the ASP page to
the current project.

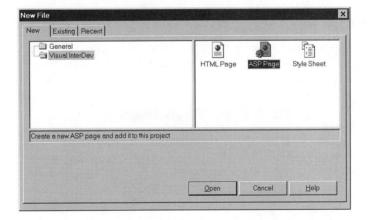

4. Click Open. Your screen should then look something like Figure 7.3.

Now you have created an ASP page. You won't do anything too exciting till you use the components that are available.

Part
II

Ch
7

FIG. 7.3
Blank ASP page in VI 6.

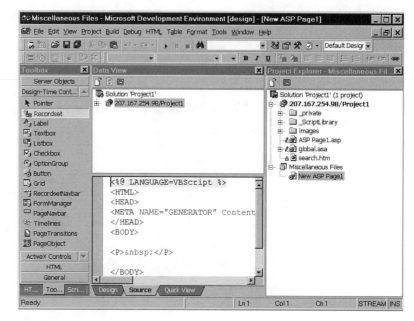

Setting ASP Page Properties

Now, as you can see, the Active Server Page is in design mode. You can easily set the ASP page properties. To do so, simply click the page in the body, right-click, and then select Properties from the context menu. The Property Pages dialog box then appears, as shown in Figure 7.4.

FIG. 7.4
Active Server Page
Property Pages. Here the
defaults for the ASP
page can be changed.

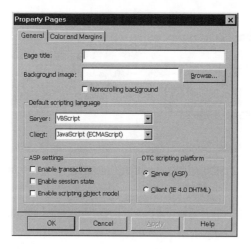

ASP Page Properties In the Property Pages dialog box, you can set the page title, the background, and the default scripting language to use on the client and Web server. You can use either JScript or VBScript. The ASP settings for transactions, sessions, object model, and the scripting platform also can be set here.

ASP Page Scripting   An ASP page script can run both on the client and on the Web server. How do you specify where the script is run? You can use the old-fashioned way of typing the code, but the quicker way is simply right-clicking the page, selecting Script Block from the context menu, as shown in Figure 7.5, and then deciding on the client or server. Then the editor puts the code there for you.

FIG. 7.5
Auto generation of Script Block for the developer to code at the server or the client.

Active Server Pages: Built-in Objects

The following built-in application objects are special because they are built into Active Server Pages and do not need to be created before you can use them in scripts:

- Application
- Request
- Response
- Server
- Session

Each of these five objects is discussed in greater detail starting with the Application object.

Application Object

The purpose of the Application object is to share data with other Web clients. An ASP-based application is defined as all the ASP files in a virtual directory and its subdirectories. Because the Application object can be shared by more than one user, Lock and Unlock methods ensure that multiple users do not try to alter a property simultaneously.

Syntax

Application.*method*

Methods   Lock, Unlock

Part
II

Ch

7

Events   Application_OnEnd, Application_OnStart

Scripts for the preceding events are declared in the GLOBAL.ASA file.

Request Object

The Request object retrieves the values that the client browser passes to the server during an HTTP request.

Syntax

Request[.*Collection*](*variable*)

Request.QueryString(*variable*)[(*index*)¦.Count]

where *variable* is the value being requested and *index* is an optional parameter for array variables.

Request.Form(*element*)[(*index*)¦.Count]

where *element* is the value in the form being requested and *index* is an optional parameter for array variables.

Request.ClientCertificate(*Key[SubField]*)

For more details on ClientCertificate browse the Net at **http://help.activeserverpages.com/iishelp/iis/htm/asp/intr8q5h.htm**.

Request.ServerVariables (*server environment variable*)

For more details on ServerVariables browse the Net at **http://help.activeserverpages.com/iishelp/iis/htm/asp/intr5vsj.htm**.

Request.Cookies(*cookie*)[(*key*)¦.*attribute*]

where *cookie* is the name of the cookie being retrieved. *Key* is an optional parameter for looking up subkeys.

Attribute is a parameter for the type of key.

For more information browse the Net at **http://help.activeserverpages.com/iishelp/iis/htm/asp/intr0z3o.htm**.

Collections   ClientCertificate, Cookies, Form, QueryString, ServerVariables

Remarks   If the specified variable is not in one of the preceding collections, the Request object returns EMPTY.

All variables can be accessed directly by calling Request(*variable*) without the collection name. In this case, the Web server searches the collections in the following order:

1. QueryString
2. Form

3. Cookies

4. ClientCertificate

5. ServerVariables

Response Object

You can use the Response object to send output to the client.

Syntax

Response.*collection¦property¦method*

Collection   Cookies

Properties   Buffer, ContentType, Expires, ExpiresAbsolute, Status

Methods   AddHeader, AppendToLogo, Binary Write, Clear, End, Flush, Write

Server Object

The Server object provides access to methods and properties on the server. Most of these methods and properties serve as utility functions.

Syntax

Server.*method*

Property   ScriptTimeout

Methods   CreateObject, HTMLEncode, MapPath, URLEncode

Session Object

You can use the Session object to store information needed for a particular user session. Variables stored in the Session object are not discarded when the user jumps between pages in the application; instead, these variables persist for the entire user session.

The Web server automatically creates a Session object when a user who does not already have a session requests a Web page from the application. The server destroys the Session object when the session expires or is abandoned.

N O T E   The Session state is maintained only for browsers that support cookies. ■

Part

II

Ch

7

Syntax

```
Session.property¦method
```

Properties   SessionID, Timeout

Method   Abandon

Remarks   You can store values in the Session object. Information stored in the Session object is available throughout the session and has session scope. The following script demonstrates storage of two types of variables:

```
<%
   Session("name") = "Sandy"
   Session("age") = 21
%>
```

However, if you store an object in the Session object and use VBScript as your primary scripting language, you must use the Set keyword, as illustrated in the following script:

```
<% Set Session("Obj1") = Server.CreateObject("MyComponent") %>
```

You can then call the methods and properties of MyObj on subsequent Web pages, by using the following:

```
<% Session("Obj1").MyObjMethod %>
```

Or you can extract a local copy of the object and use the following:

```
<%
Set MyLocalObj1 = Session("Obj1")
MyLocalObj1.MyObjMethod
%>
```

Examples

```
<%
Session("name") = "Cory"
Session("CurrentYear") = 98
Set Session("myObj") = Server.CreateObject("someObj")
%>
```

Scripting enables the developer to code applications from the ground up. It enables the developer to create the glue that keeps the application together. Now the application developer does not want to have to code low-level functions such as accessing files or databases. This is where server-side components come to the developer's rescue.

Server-Side Components

Microsoft has been kind to developers by creating server-side components, which empower you to create dynamic and interactive Web pages. The server-side components are basically functions that are pre-built for the developer to use. These functions and more will continue to evolve just as when Visual Basic was in its early versions. Basic functions have been made for the developer to access files, databases, and so forth. Two years ago, the same functionality of tying Web pages to a database that would have taken a team months of development now takes a developer only minutes to accomplish.

Here is a list of the installable ASP components. Some of the components are installed with IIS, whereas others are on the IIS Resource Kit CD. Each component is described in its own section. Some of the components are discussed in greater detail in later chapters.

- AdRotator
- BrowserType
- Database Access
- NextLink
- FileSystemObject
- Collaboration Data Objects for NTS
- Tools
- Status
- MyInfo
- Counters
- ContentRotator
- PageCounter
- PermissionChecker

AdRotator

Online advertising has taken off over the last year on the Internet. So an AdRotator object was just the object needed for automated ads. Using the AdRotator object, you can create a rotating advertisement on a Web page that automatically rotates on a specific schedule.

Adrot.dll is the AdRotator component.

Syntax

```
Set AdRotator = Server.CreateObject("MSWC.AdRotator")
```

Properties

Border	Specifies the size of the border
Clickable	Specifies whether the advertisement is hyperlinked
TargetFrame	Creates a frame to display the advertisement

Method

GetAdvertisement	Retrieves the specification from the Rotator Schedule File (RSF)

Example   The following example displays a different advertisement each time a user views the Web page:

```
<%  Set ad = Server.CreateObject("MSWC.AdRotator") %>
<%= ad.GetAdvertisement("/ads/adrot.txt") %>
```

See the Rotator Schedule File for more details on adrot.txt.

The following HTML is generated by the GetAdvertisement method and added to the page's output, displaying the next advertisement in the Rotator Schedule File:

```
<A HREF = "http://www.msn.com/isapi/adredir.asp?http://www.company.com/">

<IMG SRC="http://msnnt3web/ads/homepage/chlogolg.gif"
ALT="Check out the new Technology Center"
WIDTH=440 HEIGHT=60 BORDER=1></A>
```

The Rotator Schedule File (RSF) determines the schedule of the rotation. In the RSF file, you can set the size of the images, which images, and percentage of time for each file. The RSF file has two sections, which are separated by one line containing an * (asterisk).

Syntax

```
[REDIRECT URL]
[WIDTH numWidth]
[HEIGHT numHeight]
[BORDER numBorder]
*
adURL
adHomePageURL
Text
impressions
```

REDIRECT, WIDTH, HEIGHT, and BORDER are optional parameters.

Parameters   The parameters for AdRotator are listed in the following sections.

URL   The URL parameter specifies the path to the dynamic link library (.DLL) or application (.ASP) file that implements redirection. This path can be specified either fully (http://MyServer/MyDir/redirect.asp) or relative to the virtual directory (/MyDir/redirect.asp).

numWidth   The numWidth parameter specifies the width of the advertisement on the page in pixels. The default is 440 pixels.

numHeight   The numHeight parameter specifies the height of the advertisement on the page in pixels. The default is 60 pixels.

numBorder   The numBorder parameter specifies the thickness of the hyperlink border around the advertisement in pixels. The default is a one-pixel border. Set this parameter to 0 for no border.

adURL   The adURL parameter specifies the location of the advertisement image file.

adHomePageURL   The adHomePageURL parameter specifies the location of the advertiser's home page. If the advertiser does not have a home page, put a hyphen (-) on this line to indicate that no link exists for this ad.

Text   The Text parameter specifies alternate text that is displayed if the browser does not support graphics or has its graphics capabilities turned off.

impressions   The impressions parameter specifies a number between 0 and 4,294,967,295 that indicates the relative weight of the advertisement.

For example, if a Rotator Schedule File contains three ads with *impressions* set to 2, 3, and 5, the first advertisement is displayed 20 percent of the time; the second, 30 percent of the time; and the third, 50 percent of the time.

The following script demonstrates how you can use a Rotator Schedule File to display a variety of advertisements and how to include a Redirection File:

```
---ADROT.TXT---
REDIRECT /scripts/adredir.asp
WIDTH 440
HEIGHT 60
BORDER 1
*
http://kabaweb/ads/homepage/chlogolg.gif
http://www.bytecomp.com/
Check out the ByteComp Technology Center
20
http://kabaweb/ads/homepage/gamichlg.gif
-
Sponsored by Flyteworks
20
http://kabaweb/ads/homepage/ismodemlg.gif
http:// www.proelectron.com/
28.8 internal PC modem, only $99
80
http://kabaweb/ads/homepage/spranklg.gif
http://www.clocktower.com/
The #1 Sports site on the net
10
```

You can record how many users click each advertisement by setting the *URL* parameter in the Rotator Schedule File to direct users to the Redirection File. When you specify this parameter, each jump to an advertiser's URL is recorded in the Web server activity logs.

BrowserType

Because different browsers have different capabilities, Web developers need an object to determine which type of browser is being used. The BrowserType object allows you to do just that.

When a browser connects to the Web server, a header is sent to the server. The BrowserType object compares the header with the entries in the Browscap.ini file. If the object does not find a match for the header in the Browscap.ini file, it takes on the default browser properties. If the object does not find a match, and default browser settings have not been specified in the Browscap.ini file, it sets every property to the string "UNKNOWN". You can add properties or new browser definitions to this component simply by updating the Browscap.ini file.

Browscap.dll is the BrowserType component, and Browscap.ini is the file with the definitions of the browsers.

Syntax

```
Set BrowserType = Server.CreateObject("MSWC.BrowserType")
```

Example   The following example uses the BrowserType object to display a table showing some of the capabilities of the current browser:

```
<% Set bc = Server.CreateObject("MSWC.BrowserType") %>
<table border=1>
<tr><td>Browser</td><td>  <%= bc.browser  %>
<tr><td>Version</td><td>  <%= bc.version  %>  </td></TR>
<tr><td>Frames</td><td>
</table>
```

Database Access

Allowing developers to access databases easily is the most powerful option available to developers. This capability opens up all the information on a corporate network that ActiveX Data Objects (ADOs) allow. From corporate databases to spreadsheets, all this information is accessible via Active Server Pages.

The Database Access component uses ActiveX Data Objects to access information stored in a database or other tabular data structure. It is probably the most powerful component because it gives so much access to a legacy of data. Because this component is so powerful, an entire chapter is devoted to describing how it works. See Chapter 17, "Working with ADO and RDS," for the detailed information on this component.

NextLink

The Content Linking component creates a `NextLink` object that manages a list of URLs so that you can treat the pages in your Web site like the pages in a book. You can use the Content Linking component to automatically generate and update tables of contents and navigational links to previous and subsequent Web pages. This capability is ideal for applications such as online newspapers and forum message listings.

The Content Linking component references a Content Linking List file that contains the list of the linked Web pages. This list is stored on the Web server.

Nextlink.dll is the Content Linking component.

Syntax

```
Set NextLink = Server.CreateObject("MSWC.NextLink")
```

Methods

`GetListCount(URL)`	Returns the number of items
`GetNextURL(URL)`	Returns the URL of the next page
`GetPreviousDescription(URL)`	Returns the previous page description
`GetListIndex(URL)`	Returns the current index
`GetNthDescription(URL, Index)`	Returns a specific description
`GetPreviousURL(URL)`	Returns the URL of the previous page
`GetNextDescription(URL)`	Returns the next page description
`GetNthURL(URL, Index)`	Returns a specific URL

Example   The following example builds a table of contents:

```
<ol>
<%  Set NextLink = Server.CreateObject ("MSWC.NextLink") %>
<%  count = NextLink.GetListCount ("/data/nextlink.txt") %>
<%  I = 1 %>

<ul>
<%  Do While (I <= count)  %>
<li><a href=" <%= NextLink.GetNthURL ("/data/nextlink.txt", I)  %>  ">
<%= NextLink.GetNthDescription ("/data/nextlink.txt", I) %>  </a>
<%  I = (I + 1)  %>
<%  Loop  %>

</ul>
</ol>
```

FileSystemObject

To work with files on your computer, you must use the FileSystemObject component. The methods and properties inside this component allow you to manipulate files on your computer system.

Syntax

```
Set Object = Server.CreateObject("MSWC.FileSystemObject")
```

Methods The following are some of the useful methods for FileSystemObject. For further information on the FileSystemObject, see the VBScript Language Reference in Chapter 6, "Client-Side Scripting."

BuildPath The BuildPath method adds a path to the filename; it can be relative or absolute.

Syntax

```
object.BuildPath(path, name)
```

FileExists The FileExists method checks for a file whose existence is to be determined. A complete path specification (either absolute or relative) must be provided if the file isn't expected to exist in the current folder.

Syntax

```
object.FileExists(filespec)
```

CopyFile The CopyFile method copies a file with an optional Boolean overwrite parameter.

Syntax

```
object.CopyFile source, destination[, overwrite]
```

Collaboration Data Objects (CDO) for NTS Component

The Microsoft CDO for NTS Library (Collaboration Data Objects for Windows NT Server) version 1.2 exposes messaging objects for use by VBScript applications. The library lets you quickly and easily add to your application the ability to send and receive messages. It is not intended to run on a client process.

Part

II

Ch

7

The CDO is an extensive library of objects. For specific details on the objects then browse the Net at: **http://help.activeserverpages.com/iishelp/iis/htm/asp/amsm0hkk.htm**.

Here in Initialize Variables is a sample of the potential of CDO:

```
Set myInbox = mySession.GetDefaultFolder(CdoDefaultFolderInbox)
Set collInMessages = myInbox.Messages
Set myMessage = collInMessages.GetFirst
Set myAddrEntry = myMessage.Sender strMsg = "Sender name " & myAddrEntry.Name
strMsg = strMsg & "; address type = " & myAddrEntry.Type strMsg = strMsg &
"; e-mail address = " & myAddrEntry.Address MsgBox strMsg
```

This shows how easy it is to use CDO to send a message.

Tools

The Tools component creates a `Tools` object that provides utilities that enable you to easily add sophisticated functionality to your Web pages. Some of the tools are file existence, owner status, plug-ins, and a random number generator.

The Tools component is tools.dll.

Syntax

```
Set Tools = Server.CreateObject("MSWC.Tools")
```

Remarks   In Personal Web Server for Windows 95/98, the `Tools` object is included in the GLOBAL.ASA file in the default virtual directory. You can work with the `Tools` object as if it were a built-in object by calling `Tools.FileExists`, `Tools.ProcessForm`, and `Tools.Random`.

Methods   The following are the methods for the Tools component.

FileExists   The `FileExists` method checks the existence of a file. It returns –1 if the specified URL exists within a published directory. If the file does not exist, it returns 0.

Syntax

```
Tools.FileExists(URL)
```

Remarks   `FileExists` checks the existence of files published on your site only. Therefore, it takes a relative URL rather than an absolute URL.

Example

```
<%If Tools.FileExists("ie_animated.gif") then %>
    <p> <a href="http://www.microsoft.Com/ie/"><img src="ie_animated.gif"></a>
<% End If %>
```

Random   The `Random` method returns an integer between –32,768 to 32,767.

Syntax

```
Tools.random
```

Remarks   The `Random` method is similar to the `Rnd` function but returns an integer.

To get a positive random integer, use the Abs function.

To get a random integer below a specific value, use the Mod function.

Example

```
<% = Tools.Random %> will display a random integer between –32768 to 32767.
➥   For example, -13067.
<% = ( Abs( Tools.Random ) ) %> will display a positive random integer.
➥   For example, 23054.
<% = ( Abs( Tools.Random ) ) Mod 100 %> will display a random integer
➥   between 0 and 99. For example, 63.
```

ProcessForm   The ProcessForm method processes the contents of a form that has been submitted by a visitor to the Web site.

Syntax

```
Tools.ProcessForm(OutputFileURL, TemplateURL, [InsertionPoint])
```

Parameters

OutputFileURL	A string containing the relative URL of the file to which the processed data is written
TemplateURL	A string containing the relative URL of the file that contains the template, or instructions for processing the data
InsertionPoint	An optional parameter indicating where in the output file to insert the process data

Remarks   The template files can contain ASP scripts. A script between <% and %> delimiters is treated just like other text in the template and copied into the output file. If the output file is an ASP document, the script runs when the output file is accessed. Scripts in template files can also be put between special <%% and %%> delimiters, which cause the script to execute while Tools.ProcessForm is executing. Because these scripts are executed before the template data is saved in the output file, the results are saved in the output file, usually as standard text.

If the specified output file does not exist, the server creates it.

If the *InsertionPoint* parameter does not exist, Tools.ProcessForm replaces the entire output file. If the *InsertionPoint* parameter exists and does not begin with an asterisk (*), Tools.ProcessForm finds the *InsertionPoint* string in the output file and inserts the data immediately after it. If the *InsertionPoint* string begins with an asterisk (*), Tools.ProcessForm finds the *InsertionPoint* string in the output file and inserts the data immediately before it. If the *InsertionPoint* string exists but is not found in the output file, the data is appended to the end of the file.

Example   The following code is derived from the messageresponse.asp page used by the Microsoft Personal Web Server:

```
<%
Tools.processform("/$Received Messages/default.asp",
➥"MessageInsert.process","<SPAN>*")
%>
```

N O T E The `Owner` and `PluginExists` methods are available only on Macintosh systems. ■

Status

The Status component creates a `Status` object that has properties containing server status information. Currently, this server status is available only on Personal Web Server for Macintosh.

MyInfo

The MyInfo component creates a `MyInfo` object that keeps track of personal information, such as the site administrator's name, address, and display choices. Typically, the administrator types this information directly into the Web server interface. However, you can set the values of the properties directly using an ASP script.

Each property of a `MyInfo` object returns a string. If a `MyInfo` property has no value set, the property returns an empty string.

The `MyInfo` object can have properties in addition to the ones documented here. The properties are implemented by Personal Web Server to keep track of information entered into the Personal Web Server interface.

You can create new `MyInfo` properties by simply assigning a string value to them. For example,

```
<% MyInfo.myproperty = "StarTrek"  %>
```

creates the new property `myproperty`. These new properties are stored persistently along with the other `MyInfo` properties. You also can create new `MyInfo` properties for values that remain consistent throughout a site.

The values of `MyInfo` properties are stored in a single text file, myinfo.xml, which is installed to the \winnt\system32 directory on Windows NT and to the root directory on Windows 95. Myinfo.dll is the MyInfo component.

Syntax

```
MyInfo.property
```

You can create a `MyInfo` object once in the GLOBAL.ASA file by adding the following:

```
<OBJECT RUNAT=Server SCOPE=Session ID=MyInfo PROGID="MSWC.MyInfo">
</OBJECT>
```

Remarks   You should create only one `MyInfo` object in your site. You can create a `MyInfo` object by using the following:

```
Set MyInfoObject = Server.CreateObject('MSWC.MyInfo')
```

Counters

The Counters component creates a `Counters` object that can create, store, increment, and retrieve any number of individual counters. A counter is a persistent value that contains an integer. You can manipulate a counter with the `Get`, `Increment`, `Set`, and `Remove` methods of the `Counters` object. After you create the counter, it persists until you remove it. Counters do not automatically increment on an event like a page hit. You must manually set or increment counters using the `Set` and `Increment` methods. Counters are not limited in scope. After you create a counter, any page on your site can retrieve or manipulate its value. For example, if you increment and display a counter named `hits` in a page called Page1.asp, and you increment `hits` in another page called Page2.asp, both pages increment the same counter. If you hit Page1.asp, and increment `hits` to 34, hitting Page2.asp increments `hits` to 35. The next time you hit Page1.asp, `hits` will increment to 36. All counters are stored in a single text file, counters.txt, which is located in the same directory as the counters.dll file, which is the `Counters` component.

Syntax   You can create the `Counters` object one time on your server by adding the following to the GLOBAL.ASA file:

```
<OBJECT RUNAT=Server SCOPE=Application ID=Counter PROGID="MSWC.Counters">
</OBJECT>
```

Remarks   You should create only one `Counters` object in your site. This single `Counters` object can create any number of individual counters.

N O T E   For Personal Web Server on Windows 95 or 98, a `Counters` component is specified in the GLOBAL.ASA file in the default virtual directory. You can work with the `Counters` object the component creates as if it were a built-in object by calling `Counters.Get`, `Counters.Increment`, `Counters.Remove`, and `Counters.Set`. You should not create another instance of the `Counters` object. ■

Methods

`Get`	Returns the value of the counter
`Increment`	Increases the counter by 1
`Remove`	Removes the counter from the counters.txt file
`Set`	Sets the value of the counter to a specific integer

Example   You can create an instance of the `Counters` object in the GLOBAL.ASA file with the ID attribute set to `Counter`:

```
<OBJECT RUNAT=Server SCOPE=Application ID=Counter PROGID="MSWC.Counters">
</OBJECT>
```

You can then use that `Counters` object on one page to create all the counters you need:

```
There have been <%= Counter.Increment('defaultPageHits') %> to this site.
```

Then, on another page, you can increment the counter in the following manner:

```
You are visitor number<%= Counter.Increment('LinksPageHits') %> to this page.
```

ContentRotator

The Content Rotator component creates a `ContentRotator` object that automatically rotates HTML content strings on a Web page. Each time a user requests the Web page, the object displays a new HTML content string based on information that you specify in a Content Schedule File.

Because the content strings can contain HTML tags, you can display any type of content that HTML can represent: text, images, or hyperlinks. For example, you can use this component to rotate through a list of daily quotations or hyperlinks, or to change text and background colors each time the Web page is opened.

The controt.dll is the Content Rotator component.

Syntax

```
<% Set myobject = Server.CreateObject("MSWC.ContentRotator") %>
```

Methods

ChooseContent   Retrieves and displays a specific content string

GetAllContent   Retrieves all and displays the contents strings from the Content Schedule File

Remarks   Because the `ContentRotator` object uses a random generator to select which of the weighted content strings is displayed, a string may be repeated. This repetition is most likely to occur if few entries appear in the Content Schedule File or if one entry is weighted much higher than the others.

Example   The following example displays a different tip of the day each time a user views the Web page:

```
<%
Set Tip = Server.CreateObject("MSWC.ContentRotator")
Tip.ChooseContent("/tips/tiprot.txt")
%>
```

PageCounter

The Page Counter component creates a `PageCounter` object that counts and displays the number of times a Web page has been opened. At regular intervals, the object writes the number of hits to a text file so that in the event of a server shutdown, the data is not lost. The Page Counter component uses an internal `Central Management` object to record how many times each page in the application has been opened.

When an instance of the `PageCounter` object is created on a page by using the `Server.CreateObject` method, the object retrieves the current hit count for the specified Web page from the `Central Management` object. The object can then be manipulated with the methods it exposes.

Pagecnt.dll is the Page Counter component.

Syntax

```
<% Set oVar = Server.CreateObject("MSWC.PageCounter") %>
```

Methods

Hits	Displays the number of times a specified URL has been opened
PageHit	Increments the hit count
Reset	Sets the hit count to 0

Example   The following example uses the PageCounter object to track the number of visitors to the page and sends a special message to the millionth visitor:

```
<%
Set MyPageCounter = Server.CreateObject("MSWC.PageCounter")
HitMe = MyPageCounter.Hits

If HitMe = 1000000 Then
%>
  You are the lucky 1,000,000th Customer!!! <BR>
<% Else %>
  Sorry, you are customer #<%= HitMe %> <BR>
<% End If %>
```

PermissionChecker

The Permission Checker component creates a PermissionChecker object that uses the password authentication protocols provided in IIS to determine whether a Web user has been granted permissions to read a file.

You can use the Permission Checker component to customize an ASP-based page for different types of users. For example, if a Web page contains hyperlinks, you can use the Permission Checker component to test whether the user has permissions for the target Web pages. If the user does not have the proper permissions, you can then omit or alter the hyperlinks to those pages the user cannot access.

Syntax

```
Set myobject = Server.CreateObject("MSWC.PermissionChecker")
```

Method

HasAccess	Determines whether a Web client user has permissions to access a specific file

Example   The following example uses the HasAccess method to test whether the current user has access to a specified file. Note that you can specify either a physical or virtual path.

```
<% Set pmck = Server.CreateObject("MSWC.PermissionChecker") %>

Physical Path Access = <%= pmck.HasAccess("c:\pages\abc\default.htm") %>
Virtual Path  Access = <%= pmck.HasAccess("/abc/default.htm") %>
```

Part

II

Ch

7

Remarks   IIS supports the following three types of password authentication in any combination:

- Anonymous
- Basic
- Windows NT Challenge/Response (NTLM)

When anonymous password authentication is enabled, all users are initially logged on under the IIS anonymous user account. Because anonymous users all share the same account, the Permission Checker component cannot authenticate individual users when anonymous access is allowed.

For applications in which all users have individual accounts, such as intranet-only Web sites, you should disable anonymous authentication so that the Permission Checker component can authenticate individual users.

For applications in which some pages must be available to anonymous users and other pages need to be secure, such as mixed Internet and intranet Web sites, you should enable anonymous authentication and at least one other password authentication method, either NTLM or Basic. Then, if you deny anonymous access to a specific page, the server tries to authenticate the user by using either NTLM or Basic password authentication.

You can use either of the following two methods to deny anonymous access to a specific page:

- Set the Access Control List for the ASP-based file to exclude the anonymous user account.
- In the ASP script, check for the anonymous user account (if the LOGON_USER server variable is empty) and set Response.Status to the 401 Unauthorized error message. Setting the status causes IIS to try to identify the user by using NTLM or Basic authentication. This method is illustrated in the following example:

```
<%
If Request("LOGON_USER") = "" Then
    Response.Status = "401 Unauthorized"
End if
%>
```

If all the files in your application must be available to anonymous users, the Permission Checker component cannot distinguish individual user accounts. You can still use it, however, to ensure that the specified Web page exists and test whether the anonymous user account has access permissions for that page.

> **N O T E**   NTLM password authentication is currently supported only by Microsoft Internet Explorer and might not work over a proxy server. Thus, if users connect to your site with browsers other than Internet Explorer or through a proxy server, and your application requires a nonanonymous user context, you must also enable Basic password authentication. ■

From Here...

Now you have a taste of Active Server Page functionality and possibilities. Active Server Pages and server-side components give the developer excellent development tools. Now with VI 6.0, development will be swift thanks to the wizards and templates available to the developer. The color-coded syntax improves script writing ease, especially for the VB developer just learning Web development. Now it is time for you to get your feet wet and try VI's development environment. For more script documentation and samples browse the Net at **http://www.activeserverpages.com/docs/**.

Part

II

Ch

7

Script Debugging with Visual InterDev 6

In this chapter

In the Beginning, There Was No Debugger…   **168**

Categories of Errors   **168**

Similarities to VB's Debugger   **169**

Let's Get Debugging!   **170**

Client Script Debugging with Visual InterDev 6   **181**

Server-Side Script Debugging   **183**

Debugging Mixed Client and Server Script   **185**

Exception to the Rule: Global.asa   **187**

In the Beginning, There Was No Debugger...

I don't know how many times I've taught a Visual InterDev (VI) 1 class and been asked why there's no debugger. It has always put me in a rather awkward position because the absence of a valid VI debugging tool is an immediate turnoff to the students. Needless to say, one of the most awaited features in Visual InterDev 6 is its script debugging capabilities. This chapter discusses the debugging features introduced in Visual InterDev 6 and how they can help you support an enterprise business solution. The powerful debugging tools included with Visual InterDev 6 are intended to aid you in testing and debugging distributed code of Web applications.

N O T E   To debug script in Active Server Pages (ASP), you must be running Internet Information Server (IIS) 4.0 or later. ▪

Categories of Errors

The purpose of a debugger is to aid the developer in finding errors. Fortunately, Visual InterDev 6 and IIS 4 provide the functionality for developers to locate and correct the three categories of errors (see Table 8.1).

Table 8.1   Categories of Errors Visual InterDev 6's Debugging Tools Can Prevent and Rectify

Category	Comments
Runtime	Only surface while the program is running
Syntax	Prevent the program from running due to invalid syntax
Logic	Might not surface easily if syntax is valid

Syntax errors occur at compile-time or before the program can even run. These errors occur when you mistype a keyword, you forget to close a multi-line command, or you forget to declare a variable in an ASP that uses Option Explicit (see Listing 8.1). A syntax error causes the script not to execute and an error message to be displayed as soon as the browser or server processes the page.

Runtime errors occur when code or script attempts to execute an invalid action that could not be determined at compile-time. For example, a runtime error occurs if you try to perform a calculation on a variable that has not been initialized. If a runtime error occurs, the script either stops or performs a specified error handling routine.

Listing 8.1   A Syntax Error from Not Declaring Variables

```
<%Language=VBScript%>
<%
OPTION EXPLICIT
x = 77/7
%>
```

A logic error occurs when a script executes, but the results are not what you had intended. For example, assume a script prompts a user for his password. The user enters an incorrect password but the script allows access to the application anyway.

All three of these types of errors were more difficult to track down in Visual InterDev 1 because its debugging environment left a lot to be desired. In fact, many developers have referred to Visual InterDev 1 as "no more than a colorful HTML/ASP editor."

N O T E   Keep in mind that debugging only works if you are in the Source view of the HTML editor. ▇

Similarities to VB's Debugger

Visual InterDev 1's lack of integrated debugging tools was one of its biggest drawbacks. This left Visual InterDev 1 developers with the option of using the ASP object method `Response.Write` to display variable values. Well, I say good riddance!

For developers familiar with the Visual Basic debugging environment, you will like what Visual InterDev 6 has to offer. One of the biggest draws to Visual InterDev 6 is its debugging capabilities. In fact, the Visual InterDev 6 debugging tools only fall short of Visual Basic's tools in one major area: without restarting, you can't change your script in debug mode and continue. However, Visual InterDev 6 makes a vast improvement in its debugging tools over its previous version with several useful features:

- ▇ Watches
- ▇ Smart Breakpoints
- ▇ Dynamically setting the next line of code to execute
- ▇ Changing the value of a variable during runtime

N O T E   Fear not, all of these features listed above will be discussed in detail later in this chapter. ▇

There are many more new and great reasons to use the Visual InterDev 6 debugging tools, as we discuss throughout this chapter. In fact, after relying on `Response.Write` to aid my development efforts, I am often pleasantly surprised at how useful the Visual InterDev 6 debugging tools can be. But before you can take advantage of these features, you have to enable them for your Web project.

Let's Get Debugging!

Debugging with Visual InterDev 6 takes the anxiety out of Web development. To use these features, however, there is some background to establish first.

Enabling the Debugging Features

There are four types of debugging situations in Visual InterDev 6:

- Client-side script debugging
- Server-side script debugging
- Mixed server-side and client-side script debugging
- Debugging the Global.asa file

Each of these debugging situations is discussed in greater detail later in this chapter. Before we begin discussing these, we have to prepare our Web site for debugging.

The server-side script debugging features of Visual InterDev 6 don't do you much good unless you enable them through IIS 4. The Web server needs to allow server-side debugging for the Visual InterDev 6 tools to aid your debugging efforts. You can turn the server-side debugging features on for the entire Web site or for a particular folder/project within the Web site. For our purposes, we'll turn server-side debugging on for the entire Web site. You can do this by following these steps:

1. Open the Internet Service Manager in the Microsoft Management Console (MMC), as shown in Figure 8.1.

FIG. 8.1
The Internet Service Manager in the MMC.

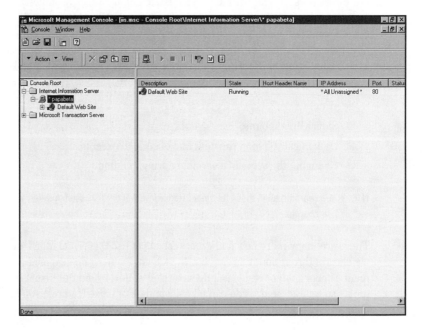

2. Right-click the Web server node in the tree view and choose Properties form the shortcut menu.

3. Select the Home Directory tab of the property sheet and click the Configuration button (as shown in Figure 8.2) to view the configuration for the entire Web site.

FIG. 8.2

The Default Web Site Properties dialog box where the Configuration button is located.

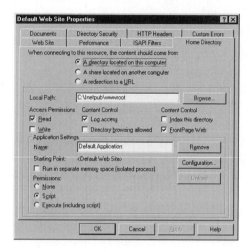

4. Choose the App Debugging tab of the property sheet as shown in Figure 8.3.

5. On this tab of the property sheet, you set the debugging features for the Web site. As shown in Figure 8.3, enable the server-side debugging features for this Web site by clicking the Enable ASP Server-Side Script Debugging check box.

FIG. 8.3

Enabling the server-side debugging features for a Web site.

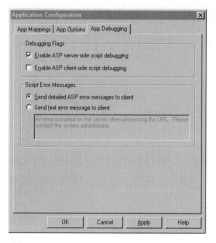

NOTE At the time of this printing, the Enable ASP Client-Side Script Debugging check box has no effect on ASP 2.0. The help documentation states that this check box is reserved for future use and that client-side debugging is always enabled for a Web site regardless of this setting. ▪

The Nuances of Debugging Scripts

You can use the Visual InterDev debugger to test scripts written in VBScript and Microsoft's version of JavaScript called JScript. Debugging Web pages can be different than debugging in traditional development environments in several key ways:

- Most Web applications consist of scripts that execute on the client in HTML files and on the server in ASP files.
- Scripts are not compiled, as opposed to Visual Basic, Visual C++, or Java components.
- One file can contain scripts in different languages.
- Scripts can be mixed with HTML.
- Many Web applications also include applets and COM objects.

 TIP Generally, it is a good idea to employ VBScript as server-side script and JavaScript as client-side script. Although VBScript is easier to use, only JavaScript is universally accepted by both the Netscape and Microsoft Web browsers. Keep in mind that VBScript will not run on Netscape browsers.

Visual InterDev 6's debugger lets you debug in all of these situations. There are limitations to debugging your scripts using the Visual InterDev debugging tools, however they are a vast improvement from the previous debugging methods. For example, you cannot change an ASP script while in debug mode and have the ASP engine recognize the change on-the-fly. In this case, you would have to stop and restart the debugging environment.

> **CAUTION**
>
> You might not want to use the Active Desktop mode of Internet Explorer 4 while you are debugging. This causes seemingly random and always aberrant behavior from the debugging environment's of Visual InterDev 6 and IIS 4.

Oh, What the Debugger Can Do!

After developing Web applications with the help of the Visual InterDev 6 debugger, you'll wonder how you ever managed without it. With the versatility of the debugging tools, there are several ways to invoke their power. For instance, you can run the file you are currently working with in your Web project or you can launch the debugger in response to a script error. The latter method is referred to as *just-in-time* debugging. Just-in-time debugging is great when you have a script that you know has an error in it but you cannot easily determine exactly where the error is occurring. With just-in-time debugging, you can run your script and the script engine breaks into the debugging environment when it attempts to perform the line in error.

Ready to Launch

So you're ready to go and you want to know how to get this debugger in gear? To launch the debugger, do the following:

1. Start at the Project Explorer and right-click an HTML (.HTM) or ASP (.ASP) file and select Set As Start Page.

2. Press the F5 key or choose Start from the Debug menu.

The script executes until the breakpoint is reached. At that point, the debugger stops and displays the source script. From here, you can check values using watches, change the values of variables, or step in/out of code.

Watches   After you've invoked the debugger, you can utilize instant watches, which now take the form of a ToolTip (see Figure 8.4). This is one of my favorite features because you can simply put your cursor over the variable, or a property, and a ToolTip appears with its value. Yes, it's a pretty basic feature these days. But aren't some of the best things in life also the simplest?

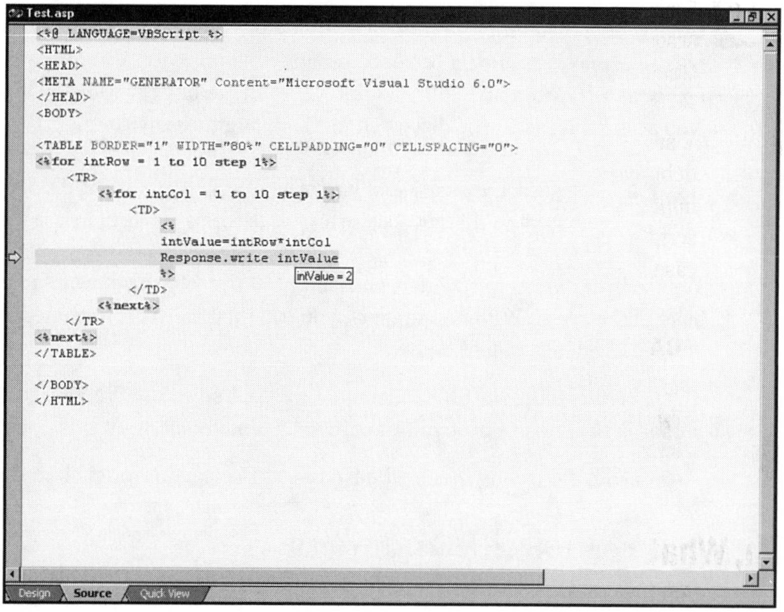

FIG. 8.4

ToolTip watches make inspecting variable values easy.

```
<%@ LANGUAGE=VBScript %>
<HTML>
<HEAD>
<META NAME="GENERATOR" Content="Microsoft Visual Studio 6.0">
</HEAD>
<BODY>

<TABLE BORDER="1" WIDTH="80%" CELLPADDING="0" CELLSPACING="0">
<%for intRow = 1 to 10 step 1%>
    <TR>
        <%for intCol = 1 to 10 step 1%>
            <TD>
                <%
                intValue=intRow*intCol
                Response.write intValue
                %>                  intValue = 2
            </TD>
        <%next%>
    </TR>
<%next%>
</TABLE>

</BODY>
</HTML>
```

Design   Source   Quick View

CAUTION

The first time you run your script and try to use a ToolTip instant watch, the ToolTip doesn't appear next to the variable. At the time of this book's printing, the first ToolTip appears at either the leftmost or topmost part of the screen. (In fact, at the time of this book's printing, the oddities of the beta product were quite hilarious at times.)

The Watch window displays the values of selected variables or watch expressions. The Watch window is only updated when execution is stopped at a breakpoint or exception. Values that have changed since the last break are highlighted. In the Watch window, you can drag a selected variable to the Immediate window or double-click a variable to edit its value. To display the Watch window, select Watch Window from the Debug Windows menu within the View menu (or press Ctrl+Alt+W).

TIP Watches used to be the way to monitor values in a debugging environment. Well, the bar has been raised with the advent of the Locals window. The Locals window displays all values of all variables and properties within the current context. Therefore, anything that is valid in the Watch window is already in the Locals window.

The Watch window shows the current watch expressions, which are expressions whose values you decide to monitor as the code runs. The Watch window only displays a value for a watch expression if the current statement is in the specified context. If it is not in the current context, then a message indicating the statement is not in context is displayed in the Watch window.

Breakpoints Another method of invoking the debugging features is to stop a script's execution by explicitly issuing a break command in your script. Visual InterDev also gives you the ability to set breakpoints in the script where the debugger will stop automatically. When you stop a script, its source is displayed in the debugging environment.

NOTE In JavaScript, you can invoke the debugger explicitly by issuing the debugger keyword in your script. In VBScript, you can achieve the same results by issuing the stop command. ■

We use breakpoints to specify a place in the script where you want to stop and examine the state of the script. With breakpoints, you can then step through, step into, or step over lines of script individually to find errors.

To set breakpoints, start by opening the file and selecting the Source view. Then, place the cursor in the line of script you want to set a breakpoint in. At this point, you have three options:

- From the Debug menu, choose Insert Breakpoint (or click in the left margin of the page).
- Right-click and choose Insert Breakpoint.
- Press the F9 key.
- Click to the right of the line of script, in the margin.

After you've applied the breakpoint, you might notice a red octagon appears to the left of the line of script. You can also clear breakpoints by following one of the same steps listed in the preceding. To clear all breakpoints at one time, choose Clear All Breakpoints from the Debug menu (or press Ctrl+Shft+F9).

They Aren't Just for Breaking Anymore Breakpoints have been vastly improved in Visual InterDev 6 from the breakpoints that Visual Basic developers are used to. For example, one new feature allows you to track the number of times a breakpoint is hit during your script's execution. In fact, there are several key features of breakpoints in Visual InterDev 6 that you can take advantage of from the Script Breakpoint Properites dialog box (see Figure 8.5).

FIG. 8.5

The Script Breakpoint
Properties dialog box.

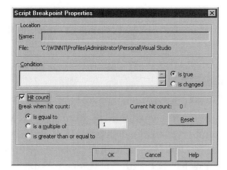

Notice the options available on the Script Breakpoint Properties dialog box in Table 8.2. Thanks to these options, breakpoints don't just stop the code anymore. Rather, they can be configured to intelligently evaluate when to stop the script.

Table 8.2 The Debugger's Breakpoint Options

Option	Description
Name	Name of the function that the breakpoint is assigned to
File	Name of the file where the breakpoint exists
Condition	Condition that must be satisfied before execution stops
Hit Count	When selected, stops execution when one of the Hit Count conditions is met

As stated in Table 8.2, the Name displays the name of the function where the breakpoint exists. The File is always read only as it displays the name of the file (ASP or HTML) that contains the breakpoint. This also shows the line in the file where the breakpoint exists.

The Condition option is really cool because you can tailor this property setting to break when a particular expression is true. What's even better is that you can configure the breakpoint to only stop when the condition changes its value. In other words, if the condition evaluates to a different value in subsequent hits of the breakpoint, the execution will stop on the breakpoint. For both the Is True and Is Changed options, if the condition is not met, the execution skips right on by the breakpoint.

As cool as the Condition options are, the Hit Count settings are equally cool. When the Hit Count check box is selected, the specified breakpoint only stops code execution when one of the conditions specified in the Hit Count settings is satisfied. The first setting, Is Equal, lets you specify the number of hits on the breakpoint that it takes for the breakpoint to stop the script's execution. The Is A Multiple Of causes the breakpoint to stop the script's execution when the breakpoint's hit count is a multiple of the number specified in the Hit Count text box. Finally, the Is Greater Than or Equal To causes the breakpoint to stop the script's execution when the breakpoint hit count is greater than or equal to the number specified in the Hit Count text box.

There is also a read only value displaying the current number of times the breakpoint has been hit. You can reset this value by clicking the Reset command button in the lower-right corner of the dialog box.

Stepping Through Your Script

As in Visual Basic, you can control the execution of individual statements and procedures by stepping through them in the debugging environment. Both stepping over procedures and stepping into procedures are supported by the debugger. However, if you are familiar with Visual Basic's debugger, you might quickly notice that the keys for these actions are different in Visual InterDev 6 (they are now F11 and F10). You also have the ability to step out of a procedure. Stepping out executes the remaining code of the active procedure without stepping line-by-line. The control then returns to the next line of the calling thread.

After the debugger reaches a breakpoint, you can use the stepping features to step into, over, and out of your script. If you reach a line of code in your script that calls another procedure, you can enter the procedure by stepping into it or execute the procedure by stepping over it. Your other option is to jump to the end of the current procedure by stepping out. With this option the script's execution proceeds to the next breakpoint (if one exists).

Let's demonstrate how you can step through some client-side JavaScript by creating an HTML file called text.htm. Edit the file so it looks like Listing 8.2.

Listing 8.2 A Simple Login Form That Uses Client-Side JavaScript to Verify a Login

```
<HTML>
<HEAD>
<META NAME="GENERATOR" Content="Microsoft Visual Studio 6.0">
</HEAD>
<BODY>
<SCRIPT LANGUAGE=javascript>
<!--
function CheckLogin()
{
        var strUserID, strPassword;
        strUserID = document.frmLogin.txtUserID.value;
        strPassword = document.frmLogin.txtPassword.value;
        if (strUserID == 'johnny' && strPassword == 'ynnhoj')
                alert ('Valid login');
        else
                alert ('Invalid login');
}
//-->
</SCRIPT>
<form method="post" name="frmLogin" action="" >
UserID: <input type="text" name="txtUserID">
<BR>
Password: <input type="password" name="txtPassword">
<BR>
```

```
<input type="button" value="Login" name="Login" onclick="CheckLogin()">
</form>
</BODY>
</HTML>
```

CAUTION

Because JavaScript is case sensitive, your HTML file must appear exactly like the script in Listing 8.2. Otherwise, your script might not execute properly.

This HTML and script combination checks to see if the UserID and password are a certain combination and then displays a dialog box stating such. At this point, continue by setting a breakpoint at the line of script that displays the submit button. You should then see a red octagon in the left margin of this line of script. When you place a breakpoint in this line of HTML, you are specifying that the script stop executing when you click the button. Now set this file to be the startup file in the project by right-clicking the file in the Project Explorer and choosing Set as Start Page. At this point, press the F5 key to execute the script, enter some values for the UserID and password, and click the Login button. After clicking the button, the debugger should launch itself and be stopped on the breakpoint we set a few moments ago (see Figure 8.6).

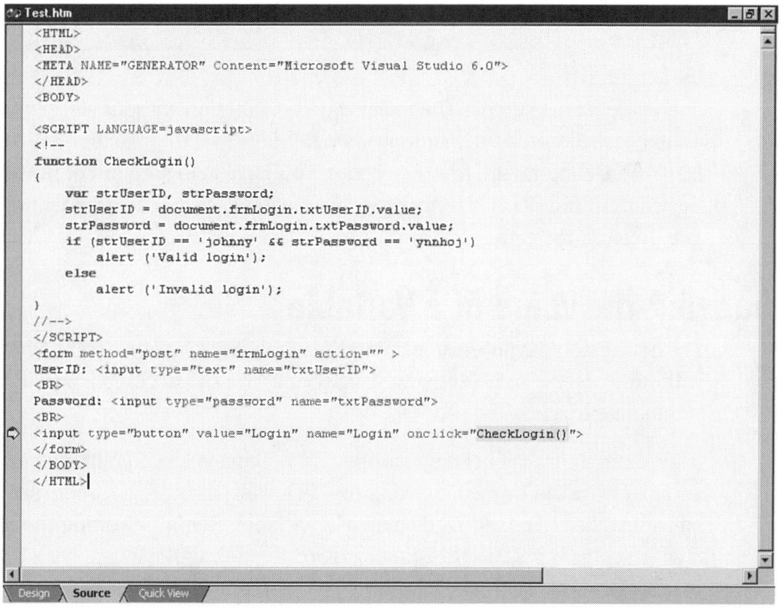

FIG. 8.6

The breakpoint set in the script.

```
<HTML>
<HEAD>
<META NAME="GENERATOR" Content="Microsoft Visual Studio 6.0">
</HEAD>
<BODY>

<SCRIPT LANGUAGE=javascript>
<!--
function CheckLogin()
{
    var strUserID, strPassword;
    strUserID = document.frmLogin.txtUserID.value;
    strPassword = document.frmLogin.txtPassword.value;
    if (strUserID == 'johnny' && strPassword == 'ynnhoj')
        alert ('Valid login');
    else
        alert ('Invalid login');
}
//-->
</SCRIPT>
<form method="post" name="frmLogin" action="" >
UserID: <input type="text" name="txtUserID">
<BR>
Password: <input type="password" name="txtPassword">
<BR>
<input type="button" value="Login" name="Login" onclick="CheckLogin()">
</form>
</BODY>
</HTML>
```

From here, you can step into the function CheckLogin() or step over it. To step into the function, press the F11 key or choose Step Into from the Debug menu. If you check the value of the variable strUserID by placing your cursor over the variable, it displays strUserID =

undefined in a ToolTip watch. This is because the variable has not been set yet. If you press F11 a few times and then recheck the value of this variable, you should see its value change (see Figure 8.7).

FIG. 8.7

The value of a variable in client-side JavaScript using a ToolTip watch.

Notice how this variable has now changed

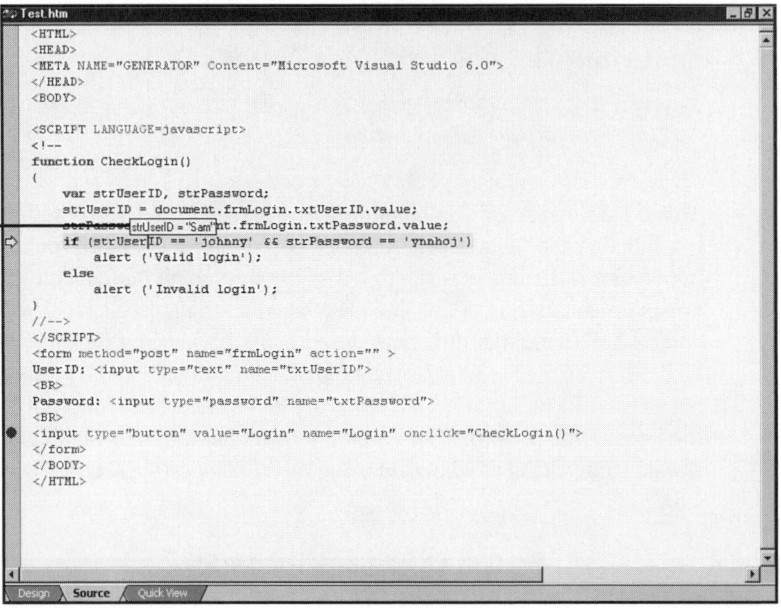

```
Test.htm                                                                        _|_|X|
    <HTML>
    <HEAD>
    <META NAME="GENERATOR" Content="Microsoft Visual Studio 6.0">
    </HEAD>
    <BODY>

    <SCRIPT LANGUAGE=javascript>
    <!--
    function CheckLogin()
    (
        var strUserID, strPassword;
        strUserID = document.frmLogin.txtUserID.value;
        strPasswo[strUserID = "Sam"]nt.frmLogin.txtPassword.value;
        if (strUserID == 'johnny' && strPassword == 'ynnhoj')
            alert ('Valid login');
        else
            alert ('Invalid login');
    )
    //-->
    </SCRIPT>
    <form method="post" name="frmLogin" action="" >
    UserID: <input type="text" name="txtUserID">
    <BR>
    Password: <input type="password" name="txtPassword">
    <BR>
    <input type="button" value="Login" name="Login" onclick="CheckLogin()">
    </form>
    </BODY>
    </HTML>

Design \ Source \ Quick View
```

You could have executed the CheckLogin() function without stepping line-by-line into its code. To execute the script as a unit, you would have had to press the F10 key or choose Step Over from the Debug menu. Another option you have is to step out of the script. If you had chosen this route (Shift+F11), the script would have finished executing without walking you line-by-line through the code.

Changing the Value of a Variable

For debugging purposes, it is sometimes helpful to be able to change the value of a variable without stopping and restarting your script. You can accomplish this with a little help from the Immediate window.

After your script has been executing and reaches a breakpoint, you can change the value of a variable from the Immediate window. Let's walk through a sample scenario that outlines the steps involved to change the value of a variable. Begin by setting the HTML file that you created from Listing 8.2 as the start page for the debugger. Then, set a breakpoint on the line of JavaScript code that looks like this:

```
if (strUserID == 'johnny' && strPassword == 'ynnhoj')
```

At this breakpoint, we'll evaluate the variable strPassword and change its value. To monitor the variable's value, you can make use of the Locals window. Go ahead and start the debugging session by pressing F5, entering values for both text boxes, and submitting the page. The Visual InterDev session stops the script at the breakpoint for you. From here, simply choose the Locals window button from the toolbar and you are presented with all variables in the current context, as shown in Figure 8.8.

FIG. 8.8

The Locals window displaying the Password and UserID values.

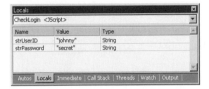

We can change the value of the variables in the Locals window and continue running the script. Figure 8.9 shows the Locals window after the value of the `strPassword` variable has been changed. Notice that onscreen the value appears in a red forecolor. From here, you can continue running to see the results of the changed value.

FIG. 8.9

The Locals window displays the changed Password in red.

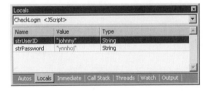

There are other ways to change a variable's value, however. Stop the debugging session and let's demonstrate how we can use the Immediate window to accomplish the same task. Continue by launching the debugger (pressing the F5 key) on the same script as in the previous example. Enter any invalid password and press the submit button. When the debugger opens the script and stops at the breakpoint, a yellow arrow appears superimposed over the red octagonal breakpoint icon in the left margin. Notice Figure 8.10, as it shows the current value of the password (which is invalid).

We can change the value of this variable to be a valid password using the Immediate window. From the View menu, select Debug Windows and then select Immediate (or press Ctrl+Alt+I). In the Immediate window, type the following and press Enter:

```
strPassword="ynnhoj"
```

To verify that you have just changed the value of the password, put your cursor back over the variable. A ToolTip watch should verify that the variable changed. From this point, you can press F5 to let the script complete its execution by validating the login.

The Immediate window is the perfect place to change the values of variables as well as display values of variables and expressions.

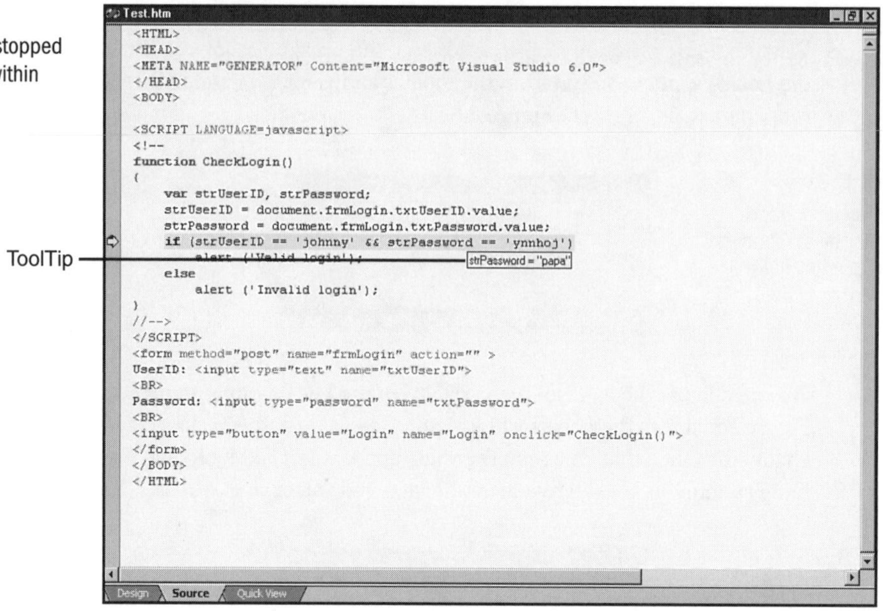

FIG. 8.10

The debugger is stopped at a breakpoint within the client-side JavaScript.

```
Test.htm
<HTML>
<HEAD>
<META NAME="GENERATOR" Content="Microsoft Visual Studio 6.0">
</HEAD>
<BODY>

<SCRIPT LANGUAGE=javascript>
<!--
function CheckLogin()
{
    var strUserID, strPassword;
    strUserID = document.frmLogin.txtUserID.value;
    strPassword = document.frmLogin.txtPassword.value;
    if (strUserID == 'johnny' && strPassword == 'ynnhoj')
        alert ('Valid login');          strPassword = "papa"
    else
        alert ('Invalid login');
}
//-->
</SCRIPT>
<form method="post" name="frmLogin" action="" >
UserID: <input type="text" name="txtUserID">
<BR>
Password: <input type="password" name="txtPassword">
<BR>
<input type="button" value="Login" name="Login" onclick="CheckLogin()">
</form>
</BODY>
</HTML>
```

ToolTip

Design   **Source**   Quick View

The Debugging Windows

By analyzing the changes in your data, you can better isolate possible problems in your script. You want to make it easier to find a problem with an expression that sets a variable or property with an incorrect value. After all, the fun of Web development is seeing the results work, not spending countless hours debugging your code. By using the Locals window, the Watch window, and the Immediate window, you can monitor the values of expressions and variables while stepping through the statements in your script.

In the previous section, we discussed how the Immediate window can aid your debugging efforts. Another debugging feature that Visual InterDev 6 employs is the *call stack*. The call stack displays a list of running procedures for the current thread of execution (which you can change).

The Locals window displays the local variables and their values in the current context. As the execution changes context by switching from procedure to procedure, the contents of the Locals window change to reflect the local variables in the current context. Keep in mind that the Locals window is only updated when execution of the script is stopped. Values that have changed since the last break in the execution of the script are highlighted in the Locals window.

The drag-and-drop features of Windows are implemented here as well. For example, you can drag a variable from the Locals window to the Immediate window or the Watch window. To access the Locals window, select Locals Window from the View menu (or press Ctrl+Alt+L).

TIP Speaking of debuggers, if you want the script debugger to automatically launch itself when an error occurs (or don't want it to launch), you can set IE 4's options to configure this. From the View menu in IE 4, choose Internet Options and select the Advanced tab (or press Alt+V+O). From here, you can check the option to Disable Script Debugging, as shown in Figure 8.11. If you disable script debugging, the Script Debugger option in the View menu in IE will not be available.

FIG. 8.11
The Internet Explorer 4 advanced options, including disabling the script debugger.

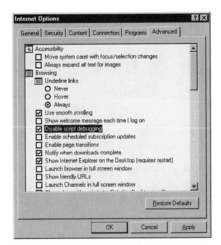

Client Script Debugging with Visual InterDev 6

There are two types of client script: global (or inline) and event-handling script. Inline scripts (see Listing 8.3) are not part of an event-handling subroutine or function and thus are parsed and executed immediately. Event-handling subroutines or functions (see Listing 8.4) are parsed right away but are not executed until they are kicked off by an event or fired explicitly by other script.

N O T E Each Web application contains a single Global.asa file. The `Application_OnStart` and `Session_OnStart` procedures in the Global.asa file are executed only once for an application and for a session, respectively. We have said that procedures are called from other procedures or inline script. However, that is not true with procedures in the Global.asa file. They are fired automatically by the Web server when the first client requests a page from the application (`Application_OnStart`) and when each new client requests a page from the site (`Session_OnStart`). Because these procedures are not triggered from other script, it is easiest to embed the debugging statements in the file (`stop` for VBScript or `debugger` for JavaScript). See the later section "Exception to the Rule: Global.asa" on debugging Global.asa files for more details. ▪

Listing 8.3   Example of Client-Side Inline JavaScript

```
<SCRIPT LANGUAGE=javascript>
<!--
    var strMessage;
    strMessage = 'This is displayed using inline or global JavaScript';
    alert (strMessage);
//-->
</SCRIPT>
```

Listing 8.4   Example of a Client-Side Event-Handling/Function Written in JavaScript

```
<SCRIPT LANGUAGE=javascript>
<!--
function DisplayMessage()
{
    var strMessage;
    strMessage = document.frmTest.txtMessage.value;
    alert (strMessage);
}
//-->
</SCRIPT>
```

CAUTION

When an error occurs in a script, you must stop the debugging session, fix the error, and then restart the debugging session. You cannot change script on-the-fly and see the effect of your changes without restarting the debugging session as you can when using Visual Basic's debugger.

Debugging a page in the Visual InterDev debugger is a simple process. There are a few general steps that you must follow to debug your scripts. First of all, open the project containing the page you want to debug in Visual InterDev. Load the page (.HTM or .ASP) into the editor and make it your project's start page. (You can do this by going to the Project Explorer, right-clicking the page, and selecting Set as Start Page.) At this point, set a breakpoint in the script and start the Visual InterDev debugger by pressing F5. Your script is now being run by Internet Explorer, however your breakpoint might not have been hit. If the breakpoint is in an event handler script (as opposed to an inline script), you have to trigger the event that contains the breakpoint. When Internet Explorer reaches the breakpoint, Visual InterDev displays the source code for the script in the editor window and puts the debugger in break mode.

 It is a good practice to get a working copy of the file before debugging it. This way, if you try to fix an error, you can save the file to the Web server.

That was easy! But there are times when you want to debug a script that is already running in Internet Explorer. In those cases, you can ask Internet Explorer to stop and debug the script using just-in-time debugging. What's even better is that you have several ways to invoke the just-in-time debugging.

The first method is to choose Script Debugger and then Break at Next Statement from the View menu of Internet Explorer (or press Alt+V+B+D). Then you simply have to trigger the event handler in your page's script that you want to debug. Another way to use Internet Explorer's script debugging options is to choose Open from the Script Debugger sub-menu from within the View menu. Visual InterDev is immediately launched as it begins a debugging session for the script.

A third method to invoke just-in-time debugging is to attach Visual InterDev to the script while it's running in Internet Explorer. This is a new feature of Visual InterDev that lets you attach to a specific process while it is already executing and bring it up in the Visual InterDev debugging environment. To use this method, from Visual InterDev, choose Processes from the Debug menu (Ctrl+Shft+R). In the Processes dialog box, select the Internet Explorer process, choose Attach, and then choose the script you want to debug. It's that simple!

When using Internet Explorer with Visual InterDev, you should also be aware that you can debug a script in response to an error. Simply choose Yes when Internet Explorer displays an error message that gives you the choice of debugging the script. Then, when Visual InterDev starts and loads the document, the line of script that caused the error will be highlighted.

Server-Side Script Debugging

Up until this point, we have mostly discussed how to debug client-side script. However, most applications couldn't run without employing some server-side script. Taking stage in ASP, VBScript has taken the Web development industry by storm. Because it is easy to learn, quick to program, and very versatile, VBScript has become the server-side scripting choice for many Web developers. However, JavaScript, with its object prowess, is a formidable scripting language that is very powerful on the server as well. Either way, feel confident that your server-side scripting choice will serve you well.

Processing Server-Side Script

Be aware that where most client-side script is event-driven, most server-side script is not. Rather, the Web server processes all server-side script when an ASP file is first requested, including all server-side script that is inline with HTML. Keep in mind when regarding client-side script that inline script is processed immediately and that event-handling script is processed only when its event is triggered.

Despite being processed immediately, not all server script is executed right away. Server-side script can include functions and subroutines that are executed only when they are called from other procedures or from within inline server-side script.

> **NOTE** Most server-side script in ASPs take the form of inline script because complex functions and procedures are executed faster from COM objects. Plus, removing the complex logic from ASPs by placing then in COM objects makes the ASP scripting easier to maintain. ■

All server-side script is processed before it reaches the client browser. That means that you can use server-side script to generate HTML. This is what has made ASP such a popular tool to bridge the gap between databases and the Web. Now, with Visual InterDev 6's debugging capabilities, Web development with ASP is made easier.

Server-Side Script Debugging

Visual InterDev 6 allows you to debug server-side script that executes on IIS 4. As long as IIS is running on your local computer, you can debug server-side script or client-side script locally. However, if the Web server is on remote computer, you can use remote debugging to find errors in the server-side script. If an ASP contains a mixture of both client and server script, you can use the Visual InterDev debugger to debug them.

To debug script on the server, debugging must be enabled for the application containing the ASPs you are working with. This can be done from within IIS 4 in the MMC. (Refer to the section "Enabling the Debugging Features" in the beginning of this chapter.)

Preparing to debug server-side script isn't much different than preparing for client-side script. In fact, except for IIS 4's server-side debugging setting, it's exactly the same. To debug server-side script from within a Visual InterDev solution, follow these steps:

1. Starting at the Project Explorer, right-click an ASP and select Set As Start Page.
2. Press the F5 key or choose Start from the Debug menu.

The ASP script executes until the breakpoint is reached. At that point, the debugger stops and displays the source script with that line (the line with the breakpoint) highlighted as the current line of execution.

> **NOTE** Keep in mind that if server debugging is not enabled for the application, all errors are displayed in the browser as HTML. ■

Listing 8.5 shows a simple ASP that is using server-side VBScript to display an HTML table. We use VBScript to code our server-side script, but JavaScript could have served our purposes just as well.

Listing 8.5   Example of Server-Side Inline VBScript

```
<%@ LANGUAGE=VBScript %>
<html>
<body>
<TABLE BORDER="1">
    <TR>
    <%
    for intCol = 1 to 5 step 1
```

```
            Response.Write "<TD> Column " & CStr(intCol) & "</TD>"
        next
        %>
        </TR>
    </TABLE>
    </body>
    </html>
```

At first glance, the first line of the ASP might jump out at you. This line of script is called the language directive as it specifies the default scripting language for the ASP. The rest of this ASP generates an HTML table's columns and data using the Response object's Write method. By placing a breakpoint on the line of script with the Response.Write statement, you can watch the ASP generate the HTML table. You can also use the other features of the debugger such as the ToolTip watches, Locals window, and Immediate window.

Debugging Mixed Client and Server Script

Many ASP pages contain both client-side and server-side script. You can set breakpoints in both client and server script, and as each script executes, it can call the debugger at breakpoints.

Keeping Track of Breakpoints

When you set a breakpoint in client-side script in a page that contains both server-side and client-side script, the debugger tracks the breakpoint even though the position of the breakpoint can change significantly in the file after server-side script has executed. If server-side script causes the client-side script to be written several times into the page, the debugger tracks each breakpoint separately.

You can set breakpoints in server script, client script, or both. If you set breakpoints in both, the debugger stops at the server script breakpoints first. When you continue to run, the page is sent to the browser, and the debugger then stops at breakpoints in client script.

Debugging Mixed Scripts

As Web developers, sometimes we want client-side script that uses values that are dynamically gathered from a database. Thankfully, this isn't rocket science when we use ASP. The ASP script in Listing 8.6 shows a sample page that uses server-side script to grab the value of a user's name and put it within JavaScript.

Listing 8.6   Example of Server-Side Inline VBScript That Is Embedded Within Client-Side JavaScript

```
<%@ LANGUAGE=VBScript %>
<HTML>
<BODY>
```

continues

Listing 8.6 Continued

```
<%strUserName = "Colleen"%>

<SCRIPT LANGUAGE="JavaScript">
function Welcome()
{
    strName = '<%=strUserName%>';
    debugger;
    alert ('Welcome, ' + strName + '!');
}
</SCRIPT>

<A href="SomeOtherPage.asp" onmouseover="Welcome()">Welcome</A>
</BODY>
</HTML>
```

When you want to debug mixed script, such as what appears in Listing 8.6, there are special circumstances. Listing 8.6's server-side script stores a user's name in a variable called strUserName. Then, inside the block of client-side JavaScript exists a block of embedded server-side script that dynamically inserts the value of the variable into a client-side JavaScript alert statement. If we want to debug this ASP, we need to follow these steps:

1. Make the page your project's start page.
2. Set the breakpoints in both the server-side and client-side lines of script that you want to debug. (Use the debugger statement to place the client-side JavaScript breakpoint.)
3. Start the debugger. The server-side script executes and stops at any breakpoint you set.
4. Continue the server script by pressing F5. The Web server sends the page to the browser to be displayed.
5. Trigger the event by placing your mouse over the hyperlink. The debugger stops at the client-side breakpoint.

CAUTION

At the time of this book's printing, Visual InterDev 6 did not explicitly break into the debugging environment for client-side JavaScript when a breakpoint was hit. You can simply bypass this flaw by issuing the JavaScript command debugger. However, in the final release, the client-side script's breakpoints will be indicated by purple octagons in the left margin.

Keep in mind that, when debugging client-side script generated by an ASP, the line numbers reported in error messages refer to lines in the HTML document currently displayed in the browser. These do not necessarily correspond to line numbers in the original ASP! The moral of the story is that any time you receive an error message in the browser's HTML text, the line number referred to is the line number in the HTML. This is true whether the HTML was static or it was generated by an ASP.

Part

II

Ch

8

N O T E Embedded server-side script within client-side script does not use the scripting language's color-coding conventions. ▨

If you set a breakpoint on the line with the embedded server script, Visual InterDev can't determine whether you want the debugger to break on the server-side script (`<%=strUserName%>`) or on the client-side script (`strName =`). In this case, you can tell Visual InterDev that you want these breakpoints to be interpreted as client-side breakpoints. If you choose to do this, be aware that the debugger doesn't break when the server is processing the embedded server-side script. You do have another option: you can tell the debugger to stop both when it processes the server-side script and when it reaches the same line while running the client-side script later.

So what happens when you want to break on a mixed script line (a line with both client-side and server-side script)? By default, Visual InterDev 6 only stops at client breakpoints. You need to enable a debugger setting if you want Visual InterDev to break on both the client-side and server-side breakpoints. The following line of code, from Listing 8.6, is an example of a mixed script line:

```
strName = '<%=strUserName%>';
```

CAUTION

Setting this option to its default state (client-side only) does not turn off server-side debugging. It only turns off server-side debugging for server-side scripting statements that are embedded within client-side scripting statements.

You can view or change this configuration setting by going to the Tools menu, selecting Options (or press Alt+T+O), and then opening the Debugger node. The option Insert Breakpoints in Active Server Pages for Breakpoints in Client Script is unchecked, by default. If you check this check box, Visual InterDev breaks on both the server-side and client-side script for mixed script lines.

Exception to the Rule: Global.asa

As with the rules of grammar for the English language, there is always an exception to the rule, and the Global.asa file is that exception to the Visual InterDev 6 debugging rules. For example, you can't use a browser to start the debugger on the Global.asa file. You cannot request the Global.asa document from the client browser. Rather, the server executes the Global.asa file and its procedures immediately when you first request any file in the ASP application (see Table 8.3).

Table 8.3   The Four Procedures in the Global.asa File and When They Are Executed

Procedure	Executes When...
Application_OnStart	First time user goes to a page in ASP application
Application_OnEnd	When the application is shut down
Session_OnStart	Once per user session
Session_OnEnd	User's session times out (or on Session.Abandon)

Because the debugger can't be explicitly invoked by requesting the Global.asa file, you don't have the option of stepping into the debugger or setting the page as your start page. So to get the Global.asa file to exist in the debugging environment of Visual InterDev 6, you have to set a breakpoint or use the explicit debugger invoking statement appropriate to the scripting language (debugger for JavaScript and stop for VBScript).

When the application starts or when a user starts a new session, the corresponding procedure in a Global.asa file executes. After the debugger breaks into the script, you can then step through the procedure employing the debugging windows and tools.

A quick way to restart the application and session is to change the Global.asa file and then publish it to the Web server. If you simply want to stop the session without restarting the application, then submit an ASP that contains the Session.Abandon statement to kill the session. Then request a page in the application to restart the session and run the Global.asa's Session_OnStart procedure. You can also close and re-open your browser. However, this method doesn't close the previous session; it only starts a new session.

From Here...

No matter what debugging techniques you require, Visual InterDev 6 can aid your Web development like no other Web development tool can. The long awaited debugging features of Visual InterDev 6 are worth the wait as Microsoft delivers the goods with this tool. Whether you want to connect and debug an Internet Explorer process, jump into mixed client-side and server-side script, or simply want to see all of the variables' values in your current context, you have the flexibility with Visual InterDev 6.

CHAPTER 9

Creating Pages with Dynamic HTML

In this chapter

Introducing the Power of Dynamic HTML   **190**

The Internet Explorer Object Model   **192**

Understanding Events and Event Bubbling   **195**

Using Style and Positioning for Better Layouts   **196**

Adding Multimedia Effects to Pages   **199**

Building Channels and Desktop Items   **203**

Creating Scriptlets   **205**

Introducing the Power of Dynamic HTML

The word *dynamic* seems to be attached to just about everything that is affiliated with the Internet these days—more often than not as a marketing ploy. What makes Dynamic Hypertext Markup Language, also called Dynamic HTML or DHTML, so important? First, it allows Web developers to extend the functionality of traditional HTML to include interactivity. It also is a standard that allows for greater control of Web page layout, formatting, and even animation.

You may be sick of hearing about the "next, latest, greatest thing" on the Internet that will supposedly launch the as-yet infant World Wide Web into the ranks of primacy along with all those other media, such as television and radio. In this case, the next, latest, greatest thing is DHTML, but don't make the mistake of assuming that it's a load of hooey. Even though the standard is still in its infancy, you can do a lot with DHTML.

The most pertinent question is then, "What is DHTML?" You can't find the answer easily, but a general response would be "A combination of JavaScript, Cascading Style Sheets (CSS), and the Document Object Model (DOM) as implemented by the 4.*x* browser version as presented by Microsoft and Netscape." Dynamic HTML is something of a misnomer because the functionality attached to it is very broad and has little to do with HTML itself. The World Wide Web Consortium considers the majority of Netscape's and Microsoft's additions as extensions to the existing standard.

N O T E The World Wide Web Consortium (W3C) is considered the standards commission of the World Wide Web and is, in fact, home to the original specification of many Internet technologies, including the original HTML standard. You can find the W3C at **http://www.w3c.org**. ■

The problem is whose DHTML to use. Both Netscape and Microsoft have battling browsers right now, both of which claim to support DHTML as each company sees it. Once again, though, these competing standards do not easily see eye to eye. In fact, some might say that they're downright incompatible. The majority of this chapter will focus on Microsoft's Internet Explorer model of DHTML, but you can find a breakdown of both companies' DHTML standards in the following sidebars.

Highlights of the Netscape Implementation of DHTML

- *Absolute Positioning*. Early in the development of Communicator 4, Netscape created its own exact positioning scheme, using the <LAYER> and <ILAYER> tags. Layers allowed users to create exact positioning and the ability to manipulate objects on the Z-axis—that is, to put one in front of the other. Unfortunately, this proved to be as popular as the <BLINK> tag was in Navigator 1.1, so the W3C rejected the standard. You can still use <LAYER> and <ILAYER> with the current release of Netscape Communicator, however.

- *CSS Positioning*. Netscape then went on to support Cascading Style Sheets (CSS) and its definition of positioning. Regardless of how you position (using CSS or <LAYER>), Communicator allows you to reference your HTML elements on the fly, creating dynamic layouts.

- *Portable Fonts.* Netscape has also built in the ability to package and transport fonts within your document, to create a specific impact when dealing with highly font-dependent layouts. (This feature really isn't a DHTML standard; it's just something neat with the new browser.)
- *Cascading Style Sheets.* Communicator supports the CSS specification as found on the W3C CSS Web site.

ON THE WEB

For a complete breakdown of the Netscape Communicator DHTML specification, including examples, investigate this site:

http://developer.netscape.com

Highlights of the Microsoft Implementation of DHTML

- *Dynamic HTML Object Model.* The flagship of Microsoft's Dynamic HTML fleet of features is its implementation of the Web Browser Object Model. The Object Model allows you to treat HTML tags as objects, with attributes and behaviors. More important, though, you can change the contents of a tag dynamically, and all on a client-side basis.
- *Dynamic Content.* Microsoft has created a dynamic content engine through its use of the Web Browser Object Model. You can link events and triggers to content on the Web page, displaying it as you choose. Once again, this activity takes place on the client side of operations and doesn't require the Web server's intervention.
- *Dynamic Styles.* You can change text style and formatting by using CSS in both Netscape and Microsoft's DHTML solutions. However, the Internet Explorer version allows you to change styles on a document-wide basis, allowing for rapid and flexible reformatting.
- *Cascading Style Sheets.* Like Netscape, Microsoft uses CSS for both positioning and formatting, according to the W3C specification. In fact, this CSS formatting is the only universal aspect of DHTML that is common to both browsers.
- *Data Controls.* The new version of Internet Explorer allows for some limited file access functionality, meaning that DHTML pages can include offline data from the Web server. Using controls like the Data Source Object ActiveX Control, you can read in textual data from a simple ASCII file.
- *Animation.* ActiveX controls are also used to add some punch to Microsoft's DHTML visually. Certain controls can add or subtract visual effects in your document, and the DirectAnimation system also gives you basic animation functionality.

ON THE WEB

You can find Microsoft's complete DHTML specification at this address:

http://www.microsoft.com/msdn/sdk/inetsdk/help

Although not a lot of agreement is going on between the two browser types, many powerful functions are being integrated into the DHTML standard. Unfortunately, getting browser agreement between the two is very difficult while still maintaining a universal code base. The only point that Internet Explorer and Netscape Navigator agree upon standards is in CSS. The rest is an open battlefield. The most common strategy for supporting both standards is to have two different copies, with a browser differentiation check at the beginning of a file. The quickest and easiest way to do so is to use the `navigator` object, as follows:

```
If (navigator.appName == "Netscape")
        {
        Communicator conditional code
        }
else
        {
        Explorer specific code
        }
```

The only other realistic method of cross-browser compatibility is to embed the Netscape `<ILAYER>` tag with Internet Explorer `ID` references, like this:

```
<ILAYER ID="Image1"><IMG ID="Image1" SRC="[...]"></ILAYER>
```

In this case, Netscape sees the `ID="Image1"` that it needs in the `<ILAYER>` tag and ignores the `ID="Image1"` in the `<IMG>` tag itself. Conversely, Internet Explorer ignores the entire `<ILAYER>` structure and reads in the `<IMG ID="Image1">` to get the information it needs. The only drawback, of course, is maintaining two sets of `ID` tags.

For the examples found later in this chapter, you'll need Microsoft Internet Explorer 4.0 or later.

The Internet Explorer Object Model

The strength of Microsoft's DHTML draws heavily upon the strength of the Document Object Model (DOM) found in Internet Explorer 4.0. Previously, the DOM existed to facilitate the use of `FORM` elements for client-side form handling. The new specification has extended that functionality to include *every single tag* found within the document. This means that the dull, static HTML page has suddenly been turned into a complex, object-oriented programming model.

Previously, the traditional Web page was a single unit, a lump sum. Now, with the extended Microsoft DOM, you can treat each tag as a module, with its own attributes and behaviors. Depending on events or user interaction, you can activate or hide certain tags as you please.

The important point to remember about the DOM is that it makes your HTML document *object-based*. This means that the document is divided into several discrete modules that can interact with or contain one another, and each module has attributes or properties that can control its behavior. The difference between the Microsoft DOM and the Netscape DOM is that the Microsoft version has far more objects to manipulate. The basic listing of objects found in the Microsoft Document Object Model are detailed in the following sections.

Window

The Window object is the actual Web browser window. It contains the following child objects:

Location. Specifies the current URL.

Frames. Can contain different window objects to make up a framed layout.

History. Specifies the browser's past locations.

Navigator. Provides browser information such as version, type, and so on.

Event. Tracks the various events occurring within the browser.

Screen. Indicates screen resolution and depth statistics.

Document

The document object, which is also a child of the window object, provides access to the entire HTML document and its attachments. The document object has the following children:

Links. Indicates the links referenced within the document.

Anchors. Lists the anchors referenced within the document.

Forms. Indicates all the form elements within the document. Each <FORM> tag has one form object.

Applets. Provides information about the Java applets within the document.

Embeds or plugins. Specifies all the information regarding the <EMBED> tag.

Scripts. Lists the scripting elements within the document.

Images. Lists the collection of images, one object per <IMG> tag.

Filters. Contains information about any filters associated with the document.

All. Accesses the entire HTML document as a whole.

Selection. Contains the current active selection, as specified by the user.

Stylesheets. Identifies the style sheets attached to the document.

Body. Allows you to access the <BODY> tag.

Note that several of these objects are, in fact, collections of other objects. For example, the links object simply contains all the hot link references within that document. The DOM treats these collections as arrays of data, which means you can use the traditional script method of calling array elements, as shown here:

```
<A HREF=http://www.mcp.com ID=MCPLink>
document.links[0]
document.links.MCPLink
document.links("MCPLink")
```

The first call (document.links[0]) says to the browser, "Give me the very first link in your links list." The second and third calls say, "Give me the link called 'MCPLink'." The first method is relative; it works only if you know for a fact that a certain link occurs within a certain order. The second and third are more exact, but using specific references can also work against you if you want to change the references later.

In the preceding example, you reference an object and one of its *properties*. In the previous case, the property was the ID, and the object was the links object, which was contained in the document object. To reference a property, you first need to state its object and any other objects that come first in the hierarchy, as in this example:

```
document.images.length
```

This line returns the number of images in the document, essentially checking how "long" the images object is. Many of the properties that you can display, you can also change. For example, you can change the MCPLink in the first example, as follows:

```
document.links.MCPLink = "http://www.mcp.com/downloads"
```

This line changes the link from **http://www.mcp.com**, as it was originally defined, to **http://www.mcp.com/downloads**. The fact that you can make this change to every single tag is a huge advantage for the Internet Explorer Document Object Model. Listing 9.1 shows you how to use the all object to list and describe every tag within a document.

Listing 9.1   9_LIST1.HTM—Using the *all* Object to Describe Every Tag in a Document

```
<HTML>
<HEAD>
<TITLE>Having your document give its 'all'</TITLE>
</HEAD>
<BODY>
<H2>A DHTML Example</H2>
<P>
Using the <B>all</B> object to manipulate a document as a whole.
This script tells you the name and amount of every tag within this document.
The relevant properties used are <B>length</B> and <B>tagName</B>,
which of course are properties of the <B>all</B> object.
</P>
</BODY>

<SCRIPT LANGUAGE="JavaScript">
total = document.all.length
for(i = 0;i < total; i++)
        document.write("Tag Number: " +(i+1) +" Tag Name =
➥    " +document.all[i].tagName + "<BR>")
</SCRIPT>
</HTML>
```

Figure 9.1 shows the output from Listing 9.1. Note that the DOM places the tags in the order they were opened.

DOM has far too many properties to list in the confines of this chapter. Suffice it to say that if you need a certain property for a certain task, the Microsoft DOM has one at your disposal.

FIG. 9.1

The all object can be an incredibly powerful tool that allows you to manipulate all the code within your document in one task.

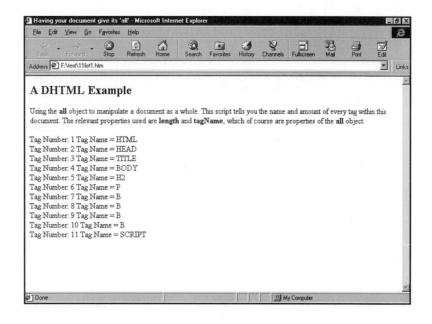

ON THE WEB

For a complete listing of all the Object Model properties, go to this site:

**http://www.microsoft.com/msdn/sdk/inetsdk/help/dhtml/references/properties/
properties.htm#om40_prop**

Understanding Events and Event Bubbling

An *event* is an action or circumstance that can trigger a process within a Web page. The idea of the event model has been around for quite a while and has been incorporated into the various scripting standards found on both browsers. Some old examples include onClick, OnLoad, and onMouseOver. The new DOM expands on these events and includes several new ones as well.

Much like properties, too many events are available to be listed adequately in the space allotted. For example, you can find several new controls for keyboard, mouse, and even window events.

ON THE WEB

For a complete listing of the Internet Explorer Document Object Model events, go to this site:

**http://www.microsoft.com/msdn/sdk/inetsdk/help/dhtml/references/events/
events.htm#om40_event**

Event declaration comes in two parts. In the first, you link the actual event to the object you want activated. The most common use of event handling is form submission, so this example links the event to the form submit button:

```
<FORM NAME="AForm">
<INPUT TYPE="BUTTON" VALUE="Submit" NAME="SubButton" onClick="thankyou()">
</FORM>
```

The second part of calling an event is defining the code that handles the event itself, as you can see in this example:

```
<SCRIPT LANGUAGE="JavaScript">
function thankyou()
        {
        alert("Thank You for your input.")
        }
</SCRIPT>
```

In this case, the submit button is linked to the function thankyou, which is called onClick of the button. After it is clicked, the button calls the thankyou function, which in turn displays an alert box thanking the user for input.

Internet Explorer goes a bit further with event handling, however. Traditionally, you had to explicitly specify an event handler for a particular event. Internet Explorer supports what's known as *event bubbling,* which is a process that allows an event to be triggered and then has an event handler "found" for it. It does so by working in order of size. If an event occurs on an <IMG> object but with no handler defined, the event bubbles up to next level. Consider this example:

```
<HTML>
<BODY>
<DIV ID=OuterDivLayer LANGUAGE="JavaScript"
➥     onmouseover="alert(window.event.srcElement.id);">
<IMG ID="AnImage" SRC="[...]">
</DIV>
</BODY>
</HTML>
```

If you move the mouse pointer over the image in the preceding example, you get an alert box saying AnImage, even though no event handler is explicitly defined for the image itself. When this event occurs, Internet Explorer immediately determines that no event handler is available for the image. It then goes up to the next hierarchical level, to the tag in which the <IMG> is contained, which in this case is the <DIV> tag. The <DIV> tag does have an event handler, and so the <IMG> tag "inherits" the mouseover event.

Using Style and Positioning for Better Layouts

Cascading Style Sheets are the essential ingredient for large-scale style and format changes in a DHTML document, and fortunately both major browser types support the basic definitions of CSS.

ON THE WEB

For the complete Cascading Style Sheets formal definition, see this site:

http://www.w3c.org/Style

The philosophy behind CSS is to divorce content from formatting in the traditional HTML page. The tags behind HTML are getting more and more complex and bloated, and the people at the W3C are trying to rein in that complexity by creating formats that don't necessarily reside within the HTML. Both CSS and DHTML are examples of this thinking.

The primary use of CSS is changing font information such as size, weight, face, and so on. However, what comes as an important breakthrough in terms of DHTML and CSS is *absolute positioning*, which is the ability to place an object on a page exactly where you want it, instead of using the macro-scale HTML tools currently available.

The following list shows the names of the CSS positional attributes, followed by possible values, and brief descriptions of what they do. The default value for these attributes is `auto`, unless specified otherwise.

- `position`

  Possible values: `absolute` | `relative` | `static`

  Controls whether the element allows you to move it further, and if so, whether it moves on an absolute scale within the browser window or relatively to the element's location on the page. If the position is set to `static` (which it is by default), then it can't be moved at all and behaves just like a traditional HTML element.

- `left`

  Possible values: `absolute length` | `percentage` | `auto`

  Determines where the left edge of the element starts, either by an absolute length or percentage.

- `top`

  Possible values: `absolute length` | `percentage` | `auto`

  Determines where the top edge of the element lies, either by an absolute length or percentage.

- `width`

  Possible values: `absolute length` | `percentage` | `auto`

  Determines the width of the element, either by an absolute length or percentage.

- `height`

  Possible values: `absolute length` | `percentage` | `auto`

  Determines the height of the element, either by an absolute length or percentage.

- `clip`

  Possible values: `bounding box` | `auto`

Part

II

Ch

9

If specified, the bounding box gives the four coordinates that define a rectangle deter-mining the visible portion of the element.

■ overflow

Possible values: scroll | visible | hidden | auto

Determines how parts of the HTML element outside the visible area (defined in clip) are displayed, if at all.

■ z-index

Possible values: stacking order | auto

Determines the three-dimensional position of the HTML elements. The higher z-index integer, the closer the element is to the viewer.

■ visibility

Possible values: visible | hidden | auto

Determines whether the element is visible.

You should note that, by default, the unit of measurement for CSS positioning is the pixel. You can define other units only by including a unit abbreviation after the number (for example, 30cm).

Listing 9.2 shows how you can place an image behind text and position both exactly using embedded CSS.

Listing 9.2   9_LIST2.HTM   Absolute Positioning and Formatting with CSSs

```
<HTML>
<HEAD>
<TITLE>CSS Positioning and Formatting</TITLE>
<STYLE TYPE="text/css">
.PictureInfo
        {
        position: absolute;
        left: 100px;
        top: 150px;
        width: 200;
        height: 200;
        z-index: 0;
        }
.TextInfo
        {
        position: absolute;
        left: 100px;
        top: 150px;
        width: 200px;
        z-index: 1;
        color: #FF0000;
        font-family: Arial;
        font-size: 24;
        text-align: left;
        }
```

```
</STYLE>
</HEAD>
<BODY BGCOLOR="#000000" TEXT="#FFFFFF">
<CENTER>
<H1>Cascading Style Sheets</H1>
<H2>Positioning and Formatting</H2>
<P ALIGN="CENTER"> 
<IMG CLASS="PictureInfo" SRC="10list2.gif" WIDTH="200" HEIGHT="200"
➥    BORDER=0 ALT="PictureInfo">
<DIV CLASS="TextInfo">
Theoretically this text will now be overwriting this mostly black image.<BR>
</DIV>
</P>
</CENTER>
</BODY>
</HTML>
```

Part
II

Ch
9

Figure 9.2 shows the results of the code. Note that the text is placed squarely over the image, and that the `width` attribute contains the text element and also defines the dimensions of the graphical element.

FIG. 9.2
The `width` and `height` attributes can also help you define how large you want your text areas to actually be.

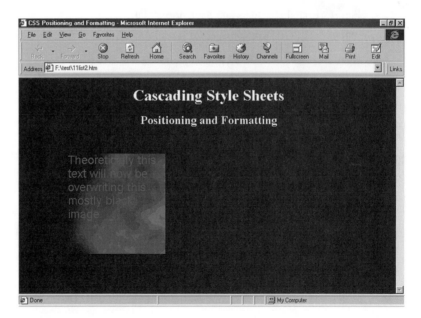

Adding Multimedia Effects to Pages

The entire approach behind the multimedia effects in Microsoft's version of DHTML has two parts: filters and DirectAnimation. Essentially, a filter puts a layer between you and the browser. What happens on that layer is entirely up to the filter. Although your page and its graphics look to be permanently changed, they're modified only temporarily while the filter is in effect. The entire concept is comparable to a colored acetate layer that goes on your monitor screen: The entire screen changes color, but you know that under the acetate your monitor is still there, good as ever.

Filters themselves are essentially ActiveX controls, which can be applied to an entire HTML document or perhaps just a single graphic. The advantage of using filters is that they leave the source graphic alone; you therefore can reuse the same graphic in different places but with different filters. Table 9.1 lists the filters that are included with Internet Explorer 4.0.

Table 9.1   Bundled Filters with Internet Explorer 4.0

Filter	Description
Alpha	Controls opacity
Blur	Blurs an object in a given direction
Chroma	Makes a certain color transparent
Drop Shadow	Creates a shadow for the object
Flip Horizontal	Flips an image horizontally
Flip Vertical	Flips an image vertically
Glow	Adds a glowing aura
Grayscale	Shows an object in shades of gray
Invert	Inverts color values
Light	Adds light sources to an object
Mask	Makes certain colored pixels transparent and applies those pixels as a mask to an object
Shadow	Creates a directional shadow
Wave	Creates a waveform distortion along the vertical axis
Xray	Changes an object's color depth and displays it in black and white

Now that you know the basic filter types, it's time to get your hands dirty and try to insert them in your code. Listing 9.3 demonstrates a simple filter effect.

Listing 9.3   9_LIST3.HTM—A Simple Application of the Blur Filter

```
<HTML>
<HEAD>
      <TITLE>CSS Blurring Filter</TITLE>
</HEAD>

<BODY bgcolor="#000000" TEXT="#FFFFFF">

<CENTER>
```

```
<DIV ID=effected Style="width:90%" style="font-family=Arial">
<P>
<B>
Filters can affect any HTML element, including text, windowless controls,
intrinsic controls, and images.
</B>
</P>
<IMG hspace=10 vspace=10 width=200 height=200 src=10list2.gif
➥    onmouseover="effected.style.filter = 'blur(direction=45,strength=15,
➥    add=0, enabled=1)';" onmouseout="effected.style.filter =
➥    'blur(enabled=0)';">
</DIV>
</CENTER>
</BODY>
</HTML>
```

Before you start getting all excited about how easily you can use filters, you should know that the application of the blur filter in Listing 9.3 is probably the most simple it can possibly get. You can find an incredibly useful demonstration of all the default filters on Microsoft's site.

ON THE WEB

For a complete listing and example of the bundled filters and how to use them, go to this address:

http://www.microsoft.com/ie/ie40/demos/filters.htm

The two parts to any filter declaration are identifying the areas affected and triggering the code. In the case of Listing 9.3, the areas affected are contained by the <DIV =effected> tag. Anything within that tag is influenced by the filter's effects, regardless of what it actually is (graphic, text, form button, what have you). The filter is triggered by using the familiar event-handling tool, the onClick function. In this case, though, an added line or so of code controls the blur effect, as well as its strength and direction. For a before and after look at the blur filter, check out Figure 9.3 and Figure 9.4.

Some of the other filters require more advanced criteria for execution, including some JavaScript interaction. However, the basic filter declaration structure remains the same, as you can see here:

```
<DIV ID=effected area name STYLE="style parameters">
        ...text
        <IMG SRC="[...]">
</DIV>
```

Without the <DIV> container, the filter doesn't know which part of the page it's influencing. After the <DIV> declaration comes the event trigger—in this case, an onmouseover event. In this example, a second trigger comes into play when the mouse rolls off the image, removing the blur effect.

FIG. 9.3
The test page before
blurring...

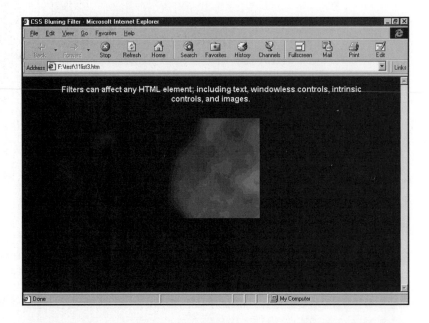

FIG. 9.4
...and after blurring.

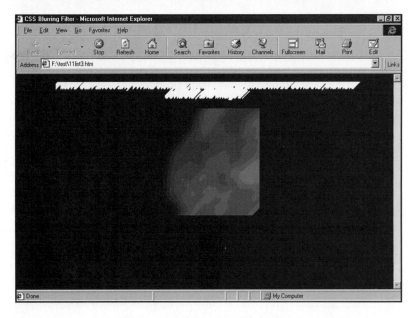

DirectAnimation is another kettle of fish entirely, having an incredibly powerful host of features and functions. Unfortunately, though, the average DirectAnimation file is usually several hundred lines of code, which is far too much to incorporate here. The principles behind DirectAnimation are nearly the same as those behind absolute position with CSS—except in this case, the objects on the screen are updated more than once. Essentially, when you use

DirectAnimation, you engage in absolute positioning, but at the rate of several times per second. The difference between them could be compared to a photograph and a video.

DirectAnimation is made up of a lot more than just CSS, of course, but the principles are the same. Microsoft offers several animation-related ActiveX objects and indeed an entire DirectAnimation API for hungry developers.

ON THE WEB

You can find the details on Microsoft DirectAnimation on its site:

http://www.microsoft.com/directx/dxm/help/da/c-frame.htm?default.htm

ON THE WEB

You also can find a good example of some simple DirectAnimation at Web Site Abstraction:

http://www.wsabstract.com/script/cut122.htm

Building Channels and Desktop Items

You're probably used to the Web by now, having to go out and get things, surfing around to various sites, generally traveling in a metaphoric sense. What if the situation were reversed, and instead of your busting your chops to get the content, it came to you? This revolutionary idea is called *push* technology because the content publishers are now actively pushing their material to the end users instead of inviting them over to chat. Surfing the Web versus using push technology is sort of like the difference between watching the football game at your buddy's house and having your own Super Bowl party.

The heart behind Microsoft's implementation of push technology is the Channel Definition Format (CDF). It actually isn't a part of any DHTML standard, as it predates DHTML by about a year in terms of release dates. In fact, the CDF format is based around XML (Extensible Markup Language), a much more powerful standard than HTML. However, CDF doesn't have nearly the same acceptance, although XML is making quiet waves in the developer world as you read this chapter.

What makes CDF so special is the level of integration you can achieve with the operating system. With the advent of Windows 98/Internet Explorer 4.0's Active Desktop, you can embed content in your own desktop. What better place for a push technology? The Channel Definition Format uses 17 basic commands, which are listed in Table 9.2.

The similarities between HTML and XML are obvious, especially concerning anchor references and the hierarchy. Here is a caveat to programmers: XML is very particular about how its tags are opened and closed. The simple example shown in Listing 9.4 should give you a good idea of how to define your own channels, especially when combined with the commands from Table 9.2.

Table 9.2   Channel Definition Format Commands

Command	Definition
?XML	The XML equivalent of <HTML>, tells potential parsers that this is an XML file.
A	Just like the HTML <A HREF>, provides a link to other documents.
ABSTRACT	Much like the *TV Guide* for channels, appears as a ToolTip like a traditional ALT tag.
CHANNEL	The rough equivalent of a <BODY> tag, defines a new channel and can contain most of the other tags.
EARLIESTTIME	States the earliest possible time a CDF can be updated.
HTTP-EQUIV	Supplies the equivalent of HTTP header information about a file.
INTERVALTIME	Determines how long an interval should pass between channel update times.
ITEM	The base unit of information within a channel, can contain several other tags.
LATESTTIME	States the latest time within a set interval that an item can be updated.
LOG	Specifies that a particular link or "hit" should be logged from the parent.
LOGIN	Provides a security layer to enforce channel memberships with a name and password.
LOGO	Contains information that represents a channel or channel item, usually graphical.
LOGTARGET	Specifies where to send a client hit log file.
PURGETIME	Indicates the expiry date on a channel or item.
SCHEDULE	Defines the schedule of a channel's update process.
TITLE	Defines a title for an item or channel.
USAGE	Indicates how an item or channel should be used. For example, you can choose from Active Desktop, Screen Saver, Channel, E-mail, Software Update, or None.

Listing 9.4   9LIST4.CDF—Sample Channel Definition Format

```
<?XML Version="1.0"?>

<CHANNEL HREF="http://www.myserver.com/mychannel.htm">

<ABSTRACT>Welcome to my Alien Abduction Channel!</ABSTRACT>
<TITLE>Jose's Alien Experiences</TITLE>
<LOGO HREF="http://www.myserver.com/mychannel/ufo.ico" STYLE="icon" />
```

```
<LOGO HREF="http://www.myserver.com/mychannel/bigeyes.gif" STYLE="image" />
<LOGO HREF="http://www.myserver.com/mychannel/starrysky.gif" STYLE="image-wide" />

<ITEM HREF="http://www.myserver.com/mychannel2.htm">
<ABSTRACT>Stories from Around the Galaxy</ABSTRACT>
<TITLE>Aliens took my little brother Ike!</TITLE>
</ITEM>

<ITEM HREF="http://www.myserver.com/mychannel3.htm">
<ABSTRACT>Experience a spine-tingling tale of supernatural horror</ABSTRACT>
<TITLE>When the Werewolf came to my backyard</TITLE>
</ITEM>

</CHANNEL>
```

To change a channel's USAGE, you need to insert the tag into the ITEM tag, like this:

```
<ITEM HREF="http://www.faboo.com/screensaver.htm">
<USAGE VALUE="ScreenSaver"></USAGE></ITEM>
```

Alternatively, you can change the entire tenor of the item or channel by making its USAGE a DESKTOP COMPONENT, CHANNEL, E-MAIL, or SOFTWARE UPDATE. The power of the XML format is that the content is almost entirely divorced from the formatting (which is admittedly limited by the Channel Definition Format).

Creating Scriptlets

Despite having such a cute name, Scriptlets are a powerful tool that extend Internet Explorer 4.0's functionality even more. Although not formally part of DHTML, Scriptlets allow you to create modular Web libraries that can be used in any Web page you make. You can create them by using standard HTML, scripting, and DHTML, and include them in a Web site by using the <OBJECT> tag.

Web developers have been looking for something with the power of Scriptlets for a long time. Because the Scriptlets are centrally located and generally called only on demand, you can put all sorts of fluid information into Scriptlets and then go back and change it. Because a Scriptlet exists in only one place, you can enact site-wide changes by editing a single file. You can also save yourself a lot of typing by simply repeating relevant scripts in your code. Some common uses for Scriptlets are repeating user interfaces, large table definitions, and repeating code segments such as button rollovers.

ON THE WEB

For all the latest information on Scriptlets and scripting generally, go to this site:

http://www.microsoft.com/scripting/

A Scriptlet is embedded into an HTML document as it's interpreted by the browser. This means that the interaction between code and user is a bit more limited than in the DHTML you've learned thus far. I'm not saying that you can't interact anymore; Scriptlets can talk to any other Web component. However, when you can talk to the Scriptlet is another matter.

A Scriptlet has two interactive events: onscripletevent, and the standard mouse clicks and keypresses. The onscriptletevent is essentially just a string and the <OBJECT> definition. The container HTML document can use the supplied string to determine its course of action and then interpret the object parameters accordingly. Only at this time do you have onscriptletevent interactivity.

The Scriptlet is referenced much like any other external Web component, with the same security precautions. If you have a Scriptlet function that you need or want to share, you preface it with public, as shown in this example:

```
<SCRIPT LANGUAGE="JavaScript">
public_Value = "This value can be seen externally"
OtherValue = "This value is still held privately"
Function public_ShowMsg(param1, param2)
       {
       [...]
       }
</SCRIPT>
```

In the preceding example, the variable prefaced with public is accessible to the container HTML file calling the Scriptlet. The variable without public is not. The procedure to call a Scriptlet from the HTML file is just as simple. Assuming you've saved the preceding example somewhere as MyScriptlet.htm, you can use it as follows:

```
<OBJECT width=300 height=300 TYPE="text/x-scriptlet" DATA="MyScriptlet.htm">
</OBJECT>
<SCRIPT LANGUAGE="JavaScript">
alert(MyScriptlet.Value)
MyScriptlet.ShowMsg(param1, param2)
</SCRIPT>
```

The height and width tags define how large the Scriptlet is within the page. The TYPE attribute must be text/x-scriptlet to let Internet Explorer 4.0 know that the object is a Scriptlet.

All this information may be well and good, but how does it relate to Visual InterDev? The Visual InterDev environment has some pretty powerful Scriptlet preview functions that allow you to develop and embed Scriptlets almost seamlessly. Just follow this procedure:

1. Create a simple HTML file like "Hello World," and add some basic text to it (why, even "Hello World!" would work well here). Save it within your Visual InterDev Web project.

2. In the Project Explorer window, right-click the name of the file you just made, and choose Mark As Scriptlet from the context menu.

3. Open an existing Web document, or create another entirely new file.

4. Press Ctrl+Alt+X, or click the Toolbox button to open the Toolbox.

5. Open the Scriptlets pane by clicking it.

6. Click and drag your first "Hello World" file into the new document. This action inserts the Scriptlet wherever you place it.

Visual InterDev's preview capability makes this feature especially powerful. Immediately after you drag the Scriptlet into the document, you see exactly what it looks like, as shown in Figure 9.5.

FIG. 9.5
Scriptlets can add automated functionality to your Web sites, but without the complex programming associated with batch commands.

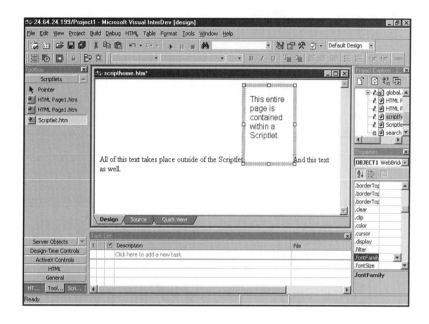

From there, you can you add and define Scriptlets as you please. Don't forget that you can change the Scriptlet's primary statistics by editing them in the Properties window, much like any other object in Visual InterDev.

From Here...

Dynamic HTML is taking Web applications a step further by adding comprehensive and powerful features to the client side. By combining server-side activation and client-side Dynamic HTML, you can create spectacular applications that your users will appreciate. For information on topics related to Dynamic HTML, consider looking to the following resources:

- Chapter 11, "Designing with Design-Time Controls."
- *Platinum Edition Using HTML 4, Java 1.1, and JavaScript 1.2* from Que.

Creating and Using ActiveX Controls

10 Using ActiveX Controls   211

11 Designing with Design-Time Controls   235

12 Building ActiveX Controls with Visual Basic   261

13 Building and Deploying Server Components   283

CHAPTER 10

Using ActiveX Controls

In this chapter

Quick Refresher on ActiveX Controls **212**

Easy Multimedia—The Animated GIF **212**

Using the Toolbox and Script Builder **215**

Multimedia ActiveX Controls **220**

Scrolling Text and Marquees **221**

The ActiveMovie Control **224**

Other Multimedia Options **232**

Quick Refresher on ActiveX Controls

In Chapter 6, "Client-Side Scripting," you were introduced to using ActiveX controls. You built a simple form in a Web page using ActiveX controls. In this chapter, your knowledge of how ActiveX controls can be used on a Web page will be expanded further.

As you might recall, ActiveX controls are components that can be placed on your Web pages to perform just about any task imaginable. An ActiveX control can be as simple as a specialized text box or as complex as the grid used on Microsoft Investor's Portfolio page (see Figure 10.1). You must remember, however, that ActiveX controls are typically specific to the Windows/Windows NT platforms. If your pages are to be used by browsers on other platforms, you should be careful in your use of ActiveX controls.

FIG. 10.1

The MSN Investor Portfolio grid is an example of a complex ActiveX control.

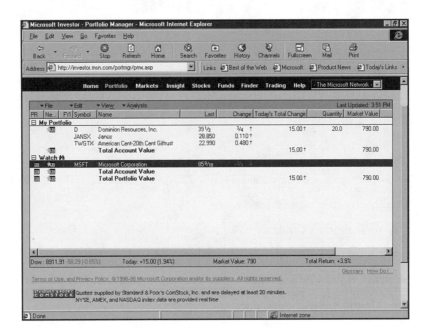

As you'll see in this chapter, Visual InterDev makes working with ActiveX controls a piece of cake. You can easily embed controls in your Web pages, set their properties, and add script code for the events they raise. You cannot, however, create an ActiveX control with Visual InterDev. For creating ActiveX controls, you need a COM development environment such as Visual Basic, Visual C++, or Visual J++. In Chapter 12, "Building ActiveX Controls with Visual Basic," you'll see how easy it is to create an ActiveX control.

Easy Multimedia—The Animated GIF

Now that I've extolled the praises of ActiveX controls, we'll take a detour and talk about an easy way to add multimedia capabilities to your Web pages: the animated GIF file.

N O T E The acronym GIF stands for Graphics Interchange Format. ▪

There are dozens of picture formats that can be used in Web pages. However, only two of these formats are in common use. First, there's JPEG, a format developed by the Joint Photographic Expert Group. JPEG supports 24-bit color and provides compression to conserve disk space and speed page downloads.

There's also the GIF format. The original format was called GIF87a and was developed by the CompuServe Information Service. Transparent GIF files (where the background of the picture blends in with the background color of the Web page hosting it) were introduced with the GIF89a format. All browsers support both the GIF87a and the GIF89a formats, as do most of the graphics packages available today. Unlike the 24-bit color available in JPEG files, GIF files are limited to 256 colors.

The GIF format has always contained the capability to provide simple animation. Animated GIF files, which are becoming increasingly popular on Web sites, contain two or more frames, each made up of a static GIF file. Each frame displays for a specified period of time and is then replaced by the next frame in the sequence. Because standard GIF files are limited to 256 colors, animated GIFs usually combine simple clip-art style graphics and colorful text to get across an advertising style message. An example is shown in Figure 10.2, which shows the various frames of a simple animated GIF.

Part
III

Ch
10

FIG. 10.2

The frames of an animated GIF.

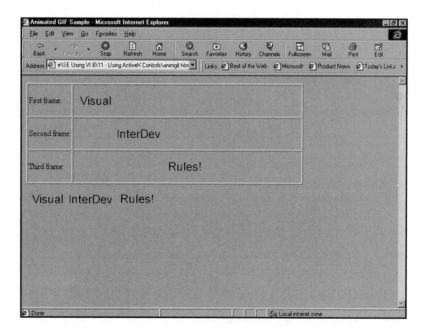

In Chapter 18, "The Image Composer and GIF Animator," you learn all there is to know about creating animated GIF files. For now, you can use the simple animated GIF included on the CD-ROM.

You insert an animated GIF into an InterDev-developed Web page the same way you insert any other image file. On either the Design or Source tabs, click where you want the animated GIF to appear and use the HTML, Image menu item or press Ctrl+Shift+W. This launches the Insert Image dialog box, shown in Figure 10.3.

FIG. 10.3

The Insert Image dialog box.

On this dialog box, you specify the location of the source image and alternative text, which is displayed if the browser doesn't have images turned on or doesn't support images. Also, some layout and spacing properties can be set from this dialog box. Click OK and the image is inserted into the Web page. Figure 10.4 shows the results of inserting the sample image into an InterDev page.

FIG. 10.4

The image shown on the Design tab.

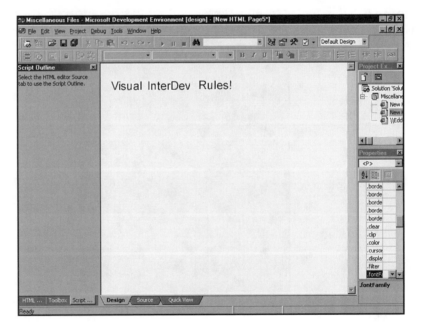

Using the Toolbox and Script Builder

ActiveX controls are inserted into Web pages using an HTML <OBJECT> tag. The design-time properties for controls are set using a <PARAM> tag for each property to be set. Here's an example demonstrating how to insert the ActiveMovie control into a Web page:

```
<OBJECT classid=clsid:05589FA1-C356-11CE-BF01-00AA0055595A id=MyMovie>
<PARAM NAME="_ExtentX" VALUE="7038">
<PARAM NAME="_ExtentY" VALUE="1958">
<PARAM NAME="EnableContextMenu" VALUE="-1">
<PARAM NAME="ShowDisplay" VALUE="-1">
<PARAM NAME="ShowControls" VALUE="-1">
<PARAM NAME="ShowPositionControls" VALUE="0">
<PARAM NAME="ShowSelectionControls" VALUE="0">
<PARAM NAME="EnablePositionControls" VALUE="-1">
<PARAM NAME="EnableSelectionControls" VALUE="-1">
<PARAM NAME="ShowTracker" VALUE="-1">
<PARAM NAME="EnableTracker" VALUE="-1">
<PARAM NAME="AllowHideDisplay" VALUE="-1">
<PARAM NAME="AllowHideControls" VALUE="-1">
<PARAM NAME="FullScreenMode" VALUE="0">
<PARAM NAME="AutoStart" VALUE="0">
<PARAM NAME="AutoRewind" VALUE="-1">
<PARAM NAME="PlayCount" VALUE="1">
<PARAM NAME="SelectionStart" VALUE="0">
<PARAM NAME="SelectionEnd" VALUE="-1">
<PARAM NAME="Appearance" VALUE="1">
<PARAM NAME="BorderStyle" VALUE="1">
<PARAM NAME="AllowChangeDisplayMode" VALUE="-1">
<PARAM NAME="DisplayForeColor" VALUE="16777215">
<PARAM NAME="DisplayBackColor" VALUE="0">
<PARAM NAME="Rate" VALUE="1">
</OBJECT>
```

Part
III

Ch
10

Most controls don't have this many properties to set, but that still leaves a lot of typing for you to do. As you might have guessed, Visual InterDev provides you with a quick and easy way to add ActiveX controls to your pages: the Toolbox. Then there's the Properties window that allows you to set the available design-time properties of the control.

Let's dissect this <OBJECT> tag a bit so you can appreciate the grunt work that InterDev saves you from. The classid element of the tag is the GUID (Globally Unique Identifier) that specifies exactly which ActiveX control to place on the page. Each ActiveX control has its own, unique identifier to distinguish it from all of the other ActiveX controls that have ever been created. So, to add the ActiveMovie control to a page, you have to know and enter its GUID into the <OBJECT> tag. That's a lot of typing, not to mention a big number to remember!

The id element specifies a unique name for this particular instance of the control within your page. The control's id value is used to reference the control from scripting code, allowing you to read or modify its properties, execute its methods, and respond to any events the control might raise.

Finally, each of the <PARAM> tags specifies a property name and value for any properties that are set at design time. The property name is specified with the name element and the value to be set for that property with the value element.

As you can see, that's a lot of typing, not to mention a lot of work just finding out *what* to enter into the <OBJECT> tag. The remainder of this section describes how to use the Toolbox with ActiveX controls. In the sections that follow, you learn how to use the Properties window effectively to specify how the control operates.

Inserting a Control

Now let's look at the first feature that InterDev provides to make working with ActiveX controls easy. Figure 10.5 shows the Toolbox with the ActiveX Controls section enabled.

FIG. 10.5

The Visual InterDev ActiveX Toolbox.

> **N O T E**   If the Toolbox isn't visible in your InterDev workspace, the <u>V</u>iew, Tool<u>b</u>ox menu item will show it (you can also use the Ctrl+Alt+X keystroke combination). ◼

You can scroll the list of ActiveX controls by using the up and down arrows found on the various section labels of the Toolbox (see Figure 10.5). To switch to a different section, such as the HTML section, click its section label. For now, though, stay on the ActiveX Controls section.

Adding a control from the Toolbox to your Web page is simple. You can add a control on either the Design tab or the Source tab of the HTML editor window. There are two methods you can use:

- ◼ In the HTML editor window, position the cursor where you want to insert the control and then double-click the control's name in the Toolbox.

- ◼ Click and drag the control's name from the Toolbox onto the HTML editor window, dropping the control where you want it placed in the page. The edit cursor moves with the mouse pointer as you drag the control around the edit window.

CAUTION

If you use the second method (double-clicking the control name), the control's <OBJECT> tag overwrites an HTML source that you have selected in the HTML editor. For example, if you highlight a paragraph of text in the HTML editor and then double-click a control name in the Toolbox, the control's <OBJECT> tag replaces the highlighted paragraph. Thank goodness there's an Undo command!

After you have the control added to the page, you can use the Properties window to modify the design-time properties for the control. If the Properties window is not visible, the View, Properties Window menu item or the F4 key will turn it on. On either the Design or the Source tabs, you must click the control for its properties to display in the Properties window (you can click on the control's name in the HTML Outline window as well).

Figure 10.6 shows the Design tab of a Web page with an ActiveMovie control added to it. Figure 10.7 shows the Source tab of the same page, but with a twist: instead of looking like HTML, the control stills shows in graphical mode.

To see the actual HTML source for the control (the <OBJECT> tag and its <PARAM> tag children), right-click the control and select Text View from the shortcut menu. The Source tab then shows the control's HTML source instead of the graphical view. However, the Properties window is now devoid of the control's internal properties. Instead, you only can edit those properties specifically related to the HTML <OBJECT> tag, such as CODEBASE and ID.

Part

III

Ch

10

FIG. 10.6

The Design tab of a Web page with an ActiveX control added.

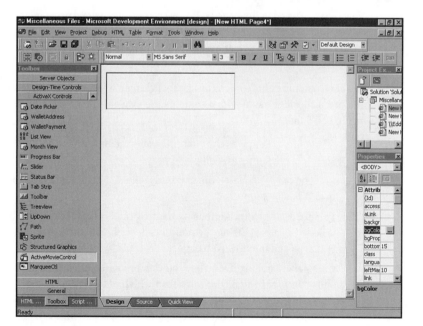

FIG. 10.7
The Source tab of a
Web page with an
ActiveX control added.

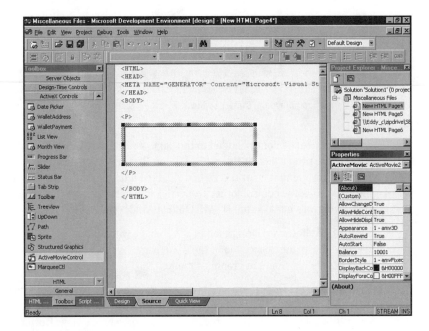

Customizing the Toolbox

Now that you've seen how easy it is to add controls to your pages using InterDev, you're probably wondering why your favorite control isn't available on the Toolbox. InterDev, by default, installs with the Toolbox loaded with the ActiveX controls most commonly used in Web pages, particularly dynamic HTML pages. However, you're not limited to this preselected list.

You can customize the Toolbox by right-clicking anywhere over the Toolbox. This activates the Toolbox's shortcut menu which contains the available customization features. On this shortcut menu, you'll find:

- Delete Item. Removes the currently selected item from the Toolbox. Only available when you right-click over a Toolbox item.

- Rename Item. Renames the currently selected item. Only available when you right-click over a Toolbox item.

- Paste. Creates a new item using the text that's on the Clipboard. Whenever this new item is added to a page using the methods described in the previous section, this Clipboard text is pasted into the Web page.

- Customize Toolbox. Launches the Customize Toolbox dialog box. On this dialog box, shown in Figure 10.8, you can select which of the Design-Time Controls and ActiveX Controls installed on your system will be available in the Toolbox. To add an item to the Toolbox, find it in the list and check its entry. If you know the location of the component's file (OCX, DLL, or EXE), you can use the Browse button to find it.

FIG. 10.8

The Customize Toolbox dialog box.

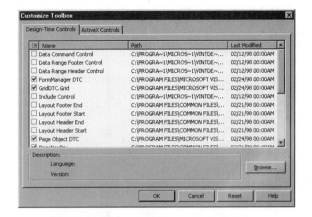

- ■ Add Tab. Creates a new tab section in the Toolbox. You simply enter a name for the new tab and add controls (using Customize Toolbox) or HTML code (using Paste) to it. You can move controls from one tab to another using drag and drop, making it easy to categorize your controls as you see fit.

- ■ List View. Toggles between List View, which displays an icon and the control's description, and non-List View, which only displays an icon. The non-List View is useful if you want to conserve screen real estate and can identify the controls by their icon. Chances are, though, that you'll always leave the List View active.

N O T E The List View setting only affects the currently selected tab's display. All other tabs/sections on the Toolbox retain their current setting for List View. ■

For now, let's add two of the controls you'll be using in this chapter. Follow these steps:

1. If it's not already active, activate the Toolbox and select the ActiveX Controls tab.

2. Right-click anywhere over the Toolbox and click Customize Toolbox to launch the Customize Toolbox dialog box.

3. Click the ActiveX Controls tab on this dialog box. There might be a slight delay as InterDev creates the list of ActiveX controls installed on your system.

4. Scroll through the list until you locate the ActiveMovieControl Object entry. Check the box next to this entry.

5. Scroll through the list until you locate the MarqueeCtl Object entry. Check the box next to this entry.

6. Click OK. Your Toolbox should now contain these additional controls and should resemble Figure 10.9.

Using the Script Builder

The final feature we'll discuss that makes working with ActiveX controls easier is the Script Builder. The Script Builder allows you to quickly create script code to respond to the events

Part

III

Ch

10

raised by the ActiveX controls you've placed on your page. This section describes how it works in this capacity. The Script Builder was introduced in Chapter 5, "Active Scripting Overview," so if you need some review that's a good place to look.

FIG. 10.9

The Toolbox with a few ActiveX controls added.

The Script Builder is a feature of the Script Outline window. If you don't see the Script Outline tab in InterDev's left hand pane (refer to Figure 10.9, for example), use the View, Other Windows, Script Outline menu item, or simply press Ctrl+Alt+S. The actual outline is only visible when the HTML editor window is on the Source tab; otherwise, the Script Outline window simply reads Select the HTML editor Source tab to use the Script Outline—explaining why you do not see an outline when the editor is on any other tab.

Using the Script Builder is simple. Drill down through the Script Outline tree until you locate the control you want to write script for. Then double-click the event you're interested in responding to and InterDev inserts the appropriate script code for you. All you have to do is write the event code itself. InterDev has taken care of the grunt work for you. Figure 10.10 shows the JavaScript stub code that InterDev created for the ActiveMovie control's StateChange event.

N O T E   The Script Builder inserts either VBScript or JavaScript code depending on the setting of the document's defaultClientScript property. To change the value of this property, select the DOCUMENT entry on the Properties window's drop-down list. ■

Multimedia ActiveX Controls

Now that you've seen some of the features that InterDev provides to support ActiveX controls, let's take a look at a few controls that provide multimedia capabilities to your pages.

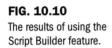

FIG. 10.10
The results of using the
Script Builder feature.

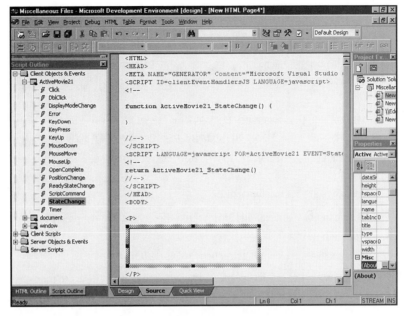

In the remainder of this chapter, you investigate the Marquee control, the ActiveMovie control, and a few of the multimedia controls provided with Internet Explorer 4. The Marquee control allows you to display any file that the browser can display within a scrolling region on the current page. The ActiveMovie control is designed to play multimedia files such as movies (.AVI, for example) and sound (.WAV, for example). Proper use of the other controls introduced is beyond the scope of this chapter, so you'll just learn about their existence and the basics of their operation.

Scrolling Text and Marquees

There are two ways to achieve scrolling text within your Web pages. The first way, using the <MARQUEE> tag, does not involve an ActiveX control. The second method is to use the Marquee control you added to your Toolbox in an earlier section of this chapter. This section discusses both of these methods but places more emphasis on the ActiveX control, because ActiveX controls are the subject of this chapter.

The *<MARQUEE>* Tag

The <MARQUEE> tag allows you to create a scrolling marquee containing embedded HTML. What the tag accomplishes is not much different from the control, as you'll see in a bit. The <MARQUEE> tag has a required end tag (</MARQUEE>) associated and displays whatever HTML is placed between the opening and ending tags. For example, to display the message Visual InterDev Rules! in a right-to-left (the default direction) scrolling marquee, use this HTML:

```
<MARQUEE>Visual InterDev Rules!</MARQUEE>
```

Part
III

Ch
10

CAUTION

The <MARQUEE> tag, as of this writing, is not an official tag according to the World Wide Web Consortium (W3C), which is the body that controls the HTML standard. Therefore, you cannot assume that the tag will be supported by any browser in particular. It is, however, supported by Internet Explorer 3.*x* and 4.*x*.

By default, the <MARQUEE> tag takes on the width of the page. To change the width, or position the marquee anywhere on the page, use the element's style properties. For example,

```
<MARQUEE height=20 style="HEIGHT:20px;WIDTH:50px" width=50>
Visual InterDev Rules!</MARQUEE>
```

displays a very small marquee.

You can place any valid HTML within the <MARQUEE> tag pair. For example, to scroll an <H3> formatted message, use

```
<MARQUEE><H3>Visual InterDev Rules!</H3></MARQUEE>
```

The <MARQUEE> tag has several properties that affect how the marquee is displayed. There's the direction property which takes the property of down, up, left, or right and defaults to left. This is the direction in which the marquee moves. If set to left, for example, the marquee scrolls from right to left. If set to up, it scrolls from bottom to top.

The behavior property can take the following values:

- **Alternate.** The contents alternate left and right (or top and bottom), causing a bouncing affect. With this setting, setting the direction values to either left or right (or to top or bottom) produce the same effect.

- **Scroll.** The contents moves in the direction specified and then loops back to the beginning. This is the default value.

- **Slide.** The contents moves in the direction specified but stops when it reaches the end. Note that if loop (discussed below) is set to -1, the contents still repeats; but instead of scrolling into the edge gracefully and repeating after the trailing edge of the contents hits the end, the repeat begins as soon as the leading edge hits the end. To have the contents slide across the marquee area and then stop, set loop to 1.

The loop property, which defaults to -1, specifies how many times the marquee should loop (that is, how many times the contents of the marquee should be displayed). The default (-1) specifies an infinite number of loops. To only loop twice, set the value of this property to 2. After the number of loops specified has been completed, the marquee's area on the page is blank, potentially leaving a big hole in your page, so use this property with caution.

To control the speed of the scrolling, adjust the scrollDelay property. The greater the value of this property, the slower the marquee scrolls. This property specifies the number of milliseconds between each successive drawing of the marquee's contents. Likewise, the scrollAmount property specifies the number of pixels separating each successive drawing of the contents.

These properties mean that the marquee's display advances by `scrollAmount` every `scrollDelay` milliseconds.

Internet Explorer 4.*x* supports a property named `trueSpeed` which specifies whether or not to use the default delay time of 60 milliseconds. The default value of this property, `False`, causes all values less of `scrollDelay` that are less than 60 to be rounded up to 60. This behavior is for compatibility with Internet Explorer 3.*x*.

The Marquee ActiveX Control

Because the `<MARQUEE>` tag is not an official part of the HTML4 specification, you might be a little wary about using it. After all, browsers that do not support the tag simply ignore it, leaving the HTML you place between the beginning and ending tags to be rendered as simple HTML. This means that content you intended to appear in a scrolling manner just sits there on the page, possibly looking odd when it's all visible at the same time.

Part

III

Ch

10

To soothe those authors who want to reach a broader audience of Web browsers, there's the Marquee ActiveX control. This control produces results that are practically identical to the `<MARQUEE>` tag. This section briefly describes the properties that are necessary to properly operate the control.

The first major difference between the control and the tag is that you do not specify the HTML to display within the `<OBJECT>` tag. Instead, there's a property named `szURL` that you set to the URL of the HTML file that is displayed within the bounds of the control. This can either be an absolute URL (of the form **http://www.mysight.com/content/marqueeStuff.htm**) or a relative URL (of the form **content/marqueeStuff.htm**).

The `ScrollDelay` property is identical to the `<MARQUEE>` tag's `scrollDelay` property: it specifies the amount of time between draws of the content. The lower the value, the faster the content moves.

The scroll direction is set by specifying the `ScrollPixelsX` and `ScrollPixelsY` properties. These specify the number of pixels to scroll the content. Specifying a positive value for `ScrollPixelsX` causes the content to scroll from left to right. A positive value for `ScrollPixelsY` scrolls the content from top to bottom. Negative values, as you probably guessed, cause the scrolling to proceed in the opposite direction. You can specify values for both of these properties, creating a diagonal scrolling effect which is pretty cool to watch.

Another cool effect can be gained by using the zoom property. Setting this to a value other than `100` causes the control to zoom in or out on the rendered HTML. For example, setting the value to `50` causes the displayed HTML to appear at half the size it would if the value were set to `100`. This allows you to display content that otherwise would not fit on the page. You could also, using Dynamic HTML and scripting, allow the user to specify the zoom factor! The HTML in Listing 10.1 accomplishes this feat (this file can be found as Marquee Control.htm on the CD-ROM accompanying this book).

Listing 10.1   Dynamically Controlling the Marquee Control's *zoom* Property

```
<HTML><HEAD>
<SCRIPT ID=clientEventHandlersJS LANGUAGE=javascript>
<!--
function zoom_onchange() {
Marquee1.Zoom = zoom.value;
}
//-->
</SCRIPT></HEAD>
<BODY>
<OBJECT classid=clsid:1A4DA620-6217-11CF-BE62-0080C72EDD2D id=Marquee1
style="HEIGHT: 100px; LEFT: 0px; TOP: 0px; WIDTH: 640px">
<PARAM NAME="_ExtentX" VALUE="16933">
<PARAM NAME="_ExtentY" VALUE="2646">
<PARAM NAME="LoopsX" VALUE="-1">
<PARAM NAME="LoopsY" VALUE="-1">
<PARAM NAME="ScrollPixelsX" VALUE="0">
<PARAM NAME="ScrollPixelsY" VALUE="10">
<PARAM NAME="ScrollDelay" VALUE="150">
<PARAM NAME="Zoom" VALUE="100">
<PARAM NAME="DrawImmediately" VALUE="1">
<PARAM NAME="Whitespace" VALUE="0">
<PARAM NAME="ocBColor" VALUE="-2147483643">
<PARAM NAME="szurl" VALUE="marqueeStuff.htm">
</OBJECT>
<select id=zoom name=zoom onchange="return zoom_onchange()">
<option value=100 SELECTED>100%
<option value=200>200%
<option value=50>50%
</select>
</BODY></HTML>
```

The results of this page, when the file marqueeStuff.htm contains Visual InterDev Rules! enclosed in an <H3> tag, is shown in Figure 10.11.

Now that you know how to use these two methods to produce scrolling text, you can decide which is best for the pages you're designing.

The ActiveMovie Control

Another useful multimedia control is the ActiveMovie control. This control lets you play many types of multimedia files from within the Web browser, including MPEG audio and video, AVI video, WAV audio, MIDI audio, and QuickTime video files.

The <OBJECT> tag for the ActiveMovie control is

```
<OBJECT classid=clsid:05589FA1-C356-11CE-BF01-00AA0055595A></OBJECT>
```

This section describes the properties, methods, and events available for the control. We'll conclude this section by building a small page that allows the user to select a multimedia file from his hard drive and play it with the ActiveMovie control. We won't attempt to cover all of the intricacies of this control. Instead, you can find the documentation in the Microsoft Internet

Client SDK or at **http://www.microsoft.com/msdn/sdk/inetsdk/help/complib/ activemovie/activemovie.htm**.

FIG. 10.11
The Marquee control
sample page resulting
from Listing 10.1.

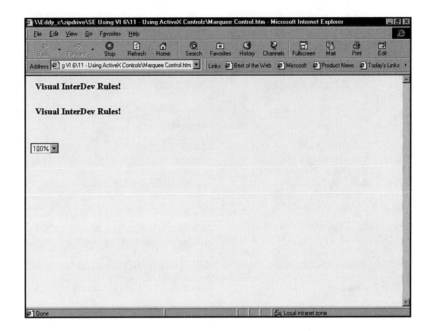

Properties

The important properties for our purposes in this chapter are CurrentState, FileName, and PlayCount. We'll discuss those in a moment. For now, Table 10.1 lists the entire set of properties that the ActiveMovie control provides.

Table 10.1   The ActiveMovie Control's Properties

Property	Description
AllowChangeDisplayMode	Indicates whether the end-user can change the display mode at runtime between seconds and frames
AllowHideControls	Indicates whether the end-user can hide the control panel at runtime
AllowHideDisplay	Indicates whether the end-user can hide the display panel at runtime
Appearance	Specifies the appearance of the display panel's border
AutoRewind	Indicates whether the multimedia stream should automatically return to the selection's starting point when it reaches the end of the selection

continues

Table 10.1   Continued

Property	Description
AutoStart	Indicates whether to automatically start playing the multimedia stream
Balance	Specifies the stereo balance
BorderStyle	Specifies the control's border style
CurrentPosition	Specifies the current position within the playback file, in seconds
CurrentState	Specifies the playback file's current state: stopped, paused, or running
DisplayBackColor	Specifies the display panel's background color
DisplayForeColor	Specifies the display panel's foreground color
DisplayMode	Indicates whether the display panel shows the current position in seconds or frames
EnableContextMenu	Indicates whether to enable the shortcut menu
Enabled	Specifies whether the control is enabled
EnablePositionControls	Indicates whether to show the position buttons in the controls panel
EnableSelectionControls	Indicates whether to show the selection buttons in the controls panel
EnableTracker	Indicates whether to show the trackbar control in the controls panel
FileName	Specifies the name of the source data file
FilterGraph	Contains the interface pointer to the current filter graph object
FilterGraphDispatch	Contains the interface pointer to the current filter graph object
FullScreenMode	Expands the area of the playback panel to fill the entire screen
MovieWindowSize	Specifies the size of the playback panel
PlayCount	Specifies the number of times to play the multimedia stream
Rate	Specifies the playback rate for the stream
ReadyState	Specifies the state of readiness for this ActiveMovie control, based on how completely the source file has loaded

Property	Description
SelectionEnd	Specifies the ending position in this multimedia stream, in seconds, relative to the stream's beginning
SelectionStart	Specifies the starting position in this multimedia stream, in seconds, relative to the stream's beginning
ShowControls	Indicates whether the controls panel is visible
ShowDisplay	Indicates whether the display panel is visible
ShowPositionControls	Indicates whether the position controls are visible
ShowSelectionControls	Indicates whether the selection controls are visible
ShowTracker	Indicates whether the trackbar is visible
Volume	Specifies the volume, in hundredths of decibels

CurrentState   This property is a read-only property that reflects the control's current state:

- 0 - Stopped
- 1 - Paused
- 2 - Running

You cannot write to this property, but can cause the same effect by using the Stop, Pause, and Run methods (respectively). Whenever the value of the CurrentState property changes, the StateChange event fires. We'll use this event in our sample.

FileName   This is the name of the multimedia file currently loaded by the control. It is read/write at both design and runtime. This means that you can specify the FileName property in a <PARAM> tag embedded within the control's <OBJECT> tag as well as change the value of the property with script code, or both. We'll use the second method in our sample.

The value can be either a path to a local file or an URL pointing to a resource on the network.

PlayCount   Another read/write property, this one specifies the number of times that the file should be played. Setting this property to 0 causes the control to continuously replay the file. Setting it to 1 causes the file to be played only once.

Methods

The ActiveMovie control has five methods: AboutBox, IsSoundCardEnabled, Pause, Run, and Stop.

AboutBox* and *IsSoundCardEnabled   The AboutBox method causes the control's About dialog box to display. Not very useful in and of itself, but could help an end-user determine which version of the control is installed on her system.

The IsSoundCardEnabled property returns a Boolean value indicating whether the computer has a working sound card. You could use this property to selectively specify the FileName property. For example, you might have a low-bandwidth file that contains no audio for use by browsers without a sound card. This could potentially decrease the download time for the file, making your page load and respond faster.

Pause, Run,* and *Stop These methods pause, run, and stop the media file, respectively. The ActiveMovie control has built-in controls that allow the user to perform the same actions, but these can be hidden from the user by setting the ShowControls property to False. In this case, you'll want to provide some other means for the media file to be controlled and you need to use these methods. You'll see an example of this in our sample page.

Events

We won't be using any of the ActiveMovie's events in our sample, but two useful events are ReadyStateChange and StateChange.

ReadyStateChange This event fires after changes are made to the FileName property. A value is passed to the event that indicates the new state of the control:

- ◼ 0—The control is asynchronously loading the file.
- ◼ 1—The FileName property has not been initialized.
- ◼ 3—The file has been loaded enough that playback can commence, but the entire file has not been loaded.
- ◼ 4—The entire file has been downloaded.

After modifying the FileName property, you should wait for the ReadyStateChange event to indicate that the file is loaded before you initiate the Run method. In our example, we'll simply check the ReadyState property before calling Run.

StateChange This event fires whenever the control's playback state changes. Two parameters, oldState and newState, are passed to the event. These indicate the previous and new values that you would read from the CurrentState property. If you want to change the browser's status bar based on whether or not the media was being played, you could do so by responding to this event.

Building a Simple Movie Player

Now that you've seen a little of the interface that the ActiveMovie control provides, it's time to build a Web page that exercises what you've learned. The results of this section are shown in Figure 10.12. The source is provided in Listing 10.2.

FIG. 10.12
The ActiveMovie sample
page.

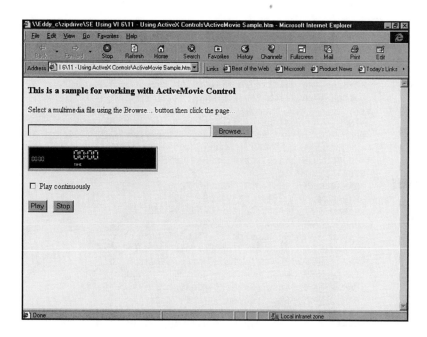

Listing 10.2 The HTML Source Code for the ActiveMovie Sample Page

```html
<HTML>
<HEAD>
<META name=VI60_defaultClientScript content=JavaScript>
<META NAME="GENERATOR" Content="Microsoft Visual Studio 6.0">
<SCRIPT ID=clientEventHandlersJS LANGUAGE=javascript>
<!--
function button2_onclick() {
if (ActiveMovie1.FileName != "")
   ActiveMovie1.Stop();
}

function checkbox1_onchange() {
if (checkbox1.checked)
    ActiveMovie1.PlayCount = 0;
else
    ActiveMovie1.PlayCount = 1;
}

function button1_onclick() {
if (ActiveMovie1.ReadyState == 4 && ActiveMovie1.FileName != "")
    ActiveMovie1.Run();
}

function file1_onchange() {
ActiveMovie1.FileName = file1.value;
}
//-->
</SCRIPT></HEAD>
```

continues

Listing 10.2 Continued

```
<BODY>
<H3>This is a sample for working with ActiveMovie Control</H3>
<P>Select a multimedia file using the Browse...
button then click the page...</P>
<P>
<INPUT id=file1 name=file1 type=file LANGUAGE=javascript
onchange="return file1_onchange()" style="HEIGHT:24px;WIDTH:377px"></P>
<P>
<OBJECT classid=clsid:05589FA1-C356-11CE-BF01-00AA0055595A id=ActiveMovie1
VIEWASTEXT>
<PARAM NAME="_ExtentX" VALUE="7038">
<PARAM NAME="_ExtentY" VALUE="1958">
<PARAM NAME="EnableContextMenu" VALUE="-1">
<PARAM NAME="ShowDisplay" VALUE="-1">
<PARAM NAME="ShowControls" VALUE="-1">
<PARAM NAME="ShowPositionControls" VALUE="0">
<PARAM NAME="ShowSelectionControls" VALUE="0">
<PARAM NAME="EnablePositionControls" VALUE="-1">
<PARAM NAME="EnableSelectionControls" VALUE="-1">
<PARAM NAME="ShowTracker" VALUE="-1">
<PARAM NAME="EnableTracker" VALUE="-1">
<PARAM NAME="AllowHideDisplay" VALUE="-1">
<PARAM NAME="AllowHideControls" VALUE="-1">
<PARAM NAME="MovieWindowSize" VALUE="0">
<PARAM NAME="FullScreenMode" VALUE="0">
<PARAM NAME="MovieWindowWidth" VALUE="-1">
<PARAM NAME="MovieWindowHeight" VALUE="-1">
<PARAM NAME="AutoStart" VALUE="0">
<PARAM NAME="AutoRewind" VALUE="-1">
<PARAM NAME="PlayCount" VALUE="1">
<PARAM NAME="SelectionStart" VALUE="0">
<PARAM NAME="SelectionEnd" VALUE="-1">
<PARAM NAME="Appearance" VALUE="1">
<PARAM NAME="BorderStyle" VALUE="1">
<PARAM NAME="FileName" VALUE="">
<PARAM NAME="DisplayMode" VALUE="0">
<PARAM NAME="AllowChangeDisplayMode" VALUE="-1">
<PARAM NAME="DisplayForeColor" VALUE="16777215">
<PARAM NAME="DisplayBackColor" VALUE="0">
<PARAM NAME="Enabled" VALUE="-1">
<PARAM NAME="Rate" VALUE="1">
</OBJECT></P>
<P><INPUT id=checkbox1 name=checkbox1 type=checkbox
LANGUAGE=javascript onchange="return checkbox1_onchange()">
Play continuously</P>

<P><INPUT id=button1 name=button1 type=button
value=Play LANGUAGE=javascript onclick="return button1_onclick()">  
<INPUT id=button2 name=button2 type=button value=Stop
LANGUAGE=javascript onclick="return button2_onclick()"></P>
</BODY></HTML>
```

To create this page, follow these steps:

1. Start a new HTML file in Visual InterDev.

2. Go to the Design tab and add the text at the top of the page.

3. If the Toolbox is not visible, turn it on using the View, Toolbox menu item. Select the HTML section of the Toolbox. Click the File Field item and drag it to just below the text. Resize it to about three-fourths the width of the page.

4. Create a new, empty line just below the file field. Switch to the ActiveX Controls section of the Toolbox. Drag the ActiveMovieControl item to the new line. If the ActiveMovieControl is not shown, follow the steps in the "Customizing the Toolbox" section earlier in this chapter.

5. Click the ActiveMovie control. Using the Properties window, change the id property to ActiveMovie1. Change the ShowControls property to False.

6. Create another blank line at the bottom of the page, switch the Toolbox back to the HTML section, and place a check box onto the page. Type **Play Continuously** immediately to the right of the new check box.

7. Press Enter to move to a new line. Drag two buttons to the page. Change the caption of the leftmost button to **Play** and the rightmost to **Stop**. You can change the caption by clicking the text in the button and typing over the existing text.

8. Whew! That was a lot of work, but now the page is ready for some script. Switch the HTML editor to the Source tab.

9. Move from the Toolbox to the Script Outline. If the Script Outline is not visible, use the View, Other Windows, Script Outline menu item, or press Ctrl+Alt+S to turn it on.

10. If necessary, expand the branch for Client Objects and Events, locate button1, and expand it. Double-click the onclick entry. Enter the following in the event's routine:

```
if (ActiveMovie1.ReadyState == 4 && ActiveMovie1.FileName != "")
    ActiveMovie1.Run();
```

11. Repeat this process for button2, entering

```
if (ActiveMovie1.FileName != "")
   ActiveMovie1.Stop();
```

12. In the Script Outline, double-click checkbox1 onchange and enter

```
if (checkbox1.checked)
    ActiveMovie1.PlayCount = 0;
else
    ActiveMovie1.PlayCount = 1;
}
```

13. Finally, for the onchange event of file1, enter

```
ActiveMovie1.FileName = file1.value;
```

14. Save the file and switch to the Quick View tab. Clicking the Browse button causes a File Open dialog box to display. Select one of the ActiveMovie control's supported files (such as an AVI or a WAV file) and click OK.

Part
III

Ch
10

15. Click anywhere in the blank area of the page. This fires the `onchange` event for `file1`. (I don't know why it doesn't fire when you actually change the contents of the control, but it just doesn't!)

16. Click the Play button. Your selected file should now play! Experiment with the Play Continuously check box and the Stop button.

Other Multimedia Options

Now that you've looked at two ways to add multimedia capabilities to your Web pages, let's look briefly at some of the DirectAnimation controls that ship with Internet Explorer 4.

The DirectAnimation library is part of the minimum install for IE4 and, as such, is available on any machine running IE4. The libraries can be accessed via an API or through the DAExpress ActiveX control (DAXCTLE.OCX). Several of these controls (Path, Sprite, and Structured Graphics) are referenced by default in the InterDev Toolbox. We'll discuss these controls in this section. You can find documentation for these controls at **http://www.microsoft.com/ directx/dxm/help/da/da_e0019.htm**.

The Path Control

The Path control allows you to animate the objects on your Web pages. You do this by specifying the path the object should follow and the amount of time it takes to complete this path. The control then takes care of moving the object for you. You can animate any page object that supports the `top` and `left` properties.

The path that the target object will take can be set to be a rectangle, an oval, a polygon, a polyline (which is an open-ended multi-line path), or a spline (which is made up of curved paths).

You can also set time markers which serve as bookmarks along the path. When a bookmark is reached during normal playback of the path, the `onPlayMarker` event fires and passes a value indicating the bookmark that was just reached.

The Sprite Control

Sprites are animated graphics similar to animated GIF files. However, the Sprite control can be moved over a background and is responsible for restoring any of the screen area that it passes over. Also, unlike animated GIF files, your script code can control the speed of playback at runtime (with animated GIFs, the speed is set when the file is created and cannot be changed). You can even combine the Sprite control with the Path control and provide some really cool graphical animations to your users, even responding to the way they manipulate your pages!

The Sprite control plays back an image strip file, which is a file created in any of the supported graphics file formats (such as GIF, JPG, or WMF). This file is created by adding each frame as a separate image, each of the same size, in a tabular format. You then tell the control how many frames there are in total, and how many frames there are across and down the image. Using this information, the Sprite control can pull out each individual frame during playback.

The Structured Graphic Control

The Structured Graphics control allows you to build graphical images using the properties of the control and script code. The Structured Graphics control builds *vector graphics*, which are created by storing the commands required to draw the image rather than the data that makes up the image. Using vector graphics allows you to create complex graphics without the larger download size of standard graphic files.

The Structured Graphic control contains methods that are used to generate the graphic that will be displayed. These include `Arc`, `Pie`, `Rect`, `SetFillColor`, `SetFillStyle`, `SetFont`, and `Text`. The results of these are pretty self-explanatory, and each takes a set of parameters that is reasonable for performing the specific task.

A sample of the use of this control can be found at **http://www.microsoft.com/directX/ dxm/help/da/DocSamps/structur.htm**. This page is also shown in Figure 10.13.

Part
III

Ch
10

FIG. 10.13
The Structured Graphics Control sample page, created entirely with the Structured Graphics Control.

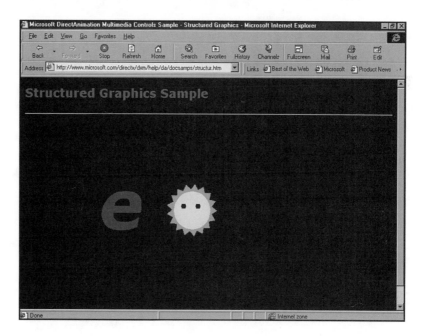

From Here...

This chapter provided you with an introduction to ActiveX controls and a few of the controls that make your Web pages more interactive. In the chapter that follows, "Designing with Design-Time Controls," you learn how to put design-time controls to use in InterDev's development environment. After that, "Building ActiveX Controls with Visual Basic" walks you through the creation of an ActiveX control. Being able to create your own controls means that you can fine-tune your Web pages to work the way you want them to.

CHAPTER 11

Designing with Design-Time Controls

In **this chapter**

Introducing Design-Time Controls (DTCs)   **236**

Controls Available in Visual InterDev 6   **237**

Inserting DTCs into Your Web Pages   **238**

The Form Controls   **244**

Data-Bound Controls   **248**

The Multimedia Controls   **256**

Introducing Design-Time Controls (DTCs)

In this chapter, you will learn how to use one of the most unique features of Visual InterDev: Design-Time Controls (DTCs). These controls are not new to Visual InterDev 6; they were available in version 1, and are present in several other development tools, including Visual Basic. Regardless, Visual InterDev 6 has transformed these controls from the interesting minor feature they were in the past into a full-blown coding technique so useful that it will quickly become a necessity in your projects. You must understand these DTCs to get the most benefit from this feature, so this chapter will provide you with the information you need.

Design-Time Controls Versus Other Components

Design-Time Controls are similar in many respects to other types of components, such as ActiveX controls, giving them a relatively quick learning curve for programmers used to working with those items. DTCs are objects designed to encapsulate a certain set of functionality; they can be placed into documents wherever you want and can be moved or deleted at any time. They have a visual interface, as shown in Figure 11.1, that is nearly identical to an ActiveX control. They also possess properties, methods, and (in some cases) events. All these similarities can quickly convince you that they are identical to ActiveX controls and should be treated exactly the same.

FIG. 11.1
Design-Time Controls have a visual interface, similar to that of ActiveX controls.

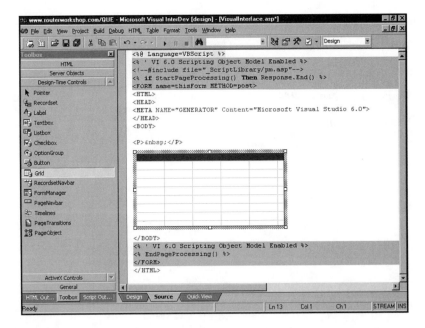

In reality, the similarity is only skin deep; Design-Time Controls are really very different. Each DTC directly represents a block of scripting code, known as its *runtime text*, and provides you with a visual interface to that text. By manipulating the properties and position of a DTC, you are really modifying the script; you're just using a nicer interface to do it. This capability is not unusual in visual programming environments. You do the same thing whenever you work with a Visual Basic form; it is the equivalent of a large DTC that represents the underlying textual definition of the form.

These controls also resemble wizards or builders; you set a series of options, and they generate the appropriate code. DTCs differ from wizards and other similar tools in that they stick around. When using a wizard, you get one chance to make your choices, and if you decide later to change those choices, you generally have to start over or attempt to make the change manually. DTCs allow you to make changes to their properties at any time, and the changes directly modify the generated code.

The Advantage of Design-Time Controls

You should use DTCs in Visual InterDev instead of regular ActiveX controls that provide similar functionality for one important reason. DTCs exist, by definition, only at design time, making them platform independent for the client. No installation is required, not even an automatic one, and no automatic restriction is placed on the Web browser software used. These features are critical in the design of Web sites, making Visual InterDev and these controls perfectly suited for each other.

N O T E A Design-Time Control is platform independent, but the script it generates may not be. No restriction is placed on that generated text. It can use any controls or technologies the creator of the DTC wants to give it, such as Dynamic HTML, and so become dependent on a specific browser as a client. ▓

Part

III

Ch

11

Controls Available in Visual InterDev 6

As discussed earlier, this release of Visual InterDev marks a major upgrade in terms of DTCs. In addition to greatly improving how you work with them, many more of them are also available. Many of these new controls are also capable of generating either client- or server-side code, making them basically two controls in one.

The significant increase in the number of Design-Time Controls available makes discussing them in groups more efficient. The following is one method of dividing them into categories based on the functions they perform, although they could be grouped in any one of several ways.

- ▓ *Form controls.* The first and largest group, these controls deal with the display and input of data. This group includes familiar controls such as the ListBox, CheckBox, TextBox, and so on.

- ▓ *Data controls.* These controls facilitate connecting and working with a database. The Recordset control, the Recordset NavBar, and the Grid control all fall into this category.

- ▓ *Multimedia controls.* These controls, the Page Transitions control, and the Timelines control are placed together because they are used to produce graphic effects.

■ *Miscellaneous controls.* As is common in any method of categorization, some items do not fall neatly into any specific group and so are grouped together for the sake of convenience. These controls include the Visual InterDev 1.0 controls (or "legacy" controls, as Microsoft calls them).

Each of these groups will be discussed individually later in this chapter, followed by a brief discussion of creating your own DTCs using Visual Basic. Before covering the controls in detail though, the next section will take you through the mechanics of inserting and manipulating DTCs in your Web pages.

Inserting DTCs into Your Web Pages

You can easily add a Design-Time Control to an Active Server Page or regular HTML by using a familiar Toolbox interface. The Toolbox window, which is generally located along the left side but can be repositioned as desired, contains several groups of objects. In the Design-Time Controls group, shown in Figure 11.2, you can find the many different DTCs available for placement in your page. The controls displayed are dependent on two factors: which DTCs are present on your machine and which ones of those are selected in the Customize Toolbox dialog box. This dialog box is the same one that allows you to select which ActiveX controls are shown on the toolbar, and is similar to the Components dialog box of Visual Basic (see the sidebar "Component References in Visual InterDev 6.0" for more information). You can open this dialog box through either one of two methods: by right-clicking the Toolbox and selecting Customize Toolbox from the context menu, or by selecting the same menu option from the Tools menu.

FIG. 11.2

The Toolbox contains various components for insertion into your Web page, including Design-Time Controls.

Component References in Visual InterDev 6.0

If you are used to working in Visual Basic or Visual Basic for Applications (VBA), you are probably familiar with the concept of *references*. When you want to use an ActiveX control in your project, you add it to the Toolbox through the Components dialog box. This method adds it to your project and allows you to place it onto a form, if you want. Unneeded references and components can cause your application to increase in size and cause additional files to be added to any distribution disks you create. Although Visual Basic 6 adds a Remove Unused option to building your project, it is still generally a good idea not to reference anything you do not need.

The Customize Toolbox dialog box in Visual InterDev does only what its name suggests—customizes the Toolbox. It adds references into your project file but uses that information only to populate the Toolbox; it has no effect on the actual Web pages. This difference means that you can freely add all the DTCs and ActiveX controls you want to your Toolbox with no ill effects.

After you open the dialog box, as shown in Figure 11.3, simply check or uncheck controls to determine which ones will be visible. After the control you want to add is on the Toolbox, you can add it to your page.

FIG. 11.3
Use the Customize Toolbox dialog box to add or remove components from your project's Toolbox.

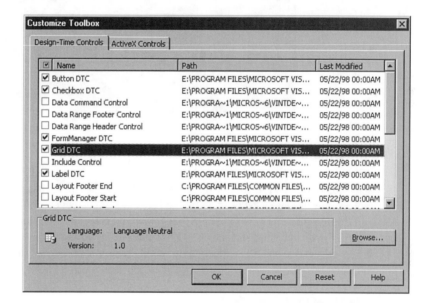

Part
III

Ch
11

N O T E If the DTCs or other items on the Toolbox appear disabled or grayed out, as in Figure 11.4, you cannot add these items to your page currently. You must have the Design or Source tab of a page open for the controls to be available. Open a new or existing page, and switch to one of these two tabs before attempting to insert a control. ■

A Design-Time Control can be added to your document in the same way as a control in Access or Visual Basic forms. You can either click and drag it onto the page, or double-click the control (place it at the current cursor position) to add it to your page.

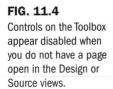

FIG. 11.4
Controls on the Toolbox appear disabled when you do not have a page open in the Design or Source views.

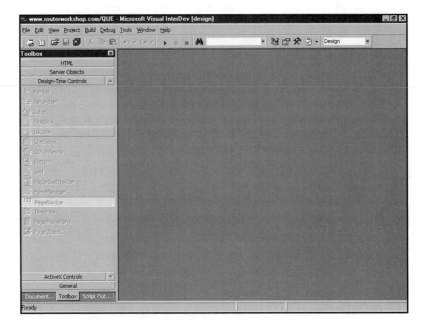

Manipulating Control Properties

After you place the control in your document, it is visible as an independent object that can be selected, moved, and resized (see Figure 11.5). When the control is selected, the Properties tool window displays a list of attributes and corresponding values. You can directly view and edit the control's properties through that list, or you can use the customized interface for that control by right-clicking and selecting Properties from the context menu. Selecting this option brings up a dialog box that allows you to modify the same properties through a more visual interface.

The Scripting Object Model

When you place certain controls into your document (such as text boxes), you are informed that the Scripting Object Model is required for these controls and asked whether you want to add them. If you select Yes, two small sections of code are added to your page; these sections are shown in Listing 11.1. Together, these two pieces of code create a wrapper around the normal processing of your page, exposing a set of events, properties, and methods for objects on that page. This wrapper enables you to use a standard event-driven style of coding against Web pages, which traditionally could not be programmed in that fashion. If you do not answer Yes to adding this code to your page, code written against the events of the DTC does not work correctly.

You can also add this object model to your page without adding any DTCs if you select the Enable Scripting Object Model option in the document's Properties dialog box. To remove this code (if you decide it is no longer needed), just deselect the same option.

FIG. 11.5

A Design-Time Control can be selected and moved as a single object.

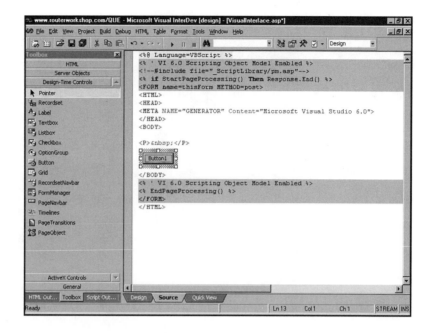

Listing 11.1 ASP PAGE1.ASP—Scripting Object Model Code Inserted at the Beginning and End of Your Document

```
<%@ Language=VBScript %>
<% ' VI 6.0 Scripting Object Model Enabled %>
<!--#include file="_ScriptLibrary/pm.asp"-->
<% if StartPageProcessing() Then Response.End() %>
<FORM name=thisForm METHOD=post>
<HTML>
<HEAD>
<META NAME="GENERATOR" Content="Microsoft Visual Studio 6.0">
</HEAD>
<BODY>
<P> </P>
</BODY>
<% ' VI 6.0 Scripting Object Model Enabled %>
<% EndPageProcessing() %>
</FORM>
</HTML>
```

Runtime Text

A Design-Time Control's purpose is to provide a visual interface to regular client- or server-side script. This is done to shield you from the complexities of that script and to allow you to work with that script only as an object. This structure is a great idea, as has already been shown with ActiveX controls and other component-based systems, but you can look into these particular components and see at least some of what is taking place.

FIG. 11.6

Runtime text can be shown for any Design-Time Control and is indicated by a gray background.

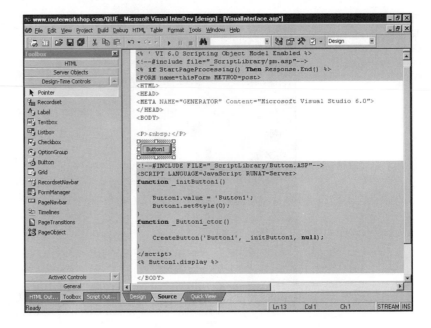

When you have a Design-Time Control selected, two commands on its right-click (context) menu allow you to look inside this control. Selecting Show Run-time Text causes a section of scripting code to become visible underneath the object, as shown in Figure 11.6. This code is shown with a gray background to indicate that it cannot be modified directly. You can hide the runtime text again by right-clicking and choosing Hide Run-time Text from the context menu.

To illustrate how the runtime text relates to the visual interface of a Design-Time Control, follow these steps:

1. Start with a new ASP document, opening a new project or using an existing one if you prefer.

2. In Source view, place the cursor somewhere between the `<body>` and `</body>` HTML tags. Double-click the TextBox DTC to add it to your page.

3. Select the text box you just added, and right-click it. Choose Show Run-time Text from the context menu. Notice the text displayed directly underneath the control and the `_initTextbox1()` function within it. (Listing 11.2 shows this function.)

4. Using the mouse, resize the text box horizontally, as shown in Figure 11.7. Notice how the argument to `textbox1.setColumnCount()` changes to match the new size of the control.

FIG. 11.7

Resizing the text box graphically modifies its runtime text.

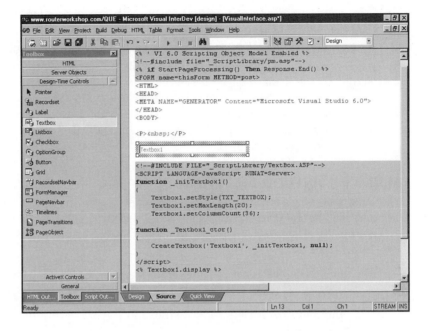

Listing 11.2   ASP PAGE1.ASP—Runtime Text for a TextBox Design-Time Control

```
<SCRIPT LANGUAGE=JavaScript>
function _initTextbox1()
{
        Textbox1.setStyle(TXT_TEXTBOX);
        Textbox1.setMaxLength(20);
        Textbox1.setColumnCount(20);
}
CreateTextbox('Textbox1', _initTextbox1, null);
</script>
```

The second command dealing with runtime text, Convert to Run-time Text, does something more permanent. Instead of merely showing you the text, this command actually removes the DTC, replacing it with its current runtime text equivalent. After you use this command, the same text is visible as with the previous command, but it no longer is shown with a gray background, and the control itself disappears. This command allows you to directly modify the code a Design-Time Control generates. In general, modifying the code this way is not a good idea, but, with a bit of work, it may be the only way to get exactly the behavior you need. To fully understand what the control's runtime text does, you need to study all the files referenced; they are stored in the _ScriptLibrary directory of your project. These files contain many functions and procedures used to produce the runtime text.

This conversion cannot be undone. If you want to go back to the original DTC, you have to restore a backup of your page, or simply insert a new control and remove all the runtime text from the old one.

The Form Controls

These Design-Time Controls allow you to build data entry forms against which you can write object-oriented, event-driven code. These controls can also be bound to a database using the Recordset control, which will be discussed later in this chapter. The following examples will illustrate the use of these controls in both server-side (ASP) and client-side (DHTML) mode. You can build these examples yourself by performing the steps one by one, or you can look at the two finished pages (ASP_FormControls.asp and DHTML_FormControls.asp) on the Web site that accompanies this book.

Example 1: Server-Side Forms

Start by creating a new ASP file named FormControls.asp. This file can be in any project you want, but the project must contain the Visual InterDev Script Library. If it does not contain that library, Visual InterDev asks whether you want to have it added when you add the first Form Design-Time Control.

1. Immediately below the opening `<body>` tag, place the following text:

   `<p>Form Controls Example</p>`

2. Directly below that line, add a TextBox DTC.

3. Select this control, and using its Properties dialog box or the Properties window, change its ID property to `txtFirstName`.

4. Add a second TextBox DTC, and set its ID property to `txtLastName`.

5. Insert the text `<br>` directly after the second text box to mark the end of the line.

6. Add a Button DTC. Change its ID to `cmdMakeFull`, and set its Caption property to `Make Full Name`.

7. Insert another `<br>` after the button.

8. Add a Label DTC, and change its ID to `lblFullName`. Erase the value in its DataField property, and set its FontBold property to `True`.

At this point, your page should resemble the one shown in Figure 11.8, and all that is left is adding the code. Each of the controls you added has a Scripting Platform property (available only through the Properties dialog boxes), which is set to Inherit from Page by default. The setting therefore is controlled by the DTC Scripting Platform property of the page. As a result, you can set the property in only one place, the Properties dialog box for the page, as shown in Figure 11.9. This setting affects all the DTCs on the page. For an ASP file, this page property defaults to Server (ASP), which is exactly what you want for this first example.

FIG. 11.8

You can position DTCs on the sample file as shown here.

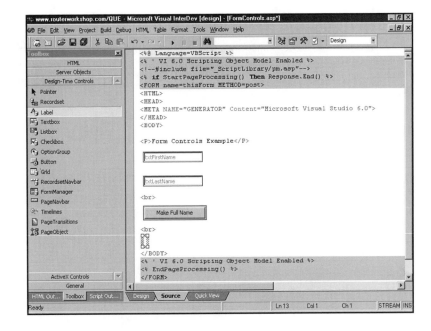

FIG. 11.9

The page-level scripting platform can be changed through the page's Properties dialog box.

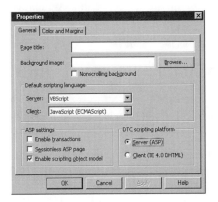

Next, you need to add code to the `onclick` event of the Button (`cmdMakeFull`) to concatenate the two text boxes, creating a full name and placing that value into the Label control. To do so, select the Script Outline tab of the Toolbox, and find the button's `onclick` event under Server Objects & Events, as shown in Figure 11.10.

FIG. 11.10
The Script Outline tab of the Toolbox window shows the events for all the objects on the page.

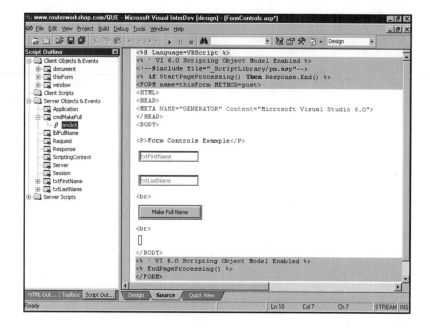

Double-click this event to begin editing the corresponding event procedure. Then enter this single line of code:

```
lblFullName.setCaption(txtFirstName.value + " " + txtLastName.value)
```

That's it; the page is done. Save it and then choose View, View in Browser. The page is then displayed in your browser and should resemble Figure 11.11. Enter your first and last name into the two text boxes, and then watch what the browser does when you click the button. Your full name should appear in bold under the button, but what is important is how this process occurred.

Regardless of the speed of your connection, you should notice that the browser has to reload the page, making a complete round-trip to the server. If it is hard to tell, try clicking the button again and watching the logo in the upper-right corner; it is animated for a moment, indicating that network traffic is taking place. The reload takes place because the page is set to use server-side script, so your onclick event is executed on the server. Every event that occurs and has an event procedure requires a reload of the page. You can imagine the effect of placing some code into the onchange event of one of these text boxes; every keypress would require a reload of the page.

N O T E One of the main reasons to use server-side code is to make your Web site platform independent, able to be viewed with any browser. If that factor is important for you, note that the DTCs included with Visual InterDev do generate some server-side code—small snippets of JavaScript that are necessary for the page to function. Browsers that do not support JavaScript cannot use your pages. ∎

FIG. 11.11

Here, you can see the finished sample page before clicking the Make Full Name button.

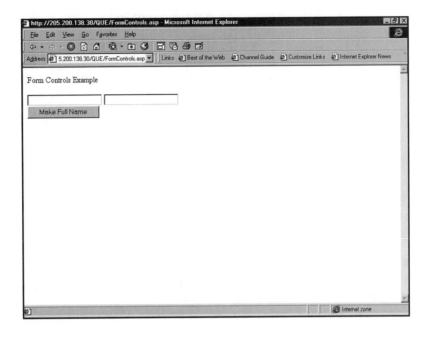

Example 2: Client-Side Script

This example illustrates the exact same functionality as the preceding one, but it is performed with client-side scripting. You could choose to begin this example with an empty page, but the beauty of Visual InterDev 6's new DTCs is that you don't have to. You can change this page to use client-side script extremely easily, with only the smallest of changes to the code.

First, you have to change the DTC Scripting Platform property of the page. Because you left the controls set to Inherit from Page, changing the page's property has the effect of changing all of them. Bring up the page's Properties dialog box, and change the Scripting Platform to Client.

Now, you need to change the `onclick` event from being server-side to client-side. You could do so by making some manual changes to the scripting block, but the easiest and most foolproof way is to use the interface. Select the Scripting Outline tab of the Toolbox again, and this time go to Client Objects & Events. Under this branch, find and double-click the desired event. Clicking this event creates an event procedure set up the way you want. Just cut and paste the one line of code from the old event procedure into your new one. Select and delete the entire script block for the old procedure, and you are done.

N O T E Not all server-side code transfers this well. Unless you explicitly change it, client-side code is in JavaScript, and server-side code is in VBScript. Many simple code statements (such as the line discussed in the preceding example) transfer with no changes, but you might need to make modifications in other cases. ■

Once again, save the page and then choose View, View in Browser. If your browser is still running from testing the previous page, refresh it to ensure that you have the latest version.

Enter some values, and try clicking the button on this new page. Notice two things: it produces the same results, and there is no network traffic; all this code is executing within the browser.

Several other Form controls were not included in the examples, but you work with them in exactly the same fashion. Each of them shares a few common properties, such as Recordset, Field, and Scripting Platform, thus reducing the amount of information you need to learn to be able to use all the available Design-Time Controls.

Data-Bound Controls

Data-bound controls are designed to simplify creating pages to display, edit, and add database information. The main control you will use is the Recordset Design-Time Control, which is always required because any data binding of DTCs takes place through it. The Recordset control itself is relatively simple to set up. For most pages, all you need to do is place the control on the page; then, using its Properties dialog box or directly interacting with the control (see Figure 11.12), you select one of the Data Connection objects from your project, and pick which table you want to link to. Through the Properties dialog box, shown in Figure 11.13, you can also enter a SQL statement to be used as the source. As long as you have a Data Connection set up, you are ready to go.

FIG. 11.12

The Recordset control supports direct interaction through its design-time interface.

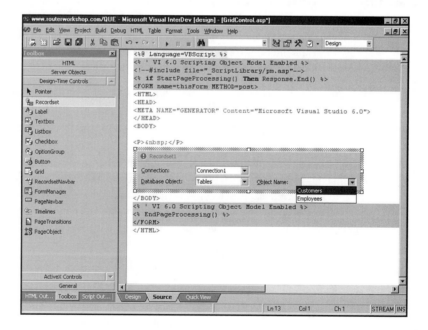

FIG. 11.13
The Properties dialog box for the Recordset control allows the entry of a SQL statement to serve as a record source.

The Data Connection

Setting up a Connection object for your Web project can be easy or difficult, depending on your development environment. When you choose Project, Add Data Connection, you are prompted to select or create an ODBC DSN. The DSN you choose is located on your machine but must also exist on your Web server. If you are developing on the Web server, having the DSN on your machine does not present an issue; the DSNs available to you are also going to be available to your server-side script.

If, as is more likely, you are developing on a different machine, perhaps even remotely, then the process can quickly become more complicated. Your first choice is to set up a DSN on both machines, with the same name, that is pointing to the same database. If such a setup is not possible—if you cannot access the same database remotely, for example—then you can move on to the second choice. Create a DSN on the server and on the development machine with the same name, but pointing to different databases. Both copies of the database should have the same structure, but they do not need to hold the same data.

The Grid Control

After you set up your Data Connection, you can move on to binding a control to your database. The example shown in the following section will focus on the Grid control. This Design-Time Control automates the creation of an HTML table that is populated with data from a Recordset control. This need is common in data-driven Web sites and becomes very simple through the use of this control. A quick example will illustrate the basic use of the Grid control, and a more detailed description of its various properties will follow.

An Example of the Grid Control   For this example, you need a Connection object set up to point to a sample database (Grid.mdb), which is included on the CD. (See "The Data Connection" earlier in this chapter for more information on how to point to a database.) After you set up the Connection, create a new ASP file and name it GridControl.asp. Add a Recordset control to the page. This control has its `Connection` property set to your new Connection object by default (unless you have multiple objects, in which case you should select the correct one). Then pick the Customers table from the drop-down list.

Add a Grid DTC to the page, directly below the Recordset. Bring up its Properties dialog box by right-clicking and selecting Properties from the context menu. The only settings on this dialog box that you need to change are on the Data tab. Select Recordset1 from the Recordset drop-down list. The Available Fields list box should be populated with the fields from the Customers table. Check Company Name, Contact Name, Region, and Country. Close the dialog box, save the page, and choose <u>V</u>iew, View in <u>B</u>rowser.

The page that is displayed, shown in Figure 11.14, contains a fully populated HTML table and a set of navigation buttons along the bottom. These buttons allow the user to move easily through pages of records, 20 records at a time. Notice the reload required every time you click any of the navigation buttons.

Grid Properties   This Grid control is very large and complex and has a correspondingly large number of properties. Going through the Properties dialog box pages in order, the following is a list of the most useful properties and descriptions of their functions.

The first page, shown in Figure 11.15, lists the properties of the control that you should modify first, the most important of which is the Autoformat information. The properties for the General tab are listed in Table 11.1.

FIG. 11.14

This full-featured data display appears without your writing any code because you use the Grid DTC.

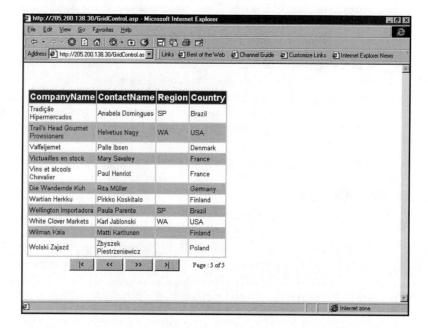

FIG. 11.15
On the General properties tab for the Grid Design-Time Control, you can modify several properties.

Table 11.1 General Properties

Property	Description
Autoformat	This property allows you to pick a predefined format for the entire table, including coloring and fonts. After picking a format here, you can customize it by using the Borders and Format pages.
Display Header Row	The state of this check box simply determines whether the control displays a row of header information.
Width/Units	This pair of properties allows you to set the width of the table to any pixel value or to a percentage of the HTML page.

The Data tab, shown in Figure 11.16, gives you control over what information is used to fill the table and allows you to build calculated fields. The properties for this tab are listed in Table 11.2.

FIG. 11.16
The Data tab of the Grid control allows you to specify data-binding information.

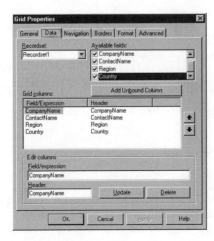

Table 11.2 Data Properties

Property	Description
Recordset	This property allows you to select which control provides the data for the grid.
Available Fields	This list is populated with all the fields from the selected Recordset control. Checking items in this list determines what fields are displayed in your table.
Grid Columns	This group of controls displays the current columns that appear in the table. The arrows on the right side allow you to manipulate the position of the columns. The Add Unbound Column button adds an additional field into which you can add a static or calculated expression.
Edit Columns	This box allows you to modify the column fields and header values. You can use script expressions to specify fields. You must click the Update button before moving to a different column; otherwise, changes are lost.

The Navigation tab, shown in Figure 11.17, controls how the grid divides data records among multiple pages. On this tab, you can add support for the selection of individual rows. The properties for this tab are listed in Table 11.3.

FIG. 11.17

The Grid Design-Time Control allows you to break up recordsets into smaller chunks, or pages.

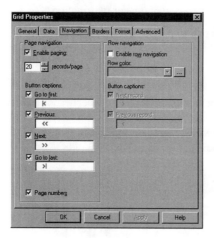

Table 11.3 Navigation Properties

Property	Description
Page Navigation	These properties allow you to control whether the grid breaks up the recordset into multiple pages, and what the next and previous page buttons look like. The Page Numbers check box determines if text is displayed next to the navigation bar in the form Page 3 of 12.

Property	Description
Row Navigation	These properties control whether the grid supports the selection of an individual row, what the highlight color is for the selected row, and what the next/previous row buttons look like. When you are dealing with server-side script, each click on the next/previous row buttons causes a reload of the page, making it very time-consuming.

The Borders tab, shown in Figure 11.18, controls the standard HTML formatting of the table borders, allowing you to specify specific colors and widths. Be sure to check any setting you create with several of your target browsers, as not all these properties are supported.

The Format tab, shown in Figure 11.19, allows you to specify font and color information for any part of the Grid. The properties for this tab are listed in Table 11.4.

Table 11.4   Format Properties

Property	Description
Font	These properties set the font face, size, and color properties for whatever section of the grid is selected (using the three toggle buttons at the top of the page). Note that the size value is not a standard font point size but refers instead to the HTML font size values.
Color	As with the Font properties, these properties affect whichever section of the grid is currently selected. Through these properties, you can control the background color of the grid cells. The Alternating Color property allows you to create the ledger-style effect of all even rows being in one color and all odd rows in another. The "alternating color" is the one used directly after the Header row and is generally the lighter of the two colors chosen.
Alignment	Most useful when you are dealing with the Specific Column choice, this property allows you to set that column to a certain alignment. This property is handy when you are dealing with a mix of numeric and text fields.

The Advanced tab, shown in Figure 11.20, allows you to specify attribute/value pairs to be inserted directly into the generated HTML. This way, you have access to any HTML feature not provided through the rest of the Grid interface. An example of an additional value to be added is the `align` attribute for the entire table, allowing you to control its positioning on your page.

FIG. 11.18

The Grid's Border properties allow greater control than standard HTML editors. Notice the ability to specify horizontal only or vertical only gridlines.

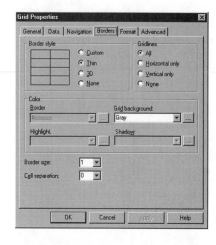

FIG. 11.19

You can create precise formatting by using the Grid Properties dialog box, which allows settings for the header row, detail rows, and even specific columns.

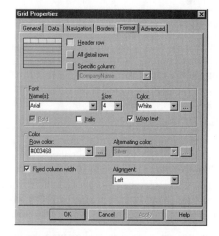

FIG. 11.20

Any HTML attributes not wrapped by the Grid's properties can be added directly through the Advanced tab.

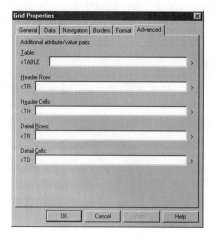

The Recordset NavBar

Using the Grid control is one way to create a tabular view of data on a Web page, but when you want to create an actual data entry form, you need to use a combination of the Recordset control and the Form DTCs. By binding TextBoxes, Labels, and other types of controls to a Recordset, you can quickly create a page that allows your users to edit, delete, or add information to a database. Each of these Design-Time Controls has two properties, Recordset and Field, that allow you to bind them to a database (see Figure 11.21). After you add a few of these controls to your page and associate them with a Recordset, all that remains is a way to handle movement between records.

FIG. 11.21

All controls that can be data-bound share the common property Recordset and, for those that bind to a single data column, Field.

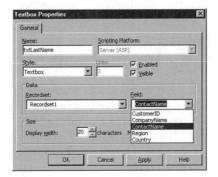

At this point, the Recordset NavBar DTC comes in. It provides the standard navigation buttons (First, Last, Next, and Previous) in a single control that you associate with your Recordset. Other than properties to control the button captions and to select an associated Recordset, the only option you need to decide on is Update on Move. This option, when selected, saves the current record whenever the user decides to navigate to a different one. Event procedures (onfirstclick, onnextclick, and so on) that allow you to execute script for each of the four buttons are available for the NavBar.

To allow more advanced functions, such as adding, deleting, and saving records, you can easily add and code your own buttons. Simply create three additional buttons on your page (assuming your Recordset is already present and functioning), and set their captions accordingly. Use the script in Listing 11.3 to provide the desired functionality. This sample assumes your Recordset control is named rsGrid, and your three buttons are cmdAddNew, cmdSave, and cmdDelete, respectively.

> **Listing 11.3 ASP PAGE1.ASP—Server-Side Script for the Addition and Deletion of Records**

```
<SCRIPT ID=serverEventHandlersVBS LANGUAGE=vbscript RUNAT=Server>

Sub cmdAddNew_onclick()
        rsGrid.addRecord
End Sub
```

continues

Part

III

Ch

11

Listing 11.3   Continued

```
Sub cmdSave_onclick()
      rsGrid.updateRecord
End Sub

Sub cmdDelete_onclick()
      rsGrid.deleteRecord
End Sub

</SCRIPT>
```

In general, by using a combination of the existing DTCs, such as the Recordset NavBar and a little of your own code, you can quickly create a fully functional data-driven Web site.

The Multimedia Controls

Most of the DTCs present in Visual InterDev 6 deal with simplifying old technology. Building data entry forms on the Web has been possible for several years, and displaying data in a formatted HTML table is nothing new. These new Design-Time Controls enable you to accomplish these tasks easily; they are timesaving features. The two Multimedia controls are the first of a new category of DTCs—a category that will be growing very quickly; they allow development using a new technology.

By providing these controls, Microsoft is removing the learning curve from some DHTML and making it quick and easy to use. It is likely that someone, either Microsoft or a third-party developer, will produce more DHTML-oriented Design-Time Controls, and over time, most of the capabilities of this powerful tool will be accessible through an easy-to-use interface.

The Page Transitions Control

The Page Transitions control allows you to create visual effects when the user moves between the pages of your site, or from a page in your site to some external URL. If you are familiar with video editing or even with Microsoft PowerPoint, you will be used to the concept of placing fades, sweeps, and dissolves between slides or clips to provide a transition. This control serves the same purpose.

Place the Page Transitions control anywhere on your Web page, and then bring up its Properties dialog box, as shown Figure 11.22. Both tabs, Site Transition and Page Transition, are nearly identical. For each, you have two events to control: Exit and Enter. Set the combo box to the type of transition you want, and then click Preview to see a simulation of the transition. Adjusting the duration controls how long the effect takes and, therefore, how much of it the user will see.

The Page Enter and Exit events occur whenever someone arrives at this page from another page within your Web site, and when this user leaves this page to go to another page within your Web site. In contrast, the Site Enter and Exit events occur during a visitor's arriving and leaving this page, but from a URL that is not within your Web site. Remember that this control affects only this page. If you want a certain transition to take effect whenever someone arrives at or leaves your entire Web site, then this Page Transitions control has to be present on every page.

FIG. 11.22
The Properties dialog box for the Page Transitions control allows you to preview effects such as an animation.

> **N O T E**   The Page Transition control provides a Duration setting for each of its effects; be sure to use this setting wisely. The most important part of a Web site is the content on the pages, not the navigation between them. If users have to wait through a 10-second dissolve every time they move to a different page, they will quickly tire of the entire experience and leave the site for good. ▪

The Timelines Control

The Timelines control, like the Page Transitions control, is client-side only. It depends on certain features of Dynamic HTML that allow scripting functions to be called based on time intervals. The possibilities for using this control are endless, but a common use is animation. You can set up a timeline that calls a series of 15 events (or the same event 15 times), once per half second, and then in your client-side event handler, move through the frames of an animation on your page. You can set up this timeline to start as soon as the page loads, or you can control it from script (using the `play`, `pause`, and `stop` methods). Imagine the interesting effects you can generate by starting a timeline playing based on selections from a form.

Setting up the control is completely visual; you use its Properties dialog box, as shown in Figure 11.23. The combo box and buttons along the top allow you to work with multiple timelines. A Web page can have only one Timelines control, but you can set up (using the New button) as many individual timelines as you want. When you create a new timeline, a dialog box is displayed, as shown in Figure 11.24, allowing you to specify the name and choose whether the timeline starts when the page is loaded. If you want to change this setting or the timeline's name later, you can use the Edit button to bring this dialog box up again.

After you select a timeline, adding events is just a matter of clicking the last item in the events list. A new event starts as a Discrete event, signifying one that just fires once at a single point in time. You can add the same event name several times to the list and therefore cause it to fire multiple times. You can change when the event fires both graphically and numerically, either by dragging the small diamond (for a Discrete event) or by changing the value in the Start Time field.

FIG. 11.23

The Timelines control has a detailed graphical interface in its Properties dialog box.

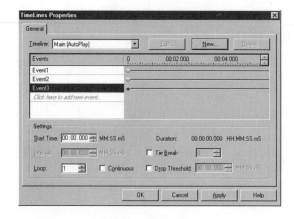

FIG. 11.24

When adding a new timeline, you can choose to have it start automatically when the page is loaded.

Events can be set as Discrete (discussed in the preceding paragraph), Continuous, or Looping. The type is controlled by the setting of three fields on the Properties dialog box. The Continuous check box specifies that the event fires once per Interval units of time for the entire time that the timeline is playing (starting at the time set in the Start Time field). The timeline is active until the user leaves the page, or until it is stopped through script. Looping events are created by increasing the Loop value to greater than one. If this is the case, the Interval property becomes enabled, allowing you to specify the time between loops. The total duration of the event is, therefore, until all loops have been completed and can be calculated as follows:

(loops − 1) * the interval value

In Figure 11.25, you can see three events. Event1 is a Discrete event that will fire once, one second into the timeline. Event2 (selected) will fire three times (Loop = 3) with one second between each occurrence, causing it to execute at two seconds, three seconds, and four seconds. The display-only Duration field gives the overall duration of the selected event. Event3, which is another Discrete event, will fire only once, at three seconds into the timeline.

In the preceding example, both Event2 and Event3 will fire at the three-second point, but both events cannot occur simultaneously. The remaining two properties on the dialog box, Tie Break and Drop Threshold, deal with multiple events occurring at once. The Tie Break value, if specified, determines which of two or more events should occur first. Lower values are considered of higher priority and are always executed first, with a value of zero (0) being the highest priority and 10 being the lowest. If Tie Break is disabled (unchecked), then the event always occurs last.

FIG. 11.25

Three events are set up for the Main timeline.

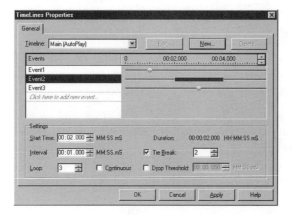

In these cases of some events firing before others, an event may not be executed exactly at the right time. For instance, in the preceding example, Event2 and Event3 are both set to execute at three seconds. If you know that the Tie Break value of Event2 is 2 and the value for Event3 is 4, then Event2's event procedure executes before Event3's. If Event2's procedure contains code that takes approximately 30 milliseconds (ms) to execute, Event3 doesn't fire until 30ms after the three-second mark. In most cases, this wouldn't really matter, but if your code is time sensitive, you can prevent late events from firing. You can set the Drop Threshold property to prevent execution if the intended time is exceeded by more than the specified amount. If this property is not enabled, then the event will fire regardless of how late it occurs.

You can easily code against the Timelines control by using the Script Outline tab. Each of the Timeline objects (not the Timelines control itself) appears as an object, and each event appears as an event under that object. Remember that they are client-side objects only and, therefore, appear under that branch of the Script Outline.

Part
III

Ch
11

CAUTION

Note that you must include script for all the events of all the Timeline objects you create, even if they do not do anything. If you do not, you receive a notice stating that an error appears in your page at Line 1, Char 1. This message is misleading because nothing is wrong with that section. The error is that some of the DTC-generated code is attempting to call functions that do not exist in the page. Simply double-click all the Timeline events in the Script Outline to ensure that at least a scripting stub exists for each function.

From Here...

Design-Time Controls open up a world of possibilities. They are really more than just tools; they are a coding methodology. The controls from Microsoft are all based around a set of concepts, such as the Scripting Object Model and the Script Library, on which they rely to produce their final results. These dependencies and interrelated systems of code make using these controls a matter of all-or-nothing. As such, using them may be difficult or inconvenient for some developers, but that is not a good reason to ignore the entire concept of Design-Time Controls. Most third-party controls will likely be designed as standalone objects because they will not be provided as part of a large, integrated system.

The purpose of these controls is to generate code, of any sort, so they can be used for almost as many different purposes as the code itself. For example, developers could bundle a DTC with their server or client ActiveX components to simplify the work required to use those components. Programmers who work on Web sites as part of a team could develop their own DTCs to provide them with a visual interface to their company's own particular mix of back office systems.

Design-Time Controls are really just specialized forms of ActiveX controls. At the following URL, you can find the detailed information required to modify a Visual Basic control project so that it can be used as a DTC inside Visual InterDev:

http://www.microsoft.com/vbasic/techmat/feature/nov97/default.htm

The information provided at this location is based on Visual Basic 5.0, and may not be 100 percent accurate for Visual Basic 6.0 or later. For detailed information on creating the ActiveX control itself, see the next chapter, "Building ActiveX Controls with Visual Basic." It provides the information Visual InterDev developers need to create a standard control for use on the client-side or as a framework for building a Design-Time Control.

For more information on the Data Environment, Data Commands, and Data Connections in Visual InterDev, see Chapter 16, "Using the Visual InterDev 6 Data Environment."

CHAPTER 12

Building ActiveX Controls with Visual Basic

In this chapter

Introducing ActiveX Controls **262**

Using Visual Basic for ActiveX **263**

Using the VB Development Environment **264**

Building Your First ActiveX Control **267**

Deploying ActiveX Controls **277**

Introducing ActiveX Controls

In Chapter 10, "Using ActiveX Controls," you were introduced to ActiveX controls and how they can be used in your Web pages. In this chapter, you'll learn how you can use Microsoft Visual Basic to create controls for use in Web pages.

The topic of ActiveX control creation is rather broad. Complete coverage would take an entire book, so I'll just scratch the surface in this chapter. However, by the time you've finished this chapter, you'll have learned how to work with the Visual Basic development environment, how Visual Basic (VB) shields the developer from the complexities of ActiveX/COM development, and you'll actually get your hands dirty creating and deploying a usable ActiveX control. Figure 12.1 shows this control embedded into a Web page (which you'll also create using the techniques discussed in this chapter). If you already have VB, the Books Online provide some great reference materials and samples of building ActiveX controls. In addition, *Sams Teach Yourself ActiveX Control Programming with Visual Basic 5* or *Sams Teach Yourself ActiveX Programming in 21 Days*, both published by Sams, are excellent books on the topic.

FIG. 12.1

The ActiveX control embedded in a Web page. You'll create both the control and the page in this chapter.

ActiveX control ⌐

Standard HTML ⌐

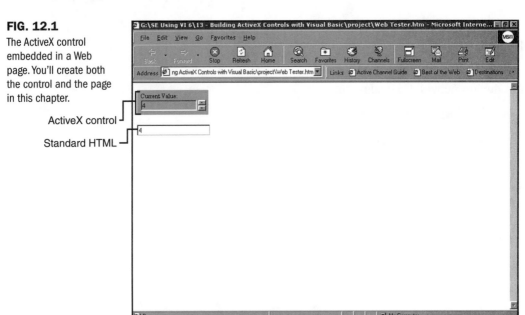

> **N O T E**   This chapter relies exclusively on Visual Basic and the ActiveX Control Interface Wizard included with most versions of Visual Basic. If you do not yet have a copy of Visual Basic, you can download the free Control Creation Edition from the VB Web site (**http:// www.microsoft.com/vbasic**). This version, however, does not include the Application Setup Wizard, which is used in the final section of this chapter. You still can create controls but have to create distribution packages for them manually. ▪

Using Visual Basic for ActiveX

One of the strengths of Visual Basic has always been that it does a lot of the grunt work for you. As a result, you are free to concentrate on the development of the business functionality of your applications without having to worry about many of the low-level implementation details. For ActiveX development, either in the form of ActiveX controls or COM components, this statement is truer than ever.

After you create the control in this chapter, I invite you to pick up a book on Visual C++ (such as *Sams Teach Yourself Visual C++ 5 in 21 Days, Fourth Edition*, published by Sams) and take a look at what's involved in building even a simple ActiveX control with C++. You'll be amazed (as I continue to be) at the number of behind-the-scenes details that Visual Basic takes care of for you in this arena.

N O T E   The Microsoft MSDN online library also has a sample of building an ActiveX control with Visual C++ at **http://premium.microsoft.com/msdn/library/devprods/vc++/tutorials/ D8/S6D99.HTM**. You need to register to use this site, but registration is free and (in my opinion) you're going to need the resources found here anyway if you're developing applications (even Web-based ones) with Microsoft tools. ■

COM Development with VB

In the olden times, people used OLE Server applications. These applications could provide objects that are accessible by other applications. Visual Basic 4 allowed you to create these OLE Servers. Today, OLE Servers haven't disappeared, but they have been renamed and enhanced. They're now called *ActiveX Components*, and they allow for a greater range of interconnectivity between applications. Another acronym used when discussing ActiveX components is *COM*, which stands for *Component Object Model*. COM is the underlying architecture upon which ActiveX rests. It is a specification defining how components are instantiated (brought to life) by the operating system and how they communicate with the operating system.

Visual Basic provides you with the following COM-centric features:

- You can create ActiveX controls, ActiveX Documents (which are applications that can be embedded into any COM container such as IE4), code components (also known as ActiveX DLLs, they cannot be embedded in a container but certainly can be used by Active Server Pages and client-side script code), and applications that provide components (Excel and Word, for example).

- Objects can raise custom events that can be trapped by their host applications. You therefore can create your own events for the controls you develop with VB and trigger them as necessary.

- You can use *friend functions,* which are visible only to code within the component but not outside the component (including other classes that may be hosted by your component). A friend function allows you to globally expose functions to code within your component without it being exposed to the outside world.

Part

III

Ch

12

■ You can use *polymorphism,* which allows your control to mimic some other code interface. You therefore can define a standard interface for working with a component and then implement that interface in different ways with different components.

■ You can specify a default property or method for your components. For example, the value property of an HTML <INPUT> element can be accessed without specifying the property name explicitly because it is the default property.

■ You don't have to write any code for registration of the component. VB takes care of this task for you, including the selection of a GUID (globally unique identifier), which is used in a Web page's <OBJECT> tag to identify the control.

■ You don't have to write any of the low-level Automation code that a COM component is required to provide. VB adds this code to your compiled modules for you.

N O T E The focus of this chapter is on developing ActiveX controls. However, you can also use Visual Basic to develop server-side code components as ActiveX DLLs. They can be instantiated from Active Server Pages and can be used to encapsulate business functionality. Moving large, commonly used code out of ASP script code and into an ActiveX DLL is often advisable. Chapter 7, "Server-Side Scripting," discusses some of the details of working with server-side components. ■

The ActiveX Control Interface Wizard

In typical VB fashion, an ActiveX Control Interface Wizard takes most of the grunge work out of creating ActiveX controls. This wizard, which is a VB Add-In component, helps you define the properties, methods, and events supported by your control. It also allows you to map these properties to any *constituent controls* you've added to your ActiveX control.

N O T E *Constituent controls* are the controls that make up the ActiveX control you're creating. You'll see how to add controls to your ActiveX control later in this chapter. ■

This wizard also helps you to set the attributes for the properties and methods that make up the public interface of your control. For example, you can easily specify that a property is read only at runtime but is read/write at design time.

> **WARNING**
> Before you use the ActiveX Control Interface Wizard, you must add all the visual elements to the control. You also must specify the name for the control.

Using the VB Development Environment

In this section, you'll take a brief tour around the Visual Basic environment. The VB user interface is fairly simple to use, so the tour won't last too long. If you want to follow along, start VB now and select ActiveX Control on the New Project dialog box (if this dialog box does not appear, choose File, New Project to launch it).

Getting Around in VB

Figure 12.2 shows what the user interface looks like immediately after starting a new ActiveX Control project. Amazingly enough, this interface looks almost identical to the standard Visual InterDev user interface. All that's missing are the tabs along the bottom of the editor window.

FIG. 12.2

The Visual Basic user interface.

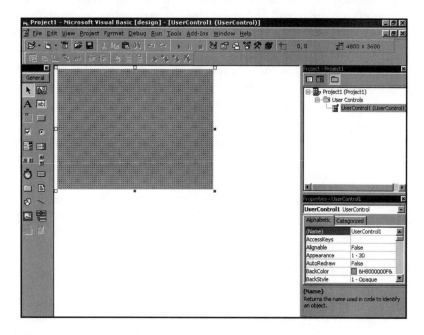

Down the left side of the screen, you can see the Toolbox. In VB, just like InterDev, you use the Toolbox to add ActiveX controls to your project quickly. You can also customize this Toolbox by adding additional controls and organizational tabs to it.

In the middle of the screen, you see the editor window. This particular example shows the form used for the ActiveX control you're creating. In VB, this feature is known as a *User Control,* as you can see in the Project Explorer window shown at the top right of the screen.

The Project Explorer shows you a tree view of all the projects and files in the current VB workspace. In version 5 and greater of VB, you can create a workspace containing more than one project, as you'll see later in this chapter.

Below the Project Explorer, you can see the Properties window. You use this window to set the properties for the selected module or control, just like you use it within InterDev.

Fiddling with the Options

To work with ActiveX controls effectively, you need to modify a few of the options provided by the development environment. A myriad of options affect not only the look and feel of the environment but also what happens when errors occur within the applications running in the environment (including ActiveX components such as the one you'll develop here).

Part
III

Ch
12

To get to the Options dialog box, choose Tools, Options. The Editor tab allows you to change settings that affect how the code editor behaves. For example, you can enable or disable automatic syntax checking or drag-and-drop editing (which allows you to highlight a section of code and drag and drop to move or copy it to another spot in the code editor window). If Require Variable Declaration is not checked, check it now. This option requires that any variables you use be explicitly declared in your code, preventing typographical errors from causing your code to misbehave.

On the Editor Format tab, you can find options that affect how the text in the code editor is displayed. You can find options for the font to be used and the colors for various types of code elements (such as comments, keywords, and variables). Change these settings to match your particular style, or just leave them as is.

On the General tab, you can find options that affect the grid used when doing the layout for user interface elements, settings for error trapping, and a few miscellaneous settings. For now, set both Grid Units Width and Height to 60, a more reasonable value for most purposes. Also, set the Error Trapping option to Break on Unhandled Errors.

The Docking, Environment, and Advanced tabs have further settings that affect the design environment and how it operates. None of them have any impact on what you'll do in this chapter, so you can click OK now to save the settings you've modified.

Activating an Add-In

The ActiveX Control Interface Wizard was mentioned briefly in the previous chapter. It is a VB Add-In module but doesn't automatically appear on the Add-Ins menu. You can check this by clicking the Add-Ins menu item. If you don't see an entry labeled ActiveX Control Interface Wizard in the menu, you need to tell Visual Basic that you want to use it.

Follow these steps to add the wizard to the Add-Ins menu:

1. Choose Add-Ins, Add-In Manager. The Add-In Manager dialog box appears (see Figure 12.3).

2. Check the box next to the entry labeled VB ActiveX Control Interface Wizard in the list box.

3. Click OK. Now look at the Add-Ins menu again. The ActiveX Control Interface Wizard entry should be present.

FIG. 12.3

The Add-In Manager dialog box.

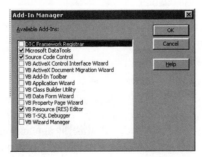

N O T E If the VB ActiveX Control Interface Wizard entry does not exist in the Add-In Manager's list of add-ins, it's probably not installed. Run the VB Setup again, select the Add/Remove Components option, and add this wizard to your VB setup. ■

Building Your First ActiveX Control

Now that you've seen what Visual Basic provides in the way of ActiveX/COM support, how the development environment works, and how to add the ActiveX Control Interface Wizard add-in to the environment, you're ready to build the ActiveX control pictured in Figure 12.1.

Mapping Out the Control

The control you're going to build is a numeric-valued text box with a spin button that can be used to increment or decrement the value. This type of control is useful for setting font size, sound card volume, and other numeric properties that typically work in close increments. The control will also allow the user to type numeric values into the text box, and will allow the programmer to specify a minimum and maximum value for the control as well as the value to increment (or decrement) by each time the spin button is clicked.

N O T E This control will be fully functioning but will be missing one important element: resizing. This means that if you place this control into a container and resize the instance of the control within the container, the individual elements that make up this control will not resize or move. For your purposes, this functionality is not a problem, but you might want to add such handling if you plan to use this control in many places. ■

Although the individual pieces that make up this control are available for use in your HTML documents created with InterDev, using an ActiveX control allows you to encapsulate all the functionality in a single component.

The individual pieces that make up this control (the constituent controls) probably are not obvious from looking at Figure 12.1. Only three controls make up this ActiveX control: a label, a text box, and an UpDown control (a new Windows common control included with Visual InterDev).

Part
III

Ch
12

Starting the Project

If you've been following along, you're already at the point where you can start creating the actual control. If you haven't been, start Visual Basic and select ActiveX Control on the New Project dialog box. If VB is already running, but you've got an existing project loaded, choose File, New Project to launch the New Project dialog box.

The UpDown control is one of the controls in the Windows Common Controls component; you need to add a reference to it to the current project. To do so, choose Project, Components. Just like InterDev's Customize Toolbox feature, this menu item launches a dialog box listing the ActiveX components installed on your system, as you can see in Figure 12.4. Your dialog box will most likely look a little different, depending on which third-party controls are installed on your system. Scroll through the list on the Controls tab until you find an entry for Windows Common Controls-2 6.0. Check the box corresponding to this entry, and click OK to create a reference to this library of controls. The Toolbox window changes to show all the individual controls contained within this library.

FIG. 12.4

The Components dialog box used to add components to your current project.

Laying Out the Constituent Controls

Now that you've got a new ActiveX control project and all the constituent controls available on the Toolbox, you can start laying out the user interface for the control. Follow these steps to create the UI:

1. Click the Label tool in the Toolbox. It's the one with the capital *A*. Click near the top-left corner of the user control form, and drag down and to the right. Keeping the mouse button pressed, pause momentarily and a ToolTip appears informing you of the width and height of the control. Size the control to 1995 pixels wide and 255 pixels high. Alternatively, you can place the control on the form and set its `Width` and `Height` properties as specified.

2. Using the Properties window, change the label's `Name` property to `lblCaption`. Change its `Caption` property to an empty string.

3. Click the Textbox control in the Toolbox (it's just to the right of the Label control). Place the control just below the label, making it 1755 pixels wide by 315 pixels high. Change its `Name` to `txtValue` and its `Text` property to `0` (this will be the default value for the control).

4. Find the UpDown control in the Toolbox. It should be near the bottom of the window and resembles a scrollbar to the right of a window. Add it to the right of the text box, sizing it to about the height of the text box. Leave all its default property values as is (it should be named `UpDown1`; if it isn't, change the `Name` property to this value to match the code you'll add in a bit).

5. Right-click over this control, and select Properties from the context menu. The Property Pages dialog box for the control appears. Click the Buddy tab. Your screen should now

resemble Figure 12.5. In the Buddy Control text box, enter `txtValue`. After you type the last character, the SyncBuddy check box and the Buddy Property list box become enabled. Check the SyncBuddy check box. The Buddy Property list box changes to (`Default`). Leave this setting as is.

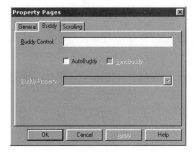

FIG. 12.5

The "Buddy control" properties of the UpDown control.

You've just tied the UpDown control to the text box. This unique control has the capability of reading and modifying the properties of another control. Using this control saves you from having to write code that responds to the UpDown control's click events and modifying the value of the text box manually.

6. Click OK. The text box is resized, and the UpDown control moves. These changes are side effects of the Buddy Control business. Simply size them and move them back to their original configuration.

7. Resize the user control form itself to approximately 2,235 pixels wide by 735 pixels high. You can do so either by clicking a blank area of the form and dragging the sizing handle at the bottom-right corner up and to the left, or you can change the `Width` and `Height` properties of the user control in the Properties window.

8. Change the `Name` property of the user control to `spinText`. If the user control is not the selected control in the Properties window, simply click in the blank area of the form to select it.

You've finished laying out the control. Your screen should now resemble Figure 12.6.

Using the ActiveX Control Interface Wizard

Now that you've got all the UI components in place, you can use the ActiveX Control Interface Wizard to define the public interface to the control (the properties, methods, and events that the outside world has access to) as well as insert code to handle most of these elements for you.

So, follow these steps to proceed with the control:

1. Choose <u>A</u>dd-Ins, ActiveX Control Interface Wizard to launch the wizard. The introductory screen describes what the wizard will do and provides a few notes about using the wizard. Click <u>N</u>ext to continue.

Part

III

Ch

12

FIG. 12.6

The finished user interface of the control.

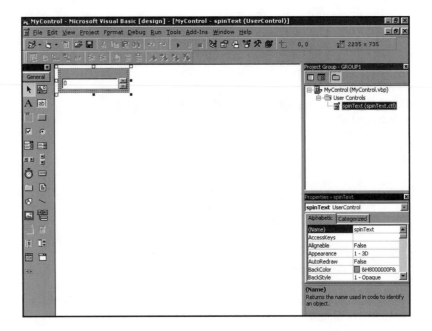

The Select Interface Members dialog box, shown in Figure 12.7, appears. In this dialog box, you specify the properties, methods, and events that the control will expose. The left-hand list box shows all the standard properties, methods, and events supported by the user control and the constituent controls you added. The right-hand list box lists the ones that will be exposed by the control.

FIG. 12.7

The Select Interface Members dialog box.

2. Remove the `BackStyle` property from the interface by double-clicking its entry in the Selected Names list box. Add the following by double-clicking them in the Available Names list box:

■ `BackColor Property`

■ `Caption Property`

- ■ Change Event
- ■ DownClick Event
- ■ ForeColor Property
- ■ Increment Property
- ■ Max Property
- ■ Min Property
- ■ UpClick Event
- ■ Value Property

3. Click Next to move to the Create Custom Interface Members dialog box. You won't be adding any custom properties, methods, or events to this control (everything you need is covered by one of the standard elements), so click Next again.

   The Set Mapping dialog box appears. As the dialog box describes, you use it to map the interface elements to the properties, methods, and events of the constituent controls.

4. By selecting the appropriate item in the Public Name list box, you can specify the mapped control and member in the Maps To frame. Table 12.1 lists the mappings you should establish. Leave all other mappings alone. Click Next after you finish.

Table 12.1   Mappings of the Public Interface to the Constituent Controls

Public Name	Control	Member
Caption Property	lblCaption	Caption
Change Event	txtValue	Change
DownClick Event	UpDown1	DownClick
Increment Property	UpDown1	Increment
KeyDown Event	txtValue	KeyDown
KeyPress Event	txtValue	KeyPress
KeyUp Event	txtValue	KeyUp
Max Property	UpDown1	Max
Min Property	UpDown1	Min
UpClick Event	UpDown1	UpClick
Value Property	txtValue	Text

Part

III

Ch

12

The Set Attributes dialog box, shown in Figure 12.8, appears. In this dialog box, you can set various attributes for the interface members. For your purposes, you need to make only two changes here. The BackColor and ForeColor properties have been set to the Long data type. There is a special OLE data type for dealing with colors. When set to this data type, many ActiveX containers that allow you to set the properties of the contained components display a special color picker dialog box when they encounter properties of this data type. For whatever reason, the wizard does not recognize that these two properties (`BackColor` and `ForeColor`) belong to this category.

5. Select `BackColor` and change the Data Type entry from `Long` to `OLE_COLOR`. For the Default Value, enter `-2147483633` (this number represents the Display Control Panel's Button Face color, which is the standard VB background color). Repeat this step for the `ForeColor` property, but do not change the Default Value. Click <u>N</u>ext.

You've made it to the final dialog box of the wizard.

FIG. 12.8

The Set Attributes dialog box.

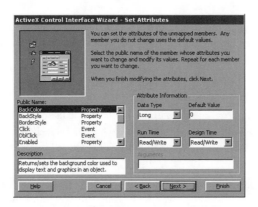

6. To see a verbose summary report of what just happened and what you should do next, leave the View Summary Report check box checked. Click <u>F</u>inish to close the wizard and let it do its work. (If you have the summary turned on, you have to close the dialog box that appears as well.)

Adding Property-Handling Code

From the looks of things, not much has changed. However, a peek at the code reveals that the wizard did quite a lot of work. Double-click in an empty area of the form, and you'll be taken to the user control's code window. Poke around in here for a few minutes to get a feel for what the wizard has done.

Basically, the wizard has added all the code necessary for the new ActiveX control to behave almost identically to the design objectives laid out previously. However, you still need to add a little bit of code to what the wizard has created. This code will give the control a more polished look and feel, and will ensure that the properties of the constituent controls are all consistent. For example, when the `BackColor` property changes, make the text box, the label, and the control's surface all change to the new color. Because the wizard can't handle this "one-to-many" mapping, you need to manually add the code that accomplishes this feat.

With the code window open, make sure that `UserControl` appears in the left-hand drop-down list (see Figure 12.9). Select `ReadProperties` in the right-hand drop-down list. The `ReadProperties` event of the user control fires whenever the control should read its persistent properties. Property names and values are stored in a "property bag" that is responsible for saving and retrieving the properties for an instance of the control. For example, when you create a Web page with an <OBJECT> tag with <PARAM> child tags, the property bag mechanism is responsible for retrieving the property values from the <PARAM> tags.

FIG. 12.9

The code window for the ActiveX control.

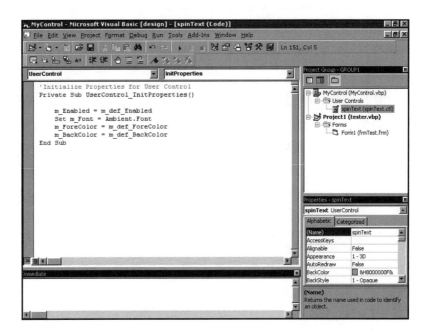

At the bottom of the ReadProperties routine, just before the End Sub line, enter the following code:

```
'set values for constituent controls
    txtValue.Enabled = m_Enabled
    UpDown1.Enabled = m_Enabled
    Set txtValue.Font = m_Font
    Set lblCaption.Font = m_Font
    Set UserControl.Font = m_Font
    txtValue.BackColor = m_BackColor
    lblCaption.BackColor = m_BackColor
    UserControl.BackColor = m_BackColor
    txtValue.ForeColor = m_ForeColor
    lblCaption.ForeColor = m_ForeColor
    UserControl.ForeColor = m_ForeColor
```

This code takes the property values read from the property bag and assigns them to the appropriate properties of the constituent controls.

Next, you need to add code to modify constituent control property values when the value of the spinText's controls properties are changed by the container. Select (General) in the left-hand drop-down list and BackColor [Property Let] in the right-hand one. This routine executes whenever the BackColor property is assigned a value. In between the two existing lines of code

Part
III

Ch
12

(ignoring the first and last lines that define the bounds of the routine), enter the following code:

```
'set values for constituent controls:
    txtValue.BackColor = New_BackColor
    lblCaption.BackColor = New_BackColor
    UserControl.BackColor = New_BackColor
```

Locate the Enabled [Property Let] entry in the right-hand drop-down list, and enter this code between the two existing lines:

```
'modify the constituent controls:
    txtValue.Enabled = New_Enabled
    UpDown1.Enabled = New_Enabled
```

For the Font [Property Set] routine, enter this code in a similar manner:

```
'set value for constituent controls:
    Set txtValue.Font = New_Font
    Set lblCaption.Font = New_Font
```

And for the ForeColor [Property Let] routine, enter this code:

```
'set values for constituent controls
    txtValue.ForeColor = New_ForeColor
    lblCaption.ForeColor = New_ForeColor
    UserControl.ForeColor = New_ForeColor
```

Coding Around User Errors

Like it or not, someone else might (and probably will) use the components you create. The world would be a wonderful place for software developers if you could make money without actually having users. However, such a nirvana does not exist (and probably won't within your lifetime), so you need to code around the foolish things a user might attempt to do with your perfect software creations.

For example, you would never type any characters except digits into your control's text box. After all, it's used as a counter. But some rogue user probably will attempt to type all sorts of things here. Although this stray information won't necessarily affect the operation of the control itself, some script code could respond to the events raised by the control, and having characters in the Value property could cause a problem. So, in this section, you'll add some code to the control to prevent this and other mistakes from happening.

With the code window still open, select txtValue in the left-hand drop-down list. Select KeyPress in the right-hand drop-down list. Insert the following lines of code before the line that starts with RaiseEvent:

```
'only accept digit keys or Backspace key:
If (Chr$(KeyAscii) < "0" Or Chr$(KeyAscii) > "9") And _
    KeyAscii <> 8 Then
    Beep
    KeyAscii = 0
    Exit Sub
End If
```

```
'check value:
If KeyAscii <> 8 Then        'let the backspace through no matter what
    If Val(txtValue.Text & Chr$(KeyAscii)) > Max Or _
        Val(txtValue.Text & Chr$(KeyAscii)) < Min Then
        Beep
        KeyAscii = 0
        Exit Sub
    End If
End If
```

This code filters out all keypresses except those that are digits or the Backspace key. Note that pressing the Delete key is handled by the text box control, and the KeyPress event is not raised, so you don't have to code for that one here. It also ensures that the value doesn't exceed the bounds set by the Min and Max properties of the control.

Next, select (General) and Value [PropertyLet]; then enter the following before the existing lines of code:

```
If IsNumeric(New_Value) = False Then
    Err.Raise 380, "spinText", "Invalid property value. Must be numeric!"
End If
```

This code ensures that if the Value property is set to a new value, it is a numeric value. Otherwise, the standard Property value is invalid error is raised. Note that no code in this routine executes after the Err.Raise line is executed. In this case, execution is immediately passed back to the routine that set the property value.

Creating a Tester Application

The control is functionally complete. You can now test what you've done, without having to compile the control, by adding a new project to the VB workspace. This new project will serve as a tester application for the control. You can place an instance of the control onto a form, set some properties, and run the program. Then you can finally see your control in action. Here's how to get started:

1. Close the code and user control windows.

2. Choose File, Add Project to launch the Add Project dialog box. On this dialog box, select Standard EXE and click Open. A new project appears in the Project Explorer, and a blank Form file is created and opened.

3. Because the Toolbox already contains a button for the ActiveX control (it's placed just before the Windows Common Controls' buttons), click it (its ToolTip reads spinText if you let the mouse pointer hover over the button in the Toolbox). Then place the control onto the new form.

> **CAUTION**
>
> The usercontrol window must be closed before you can add the control to your test form. If the Toolbox button for the control is grayed out, you can check the Window menu to see if the usercontrol window is open. Likewise, sometimes VB also disables the button if the code window for the control is open.

4. Save everything to an appropriate folder on your machine. Name the control's project file `MyControl.vbp`, and accept the default file name for the user control file (`spinText.ctl`). Accept the defaults for the tester application as well.

5. Press F5 to run the project. Click the up and down spin buttons to watch the value in the text box change. Try typing in the text box. Everything should work as advertised. If not, retrace your steps to find the missing element. After a few clicks of the spin button, your form should appear similar to Figure 12.10.

FIG. 12.10

The spinText ActiveX control in action on a Visual Basic form.

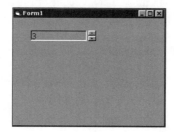

Compiling the Control

Now you're ready for the big step: actually compiling the control into an ActiveX control file that can be used by Web pages or other ActiveX containers. Actually, it's not that big of a step, but I like to finish a major section such as this with a little drama if possible.

Double-click the `spinText.ctl` entry in VB's Project Explorer to set the active project to the control (VB's project-related functions operate only on the active project). Choose File, Make MyControl.ocx. You then are prompted for a filename and folder to write to. Either accept the defaults or make the changes you want, and click OK. Clicking this button starts the compiler and quickly moves on to writing the OCX file (the status is displayed in VB's toolbar area).

This task finishes unceremoniously, without so much as even a piece of status bar text informing you of a successful completion. In this case, no news is good news. The compiler most definitely lets you know about any problems it encounters along the way. And with this compiler, unlike many others, you must deal with any problems one at a time: fix a problem, compile, get a new error message, fix, compile, and so on.

Now for some housekeeping details: When you build a COM component such as the ActiveX control you just built, or when you register a new component on your system, Windows needs to store some information about the component in the system registry. At this point, the GUID I talked about earlier comes into play.

The GUID is used as a class identifier (or CLSID) to uniquely identify the component and its classes. (In this case, `MyControl` is the component and `spinText` is the class.) This identification must be unique not only on your system but also on all computers in the world: this is the only way for Windows to keep straight what classes go with what implementation file (in this case, the MyControl.ocx file). So, you need to make sure that if you compile the control again, it has the same GUID. Otherwise, any code (including HTML <OBJECT> tags) that references the control has to be modified to reference the new GUID.

Of course, Visual Basic hides most of the nasty details of all this from you. You can modify one setting to tell VB whether to reuse the GUID next time you compile the project. To see this setting, choose Project, MyControl Properties. When the Project Properties dialog box appears, click the Component tab. Near the bottom of the dialog box is a frame labeled Version Compatibility. This frame contains three option buttons:

- *No Compatibility.* When this option is selected, VB does not enforce version compatibility rules and creates a new GUID each time the project is compiled. You will almost never select this one unless something has gone drastically awry in your component and you want to "flush" out all the Automation-specific information stored in the registry about this component.

- *Project Compatibility.* When this option is selected, VB uses the same GUID each time the component is compiled. However, the compiler does not check for consistency between the current version of the component's public interface (the one that's in the previous compile of the component) and the version you're about to compile. This means that if you've changed the parameters of a method, for example, you don't get a warning when you compile the component, but any application that calls this method of the component has to be recompiled to use the new parameter list. This setting is fine when you are developing the component for your own use but should be changed to the next setting when you officially "publish" your component.

- *Binary Compatibility.* When this option is selected, VB ensures that your component's public interface matches the previous compiled version. You cannot make any changes to the interface that would cause applications using your component to have to be recompiled. The GUID, of course, is not regenerated. Use this setting after you have published your component.

The text box below the option buttons specifies the file to which the project should be compatible. Leave the default as is most of the time. Someday you might want to go back a few versions to be compatible to an earlier version, but doing so is typically necessary only when you're developing a component-based application in a team environment.

Part
III

Ch
12

Deploying ActiveX Controls

Now that you've created and compiled the control, you can prepare a deployment package for it. As far as ActiveX controls and the Web are concerned, this activity involves creating a CAB file for the control. You'll also look at how to add the new control to a Web page using the Visual InterDev environment.

Using the Application Setup Wizard

The easiest and cheapest way to create a distribution package for a simple ActiveX control such as the one created in this chapter is to use the Application Setup Wizard. This wizard is included in the Professional and Enterprise Editions of Visual Basic. If it doesn't appear on the Visual Basic Start menu, you probably need to install it by running the VB Setup, selecting Add/Remove Components, and adding the Application Setup Wizard to your configuration.

> **N O T E**   Other distribution/setup creation applications are available on the market. Two that I recommend are the Wise Installation System (**http://www.glbs.com**) and InstallShield (**http://www.installshield.com**). ■

To create the CAB file necessary for distribution of the control on a Web page, follow these steps:

1. Close Visual Basic, saving any changes.

2. Launch the Application Setup Wizard from the Visual Basic 6 Start menu. Click Next on the introduction screen that appears. The Select Project and Options dialog box, shown in Figure 12.11, then appears.

3. Click the Browse button, and locate the MyControl.vbp file you saved earlier.

FIG. 12.11

The Select Project and Options dialog box of the Application Setup Wizard.

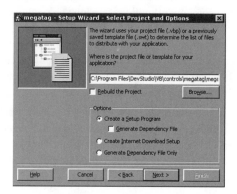

4. In the Options section of this dialog box, select the Create Internet Download Setup option button. Click Next.

5. On the dialog box that appears, specify the location to which the wizard should store its output. The default is the subdirectory beneath your temporary files folder. You can either leave the default or select a different folder. If you want to make your control available on a Web server, you need to copy the CAB file that will be stored in this directory to a directory accessible by the server. Then click Next.

6. On the Internet Package dialog box that appears next, specify some settings particular to Internet downloading. Unless you have the CAB files containing the Visual Basic runtime, leave the Download from the Microsoft Web Site option button selected.

7. Click the Safety button. On the Safety dialog box, check the boxes labeled Safe for Initialization and Safe for Scripting. Selecting these options prevents the Internet Explorer security warning dialog boxes from activating when the control is used in a Web page. Click OK.

8. Click <u>N</u>ext. Click <u>N</u>ext three more times to accept the defaults on all the dialog boxes. (You also can click <u>F</u>inish, but you need to save your work, which you can do only on the final dialog box.) Click the <u>S</u>ave Template button, enter `MyControl` in the File <u>N</u>ame text box, and click <u>S</u>ave. Now click the <u>F</u>inish button.

After the wizard churns away for a minute or two, it leaves a file named MyControl.CAB and one named MyControl.HTM in the output directory. If you open MyControl.HTM with Internet Explorer, you see the control embedded in a Web page. If you created Web pages by hand, you can manually type or copy the `<OBJECT>` tag contained in this file into your pages. However, because you're using Visual InterDev, you don't need to concern yourself with this brain-dead task, as you'll see in the next section.

 You can find additional information about deploying controls on the Internet at **http:// premium.microsoft.com/msdn/library/techart/msdn_deplactx.htm** (another page in the MSDN online library).

Using the Control with Visual InterDev

Now that you've got a compiled control and a distribution package (the CAB file), you're ready to go over the steps necessary to create the Web page shown in Figure 12.1 using Visual InterDev.

So, to create the Web page in Figure 12.1, follow these steps:

1. Start Visual InterDev. Create a new HTML file by choosing <u>F</u>ile, Ne<u>w</u> File. Activate the Toolbox (press Ctrl+Alt+X if it's not visible).

2. Either right-click over the Toolbox and click Customize Toolbo<u>x</u>, or choose <u>T</u>ools, Customize Toolbo<u>x</u> to launch the Customize Toolbox dialog box. Click the ActiveX Controls tab.

3. Scroll through the list of available controls until you find the entry for `MyControl.spinText`. Select this control by checking its box. Click OK, and the control is added to the Toolbox.

4. Drag the control's entry from the Toolbox onto the Design tab of the HTML file. Your screen should now appear similar to Figure 12.12. Click the Quick View tab, and you can work with the control just like you could with the tester application developed earlier.

5. Switch to the Source tab. Click the spinText control, and change its `Caption` property to `Current Value`. Change the `Max` property to `100`.

6. Insert a text box from the HTML section of the Toolbox. Put it below the spinText control.

7. Switch to the Script Outline (press Ctrl+Alt+S if it's not visible). Expand the Client Objects & Events branch and then the spinText1 branch (if necessary). Double-click the entry for the `Change` event under spinText1. In the code window, enter the following code if the script section is JavaScript:

```
text1.value = spinText1.value;
```

If it's VBScript, leave off the trailing semicolon.

FIG. 12.12

The ActiveX control inserted into a Web page using the InterDev Design tab.

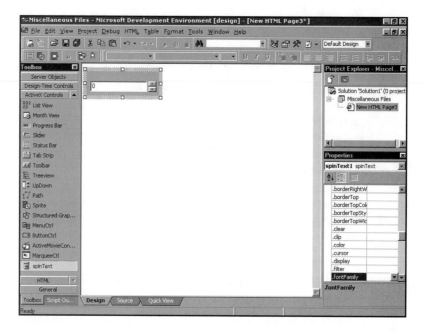

8. Switch to the Quick View tab again. Click the spin button, and notice that the text in both text boxes (the one in the spinText control and the one on the page) changes. The control is raising events that the Web page fis capturing. Figure 12.13 shows the results.

FIG. 12.13

Almost there. The control working its magic on a Web page.

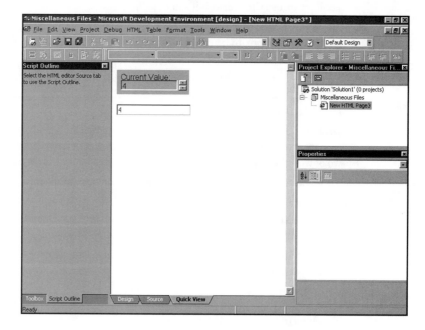

9. Now for a lesson in ActiveX containers. Did you notice that the font size of the constituent controls seems to be a little large? Switch to the Source tab, select the spinText control, and modify the `Font` property. Things look fine now, right? Well, switch back to the Quick View, and it appears your changes didn't stick. In fact, they didn't. Instead, switch back to the Source tab, select the control again, but this time change the `.font-size` property (found under the Style category) to `x-small`. Now when you return to the Quick View tab, the font appears reasonable. You get these results because InterDev, as the container for the control, is controlling the font properties based on the Style settings for the HTML `<OBJECT>` element. Your screen should now more closely resemble Figure 12.1.

From Here...

In this chapter you learned about using Visual Basic to create ActiveX. The controls you create with VB can be used in any COM container application, including Internet Explorer. This means that you can customize any Web page to meet your specific needs by building an ActiveX control that fits the bill.

Other books on this topic include *Sams Teach Yourself ActiveX Control Programming with Visual Basic 5*, *Sams Teach Yourself ActiveX Programming in 21 Days*, and *Sams Teach Yourself Visual C++ 5 in 21 Days, Fourth Edition*, all published by Sams.

In the chapter to follow, "Building and Deploying Server Components," you'll learn the details of creating server-side components that can be used in Active Server Page programming.

Part

III

Ch

12

CHAPTER 13

Building and Deploying Server Components

In this chapter

Life Before the Web   **284**

Brief History of ActiveX   **287**

Creating Components with Visual Basic   **292**

Using the Component   **296**

Components and Microsoft Transaction Server   **301**

Life Before the Web

Before delving deeper into the features of Visual InterDev, it's important to understand some of the background behind writing server components. By understanding the techniques for creating server-side components, you can quickly see how Visual InterDev can ease Web site development using these components.

You might find it hard to believe, but some enterprise and worldwide applications were actually written before the huge success of the Web and Internet technologies. In the past, many of these applications were written and designed to work on large mainframe computer systems that hosted multiple terminals from around the office or around the world. Although mainframe technology seems similar to a Web server and browser environment, it was really a single computer solution. Albeit this single computer was a very large machine, it was still a single computer. The terminals that programmers and clients used to update and access information on these systems were basically dumb machines that simply provided a gateway to the supercomputer. These terminals had no "intelligence" of their own; they simply passed keystrokes from the operator to the mainframe machine over network lines and displayed the results that were generated from the mainframe.

As these client terminals began gaining intelligence—thanks to the onslaught of the personal computer revolution—the industry quickly realized that some problems were best solved when multiple players were working on the solution. Now that the terminal machines or clients had better computation power, work could be divided on these machines as well as the larger server machines. This implementation quickly became known as *client/server technology* because client machines spoke to a host server. The key difference with this implementation is that the local machines also did some work. For example, when a user entered a date field in the wrong format, the client machine began doing basic confirmation and automation before sending data back to the server. Likewise, the important data was stored on the server, a machine that had ample power for information storage as well as defined procedures for backing up that information and maintaining integrity. Any processing that required direct access to a database or power for crunching time-consuming tasks could be isolated on a server and the results passed to the client when ready.

As usual, the more things change, the more they stay the same. Although client/server technology became a hugely popular buzzword within the computer industry, it was not long before it was overshadowed by a much more marketable technology: the Web. Although the Web seemed like a large step forward in computer technology at first, the original Web was more like the older mainframe computers of the past. Remember that the first Web browsers that were available for viewing information had no intelligence of their own. They basically acted as gateways to computer servers on the Internet by displaying the information passed by the Web server and allowing users to enter data on forms that routed back to the server. If you think about this process, the basic Web browser acted similarly to the mainframe terminal.

Fortunately, like the terminal, the Web browser matured and began inheriting intelligence of its own. With innovations such as Java and ActiveX components, client-side scripting, and other advancements, the browser was suddenly much more than a "thin" client. Yet more important, it was suddenly a more powerful component that helped reintroduce client/server technology on a broader network.

Beyond Client/Server

After examining the evolution of client/server technology, you might begin to think that it is the panacea of computing and that there is no room for improvement. Although separating tasks that should run on a client's machine and those that execute on a server is easy and convenient, on some occasions, more layers are required.

Consider, for example, a database application that can be accessed from a Web browser. For a typical static, page-based Web site, a simple client/server type of technology is used. The browser downloads page information from the Web server, renders the content, and perhaps waits for form input from the user. If data is entered within a form, that information may undergo basic validation checking or other script functions and then be routed back to the Web server. At this level, you are talking about a basic 2-tier architecture: the client and the server.

In the example, what should the Web server do with the information passed to it by the Web browser? In some cases, the data may be written to a file on the actual Web server for future access. Yet more recently, this information is imported into a database system, which can more efficiently manage volumes of information. In this case, the addition of a database server introduces another layer in the architecture. Instead of simple client/server technology, you are now looking at a 3-tier architecture: the client or browser, the Web server, and the database server. An important issue to remember is that a system such as this allows for information to be processed at more levels than previously possible. In a 3-tier system, processing can occur at the client level, on the Web server itself, or within the confines of the database server. An example is a basic order entry form displayed within a Web browser. A Web browser can perform basic data validation and send the information to an Active Server Page (ASP) on the Web server. This page can then perform some additional logic to update the content of the database system. In some cases, though, an entry to one database table may trigger an event to occur to add the same item to another table. In this scenario, computation can be performed at each level of the system.

Like the term *client/server*, *3-tier development* became the buzzword in the industry as the Internet matured into a fully capable, database-enabled environment. In reality, however, there can be an infinite number of levels for processing. Therefore, the terminology has been tweaked slightly and is now often referred to as *N-tier* development. In a volatile environment such as the Internet, many requirements are in place for safeguarding information that is passed between machines. As you will see later in this chapter, technologies that protect events that occur on and between servers are required for creating robust and reliable Web-based applications or "weblications." For example, adding a transaction component server between the Web server and the database server introduces a fourth tier to the application's architecture. And there is no reason why additional tiers cannot exist to complete a system.

Part III

Ch 13

N O T E Remember that, in an N-tier system, each server can act as a client to another server. For example, a Web server creates database objects, in which case the Web server script becomes the client to the database server component. ▪

N O T E In most discussions of multi-tier environments, most people assume that multiple physical server machines are required. However, remember that multiple types of servers can exist on one physical machine and still be considered an N-tier environment. The physical number of machines is not what determines the number of levels. ■

Advantages and Disadvantages of N-Tier

Now that you have a basic appreciation of what N-tier architecture is, you need to understand that this type of development presents some basic advantages as well as disadvantages. More often than not, any disadvantages are not really hindrances but are basically issues that you should be aware of when creating multiple-level systems. In addition, many of these issues are correctable through your use of other software components or by your simply being aware of the issues and programming responsibly.

Multiple-tier architecture is advantageous for many reasons:

- *Performance.* When components are distributed correctly across the appropriate servers, the entire system can execute more efficiently. The key here is to place the right components on the right servers to optimize overall system performance. For example, placing database dependency logic in the database system as triggers may be more appropriate than placing it in an Active Server Page.

- *Reusability.* If a particular piece of the system is useful to completely different applications, it can sometimes be more accessible when used in an N-tier environment. For example, an ASP program can be called from more than one Web page because it is not embedded within the Web page and is available at a central location.

- *Isolation.* When pieces of an application are distributed across different physical servers, they become slightly isolated from each other. In some instances, this isolation can be beneficial, especially if a portion of the system fails. For example, if a database server becomes unavailable, the Web server may still be available for clients to access. Although the application is crippled, it is still somewhat functional.

- *Redundancy.* Again, when pieces of a system are distributed across physical machines, adding a level of redundancy to an application is possible. Two systems can perform similar tasks to ensure some action is still completed, even in the event of a failure. For example, a Web server application can write information to a file on the system when a database server becomes unavailable.

- *Multi-Developer.* Controlling several developers on a project becomes difficult, especially if more than one developer alters the same file. Besides the obvious use of source control applications to address this issue, N-tier development offers a tacit solution to this problem as well. With multiple levels of an application, developers can be assigned to each layer of the system without intruding on the other layers.

In addition to these advantages, you must consider several issues when developing multi-tier systems:

- *Security.* Security is a tremendously important issue. Although it has always existed, it has increasingly become a priority in application development because of the issues surrounding it with the public Internet and the Web. When components of a system are distributed across multiple machines, the only method available for the computers to communicate with each other is through the network. In a world of hackers where information can be plucked from network lines, you must remember to ensure the protection of data as it moves around the network.

- *Network Stability.* Networks are exceedingly important for allowing systems to communicate with each other and are essential for distributed components of an application. If the network fails for any reason, machines cannot communicate with each other. To prevent disasters in a multi-tier environment, you must consider the possibilities and implement solutions. Fortunately, software is available to help with some of these problems. As you'll see later in this chapter, Microsoft Transaction Server (MTS) helps guarantee that an entire batch of information is either stored or aborted. Similarly, products such as Microsoft Message Queue guarantee delivery of information across networks by queuing requests when connectivity is unavailable and later processing those requests when the network is restored.

- *Maintenance Complexity.* Future maintenance of applications is a constantly overlooked item. In a system in which multiple components can exist across several machines using different software with different platform installations, you can easily forget which pieces were required to create the application and just how the pieces are to be assembled. This issue can be easily addressed with adequate and updated documentation of the system.

Brief History of ActiveX

Several years ago, discussions began to rumble in the computer development industry about component technology and reuse. In particular, companies such as Microsoft began illustrating the reuse of components within larger systems. A great example of this was the use of spell-checking software within a larger office suite application. Instead of including the spell-checking algorithm in each of the suite's products, the spell checker was extracted as a single component and reused as necessary within the context of the appropriate application.

Originally, this separation and reuse of common components was encapsulated by the use of dynamic link library (DLL) files within the Windows system. Yet the development community was becoming entrenched in a fairly new programming paradigm referred to as *object-oriented programming* (OOP). This new programming practice began separating pieces of an application into components or objects, with each accomplishing its own task. Additionally, the inner working of these objects was hidden from developers who reused these components for security reasons, manageability, and ease of implementation. The developers merely accessed functions or set attributes on the object as necessary and no longer required an intimate knowledge of how the component worked.

Microsoft quickly invested in this technology and introduced it within its set of applications as *Object Linking and Embedding* (OLE), which you remember reading about in the last chapter. If

Part

III

Ch

13

you remember, this technology allowed users to take objects from one Microsoft Office application and embed them within another. For example, the charting piece that was common in Microsoft Excel could easily be placed as a component within a Microsoft Word document or Microsoft PowerPoint slideshow presentation.

What became more important than simply embedding component pieces into other applications, however, was interacting with those components. Soon it became apparent that the true power lay in using these components, but tying them to scripts that could interact and control these objects. If you remember the earlier versions of Visual Basic, then you'll recall the use of VBX files or Visual Basic extensions. In Visual Basic, like other rapid application development environments, dragging and dropping controls such as buttons or entry fields from a toolbox onto a window was easy. You could then easily write code to interact with those objects you placed on the window. However, a need to allow other objects to be added to a project other than the basic intrinsic Windows controls became quickly apparent. VBX extensions provided a method by which developers could create unique and reusable components that could be easily embedded within Visual Basic projects.

Microsoft named the underlying technology for building reusable objects COM or the Component Object Model. This model outlined how to create objects that were reusable in the Win32 operating system architecture. It also defined the use of methods or exposed functions of objects, properties or settings for objects, and events that could be triggered from objects. This technology was further marketed as ActiveX technology when Java threatened to be the overall object-oriented solution for the Internet. *ActiveX technology* may be a new marketing term for COM, but more important, it is a refined version of COM sometimes referred to as Distributed COM, or DCOM. ActiveX components or OCX files in newer versions of Visual Basic are slimmer controls than their OLE ancestors were, adhere to a standard and common interface that can be exploited by any program, and are optimized to be version-controlled, which is particularly useful for component registration via the Internet.

Client/Server ActiveX

With the capability to wrap common functionality into reusable objects or components, ActiveX technology can be very useful in creating robust applications quickly and efficiently. For example, with ActiveX controls on the client of a Web browser that understands ActiveX, a Web page can embed objects that extend the normal capabilities of the Web browser. For example, a video playback ActiveX control can allow a Web page developer to embed a video on a Web page, invoke methods such as "play" on the control, read or set properties like "current position," and receive events such as "content not found" warnings. A great example of this control was covered in Chapter 10, "Using ActiveX Controls."

Contrary to popular belief, however, ActiveX technology does not need to exist solely in the Web browser. ActiveX controls are available for use within many application development environments, such as Visual Basic, Delphi, PowerBuilder, and more. Therefore, the same functionality available to a Web browser can be exploited in other custom-developed applications. Even more important, though, Active components can be reused on any Win32-based platform, including server machines. Although you can clearly see the advantage of creating reusable objects such as video players for use in client applications or Web pages, you may not see immediately the need to implement this type of technology on servers. After all, servers do not typically exploit interactive controls because commonly users do not watch over the machine at all times.

At this point, it is extremely important to notice that ActiveX technology does not refer just to interactive controls, but to any functionality that can be reused and separated as an object. There is no reason why you cannot create a mathematical object that contains numerous functions not commonly found in programming languages. These functions could be exposed as methods for that object, and that object could be reused in client-based applications or on portions of a system that executes on the server. In the world of database intranet and Internet applications, making reusable programming logic available to all applications that require it has become increasingly desirable.

More often than not, some components in a business system can be reused in other systems. Consider, for example, currency conversion logic; this technology could very well be used by many other financial systems in the business other than just a single application. If this currency system were properly encapsulated in a separate component, it could also be made available to not only intranet servers but also to Visual Basic applications or other server applications. When core components are written explicitly for use in business, they are said to be "business logic" components. In the popular world of intranet and Internet business, the recommendation is to use business components for wrapping this logic rather than embedding it and dispersing it across other technologies such as Active Server Pages. Later in this chapter, you'll see why placing business logic in a server component is more beneficial than writing it in an Active Server Page.

The Different Flavors of ActiveX

At this point, you can clearly see a plethora of uses for ActiveX components and a variety of ways to use them. However, you should note that ActiveX components actually come in several flavors, each which has a slightly different technical capability.

ActiveX Controls   By far, the most popular forms of ActiveX components to date are those that are used in development of applications or Web pages. These ActiveX controls allow developers to incorporate rich objects in their applications designed in products such as Visual Basic or in Web pages to add enhanced functionality. These components compete directly with other technologies such as Java applets or plug-in technology.

Part

III

Ch

13

Clearly, these ActiveX controls are well known for their visible enhancements to a Web page or application and are therefore usually highly interactive. However, this is not necessarily always the case. For example, the Internet control included with the most recent versions of Visual Basic allows developers to attach to Internet servers easily and perform a variety of functions. Usually, functions such as uploading a file to an FTP server are not necessarily visible. They may be invoked by a visible interface that allows users to choose files to upload, but the Internet control that establishes a connection and performs the move is not necessarily visible.

Although server applications or applications that do not rely upon user interaction can certainly use ActiveX controls, it is recommended that these types of controls be carefully crafted. For example, if an error condition occurs, you cannot rely upon a message box indicating the error. In a server application, this message would appear on the server machine, which is not usually watched. Likewise, you, as the developer, will not be able to see the condition that occurs.

When you are creating ActiveX controls for server processes, remember to write errors to a log file and not rely upon a user interface.

ActiveX Documents   A version of ActiveX components that is perhaps a little less known is the ActiveX Document. This control is similar to an ActiveX control in that it is almost exclusively used for visible enhancements to an application. The ActiveX Document allows developers to use document files that they create in their own proprietary format and provide interfaces that allow these documents to be formatted properly in other applications. Basically, the ActiveX Document enables the client to read and edit a document type. Being an ActiveX component, though, this control can easily be embedded in other applications.

A prime example of this technology in use is with Microsoft's Web browser, Internet Explorer. As you browse the Web, you may come across many document types in addition to HTML files. You can click a link on a Web page that points to a standard Word document (DOC file). Under normal circumstances, clicking this link displays a window prompting you to download the file to your local system, or at best associating the file with an appropriate viewer. In this case, the Word document is either downloaded to your local hard disk, or downloaded and automatically opened with its respective viewer: Word. If you have Microsoft Office 97 installed on your computer, however, and use Internet Explorer version 3.0 or higher with ActiveX, the document is still transferred. Instead of being simply downloaded or displayed in a full-window application such as Word, however, the document is displayed within the context of the Web browser in this case. This document essentially replaces the main document window of the browser. In addition, the menus and toolbars that you commonly use for navigating the Web change to provide the capabilities of Microsoft Word as well. In a sense, you are running Word within Internet Explorer.

In-Process and Out-of-Process   Other ActiveX components are those intended for use as shared code components such as those found on a server. These components typically do not have any user interface capabilities whatsoever because they are optimized for performance on a server machine that has no user interaction. Therefore, to use these components in your custom applications, you cannot expect to add them to a component toolbox. Instead, you must use the CreateObject method found in the VBScript language or the <OBJECT> syntax in either VBScript or JavaScript to create an object.

These components, as you will see later in this chapter, are compiled as either executable files (EXE) or dynamic link libraries (DLL). The difference is whether the component is to be used in-process or out-of-process. This difference is subtle but important to understand.

In-process components are those that share the same physical resources with the application that uses the component and possibly other components. They are compiled as a sharable dynamic link library file. Typically, in-process components are faster because their resources do not quickly terminate. For example, database connections may stay available for the entire use of a component, until it is destroyed. Although this effect is positive, a negative is that they are not truly independent components. If one piece of the application that uses a component fails, that component fails as well because it shares the same memory space. Unless they are properly managed, these components can easily hog resources on the system.

Out-of-process components are, therefore, the opposite of in-process components. These components cause the system to execute independent processes for each component used. This often implies a slight degradation in performance because of the extra overhead required initializing and destroying the component each time it is requested. Likewise, any resources associated with the component are lost each time the component is destroyed. A benefit to this approach, however, is that each component executes in its own space, and therefore other instances of the component can crash without having an impact on other instances.

Choosing the correct form of process for your ActiveX component depends on a variety of factors, especially on the architecture of your application. Depending on your requirements for the application, each process can be used for a variety of reasons.

The Advantages and Disadvantages of ActiveX

As with any computer technology, you will discover positive reasons for using ActiveX components as well as many issues that may have an impact on the use of such components. You can find many good reasons for using ActiveX components on the server, and they are similar for using any object-oriented technology:

- *Reuse.* If an ActiveX component is designed to be generic enough to be used in other parts of the system or in completely different systems, then reusability becomes an important advantage. A single component can be easily reused when it is bundled as an object because its logic does not need to be replicated constantly throughout all calling scripts.

- *Speed.* ActiveX components are always compiled applications. Typically, they are written using Visual Basic, Visual C++, Visual J++, or some other development environment. When they are deployed, they are compiled into a single executable file or dynamic link library. Because they are compiled into native machine code or at least optimized byte-code, they execute much more quickly than interpreted scripts such as those in Active Server Pages.

- *Security.* In a way, ActiveX objects are more secure because they are compiled executables. Disassembling the logic of a compiled application is much more difficult than reviewing the raw source code embedded within other methods such as Active Server Page scripts.

- *Ease of Use.* With basic methods and properties exposed by objects for use in other applications, a tremendous level of complexity is removed from the developer. To adequately use the advantages of a component, the developer needs to know only the syntax of exposed methods or properties for the object. The complexities of the actual code required to implement those features in a component are hidden from the developer.

- *Ability to Be Updated.* When systems use components to implement portions of the application, components can be updated easily because of their inherent isolation from the calling scripts. If a component contains a bug, only it needs to be repaired and redistributed. As long as the implementation of methods and properties for the object remains the same, only updating the object itself is required, not the calling scripts.

- *Current Expertise.* With a variety of development tools available to create ActiveX components, methods for creating objects are available for developers comfortable with just about any programming language. Also, because ActiveX technology is based on the Win32 architecture, many of the routines and components developed for client/server applications written with Visual Basic can be reused.

With all the positive reasons for using objects such as ActiveX components, thinking of many negatives is hard. In the world of object-oriented programming, you will find really no significant negatives. The primary concern with using ActiveX components is that they are heavily dependent upon Microsoft's technology. Therefore, to implement solutions using ActiveX components, you are required to use Win32 systems. This also implies that you need to consider NT as a server platform and Internet Information Server (IIS) as a Web server.

Creating Components with Visual Basic

Now that you understand what ActiveX component technology is and how it can be used effectively, you're ready to look at just how to get started creating such components. As I stated earlier, you can use a variety of development tools to create ActiveX server components. However, in this chapter, you will review the basic use of Visual Basic 5.0 to create server-side components. A complete review of ActiveX control creation is covered in-depth in Chapter 12. It is recommended that you first familiarize yourself with creating typical client ActiveX components; this will help prepare you for creating server-side components.

Creating the Project

To start building an ActiveX component in Visual Basic, you should first consider the type of ActiveX component you want to build. In this example, you will look at creating an ActiveX server component that runs out-of-process. Therefore, you begin by creating a brand-new project and selecting the appropriate *ActiveX EXE* project from the dialog window. Figure 13.1 illustrates the different project types presented by Visual Basic when a new project is started. Chapter 12 also covers in much more detail the actual creation of ActiveX components using Visual Basic and these different project options. Remember, Chapter 12 reviews in depth these Visual Basic projects and the use of each.

If you decide to change the type of ActiveX component the project should be at a later time, you can do so quite easily by tweaking the parameters in the project's property page. For example, you might decide that an ActiveX object needs to be recompiled as an in-process component for use with Microsoft Transaction Server.

FIG. 13.1

When you start a new project in Visual Basic, you can choose from several ActiveX projects types.

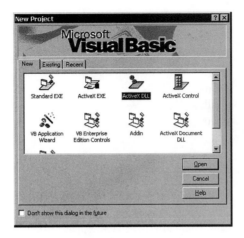

The sample project is going to be a simple utility component that features capabilities for searching and replacing text within a string. More often than not, developers need to create their own functions for searching recursively through text to find all instances of a string pattern and replace that pattern with a new pattern. So that you can avoid rewriting this logic into every application, this component will encapsulate this logic into an object that can be easily included with any project.

The sample component will provide a single method for searching and replacing content within a string. It will also host a single property for instructing whether this method should perform the substitution on all strings or simply the first occurrence it encounters.

Reviewing the Component's Properties

After you initialize the project, Visual Basic adds a single class named Class1 to its project window. Before you examine the code necessary for implementing the search and replace routine, first review the project properties as well as the importance of the name of this class.

If you review the project properties by choosing Project, Properties, you see a screen similar to the one shown in Figure 13.2.

First, notice the name of the project. You must set this value to something more appropriate than Project1. This value is used to help identify ActiveX controls in the system. Recall that the CreateObject command is required to include components into Active Server Pages or VBScript applications. This CreateObject statement returns a pointer to the newly created object so that it can be referenced later in your custom code. It also accepts one parameter, however, the name of the object to instantiate. This name is commonly denoted using "dot" (.) notation—for example, Business.Object. Often objects are identified by the name of the company that created them followed by the name of the object to use.

Part

III

Ch

13

FIG. 13.2

The numerous properties for any ActiveX project are used to identify the object.

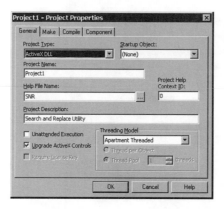

The name of the project being created in Visual Basic equates to the business name in the preceding example, or a higher-level identifier. In the case of this search and replace component, you can name the project SNR, short for "Search aNd Replace." Likewise, the name of the class created in the project is equally important. You can find this name in the Property Inspector, which is usually found in the lower-right corner of the Visual Basic environment. You can easily change this name by using the Property Inspector. It is equivalent to the second portion of the name of the ActiveX component, the piece that follows the period (.). For this simple example, name it SearchNReplace.

Reviewing the Code

Performing a basic search and replace in Visual Basic is relatively simple. To replace all instances of a search pattern within a given string, the code must use a loop to iterate through the string and the instr function inherent in Visual Basic to actually find the first instance of a substring within the main string. Listing 13.1 shows the function necessary for performing a basic search-and-replace algorithm.

Listing 13.1 An ActiveX Server Component Can Be as Simple as a Search-and-Replace Algorithm with a Single Method and Property

```
Public ReplaceFirstOnly As Boolean

Public Function SearchNReplaceString(ByVal sourceString As String,
                                     ByVal searchString As String,
                                     ByVal replaceString As String
                                     ) As String
    p = 1
    Found = False

    While p > 0 And Not Found
        p = InStr(p, sourceString, searchString)
        If p > 0 Then
            sourceString = Left(sourceString, p - 1) + replaceString
                        + Mid(sourceString, p + Len(searchString))
            If ReplaceFirstOnly Then
                Found = True
```

```
            End If
         End If
      Wend
      SearchNReplaceString = sourceString
   End Function
```

Initially, you might review this source code and think that nothing is special about it. In reality, it contains a very basic function and a single global variable. However, I should point out a few things about this sample of code.

Going Public   If you're already quite familiar with the object-oriented concepts of Visual Basic, then you'll recognize quickly that the public statement before a function makes it accessible or viewable by other objects. Conversely, the private statement declares functions that can be accessed only within the scope of the object in which the function exists. This public parameter before a function or subroutine essentially indicates that a particular routine in Visual Basic is to be exported as a method for the object being created. The method takes on the name of the routine being defined publicly.

Similarly, you can easily create public properties for an object by defining public variables. The simplest way to do so is to define a global variable and make it publicly available. However, you may rather use functions to set properties for the application. With methods, you can verify the properties being set for inconsistencies or errors. In the search and replace example, you defined one global variable as public, which determines whether the replace algorithm should replace *all* instances of a pattern or just the first match.

One if *ByVal*, Two if *ByRef*   Another thing you'll notice immediately in the source code of Listing 13.1 is the use of the ByVal statement. You can pass parameters to functions in one of two ways in Visual Basic: ByVal or ByRef. ByVal indicates that the actual data is passed into the function. For example, if a string is passed in, the actual textual contents of that string are passed. In reality, a copy of the data is made for use within the subroutine. This method for passing information into subroutines or functions is often preferred. By using ByVal, the client invoking the method of the object does not need to explicitly cast the data in the appropriate data type for the component's routine. Otherwise, the client may need to purposely convert data into its respective Integer (CInt), String (CString), or other data type for the respective parameters of the method.

In particular instances, you might prefer to use ByRef within your method's parameters. ByRef is usually used for passing large amounts of information into the method—for example, passing a text block that far exceeds the limits of a string data type in Visual Basic. In reality, ByRef gets is name because, unlike ByVal in which the actual value is passed to the routine in your object, ByRef passes a pointer in memory that points to the data being passed. The actual data is never passed; only the data's reference is passed.

Dynamic Help   In Visual Basic version 5.0/6.0 and Visual InterDev version 6.0, you can now quickly see the methods and properties available for any given object in the project by typing the object's name in your code, followed by pressing the . (period) key to access the dynamic help. (It's not exactly dynamic help, but you get the idea.) After you press the period key, a list box appears next to the object's name listing all valid methods and properties for the respective object.

Part

III

Ch

13

In a similar manner, when you choose to implement a method, you may be required to pass additional parameters into that method. The same technology that helps you to decide methods and properties for an object briefly displays the syntax for the parameters of the method as a ToolTip. Therefore, you should make your parameter names clear to understand and include their data types. In the SearchNReplaceString function in Listing 13.1, notice that each parameter is named a logical variable name so that it will make sense to developers who will see these parameters presented in their development tool's pop-up windows. Each parameter's data type is also defined, even though doing so is optional in Visual Basic.

 TIP When you are creating methods for your objects, you should perform a high level of error trapping. If errors occur during the execution of your object's method, undesirable effects may ensue. To start, use the on error goto errHandler syntax and an error handling code block (errHandler) at the end of each routine. This way, you can give your object a chance to recover from potentially serious errors. But, more important if you use functions for methods, you will be able to return an error status to the client that invoked your object. The client application can then handle the error appropriately.

N O T E Remember that server applications that execute on server machines do not have users interacting with the objects. Therefore, you should not send information to the server machine's display or expect input from the server machine's terminal. Instead, consider writing errors and other messages to log files that you and other developers can access. ■

Making the Cut

After you finish working with your project, be sure to compile it. Depending on the choice you made when the initial project wizard dialog box appeared, this final result may be either an executable file (EXE) or a dynamic link library file (DLL). When you are ready to create the final application for testing or use, simply compile the component as you would any Visual Basic application: Choose File, Make.

Using the Component

After you successfully create your component, you need to test and use it. In the following sections, you'll see how to incorporate custom ActiveX components within your own applications after registering these objects on the server. You'll look at registering components on the server through traditional means as well as using Visual InterDev.

Using Components in Visual Basic

The easiest way to get started is to test your custom component using Visual Basic. To do so, you need to first create a separate application, which will act as the base client for incorporating and using your new ActiveX component. You can create another project by simply choosing File, Add Project, or by starting another instance of Visual Basic and creating a standard executable project.

In either case, once your project has started and you have a blank form, you can begin adding code to incorporate your new component. For example, to test the search and replace component that you created earlier in Listing 13.1, you can use the code in Listing 13.2 in an onclick event for a button on the form.

Listing 13.2   To Invoke a Custom ActiveX Component, You Should Remember the Original Object's Project and Class Names to Identify the Object

```
Private Sub Command1_Click()
    strSource = txtSource.Text
    strSearch = txtSearch.Text
    strReplace = txtReplace.Text

    Set obj = CreateObject("SNR.SearchNReplace")

    If chkReplace.Value = 1 Then
        obj.ReplaceFirstOnly = True
    Else
        obj.ReplaceFirstOnly = False
    End If

    strResult = obj.SearchNReplaceString(strSource,
                                         strSearch,
                                         strReplace)

    txtSource.Text = strResult

End Sub
```

The fragment of code listed in Listing 13.2 demonstrates the Replace button in the form for the application pictured in Figure 13.3.

FIG. 13.3

The search and replace ActiveX component can be tested in another Visual Basic application.

The key syntax to examine in Listing 13.2 is the CreateObject syntax. Recall that the search and replace object was designed for use without a user interface. Therefore, the object is missing much of the information necessary for adding it as a control to the Visual Basic component toolbox. To include the component in another Visual Basic application, you use the CreateObject command, which specifies which component to embed and returns a reference to that object.

You'll recall that the name of the control for which you want to create an instance is determined by that ActiveX component's project and class names. So, in the search and replace example that you explored earlier, the project name was SNR and the class was SearchNReplace. Therefore, the CreateObject command attempts to instantiate the component using the SNR.SearchNReplace name.

After the object is created, you need to reference the component to invoke methods or set properties. Therefore, the CreateObject syntax returns a reference to this object that can be set to a variable for future reference in your scripts. Then, as you want to invoke methods or modify properties, you can reference the new ActiveX component by its variable name in your code. Using the object's variable name in the code then allows the Visual Basic development environment to treat the object as it does other ActiveX control objects. Pressing the period key after the component's name should list valid methods and properties for the component. Likewise, when you are invoking a method, the ((open parenthesis) displays the order and expected variables to be passed as parameters.

Using Components on the Server

ActiveX components are peculiar creatures in some respects. One idiosyncrasy with ActiveX technology is that the component's software must be installed on the machine from which it will execute. Usually, when you view ActiveX objects within the context of a Web browser, these controls self-register. That is, they are automatically downloaded and installed if they are not already present on your system. When the component is installed, it is not only copied locally onto your hard disk, but also registered in your system's Registry.

If an ActiveX component is to execute on a server, there is no exception to this rule. Every component that runs on a server machine must be installed and registered there as well. Although this process sounds painful at first, in reality it really is not very difficult. In fact, you can manually register components on the server, or you can let Visual InterDev do the work for you.

Manually Registering Components To register a component by hand on a server such as an NT-based Internet Information Server, you can either create a setup application for your component, or manually copy the files and register the component in the server's System Registry. In either case, this process obviously requires that you have access to the server to copy files and change the Registry database.

One simple solution is to create an installation for your custom component, just as you would for any other regular Visual Basic application. To do so, you simply need to run the Visual Basic installation wizard, which can typically be found in the same group off the Start menu as your Visual Basic application. Stepping through the wizard and including the ActiveX executable or dynamic link library in the setup ensures that the file is copied onto its destination machine as well as registered in that machine's database.

A second method is to copy the file manually onto the destination machine. After it is there, you can easily register it by using one of the following methods:

■ *ActiveX EXE Components.* To register an executable component, you simply can run that application on the destination machine. Running the object starts it and automatically registers it in the Registry. You also can specify the /regserver parameter after the executable if you want, but it will have the same effect.

■ *ActiveX DLL Components.* Registering a dynamic link library or in-process component just takes a tad bit more work. Dynamic link libraries cannot be executed by themselves; therefore, you must run the DLL file as a parameter to the regsvr32.exe program—for example, regsvr32 SearchComponent.dll.

Using InterDev to Register the Component   Although the processes described in the preceding section for copying and registering an ActiveX component to execute on the server are not terribly complicated, you may prefer to use a client development tool such as Visual InterDev to do the work for you. One primary reason is that, more often than not, you probably don't have the administrative rights to access and register servers. If this is the case, you can set up procedures for server administrators to register components, or you can more efficiently use the built-in capabilities of Visual InterDev and still register the components yourself.

To register components through Visual InterDev, you simply add your component to a current Visual InterDev project. For example, you can choose to add the DLL or EXE file that you created for an ActiveX component to a project. After it is added and appears in the project file list toward the right side of the InterDev screen, you can choose to set properties on the ActiveX DLL or EXE file. Doing so reveals a dialog box similar to the one shown in Figure 13.4.

FIG. 13.4
Components can be easily registered or unregistered through the Visual InterDev interface.

Within the Component Installation tab of this dialog box, you can clearly see options for registering the component on the client as well as the server. If you simply click the appropriate check box, the component is installed correctly in the server's Registry database.

Uninstalling Components   In some cases, you might need to remove components that have been previously installed on the server. Fortunately, uninstalling is about as easy as registering the components in the first place. Again, you can choose to perform this action either manually or with the help of Visual InterDev. If you choose the manual route, you can use one of the following commands, based on the type of ActiveX component you want to uninstall:

■ *ActiveX EXE Components.* To remove an out-of-process component from the server, you can simply run the executable again, but with the /unregserver command-line parameter.

Part
III

Ch
13

■ *ActiveX DLL Components.* Removing in-process components requires running the familiar regsvr32.exe program again. However, this time the name of the DLL file to be removed from the Registry must be prefaced by the /u switch—for example, `regsvr32.exe /u SearchComponent.dll`.

When using the flexibility and ease of management of Visual InterDev for ActiveX objects, you can simply recall the property page for the ActiveX DLL or ActiveX EXE file. On the Component Installation tab, the option for registering the component on the server should be checked. Unchecking it removes the component from the server's Registry.

To install components to the server via Visual InterDev, you need to install several key components on the server. First, you need to install the FrontPage extensions; otherwise, you cannot copy files onto the server. Second, you must make sure that you have installed the Visual InterDev RAD Component Deployment option that is included with either your Personal Web Server or Internet Information Server installation. Without it, you cannot register components correctly into the server's Registry.

Using the Component in ASP

After you successfully install the ActiveX component on a Web server, you can create an Active Server Pages script that will invoke the component on the server. Because you have already reviewed the implementation in Visual Basic, the Active Server Page version using the VBScript language will not differ greatly. Listing 13.3 illustrates a simple Active Server Page that creates the object using the same `CreateObject` function discussed earlier in the Visual Basic example.

Listing 13.3   Active Server Pages Can Use VBScript in the Same Fashion as Visual Basic to Initialize ActiveX Components

```
<HTML>
<BODY>
<H1>SearchNReplace</H1>
This page tests the SearchNReplace Server-side ActiveX Component
to make sure that it works properly with ASP.

<%
    result="This is a test program."

    Set objTrans = CreateObject("TxCtx.TransactionContext")
    Set obj = CreateObject("SNR.SearchNReplace")

    obj.ReplaceFirstOnly = False
    result=obj.SearchNReplaceString("This is a test program.",
➥                                    "program",
➥                                    "ASP Page")

    objTrans.Abort
%>

<FONT COLOR=#000099>
    <%= result  %>
```

```
</FONT>
</BODY>
</HTML>
```

The example in Listing 13.3 replaces all spaces with a plus sign (+) instead. Although adding plus signs does not seem practical at first, imagine requesting data from a user and publishing it as HTML content. You could easily use this ActiveX component to replace all carriage-return characters with equivalent <P> tags in HTML.

Components and Microsoft Transaction Server

Now that you are comfortable with creating and using ActiveX components, I'm sure you think that you've mastered all you need to know about component development. For most development projects, this point may indeed be as far as developers will go. For some large projects, however, you can imagine how quickly problems can begin to arise as multiple components are strung together to create a total solution. If you cannot picture it, you should review a possible situation in which ActiveX components lose synchronicity.

Imagine for a minute that you work for a banking company. Your boss requests that you write a new Web-based front-end for the bank's customers to perform transactions over the Internet. These transactions will include the withdrawal of money via electronic payment and deposits of money via electronic transactions. In addition, the customers would need a basic ability to move money between accounts such as a checking and savings account. So, you decide that a single object with a basic transaction component will suffice. After all, every transaction will be a particular amount of money, either positive for deposits, negative for withdrawals, or a combination of both for moving money out of one account and into another.

Now assume that a customer is going to move $100 from savings into a checking account. Obviously, this process requires a negative transaction on the savings account and a positive transaction on the checking account. If you assume that each transaction requires an instance of an ActiveX component, the information can potentially be out of sync.

If the components perform database updates, one transaction could be complete and the second might not. For example, assume that the application first removes the $100 from the client's savings account. After the transaction is accomplished, the next step is to add $100 to the respective checking account. However, assume that the database connection fails in between the withdrawal of the savings account and the deposit into the checking account. If this were the case, the application would fail and the client would lose $100. And nobody likes to lose money!

To help guarantee against such incidents, the concept of *transactions* was introduced. With transactions, you can define a group of application components or pieces that must work together. In the event that one piece of the transaction fails, the entire transaction is then forced to fail. It's basically an all-or-nothing approach that helps solve the problem.

Part

III

Ch

13

In the example with the client moving $100 between accounts, assume that the database fails halfway through the entire transaction. In this case, the transaction is the entire process for moving money, including each piece of removing money from one account and depositing money in a second account. Therefore, in the example, the money is successfully withdrawn from the savings account, and the attempt to add money to the checking account fails. With transaction management in effect, the second component fails, and thus the entire action fails. As a result, the money withdrawn from the original account is rolled back as if it were never removed. The entire transaction fails, and all pieces involved in the transaction are aborted; if they have already executed, they are restored to their original state.

Usually, implementing such a complex system for committing and rolling back changes across several components requires an extensive amount of code and logic. Fortunately, Microsoft provides a solution to this problem with the Microsoft Transaction Server (MTS). With just a few additional lines of code and settings added to the transaction management explorer, transactions can be completely aborted or completed.

N O T E In transaction management, changes that were committed to a database are reverted back to their original state. Remember that such rollbacks are currently available only for controlling content in databases. Transaction Server cannot be used to revert file system changes or other modifications to the system; only databases can be affected by the aborted results of Transaction Server. ■

A second reason for using Transaction Server management is for scalability. In many older systems, you could easily write client/server applications because maybe only a few hundred users required access to the system. In the world of the Internet, however, you quickly see that the number of potential users accessing the system could be in the thousands or more. A large number of concurrent accesses could quickly consume resources for databases and other actions. Transaction Server helps relieve this stress by automatically freeing components and their connections as it can. Transaction Server also helps to manage these connections so that the next time an object requests a connection, it can be made readily available. The server basically helps with the pooling of information resources.

Installing Transaction Server

When you install Internet Information Server, you see an option for installing Microsoft Transaction Server. This component is included by default to help manage the actual processes and server pages used within IIS, so Transaction Server will probably be installed on your server. After it is installed, however, you need to check and install a few additional components on the server if they are not already there.

As I mentioned earlier in this chapter, you need to make certain that the FrontPage extensions are installed on this server to facilitate the movement of content from the Visual InterDev environment to the server. Likewise, the Visual InterDev RAD Component Deployment option must be installed so that Visual InterDev can communicate with ActiveX components registered on the server.

After all the Transaction Server components are installed, they are invoked automatically as required when components that are registered with the server are instantiated. To help you manage the components that are under Transaction Server control, the server provides a management console screen that attaches as a snap-in to the Microsoft Management Console. This console is the same interface used to manage Internet Information Servers.

Registering Components with MTS

After you create your ActiveX components and decide which should be included in transaction management routines, you need to register those components with the Microsoft Transaction Server. Fortunately, registering components with MTS is fairly simple and can be accomplished using one of two methods: the MTS Explorer included in the Microsoft Management console or Visual InterDev.

Registering with MTS Explorer   To register a component within the MTS Explorer interface, you merely need to navigate through the hierarchy of folders to the list of packages for the computer on which you want to register a component. At this point, you can add a component by first creating a new package. A *package* is basically a term for the bundle of components that work together to form a complete transaction. When creating this package, you can give it a unique name for the project you are working on and define security properties for invoking this package if necessary. Figure 13.5 illustrates a typical MTS Explorer window.

FIG. 13.5

The Microsoft Transaction Server includes an Explorer-type interface for controlling packages on the server.

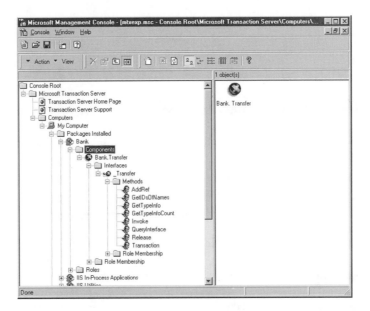

After the package is created, you can begin adding components. When you choose to create a component within a package, a wizard screen appears, asking whether you would like to import an existing component into MTS or install a new one. If you already installed and registered your ActiveX component on the server, you can choose it from the Registry list. However, even if you did already register the component, you should probably still install the component. While using MTS, I found that the options for installing new components worked better than importing existing components. When installing the components, you can browse for the ActiveX EXE or DLL files that you compiled. The dialog box that appears after you pick an appropriate ActiveX control file is depicted in Figure 13.6.

FIG. 13.6

You can easily choose and install components with the Microsoft Transaction Server explorer.

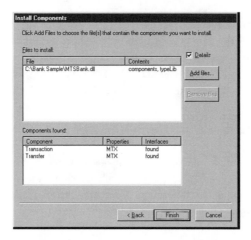

After you pick the component to register in Transaction Server, you can pick the transaction properties for the component. For example, you can specify that a component requires transactions, requires new transactions, or other properties. These properties are described in Table 13.1.

Table 13.1   Transaction Properties for MTS Components

Transaction Property	Description
Requires a transaction	Object must execute within the transaction's scope.
Requires a new transaction	An object must execute within its own unique transaction.
Supports transactions	The base client's transactional scope is used for transactions on the component.
Does not support transactions	Objects should not run within a transactional scope.

Registering with Visual InterDev   You can also easily register components if you want to use the Visual InterDev interface. Using Visual InterDev to register components with Transaction Server is effective, especially when you do not have direct access to the management tools included on the server.

To add a component to the Transaction Server via Visual InterDev, you follow a similar routine as you used for registering components on the server. You basically add the ActiveX component to your Visual InterDev project and view the properties for that file. After the Properties dialog box appears, you will see a tab marked for installing the component. In the contents of that tab are the options for registering the component on the client, server, or with Transaction Server. When you select the check box for registering with Transaction Server, you need to name the package with which you want to register the component in Transaction Server as well as the transaction properties for the component. To add to a preexisting package, you can simply use the name of the already-created package. To create a new package, simply choose a unique name for the package.

 TIP Because you cannot browse all packages that are currently created under MTS, you might want to devise a standard method for naming packages. For example, you can use the name of the project itself, or if the project has multiple packages, you can use the project name followed by an underscore (_) and a name for the subcomponent of the system. Whatever you decide, the naming method should ensure that no two developers accidentally use the same name for packages.

N O T E When you are creating ActiveX components for use with Transaction Server, they must be in-process components. That is, they must be compiled as dynamic link library files. Transaction Server does not handle other component types. ■

Component Context

Registering a component in Transaction Server is all that is required to perform transaction management on a component. Simply having the control registered automatically gives the control the scalability and reliability for transactions. Unless you carefully craft all your transactions into a single component, this simple addition to Transaction Server is not enough. Because using object-oriented computing and reusable components is stressed, you need a provision for linking together multiple ActiveX components as part of a single, larger transaction.

In the earlier banking example, you invoked two components: one for removing money from savings and one for adding money to checking. In reality, this is one component used twice. Although you can add the component to Transaction Server, that alone does not suffice to create both instances of the object as one transaction. You need to create a base client for the larger transaction, and this client invokes the two instances of the banking component. This way, you can register the basic component and this base client component in the Transaction Server and maintain state across the entire transaction. Basically, when a base client invokes multiple components, each of the components is instantiated within the scope of the base client. This process is referred to as maintaining the component context, and with it, one component can affect the outcome of other components. For the banking example, this process is required to maintain consistency across all objects involved.

Using *GetObjectContext* For components to work together in a transaction, they must be created within the context of the transaction. To understand how components can interact with each other, consider Listing 13.4. This example contains the logic for controlling withdrawals or deposits to the account passed in as a parameter to the method.

Listing 13.4 Using *GetObjectContext* Can Help ActiveX Controls Understand the Context of a Transactional Environment

```
Public Function Transaction(ByVal Account As String,
                            ByVal TransAmount As Integer) As Integer
    On Error GoTo errHandler

    Set objDB = CreateObject("ADODB.Connection")
    objDB.open "Bank"

    ExecuteString = "select * from " + Account
    Set dbResults = objDB.Execute(ExecuteString)
    Amount = (dbResults("amount"))

    If Amount + TransAmount < 0 Then
        ' Trying to withdraw when balance is < $0
        Transaction = -1
    Else
        newAmount = Amount + TransAmount
        ExecuteString = "UPDATE " + Account + " SET Amount = " +
                        Str(newAmount) + " WHERE ID = " +
                        Str(dbResults("ID"))
        objDB.Execute (ExecuteString)
        Transaction = newAmount

    End If

    ExecuteString = "select amount from " + Account
    Set dbResults = objDB.Execute(ExecuteString)
    Amount = (dbResults("amount"))

    dbResults.Close
    objDB.Close
    GetObjectContext.SetComplete
    Exit Function

errHandler:
    GetObjectContext.SetAbort
    fHandle = FreeFile
    Open "c:\mtsbank.log" For Output As #fHandle
    Print #fHandle, Str(Err) + " - " + Error$
    Close #fHandle
    Exit Function
End Function
```

Listing 13.4 contains the source code for the banking component that controls the database. Remember that this object is invoked twice—once with the "savings" account parameter passed and a negative value, and again with the "checking" account parameter passed and a positive value. These two individual instances of the component need to be tied together to form a complete transaction. Therefore, a base client component is developed to incorporate these two instances of the banking component in Listing 13.4. Listing 13.5 demonstrates the base client that can be used to create a `transfer` function that uses the transaction components.

N O T E To invoke the context for transaction management, Listing 13.5 creates an instance of the banking component using the `GetObjectContext.CreateInstance` method instead of just using `CreateObject`. ▨

Listing 13.5   To Group Related Components Together, You Must Use a Base Client Such as This One

```
Public Function Transfer(ByVal FromAccount As String,
                         ByVal ToAccount As String,
                         ByVal Amount As Integer) As Integer
    On Error GoTo errHandler

    Set objTransaction =
        GetObjectContext.CreateInstance("MTSBank.Transaction")
    result = objTransaction.Transaction(FromAccount, -1 * Amount)
    result = objTransaction.Transaction(ToAccount, Amount)
    GetObjectContext.SetComplete
    Exit Function

errHandler:
    GetObjectContext.SetAbort
    fHandle = FreeFile
    Open "c:\mtsbank.log" For Output As #fHandle
    Print #fHandle, Str(Err) + " - " + Error$
    Close #fHandle

    Exit Function
End Function
```

N O T E To use the `GetObjectContext` function, you must remember to add references to your Visual Basic project for Transaction Server. Under the Project menu, you will find a References item. By choosing it, you can add additional references by picking DLL files. Several DLL files such as mtsas.dll are associated with Transaction Server. These libraries, when added to your project, give you the `GetObjectContext` function, among other capabilities. ▨

As a result of the new code in Listings 13.4 and 13.5, you have enabled the components to work in a transactional environment. After these components are registered in the Transaction Server, you can create a Web page that points to the base client to complete the demonstration. Listing 13.6 shows a basic Web page that invokes the base client component.

Part

III

Ch

13

Listing 13.6   Any Source Such as a Web Page Can Invoke the Transactional Base Client

```
<%@ LANGUAGE=VBScript %>
<HTML>
<HEAD>
<META NAME="GENERATOR" Content="Microsoft Visual Studio 6.0">
</HEAD>
<BODY>
```

continues

Listing 13.6   Continued

```
<H2>Transfer $100 of Money from Savings to Checking</H2>

<%

Set objTransfer = CreateObject("MTSBank.Transfer")
result=objTransfer.Transfer("Checking","Saving",100)

%>

</BODY>
</HTML>
```

The Results   Assuming that everything is registered properly on the server, this application should work properly. If a client decides to move $100 from a savings account into a checking account, and the process fails, the customer no longer loses money because the Transaction Server recognizes the failure and reverts changes to the database.

This system actually works because the component that performs the database moves does some error validation, and if an error is encountered, the Abort method is called for the transaction context. Conversely, if the component works flawlessly, the Commit method is invoked. These basic functions instruct the Transaction Server what to do. In the event of an abort, all database actions are rolled back. So, in the example, when money is removed from savings and a failure occurs during the deposit to checking, the Abort method in the error handling routine instructs Transaction Server to revert all changes in the system.

From Here...

In this chapter, you received a brief introduction to server-side ActiveX components and how to use them in a transactional environment. With some practice, you will discover that these techniques will prove to be extremely valuable in creating highly reliable applications in the future.

The next section of this book continues your knowledge of Visual InterDev by introducing the concept of database programming. In this chapter, you were quickly introduced to some of the anomalies that occur when writing complex database applications. In the next section you learn how to use databases more effectively and will be able to understand the code covered in this chapter for database access more fully. With the knowledge you gain throughout the rest of this book, you will see how to write truly useful and functional Web sites with Visual InterDev.

PART IV

Database Programming Basics

14 Database Programming Basics 311

15 Setting Up a Database 327

16 Using the Visual InterDev 6 Data Environment 345

17 Working with ADO and RDS 359

CHAPTER 14

Database Programming Basics

In this chapter

What Is a Relational Database?   **312**

Creating Database Indexes   **316**

Normalized Database Development   **317**

Referential Integrity   **325**

What Is a Relational Database?

The database has long been the most difficult aspect of Web development, with several different methods of database access being developed over the years. Adding a database back end to your Web site can radically change its maintenance, appearance, and speed. The problem with databases is the fact that they're traditionally the realm of the technologically inclined, which is something that Web developers are not usually considered.

If you look at the latest versions of desktop database programs such as Microsoft Access, Microsoft Visual FoxPro, Borland Paradox, and Lotus Approach, you will find that each of these programs uses HTML conversion wizards to convert forms and reports to HTML format. On the high end of the database spectrum, Microsoft SQL Server, Oracle, and others incorporate HTML conversion wizards as well. Clearly, modern intranet and Internet professionals have to learn database programming and development.

 Databases represent the lifeblood of companies. A poorly designed database can easily cause financial havoc, among other things, to an otherwise stable company. Therefore, the importance of proper database development practices cannot be stressed enough: No amount of programming code, Web page elegance, or ActiveX controls can salvage the damage that can come as a result of a poorly designed database.

The purpose of a database is to store information for quick and easy retrieval. You are seeing a marriage made in heaven: A medium designed for the exchange of information (the Internet) is being merged with a tool to store and retrieve information (databases).

Understanding relational database design is essential to employing this cutting-edge technology that will revolutionize how information is served to the public. The origin of relational database design has been repeated in every book that talks about databases, so this section will very briefly describe the origin of the relational model.

In the mid-1970s, E.F. Codd, who was working for IBM at the time, wrote *A Relational Model of Data for Large Shared Data Banks*. This document revolutionized the database industry. It provided a model for database organization that was a major contrast to the other theories of the time. It is on this model that the majority of databases are based.

The Relational Database Model, unlike previous database models, deals only with how the data is presented. This model does not deal with how the data is actually stored. The data is to be presented as tables, discussed next. Each column is considered a field. Each row is considered a record. The only redundant data resulting from this model are columns that are common to two or more tables. These columns provide for the joining of two tables. Note that the term *relational* is used to state that one group of related information is placed in one table.

Introducing Tables

If you have already installed Visual InterDev or any other piece of commercial software, you probably understand what tables are and how they work. During the installation process, you were required to enter the serial number or CD-key that identifies your copy of Visual InterDev as unique. Somewhere in Microsoft's database, possibly in the Products table, is the serial number and the product description—Visual InterDev. In a relational database, *a table is a collection of unique instances of similar data.*

In practical terms, a table is a set of *columns* and *rows.* Columns describe the attributes or characteristics of the *primary key* (discussed later). In the example of a Products table, one column might be called CDKey_ID; another might be called Description. Each row of values, divided into columns, always contains at least one unique value. These rows are called records. A column is a vertical collection of fields; a row is a horizontal collection of fields. Figure 14.1 shows an example of a typical table.

FIG. 14.1

Designing a table in MS SQL Server 6.5.

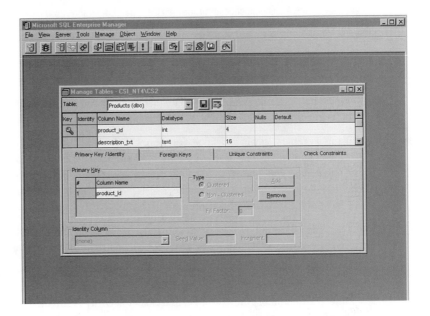

Adding Fields   A *field* is a single unit of information. Normally, you refer to a specific column in a row as the CDKey_ID field or the Description field. At the field level, the user interacts with the table by inputting data. After the user inputs data into a field, it is then evaluated to see whether it is of the correct data type. If it is not the correct data type, an error occurs and the database prevents the user from leaving the field until a value of the correct data type is input.

What type of data is stored in a table column? When you create a new column, database programs such as Microsoft SQL Server, Oracle, and DB2 require you to choose the data type from `binary`, `datetime`, `decimal`, `image`, or `varchar`, just to name a few. This information tells the database how it is to interpret the data in the column.

Part

IV

Ch

14

> **CAUTION**
>
> Choosing the correct data type is very important. A common mistake is to store the zip code, for example, as a type of `number`. Numbers do make up a zip code, but the zip code itself is not a true number. When you implement Zip+4, this becomes obvious. Now you are storing a hyphen (-) in the field. If the zip code were a number, you would be subtracting a four-digit number from a five-digit number, and your package or letter would not arrive at the correct address. The more accurate data type to use for a zip code is a `char`.

 The whole idea around choosing the correct data type is to choose the type that is closest to the description of the data. For example, you can store a dollar amount as a `number`, but `money` is a closer description. You should choose `number` as the type of data only if you plan to make calculations on the data.

Using Primary Keys   *Primary keys* are often called "row identifiers" because they uniquely identify rows. Without a primary key, relational database design is all but lost.

Each table has only one primary key. The primary key can be made of multiple fields; in this case, it is known as a *composite key*. A *simple key* is a primary key comprising a single field.

Choosing a primary key is a difficult decision. Of all the fields that will be entered into a record, you should have at least one candidate field from which to choose a primary key. As its name suggests, a *candidate field* is a field that is a candidate to be a primary key. Another issue in the decision of choosing a primary key is that primary keys cannot have null values. A primary key should also contain unique data for each record it represents.

Consider this information in the context of a customer table. If you look at Figure 14.2, you will see the names of several customers. (Any Social Security number corresponding to the ones shown is purely coincidental.)

The following fields in the customer table shown in Figure 14.2 are candidate fields: CustomerID, Customer Name, Phone, and Social Security Number. Choosing any one field as a simple primary key poses both advantages and disadvantages. You don't need to choose a composite key because you have at least one candidate field.

The primary key marks a particular record as different from all the others. The primary key references this record in this table with another record in another table. What makes a field a good candidate field? If the field is unique, unambiguous, data-less, and unchanging, it is a good candidate field.

The CustomerID field is the field that is most often chosen as the primary key by developers. This method guarantees that the data is unique. The problem is that one customer could have two CustomerIDs. For example, you can have two records that identify the same person, as you can see in Figure 14.2. A large software company's customer database may commonly contain 12 different CustomerIDs for one customer. If you are at all interested in keeping a history, using more than one CustomerID for the same person is not a good solution.

FIG. 14.2
Choosing a primary key requires effort.

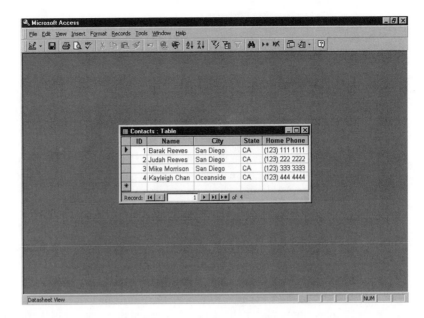

The Customer Name is a good candidate field. A major problem with it is that if you look in your phone book, you can find many John Smiths, for example. Another problem, although lesser, deals with the possibility of name changes. These changes more commonly occur with female customers who change their names because of marriage.

The Phone field is also a good candidate field. It is a better candidate than a Customer Name in that a phone number can belong to only one household. However, problems can occur; phone numbers do change, so you either need to build a system that can reflect these changes or create another database entry. Another problem is that if Jose orders something and his wife Jane orders something later, your records do not reflect an actual customer, but a household. An added problem is that of new area codes. As populations grow in many cities, new area codes are being added to prevent duplication of numbers.

The Social Security number is a phenomenal candidate field if it is applicable to your business. A Social Security number can refer to only one person. The chance of a person having it changed is virtually nil. Using the Social Security number as the primary key does pose some difficulties, however. The main difficulty is in having your customers reveal their Social Security numbers. Unless you work in the medical or financial field, people are reluctant to give out their Social Security numbers.

The best primary key is usually one you generate yourself and then assign to a customer. Ideally, you would use the existing national primary key, the Social Security number, but client reticence prevents that use.

Using Foreign Keys   A *foreign key* is a primary key from another table. Therefore, the values of the foreign key column match that of a primary key column of another table. For example, in an invoice table, you store an invoice number and a customer number. The customer number is

Part
IV

Ch
14

a foreign key because this value is the primary key of a customer table. This information will have more meaning to you after you read the next few sections.

Creating Database Indexes

Indexes are used to increase the speed of information retrieval from a database, at the expense of hard drive space. Indexes are based on the values of a particular column. The database stores a list of values in a column and the location of those values in a particular table. By storing information this way, the database can search an index for a value, instead of the entire table. In addition to the increased disk space required for an index, insertion, updating, and deletion of data are slowed. These procedures are slowed because, when the database updates its source data, it also has to go through and update whatever indexes mirror that data. When choosing to use an index, you must consider the following factors:

- If a table is used for many insertions, updates, or deletions, indexes must be maintained constantly. Moreover, if that field is not part of the criteria of a query, an index does not improve performance. This consideration is the most important.

- If a column has many records with the same value, it is a good candidate for indexing. An index stores a list of the unique values and the locations of these values. If a large range of data must be indexed, the performance increase is minimal.

- If a table has few records, an index causes more overhead than the database takes to simply scan through a table. Considering this factor along with the preceding item, having very few unique values and a large number of records in a table would be good.

- The width of the column refers primarily to column or text fields. If a column is particularly wide, it requires additional storage space and causes longer search times. In general, indexing only text columns that have 25 characters or fewer is better.

When you deal with higher-end database applications, such as Microsoft SQL Server, Oracle, and DB2, you are given a choice of index types: clustered and nonclustered.

Clustered Indexes

A clustered index actually stores the data in a logical order. For this reason, only one clustered index is allowed per table. In general, this type of index is the fastest. However, the data takes up 20 percent more space in the database than if the data did not have a clustered index. Desktop databases such as Microsoft Access and Borland Paradox use the primary key as a clustered index.

Clustered indexes are best for queries returning the following:

- Large amounts of data
- Ranges
- Data grouped together
- Data in a certain order

In addition, they work well for keyed fields, primary keys being the best.

Nonclustered Indexes

A nonclustered index stores pointers to the actual data. The index tells the database every location of a particular value. Unlike the clustered index, more than one nonclustered index is allowed. This type of index uses less disk space but is faster than scanning the entire table. Desktop databases such as Microsoft Access and Borland Paradox use nonclustered indexes for nonprimary keyed fields.

Even though databases allow many nonclustered indexes, you should have fewer than four indexes per table.

Nonclustered indexes are best for the following:

- Returning a small amount of data
- Foreign keys
- When the primary key is numbered sequentially

Normalized Database Development

In this section, you will learn about the single most important part of database design: data normalization. *Data normalization* is the breaking up of data into tables of related data, keeping repeats and redundancy to minimal levels. You will see from the first two rules of data normalization (discussed later) that the terms *repeats* and *redundancy* are not redundant in themselves.

Normalization provides the following benefits:

- The tables are smaller because you eliminate repeating data. Moreover, because the fields in a table describe only the primary key, fewer fields appear in a table. This number provides additional performance enhancement in querying the data.
- The data is easier to maintain. For example, if a customer were to change his or her address, you need to change the data only once.
- The program is easier to maintain because of the preceding point; the program has to deal with data in only a single place instead of having multiple instances of the same data.

> **CAUTION**
>
> You will find no substitute for proper data normalization. Without it, your database will prove to be unwieldy, buggy, fragile, liable to crash, and miserable to maintain. In addition, lack of data normalization has resulted in inaccurate data reporting and data errors. Cute buttons, music, and animation on your company's Web site cannot help your database. You don't need to panic; I am simply expressing the importance of following good database design.

Part
IV

Ch
14

There are 12 rules and 333 subsets for The Relational Data Model. I will provide suggestions and give you plenty of examples of how to follow these rules, simplified into five steps, which are described in the next section. Before normalizing your database, you can follow these steps to make the normalization process faster:

1. Develop a list of all the fields you will be storing in this database. Leaving room for more fields would be a good idea because getting requests near design completion for more data to be stored in the database is common. Be sure to confirm that all the fields your company wants in the database are present before any data is imported or input.

2. Find your static data. *Static data* is data that rarely changes. If you call it a type, status, or priority, it is static data. You will probably have varying degrees of staticity. *Staticity* is the condition of being static or unchanging. For example, the probability of the United States adding any more states is low, so a table of states has a high staticity rating. Make a table for these highly static items. For example, create a table that stores the status of a project, a table storing types of insurance, and table storing the names and abbreviations of the States of the Union. They are called lookup tables.

3. Group your data together in related sets. For example, in an order entry database, you can have product data in one table, customer data in another, and invoice data in yet another.

4. Go through your list and find everything that will have multiple items. For example, one invoice can have many items but only one total. Separate this data. You should be aggressive in finding this data.

Be Aggressive When Separating Data into Tables

When you're working with databases, all it takes is for one item suddenly to become two to ruin your whole day. Case in point: I was working on a construction defect project. A law firm wanted a database of document summaries. The firm wanted to store document IDs, the author names, the issues, the names of the recipients, and later the storage location. Now, from reading the preceding sentence, you might assume that you should separate the issues and the recipients from the main document data. Yes, that is correct. Yet there is more to consider. It turns out that a one-page letter really can have more than one author. Who knew? What is more, the company would make copies of the documents and put them in separate locations so that certain documents would stay together. Don't learn this lesson the hard way; be aggressive in separating data. You are probably wondering what I did to solve the problem. I made a few queries to separate the data, and I was back in business—after some significant reprogramming.

After you perform the preceding steps, you can go through the database normalization rules. These steps should eliminate 90 percent of the work required to implement the 12 rules of data normalization.

Normalizing Data

The following five steps provide an easy way to follow the 12 rules of data normalization. Each of the steps corresponds to the widely accepted rules of data normalization.

Step 1—Eliminate repeating data. When you are dealing with invoices, for example, you may have ship-to data, product data, and the total invoice amount, as well as other data. Figure 14.3 shows a table that is in desperate need of normalization.

FIG. 14.3

This table really needs to be normalized.

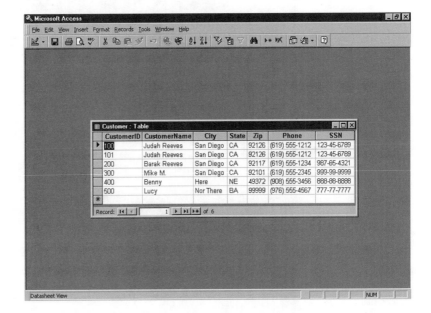

Notice the repeating data in Figure 14.3; it is confusing. Is the freight for each item, or is that the total freight? This table is a nightmare, so it is perfect for this demonstration. The following fields are repeated: OrderID, CustomerID, OrderDate, ShipName, and FreightCharge. Something needs to be separated. From this one table, you can create another table. Then you will have two invoice tables: Invoice Header and Invoice Footer. You can store the following fields in Invoice Header: OrderID, CustomerID, OrderDate, ShipName, and FreightCharge. In Invoice Footer, you can store OrderID, ProductID, ProductDescription, ProductSupplier, Quantity, UnitPrice, and LineTotal. Figure 14.4 shows the two described tables. Notice that the Invoice Footer still has repeating data in the form of an OrderID. This result is completely unavoidable because it is a detail table.

Step 2—Eliminate redundant data. Notice that the Invoice Footer has both a ProductID and a ProductDescription. The ProductID should refer to ProductDescription. Therefore, the data is redundant and needs to be removed. You can now create a Product table to store the ProductID and the ProductDescription. Figure 14.5 shows the new Invoice Footer and Product tables.

FIG. 14.4

Order table after Step 1 has been applied.

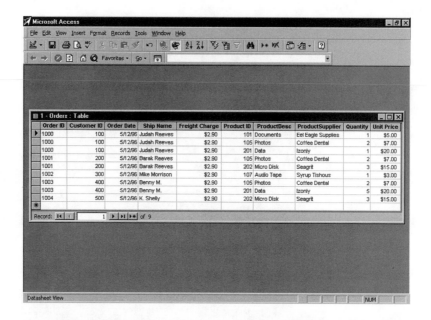

FIG. 14.5

New Invoice Footer and Product tables.

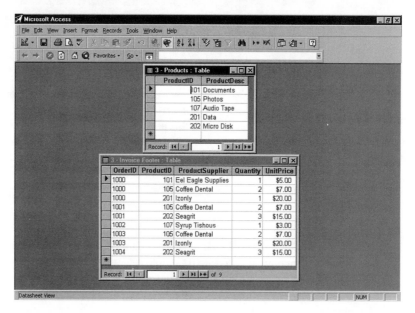

Step 3—Eliminate columns that do not describe the key. Now you need to review the keys. Look at the current tables in Figure 14.6 so that you can identify the key fields.

Remember that the key field is the unique identifier for a record. Both Invoice Header and Products are easy for selecting key fields. For the Invoice Header, the key field is the OrderID. For the Products, it is the ProductID. In the Invoice Footer, no one field is unique for all the records (yes, I created them that way on purpose). Therefore, you have to select two fields for a composite key. In this case, select OrderID and ProductID. Actually, the keys should be selected before you get to this point. If you look at the Invoice Footer, you will notice a ProductSupplier field. It has absolutely nothing to do with the Invoice. It does relate to the Product, though, so move it to that table, as shown in Figure 14.7.

FIG. 14.6

Identifying primary keys.

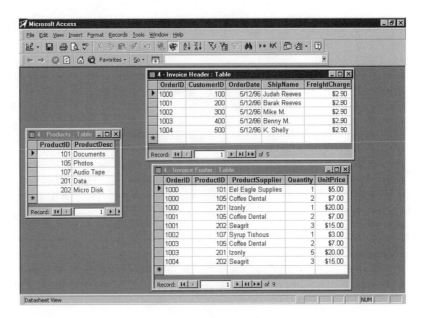

FIG. 14.7

Product with Supplier data.

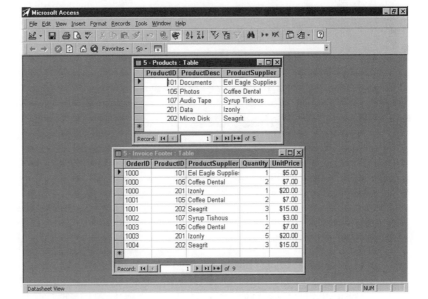

Step 4—Eliminate multiple relationships. Say that Red Descent wants to get a market share of Seagrit's Micro Disk. They both sell the same exact product but have different prices. Having two "201" products in the Products table would be a violation of Step 1. Therefore, you can create a Product-Suppliers table. This table allows for many suppliers for one product, as illustrated in Figure 14.8.

FIG. 14.8
Product and Product-Suppliers tables.

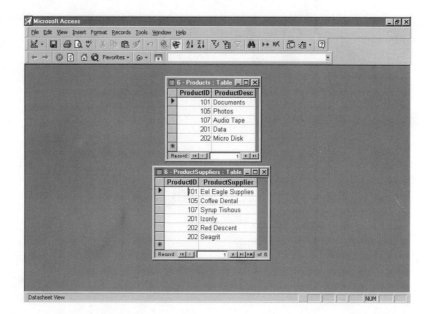

Step 5—Eliminate related multiple relationships. This particular rule is rarely needed and is usually provided for in Step 4. The example used for Step 4 also applies to this rule because the product relates to the supplier. You can take that example a step further by storing the manufacturer information as well. Then if some regulation is passed stating that, for instance, if a supplier supplies one product from a manufacturer, it must supply all products from a manufacturer, you are ready. In such a case, Step 5 makes inserting data faster.

Denormalized Database Development

Why would you denormalize a normalized database? Did you notice that the Customer table does not follow Step 3? It does not follow because the city and state are not required. The zip code already describes a city and state. On that basis, you have a Customer table with a street address and a zip code. In addition, you have a zip code table that describes the zip code's city and state. However, implementation of this table would be a headache and would degrade performance. Therefore, the main reason for denormalization is performance.

You have to be very careful if you choose to store your data in a denormalized format. When you denormalize, you create redundant data. If you update data a lot, your database has to maintain two copies of the data. Having two copies causes performance degradation. So, denormalize only when you know you will have performance improvements. In short, normalized data is standard and provides for the fastest insertions, updates, and deletions. Denormalized data, if denormalized properly, provides for the fastest retrieval.

Data denormalization provides for easier creation of ad hoc reports by end users. Because the data is duplicated, complex queries on which to base a report are not required.

> **CAUTION**
>
> Denormalizing a database is a major undertaking. It is recommended that denormalization be performed by experienced database personnel only.

 One easy approach to denormalization is to create a summary table for values that are not likely to be updated. For example, you can create a table to store aggregates of weekly sales figures. The summary data can be computed and inserted after all the appropriate values have been entered.

Overnormalization in Database Development

Overnormalization is a technique to increase database performance. It is easier to employ than denormalization. Overnormalization involves splitting tables; horizontal partitioning and vertical partitioning are the two techniques of overnormalization. In general, overnormalization is much easier to maintain than denormalization. Furthermore, of the two overnormalization techniques, vertical partitioning is the easier because horizontal partitioning requires a decision on which table to insert, update, delete, or retrieve fields from. For example, you might retrieve name and address information from one table and other information from another table. On the other hand, when you use vertical partitioning, making a decision on which table to insert a particular record into is much easier. For example, you have to decide only which of two tables to deal with all information on a customer.

Horizontal partitioning involves splitting a table by row. This approach reduces the number of rows per table. Implementation is based on the table you choose. Most tables have a type of control number as a primary key. By having a certain range of numbers in one table and the remaining numbers in a second table, a horizontal partition is made. For example, in an Invoice History containing one million records, you can place invoice numbers 1 to 500,000 in one Invoice History table, and records 500,001 to 1,000,000+ in a second Invoice History table. You can adjust this number to account for a certain date, so you can create a report comparing last year's sales with this year's sales faster. Figure 14.9 shows an example of horizontal partitioning.

Vertical partitioning involves splitting a table based on column. This approach reduces the number of columns per table. Implementation is based on the table you choose. A decision must be made as to which columns are used more than others. From there, you can create one table of data that is used more often and another to store the data that is used less often. For example, you can store a property name, number, type, and reference code in one table, and its address, statistics, and other less-used information in a separate table. Figure 14.10 shows an example of vertical partitioning.

FIG. 14.9

Customer IDs numbered 100 to 250 have been moved left in the original Customer table. Customer IDs numbered 251 to 750 have been moved to a new Customer table.

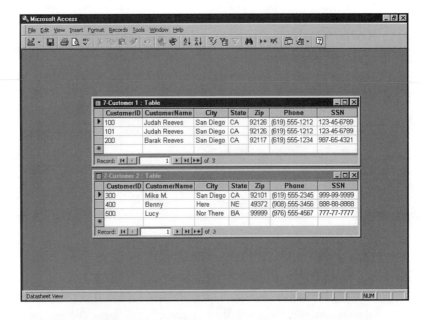

FIG. 14.10

This example shows how security can be implemented by splitting confidential information from public information.

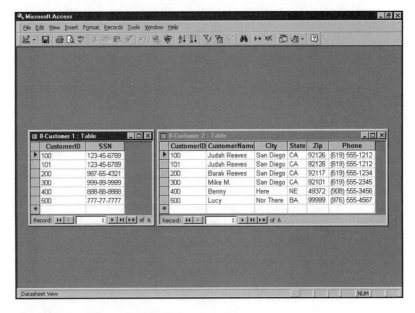

TIP Vertical partitioning can also be used to help implement security. For example, you can split a single table into one confidential information table and one nonconfidential information table. This way, you can protect information that you do not want to divulge by allowing most users to see the nonconfidential information and the users with higher security to access the confidential data. Moreover, you can allow most users to deal only with customers' reference numbers, and give those users with higher access the ability to view the more descriptive data such as names and addresses. Refer to Figure 14.10 for an example.

Referential Integrity

After you have set the proper amount of normalization, you can set up referential integrity. Referential integrity keeps your data together. Say your Invoice Footer table has Invoice Number 118, but your Invoice Header table does not. In this case, you have an orphaned piece of data. I prefer to use the term *illegitimate* because it makes the situation sound as bad as it is. This illegitimate data is completely useless to you because you do not know to whom the product was sent; you do not know when it was ordered. Referential integrity prevents this travesty. Note that this is acceptable if it involves lookup data. For example, if you have an employee table and an employee leaves, you can remove that employee's name from the lookup table so that it is not used in future records. However, it is a travesty for things such as Invoice Numbers, Customer Numbers, and other critical data that must be linked together.

Referential integrity uses the primary key and the foreign key of different tables. It requires data that is in a foreign key to be present in a primary key of a different table. In Figure 14.11, notice that at the center of all other tables is tblProperty. The prefix *tbl* tells anyone who looks at this that it is a table.

Note that Figure 14.11 is a graphical representation of relationships between tables. The graphical relationship design was created in Microsoft Access. High-end databases such as Microsoft SQL Server and Oracle do not have the benefit of graphical relationship design. Their relationships are set programmatically or at table design. In Microsoft SQL Server, these relationships are called *constraints*.

FIG. 14.11
Despite its appearance, this relationship is the cleanest for the number of tables shown.

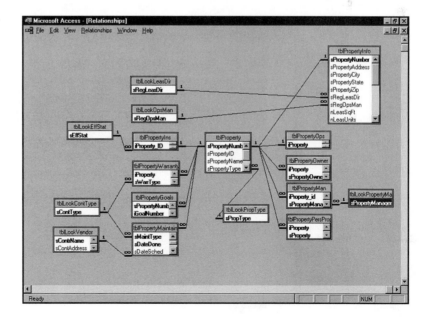

Part
IV

Ch
14

Lines coming out of tblProperty connect it to nine different tables: tblPropertyIns, tblPropertyWarranty, tblPropertyGoals, tblPropertyMaintain, tblPropertyOps, tblPropertyOwner, tblPropertyMan, and tblPropertyPersProp. Notice that at each end of the line is either a 1 or a 0.

From Here...

A strong understanding of databases is integral to creating a successful data-based Web application. Too many Web developers approach databases without the care and attention the database deserves. Databases are complex beasts and require you to carefully plan and implement a solid architecture for your application to use. The following chapters continue the exploration of databases and Visual InterDev, and how to use them in your applications.

- Chapter 15, "Setting Up a Database," steps you through the process of planning your database and implementing it with Visual InterDev.

- Chapter 16, "Using the Visual InterDev 6 Data Environment," explores the Visual InterDev interface for databases, called the Data Environment.

- Chapter 22, "SQL Server Basics," is a useful chapter if you plan on using a Microsoft SQL Server as your database server. Here you can learn how to add users, modify your databases, and implement the all important backups.

CHAPTER 15

Setting Up a Database

In this chapter

Introducing Visual InterDev 6 and Databases   **328**

Connecting to Databases with ODBC   **328**

Using SQL Server Databases   **330**

Creating a Data Connection to Use Access Databases   **340**

Using FoxPro Databases   **342**

Introducing Visual InterDev 6 and Databases

One of the main reasons you might want to use Visual InterDev 6 is to set up existing databases on the Web. The ease with which you can put these databases on the Web will astound you. No longer do you need a team of developers to develop APIs to access your legacy databases. Visual InterDev allows you to open any ODBC/OLE DB–compliant database on the Web. You can simply create an Active Server Page (ASP) and insert a data connection, and you are ready to start customizing your data-aware Web page. This capability is one the most important differences between Visual InterDev 1.0 and Visual InterDev 6. The design environment in Visual InterDev 6 allows you to customize the Web page easily with the data connection. The development environment is progressing as Visual InterDev is maturing as a development tool.

To set up existing databases, you must consider a few important factors. The Web server that accesses the database must have the database driver installed. Keep in mind that the database need not be on the same machine as the Web server; the database can reside on a completely different machine. Splitting the Web server and the database server may improve overall performance, depending on the number of Web clients and database servers implemented. Depending on the database being accessed, you need to consider different issues specific to the database.

Connecting to Databases with ODBC

If you want to put a legacy database on the Web, the easiest way is to first create a Data Source Name, or DSN. In Windows 95 or NT, go to the Control Panel, and open the item called 32bit ODBC (see Figure 15.1).

FIG. 15.1
The 32-bit ODBC Data Source Administrator in Windows 95.

If you have version 3.6 of ODBC Data Source Administrator, you have more control on how you can set up the DSN than you would have with older versions of the ODBC Administrator. If you want to download the latest version of ODBC, browse the Net at this address: **http://www.microsoft.com/data/**.

Next, you'll learn about the different tabs in the ODBC Data Source Administrator, which is shown in Figure 15.2.

FIG. 15.2
The ODBC Data Source Administrator tabs.

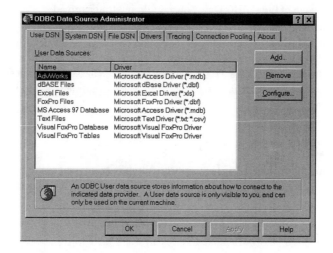

You can select from the following seven tabs. You use some tabs to configure the database locations and accessibility. You can use some to debug database connection problems. You will learn about each in more detail in the following sections.

- User DSN
- System DSN
- File DSN
- Drivers
- Tracing
- Connection Pooling
- About

The User DSN

In the User DSN tab of the ODBC Data Source Administrator, you can set up DSNs specific to a user. The user of the machine therefore can access only this database.

The System DSN

In the System DSN tab of the ODBC Data Source Administrator, you can set up DSNs for all users of this machine.

The File DSN

The File DSN tab of the ODBC Data Source Administrator provides Microsoft's latest DSN, which is recommended for future use as DSNs are easily transferable from one machine to another.

Drivers

The Drivers tab of the ODBC Data Source Administrator provides the list of drivers available on this machine. If you do not see the driver for your database here, you have to get the driver from the vendor.

> **N O T E** Drivers and versions are listed in the Drivers tab. Having the latest driver supported by the vendor is very important. Many database problems arise from having incorrect versions of database drivers. ■

The Tracing Tab

The Tracing tab of the ODBC Data Source Administrator is a great new feature; it tracks calls to the ODBC driver and stores this information in log files. The Vista tracing feature has more events that may prove more useful than the Basic tracing feature.

The Connection Pooling Tab

The Connection Pooling tab is for advanced use; on this tab, you can set the connection timeouts and combine pooling to save the number of calls to the server. I suggest making the timeouts within the application instead of setting the timeouts here.

The About Tab

The About tab of the ODBC Data Source Administrator tells you which ODBC Data Source Administrator version is installed on this machine.

Using SQL Server Databases

Microsoft's Enterprise Database is SQL Server, which will be upgraded from version 6.5 to 7.0 this year. Visual InterDev 6 has an excellent interface with MS SQL Server. Visual InterDev has an array of capabilities for manipulating MS SQL Server within its own development environment, and the integration is quite extensive.

Setting Up an Existing SQL Server Database

You can have a data-aware application in minutes. In the following sections, you'll learn how to create your own data connection.

Creating a Data Connection   You can add a data connection in Visual InterDev by simply following these steps:

1. Create a blank Web project in Visual InterDev.
2. Right-click on the Web project, and select Add Data Connection from the context menu, as shown in Figure 15.3.

FIG. 15.3

Choosing Add Data Connection in Visual InterDev 6.

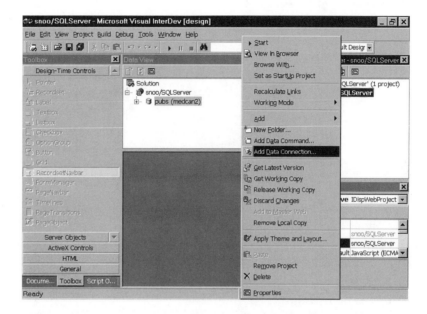

Visual InterDev brings up the ODBC DSN selection screen called Select Data Source, as you can see in Figure 15.4.

FIG. 15.4

Selecting the ODBC DSN.

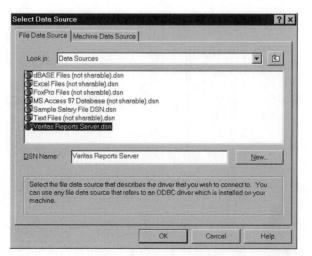

3. Select your SQL Server DSN database. In Figure 15.4, you can see the example of Veritas Reports Server DSN. If your database does not already have a DSN set up, click New and create your DSN as shown in the following section.

Creating an MS SQL DSN For MS SQL Server, the DSN creation is specific to the database. Picking up where you left off in the preceding section, follow these steps to create a MS SQL DSN:

1. In the Create New Data Source dialog box, shown in Figure 15.5, select the SQL driver, and click Next.

FIG. 15.5

Selecting the MS SQL driver.

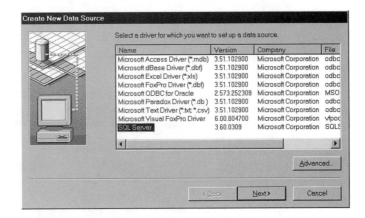

2. In the next dialog box, enter a descriptive name for your DSN. Using a combination of the database and table name is a good idea so that it is descriptive of the purpose of this DSN. Because this is just an example, use MySQLDSN as the DSN name, as shown in Figure 15.6.

FIG. 15.6

Adding a descriptive DSN name.

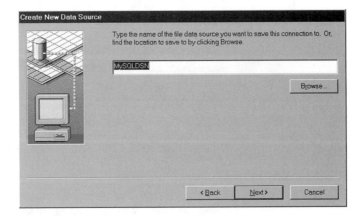

Part

IV

Ch

15

3. Click Next and then click Finish to go to the SQL-specific configuration screen.

4. In the resulting dialog box, enter a description of the DSN and the database server name, as shown in Figure 15.7.

FIG. 15.7

Entering a description and the database server name.

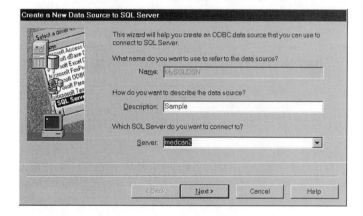

5. Click Next to continue.

6. In the next dialog box, shown in Figure 15.8, configure how the client machine will communicate with SQL Database Server. You should communicate with the SQL Server Database Administrator (DBA) on which manner to configure the client machine. The DBA can inform you whether to use NT authentication or SQL Server authentication.

FIG. 15.8

Setting SQL Server authentication and client configuration.

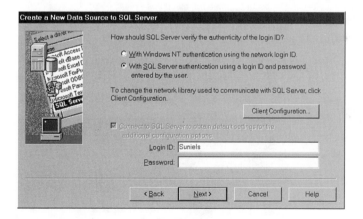

N O T E The SQL Server can communicate by using different protocols such as TCP/IP or Named Pipes. TCP/IP and Named Pipes are interprocess communication mechanisms that SQL Server and workstation data services use to provide communication between clients and servers. Protocols are the network languages used for communication between the client and server. Again, the DBA will let you know which protocols are available to be used.

On this screen, to change the protocol being used, click Client Configuration, and then click the Net Library tab on the resulting dialog box, as shown in Figure 15.9.

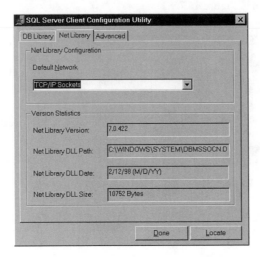

7. Click the Default Network pop-up list, and then select the appropriate protocol.

N O T E The default network you select must be installed on the SQL Server; otherwise, no communication will occur between the client and the database server. This situation is like one person speaking Spanish and the other speaking French. With no common network or language, no communication can occur between the machines. ∎

8. Click Done on the client configuration dialog box to return to the SQL-specific page.

9. Select the appropriate authentication, and if necessary, enter the username and password. Then click Next for some more MS SQL-specific configuration details, as shown in Figure 15.10.

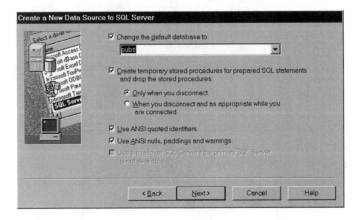

10. On this screen, specify the default database. Specifying the database that is going to be used here is a good idea so that you don't have to change the database through code.

   For the other parameters here, you should communicate with the DBA, who will let you know how the database is set up and how best to set up the connection parameters such as stored procedures quoting nulls and warnings needed.

11. Click Next to continue. You then see the dialog box shown in Figure 15.11.

FIG. 15.11

Setting the ODBC driver configuration.

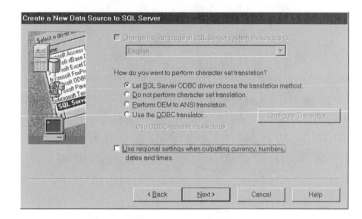

12. Configure how the ODBC layer will communicate with SQL Server. These details are important, especially when you are dealing with international machines. For example, how are regional settings being used? Does your database handle foreign languages or only English characters? Here, you can set up the ODBC to handle these options and translation methods.

13. Click Next to continue. You then see the dialog box shown in Figure 15.12.

FIG. 15.12

Choosing log files for ODBC.

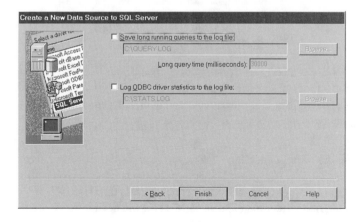

14. Set up log files for debugging or usage purposes in this dialog box.

15. Click Finish to continue. The ODBC connections are summarized, as shown in Figure 15.13. Testing the connection to confirm it is a good idea.

FIG. 15.13

Viewing the summary of ODBC connections.

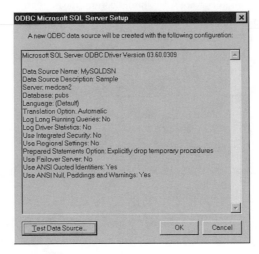

16. Click OK to continue.

17. Now that you have created the DSN, select the DSN and click OK to continue.

    After you select your SQL Server DSN, the username/authentication screen is displayed, as shown in Figure 15.14.

FIG. 15.14

The SQL Server authentication screen.

Here, you can select Use Trusted Connection if your database is already set up with NT integration; otherwise, enter your username and password. You can always change the username and password later in the design environment, if necessary. You also can click Options to access more options, such as the default database to use (see Figure 15.15). The example uses the pubs database.

Using the Data Connection   Okay, you've created the data connection, but how do you put the data on your Web page? The process just gets easier as you go. Just add a blank ASP to the Web project. Then drag the recordset object from the Design-Time Controls from the Toolbox onto the ASP, as shown in Figure 15.16. Now, you need to configure the recordset.

FIG. 15.15
Setting options for the
SQL Server.

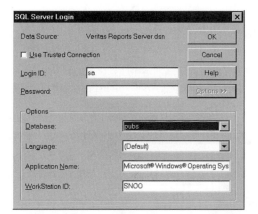

FIG. 15.16
Configuring a recordset
object.

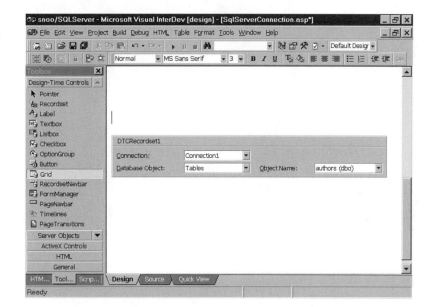

The following three items are visible immediately without going into the properties of the recordset object:

- Connection
- Database Object
- Object Name

Connection Connection provides a pop-up list of connections available to the Visual InterDev project. If only one connection has been made, and the default name is used, Connection1 is the only item available in the list. Select Connection1 for this example.

Database Object Database Object provides a pop-up list of object types for the recordset. Some of the different types are Tables, Views, and Stored Procedures. Select Tables for this example.

Object Name Object Name provides a pop-up list of available names of that object type. If Table is selected for the Database Object, then the list of available tables is shown. Select the Authors Table for this example, as shown in Figure 15.17.

FIG. 15.17
Selecting the Object Name.

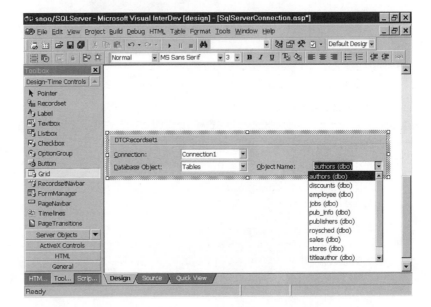

Setting the Properties of the Recordset Now the basic parameters for the recordset are selected; however, you can still make a lot more choices within Visual InterDev. Right-click the properties of the recordset to open the Property Pages dialog box, as shown in Figure 15.18.

FIG. 15.18
Setting the properties of the recordset.

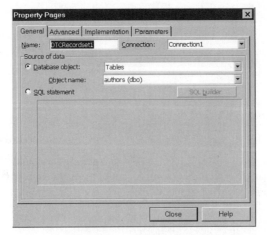

You can set properties on the following tabs of the Property Pages dialog box:

- General
- Advanced
- Implementation
- Parameters

General Tab   On the General tab, you can set the name of the recordset, the connection, database object, object name, and SQL statement. If you want to create your own special view for your Web page, you can simply enter your SQL statement here or use the SQL Builder.

Advanced Tab   On the Recordset Management section of the Advanced tab, you can select the cursor type, cursor location, locking type, and cache size. The Command configuration is also available; it enables the timeout for the command number of rows to be returned.

Implementation Tab   On the Implementation tab, you can set the scripting platform, recordset cache, and the option to open the recordset automatically.

Parameters Tab   On the Parameters tab, you can set the parameters to be passed to the database object. For example, you can set a parameter for a stored procedure.

Setting Up the Controls on the Web Page   Now that the recordset is set up, you can add data-aware controls to the Web page that will communicate with the recordset object.

If you select from the Design-Time Controls tab in the Toolbox, objects such as a text box, list box, or grid control are easily connected to the database with no coding whatsoever. For example, drag three text boxes to the ASP. Enter a hard return to space one below the other. Then right-click the properties of the text box on the ASP. The properties available are Name, Scripting Platform, Style, Lines, Enabled, Visible, Recordset, Field, Display Size, and Field Sizes.

To connect the text box to the recordset, all you have to do is select the recordset and the field name. Do the same to all three text boxes, but select a different field name for each text box.

Moving Between Records   Now that the fields appear on the Web page, how do you manipulate the records?

A simple solution is to use the RecordSetNavBar. Simply drag the RecordSetNavBar to the ASP. Right-click the properties. The properties available are Name, Scripting Platform, Recordset, and Update on Move. Select the recordset, and choose the Update on Move option if you want to update the records in the table. Save your changes, and release your working copies to the Web site.

If you try to use Quick View, it doesn't show anything because these controls work only with the server. So, select the ASP, right-click, and then select Preview in Browser from the context menu. Voilà, you are rewarded with a data-aware page in minutes with no coding.

You could have performed the same process in Visual InterDev 1.0; however, you now have so much more extensibility available to you. The developer can now modify the Web page without re-creating the page. In Visual InterDev 1.0, it was a chore to modify the page after the page was created. Microsoft has added some great features for you to take advantage of the SQL Server Database features within a Web project. Not many development environments have this integration.

Creating a Data Connection to Use Access Databases

To create a data connection so that you can use Access databases, create a new Web project within Visual InterDev. Then select the Web project from the Project Explorer, and right-click. Next, select Add Data Connection from the context menu to open the ODBC/DSN screen named Select Data Source, as shown in Figure 15.19. Select your Access DSN from this dialog box. This example uses Access Example.DSN. Then click OK.

FIG. 15.19

Selecting the Access DSN.

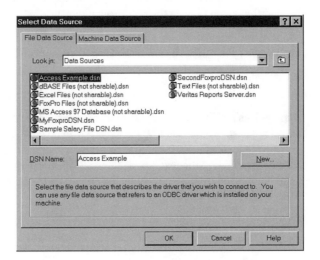

The Connection Properties dialog box then appears, as shown in Figure 15.20. Here, you can test the connection to confirm that you are accessing the database with no connection errors. You also can enter a more descriptive name than the default Connection#. This example uses AccessSalary.

The Connection Properties page has three tabs: General, which you used here, Authentication, and Miscellaneous. Next, delve into those other two tabs.

Authentication

The Authentication tab of the Connection Properties dialog box has two sections, Design-Time and Run-Time Information, which is a plus for you, as the developer. You can set different usernames and passwords for design- and runtime situations. This way, you can save your password to save time so that you don't have to reenter your username and password in the design environment, thus leaving the runtime with its own authentication.

FIG. 15.20
Naming the connection.

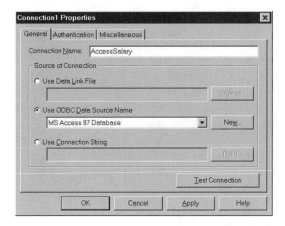

Miscellaneous

The two sections of the Miscellaneous tab of the Connection Properties dialog box are Timeouts and Other, as shown in Figure 15.21.

FIG. 15.21
The Miscellaneous tab of the Connection Properties dialog box.

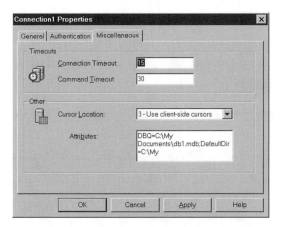

This tab is important for the Web application and its behavior. These timeouts dictate how long the Web application should wait for the database to perform the query. When the load on the Web server becomes great, the time for the query to run may increase; therefore, you might need to increase these timeouts. Otherwise, Web clients may see only timeout errors instead of the data.

Using the Data Connection

Now that you have your Access connection set up, you can set up the recordset object just as you did with MS SQL Server earlier in this chapter. There are no differences in the implementation within Visual InterDev. You simply drag the recordset object onto the ASP and similarly drag the data-aware controls.

Web Clients MS Access and MS SQL Server

The number of clients supported by MS Access should not be over 75 simultaneous users, whereas MS SQL Server can be used with hundreds of simultaneous users. This number will grow with the new robust SQL Server 7.0, which has been redesigned for greater numbers. The speed of the database depends on few factors other than just the database chosen. Hardware factors such as processor, hard disk type, network card, and Internet connection of the Web server and database server have a huge impact on performance. When you are implementing the Web application, make sure that you think through all these factors, or your users will be simply waiting for results instead of getting them.

Using FoxPro Databases

Microsoft continues to support FoxPro and will release a new version. Microsoft recognizes the number of FoxPro users, so the development of FoxPro is still a priority. The setup of FoxPro databases is similar to MS Access. You create a blank Web project and add a data connection and an ASP. You then drop in the recordset object and select the objects to work with the recordset.

N O T E Different FoxPro drivers are available. The FoxPro driver for DBF files is called Microsoft FoxPro Driver. When the ODBC connection is created for the FoxPro database, the database file is not selected. You must select the directory for the FoxPro database, as shown in Figure 15.22. ■

FIG. 15.22
Selecting the directory of DBF files.

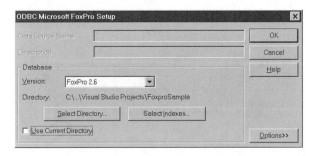

The latest FoxPro driver is called Microsoft Visual FoxPro Driver, which is for FoxPro databases with the .DBC extension. The Microsoft Visual FoxPro driver works with a database file, not a directory. You can see its setup screen in Figure 15.23.

FIG. 15.23
Selecting Visual FoxPro databases.

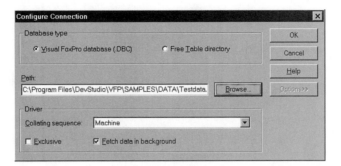

From Here...

Now that you have seen how easily you connect your databases to the Web, from MS Access to SQL Server, you can develop data-aware Web applications with ease. Now you can view data, modify it via the Web in a secure fashion, and create it with tremendous ease by using Visual InterDev 6. No longer do you need a team of developers to set up your Web database applications. As a result, corporations can deliver Web database applications to end users much more cost effectively. Now you can show them what you can create!

CHAPTER 16

Using the Visual InterDev 6 Data Environment

In this chapter

The Data Environment   346

Controlling Database Views   352

Using Stored Procedures   354

The Data Environment

Databases are at the heart of the most powerful Web applications. Visual InterDev 6 provides you with a comprehensive and effective integrated solution for database development without your having to leave the Visual Studio environment. This aspect of Visual InterDev, called the *data environment,* provides you with the tools for the most common aspects of database development: direct manipulation of tables and views, the creation of stored procedures, and the creation of indexes. When used alone, the data environment gives you a means to create database applications with minimal effort. When it is combined with other data development tools from your database of choice, you are given a powerhouse of unequaled capabilities.

Microsoft bills the data environment as "a repository in your Visual InterDev Web project for the information required in a server script to connect and manipulate data in databases." You can use this standard interface to create reusable data-related objects to use within your Web applications. Remember that the data environment is server-based and is not available from the client side. In essence, the data environment acts as an easy-to-use wrapper around ActiveX Data Objects (ADO) for communication with databases in your scripts. The environment provides easy access to these standard database objects:

- Tables
- Views
- Stored procedures
- SQL commands

▶ **See** "Working with ADO and RDS" on **p. 359** for more information about ADO.

Data Environment Contents

The data environment acts like an explorer tree, working with multiple branches. At its root level, the primary component of the data environment is the *data connection.* Data connections represent the information required to connect to a single database. For each database that your application communicates with, the data environment requires a database connection. Below the data connection are *data commands.* Data commands are command objects within each data connection. These commands define a set of data to work with, such as a table, query, view, stored procedure, or SQL command. You will likely have many data commands for each data connection in your data environment.

Data commands are accessible throughout your Web application, meaning that they can be called from any page in your site. These objects are reusable, and only the original object requires changes when the database is modified; typically, you don't need to change each individual page that uses the object.

Each command, in turn, can display the database object it references. For example, a database command that references a stored procedure can contain the columns involved in the procedure or perhaps the procedure's parameters. Regardless, each command appears as a node under the DataEnvironment folder in the Project Explorer. The DataEnvironment folder, in turn, is added as a node under the GLOBAL.ASA file in your project. As you create additional data connections, they appear in the DataEnvironment folder. However, you can have only one DataEnvironment folder. Figure 16.1 illustrates the data environment in the Project Explorer.

> **N O T E**   The GLOBAL.ASA file is used by Internet Information Server to keep track of all settings and database connections that are available to your entire Web application. IIS reads the GLOBAL.ASA when a visitor first arrives at your Web site. This allows it to establish any required setup for the Web application, including (but not limited to) database connections, global variables, and session setup commands. ▪

FIG. 16.1

The DataEnvironment folder in the Project Explorer houses your data connections and commands.

> **N O T E**   These instructions assume that you already have a data source created. Your data source could be a simple Access database or an enterprise-level SQL Server or Oracle instance. You should create your data source first, before proceeding with these steps, if you have not already done so. ▪

Before you can proceed with adding data commands to your Web application, you must have a data connection. Creating a data connection requires that you already have a data source created. Data connections use standard ODBC DSN (Data Source Name) references, and can be a machine, system, or file reference depending on the installation of your Web server and your data. To create a data connection, follow these steps:

1. Right-click on your project name in the Project Explorer.
2. Choose Add Data Connection... from the context menu.
3. The standard ODBC Select Data Source dialog box appears. Select your data source from the appropriate tab (File Data Source or Machine Data Source).
4. Click the OK button.

When you add a connection to your data environment, the Data View window appears, as shown in Figure 16.2. This window displays the data connection's objects that can be added to your environment.

> **N O T E**   If you need to create a new ODBC DSN, refer to the ODBC control panel and its online help pages for information specific to your ODBC drivers. ▪

FIG. 16.2

The Data View window employs a tree-based approach to display your data connection's objects, which include tables, views, and stored procedures.

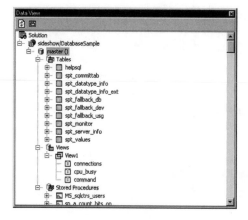

Creating a Data Command

Data commands represent your database actions. Most of your commands include queries or inserts into your data source. The most basic command is a query command. Follow these steps to create this type of command:

1. Locate your data connection in the data environment. Right-click the data connection, and choose Add Data Command from the context menu. The Command Properties dialog box, shown in Figure 16.3, appears.

FIG. 16.3

In the Command Properties dialog box, you can create your data command.

2. Enter a name for your command in the Command Name text box. This name is used within your application to refer to this command.

3. Select your data connection from the Connection drop-down list box. Selecting a connection is especially important if you have multiple connections in your project.

4. From the Database Object drop-down list box, select the object type you want to use as the origin for your data. It can be a stored procedure, table, view, or synonym.

5. Based on your selection in the Database Object drop-down list box, the Object Name drop-down list box refreshes to provide you with the individual objects available to you. Select the object you want to query.

6. If you selected a stored procedure in step 4, click the Parameters tab. The Microsoft Data Environment prompts you, as shown in Figure 16.4, to execute the stored procedure to retrieve the data. Click Yes.

FIG. 16.4

This prompt warns you that the stored procedure must be executed to retrieve data for parameters.

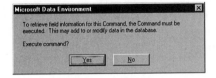

> **CAUTION**
>
> When you execute a stored procedure, you run the risk of damaging your data and causing problems on your database server. Always consider the results of your actions!

7. After the stored procedure is executed, the Parameters tab displays the parameters appropriate for the selected stored procedure, as shown in Figure 16.5. Adjust the parameters according to your procedure's requirements.

FIG. 16.5

Stored procedure parameters are like program arguments; they are used to augment or operate the stored procedure's actions.

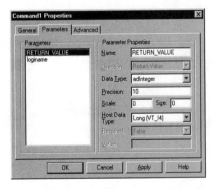

8. Click OK to close the dialog box and add your command to the data environment.

Creating a Data Command Using SQL Statements

Creating data commands using SQL statements provides you with a level of flexibility and power. You can use these statements to create intricate and powerful commands that accomplish specific tasks. You can either code the SQL statements manually or use a database diagram in the Query Builder to design your commands. To create a command using SQL statements, follow these steps:

1. Locate your data connection in the data environment. Right-click the data connection, and choose Add Data Command from the context menu. The Command Properties dialog box, previously shown in Figure 16.3, appears.

2. Enter a name for your command in the Command <u>N</u>ame text box. This name is used within your application to refer to this command.

3. Select the <u>S</u>QL Statement radio button. Selecting this button opens the SQL Statement text box for editing.

4. You can manually enter your SQL statement into the SQL Statement text box, or you can click the SQL <u>B</u>uilder button to create your statement visually. Click the SQL <u>B</u>uilder button to create your statement now. The Query Builder appears, as shown in Figure 16.6.

5. From your data connection in the Data View window, drag the tables or views to which you want to refer into the diagram.

FIG. 16.6
With the Query Builder, you can create complex commands using either a database diagram or raw SQL statements.

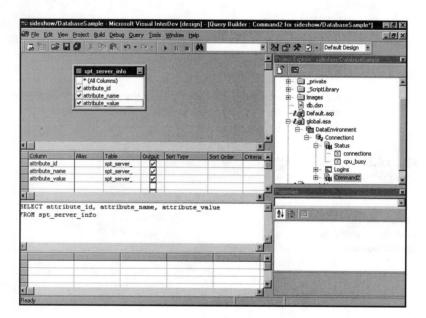

6. The SQL Pane immediately refreshes to reflect the statement required to carry out the actions you have requested. In the Grid Pane, modify the output of your query, such as the sorting options and criteria.

7. Each box represents an individual table, and each check box represents a column inside that table. Select the columns you want to include in your view by selecting the appropriate check boxes.

8. You can change the type of SQL command (from Query to Insert, Update, or Delete) by using the Query toolbar, shown in Figure 16.7.

9. When you are satisfied with your command, click the Verify SQL Syntax button on the Query toolbar. Clicking this button tells VID to confirm that your SQL statement contains no errors. A dialog box appears to inform you of the statement's validity.

10. Click OK to close the dialog box and return to the Query Builder.

FIG. 16.7
The Query toolbar lets you display the different panes of the Query Builder, as well as modify the type of action you are developing.

11. Choose File, Save Command.

12. Close the Query Builder window. Your SQL statement then is added to your command.

T I P You can modify your SQL statement at any time by opening the command's properties from the data environment.

Dragging and Dropping from the Data Environment

One of the most important features of the data environment is the drag-and-drop simplicity. You can drag objects to and from the environment to add database access to your applications. You also can create new commands by dragging objects from the Data View window into the data environment, and you can add data-bound controls to your pages by dragging commands and fields from the environment onto your pages. Table 16.1 identifies how you can use drag and drop in the data environment.

Table 16.1   Data Environment Drag-and-Drop Usage

Drag What Object?	From Where?	Onto What?	To Do What?
Database object	Data View	Data Environment	Create a command object for the database object that was dragged. For example, dragging a table creates a command with a database object type of table.
Command object	Data Environment	Web page	Create a data-bound control to the command.
Field object	Data Environment	Web pages	Create a data-bound control to the field.

When you drag a data command from the data environment onto a Web page, you see a display similar to the one shown in Figure 16.8.

FIG. 16.8
Data records are the visible representations of data commands in the source and design editors of VID.

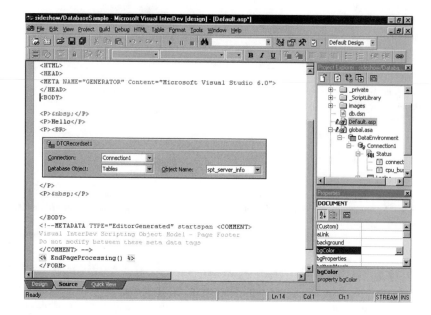

Controlling Database Views

In database parlance, a *view* is a virtual table created by a database query stored in a database. Views can define multiple columns and are often used to limit access to certain information. Views can be treated like tables for most database operations, such as Select queries. This functionality also can be extended to Update, Insert, and Delete queries. Operations performed on views actually affect the data in the respective tables on which the views are based.

Using views for Web applications makes a great deal of sense. You can use views to group data from the database for your application, without directly accessing numerous tables. Views can be used for ease of development and speed of deployment. The Visual InterDev data environment provides you with a means of defining and controlling views without relying on additional software. Figure 16.9 provides a conceptual representation of views.

The process for creating a view is almost identical to the process for creating a query. You must have a data connection established in your data environment to create a view. To begin, follow these instructions:

1. Open the Data View window if it is not already open. You can do so by double-clicking your data connection in the DataEnvironment folder of the Project Explorer.

2. Expand the Data View tree until the Views node is visible.

3. Right-click the Views node, and choose New View from the context menu. The Database Design View appears, as shown in Figure 16.10.

4. From your data connection in the Data View window, drag the tables to which you want to refer into the Database Design View diagram, as shown in Figure 16.11.

FIG. 16.9
Views are used to access data from several different columns and tables to create a virtual table for data access.

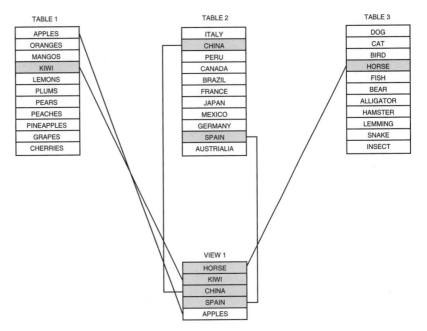

FIG. 16.10
Using Database Design View, you can create your view much like you would a conventional query.

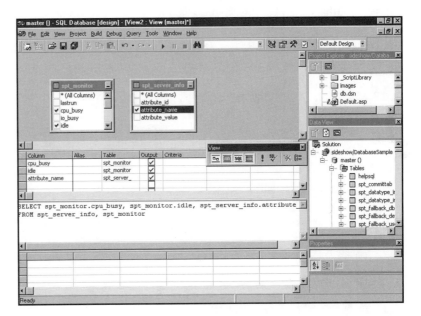

FIG. 16.11

Each table represents a grouping of columns that you can add to your view.

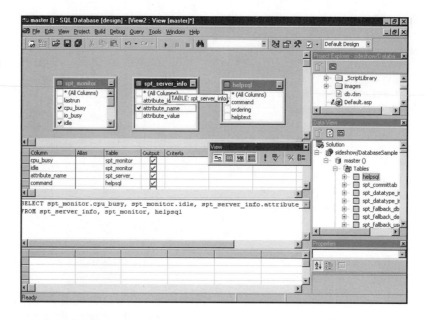

5. Each box represents an individual table, and each check box represents a column inside that table. Select the columns you want to include in your view by selecting the appropriate check boxes.

6. Choose File, Save View. The Save New View dialog box then appears, as shown in Figure 16.12. Save your view by entering the view name and click OK.

FIG. 16.12

In the Save New View dialog box, you can name your view in the database.

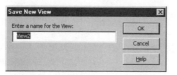

7. Close the database diagram.

TIP Database views can be a great help for your applications when you are working with multiple databases. You can create views that link the required tables into one virtual table used for your queries. Consider using views whenever you have a group of data you frequently need to return.

Using Stored Procedures

Stored procedures are collections of precompiled SQL statements that have flow control provisions for logic, conditional execution, and declared variables. These procedures are stored within the database and can be executed by calls in an application. You can use stored procedures to carry out tasks within your database, such as data manipulation or propagation. Traditionally, stored procedures (or stored procs) are created using database development and administration tools. Visual InterDev provides you with a means of creating stored procedures on remote databases that support them (such as SQL Server and Oracle).

The following is a list of a few possible uses for stored procedures in your Web applications:

- Control management of your database and the displaying of information
- Execution of a series of SQL statements in one action
- Massaging of data after it has been submitted to the database
- Expiration of data in the database that is no longer valid
- Data auditing

To create a stored procedure, follow these instructions:

1. Open the Data View window if it is not already open. You can do so by double-clicking your data connection in the DataEnvironment folder of the Project Explorer.
2. Expand the Data View tree until the Stored Procedures node is visible.
3. Right-click the Views node, and choose New Stored Procedure from the context menu. A stored procedure template is opened for editing, as shown in Figure 16.13. The template contains the skeleton SQL commands required for creating your procedure.

FIG. 16.13
Using the stored procedure template, you can define your procedure so that it can be compiled on the database server.

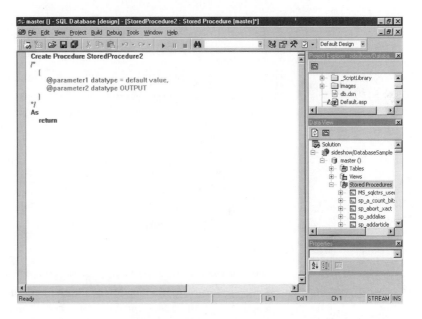

4. The first line of the procedure should look similar to the following:

```
Create Procedure StoredProcedure1
```

Replace StoredProcedure1 with the name of your stored procedure. For example, enter the following:

```
Create Procedure MyStoredProcedure
```

N O T E Remember that stored procedures, as database objects, require unique names. If you specify a name that is already in use, a SQL error occurs when the procedure is compiled and executed. ▪

5. Enter the procedure's remaining SQL statements in the template. Make sure that you are using the SQL statements specific to your database type. For example, use the following SQL statements for checking the users and activity on the SQL server:

```
declare    @low         int
   ,@high        int
   ,@spidlow    int
   ,@spidhigh   int
select    @low       =     0
   ,@high      = 32767
select    @spidlow   =     0
   ,@spidhigh    = 32767
if (    @loginame is not NULL
   AND    upper(@loginame) = 'ACTIVE'
   )
   begin
   select spid ,status
             ,loginame=substring(suser_name(suid),1,12)
          ,hostname ,blk=convert(char(5),blocked)
          ,dbname=substring(db_name(dbid),1,10),cmd
   from    sysprocesses
   where suid >= @low       and suid <= @high
   and    spid >= @spidlow and spid <= @spidhigh
   AND    upper(cmd) <> 'AWAITING COMMAND'
   end
else
   begin
   select spid ,status
             ,loginame=substring(suser_name(suid),1,12)
          ,hostname ,blk=convert(char(5),blocked)
          ,dbname=substring(db_name(dbid),1,10),cmd
   from    sysprocesses
   where suid >= @low       and suid <= @high
   and    spid >= @spidlow and spid <= @spidhigh
   end
return (0)
```

6. Choose File, Save StoredProcedure As to save your stored procedure.

7. To test your stored procedure, locate it in the Data View under the Stored Procedures node. Right-click the procedure name, and choose Execute from the context menu. The Output dialog box, shown in Figure 16.14, appears, displaying the results of your new procedure.

FIG. 16.14

The Output window displays the results of your stored procedure. You can use this window to see what will be returned from your procedure.

N O T E   Stored procedures require careful attention because you are directly interacting with your database on the database server itself. Exercise caution when altering your tables to avoid unexpected results. ▪

Debugging Stored Procedures

Developing stored procedures is much like developing server-side scripts. Because debugging complex procedures can be awkward and difficult, Microsoft has included a SQL Debugger with Visual InterDev. This SQL Debugger can be used to debug stored procedures and triggers on a SQL Server database. You must have the SQL Server Debugging Components installed and have Visual InterDev configured for remote debugging. For information on doing so, refer to the Microsoft documentation included with Visual InterDev.

The key difference between debugging stored procedures and client or server scripts is the approach. Unlike other processes, stored procedures and triggers are not debugged while they are running. Instead, they are debugged within the editor itself. To do so, follow these steps:

1. In the Data View window, right-click your stored procedure, and choose Debug from the context menu. Your stored procedure is opened in the editor. The key difference between this and traditional editing is the Debug menu.

2. From the Debug menu, use the debugger commands as you would in client- or server-side scripting. Use features such as breakpoints to step through procedures. You can also monitor variables and parameters through the Locals window.

3. Drag expressions into the Watch window to track the individual steps in your stored procedure. All SQL PRINT statements are displayed in the Output window.

You can carry out the debugging process whenever changes are made to your stored procedures.

From Here...

The Visual InterDev data environment makes working with databases much less of a strain for developers. You no longer need to rely on several different tools and arcane command files to complete your database development. For more information on database development in your Web application, take a look at these chapters:

Part
IV

Ch
16

- Chapter 15, "Setting Up a Database."
- Chapter 17, "Working with ADO and RDS."
- Chapter 22, "SQL Server Basics."

Working with ADO and RDS

In this chapter

What Is ADO (ActiveX Database Objects)? **360**

ADO Features **360**

Methods, Objects, and Properties of ADO **361**

Tuning ADO for Performance **382**

Debugging ADO-Based Applications **383**

ADO Error Codes **383**

What Is ADO (ActiveX Database Objects)?

Microsoft's new Digital Nervous System is built on universal data access. ActiveX Database Objects (ADO) is Microsoft's latest data access tool for high speed, ease of use, and small overhead for universal data access through an OLE DB provider. This layer is used between the application and ODBC so that, as the developer, you have access to all sorts of data without having to learn any specific API. Data Access Objects (DAO) and Remote Data Objects (RDO) are older tools that enabled you to have similar access.

Do you have to rewrite all your previous applications that used DAO and RDO? Currently, the answer is no. If it isn't broke, then don't fix it. ADO is for new and future application development. It can reach more data sources than DAO and RDO, and as ADO matures, it will have more features than DAO and RDO. Currently, the release version is 1.5; however, ADO 2.0 will be released with Visual Studio 6.0. This chapter is based on information from Microsoft's Web site for ADO documentation at **www.microsoft.com/data/ado/adords15**. The ADO application model is illustrated in Figure 17.1.

FIG. 17.1
The ADO application model.

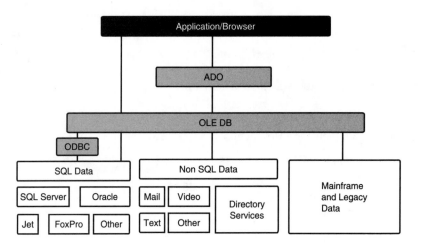

ADO Features

ADO supports key features for building client/server and Web-based applications, including the following:

- Independently created objects. With ADO, unlike DAO or RDO, you no longer have to navigate through a hierarchy to create objects because most ADO objects can be created independently. This capability allows you to create and track only the objects you need, and also results in fewer ADO objects and thus a smaller working set.

- Batch updating, which helps improve performance by locally caching changes to data and then writing them all to the server in a single update.

- Support for stored procedures with parameters and return values.
- Different cursor types, including support of back-end–specific cursors to databases such as SQL Server and Oracle.

You also can limit the number of returned rows and other query goals for performance tuning.

Multiple recordsets returned from stored procedures or batch statements also are supported.

Methods, Objects, and Properties of ADO

Every developer knows that using examples is always a good way to learn a new technology. Here, you'll learn about the methods, objects, and properties of ADO.

Listing 17.1 demonstrates the Value property with Field and Property objects by displaying field and property values for the Employees table.

Listing 17.1 The *Value* Property with *Field* and *Property* Objects

```
Public Sub ADOExample()
      Dim rstEmployees As ADODB.Recordset
      Dim fldLoop As ADODB.Field
      Dim prpLoop As ADODB.Property
      Dim strCnn As String

      ' Open recordset with data from Employee table.
      strCnn = "driver={SQL Server};server=srv;" & _
            "uid=sa;pwd=;database=pubs"
      Set rstEmployees = New ADODB.Recordset
      rstEmployees.Open "employee", strCnn, , , adCmdTable

      Debug.Print "Field values in rstEmployees"
      ' Enumerate the Fields collection of the Employees
      ' table.
      For Each fldLoop In rstEmployees.Fields
            ' Because Value is the default property of a
            ' Field object, the use of the actual keyword
            ' here is optional.
            Debug.Print "        " & fldLoop.Name & " = " & fldLoop.Value
      Next fldLoop

      Debug.Print "Property values in rstEmployees"
      ' Enumerate the Properties collection of the
      ' Recordset object.
      For Each prpLoop In rstEmployees.Properties
            ' Because Value is the default property of a
            ' Property object, the use of the actual keyword
            ' here is optional.
            Debug.Print "        " & prpLoop.Name & " = " & prpLoop.Value
      Next prpLoop

      rstEmployees.Close

End Sub
```

Objects in ADO

You can find seven objects in ADO:

- Connection—The connection to the data source (required)
- Command—The query or statement object (optional)
- Parameter—The parameter of the command (optional)
- Recordset—The improved cursor functionality
- Field—A column in a recordset
- Error—A storage place for multiple errors from the data source
- Property—A Property object represents a dynamic characteristic of an ADO object that is defined by the provider

You'll learn about these objects in more detail in the following sections.

Connection Object A Connection object represents an open connection to a data source. A Connection object represents a unique session with a data source. In the case of a client/server database system, it may be equivalent to an actual network connection to the server. Table 17.1 provides information on the methods of the Connection object, and Table 17.2 provides information about the properties.

Collections Errors, Properties

Table 17.1 *Connection* **Object Methods**

Method	Syntax	Parameters	Comments
BeginTrans CommitTrans RollbackTrans	*Object*.BeginTrans() *Object*.CommitTrans() *Object*.RollBackTrans()	None.	Manages transactions on the open connection, including nested transactions if the provider supports them, with the BeginTrans, CommitTrans, and RollbackTrans methods and the Attributes property. This feature is great.
Open,Close	*Object*.Open *ConnectionString*, *UserID*, *Password* *Object*.Close	*ConnectionString* optional; a string containing connection information. See the ConnectionString property for details on valid settings.	Opens and closes the connection.

Method	Syntax	Parameters	Comments
		UserID optional; a string containing a username to use when establishing the connection.	
		Password optional; a string containing a password to use when establishing the connection.	
		None for Close.	
OpenSchema	Set recordset = connection.OpenSchema (QueryType, Criteria, SchemaID)	QueryType; the type of schema query to run.	See Microsoft Web site at **http://www.microsoft.com/ data/ado/adords15/** for more details on OpenSchema.
		Criteria optional; an array of query constraints for each QueryType option, as listed below.	
Execute	Set recordset = Object.Execute (CommandText, RecordsAffected, Options)	CommandText; a string containing the SQL statement, table name, stored procedure, or provider-specific text to execute.	Executes the specified query, SQL statement, stored procedure, or provider-specific text.
		RecordsAffected optional; a Long variable to which the provider returns the number of records that the operation affected.	
		Options optional; a Long value that indicates how the provider should evaluate the CommandText argument.	

Part

IV

Ch

17

Table 17.2   *Connection* **Object Properties**

Property	Comments
Attributes	Indicates one or more characteristics of an object.
CommandTimeout	Indicates how long to wait while executing a command before terminating the attempt and generating an error.
ConnectionString	Contains the information used to establish a connection to a data source.
ConnectionTimeout	Indicates how long to wait while establishing a connection before terminating the attempt and generating an error.
CursorLocation	Sets or returns the location of the cursor engine.
DefaultDatabase	Indicates the default database for a Connection object.
IsolationLevel	Indicates the level of isolation for a Connection object.
Mode	Indicates the available permissions for modifying data in a connection.
Provider	Indicates the name of the provider for a Connection object.
State	Describes the current state of an object.
Version	Indicates the ADO version number.

Remarks

N O T E   To execute a query without using a Command object, pass a query string to the Execute method of a Connection object. However, a Command object is required when you want to re-execute the command text or use query parameters. ■

You can create Connection objects independently of any other previously defined object.

Example   Listing 17.2 demonstrates the Provider property by opening two Connection objects using different providers. It also uses the DefaultDatabase property to set the default database for the Microsoft ODBC Provider. This is an excellent feature.

Listing 17.2   Opening Two *Connection* Objects with Different Providers

```
Public Sub ConnectionExample()

    Dim cnn1 As ADODB.Connection
    Dim cnn2 As ADODB.Connection

    ' Open a connection using the Microsoft ODBC provider.
    Set cnn1 = New ADODB.Connection
    cnn1.ConnectionString = "driver={SQL Server};" & _
        "server=bigsmile;uid=sa;pwd=pwd"
```

```
cnn1.Open strCnn
cnn1.DefaultDatabase = "pubs"

' Display the provider.
MsgBox "Cnn1 provider: " & cnn1.Provider

' Open a connection using the Microsoft Jet provider.
Set cnn2 = New ADODB.Connection
cnn2.Provider = "Microsoft.Jet.OLEDB.3.51"
cnn2.Open "C:\Samples\northwind.mdb", "admin", ""

' Display the provider.
MsgBox "Cnn2 provider: " & cnn2.Provider

cnn1.Close
cnn2.Close

End Sub
```

Command Object   A Command object is a definition of a specific command that you intend to execute against a data source. Use a Command object to query a database and return records in a Recordset object, to execute a bulk operation, or to manipulate the structure of a database. See Tables 17.3 and 17.4 for information on the Command object's methods and properties, respectively.

Collections   Parameters, Properties

Table 17.3   *Command* Object Methods

Method	Syntax	Parameters	Comments
CreateParameter	Set parameter = command. CreateParameter (Name, Type, Direction, Size, Value)	Name optional; a string representing the name of the Parameter object.	Creates a new Parameter object with the specified properties.
		Type optional; a Long value specifying the data type of the Parameter object. See the Type property for valid settings.	If you know the names and properties of the parameters associated with the stored procedure or parameterized query you want to call, you can use the CreateParameter method to create Parameter objects with

continues

Table 17.3   Continued

Method	Syntax	Parameters	Comments
		Direction optional; a Long value specifying the type of Parameter object. Size optional; a Long value specifying the maximum length for the parameter value in characters or bytes. Value, varValue optional; a Variant specifying the value for the Parameter object.	the appropriate property settings and use the Append method to add them to the Parameters collection. This way, you can set and return parameter values without having to call the Refresh method on the Parameters collection to retrieve the parameter information from the provider, a potentially resource-intensive operation.
Execute	Set recordset = command.Execute (RecordsAffected, Parameters, Options)	RecordsAffected optional; a Long variable to which the provider returns the number of records that the operation affected. Parameters optional; a Variant array of parameter values passed with a SQL statement. Options optional; a Long value that indicates how the provider should evaluate the CommandText property of the Command object.	Using the Execute method on a Command object executes the query specified in the CommandText property of the object. If the CommandText property specifies a row-returning query, any results the execution generates are stored in a new Recordset object. If the command is not a row-returning query, the provider returns a closed Recordset object. Some application languages allow you to ignore this return value if no Recordset is desired.

Table 17.4 *Command* Object Properties

Property	Comments
ActiveConnection	Indicates to which Connection object the specified Command or Recordset object currently belongs.
CommandText	Contains the text of a command that you want to issue against a provider.
CommandTimeout	Indicates how long to wait while executing a command before terminating the attempt and generating an error.
CommandType	Indicates the type of a Command object.
Name	Indicates the name of an object.
Prepared	Indicates whether to save a compiled version of a command before execution.
State	Describes the current state of an object.

Remarks

N O T E To execute a query without using a Command object, pass a query string to the Execute method of a Connection object or to the Open method of a Recordset object. However, a Command object is required when you want to re-execute the command text or use query parameters. ▪

To create a Command object independently of a previously defined Connection object, set its ActiveConnection property to a valid connection string. ADO still creates a Connection object, but it doesn't assign that object to an object variable. However, if you are associating multiple Command objects with the same connection, you should explicitly create and open a Connection object; doing so assigns the Connection object to an object variable. If you don't set the Command object's ActiveConnection property to this object variable, ADO creates a new Connection object for each Command object, even if you use the same connection string.

To execute a Command, simply call it by its Name property on the associated Connection object. The Command must have its ActiveConnection property set to the Connection object. If the Command has parameters, pass values for them as arguments to the method.

Example Listing 17.3 uses the ActiveConnection, CommandText, CommandTimeout, CommandType, Size, and Direction properties to execute a stored procedure.

Listing 17.3 Using *Command* Object Properties to Execute a Stored Procedure

```
Public Sub CommandExample()

    Dim cnn1 As ADODB.Connection
    Dim cmdByRoyalty As ADODB.Command
    Dim prmByRoyalty As ADODB.Parameter
    Dim rstByRoyalty As ADODB.Recordset
    Dim rstAuthors As ADODB.Recordset
    Dim intRoyalty As Integer
    Dim strAuthorID As String
    Dim strCnn As String

    ' Define a command object for a stored procedure.
    Set cnn1 = New ADODB.Connection
    strCnn = "driver={SQL Server};server=srv;" & _
          "uid=sa;pwd=;database=pubs"
    cnn1.Open strCnn
    Set cmdByRoyalty = New ADODB.Command
    Set cmdByRoyalty.ActiveConnection = cnn1
    cmdByRoyalty.CommandText = "byroyalty"
    cmdByRoyalty.CommandType = adCmdStoredProc
    cmdByRoyalty.CommandTimeout = 15

    ' Define the stored procedure's input parameter.
    intRoyalty = Trim(InputBox( _
          "Enter royalty:"))
    Set prmByRoyalty = New ADODB.Parameter
    prmByRoyalty.Type = adInteger
    prmByRoyalty.Size = 3
    prmByRoyalty.Direction = adParamInput
    prmByRoyalty.Value = intRoyalty
    cmdByRoyalty.Parameters.Append prmByRoyalty

    ' Create a recordset by executing the command.
    Set rstByRoyalty = cmdByRoyalty.Execute()

    ' Open the Authors table to get author names for display.
    Set rstAuthors = New ADODB.Recordset
    rstAuthors.Open "authors", strCnn, , , adCmdTable

    ' Print current data in the recordset, adding
    ' author names from Authors table.
    Debug.Print "Authors with " & intRoyalty & _
          " percent royalty"
    Do While Not rstByRoyalty.EOF
          strAuthorID = rstByRoyalty!au_id
          Debug.Print , rstByRoyalty!au_id & ", ";
          rstAuthors.Filter = "au_id = '" & strAuthorID & "'"
          Debug.Print rstAuthors!au_fname & " " & _
                rstAuthors!au_lname
```

```
        rstByRoyalty.MoveNext
    Loop

    rstByRoyalty.Close
    rstAuthors.Close
    cnn1.Close

End Sub
```

***Parameter* Object**   A `Parameter` object represents a parameter or argument associated with a `Command` object based on a parameterized query or stored procedure. Table 17.5 describes the `Parameter` object's methods, and Table 17.6 describes its properties.

Collections

Properties

Table 17.5   *Parameter* Object Methods

Method	Syntax	Parameter	Comments
AppendChunk	*object.* AppendChunk Data	Data; a Variant containing the data you want to append to the object.	Use the AppendChunk method on a Field or Parameter object to fill it with long binary or character data. In situations where system memory is limited, you can use the AppendChunk method to manipulate long values in portions rather than in their entirety.

Table 17.6   *Parameter* Object Properties

Property	Comments
Attributes	Indicates one or more characteristics of an object.
Direction	Indicates whether the Parameter represents an input parameter, an output parameter, or both, or if the parameter is the return value from a stored procedure.
Name	Indicates the name of an object.
	Sets or returns the name of a parameter with the Name property.

continues

Table 17.6 Continued

Property	Comments
NumericScale	Indicates the scale of Numeric values in a Parameter or Field object.
Precision	Indicates the degree of precision for Numeric values in a Parameter object or for numeric Field objects.
Size	Indicates the maximum size, in bytes or characters, of a Parameter object.
Type	Indicates the operational type or data type of a Parameter, Field, or Property object.
Value	Indicates the value assigned to a Field, Parameter, or Property object.
	Sets or returns the value of a parameter with the Value property.

Remarks   Many providers support *parameterized* commands. With these commands, the desired action is defined once, but variables (or parameters) are used to alter some details of the command. For example, a SQL SELECT statement can use a parameter to define the matching criteria of a WHERE clause and another to define the column name for a SORT BY clause.

Parameter objects represent parameters associated with parameterized queries, or the in/out arguments and the return values of stored procedures. Depending on the functionality of the provider, some collections, methods, or properties of a Parameter object may not be available.

Recordset Object   A Recordset object represents the entire set of records from a base table or the results of an executed command. At any time, the Recordset object refers only to a single record within the set as the current record. See Tables 17.7 and 17.8 for details about the Recordset object's methods and properties, respectively.

Collections   Fields, Properties

Table 17.7 *Recordset* Object Methods

Method	Syntax	Parameters	Comments
AddNew	recordset. AddNew *Fields*, *Values*	*Fields* optional; a single name or an array of names or ordinal positions of the fields in the new record.	Creates a new record for an updatable Recordset object.

Method	Syntax	Parameters	Comments
		Values optional; a single value or an array of values for the fields in the new record. If *Fields* is an array, *Values* must also be an array with the same number of members; otherwise, an error occurs. The order of field names must match the order of field values in each array.	
CancelBatch	*recordset*.Can celBatch *AffectRecords*	*AffectRecords* optional; an AffectEnum value that determines how many records the CancelBatch method will affect.	Cancels a pending batch update.
CancelUpdate	*recordset*.Can celUpdate	None.	Cancels any changes made to the current record or to a new record prior to calling the Update method.
Clone	Set *rstDuplicate* = *rstOriginal*. Clone()	None.	Creates a duplicate Recordset object from an existing Recordset object.
			Use the Clone method to create multiple, duplicate Recordset objects, particularly if you want to be able to maintain more than one current record in a given set of records. Using the Clone method is more efficient than creating and opening a new Recordset object with the same definition as the original.

continues

Table 17.7   Continued

Method	Syntax	Parameters	Comments
Close	*object*.Close	None.	Closes an open object and any dependent objects.
Delete	*recordset*. Delete *AffectRecords*	*AffectRecords* optional; an AffectEnum value that determines how many records the Delete method will affect.	Deletes the current record or group of records.
GetRows	*array = recordset*. GetRows(*Rows, Start, Fields*)	*Rows* optional; a Long expression indicating the number of records to retrieve. Default is adGet RowsRest (-1). *Start* optional; a String or Variant that evaluates to the bookmark for the record from which the GetRows operation should begin. *Fields* optional; a Variant representing a single field name or ordinal position or an array of field names or ordinal position numbers. ADO returns only the data in these fields.	Retrieves multiple records of a Recordset into an array.

Method	Syntax	Parameters	Comments
Move	*recordset*. Move *Num Records*, *Start*	*NumRecords*; a signed Long expression specifying the number of records the current record position moves. *Start* optional; a String or Variant that evaluates to a bookmark.	Moves the position of the current record in a Recordset object.
MoveFirst MoveLast MoveNext MovePrevious	*recordset*. MoveFirst *recordset*. MoveLast *recordset*. MoveNext *recordset*. **MovePrevious**	None.	Moves to the first, last, next, or previous record in a specified Recordset object and makes that record the current record.
NextRecordset	Set *recordset2* = *recordset1*. NextRecordset (*Records Affected*)	*RecordsAffected* Optional; a Long variable to which the provider returns the number of records that the current operation affected.	Clears the current Recordset object and returns the next Recordset by advancing through a series of commands.
Open	***recordset*.** Open *Source*, *Active Connection*, *CursorType*, *LockType*, *Options*	*Source* optional; a Variant that evaluates to a valid Command object variable name, a SQL statement, a table name, or a stored procedure call.	Opens a cursor.

Part

IV

Ch

17

continues

Table 17.7   Continued

Method	Syntax	Parameters	Comments
		ActiveConnection optional; either a Variant that evaluates to a valid Connection object variable name, or a String containing ConnectionString parameters.	
		CursorType optional; a CursorTypeEnum value that determines the type of cursor that the provider should use when opening the Recordset.	
		LockType optional; a LockTypeEnum value that determines what type of locking (concurrency) the provider should use when opening the Recordset.	
		Options optional; a Long value that indicates how the provider should evaluate the *Source* argument if it represents something other than a Command object.	
Requery	*recordset.* Requery	None.	Updates the data in a Recordset object by re-executing the query on which the object is based.

Method	Syntax	Parameters	Comments
Resync	*recordset.* Resync *Affect Records*	*AffectRecords* optional; an AffectEnum value that determines how many records the Resync method will affect.	Refreshes the data in the current Recordset object from the underlying database.
Supports	*boolean =* *recordset.* Supports(*CursorOptions*)	*CursorOptions*; a Long expression.	Determines whether a specified Recordset object supports a particular type of functionality.
Update	*recordset.* Update *Fields*, *Values*	*Fields* optional; a Variant representing a single name or a Variant array representing names or ordinal positions of the field or fields you want to modify. *Values* optional; a Variant representing a single value or a Variant array representing values for the field or fields in the new record.	Saves any changes you make to the current record of a Recordset object.
UpdateBatch	*recordset.* UpdateBatch *AffectRecords*	*AffectRecords* optional; an AffectEnum value that determines how many records the UpdateBatch method will affect.	Writes all pending batch updates to disk.

Part

IV

Ch

17

Table 17.8 *Recordset* Object Properties

Property	Comment
AbsolutePage	Specifies in which page the current record resides.
AbsolutePositon	Specifies the ordinal position of a Recordset object's current record.
ActiveConnection	Indicates to which Connection object the specified Command or Recordset object currently belongs.
BOF	BOF indicates that the current record position is before the first record in a Recordset object.
Bookmark	Returns a bookmark that uniquely identifies the current record in a Recordset object or sets the current record in a Recordset object to the record identified by a valid bookmark.
Cachesize	Indicates the number of records from a Recordset object that are cached locally in memory.
CursorLocation	Sets or returns the location of the cursor engine.
CursorType	Indicates the type of cursor used in a Recordset object.
EditMode	Indicates the editing status of the current record.
EOF	EOF indicates that the current record position is after the last record in a Recordset object.
Filter	Indicates a filter for data in a Recordset.
LockType	Indicates the type of locks placed on records during editing.
MarshalOptions	Indicates which records are to be marshaled back to the server.
MaxRecords	Indicates the maximum number of records to return to a Recordset from a query.
PageCount	Indicates how many pages of data the Recordset object contains.
PageSize	Indicates how many records constitute one page in the Recordset.
RecordCount	Indicates the current number of records in a Recordset object.
Source	Indicates the source for the data in a Recordset object (Command object, SQL statement, table name, or stored procedure).
State	Describes the current state of an object.
Status	Indicates the status of the current record with respect to batch updates or other bulk operations.

Remarks   You use Recordset objects to manipulate data from a provider. When you use ADO, you manipulate data almost entirely using Recordset objects. All Recordset objects are constructed using records (rows) and fields (columns). Depending on the functionality supported by the provider, some Recordset methods or properties may not be available.

Recordset objects can also be cached locally. For example, in a Web-based application, you can open a Recordset on the client, using the progID ADOR. The Remote Data Service provides a mechanism for local data caching and local cursoring of remote Recordset data. A client-side Recordset can be used in the same way as a server-side Recordset, and supports almost all the normal Recordset methods and properties. Recordset methods and properties that aren't supported on a client-side Recordset, or that behave differently, are noted in the Help topics for those properties and methods.

Four different cursor types are defined in ADO:

- Dynamic cursor—Allows you to view additions, changes, and deletions by other users, and allows all types of movement through the Recordset that don't rely on bookmarks; allows bookmarks if the provider supports them.

- Keyset cursor—Behaves like a dynamic cursor, except that it prevents you from seeing records that other users add, and prevents access to records that other users delete. Data changes by other users will still be visible. It always supports bookmarks and therefore allows all types of movement through the Recordset.

- Static cursor—Provides a static copy of a set of records for you to use to find data or generate reports; always allows bookmarks and therefore allows all types of movement through the Recordset. Additions, changes, or deletions by other users will not be visible. This is the only type of cursor allowed when you open a client-side (ADOR) Recordset object.

- Forward-only cursor—Behaves identically to a dynamic cursor except that it allows you to scroll only forward through records. This capability improves performance in situations in which you need to make only a single pass through a recordset.

Set the CursorType property prior to opening the Recordset to choose the cursor type, or pass a CursorType argument with the Open method. Some providers don't support all cursor types. Check the documentation for the provider. If you don't specify a cursor type, ADO opens a forward-only cursor by default.

When Recordset objects are used with some providers (such as the Microsoft ODBC Provider for OLE DB in conjunction with Microsoft SQL Server), you can create Recordset objects independently of a previously defined object by passing a connection string with the method. ADO still creates a Connection object, but it doesn't assign that object to an object variable. However, if you are opening multiple Recordset objects over the same connection, you should explicitly create and open a Connection object; this way, you can assign the Connection object to an object variable. If you don't use this object variable when opening your Recordset objects, ADO creates a new Connection object for each new Recordset, even if you pass the same connection string.

You can create as many Recordset objects as needed.

Field Object   A Field object represents a column of data with a common data type. A Recordset object has a Fields collection made up of Field objects. Each Field object corresponds to a column in the Recordset. You use the Value property of Field objects to set or return data for the current record. Depending on the functionality the provider exposes, some collections, methods, or properties of a Field object may not be available. Table 17.9 provides information about the Field object's methods, and Table 17.10 details its properties.

Collections

Properties

Table 17.9 *Field* Object Methods

Method	Syntax	Parameters	Comments
AppendChunk	*object*.Append Chunk *Data*	*Data*; a Variant containing the data you want to append to the object.	Appends data to a large text or binary data Field or Parameter object.
GetChunk	*variable* = *field*.GetChunk (*Size*)	*Size*; a Long expression equal to the number of bytes or characters you want to retrieve.	Returns all or a portion of the contents of a large text or binary data Field object.

Table 17.10 *Field* Object Properties

Property	Comments
ActualSize	Indicates the actual length of a field's value.
Attributes	Indicates one or more characteristics of an object.
DefinedSize	Indicates the defined size of a Field object.
Name	Indicates the name of an object.
NumericScale	Indicates the scale of Numeric values in a Parameter or Field object.
OriginalValue	Indicates the value of a Field that existed in the record before any changes were made.
Precision	Indicates the degree of precision for Numeric values in a Parameter object or for numeric Field objects.
Type	Indicates the operational type or data type of a Parameter, Field, or Property object.
UnderlyingValue	Indicates a Field object's current value in the database.
Value	Indicates the value assigned to a Field, Parameter, or Property object.

***Error* Object**   An `Error` object contains details about data access errors pertaining to a single operation involving the provider. Any operation involving ADO objects can generate one or more provider errors. As each error occurs, one or more `Error` objects are placed in the `Errors` collection of the `Connection` object. When another ADO operation generates an error, the `Errors` collection is cleared, and the new set of `Error` objects is placed in the `Errors` collection. The `Error` object's properties are described in Table 17.11.

Table 17.11   *Error* Object Properties

Property	Comments
Description	A descriptive string associated with an `Error` object.
HelpContext	Indicates the help file and topic associated with an `Error` object.
HelpFile	Indicates the help file and topic associated with an `Error` object.
NativeError	Indicates the provider-specific error code for a given `Error` object.
Number	Indicates the number that uniquely identifies an `Error` object.
Source	Indicates the name of the object or application that originally generated an error.
SQLState	Indicates the SQL state for a given `Error` object.

Part
IV

Ch
17

Remarks

N O T E   Each `Error` object represents a specific provider error, not an ADO error. ADO errors are exposed to the runtime exception handling mechanism. For example, in Microsoft Visual Basic, the occurrence of an ADO-specific error triggers an `On  Error` event and appears in the `Err` object. For a complete list of ADO errors, see the "ADO Error Codes" section later in this chapter. ■

When a provider error occurs, it is placed in the `Errors` collection of the `Connection` object. ADO supports the return of multiple errors by a single ADO operation to allow for error information specific to the provider. To obtain this rich error information in an error handler, use the appropriate error-trapping features of the language or environment you are working with; then use nested loops to enumerate the properties of each `Error` object in the `Errors` collection.

In VBScript, if no valid `Connection` object is present, you need to retrieve error information from the `Err` object.

Just as providers do, ADO clears the `OLE Error Info` object before making a call that could potentially generate a new provider error. However, the `Errors` collection on the `Connection` object is cleared and populated only when the provider generates a new error, or when the `Clear` method is called.

Some properties and methods return warnings that appear as Error objects in the Errors collection but don't halt a program's execution. Before you call the Resync, UpdateBatch, or CancelBatch methods on a Recordset object, or before you set the Filter property on a Recordset object, call the Clear method on the Errors collection so that you can read the Count property of the Errors collection to test for returned warnings.

Property Object   A Property object represents a dynamic characteristic of an ADO object that is defined by the provider. Property object properties are detailed in Table 17.12.

Table 17.12   *Property* Object Properties

Property	Comments
Attributes	Indicates one or more characteristics of an object. The Attributes property is a long value that indicates characteristics of the property specific to the provider.
Name	Indicates the name of an object.
Type	Indicates the operational type or data type of a Parameter, Field, or Property object. The Type property is an integer that specifies the property data type.
Value	Indicates the value assigned to a Field, Parameter, or Property object. The Value property is a variant that contains the property setting.

Remarks   ADO objects have two types of properties: built-in and dynamic. Built-in properties are those properties implemented in ADO and immediately available to any new object, using the familiar MyObject.Property syntax.

Built-in properties don't appear as Property objects in an object's Properties collection, so although you can change their values, you cannot modify their characteristics or delete them.

Dynamic properties are defined by the underlying data provider, and appear in the Properties collection for the appropriate ADO object. For example, a property specific to the provider may indicate if a Recordset object supports transactions or updating. These additional properties appear as Property objects in that Recordset object's Properties collection. Dynamic properties can be referenced only through the collection, using the MyObject.Properties(0) or MyObject.Properties("Name") syntax.

Errors Collection

The Errors collection contains all the Error objects created in response to a single failure involving the provider. Errors collection methods are described in Table 17.13; properties are described in Table 17.14.

Table 17.13 *Errors* Collection Methods

Method	Syntax	Parameter	Comments
Clear	object.Clear	None.	Removes all the objects in a collection.
Item	Set *object* = *collection*. Item (*Index*)	*Index*; a Variant that evaluates either to the name or to the ordinal number of an object in a collection.	Returns a specific member of a collection by name or ordinal number.

Table 17.14 *Errors* Collection Properties

Property	Comment
Count	Indicates the number of objects in a collection.

Remarks   The set of Error objects in the Errors collection describes all errors that occurred in response to a single statement. Enumerating the specific errors in the Errors collection enables your error-handling routines to more precisely determine the cause and origin of an error, and take appropriate steps to recover.

See the "Error Object" section earlier in this chapter for a more detailed explanation of the way a single ADO operation can generate multiple errors.

Fields and *Properties* Collections

A Fields collection contains all the Field objects of a Recordset object. A Properties collection contains all the Property objects for a specific instance of an object. The Fields and Properties collections' methods are detailed in Table 17.15; properties are detailed in Table 17.16.

Table 17.15 *Fields* and *Properties* Collections Methods

Method	Syntax	Parameter	Comment
Item	Set *object* = *collection*. Item (*Index*)	*Index*; a Variant that evaluates either to the name or to the ordinal number of an object in a collection.	Returns a specific member of a collection by name or ordinal number.

continues

Table 17.15   Continued

Method	Syntax	Parameter	Comment
Refresh	*Collection.* Refresh	None.	Updates the objects in a collection to reflect objects available from and specific to the provider.

Table 17.16   *Fields* and *Properties* Collections Properties

Property	Comment
Count	Indicates the number of objects in a collection.

Remarks   A Recordset object has a Fields collection made up of Field objects. Each Field object corresponds to a column in the Recordset. You can populate the Fields collection before opening the Recordset by calling the Refresh method on the collection.

See the "Field Object" section earlier in this chapter for a more detailed explanation of how to use Field objects.

Some ADO objects have a Properties collection made up of Property objects. Each Property object corresponds to a characteristic of the ADO object specific to the provider.

See the "Property Object" section earlier in this chapter for a more detailed explanation of how to use Property objects.

Tuning ADO for Performance

The key to tuning ADO for performance is bytes. Yes, it always comes down to the amount of data used by ADO. The fewer bytes needed, the better. Indexes and Recordset Types are key; however, a developer's method may improve performance as well. Use only the necessary fields; using unnecessary fields means wasting bytes and increasing the stress on the database server. Calculated fields are time consuming, so minimize their use. Here is a quick example. Let's say you have to calculate the average salary for managers in a company with 10,000 employees and 20 managers. If you first calculate the average salary of all the employees and then filter the list for only managers, an extraneous 9,980 average calculations are done. If you first filter the list and then average only the 20 managers, the calculations for the 20 managers are done, resulting in a big performance gain. Always think about how you create your queries.

An excellent tool is coming out in SQL 7.0 that enables you to graphically show the plan of your query. If you are using a combination of ADO and SQL Server 7.0, use the showplan tool. The showplan tool will even suggest and implement improvements.

Indexes

Use indexed columns for searching recordsets. The database can process the requests more quickly in a properly indexed table.

Recordset Types

Use the appropriate locking and cursors when creating recordsets. If you don't need an updatable recordset, make sure that it is read-only. This way, you get less overhead and better performance. The same is true for cursor types: If you don't need a scrollable cursor, just use a forward-scrolling cursor to decrease the load and increase performance.

Debugging ADO-Based Applications

Ninety percent of ADO problems occur with the connections to the database. To solve these problems, make sure that all required software and hardware are being used, all database drivers are working on the Web server, and proper protocols are installed and being used to communicate with the Web and database server.

By testing your applications, you can debug any ADO bugs or errors. Watch out for locking errors that become evident only after concurrent usage. Also, check for load problems with high usage and large data manipulation such as audio, video, or memo files.

Part
IV

Ch
17

ADO Error Codes

In addition to the provider errors that are described in the "Error Object" and "Errors Collection" sections, ADO itself can return errors to the exception-handling mechanism of your runtime environment. Both decimal and hexadecimal error code values are shown in Table 17.17.

Table 17.17   ADO Error Codes

Constant Name	Number	Description
AdErrInvalidArgument	3001 x800A0BB9	The application is using arguments that are of the wrong type, out of the acceptable range, or in conflict with one another.
AdErrNoCurrentRecord	3021 800A0BCD	Either BOF or EOF is True, or the current record has been deleted; the operation requested by the application requires a current record.

continues

Table 17.17 Continued

Constant Name	Number	Description
AdErrIllegalOperation	3219 x800A0C93	The operation requested by the application isn't allowed in this context.
AdErrInTransaction	3246 x800A0CAE	The application may not explicitly close a Connection object while in the middle of a transaction.
AdErrFeatureNotAvailable	3251 x800A0CB3	The operation requested by the application isn't supported by the provider.
AdErrItemNotFound	3265 x800A0CC1	ADO could not find the object in the collection corresponding to the name or ordinal reference requested by the application.
AdErrObjectInCollection	3367 x800A0D27	The application cannot append the object; the object is already in the collection.
AdErrObjectNotSet	3420 x800A0D5C	The object referenced by the application no longer points to a valid object.
AdErrDataConversion	3421 x800A0D5D	The application is using a value of the wrong type for the current operation.
AdErrObjectClosed	3704 x800A0E78	The operation requested by the application isn't allowed if the object is closed.
AdErrObjectOpen	3705 x800A0E79	The operation requested by the application isn't allowed if the object is open.
AdErrProviderNotFound	3706 x800A0E7A	ADO could not find the specified provider.

Constant Name	Number	Description
AdErrBoundToCommand	3707 x800A0E7B	The application cannot change the property of an object with an object as its source.
AdErrInvalidParamInfo	3708 x800A0E7C	The application has improperly defined a parameter object.
AdErrInvalidConnection	3709 x800A0E7D	The application requested an operation on an object with a reference to a closed or invalid Connection object.

From Here...

ADO is a key component of Microsoft's Universal Data Access. ADO will replace RDO and DAO in Microsoft's development suite of tools. It is a powerful, robust component for Web site developers because it enables an easy-to-use, powerful, and lightweight database interface. The possibilities are endless.

Visual InterDev 6 Creativity Tool

18   The Image Composer and GIF Animator   389

The Image Composer and GIF Animator

In this chapter

The Image Composer   **390**

Key Features of Image Composer 1.5   **390**

Using Image Composer with Visual InterDev   **391**

Getting Started with the Image Composer Interface   **391**

Creating and Editing Your First Sprites   **393**

Changing and Copying Sprites   **395**

Using Composition Guides   **396**

Using Clip Art and Buttons   **397**

Using the GIF Animator   **398**

The Image Composer

Image Composer is a step beyond "pixel-pushing" paint programs such as Adobe Photoshop. Using an object-oriented approach to electronic painting, Image Composer stands head and shoulders above other paint programs. Working with pictures as objects, you can specify how transparent each object is, and the underlying objects show through automatically. When you are finished with a composition, you can flatten it into a standard image format such as GIF or JPEG. The tutorials in this chapter give you a good taste of working with an object-oriented painting program.

Key Features of Image Composer 1.5

The original release of Visual InterDev included Image Composer 1.0. Visual InterDev 6 includes the newest release of Image Composer, version 1.5. This new version has seen some improvements and enhancements to improve usability and functionality. The following are the new elements or changes in Image Composer 1.5:

- *Button Wizard and Editor.* Now you can easily create stylized buttons for your Web site by using the new Button Wizard and Editor. Using the Button Wizard, you can create from 1 to 20 buttons in one session.

- *Editable Text Sprites.* You can now make changes to text sprites that have already been created.

- *Cutout Tools.* New tools on the Cutout palette make it easier for you to create masks and sprites from portions of existing sprites.

- *Object Smoothing.* Unlike the previous version, Image Composer 1.5 now gives you the option of whether you want to antialias jagged edges in sprites.

- *Select Button.* The new Select button in the Toolbox lets you select multiple sprites when you are working with a tool or dialog box.

- *Continuous Crop.* The Crop tool is now continuously active in the Arrange palette. It lets you make step-by-step changes in a sprite's cropping as you work.

- *Variable Drop Shadows.* Now you can create shadows for your sprites with a diffused or well-defined edge.

- *Save for the Web Wizard.* This new wizard helps you save your images for your Web site. You can use it to control transparency and image quality, and monitor download times for your pictures.

- *New File Formats.* Image Composer supports Graphic Interchange Format (GIF), JPEG (JPG), Portable Network graphics (PNG), .MIX, and FlashPix (FPX) formats for emerging standards.

- *User Interface Changes.* The Image Composer interface has been redesigned for more accessible workspace and composition space, new tool palettes, direct links to the GIF Animator, and more.

Using Image Composer with Visual InterDev

Image Composer acts as an extension to Visual InterDev, allowing you to create and manipulate graphics for your Web sites. To use Image Composer as your image editing tool in Visual InterDev, you must first define Image Composer as the default editor for graphic files. To do so, follow these steps:

1. Right-click an image file (such as a .GIF file) in your Web project. From the context menu, choose Open With…. This opens the Open With dialog box.

2. Click the Add… button to add Image Composer to the list. This opens an Add Program dialog box.

3. Click the Browse button to select the Program Name. Locate the executable for Image Composer on your file system.

4. Enter a Friendly Name in the text box, such as Image Composer.

5. Click OK to return to the Open With dialog box.

6. Select Image Composer (or the Friendly Name you entered in step 4) and click the Set as Default button. This informs Visual InterDev to use Image Composer as the default editor for the file type you selected.

7. Click the Open button to open the image in Image Composer.

You can repeat this process for each image type that you want Image Composer to be the default editor for (keeping in mind the file formats Image Composer supports, of course). By setting Image Composer as the default editor for these file types, Visual InterDev recognizes that it should use Image Composer as the associated program whenever you double-click an image file in the Project Explorer.

Getting Started with the Image Composer Interface

Image Composer's interface is much like any other Windows-oriented program, with the unique twists needed for a graphic manipulation utility. What makes Image Composer shine is its selection of tools and utilities, all available in easily accessible forms such as toolbars and palettes.

You'll be spending most of your time using the primary toolbar, which runs along the left side of the screen. These 12 options, which encapsulate Image Composer's functions almost entirely, are displayed in Figure 18.1.

Most of the tools in this toolbar spawn a palette of their own if you click them. This way, the Image Composer interface never gets too cluttered, because you can never have more than one type of palette open at once. The tools and the palettes they spawn are listed in the following, from the top of the left-hand toolbar to the bottom:

FIG. 18.1

By using the primary toolbar, you can create effective graphics within Image Composer.

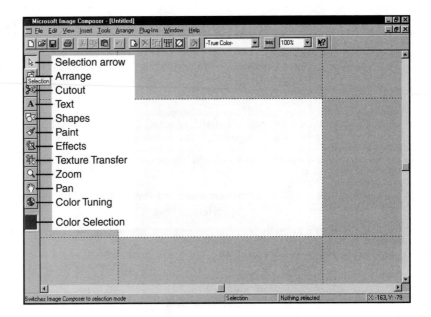

- The *Selection* arrow turns Image Composer into selection mode. From here, you can select and deselect a variety of objects, all to be manipulated later. If the selection controls seem a bit too simple, that's because Image Composer is a sprite-based system; sprites remain separate until combined. Because each sprite is usually a discrete object, all you really need to select one is a simple arrow pointer.

- The *Arrange* button brings up the Arrange palette. From here, you can engage in a variety of activities, including warping, aligning, flipping, scaling, and cropping. The align tools especially are quite flexible, with 12 different options such as Align Centers, Lower Left Corner, Horizontal Centers, and Touch Edges. The Arrange tool is essentially a macro-manipulator; it operates on a sprite-wide scale to create larger changes within a picture.

- The *Cutout* button spawns the Cutout palette. The Cutout tool is actually more powerful than the button image that a pair of scissors implies. Here, you can find the complex selection tools allowing you to work on a pixel-by-pixel basis or select parts of objects based on color.

- The *Text* button generates the Text Control palette. From here, you create text objects to make up your headlines, articles, and menus. You can control all the important attributes such as text alignment, font size, style, and color. Note that you can go back and edit the text after it has been placed with this program, as opposed to bitmap programs such as Photoshop or Fractal Paint.

- Next comes the *Shapes* button, spawning the Shapes palette. The Shapes palette generates and edits basic geometric forms. From here, you can create and control several shapes using Bezier curves. You can also set options such as the shape's color, opacity, line weight, and so on.

N O T E A *Bezier curve* is a simple object-based shape. You can create the curve by placing "points," with a line connecting each point. By moving one of the points, you can influence the behavior of the line. ■

- Clicking the *Paint* button produces the Paint palette. From here, you can manage Image Composer's several painting tools, such as an airbrush, traditional paintbrush, and pencil. However, you can also access several other tools, such as the Dodge/Burn tool and the Contrast and Tint controls. Finally, you can define brush sizes and attributes.

- The *Effects* button brings up the powerful Effects palette. The Effects palette is the "gizmo-laden" segment of Image Composer. From here, you can apply effects to your sprites such as Charcoal, Colored Pencil, Vortex, and a host of others. You can also control the behaviors of these various effects by clicking over to the Details tab and changing any of the values found therein.

- Selecting the *Texture Transfer* button brings up the Texture Transfer palette. This powerful feature lets you combine two different sprites in a variety of ways. The Texture Transfer palette lets you control how the sprites merge. Possible merge types include Glue, Snip, Tile, and many more.

- Next comes the *Zoom* button, which doesn't actually have an associated palette. However, it's just as valuable a tool as any of the others. Simply select the Zoom tool and click a desired area to zoom in on it. Hold down the Ctrl key and click to zoom out.

- Like the Zoom button, the *Pan* button doesn't summon a new palette. Instead, it lets you position your viewpoint. This capability is especially handy when you have zoomed in and need to move a picture around so that certain parts of it are visible.

- The Color Tuning palette is brought to the front by selecting the *Color Tuning* button, second from the bottom. These powerful tools let you control the color values for a particular sprite. You can also adjust the Highlight/Shadow depth, as well as define the upper and lower ranges of intensity in the Dynamic Range tab.

- Finally comes the Color Selection square, firmly situated on the bottom of the toolbar. By clicking here, you can change the current color to whatever you please. More important though, you can set and import color palettes, ensuring that your Web graphics share the same colors.

Just about every single palette needs to have a sprite selected in order to be effective. You'll find that many of the options you want to pursue are mysteriously grayed out until you actually make a selection. Although you can select multiple sprites, not all of the preceding tools work on them *en masse*. The tools that can influence multiple sprites at once are Effects, Texture Transfer, and Arrange. The rest either work on an individual basis or simply create new sprites.

Part

V

Ch

18

Creating and Editing Your First Sprites

As you may have guessed, sprites form the basis of Image Composer's design philosophy. Sprites are Image Composer's representation of grouped graphical objects. Sprites may be made up of many different components, creating a complete object. You can simply think of a sprite as an object within Image Composer, and that no image can exist without being composed of objects. If you just start Image Composer and try to start painting, you'll find that you can't. Most of the available options are grayed out and are inaccessible. They are unavailable because you don't have a sprite to act upon, and in Image Composer even the background is a sprite.

Put another way, a new Image Composer document is an entirely clean slate. Traditionally, in graphics programs, you have a default blank "page" to start with, and you can then set up the page attributes as you want. Image Composer lets you create your own background, granting a degree of control not seen in many other programs. You also should note that the background is not differentiated from any of the other sprites; it is in no way special or unique.

N O T E Despite what you may think, a sprite in this context is *not* an animation term. Although animators have (and still do) referred to sprites in their jargon, Microsoft has settled on a different definition. Image Composer sprites are graphical entities—a logical grouping of elements to create a graphical object. Sprites also have nothing to do with mythology. ▪

Obviously, then, you need to create a sprite of some kind before you can proceed. Remember that a sprite is basically anything that appears in your document. A sprite is usually a geometric primitive that has been modified somehow, be it by a size change or by having something painted on it. Every sprite that you'll be making yourself will likely originate from the Shapes palette. To create a sprite, you must follow these steps:

1. Click the Shapes button to bring up the Shapes palette.
2. Decide what variety of shape you want. You can choose from Rectangle, Oval, Curve, or Polygon. For example, choose the oval button to create a circular object.
3. Draw the shape to the size you want on your screen. Note that you can change the attributes of the shape, and the figure you've just drawn isn't the "final" version.
4. Set the Opacity option to determine the shape's translucence. Set how hard or soft you want the edges by using the Edge control. Change the spline options by using the Curve and Polygon Options.
5. If you haven't done so already, choose a color from the Color Picker.
6. Click the Create button to render your shape. Your shape should appear similar to the one shown in Figure 18.2.

So now that you've got your sprite, you can make some basic changes to it. At this point, the rest of the tools come into play. If you want to change your sprite's facing, alignment, or scale, select it and click the Arrange button. However, if you're creating your sprite from scratch and not importing an existing image, you may want to paint on it. To paint on a sprite, follow these steps:

1. Select the sprite by using the Selection arrow. You can click the button on top of the toolbar, or just click anywhere that isn't a sprite in the document window. The Selection tool is chosen by default.
2. Click the Paint button, bringing up the Paint palette, shown in Figure 18.3.

FIG. 18.2

Your new sprite is now visible. Sprite creation is at its heart very easy; it can become more complex if you choose to create more intricate sprites.

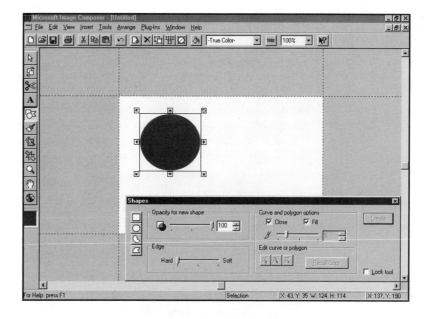

FIG. 18.3

You use the Paint palette to carry out the fine art of painting on your sprite.

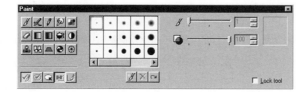

3. Choose a color to use, and select the Paintbrush, Airbrush, or Pencil icon. Now select a brush size, preferably something smaller than your actual sprite.

4. Draw or paint whatever you want on the sprite.

If you make a mistake, you can always use the Eraser tool to remove it. However, the eraser doesn't just erase whatever you've applied to the sprite; it erases the sprite itself. For example, if you create a solid black rectangle, you can erase parts of it to create a transparency effect. The problem with using this approach is that you can't paint over the transparent areas, as they cease to exist as active areas within the sprite. If you want to restore the transparent area, you need to re-create the sprite or use the Undo option from the Edit menu. Simply using the Color Fill paint bucket icon to cover up painting mistakes is actually a better idea; this way, you can start over.

Changing and Copying Sprites

You've learned how to create and change the appearance of a sprite. Now you're ready to learn how to manipulate and change a sprite's attributes. Image Composer treats each sprite as a single discrete unit, and therefore you can make changes on the sprite level. For example, each sprite has a relative position to other sprites. Because Image Composer is a two-dimensional program, images have no actual depth, but sprites can be layered behind one another. Layered positioning is just one of the aspects you can change about a sprite.

Another aspect you can modify is the sprite's size. Note the handles around each sprite, illustrated in Figure 18.4. By clicking and dragging one of these handles, you can elongate or shrink the selected sprite, and by clicking the upper-right handle, you can rotate it. These handles may change the sprite's size, but what if you want to actually crop or expand the sprite's area without affecting the image? To do so, you must follow these steps:

FIG. 18.4
The handles on a sprite allow you to change the sprite's dimensions or rotate it on the x- and y-axes.

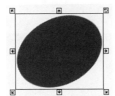

1. Right-click the sprite you want to modify.
2. Choose Crop from the pop-up menu that results.
3. Either expand or shrink the sprite's display area as you want by dragging the cropping handles.
4. Make sure that you get out of Cropping mode by clicking elsewhere in the document. You don't want to inadvertently crop the sprite twice.

Sprites are incredibly malleable objects. You can bend, pull, warp, and scale them all that you want. The important point to remember when you are manipulating sprites is that they're objects; their attributes are not set in stone like a pure bitmap image. Once you start to take advantage of this flexibility, you'll realize that there's little you cannot create within Image Composer's boundaries.

Using Composition Guides

If you look closely at a newly created document, you'll notice a white square bounded by four dotted lines. Those dotted lines are your Composition Guides. At first glance, they may appear to be nothing more than traditional rulers that help you position objects. However, Composition Guides actually control a great deal more.

The Composition Guides delineate your active space. You can change how much room you have to work with by dragging the guides around your document. In traditional desktop publishing programs, you set your space by an exact size because your work has to adhere to a standard size. In Image Composer, you don't have to set the size. A means for setting the exact size of your working space is still available, but when you are preparing graphics for the Web, there isn't as much emphasis on the precise area.

This point, too, may not seem important, but the Composition Guides determine what appears in the final graphic and what doesn't. When you're creating an image, you can draw sprites outside the composition area. When you save the file into a non-MIC file, the material outside the composition area is thrown out. As a result, you can create several fringe and bordering effects.

Using Clip Art and Buttons

Sprites, as you've experienced them thus far, are simple geometric primitives. However, you can do more with them than that, as you can import already-existing graphics. This capability grants a particular degree of flexibility when you are creating new compositions because it lets you use some of your already-existing work.

All the tools within Image Composer work just as well with an imported image as they do with an existing object because they are both classified as sprites. Although you cannot stretch and warp a bitmap with the same impunity that you could a simple sprite, you can apply effects to much greater effect. Follow these steps to import an existing graphic into Image Composer:

1. Choose Insert, Clip Art.
2. When the Microsoft Clip Gallery appears, choose from a variety of existing clip art.
3. After you select an image, click the Insert button.
4. After the image is inserted into your document, size and modify it as you like.
5. Alternatively, you can just drag the clip art out of the gallery and into your document to add the image.

Part

V

Ch

18

As a general note, the Insert menu can be used to add nearly any kind of image to your document. If you want to add an image from a Photo CD, for example, you follow roughly the same procedure as shown here, but you select From Photo CD instead of Clip Art. The ability to import and insert existing graphics into a document turns Image Composer from a glorified paint program into a powerful graphic utility.

You can choose from six different formats when inserting objects. The first is the simple File insertion. Basically, all it does is let you insert any of the supported file graphics formats into your composition. Essentially, it is the equivalent of an import function. Second, you can import from a Kodak Photo CD directly by using the From Photo CD menu item. Third, you can insert a button, bringing up the powerful Button Wizard. To create a button, follow these steps:

1. Choose Insert, Button.
2. Select the style of button you want to create, as shown in Figure 18.5, and click Next.
3. Select how many buttons you want to create, and click Next.
4. Name your button, and if you want a graphic label instead of a textual one, click the Image check box (see Figure 18.6). Then select the graphic you want on the button by browsing.

FIG. 18.5
You can create an amazing array of buttons with the Button Wizard.

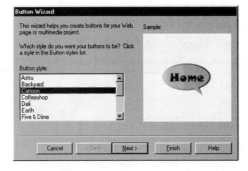

FIG. 18.6
By adding the ability to map graphical labels onto buttons, the Button Wizard allows you to escape the traditional textual look and feel of a Web page.

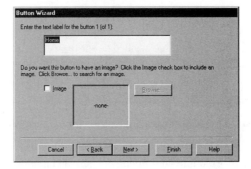

5. Click the size of button you want. If you want the button to be the size of its label, click the Exact Fit for Each Button radio button. If you want all the buttons to be the same size, click the Same Size for All Buttons radio button. The Same Size button also lets you specify a size if you don't want to use the minimum fit size.

6. Click Finish to create your button(s), while keeping in mind that you can edit them from the Image Composer with as much control over the eventual result as you had when creating them.

Using the GIF Animator

Although beautiful images certainly make your Web sites more appealing, it's animation that gives them that added touch. On the Web, you can accomplish animation in a number of ways, but the easiest is through using an animated GIF file. An animated GIF file contains a number of images instead of one, and Web browsers automatically cycle through these images, thus creating animation.

N O T E Always consider your target audience when incorporating animated GIFs. Only newer versions of most Web browsers support animated GIFs. Browsers that do not support animated GIFs typically see the first frame of your GIF, and nothing else. ■

Microsoft has included a simple utility called the GIF Animator, which enables you to create animated GIF files easily. All you have to do is launch GIF Animator from the Start menu and drag and drop sprites from Image Composer into cells in the animator. You can also launch the GIF Animator, shown in Figure 18.7, from the Tools menu (by choosing Tools, Microsoft GIF Animator).

FIG. 18.7
The GIF Animator tool is a straightforward utility for assembling the frames that make up your animation.

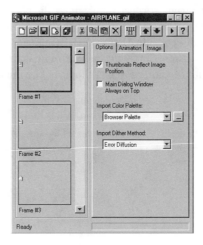

In the following steps, you create a simple animation showing the handles of the scissors cycling through a number of colors:

1. If you still have the previous tutorial loaded into Composer, go to step 2. Otherwise, click the Insert Image File button on the toolbar, and select the file SCISSOR1.MIC.

2. Choose Tools, Microsoft GIF Animator to load the GIF Animator. After it loads, drag it to the right of the screen so that it is visible at the same time that Composer is visible.

3. Click the scissors, and drag them to an empty cell in the GIF Animator. A thumbnail of the GIF image appears in the GIF Animator cell.

4. In Composer, choose the Color Tuning/Color Shifting palette, and drag the Hue slider to the right to a setting of about 40. Click Apply. The handles of the scissors change from orange to yellow.

5. Repeat steps 3 and 4 four times to create four frames, each with the scissors having handles of a different color.

6. In the GIF Animator, select the Animation tab and turn on Loop and Repeat Forever.

7. To preview your new GIF animation, click the Play button in the GIF Animator toolbar. You then see the animation playback with the handles of the scissors cycling through the four colors.

Again, if you want to save your animated GIF, choose File, Save and give it a filename. To embed it in a Web page, simply insert it as you would any GIF image. The client's browser will download the entire GIF and then cycle through its frames.

Part
V

Ch
18

> **CAUTION**
>
> Be careful not to make your animated GIFs too large. Keep in mind that the target size for a single Web page should be 100KB or less.

You can also create animation of moving sprites. Simply move the objects in a sprite, drag it to the GIF Animator, and then move the objects again, dragging each succeeding frame to the GIF Animator. You can drag files directly into Microsoft GIF Animator from any program that supports OLE drag-and-drop operations. Currently, the GIF Animator supports TIFF, JPEG, and MIC format images along with any other formats supported by Image Composer.

> **CAUTION**
>
> When you are creating an animation by dragging sprites, be aware of the sprites' bounding box size. Using frames of varying sizes can cause unpredictable results because GIF Animator aligns every frame to the left edge automatically.

From Here...

You can use Image Composer to create or modify images for your Web site without expending considerable effort. When working with images in your Web site, it is important to consider the impact they will have on your site structure and performance. Consider reading these chapters for more information:

- Chapter 25, "Designing and Organizing Web Sites."
- Chapter 27, "Increasing Site Performance."

Administrating Visual InterDev 6

19 Windows NT Server Basics   403

20 Using the Internet Information Server (IIS)   433

21 Working with Site Server Enterprise Edition   455

22 SQL Server Basics   465

23 Understanding Visual InterDev 6 Security   481

24 Using Developer Isolation and Visual SourceSafe   497

CHAPTER 19

Windows NT Server Basics

In this chapter

NT Server Configuration for Visual InterDev 6 **404**

The NT Server 4.0 Advantages **404**

Setting Up User Accounts and Security **407**

Administering Windows NT **412**

Windows NT Performance Tuning **412**

NT Server Configuration for Visual InterDev 6

It's no secret that the Internet is exploding in popularity. Among the aftershocks of this explosion is an incredible growth in the number of computers required for dispensing information. In the past, these machines (servers) were primarily UNIX or UNIX-derivative systems. With the advent of low-cost PC servers (as opposed to pricey high-end systems) and the evolution of the Microsoft Windows NT Server operating system, a powerful alternative to existing server options is now available. Coupled with Visual InterDev, Windows NT Server is an attractive and powerful framework for Internet applications. This chapter highlights basic administration related to Visual InterDev and outlines a few of the advantages to NT Server 4.0.

The NT Server 4.0 Advantages

Microsoft Windows NT has grown from its humble LAN-based heritage to a capable WAN-based server platform. NT Server 3.51 saw the maturation of NT as an Internet-capable platform, which could then be expanded to serve any variety of roles on the Internet. With NT Server 4.0, Microsoft has created a platform that, out of the box, provides almost everything people need in a network server.

Aware of several shortcomings in previous versions of Windows NT Server, Microsoft has released a product with many benefits. The new server is easier to install, use, and manage than any previous version. By adopting the standard Windows 95 Explorer interface, a pleasant (and easier to use) new face has been added to the operating system.

Integration

NT Server 4.0 provides a significant change in the underlying structure of the Windows NT architecture. By rewriting the root levels of the operating system, Microsoft was able to bring considerable enhancements in speed and stability to the operating system. Continuing beyond a reworking of the NT internals, Microsoft united software titles that were add-ons in the past. They were then incorporated into the operating system.

Previously, content-serving software for the Internet, such as Web servers, was delivered as third-party packages to build on existing transport layers of NT. In NT Server 4.0, this changes with the combination Internet Information Server 4.0, which empowers servers with the capability to host demanding and effective Internet and intranet sites. By designing the architecture of NT 4.0 around these services, Microsoft was able to coax tremendous performance over traditional services of the previous model.

Integration within NT Server 4.0 is not limited to Internet services. Network interoperability also received considerable enhancements at the root of NT. With improvements not only to the NT Server content-provision, but also to the lowest level transport layers of the operating system, NT now provides some of the fastest and most stable network services available on modern network operating systems.

Not content with merely upgrading the core of NT, Microsoft continued the improved integration of the administrative tools present in the operating system. Unlike most UNIX systems, NT offers a set of centralized tools for monitoring and managing the server. Because NT provides a standardized interface and common tools, the previously daunting task of maintaining a network server is now simplified. Because only one program is ever available for use, an administrator's learning curve and workload lessens considerably. The NT administration tools allow an administrator to control almost any aspect of the server including (but not limited to) Performance Monitoring, System Diagnostics, Disk and Device Management, Security and User Management, Internet Services, Task and Process Control, DNS/WINS Name Services, System and Application Events, Security Events, and Connection Status.

Scalability

Windows NT Server 4.0 also offers improvements in the expandability of the operating system to suit growth requirements. NT Server 4.0 delivers scalability through support for multiprocessor systems and symmetric multiprocessing (SMP) for over four processors. In addition to processor expansion, NT Server 4.0 provides improved throughput and scalability for applications that demand considerable overhead.

NT Server 4.0's framework has allowed for system clustering using several industry vendors and the Microsoft WolfPack. By using multiprocessing systems in a clustered environment, sizable network installations can grow or shrink as needed. As the cost of systems decrease, installation can be expanded quickly.

Fault Tolerance

Because reliability is a key requirement in any installation, NT Server uniformly handles all hardware and software faults. By having fault-tolerant technologies for reliability built into the core of NT, there is greater insurance that data has better protection. While maintaining the safety of the data and the system, NT also maintains the availability of system services and resources over the network.

Protected Subsystems and Error Handling   Windows NT Server employs protected subsystems in its design. In case of a fault (program error or crash), properly designed software reports an error to the system reporting service (Event Viewer) and gracefully exits. This capability ensures that the operating system is not brought to its knees by an application exception. With this capability, new server-based applications can be run with less risk of downing the server.

Recoverable File System   The Windows NT File System (NTFS) excels at recovering from disk and system faults. By using unique transaction records for each I/O operation, NT stores both redo and undo information in the Log File Service. If a transaction is completed properly, the update is completed. In the event of a fault such as a disk failure, NTFS rolls back the transaction using the undo information. Additionally, NTFS supports "hot fixing" if a physical error is encountered because of a bad sector on the device. Hot fixing forces NT to relocate the data to a different sector on the device and marks the original as bad, never to be used again.

Automatic Restarts   Through the use of protected subsystems and error handling, system failures are extremely rare. In case a system-wide failure does occur, NT can be configured to restart itself automatically to reduce downtime. With NT systems, like UNIX systems, administrators have the option of having NT transfer the complete memory contents to disk, similar to a "core dump." This feature provides a wealth of debugging information for skilled administrators and programmers in the event of a problem.

Backup Support   Integral to any fault-tolerant system are regular backups. NT's backup has tape support built into it. NT backup allows you to create multiple-set backups with standard, incremental, and even differential archival methods. The basic NT Server backup service can be extended through third-party products to provide additional functionality.

Uninterruptible Power Supply Support   Using Uninterruptible Power Supply (UPS) guarantees less downtime for any server during a power failure. The NT UPS service can detect a loss of power and warn all connected users. After the service notifies currently connected users, predefined commands can be executed before a graceful shutdown of the system. This feature ensures that all data is safely stored and applications end normally.

RAID Support   Another key element of the scalability of NT Server 4.0 is its robust support for high-capacity, expandable storage devices using Redundant Array of Inexpensive Disks (RAID). RAID enables you to create a large information store that spans multiple physical drives. When using RAID, you are employing a series of (relatively) inexpensive hard disk drives using in-groups to store your data. In a RAID system, not all data is necessarily stored consecutively on the first hard drive. Instead, RAID may scatter your data across several devices to increase efficiency and access time.

One of the main appeals of NT's support for RAID, aside from its storage expandability, is the nature of fault-tolerant disk systems. RAID systems are categorized into six levels, RAID 0 through 5. By using a different algorithm to implement its fault tolerance, each level provides differing performance and reliability. Briefly, the six RAID levels are as follow:

- *Level 0.* RAID 0 is also known as *disk striping*. If you use a file system known as a stripe set, data is split across all disks in the array in blocks. This approach is primarily used for speed reasons so that access can be done independently of each device.

- *Level 1.* This level is known as *mirroring*, or *disk mirroring*. Here, identical copies of selected disks are created. When the primary disk is modified, the change is duplicated on the mirror. Because duplicate copies of the data are available, read access is improved but write access is typically slower.

- *Level 2.* Disk striping with error correcting is the basic idea of this level. Error correction in RAID 2 uses multiple drives. Due to the marginal improvements and increased costs, this level is rarely used.

- *Level 3.* Unlike RAID Level 2, this disk-striping alternative requires only one disk for error correction using parity data.

- *Level 4.* Using larger segments than Levels 2 and 3, RAID 4 uses disk striping and keeps user data away from error-correcting data. Because it is not efficient in comparison to other levels, it is rarely used.

- *Level 5.* RAID 5 is one of the most popular RAID designs. Also known as *striping with parity*, it stripes data in large blocks across all disks in the array. As in Level 4, data and parity information are always arranged in the array, so they are on separate disks.

RAID technology provides considerable flexibility for systems to grow. Because RAID spans multiple devices while yielding performance improvements, you have few effective limits on your system. One thing to keep in mind is that system-based RAID performs slower than hardware-based RAID systems. As the server must use CPU cycles to handle the RAID array, expect slowdowns on software-based RAID setups.

Setting Up User Accounts and Security

At the heart of many of your Web applications will be users. Internet Information Server 4.0 directly interfaces with the Windows NT Server Security Accounts Manager (SAM) Database, allowing you to use the Windows NT accounts on your server or domain for application access control. Using these accounts, you can then enforce specific security restrictions on individual users or groups of users, down to the file level (a comprehensive discussion on security, the Windows NT file system, and other security considerations is located in Chapter 23, "Understanding Visual InterDev 6 Security").

Windows NT user accounts are used to uniquely identify an individual using the services accessible on your network. Similar user accounts (such as all users needing access to a particular resource) can be combined into a security "group," sharing security and access traits. A user account can be a member of more than one group in a Microsoft network (Windows Network), allowing you to create special combinations of access that may cross one traditional group's access. All user and group management is carried out using the *User Manager for Domains*, shown in Figure 19.1.

One of the distinct advantages in creating individual user accounts and groups with Windows NT is that your users need to use only one user account or username to access the resources present on your entire network (assuming that all your network resources belong to the same Windows NT security domain). This way, you can manage access restrictions without having to create multiple usernames for each different system and expect your users to remember them.

FIG. 19.1

The User Manager for Domains is used to create and manage user accounts, as well as security groups. It is also used to establish security audits and access permissions.

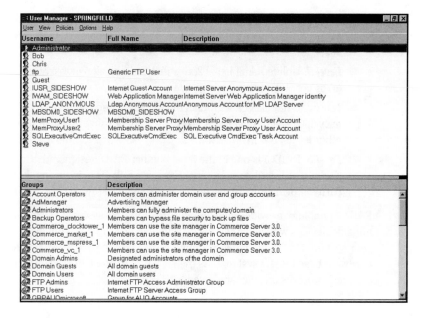

Creating a User

The process of creating a user in the User Manager for Domains takes little effort but does require you to be careful of the security permissions you assign. To begin, open the User Manager for Domains tool. By default, it is located in the Start menu under Administrative Tools (Common). With the tool open, follow these instructions:

1. Choose User, New User to open the New User dialog box, shown in Figure 19.2.

FIG. 19.2

The New User dialog box is a snapshot look at your user's basic information. From this dialog box, you also assign your user to groups and establish default information and other security elements.

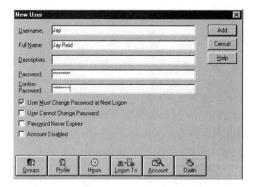

2. In the Username text box, enter the name your user will use to connect to resources and services on your network. Your user will be recognized by this name on your network and can follow whatever naming conventions you already have in place. For example, one popular scheme is to use the first initial, last name, plus a digit, such as sbanick1.

3. Enter your user's full name into the Full Name text box. This name is used for visual identification of your user so that you don't have to memorize which username represents which user.

4. Enter a description for this account in the Description text box. The description is used for your own reference, to record a reason for this account. For example, you can enter IT Specialist.

5. Each user should have a password. Enter the user's password into the Password text box. Remember that passwords are *case sensitive* and must be entered exactly as they are typed.

6. To ensure that the password has been entered correctly, retype the user's password into the Confirm Password text box. If you make an error in either box, and the passwords do not match, an error message appears, instructing you to retype the password.

7. If you want your new user to change his or her password when first logging on using this account, select the User Must Change Password at Next Logon check box. This option forces the user to change the password the next time he or she logs in to the network.

8. If you want to prevent your user from being able to change the password (for example, if the account is shared), select the User Cannot Change Password check box.

9. You can enforce password expiry, forcing users to change their passwords after a selected time period. To exempt your user from having the password expire, select the Password Never Expires check box.

10. To prevent this user account from logging in or using any network services, select the Account Disabled check box.

11. Click the Add button to create this user account.

12. Click the Close button to close the New User dialog box.

Groups: Adding and Removing Users

By default, all new users are immediately added to the Domain Users group to allow access to network resources. You can control the groups that a user belongs to from the User Manager for Domains. To control a user's membership to a group, follow these steps:

1. From the User Manager for Domains list of users, double-click the appropriate username. This action opens the User Properties dialog box, which is identical to the New User dialog box shown in Figure 19.2.

2. Click the Groups button to open the Group Memberships dialog box, shown in Figure 19.3.

3. To add your user to a particular group, double-click the group name in the Not Member Of list on the right side of the dialog box. Clicking this name adds the group name to the list of groups the user belongs to on the left side of the dialog box.

4. To remove a user from a particular group, double-click the group name in the Member Of list on the left side of the dialog box. This action removes the group from the list of groups the user belongs to and adds it to the list on the right side of the dialog box.

Part

VI

Ch

19

FIG. 19.3

The Group Memberships dialog box lets you add and remove a user from individual groups. Groups that the user belongs to are listed on the left side, and all groups in the Windows NT security domain are listed on the right.

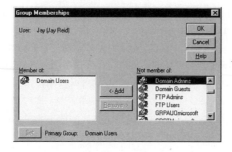

N O T E A user must always belong to at least one group. ■

5. To establish the primary group that the user belongs to, select the group from the list of groups on the left side of the dialog box, and click the Set button. Clicking this button updates the primary group the user belongs to.

6. Click OK to close the Group Memberships dialog box.

7. Click Close to close the User Properties dialog box.

Setting Access Rights

Security on accounts is not limited to group memberships and file-level security. You can establish and modify the access rights of user groups and accounts using the User Manager for Domains. To do so, open the User Manager for Domains and follow these instructions:

1. Choose Policies, User Rights to open the User Rights Policy dialog box.

2. From the Right drop-down list box, select the access right from which you want to add or remove your user or group.

Standard User Rights

The default user rights for Windows NT Server are listed here. Additional rights, called Advanced User Rights, can also be modified by selecting the Show Advanced User Rights check box. They should be modified with caution.

Access This Computer from Network. Allows the user or group to access services and resources offered by the local computer.

Add Workstations to Domain. Allows the user or group to add a new workstation to the domain without an administrator.

Back Up Files and Directories. Allows the user or group to archive files and directories that he or she/they may not normally have access to.

Change the System Time. Allows the user or group to reset the system clock.

Force Shutdown from a Remote System. Allows the user or group to shut down a system or server remotely.

Load and Unload Device Drivers. Allows the user or group to add or remove device drivers to a system without administrator privileges.

Log On Locally. Allows the user or group to log in to the local server or workstation interactively. This right also applies for FTP and Web connections.

Manage Auditing and Security Logs. Allows the user or group to modify the properties of audit and security logs.

Restore Files and Directories. Allows the user or group to restore files and directories of the computer. This right supersedes files and directory permissions.

Shutdown the System. Allows the user or group to shut down the system locally.

Take Ownership of Files or Other Object. Allows the user or group to take ownership of files or objects owned by other users.

3. To add a user or group to a user right, click the <u>A</u>dd button to open the standard Add Users and Groups dialog box, shown in Figure 19.4.

FIG. 19.4
The Add Users and Groups dialog box is used throughout Windows NT for permissions. The bottom half of the dialog box lists the selected groups and users.

4. Double-click each group you want to add from the <u>N</u>ames list to add it to the user right. To display user accounts, click the Show <u>U</u>sers button to display usernames along with group names.

5. Click OK to commit your changes and return to the User Rights Policy dialog box.

6. To remove a user or group from the access right, select the appropriate item in the <u>G</u>rant To list, and click the <u>R</u>emove button.

7. After you finish modifying the user rights, click OK to commit your changes and close the dialog box.

CAUTION
Modifications of user rights should be carried out with caution. Most Web applications require a user to have the Log on Locally user right enabled. Refer to the Windows NT Server online help for more information on user rights and their impact.

Administering Windows NT

Although your server is set up and operational, your job is not done yet. The ongoing administration and support for a server can be a rigorous task. By using the following Windows NT administration tools, you have simple utilities for server management:

■ *Performance Monitor.* Curious as to how the server is holding up? The Performance Monitor provides a graphical chart of almost every aspect of the server and the services running on it. You can also create stored charts that can be modified as you see fit.

■ *Event Viewer.* The Windows NT Event Viewer allows you to examine detailed logs of what happens in the server. These logs are split into three categories: System, Security, and Application. Sorting events by these categories reduces those dauntingly long log files.

■ *User Manager.* If you want secured areas on the server, you can use the User Manager to create and modify user accounts and groups. By grouping users into logical arrangements, you can assign security permissions and accessibility in a large bundle as opposed to one user at a time.

■ *Explorer.* File and directory maintenance, including security permissions, uses the standard Windows (95/98) GUI file management utility called Explorer.

In addition to these basic utilities, several other tools may prove useful to you, depending on your installation:

■ *Microsoft Domain Name System (DNS).* If you are maintaining your own DNS service, you can use Microsoft's implementation of the standard naming service. DNS benefits from a simplified GUI interface, as opposed to configuration files and command-line utilities.

■ *Windows Internet Name Service (WINS) Administrator.* If you are using a Windows NT wide area network over a TCP/IP network, you need the WINS naming service.

■ *Dynamic Host Configuration Protocol (DHCP) Administrator.* If you require dynamic IP allocation on your network, the DHCP service is an industry standard method for handling IP address management for clients.

■ *Server Manager.* When you are dealing with multiple servers, the NT Server Manager allows you to control and monitor all the computers on your network. The Server Manager lets you control directory shares, connected users, services, and event alerts.

If you need help with any of these utilities, refer to the provided documentation or their online counterparts.

Windows NT Performance Tuning

The first stop on your hunt for better performance is the server, but where do you begin? Establishing just where you need to improve your server can be a difficult task. Windows NT fortunately includes several tools intended for administrators to tune their servers. Without these tools, the job could prove difficult, but with your small toolkit in hand, you can get started.

Performance Monitor: Your Window to Your Server's Health

The first tool you should examine is the Windows NT Performance Monitor. Included with both Windows NT Server and NT Workstation, the Performance Monitor is a gauge to your server's overall activity and resources. The monitor, shown in Figure 19.5, is fully customizable. By adding *counters*, you can track almost every aspect of your server with visual graphs. Performance Monitor also includes facilities for reporting and alerting based on ongoing activity. Like most NT administration tools, the Performance Monitor also lets you connect to other machines on your network to evaluate their performance.

FIG. 19.5

The Windows NT Performance Monitor is a graphical tool for measuring your server's health and ongoing activity.

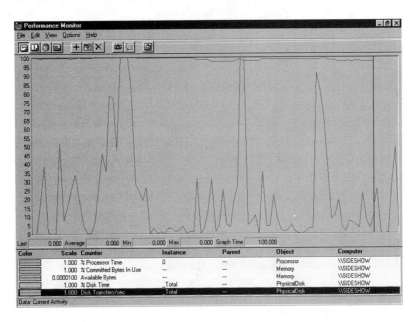

Part

VI

Ch

19

Because the Performance Monitor is so customizable, deciding on the criteria you want to monitor can take some time. A wealth of information, in the form of objects, is available for you to monitor. Most NT-based services add their own object to the monitor, and each object has its own variety of counters. You can customize each counter with a unique color, scale, style, and line width for the graph. Each counter also includes a description, letting you decide easily and quickly what to choose. Each chart that you create can be saved to disk, thereby letting you quickly load different settings and counters for observation.

You can easily start using the Performance Monitor. You don't need to specifically install the monitor; it is automatically installed with other administrative tools when you first install Windows NT. To begin, locate the Performance Monitor icon in your Start menu. Select the icon to launch the program. When first launched, the Performance Monitor opens a blank chart, as shown in Figure 19.6.

N O T E By default, the Performance Monitor is grouped with other Windows NT administrative tools in the common Administrative Tools program group. This setup may vary among machines, especially if you have spent any time customizing your Start menu. ■

FIG. 19.6

The Performance Monitor window is dominated by the chart region in the center.

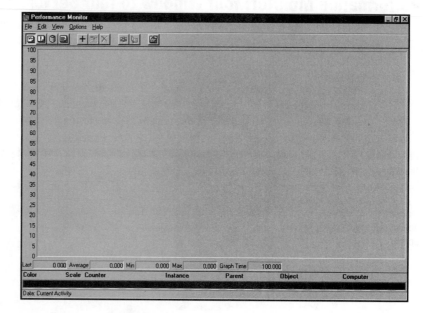

As in most Windows programs, a standard hierarchical menu bar appears along the top of the window. Below the menu bar is the toolbar, which contains several small icon buttons that act as shortcuts to menu bar functions. More noticeably, the large chart area is visible in the center of the window. The vertical labels are represented on the left side of the chart, with an updated display at the bottom of the chart called the *value bar*. The display shows the selected counter's information (including the last reading, average reading, minimum and maximum reading, and the graph time). Below the display is a legend, providing the counter color, scale, object, instance, and computer.

Making a New Chart   To begin using Performance Monitor, you must add counters to your new chart. After you add counters to your chart, their progress is updated on the display. To add a counter, follow these steps:

1. Click the Add Counter toolbar button, which is represented by a large plus sign icon. You can alternatively choose Edit, Add to Chart. The Add to Chart dialog box appears, as shown in Figure 19.7.

2. Click the Explain button on the right side to expand the dialog box. The Counter Definition box appears at the bottom of the dialog box.

3. From the Object drop-down list box, select an object you want to monitor. For the sake of this example, choose the Processor object.

FIG. 19.7

The Add to Chart dialog box contains a list of all objects on your server from which counters can be used.

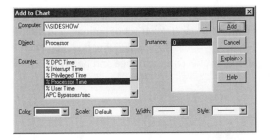

4. After the Counter list box updates with the currently selected object's counters, select a counter that you want to monitor. For this example, select %Processor Time.

5. If more than one instance of an object (such as more than one processor) exists, the Instance list box displays the available instances. Select the appropriate instance you want to monitor.

6. The Color drop-down list box displays the color used to represent this counter in the graph. Select the color you want to use for this counter.

7. The Scale drop-down list box defines what scale your counter uses, according to the legend. This value ranges from 0.0000001 to 100000.0. Select the scale you want to use, or select Default.

N O T E What is the *scale*? The vertical labels on the left of the chart provide a numerical representation to reflect change in the chart. By changing the scale value, you can change how the counter is represented on the chart. The lower the scale, the smaller the visible change on the chart. You can use the scale to fine-tune your counter monitoring. ▦

8. With a large number of counters to monitor, you may want to make some stand out more than others. Using the Width drop-down list box, select the line width you want to use for this counter.

9. Instead of line widths, you can instead use line styles to differentiate counters on the chart. Use the Style drop-down list box to select a line style for this counter.

10. After you set up your counter, click the Add button to commit your changes and add the counter to the chart. If you have no more counters to add to the chart, click the Done button.

Your new counter now appears in the display area of the chart, with its information updated in real-time. The counters list at the bottom of the Performance Monitor window also lists your new counter, including the instance and scale. Use the legend's counter list to quickly identify the counters in your chart. When you select a counter from the counter list, the value bar below the chart changes to reflect the currently selected item. You can also double-click the selected counter to change its properties in the chart.

You can freely add and remove counters to change your chart. You can also save your current chart by choosing File, Save Chart Settings. You then can choose File, Open to open your chart at another time to resume your monitoring.

Part
VI

Ch
19

You can modify the display and behavior of your chart by choosing Options, Chart. Each aspect of the Performance Monitor has its own set of options, and the Chart options let you choose how the chart looks. The Chart Options dialog box, shown in Figure 19.8, provides you with a few options to alter your chart's appearance and behavior. The following check boxes alter the chart display:

FIG. 19.8

The Chart Options dialog box lets you alter your chart's appearance and behavior.

- *Legend.* The legend acts as a counter list for your chart. Each counter you add to your chart appears with its attributes in the legend. You can use the legend to select individual counters (which, in turn, update the value bar) and change their properties.

- *Value Bar.* When you select a counter from the counter list, the counter's values are displayed in the value bar below the chart. If you do not use this feature, you can remove the value bar for additional screen space. If you choose to remove the legend from the display, the value bar is automatically removed.

- *Vertical Grid and Horizontal Grid.* These two check boxes let you add (or remove) a vertical or horizontal set of lines to compose a grid. These grids can be used to create more distinct visual references for change on your machine's performance.

- *Vertical Labels.* The vertical labels on the left of the chart display are used to reference changes in your chart. If you find that these labels obstruct your chart, you can remove the legend from the display.

In addition to the five check boxes, a few other options are available to you:

- The Gallery radio buttons let you change the type of display that is used for your chart. The Graph option displays a familiar graph, plotting each point of change of a counter in the chart. If you prefer, you can use the Histogram option instead to display a vertical bar for each counter.

- In the Vertical Maximum text box, you can define the upper limit of the vertical label. If you find that your counters rarely hit the upper-level limit, lower the value to create a clearer display. Alternatively, if your counters are always peaking, extend the upper limit by entering a higher value.

- The Update Time radio buttons define how your chart is updated to reflect changes in performance. The first option, Periodic Update, lets you define an Interval (in seconds) between automatic updates to your chart. If you prefer to update your chart yourself, you can choose Manual Update instead.

Using Alerts   Another aspect of Performance Monitor that is incredibly useful is the Alerts facility. Say that you want your machine to warn you if your available memory falls dangerously low. You can create an alert inside the Performance Monitor that constantly monitors your system's condition and executes a specified program in the event that an alert is triggered. This program could be a batch file that sends an alert message to your screen or event log, or perhaps a more drastic program that shuts down your machine until you return to look at it. Alerts are incredibly simple in behavior. They simply wait for the trigger to be hit and then launch the program. If no trigger is hit, the alert sits idly by and waits for it to happen.

N O T E   The Performance Monitor must be running on your server for the alert to take place. ▪

To switch to Alert view, click the Alert View button on the toolbar (the second button, a pad of paper with an exclamation mark on it). Alternatively, you can choose View, Alert . The display changes to Alert view, which differs considerably from the Chart view. The display is dominated by the Alert Log in the center of the screen, with an Alert Interval listed above it, and the Alert Legend listed below. This display is shown in Figure 19.9.

FIG. 19.9

The Alert view display is Spartan in comparison to the Chart view. The Alert Log lists every triggered alert that has occurred.

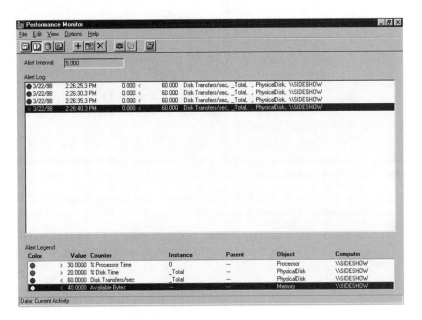

Part
VI

Ch
19

Adding counters for an alert is similar to adding counters to a chart. To add an alert counter, follow these steps:

1. Click the Add Counter button on the toolbar, or choose Edit, Add to Alert. This action opens the Add to Alert dialog box, as shown in Figure 19.10.

FIG. 19.10

The Add to Alert dialog box differs slightly from the Add to Chart dialog box. The focus of this dialog box is to define the actions in an alert situation.

2. Just as you do in the Add to Chart dialog box, select an object to monitor from the Object drop-down list box. For this example, choose Memory. If more than one instance of your object exists, be sure to specify it.

3. After the Counter list box updates with the currently selected object's counters, select the counter you want to monitor for an alert. For this example, choose Available Bytes.

4. From the Color drop-down list box, choose the color with which you want to identify this counter.

5. The Alert If radio button group defines how your alert works. You can choose to trigger the alert if the counter is over or under the value you specify in the text box. Specify a value for the trigger, and define the range by selecting either Over or Under. For this example, choose Under and enter the value 1000 to warn if your available bytes fall below 1,000.

6. The Run Program on Alert text box and radio button group define what happens when the alert is triggered. You can launch a selected program either the first time the alert is triggered or every time. In the text box, specify the program to launch (complete with the path, if it is not in the environment path). Then choose when the program will be launched. For this example, in the text box enter **net send administrator alert!** and select First Time.

7. After you define your alert, click the Add button. When you are done, click the Done button to close the dialog box.

Your new alert appears in the Alert Legend. When an alert is triggered, it is added to the Alert Log so that you can visually track what has happened. Alerts can prove useful warnings of dangerous situations, such as low storage space, memory, or processing power.

Just like Chart view, Alert view provides you with options to alter alert behavior. The Alert Options dialog box, shown in Figure 19.11, provides you with the following options:

FIG. 19.11

The Alert Options dialog box lets you change how alerts behave.

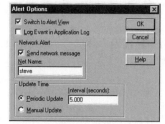

- *Switch to Alert View.* With this check box selected, the Performance Monitor automatically switches to the Alert view in the event that an alert is triggered. This feature is useful for studying the Alert Log for triggered alerts.

- *Log Event in Application Log.* The Windows NT Event Viewer (see "Event Viewer: Your Server's Own News Service" later in this chapter) is used to record events and alerts for your server. You can select this check box to have your alert recorded in the application log of the Event Viewer to create a more permanent record of your triggered alert. This capability is useful if you are away from your computer and an alert is triggered.

- *Network Alert.* Using this check box and text box, you can send a network alert message to a specified user when an alert is triggered. By selecting the check box and entering a network username, the message dialog box appears on that user's screen if he or she is logged in.

- *Update Time.* This radio group behaves exactly like the radio group in the Chart Options dialog box. You can alter the frequency that the Performance Monitor updates the counters to monitor for triggers by selecting Periodic Update and specifying an Interval in seconds, or you can choose Manually Update the Alerts.

Log Files　When you want to store the activity of your server and look back on it later, you can use the Performance Monitor's Log view. To switch to Log view, click the View Output Log File Status toolbar button (the third icon, represented by a cylinder), or choose View, Log. The display changes to the Log view, as shown in Figure 19.12. This display is dominated by the legend list box at the bottom of the display, with the log file information appearing above it.

FIG. 19.12

Outputting your performance monitoring to a log lets you study the results later.

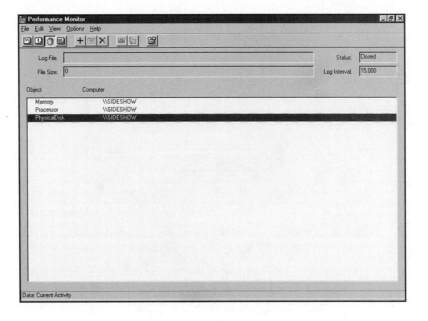

Instead of logging individual counters, Performance Monitor logs entire object activity. This way, you can use the log data at a later time to create charts of individual counters. To create a log file, you must define the objects to be monitored:

1. Click the Add Counter icon, or choose Edit, Add to Log. The Add To Log dialog box appears, as shown in Figure 19.13.

FIG. 19.13

The Add To Log dialog box lets you add complete objects to be logged.

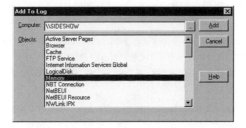

2. From the Objects list box, select the object you want to have logged. Remember that each object's counter is included in the logging.

3. Click the Add button to add the object. After you finish adding objects, click the Done button to close the dialog box.

The objects you add appear in the display's legend. Before logging begins, you must set the Log Options. To do so, open the Log Options dialog box, as shown in Figure 19.14, by choosing Options, Log.

FIG. 19.14

In the Log Options dialog box, you can set the log file's name and location, as well as the frequency of the updates.

The Log Options dialog box is a specialized file selector, letting you choose the location and name of the log file. To begin your log file, follow these steps:

1. Using the Explorer interface within the dialog box, locate the directory where you want the log file to be stored. Alternatively, you can enter the path with the filename.

2. Enter the log file's name in the File Name text box, ending with the .LOG extension.

3. Set the update time in the Update Time radio button group at the bottom of the dialog box. For automatic updates, choose Periodic Update and enter an Interval (in seconds) in the text box. Otherwise, choose Manual Update.

4. To begin logging immediately, click the Start Log button. If you do not want to begin logging yet, click the Save button (you will need to return to this dialog box to start the logging later).

When the logging begins, the upper display changes to reflect the filename and location, the status (either opened or closed), the interval (in seconds), and the size of the log file. After you finish logging, you must return to the Log Options dialog box and select Stop Logging to close the log.

After you save a log file to disk, you can use that log within the Performance Monitor whenever you want. To load your log data into the Performance Monitor, follow these steps:

1. Choose Options, Data From to open the Data From dialog box, as shown in Figure 19.15.

FIG. 19.15
The Data From dialog box lets you specify what data the Performance Monitor uses.

2. Select Log File, and enter the log file path in the text box. Alternatively, use the browse button beside the text box to select the log file using the Explorer interface.

3. Click OK to close the dialog box and load the data.

After you load the data, your charts use the logged information. You must add your counters as before, but the logged information is used rather than the current activity. Note that certain options (such as intervals) may not be available in all dialog boxes. To return to using the current activity in Performance Monitor, follow these steps:

1. Choose Options, Data From to open the Data From dialog box.

2. Select Current Activity.

3. Click OK to close the dialog box.

Performance Monitor Reports   Reports reflect current conditions on your server. Instead of using a chart to display the information, reports use numerical representation. To switch to Reports view, click the View Report Data button on the toolbar (the fourth icon, represented by a pad of paper with lines on it), or choose View, Report. This action changes the display to Report view, as shown in Figure 19.16.

Part
VI

Ch
19

FIG. 19.16
You can use Report view
to get an overall status
of your server without
using charts.

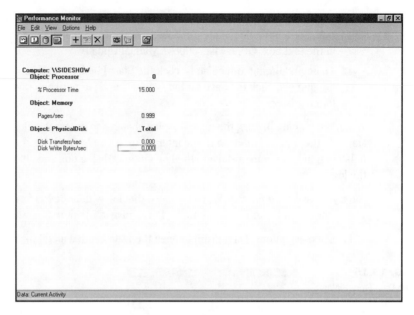

Reports display information in columns for each individual instance of an object. You can create a report on all the counters for a given object and then watch them change under various conditions. To add counters to your report, follow these steps:

1. Click the Add Counter button, or choose Edit, Add to Report. This action opens the Add to Report dialog box, as shown in Figure 19.17.

FIG. 19.17
The Add to Report
Dialog box continues in
the same vein as the
Add Chart dialog box.

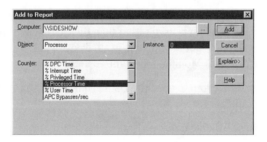

2. From the Object drop-down list box, select the object you want to monitor. For this example, choose Physical Disk. If more than one instance of an object (such as more than one physical disk drive) exists, specify the instance to monitor in the Instance box.

3. After the Counter list box updates to represent the counters for the current object, select the counter to add to your report. For this example, choose %Disk Time.

4. After you select your counter, click the Add button. If you are done adding counters, click the Done button to close the dialog box.

Your new counters are added to the Report view, listed according to object and instance. To modify the update interval for your report, open the Report Options dialog box by choosing

Options, Report. In this dialog box, as shown in Figure 19.18, you can change the update time. You can have the report updated automatically by choosing Periodic Update and specifying an Interval (in seconds) in the text box. If you would rather update the report manually, you can choose Manual Update.

FIG. 19.18

The Report Options dialog box lets you change only the frequency of the report updates.

N O T E There is much more to Performance Monitor than meets the eye. You should explore Performance Monitor further by experimenting with the tool and referring to the Microsoft documentation. One of the key aspects of Performance Monitor not covered here is its capability to monitor multiple computers over a network. If you are monitoring more than one server over a network, you are bound to find these features useful. ■

Event Viewer: Your Server's Own News Service

If the Performance Monitor is the window inside your server, the Event Viewer is the narrator. The Windows NT Event Viewer, shown in Figure 19.19, is automatically installed when you first set up Windows NT Server and Workstation. It records events and audits situations on your machine that may require your attention. The Event Viewer should be monitored closely, as it often provides the first clues of possible problems.

Part

VI

Ch

19

FIG. 19.19

The Event Viewer is an invaluable tool for administrators. You can customize what events will be recorded.

Date	Time	Source	Category	Event	User	Computer
3/22/98	2:15:00 PM	Application Popup	None	26	N/A	SIDESHOW
3/22/98	9:13:16 AM	Print	None	10	Steve	SIDESHOW
3/21/98	10:48:08 PM	Srv	None	2013	N/A	SIDESHOW
3/19/98	9:59:44 PM	Print	None	10	Steve	SIDESHOW
3/19/98	9:52:50 PM	Print	None	13	Steve	SIDESHOW
3/19/98	9:52:50 PM	Print	None	10	Steve	SIDESHOW
3/19/98	9:50:20 PM	Print	None	10	Steve	SIDESHOW
3/19/98	7:56:43 PM	WAM	None	201	N/A	SIDESHOW
3/18/98	10:04:49 PM	Print	None	10	Steve	SIDESHOW
3/17/98	11:24:02 PM	Rdr	None	3013	N/A	SIDESHOW
3/17/98	11:08:08 PM	Srv	None	2013	N/A	SIDESHOW
3/17/98	6:14:54 PM	DCOM	None	10005	SYSTEM	SIDESHOW
3/17/98	6:14:48 PM	W3SVC	None	115	N/A	SIDESHOW
3/17/98	6:14:48 PM	W3SVC	None	113	N/A	SIDESHOW
3/17/98	6:14:47 PM	MSFTPSVC	None	101	N/A	SIDESHOW
3/17/98	6:14:16 PM	BROWSER	None	8015	N/A	SIDESHOW
3/17/98	6:14:16 PM	BROWSER	None	8015	N/A	SIDESHOW
3/17/98	6:14:16 PM	BROWSER	None	8015	N/A	SIDESHOW
3/17/98	6:14:16 PM	BROWSER	None	8015	N/A	SIDESHOW
3/17/98	6:14:05 PM	BROWSER	None	8021	N/A	SIDESHOW
3/17/98	6:12:45 PM	EventLog	None	6005	N/A	SIDESHOW
3/17/98	6:11:26 PM	BROWSER	None	8033	N/A	SIDESHOW
3/17/98	6:11:24 PM	BROWSER	None	8033	N/A	SIDESHOW
3/17/98	6:11:24 PM	BROWSER	None	8033	N/A	SIDESHOW
3/17/98	6:11:24 PM	BROWSER	None	8033	N/A	SIDESHOW
3/16/98	10:58:15 PM	Print	None	10	Steve	SIDESHOW
3/15/98	3:47:37 PM	Srv	None	2013	N/A	SIDESHOW
3/15/98	3:47:34 PM	SMTPSVC	None	416	N/A	SIDESHOW
3/15/98	3:47:34 PM	SMTPSVC	None	534	N/A	SIDESHOW
3/15/98	3:47:26 PM	NNTPSVC	None	86	N/A	SIDESHOW
3/15/98	3:47:24 PM	NNTPSVC	None	94	N/A	SIDESHOW
3/15/98	3:44:38 PM	DCOM	None	10005	SYSTEM	SIDESHOW

Event Viewer - System Log on \\SIDESHOW

Log   View   Options   Help

As defined by the Microsoft Event Viewer online help, an event is "...any significant occurrence in the system or in an application that requires users to be notified...". Events that do not require immediate attention by the user are recorded to the Event Viewer, whereas critical events are usually recorded to the Event Viewer and brought to the attention of the user with an onscreen message. The Event Viewer splits events into three separate logs:

- *System*. System events directly apply to the underlying system functions of Windows NT. They include device drivers and system components. Any problems of this nature are recorded to the system log.

- *Security*. Security events are situations that may indicate possible breaches to the security of your system. You can use the security log to record both successful and unsuccessful security events.

- *Application*. For programs that encounter errors, typically while running invisible to the user, the application log is used. Services report status and error messages to the application log for your reference.

Within each log, events are displayed by a single line. Each line contains the following:

- *Date and Time*. The actual date and time that the event occurred is recorded in the Event Viewer log.

- *Source*. The source of the event is the software that reported the condition. It can be either an application or a component of the system, such as a device driver.

- *Category*. Events are classified by the source, for easier sorting. Sample categories may be logons and logoffs for security, for example.

- *Event*. To assist in diagnosing events, particular events have event numbers to identify situations.

- *User*. If a user account was involved, such as a service running under a specific user, the user's name is provided.

- *Computer*. The computer on which the event occurred is listed.

- *Type*. Beside each event entry is a colored icon representing a classification for the event. Sample classifications include Error, Warning, Information, Success Audit, and Failure Audit.

To move between logs, you can choose the log of your choice from the Log menu. When you choose a different log, the display changes to represent the current log's contents.

Examining an Event   To look more closely at an event, select it from the log and double-click it to open the Event Detail dialog box, as shown in Figure 19.20.

FIG. 19.20

The Event Detail dialog box provides you with more specific information on the event, including a data breakdown.

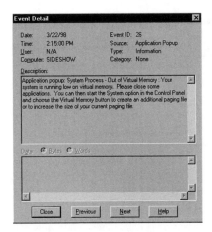

The Event Detail dialog box provides you with more comprehensive information on the event:

- The upper third of the dialog box displays the event time and date, user, source, type, category, and computer. This information is a mirror of the information displayed in the log.

- The Description box, in the center of the dialog box, displays a text report of the event. This message varies according to the event but usually provides specific information on what happened to the source involved.

- Below the Description box is the Data box. It lists a data breakdown of the event for debugging. You can choose to see this in the form of Bytes or Words.

- Along the bottom of the dialog box is a row of buttons, including a Close button to close the dialog box, a Previous button to move to the preceding event in the log, and a Next button to move to the following event in the log.

Your ability to move to the next and previous events depends on how your log is being sorted. From the View menu, you can choose the Newest Events Listed First or Oldest Events First options.

Filtering Your Log   In addition to choosing what order your events will appear, you can choose to list all events or filter the events to view only specific messages. To filter your log view, follow these steps:

1. Choose View, Filter Events to open the Filter dialog box, as shown in Figure 19.21.

FIG. 19.21

The Filter dialog box lets you choose which events will appear in your log view.

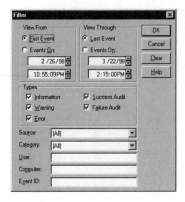

2. The top two grouping boxes let you specify where your view will begin and end. You can choose to view from the First event to the Last event, or specify particular starting and ending dates and times (Events On for starting, Events On for ending). Specify the starting and ending criteria for your view.

3. The center box provides you with five check boxes that represent event types. Select the check boxes for the types of events you want to include in your view.

4. The Source drop-down list box lets you specify the event source that the view will contain. This lengthy list includes every source on your server. Select the source that you want to view.

5. The Category drop-down list box lets you select the event category (if applicable) to view. Select the category you want to view.

6. If you want to view all events belonging to a particular user, enter the username in the User text box.

7. Because you can monitor events from more than one machine, you may want to specify a particular computer to monitor. To do so, enter the computer name in the Computer text box.

8. The Event ID text box lets you specify a particular event number to view. If you want to filter based on an event ID, enter the number in this box.

9. If you are satisfied with your filter criteria, click OK. Otherwise, click the Clear button to reset the criteria or the Cancel button to abort the filter.

Log Settings   Logs can become cumbersome and large to sort through. Fortunately, the Event Viewer provides you with a few options for making your job easier. You can open the Event Log Settings dialog box, as shown in Figure 19.22, by choosing Log, Log Settings.

FIG. 19.22

The Event Log Settings dialog box lets you limit the size of a log file and control how events are overwritten.

This dialog box lets you control the overall size of each log, as well as how the log manages overwriting old events. To modify a log's settings, follow these steps:

1. From the Change Settings For drop-down list box, choose the log that you want to modify. You can choose the System, Security, or Application Log.

2. In the Maximum Log Size text box, enter a maximum size for the selected log. The log size must be defined in 64-kilobyte increments. You optionally can use the spin buttons on the side of the text box to control the size.

3. The Event Log Wrapping radio group controls how old events are overwritten in the log. If you want the Event Viewer to overwrite events as it needs, choose Overwrite Events as Needed. If you prefer to have the events overwritten after so many days, choose Overwrite Events Older Than and specify the number of days in the text box. You optionally can use the spin buttons on the side of the text box to set the number of days. Finally, if you prefer to clear the events manually, choose Do Not Overwrite Events.

4. Repeat steps 1 through 3 for each log. When you are satisfied with your changes, click OK to accept them. If you prefer to return to the defaults, click the Default button.

If you reduce the maximum size of the logs, your change does not take effect until the log is first cleared.

Clearing Your Log   When a log is filled with outdated information, or if you have changed the maximum size of the log, you may want to clear the log contents and start fresh. You can clear your log by following these steps:

1. From the Log menu, choose the log that you want to clear.

2. Return to the Log menu and choose Clear All Events to open a confirmation dialog box.

3. You are asked whether you want to save the contents of this log before clearing its contents. Click Yes to save the log using a standard file selector. To clear the log without saving, click No.

4. A final warning and confirmation dialog box appears, warning you that the clearing of a log is irreversible. If you are still sure that you want to clear this log, click Yes; otherwise, click No.

Part

VI

Ch

19

Your log file is cleared and records any new events. You may need to refresh your log to see any new events. You can do so by choosing View, Refresh.

Task Manager: Real-Time Server Monitoring

One other useful tool to manage server performance is the NT 4 Task Manager, shown in Figure 19.23. The Task Manager displays all the ongoing tasks and threads on your machine, as well as their resource usage. You can use the Task Manager to switch tasks, launch new tasks, or end processes.

FIG. 19.23

The Task Manager can be your front-line tool for checking up on server performance.

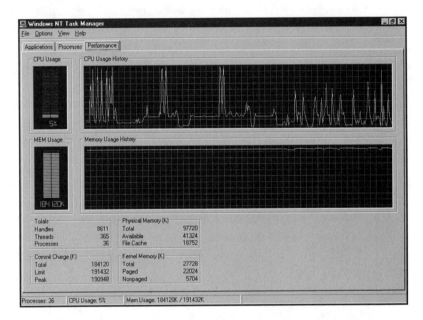

The Task Manager window is broken into a few different areas. Along the top is the obligatory menu bar. Below that is a row of three tabs, with which you can switch views (more details on that subject in a second). Below the tabs is the current view, which displays the constantly updated information appropriate to the selected view. Finally, a status bar lies at the bottom of the window. This status bar displays the current number of running processes, percentage of processor usage (CPU), and memory usage (in the form of physical memory followed by kernel memory).

The Task Manager has three views: Applications, Processes, and Performance. These views are discussed in the following sections.

Applications View If you think of applications as programs running in the foreground of your computer (that is, you can interact with it), the Applications view lets you control these programs. As shown in Figure 19.24, the Applications view lists all the currently running application tasks and the status of each one. You can select a currently running program and use the End Task button to close the program, or the Switch To button to move focus to that program. Otherwise, you can use the New Task button to launch a new program.

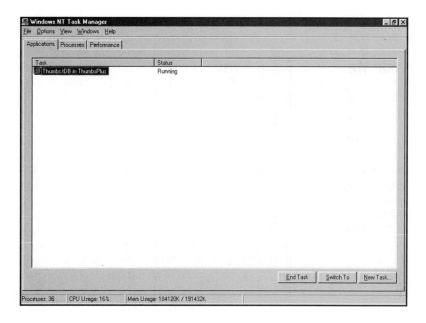

Processes View

When you consider that all activities on your computer are broken up into processes, your machine is filled with a lot of them. Each program has one or more processes running, and most of them are invisible to you. Processes view, shown in Figure 19.25, lets you see what processes are currently running on your machine and what resources they are using. You can select a process from the list and click the End Process button to close the task (if possible).

You also can control the process *priority*. Certain processes on your server may be of greater importance than others; thus, they may be running with more resources allocated to them. This is called priority. You can control the priority of a process by right-clicking its name in the list and choosing Set Priority from the context menu. From there, you can choose to have the process operate in one of these different priorities:

- *Realtime*. If a program relies on instantaneous response and no delay, select Realtime. This option allocates the highest priority to the process.
- *High*. If you want a process to run at better-than-normal performance, choose the High priority to allocate more resources to the task.
- *Normal*. If you want a process to run without any resource boosts or special priority, select Normal. As the computer slows down or speeds up, so does the process.
- *Low*. When you have a task that is not very important, such as an idle program in the background, you may want to move it to a low priority. Do so by choosing Low.

The changes you make in the process's priority is effective only while the process is running. If you end the process and restart it, or restart your machine, you need to adjust the priority.

Part
VI

Ch
19

FIG. 19.25

Processes view lists every process currently running on your machine.

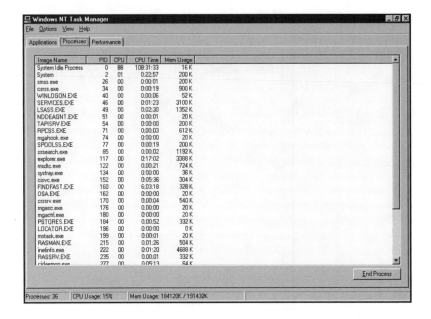

Performance View   Performance view, as shown in Figure 19.26, does not involve any interaction. It displays the status of your machine, including the percentage of CPU usage, memory usage, as well as total processes and threads. In addition, a visual graph depicts both CPU usage history and memory usage history. This view can help you keep an eye on how your computer is behaving.

FIG. 19.26

Performance view acts like a dashboard, giving you a constant readout as to what is going on underneath the hood.

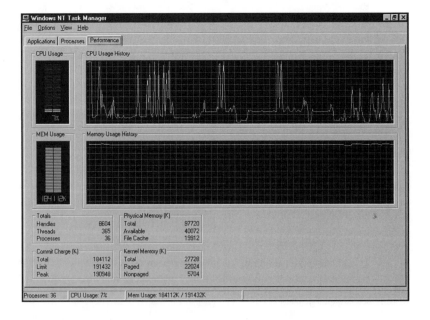

N O T E Task Manager provides minimal customizability, mostly in the form of update intervals. This tool is most useful for taking a quick look at how your machine is doing. For comprehensive studying of your machine, Performance Monitor is more ideally suited. Of course, Task Manager is the only tool to enable you to end processes and adjust their priority instantly. ▪

Resource Management

The tools mentioned in the preceding sections are used for monitoring your server. The actual task of keeping your server afloat relies on the management of your server's resources. Using the information given to you through the Performance Monitor, Event Viewer, and Task Manager, you can make educated decisions on where you need to adjust your server's resources. You can look into the following essential areas:

- *Storage.* Everyone knows that you can never have too much disk space. This axiom holds especially true when you are delivering content to the Internet or an intranet. As you need to increase your storage, you can begin by adding hard disk space to your server. This process and the limitations depend on your hardware platform. Beyond simply adding hard disk space or removing files, you can look to larger storage solutions such as RAID arrays.

- *Memory.* The only commodity more valuable than disk space is RAM. As your server's load increases, expanding your system's memory can add relief in many ways. If you increase RAM, your server can not only deliver content to more people, but also deliver more content faster.

- *Processing power.* If you've looked into adding more memory and that simply hasn't helped the growing pains, you may want to look to a faster processor, or even multiprocessor options. NT's support for multiple processors and symmetric multiprocessing makes it a great platform for delivering content in high-volume sites.

- *Distributing the load.* Growing your one server may be a losing battle when you may be better off moving some services to separate servers. Windows NT's network operating system (NOS) heritage enables you to distribute your services to other NT Servers running within the same NT "Domain" (no relation to Internet domains). If you select one server in your pool to become the Primary Domain Controller (PDC) and each subsequent server as a Backup Domain Controller (BDC), your servers can take advantage of shared user accounts and permissions. If you are running several systems with different user bases, you may want to look at setting up multiple PDCs.

- *Clustering.* So, you've tried more storage, more memory, more processors, and more servers. Those solutions still don't do the trick? Maybe you need to look at clustering. Clustering is the powerful ability to group similar—or even dissimilar—servers to share the load. Clustering allows an entirely new level of fault tolerance for servers, as well as performance increases. Clustering is available through third-party products, such as Digital Clustering from Digital Equipment and from the Microsoft WolfPack Clustering API.

Part
VI

Ch
19

From Here...

Having a healthy server that performs well is integral to all of your Web application development with Visual InterDev. These chapters continue the discussion of server-oriented concepts:

- Chapter 20, "Using the Internet Information Server (IIS)."
- Chapter 23, "Understanding Visual InterDev Security."
- Chapter 27, "Increasing Site Performance."

Using the Internet Information Server (IIS)

In this chapter

IIS **434**

What's New with IIS 4.0 **434**

Using the Management Console to Build Web Sites for VID **436**

Introducing Index Server 2.0 for Visual InterDev **444**

Incorporating Microsoft Transaction Server **447**

Using the SMTP Server **449**

Using the NNTP Server **451**

IIS

At the heart of every Web application is the Web server hosting it. Microsoft's Internet Information Server (IIS) product has evolved a great deal since its introduction a few years ago. The IIS architecture is one of the most highly regarded Web servers available on the market today, and it continues to revolutionize how Web servers should work. The most recent version of IIS, version 4.0, has seen a radical change in its architecture and management features. IIS 4.0 is a truly advanced platform for deploying Web applications and next-generation Web sites.

N O T E   The following section is intended for use as a quick reference for frequently used features and actions in IIS 4.0 when you are working with Visual InterDev. For comprehensive information on using and administering IIS 4.0, refer to the Windows NT Option Pack documentation and other references, such as *Special Edition Using Internet Information Server 4.0* from Macmillan Computer Publishing. ▪

What's New with IIS 4.0

Since its introduction in version 1.0 as a Windows NT Server 3.51 extension, Internet Information Server has continued to evolve at a frantic pace. Each release of IIS has brought significant enhancements and innovations in network hosting and development. IIS 4.0 is no exception; in fact, it is a revolutionary upgrade to the IIS product. Users of previous versions may not even recognize the product through all these changes. Major changes include new administrative interfaces for both Windows-based systems and a powerful Web interface, integration of the Microsoft Transaction Server for creating definitive applications that require transactional processing, addition of both NNTP (news) and SMTP (outgoing email) servers, an upgraded index server for searching your Web site and your documents, and a new Active Server Pages engine for server-side scripting.

Also key to the enhancements in IIS 4.0 are the improvements for developers. Microsoft bills these additions as "reliable application services." They include crash protection to prevent a single site from crashing an entire Web server, script debugging for server-side development, integrated message queuing to send and receive messages reliably over a network, and server-side Java 1.1 support. The following is a list of major improvements and additions to IIS as of version 4.0:

- *Crash Protection.* Anyone who has run multiple Web sites from one Web server is likely to be familiar with the cascading effect when one Web site goes astray. With crash protection, each Web site on the server operates in its own protected space; this way, if the application (server-side scripting, or programs) crashes, it does not dramatically affect the other sites on the server. An added benefit is that IIS 4.0 can restart the failed application at the next request, minimizing the possibility of downtime. This makes real-time development with Visual InterDev a snap.

- *Transacted Active Server Pages.* Primarily used when you are working with database applications, Transacted (or Transactional) Server Pages allow your Web applications (both pages and components) to carry out multiple actions together, or perhaps none at all, depending on the state of the transaction. With Transacted Active Server Pages, you can assure the integrity and quality of the data by mapping your work flow through transactions that require processing before they are approved and committed.

■ *Script Debugging*. Server-side scripting development can be torturous, especially when something goes wrong. IIS 4.0 now has direct hooks into the Microsoft Script Debugger, which allows you, as a developer, to establish breakpoints and conditions for debugging. With this capability in hand, you can now accelerate your development process by catching problems quickly at the development stage rather than at the point of release. This is an important extension to Visual InterDev, allowing you to develop code and immediately see the results.

■ *Java Virtual Machine*. Microsoft's speedy Java 1.1 Virtual Machine has been paired with a new set of Java classes for development of server-side components. Paired with Active Server Pages and Transacted Active Server Pages, your server-side Java components can perform much faster in a demanding environment.

■ *Improved Site and Server Administration*. New to IIS 4.0 is Microsoft's Management Console. You can use this tool to manipulate and control your entire server from one point. You now can create and configure independent sites (for example, Web, FTP, news, or mail) on a per server basis. You can also isolate settings, virtual directories, applications, and conditions on a server, site, or file level. Administration has also been extended to include a powerful Web interface, allowing you to control your site remotely from your browser. You can also use this tool to grant "site operators" permission to manage their own Web sites, independent from your control but within your security constraints.

■ *Content Management and Site Analysis*. IIS 4.0 includes a scaled-down version of Microsoft's Site Server product, called Site Server Express. Site Server Express gives you tools for managing your site, monitoring its traffic, and analyzing patterns of your site's usage and structure.

■ *New Technologies and Standards*. Incorporating the newest of technologies, IIS 4.0 provides support for HTTP 1.1, management of X.509 digital certificates, and communication with NNTP and SMTP servers.

■ *Security Enhancements*. Now administrators can control Web sites on a file and directory level by using the existing Windows NT Security coupled with IIS's unique capability to support several security standards, including 128-bit encryption and X.509 digital certificates that can be mapped to individual users.

■ *And More*. IIS 4.0 includes many other advances and special features that make development site hosting easier, more rewarding, and more productive.

Part
VI

Ch
20

N O T E Internet Information Server 4.0 is available only on the Windows NT Server platform. Unlike previous versions of IIS, the NT Workstation edition is not as closely comparable to the Server product. Users with NT Workstation and Windows 95 can use Microsoft Personal Web Server (PWS). PWS includes many of the features provided in IIS 4.0 but is intended for a small audience (10-user) environment and developers. To take full advantage of these new enhancements, you must be working with an NT Server using the complete IIS 4.0 product. ■

ON THE WEB

For more information on Internet Information Server 4.0 and Microsoft Personal Web Server 4.0, visit the IIS Web site at this address:

http://www.microsoft.com/iis

Product information is available for both products in the IIS family.

Using the Management Console to Build Web Sites for VID

The Microsoft Management Console application is a new tool that is used for creating and managing Web sites under IIS 4.0. With this new program, you can create, maintain, and secure all aspects of your Web site under IIS. Before you can build a Web site, however, you first need to understand the console program.

Introducing the Management Console

The original Internet Service Manager has been replaced with a new administrative tool: the Microsoft Management Console (MMC). The MMC is a consolidated tool for administering your server from one convenient interface. The Management Console has been designed to become the standard for administration of all Microsoft Server products by using "snap-ins" to add support for new products. In fact, Windows NT 5.0 uses the MMC for administration of all aspects of the system. The Management Console, shown in Figure 20.1, is a straightforward tool resembling the Windows Explorer interface.

FIG. 20.1

The Microsoft Management Console is the new standardized administrative tool for future products from Microsoft, including Windows NT 5.0.

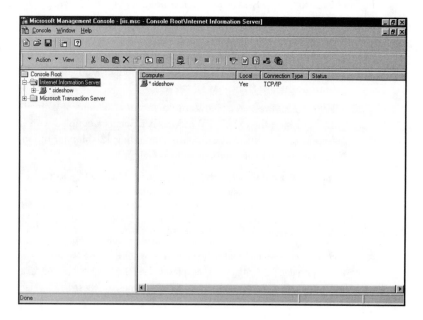

The Management Console's interface is divided into three key areas. Along the top of the console are the traditional menu bar and toolbar. The toolbar dynamically changes to represent the particular service that you are working with at that moment. On the left side of the MMC window is the *scope pane*. The scope represents the specific service or site that you are interacting with. The scope is presented as an Explorer-like "tree" called the *namespace*, descending from the root level. Each "snap-in" represents a particular service (or set of services) in the namespace and is indicated by a root-level folder in the scope pane. As you expand down from the root-level folder, additional "leaves" are displayed. In the case of the IIS snap-in, the root level indicates the IIS service. As you expand the tree, you expand to include servers, services, and then individual sites.

As you select leaves from the namespace, the *results pane* on the right side of the MMC updates to display your selection. Leaves are analogous to folders in the Windows Explorer. What is presented in the results pane is entirely dependent on what you select from the namespace. If you select a specific server in the namespace, the results pane updates to display the services on that server, as shown in Figure 20.2. However, if you select a virtual directory from a Web site in the namespace, the results pane updates to display the files contained in that virtual directory, as shown in Figure 20.3.

FIG. 20.2

When a particular server is selected from the namespace, the results pane updates to display the services on that server for the IIS snap-in.

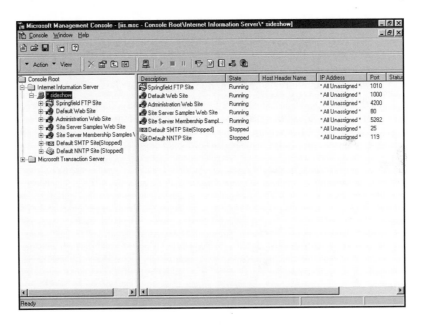

T I P You can customize the MMC namespace easily to create your own personalized console. Choose Console, Add/Remove Snap-In. From the Add/Remove Snap-In dialog box that appears, you can extend your console with the snap-ins you frequently use. You can also add ActiveX objects or URLs. In this dialog box, you can even add the IIS documentation to the namespace, allowing for convenient access.

Part
VI

Ch
20

FIG. 20.3

With a virtual directory selected from a Web site in the namespace, the results pane displays the files and directories located in that virtual directory. This pane is updated dynamically to reflect current changes.

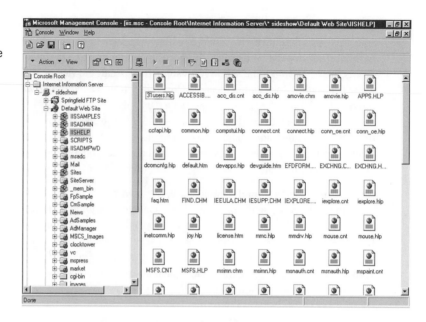

When you select a leaf from the namespace, you are provided with varying *actions* that can be carried out. The actions available to you are dependent on the type of leaf that you select from the namespace. Actions are listed in both the Action drop-down menu in the toolbar (see Figure 20.4) and in the context menu that appears when you right-click the leaf in the namespace (see Figure 20.5). Typical actions include adding items (such as new sites) to or removing them from the namespace, modifying the properties of a selected item, or opening a Web browser at the currently selected item.

FIG. 20.4

This list shows available actions for the item selected.

The Management Console is a straightforward tool for manipulating the different aspects of IIS 4.0. Typically, you will be dealing with the properties of different leaves from the namespace (such as a particular Web site).

FIG. 20.5

Right-clicking an object displays a list of possible actions.

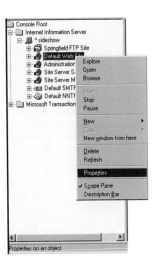

Setting Up Virtual Directories   Virtual directories are common elements in Web sites. Due to many considerations including storage, security, and logistics, having a content directory in the Web site's home directory is not always possible (or desirable). When you want a directory to *appear* as if it is within the site's home directory, you can create a *virtual directory*. A virtual directory acts as an alias to a physical directory that can be on the same server or located on a network drive, transparent to users of your Web site. For example, say that your Web site's home directory is located in c:\inetpub\wwwroot and its URL is **http://www.mydom.dom**. You want to add a directory for your script files, but they are currently located in c:\inetpub\scripts. Rather than physically move the scripts directory into the wwwroot directory, you can create a virtual directory named *scripts* that mimics the path and create a URL of **http://www.mydom.dom/scripts**. In actuality, the location of scripts never moves, but a user on your Web site would never know its true location.

IIS 4.0 lets you create virtual directories on a per site basis. Therefore, a virtual directory you create for Site A is not available in Site B, unless you create the same virtual directory for Site B. You can create a virtual directory by following this simple process:

1. With the Microsoft Management Console open, select your Web site from the namespace tree.

2. From the Actions drop-down menu, choose New, Virtual Directory. Alternatively, right-click the name of your Web site and choose New, Virtual Directory from the context menu.

3. When the New Virtual Directory Wizard dialog box appears, as shown in Figure 20.6, enter the name of your virtual directory's alias into the text box. This is the name of the virtual directory that will be used in your URL.

Part
VI

Ch
20

FIG. 20.6

The New Virtual Directory Wizard lets you quickly create your virtual directories on a site-by-site basis.

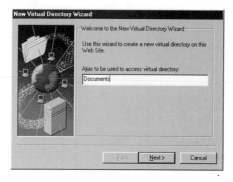

4. Click the Next button to proceed to the next page of the wizard, shown in Figure 20.7.

FIG. 20.7

Although the dialog box asks for a physical directory path, the path can instead be a network path using Universal Naming Conventions (UNC).

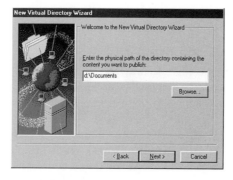

5. Enter the path to the directory you want to use as your content directory. It can be either a physical directory path (C:\Directory) or a UNC path (\\Server\Share). You optionally can click the Browse button to select the directory using a GUI explorer.

6. Click the Next button to proceed to the next page of the wizard, shown in Figure 20.8.

FIG. 20.8

You can set virtual directory access permissions here.

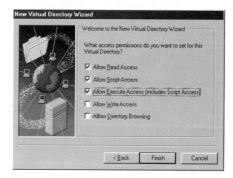

7. The third page of the New Virtual Directory Wizard lets you select the access permissions for the virtual directory. From the five check boxes, select the access permissions you want to grant to all users.

Virtual Directory Access Permissions

The five check boxes in the third page of the New Virtual Directory Wizard represent different permissions that users can have in your virtual directory. By default, the top two check boxes are selected. The choices are as follow:

- *Allow Read Access*. Users can access and view files located in this directory.
- *Allow Script Access*. Active Server Pages located in this directory are allowed to execute their respective server-side scripts.
- *Allow Execute Access*. Server-side programs are allowed to execute when accessed by a user. This option also enables script access for the directory.
- *Allow Write Access*. This option permits writing to the directory via scripts or HTTP upload facilities.
- *Allow Directory Browsing*. This option allows users to view the contents of a directory if a default document is not loaded for the requested URL.

You can use combinations of these check boxes to create access permissions ideal for your virtual directory's needs.

---

8. Click the Finish button to commit your changes and close the New Virtual Directory Wizard.

You can modify the attributes of your virtual directory at any time by selecting it from the namespace in the scope pane and choosing Properties from the Action menu or from the context menu that appears when you right-click.

Setting Up Virtual Domains   Virtual domains are distinct Web sites located on the same physical Web server. With virtual domains, you can host more than one Web site with the same IIS 4.0 server, without users ever realizing they are dealing with the same machine. IIS's support for virtual domains has evolved a great deal from previous versions. As of IIS 4.0, virtual domains are referred to as *Web sites* in the Microsoft Management Console. Each site has its own tree in the IIS namespace and its own attributes. Properties for individual sites can be modified as required, without affecting the operation of others. This flexibility has created a powerful platform for administrators and developers alike: Administrators can freely isolate Web sites so that they do not disrupt other services on the server, and developers have the freedom to experiment without fearing damage to other virtual domains.

Creation of new virtual domains or Web sites requires careful attention to two details:

- The IP address for the virtual domain must already be assigned and functioning on the NT Server.
- If the new Web site uses a unique domain name, the fully qualified domain name (FQDN) must be updated in the domain's Domain Name Services (DNS) records. It can

Part
VI

Ch
20

be managed by your Internet service provider, network administrator, or even by yourself.

If these points are not taken care of, your users may not be able to access your new site. After these points are resolved, you can create your virtual domain. To create the site, follow these steps:

1. Select your server from the IIS namespace tree.

2. From the Action menu, choose <u>N</u>ew, Web Site. Alternatively, right-click the server name and select <u>N</u>ew, Web Site from the context menu.

3. When the New Web Site Wizard appears, as shown in Figure 20.9, enter a description of your new virtual domain in the <u>W</u>eb Site Description text box. This description identifies your site from a list in the MMC. For example, a new marketing Web site may have a description that reads: `Marketing Dept's Promotions Web Site`.

FIG. 20.9

The New Web Site Wizard simplifies the site creation process.

4. Click the <u>N</u>ext button to advance to the second page of the wizard, shown in Figure 20.10.

FIG. 20.10

Here, you can assign a new IP address to your virtual domain.

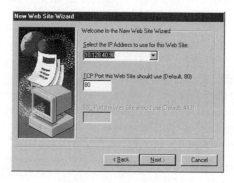

5. From the <u>S</u>elect the IP Address to Use for This Web Site drop-down list box, choose the IP address that corresponds to your new virtual domain. If you do not specify an IP address, your new site will respond on any IP address bound to the server that has not been assigned to another Web site.

6. Enter the port for your new Web site to use in the TCP Port This Web Site Should Use text box. The default port for all Web sites is 80; however, you may require a different port number for your new site.

7. If you have a Secure Sockets Layer (SSL) certificate present on your NT Server, you can enable SSL encryption for your Web site. Enter the port that SSL connections should use in the SSL Port This Web Site Should Use text box. The default port for SSL is 443.

8. Click the Next button to advance to the next page of the wizard. This page is shown in Figure 20.11.

FIG. 20.11
Here, you can enter the new home directory for the new Web site.

9. Enter the directory path for your Web site's home directory in the Enter the Path for Your Home Directory text box. Optionally, you can click the Browse button to use a GUI explorer to select the directory. This directory can be either a local directory or a network share on another server.

10. If you want to allow any visitor access to your Web site (the default), select the Allow Anonymous Access to This Web Site check box. However, if you want to restrict access to allow only authorized users, make sure that this check box is not selected.

11. Click the Next button to proceed. On the next page, shown in Figure 20.12, you can determine access permissions for your new site.

FIG. 20.12
The access permissions for the Web site are identical to those given for virtual directories.

Part
VI

Ch
20

12. From the five check boxes, select the access permissions you want to be used for your Web site. These access permissions are identical to those used for virtual directories (see "Setting Up Virtual Directories" earlier in this chapter).

13. Click the Finish button to commit your changes and create the site.

You can modify the attributes of your new Web site as the need arises. To do so, select the site's icon from the namespace in the scope pane, and select Properties from the Action menu. You can also select Properties from the context menu that appears when you right-click the site icon.

Introducing Index Server 2.0 for Visual InterDev

These days, nearly everyone has first-hand experience with a search engine on the World Wide Web. Index Server was introduced as Microsoft's offering for IIS-powered Web sites, providing searching not only of Web site contents but also other document types (such as Microsoft Word and Excel files). Index Server, as its name implies, indexes the contents and properties of selected content files. Using the Index Server's database, you can create customized "search forms" for your Web site's users to search for specific material. Index Server 2.0 is, like its previous version, an IIS-specific extension. Coupled with the power of the IIS application platform, Index Server lets you create complex applications and searchable contents.

Getting Started with Index Server

With Index Server installed (refer to the Windows NT 4.0 Option Pack documentation), setting up your first index is a relatively painless process. Before your site's users can actually begin searching your site, you must create an index for them to access. An index can represent individual files, a local physical directory, a network share, or even a virtual directory on your Web site. Index Server uses the term *scope* to represent the set of documents that are to be searched. You can establish multiple scopes for your Web sites, allowing certain pages and users access to particular searches. To enable indexing for your Web site and/or specific physical or virtual directories, follow these steps:

1. In the Microsoft Management Console for Internet Information Server (Internet Services Manager), select your Web site, directory, or virtual directory from the namespace.

2. Choose Action, Properties to open the Site Properties/Virtual Directory Properties dialog box. Alternatively, you can right-click the icon in the namespace and select Properties from the context menu.

3. For Web sites, click the Home Directory tab to view the page shown in Figure 20.13. Directories and virtual directories default to identical pages titled Directory and Virtual Directory, respectively.

4. To index this Web site (including its home directory and subdirectories), directory, or virtual directory, select the Index This Directory check box. This option instructs the Index Server that this directory should be indexed and made searchable.

FIG. 20.13

Here, you can set the attributes for your Web site's home directory.

5. Click OK to commit your changes and close the Site Properties/Directory Properties dialog box.

Identifying the scope of your index does not necessarily mean that the search will be immediately available to your users. You must create the initial index. The Index Server indexes your new scope; however, this process may take some time. To force an immediate scan of your new index, follow these steps:

1. Open the Index Server Manager MMC from the Start menu. (You optionally can choose to add the Index Server snap-in to your existing MMC window.)

2. Select the Directories leaf from the namespace tree in the scope pane. The results pane refreshes to resemble the one shown in Figure 20.14.

FIG. 20.14

Selecting Directories lists all the local directory paths that Index Server is responsible for indexing on your server.

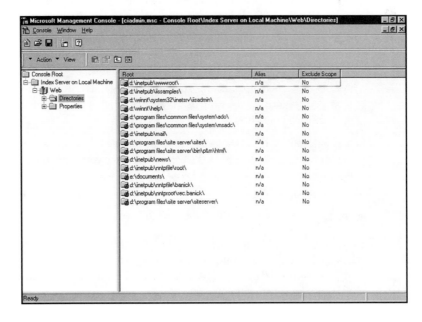

3. Locate and select the physical directory path that represents your site, directory, or virtual directory under the Root column.

4. Choose Action, Rescan. Alternatively, right-click the path and select Rescan from the context menu.

5. When the Full Rescan? dialog box, shown in Figure 20.15, appears, click the Yes button to force the rescan of the index. If you force a rescan of a directory that is filled with content, it may take some time for the indexing to finish. Always weigh the importance of a fresh index versus server performance.

FIG. 20.15

Choose whether you want a full rescan for building a new index list.

6. Repeat these steps as needed for each index you want to force. When you are done, close the Index Server Manager MMC window.

After the Index Server finishes rescanning your directory, the index is available for searching.

Creating the Search Form

Visitors to your Web site interact with the Index Server through a search form. With Index Server, you can customize the search form to suit your needs and your site's appearance. You can also customize how the results returned from the Index Server will appear. The Index Server provides three default files for use in searching on your site:

- *Query.htm.* The search form itself. Your site's visitors use this page to search your index. By default, this file is located in /iissamples/issamples/query.htm.

- *Query.idq.* The configuration file for the query. This file is used to establish the scope of your search. A typical scope is a physical directory or a virtual directory. By default, this file is located in /iissamples/issamples/query.idq.

- *Query.htx.* The output of your search. This page determines how the results of your search are formatted for the users. By default, this file is located in /iissamples/issamples/query.htx.

You can customize each of these files to suit your needs. Ideally, you should copy these files into your own Web site and leave the originals in case you need them later. To begin, copy the Query.htm file into your Web site's home directory with the name search.htm. Copy the query.idq and query.htx files to new files named search.idq and search.htx, respectively.

Begin by customizing your search form, as follows:

1. Open the search.htm file in your Web site's directory for editing.

2. Customize the page's appearance to suit your needs. For example, replace the page's title (Sample HTM/IDQ/HTX Search Form) with your own title, and replace the Index Server Logo with your own title.

3. Search for the line that reads

```
<FORM ACTION="query.idq" METHOD="GET">
```

4. Replace the preceding line with

```
<FORM ACTION="/iissamples/issamples/search.idq" METHOD="GET">
```

5. Search for the line that reads

```
<INPUT TYPE="HIDDEN" NAME="HTMLQueryForm" VALUE="query.htm">
```

6. Replace the preceding line with

```
<INPUT TYPE="HIDDEN" NAME="HTMLQueryForm" VALUE="/search.htm">
```

7. Save your changes, and close the search.htm file.

With your search form customized to suit your needs, you now must configure the search to refer to the proper scope:

1. Open the search.idq file in an editor. This file is typically located in the InetPub\iissamples\Issamples directory.

2. Locate the line that reads

```
CiScope=%CiScope%
```

3. Edit the line to read

```
CiScope=/<Site or Directory Name>
```

For example, your line might read

```
CiScope=/Marketing
```

4. Save your changes to the search.idq file, and close it.

Now test your search by opening the search.htm page via your Web browser. Your search should return matches from the specified index. Figure 20.16 displays a sample search form.

 TIP By default, Index Server uses the HTM, IDQ, and HTX files for searches. You can augment or replace these files with Active Server Pages. This way, you can create dynamic applications that directly interact with the Index Server. Refer to the Windows NT 4.0 Option Pack documentation for information.

Part
VI

Ch
20

Incorporating Microsoft Transaction Server

Developers can look at Microsoft Transaction Server (MTS) as the plumbing that makes powerful Web applications possible. Microsoft bills MTS as a product that "...handles many of the complexities of developing secure, scalable and reliable client/server and Web applications." Using MTS, you can concentrate on the core of your application: the workflow and business logic. When you use MTS, complex projects require less development time and less complex programming. IIS 4.0's integration with MTS offers three key benefits:

- A three-tier application model
- Transacted Active Server Pages
- Application services

FIG. 20.16
By using the search.htx
file, you can customize
how your search results
appear to the user.

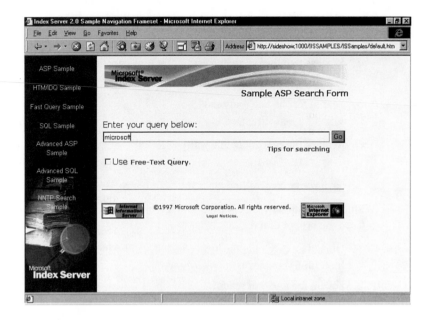

Transacted Active Server Pages

IIS 3.0 introduced Active Server Pages (ASP) to developers. ASP enabled developers to create and deploy server-side logic quickly in a Web site without relying on compiled languages. This capability made development and changes quick and relatively painless. The addition of Transacted Active Server Pages (or Transactional Server Pages) adds another layer of power to developers. The key feature missing in server-side scripting was the ability to ensure the integrity of the script's results. Using Transacted Active Server Pages, you can create server operations that involve many steps using checkpoints. These checkpoints can monitor the quality of your transaction and abort the process should any of the intermediary steps fail to deliver the required information.

Applications such as ordering, billing, and checking inventory rely on transactions to make sure that the data is accurate and no mistakes have been made through the process. Transacted Active Server Pages let you create complex workflow engines and logic to manage your Web applications. With this flexibility, Web applications can realistically take their place alongside traditional client/server applications.

Application Services

To support MTS and transactional services, IIS must have the support infrastructure to support these features. With IIS 4.0 and Microsoft Transaction Server, developers can package components so that they run with transactions. The following are some of the benefits:

- Support for components created in nearly any language (Visual Basic, Visual C++, or Visual J++, for example). This support translates into support for ActiveX components and Java applets on the server level.

- Simple interfaces for developing transactions. MTS provides two main Application Programming Interfaces (APIs) for developing transactional server components.

- Process and thread management that is automatically handled by IIS and MTS. Low-level system resources are taken care of so that your components can operate properly in a multiuser environment without added complexity.

- Component packaging handled by MTS so that you do not have to deploy your components manually as you would in a traditional application. This benefit directly translates into less time deploying and more time doing what needs to be done.

- A shared property manager that is present in Microsoft Transaction Server, making it easy to share data among concurrent components and applications. MTS manages the complexities of state-sharing and synchronization of data.

N O T E For more information on the Microsoft Transaction Server, refer to the MTS documentation included in the Windows NT Option Pack documentation. ▤

Using the SMTP Server

With email being a large part of the Internet, Microsoft elected to include a solid outgoing (not incoming) mail server using the Internet-wide standard Simple Mail Transfer Protocol (SMTP). Because it is integrated into IIS 4.0, you can create and manage individual mail sites for delivering mail over the Internet or an intranet. This mail server is intended for outgoing mail only, not incoming; it does not provide a facility for picking up mail after it has been received. The SMTP server uses a "directed mail drop and pickup" approach, letting you use the SMTP server to send and receive mail messages as a mail transfer agent, while using another package (or perhaps a Web application) such as Microsoft Exchange Server to manage the delivery of the mail to individual users using a mail client such as Microsoft Outlook.

Like the other services included with IIS 4.0, the SMTP server can be administered directly from the Microsoft Management Console or from the HTML administration interface. It also offers advanced security options, including Transport Layer Security (TLS) for encrypting transmissions. With the SMTP server's approach, it is a scalable application that can service several hundred client connections in a single server setting.

Key Components to the Microsoft SMTP Service

As far as the SMTP Service is concerned, the Microsoft Management Console has four main components. The following components, all located in the namespace, represent different levels of interaction with the SMTP server itself:

- *Computers*. The main administrative component of IIS, the computer, represents a physical server. Each server can have several different IIS services installed on it.

- *SMTP Site*. On the SMTP Service scale, this is its main administrative component. Properties set for the SMTP Site affect all the *domains* that it handles.

Part
VI

Ch
20

■ *Domains.* Acting as an organizational component, each domain is a particular domain for which the SMTP Service accepts mail. For example, **microsoft.com** services all users who have email addresses like **user@microsoft.com**.

■ *Current Sessions.* Providing you with status information on your service, the Current Sessions component lists each established connection to your SMTP Service, its duration, and its origin.

On the physical directory level, all SMTP Service mail is located in a *mail root*. The mail root, by default, is located at root:\Inetpub\Mailroot. Within the mail root directory are several subdirectories that store the individual mail files dependent on their status. These subdirectories are as follow:

■ *Badmail.* This directory contains undeliverable mail that cannot be returned to the original sender.

■ *Drop.* All incoming mail for the hosted domains is located in a Drop directory.

■ *Pickup.* Outgoing mail that has completed processing is placed in this directory and then delivered by the SMTP Service.

■ *Queue.* Pending deliveries are placed in the Queue directory. Messages that cannot be delivered because of a busy server or network outage remain here, and delivery attempts are tried at different intervals.

Creating an SMTP Mail Domain

Creating a new SMTP mail domain is a straightforward process in the Microsoft Management Console. First, open the MMC, and then follow these steps:

1. In the IIS namespace, select the Default SMTP Site.

2. From the Action menu, choose New, Domain. Alternatively, right-click the Default SMTP Site and select New, Domain from the context menu. The New Domain Wizard appears, as shown in Figure 20.17.

FIG. 20.17
The New Domain Wizard lets you easily create mail domains for use on your IIS server.

3. Determine whether the mail server will deliver inbound mail (acting as an endpoint) or send mail to another server (outgoing) by selecting either Local or Remote, respectively.

4. Click the <u>N</u>ext button to proceed to the second page of the wizard, shown in Figure 20.18.

FIG. 20.18
Here, you can select a name for your domain.

5. Enter the name to be used for the new domain in the text box. Make sure that it is a valid domain name that has been configured in a DNS server.

6. Click the Finish button to commit your changes and close the dialog box.

N O T E For more information on the Microsoft SMTP Service, refer to the Windows NT Option Pack documentation. ▓

Using the NNTP Server

Using newsgroups is a commonly accepted method for communication on the Internet. Newsgroups also provide an ideal way to share information on an intranet. Using the NNTP Service and IIS 4.0, you can create discussion groups for your organization or your Internet site. Conversations can be grouped, allowing individuals to post articles relating to a particular topic so that others can access them. The Internet standard Network News Transfer Protocol (or NNTP) is the heart of Microsoft's NNTP Service. This service, which has a scalable architecture, offers you a reliable and secure means of allowing many different clients to share information.

The NNTP Service is directly integrated with IIS 4.0 and the Microsoft Management Console. Like the SMTP Service, it also offers enhanced security. The NNTP Service supports anonymous access, standard NNTP security (using a name and password), Windows NT Challenge/Response protocol, and Secure Socket Layers for encryption.

Creating an NNTP Newsgroup

The Microsoft NNTP Service views individual newsgroups as virtual directories. By creating a virtual directory in the NNTP Service namespace, you are, in fact, creating a new newsgroup for use by your clients. To create a new newsgroup, follow these steps:

Part
VI

Ch
20

1. Open the Microsoft Management Console for Internet Services Manager.

2. Select the Default NNTP Site icon in the namespace.

3. From the Action menu, choose New, Virtual Directory. Alternatively, right-click the Default NNTP Site icon and choose New, Virtual Directory from the context menu.

4. When the New Virtual Directory Wizard dialog box, shown in Figure 20.19, appears, enter the name of your new newsgroup in the text box. For example, enter `alt.microsoft`.

FIG. 20.19
The name you select for your virtual directory is how it will appear in your users' NNTP clients.

5. Click the Next button to proceed to the second page of the wizard, shown in Figure 20.20.

FIG. 20.20
Here, you can enter the path where the news content should be stored.

6. Enter the physical directory path that will be used to store the articles for this newsgroup. Alternatively, click the Browse button to select the directory using a GUI explorer. The Microsoft NNTP Service considers virtual directories within itself as newsgroups.

7. Click the Finish button to commit your changes and close the dialog box.

Controlling Access in Your Newsgroup

With your newsgroup created, you may want to limit access inside it. To control the access permissions and properties for your newsgroup, open the Internet Services Manager MMC and follow these steps:

1. Select your newsgroup from the MMC namespace.

2. Choose Action, Properties. Alternatively, right-click the newsgroup's icon and select Properties from the context menu.

3. The newsgroup Properties dialog box appears, similar to the one shown in Figure 20.21. This dialog box lets you control the access restrictions to your newsgroup, its local path, and secure communications.

FIG. 20.21

The newsgroup Properties dialog box specifies the settings for your new group.

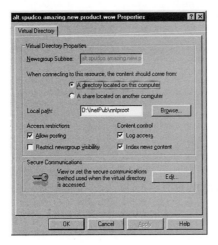

4. By default, newsgroups allow posting. If you want this newsgroup to be a read-only group, deselect the Allow Posting check box.

5. If you want to hide your newsgroup from view for those who do not have access, select the Restrict Newsgroup Visibility check box.

6. To allow your newsgroup's contents to be searchable, select the Index News Contents check box.

7. To keep a log file with the details of users accessing your newsgroup, select the Log Access check box.

8. If you have an SSL certificate on your server and want to enable SSL for your newsgroup, click the Edit button to open the Secure Communications dialog box, and specify your SSL information.

9. Click OK to close this dialog box and commit your changes.

Part
VI

Ch
20

With your newsgroup created and the access permissions modified, it is ready for use. Open your NNTP news client, and post a few test messages to verify that everything is functioning correctly.

N O T E For more information on the Microsoft NNTP Service, refer to the Windows NT Option Pack documentation. ■

From Here...

Internet Information Server is the core of your Web application. Having a happy and healthy Web server is dependent on the condition of your server and your Web application. Look to the following chapters for more information related to your server:

- Chapter 25, "Designing and Organizing Web Sites."
- Chapter 27, "Increasing Site Performance."

CHAPTER 21

Working with Site Server Enterprise Edition

In this chapter

What Is Site Server? **456**

Working with the Publishing Features of Site Server **457**

Site Indexing with Site Server Search **459**

Delivering Content with Site Server **460**

Site Server Commerce Edition **463**

What Is Site Server?

Internet Information Server 4.0 alone is a powerful platform for developing Web applications. Using IIS, combined with the extended capabilities of Microsoft Site Server, you can create and manage large sites and applications with reduced effort. Site Server 3.0 is focused primarily on intranet sites, although it is equally applicable for Internet sites. Microsoft bills Site Server as a tool that "…allows users and administrators to publish information easily by providing authors with a structured content submission, posting, and approval process." Site Server extends the capabilities of IIS to include important management and analysis tools, as well as intriguing features that can be implemented into any site. In addition to Site Server 3.0 Enterprise Edition, Microsoft offers a Site Server 3.0 Commerce Edition. The Commerce Edition extends the Enterprise Edition with business-minded features, making advertising and sales management over a Web application easier. This chapter briefly explores Site Server Enterprise and Commerce Editions to demonstrate the capabilities each one has, and how you can use them to compliment Visual InterDev.

So what is Site Server? Microsoft Site Server is a set of extensions to IIS 4.0, primarily geared toward intranet development. Site Server focuses on extending the capabilities of IIS to make development, deployment, and management of a site easier. Several new services and tools are included with Site Server Enterprise Edition to make development and administration easier. The features of Site Server can be broken up into four distinct categories:

- *Publishing*. When you are working with large sites involving many contributors, a structured publishing process is a necessity. Site Server implements a structured process for managing submissions from multiple authors. Users appointed as *site editors* can then approve, edit, and enforce guidelines for all content before it is posted to the site. This frees you from having to establish informal guidelines from within Visual InterDev—insuring that only those who are allowed to can alter certain aspects of your site.

- *Staging*. Site Server takes development work to production through a staging process. Staging may involve moving content from a staging directory on the production server or moving data between multiple staging servers to the production environment. Using the staging process, you can filter and control the quality of all material before it is deployed live on your endpoint server, be it a Windows NT server or a UNIX server. This allows you to use Visual InterDev to develop your Web site, and use Site Server to stage it to another server.

- *Content Tagging*. Microsoft considers *content tagging* as the development of a standardized and structured site-wide vocabulary that authors can use to classify developed content. Using content tagging, you can then provide a more effective search engine to your users for expedient information retrieval. You can also use content tagging to create intricate and organized indexes of your site. This frees you from having to establish informal guidelines from within Visual InterDev—insuring that only those who are allowed to can alter certain aspects of your site.

■ *Web Site Analysis.* One of the ongoing struggles for nearly every Web site administrator and developer is getting an understanding of how the site is used. Site Server provides you with the tools to analyze your site's traffic, usage, and content trees. With this data, you can map usage data and see which parts of your site and content are proving the most popular. Microsoft states "…by measuring the effectiveness of your site, you can ensure it is meeting its business objective."

Microsoft Site Server Enterprise Edition introduces content management and deployment features that map to a four-step publishing process:

1. Content submission
2. Content tagging
3. Editor approval
4. Content deployment

After the deployment is completed, you can then use Site Server to analyze your site for the following:

■ Usage information based on particular areas of your site or content types

■ The content on your site, based on content tagging

■ The type of audience visiting your site—in particular, the users' browser capabilities

■ The effectiveness of your site

Working with the Publishing Features of Site Server

Site Server provides you with a number of publishing features to make your site development easier. This works in conjunction with Visual InterDev's publishing features that you use on an ongoing basis to develop your content. Keeping in mind that Site Server is geared toward multiple-author environments, these features may or may not prove beneficial to a single developer. Of particular benefit to multiple-author environments are

■ Customizable starter sites

■ Content management

■ Content deployment

Customizable Starter Sites

Site Server Enterprise Edition includes three customizable sites that you can use as a starting framework for your own site. Each site is an example of a powerful Web application that can be deployed in minimal time using the features of Site Server. Depending on your goals, you can add or remove elements and sections to the sites. The following sample starter sites benefit from easy customization using Visual InterDev 6 or Microsoft FrontPage 98, as well as easy implementation of the Site Server technologies:

■ *Business Internet Site*. The most common commercial Web site on the Internet is the business Internet site, representing a company to the diverse audience of the Internet. The business Internet site is focused on targeting potential customers and communicating information about your company's products and services. This site includes features such as data sheets, frequently asked questions, and media releases. A powerful survey feature is also included to poll visitors to the site for information. In addition to the survey feature, the business Internet site also includes a members' forum for information exchange and community-minded discussion. The business Internet site uses the personalization, membership, push, search, content deployment, content tagging, and content analysis features of Site Server.

■ *Enterprise Information Site*. Intranets are becoming more predominant, as they allow your company to distribute information effectively across geographical boundaries with limited costs. The enterprise information site offers several key intranet features that can be customized to suit your needs. Internal directories, event calendars, job postings, and information bulletins are smoothly integrated into this sample using the personalization, content management, content deployment, content tagging, content analysis, and usage analysis features of Site Server. This sample site also includes a demonstration on how effectively reports can be distributed online by using IIS 4.0 and Site Server.

■ *Online Support Site*. One of the best ways of showcasing Site Server is by using the online support site. This site demonstrates the power of electronic helpdesks to lower traditional support costs by using preconfigured support areas and information. A transactional electronic helpdesk is present in this site, allowing users to request information from support personnel and posting of information by the same support personnel for specific users. A functional knowledge base engine demonstrates Site Server's advanced search capabilities. The online support site uses Site Server's personalization, content management, content deployment, content tagging, content analysis, and usage analysis features.

You can use each of these starter sites as the launch pad for your own projects. Review these sites, even if you do not plan to use them. They are ideal examples of how Site Server works and what it offers to developers and administrators alike.

Content Management

Effective site publishing relies on effective management of the site's contents. Using the content management features of Site Server, multiple developers, authors, and editors can contribute to a site while maintaining consistency and accessibility for the users or visitors. Content management relies on several stages:

1. *Content Submission*. Typically acting from a remote site, content authors submit site content using a Web browser, such as Microsoft Internet Explorer. Content is dragged and dropped onto the Web interface provided by Site Server. Content can be of multiple file types, including traditional Web documents and Microsoft Office documents. The Web interface enforces security using defined roles such as "author," "editor," or "user."

2. *Content Tagging*. When authors submit their content, they can then assign content tags to the content. Content tags identify what type of content is being submitted. Site editors can define content tags to include any data required, such as author, expiration information, section, and owner. These tags are used to establish a consistent vocabulary throughout the site and can be modified by the editors. These tags are considered *metadata* and are used to index the site and analyze data.

3. *Editorial Approval*. With the content categorized and tagged, the site editors can then evaluate the material and determine whether it is appropriate to be published. The editors can define more attributes to the content, adding to the metadata for the material. This activity streamlines the publishing process and makes it easier to ensure quality control.

4. *Separation of Production and Presentation Format*. Due to Site Server's publishing process, authors can use whatever tools they want to create content. Site Server can use the metadata and content tags to determine how the content should be presented to the end users.

Content Deployment

The Content Deployment service of Site Server was formerly known as the Content Replication System, found in the Microsoft Commercial Internet System suite of tools. The Content Deployment service lets sites and organizations perform secure and reliable remote deployment of content between Web servers. The deployed content can be Web-specific content, components, or even Microsoft Office documents. You can use content deployment as a means of staging between multiple development servers to a production environment, or for mirroring content throughout multiple sites. Content can be deployed to dissimilar servers—for example, from Windows NT servers to UNIX servers. You can even use content deployment on the same server to automate the process of moving from a staging directory to production.

Site Indexing with Site Server Search

Although IIS 4.0 includes a powerful indexing and search engine, it may not fulfill all the requirements in many environments. Site Server Search takes the already powerful Index Server and adds expansive support for more data sources, filtering, crawling, language mapping, and advanced features. Site Server also can create a catalog of your information assets, based on content tagging, that lets users quickly locate the information they are looking for—as opposed to searching through Index Server results. Site Server Search included the following features:

- The ability to index not only local file system documents, but also Web resources, Exchange Server folders, ODBC Databases (such as SQL Server), and Microsoft NNTP service
- The ability for users to search across multiple data sources using a single query
- Automatic language detection for both content and user queries
- Higher fidelity searches using content tagging

- Fault-tolerant and incremental crawling searches
- URL mapping
- Distributed architecture
- Control over the information stored in the index, including data of certain formats, certain types, and subdirectories; inclusion or exclusion of meta tags, OLE properties, and file system properties
- Secure indexes using NTLM and basic authentication, as well as file-system level access control using file ACLs
- Personalized searches, using Site Server personalization features
- Adherence to "Robot Exclusion Rules" when site crawling

Site Server Search continues in the same fashion as IIS 4.0 with both Microsoft Management Console–based administration and a Web-based HTML administrator, for cross-platform control.

Delivering Content with Site Server

Using Site Server, you can gather information from different sources and target it to your users through focused delivery or precise searching. Site Server aims to deliver content to users at the right time or enable users to locate the information easily when they need it. With this capability, coupled with content tagging and Site Server Search, users should be able to locate the data they need when they need it. Site Server delivery features are broken down into four categories:

- Knowledge Manager
- Push
- Personalization and Membership Services
- Analysis Tools

Site Server Knowledge Manager

Using the Site Server Knowledge Manager, you can create a central resource for knowledge and information contained in your site whenever content is added or changed. The Knowledge Manager uses content tagging to organize site content and keep a categorical database. Users can then search or browse for the information they need based on a common site vocabulary. The Knowledge Manager can also be used to create *Briefing Centers*, which let you deliver to users *knowledge briefs* that are organized by specific topics. *Shared briefs* can be delivered or shared among many users, when information must be sent to more than one individual. After a brief is defined, users can opt to visit your site for updates, or have updates delivered to them via email or push publishing.

Knowledge Manager also creates a *Channel Center*, which acts as a central repository for information on push channels available to users. Users can specify which channels they want to receive or personalize. Coupled with Briefing Centers, the Channel Center can be used to deliver focused information to already-interested users. This concentrated information delivery reduces the need for users to consciously seek out the information they need and lets them get on with their work.

Push Publishing

With the introduction of Internet Explorer 4.0, Microsoft entered the "push publishing" arena. Push publishing lets content developers deliver content to interested users directly rather than rely on the users to visit the site every time an update is added or a change made. Push publishing relies on visiting users subscribing to the content in the form of a channel. At a schedule determined by either the publisher or the users, the users' clients retrieve updated information. In essence, push publishing is more analogous to "smart pull" because it still relies on the users to initiate the subscription and the users' clients to retrieve the content. Site Server's "push solution" includes the following:

- *Active Channel Server.* Using the Active Channel Server, administrators can manage and update channels in a project-oriented fashion. In addition to creating Channel Definition Format (CDF) files that comprise push channels for Internet Explorer 4.0, you can also use the Active Channel Server to establish the frequency of updates for each channel.

- *Active Channel Multicaster.* For multicast-capable networks (typically LANs), channels can be delivered to multiple desktops using one stream of data. This capability minimizes the amount of network congestion created by multiple transmissions to users in close network proximity.

- *Active Channel Agents.* Site Server can automate the addition of content to channels using Active Channel Agents. Active Channel Agents are scripts that retrieve content from any supported data source (file directory, ODBC database, Index Server catalog, Site Server Commerce databases, Site Server Search catalogs, and Knowledge Manager knowledge briefs) and place the content into channels.

You can use Site Server's push capabilities any time that data must be reliably and efficiently delivered to multiple users without manual intervention. Typical examples include departmental updates, subscription services, and news provisioning.

Personalization and Membership Services

The Personalization and Membership Services, also carried over from the Microsoft Commercial Internet System suite, enable developers to create customizable sites and applications. The Personalization and Membership Services manage the complexities of storing information for each visitor so that Web applications can be more easily created using Visual InterDev. A Web site can "remember" what site users last visited and what information may be important to them. Using that information, a more focused site is accessible to the users. The site can adapt itself to the users' behaviors rather than force the users to interact to suit the site. This is an incredible benefit for Visual InterDev developers.

Part
VI

Ch
21

Site Server's enhancements to the Personalization and Membership Services include the following:

- *Rule Manager.* Using a marketing-oriented perspective, the Rule Manager lets an administrator (or marketing person) directly interact with the Web site. Using a point-and-click interface, you can build or modify content targeting rules without requiring extensive development. For example, on a whim you could change the focus of certain areas of your Web site based on who is viewing the pages.

- *Direct Mail.* Using the Membership database, sites can establish a connection with users with personalized email. On either an ad hoc or scheduled basis, electronic mail messages (in a variety of formats) can be sent to users or customers to alert them of important information or changes. Direct mail also supports the sending of file attachments, for automated delivery of important files.

- *Analysis.* Using Site Server Analysis and the Membership database, you can also create rich user profiles and analyze who is visiting your site. With this information in hand, you can then modify the flow of your site and target your content to the users, even with direct mail.

Site Server Analysis

Without an effective means of measuring your site's usage and visitors, Web sites are gambles at best. Site Server provides extensive analysis tools for examining exactly who is using your site, why, and what content is most popular. Using the information provided through the analysis tools, you can refine your content to suit the needs of your users. You can also use this information to map out possible trends and predict what path you should take in the future. Analysis in Site Server is not limited to usage analysis, however; it also provides extensive support for content analysis. If you use content tags in your site, content analysis ensures quality and consistency throughout your site. If an element in your site does not conform to your requirements (such as load sizes, for example), you can then take action on it. Site Server's analysis features offer the following:

- *Usage Analysis.* Traditional analysis for a Web site monitors the site's traffic or usage. Usage analysis often determines the return on investment for a site and exactly how popular sections of your site are. Each interaction with your site records a "hit." By monitoring the hits throughout your site, you can determine where your traffic is coming from, what sections of your site are proving the most popular, and where users are returning to. With this information, you can then determine what course to take with your Web site: Are sections being underused? Are you seeing a lot of traffic from a particular service provider? You can use these measures to determine the success of your site.

- *Content Analysis.* As mentioned previously, content analysis lets you run a tight ship. Using content analysis, you can monitor for content quality, consistency, and conformance to site policy. Content analysis lets you better judge your site and see where improvements need to be made.

■ *User Analysis.* Directly integrated with the Membership database, the ability to analyze your audience is perhaps the most beneficial. Armed with information on your users, you can establish stronger relationships by delivering content that fulfills their needs and expectations. Additionally, this information can provide you with the means for more focused commercial targeting. User analysis builds on your information by detailing the effectiveness of your efforts and creating targeted user lists for direct mail campaigns.

Site Server Commerce Edition

The Site Server Commerce Edition builds on the Site Server Enterprise Edition by providing features that are of interest to commercial Web sites. Emphasizing the business nature of Web sites, the Commerce Edition provides many important enhancements for those who plan to do sales over the Web. Site Server Commerce Edition focuses on three areas that commerce Web sites require: engaging customers, transacting with customers, and analyzing the results. Site Server Commerce Edition requires Site Server Enterprise Edition for operation.

Engaging Customers

The key to successful Web commerce is to attract and retain customers with an online relationship. A cost-effective commercial site relies on targeted online advertising and personalized promotions to entice new customers to the door. Site Server Commerce Edition provides you with several sample commerce sites, as well as site authoring wizards to help you create engaging Web sites that draw consumers. These wizards and samples help remove the complexity in creating a commercial site, which you then can easily customize by using Visual InterDev. These wizards and sample sites enable you to do the following:

■ Build a complete database schema to house the commercial information

■ Write script and HTML code for the store front

■ Provide cross-selling and price promotions

■ Create stores with multilevel departments

■ Include products with varied attributes

■ Support E-Commerce initiatives, such as Microsoft Wallet

In addition to the site wizards and samples, the Commerce Edition includes a comprehensive solution for online advertising: the Ad Server. The Ad Server supports targeted advertising with scheduling and exposure limits. Using the Ad Manager, administrators can create, schedule, and configure ad campaigns and rotations, as well as request reports on individual online advertisements. Use of these advertisements can grow based on your needs and even be served across multiple Web servers. The Ad Server also supports *Buy Now*, which is a powerful solution for sales over the Web. Buy Now lets administrators embed product information and order forms into other sites, even online advertisements, and it allows consumers to purchase products or services without requiring the customers to visit your site first.

Part

VI

Ch

21

By using the established trends and user information, the Commerce Edition also offers *Intelligent CrossSell*. Intelligent CrossSell recommends to the consumers items that they may not have originally considered, based on their existing selections. It can also adapt to the buying patterns of the consumers in a particular session or over time. CrossSell lets commercial Web sites adopt an adaptive advertising strategy that could drive sales in a different way than originally anticipated. CrossSell and BuyNow can also be directly implemented with push publishing in Site Server.

Transacting with Customers

The mechanics of online sales are handled directly by the Site Server Commerce Edition. The Commerce Edition uses technologies established in Microsoft Commerce Server for handling the processing of transactions with customers. The transactional process is fully extensible using an application programming interface (API) and can be integrated with third-party components to suit a site's specific needs. Throughout the entire transaction, security is very closely monitored by using strict account policies and encrypted data; these policies and data use Secure Sockets Layer (SSL) and Secure Electronic Transaction (SET). The Commerce Edition also directly supports the Microsoft Wallet, enabling businesses to provide customers with a convenient and secure method for online payment.

Analyzing the Results

Coupled with Site Server's already impressive analysis facilities, the Commerce Edition adds the capability for real-time order reporting and customer order history. The Order Manager lets you analyze purchases in real-time, ordered by the time period, product, and shopper. Using this information, you can then identify changes in customer demand and products that are not meeting expectations. The Store Builder Wizard adds the capability to store each customer's order history and receipt information for future access. This storehouse of information lets customers review their previous purchases at any time. You can also use the Commerce Server to provide purchase confirmations for customers so that the customers or customer service representatives can quickly access a particular customer's order history on demand. Armed with the information about your customers and what they are interested in, you can quickly adapt your strategy to suit their needs.

From Here...

This chapter has acted as an introduction to what Site Server can offer you. Closely tied with Site Server are Internet Information Server and Active Scripting. The following chapters detail information on extending Web applications by using scripting and the facilities of Internet Information Server:

- Chapter 5, "Active Scripting Overview."
- Chapter 7, "Server-Side Scripting."
- Chapter 20, "Using the Internet Information Server."

CHAPTER 22

SQL Server Basics

In this chapter

Introducing SQL Server   **466**

Setting Up User Accounts and Security   **466**

SQL Server Administration   **473**

SQL Server Performance Tuning   **478**

Introducing SQL Server

At the heart of most truly powerful Web applications is the database. Microsoft's answer for demanding database-driven environments is SQL Server. A smoothly running SQL Server is crucial to a successful database-driven application. If a weak link exists in the chain, the database is likely to be it. The database can be your Achilles heel if it is not properly set up and maintained. Typically, the role of database administration is demanding enough to warrant a specialized database administrator, or DBA; the DBA's responsibility is to ensure the reliability and performance of the database. However, you may be personally responsible for your SQL Server or want to involve yourself in some of its operations. This chapter outlines the rudimentary basics of SQL Server that directly pertain to Web applications:

- User accounts and security
- Basic administration
- Performance tuning

Setting Up User Accounts and Security

Just as Windows NT requires a user account to identify who is accessing resources, so do databases. A database user account is used to establish the security rights and access permissions for those using the database. Access can be restricted to read-only in certain database tables or perhaps modification rights in others. Failure to establish the security rights properly for your user accounts could result in erratic and unpredictable behavior in your Web applications—if they are able to communicate with your database at all. You can create your SQL Server user accounts through the Microsoft SQL Enterprise Manager, shown in Figure 22.1.

FIG. 22.1

The Enterprise Manager is the central tool used for administration in a SQL Server environment.

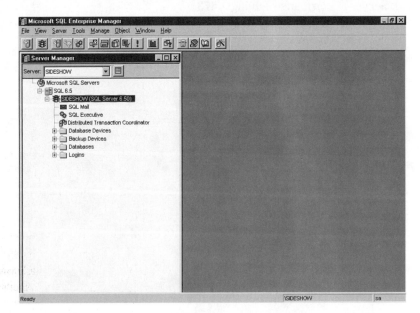

One of the powerful advantages to SQL Server is its capability to tie into existing Windows NT domain user accounts for access to the SQL Server database. This capability requires users to remember only one username and password, while still enforcing security on the database itself. In actuality, the users are indeed using two separate logins (one for LAN resources, one for database resources), but the logins are handled transparently for the users. Simplicity is the key. This simplicity can be extended to your Web applications, in which you may already be using specific NT usernames for interaction with the application. In a corporate LAN or intranet environment, this process may be as simple as requiring each user to log in to the intranet itself. This information is then used for the database communications as well.

Adding SQL Server Logins

SQL Server refers to accounts and account names as *login IDs*, or *logins*. If a server is configured to do so, it can map to the existing Windows NT security database without requiring an ID to be created for each user. An NT security account can be used only from a *trusted* connection, which is typically a LAN or local connection. Nontrusted connections require that a specific login be created in SQL Server.

> **N O T E** What is a *trusted* connection? In Windows NT-based networks, groups of similar systems are organized under *domains*. These domains share no similarities with Internet domains, and in fact are more like Novell Netware trees and contexts. Windows NT establishes security between domains (groups of systems) based on *trust relationships*. A trust relationship essentially says that "Domain A" can freely talk to "Domain B." Without a trust relationship, the two domains do not communicate openly. Trusted connections occur within a trust relationship, and can be extended into SQL Server. SQL Server trusts the connections coming from a particular domain or group of users and allows them to interact with the database. ∎

If you have not yet registered your SQL Server with the Enterprise Manager, you should do so by following these steps:

1. Open the Microsoft SQL Enterprise Manager from the Start menu. The Register Server dialog box appears.
2. In the Serve textbox, enter the machine name of your SQL Server. You may also click on the Servers button to see a refreshed list of the available servers on your network.
3. Enter your sa username and password into the Login ID and Password textboxes, respectively, or choose to Use Trusted Connection.
4. Click the Register button to add your server to the Server Group list.
5. Click the Close button to dismiss the dialog box and enter the Enterprise Manager.

To create a new SQL Server login ID, follow these instructions using the Microsoft SQL Enterprise Manager. You must already be connected to a registered server in the Enterprise Manager to complete these steps:

1. Select your SQL Server from the Microsoft SQL Servers tree in the Server Manager window, and expand the tree to display the Logins folder.

2. Right-click the Logins folder, and select New Login from the context menu. This action opens the Manage Logins dialog box, shown in Figure 22.2.

FIG. 22.2

The Manage Logins dialog box allows you to add and edit login IDs.

3. Enter the new login name in the Login Name text box. If you want to modify an existing login, select it from the drop-down list box.

4. Enter the new login's password (which is case sensitive) in the Password text box.

5. Select the user's default language from the Default Language drop-down list box.

6. The Database Access panel displays each database in your SQL Server. To grant access to the database for this user, click in the Permit column for the appropriate database(s).

7. The subsequent columns in the display update to reflect the selected default database. Additionally, the ID is assigned a username and group name for each selected database. Modify the username and group name as you need.

8. If, instead, you want this login to be an alias for an existing login, select it from the list by clicking in the Alias column for the database.

9. Click the Add button to add the user.

10. Repeat steps 1 through 9 for additional users. If you are finished, click the Close button to close the dialog box and return to the Enterprise Manager.

Using Windows NT Accounts in SQL Server

To enable *trusted* mode, which allows access using existing Windows NT domain accounts, follow these instructions using the Microsoft SQL Enterprise Manager. You must already be connected to a registered server in the Enterprise Manager to complete these steps.

1. Select your SQL Server from the Microsoft SQL Servers tree in the Server Manager window.

2. Choose Server, SQL Server, Configure to open the Server Configuration/Options dialog box, shown in Figure 22.3.

FIG. 22.3

The Server Configuration/Options dialog box controls the behavior for your SQL Server on a global level. Individual databases have their own properties.

3. Select the Security Options tab to display the page shown in Figure 22.4.

FIG. 22.4

The Security Options tab determines the security mode for the entire SQL Server. Here, you also can specify security audit levels, the default domain, and the default login typically used by guests.

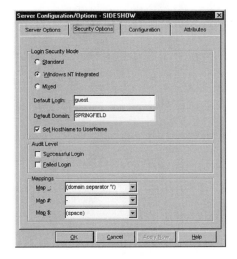

4. To fully integrate the Windows NT Security information, select the Windows NT Integrated check box.

5. To have a mixed environment with both Windows NT accounts and standard SQL Server login IDs, select the Mixed check box.

6. Specify the default Windows NT security domain you want to use for the SQL Server in the Default Domain text box.

7. Click OK to close this dialog box and establish your changes.

> **CAUTION**
>
> You can grant Windows NT accounts to the SQL Server database on a group level for privileges. Individual accounts cannot be added or removed. If you have special security considerations, you should create a SQL Server Users group to grant access to only those users you want to have access.

After you select the integrated or mixed security mode, you need to grant the individual Windows NT Security accounts access to the SQL Server. To do so, open the SQL Security Manager tool from the SQL Server program group. Connect to your SQL Server, and follow these steps:

1. With the SQL Security Manager open, as shown in Figure 22.5, choose View, User Privilege. This action selects standard user permissions for the SQL Server.

FIG. 22.5

The SQL Security Manager maps Windows NT accounts into the SQL Server security database.

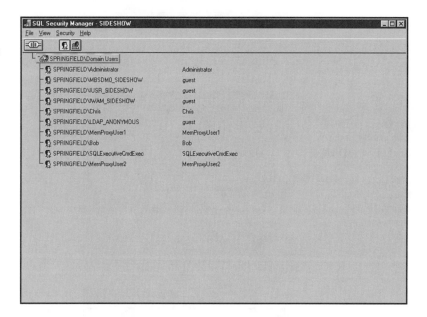

2. Choose Security, Grant New to open the Grant User Privilege dialog box, shown in Figure 22.6. You can grant NT accounts user privileges and/or administrator sa privileges.

3. The Grant Privilege list displays the groups that can be granted access. To display only local groups, you should select the Local Groups radio button. To display all the groups in the default domain, select the Groups on Default Domain radio button.

4. To create login IDs for each NT user account in the selected group, select the Add Login IDs for Group Members radio button. If this button is not selected, users are required to use the default login (guest) ID to connect.

FIG. 22.6

Using the Grant User Privilege dialog box, you can grant access to Windows NT security domain groups and specify the default database for the groups.

Part

VI

Ch

22

5. To assign a default database, select the Add Users to Database radio button, and select the database from the drop-down list. If a default database is not selected, the *master* database is used.

 You should not grant default access to the master database so that you can discourage users from creating database objects in the master database. You should always set the default database to the same database the users will interact with on a regular basis.

6. Click the Grant button to execute your selections. The Adding SQL Server Login IDs/Users dialog box appears to reflect the status of the additions to your database, as shown in Figure 22.7. These changes may take a while if you are adding a group with many users.

FIG. 22.7

The Adding SQL Server Login IDs/Users dialog box displays the status of your changes.

7. To display the error messages of the addition, if any, click the Error Detail button. Clicking this button expands the dialog box to display the error details, as shown in Figure 22.8. Remember that just because an error was generated, it does not mean the users were not added.

8. Click the Done button to close the dialog box.

9. If you want to add another group to the SQL Server database, repeat steps 1 through 8. If you are finished, click the Done button to close this dialog box and return to the SQL Security Manager.

FIG. 22.8

If your additions result in errors, you can use the Error Detail to examine the problem closely.

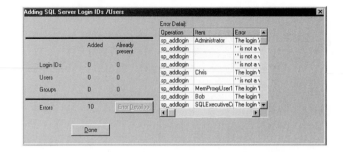

N O T E You can use the SQL Security Manager to grant Windows NT groups sa database administrator access by choosing View, Sa Privileges. sa is the standard method of referring to the
database administrator account. sa is directly analogous with "Administrator" under Windows NT and
"root" in a UNIX environment. This option should be used with extreme caution but can be used to add
site operators to the list of users who have administrative rights to the database. ■

To modify the attributes of a user who has been added using the SQL Security Manager, follow
these steps within that tool:

1. Select the user account from the list of users in the SQL Security Manager display.

2. Choose Security, Account Details to open the Account Detail dialog box, shown in
   Figure 22.9.

FIG. 22.9

The Account Detail dialog box shows specific information on the mapped NT account.

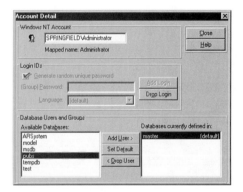

3. To set a password for the user account when a nontrusted connection is established,
   deselect the Generate Random Unique Password check box, and enter the password in
   the (Group) Password text box. This password is used for the entire group.

4. Click the Close button to close this dialog box.

5. Repeat steps 1 through 4 for each user or group as required. When you are finished, exit
   the SQL Security Manager tool.

Removing Logins from SQL Server

At some point, you may want to remove users from the SQL Server to prevent them from accessing your database. Deleting logins is considered "dropping" logins and can be completed from the Microsoft SQL Enterprise Manager using the following steps:

1. Select your SQL Server from the Microsoft SQL Servers tree in the Server Manager window, and expand the tree to display the contents of the Logins folder.

2. Select the login ID you want to remove.

3. Right-click the login ID, and select Drop from the context menu. A confirmation dialog box appears, asking whether you are sure you want to remove the selected login.

4. To remove the login (with no recourse), click the Yes button. To cancel, click the No button.

SQL Server Administration

The ongoing maintenance of your SQL Server can be a monumental task. You will likely encounter several ongoing administrative issues at one time or another in the future. This section briefly outlines the most common administrative issues you need to take care of:

- Creating a new database
- Removing an unneeded database
- Adding a new database storage device
- Adding a backup device
- Backing up a database
- Restoring from a backup

Creating a New Database

SQL Server itself is an engine for database management. Individual databases store the actual data with which your Web applications interact; SQL Server can handle multiple databases. During your Web application's life cycle, you may want to create a new database to store different types of data. Follow these instructions in the SQL Enterprise Manager to create a database:

1. Open your SQL Server from the Server Manager window.

2. Right-click the Database folder, and select New Database from the context menu. This action opens the New Database dialog box, shown in Figure 22.10.

3. Enter the new database's name in the Name text box.

4. Select the database device on which the database will reside from the Database Device drop-down list box.

5. Specify the starting size for this database in megabytes in the Size text box. The database size can be modified later (see "Resizing Databases" later in this chapter).

FIG. 22.10

In the New Database dialog box, you can specify the database's physical size and log device.

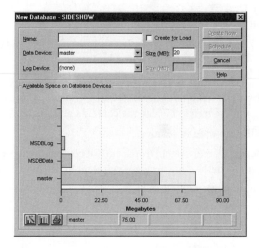

6. Click the Create Now button to create the database immediately. If you want to schedule the creation for an off-peak period, click the Schedule button to specify creation parameters.

Removing a Database

In the life cycle of a Web application, you likely will find that some databases outlive their usefulness. You can easily remove a database from your SQL Server to conserve space by following these steps using the SQL Enterprise Manager:

1. Select your SQL Server from the Microsoft SQL Servers tree in the Server Manager window, and expand the tree to display the Databases folder.

2. Select the offending database from the Databases list.

3. Right-click the database, and select Delete from the context menu. A confirmation dialog box appears to confirm the deletion of this database.

4. Click Yes to remove the database, or click No to cancel and keep the database.

Adding a New Database Device

Databases house data, whereas database devices house databases. Typically, database devices represent physical data storage locations or similar database types. For example, your Web application may have a data device for customers, with a database for purchase history and another database for contact information. Database devices establish the physical location and size constraints for the databases they house. To create a new database device, follow these instructions using the SQL Enterprise Manager:

1. Select your SQL Server from the Microsoft SQL Servers tree in the Server Manager window, and expand the tree to display the Database Devices folder.

2. Right-click the Database Devices folder, and select New Device from the context menu. This action opens the New Database Device dialog box, shown in Figure 22.11.

FIG. 22.11

The New Database Devices dialog box establishes the physical location and size constraints for the databases the device houses.

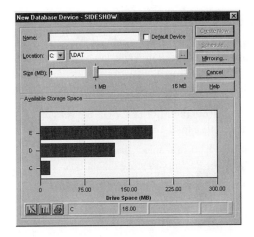

3. Enter the name for the new database device in the Name text box.

4. Select the physical location for the database device using the Location text box. You can select the physical drive from the drop-down list box or use the ... (ellipses) button to open a directory selector.

5. Establish the size for the database device by entering the size in megabytes in the Size text box or by dragging the slider bar to the right of it.

6. Click the Create Now button to create the database immediately. If you want to schedule the creation for an off-peak period, click the Schedule button to specify creation parameters.

Creating a Backup Device

To prevent the loss of data in unexpected events, you should regularly back up your databases. To do so, you must have a backup device created for SQL Server to use. The backup device establishes the physical location of the backup, be it a tape drive or a file on a local hard disk. To create a new backup device, follow these steps:

1. Select your SQL Server from the Microsoft SQL Servers tree in the Server Manager window, and expand the tree to display the Backup Devices folder.

2. Right-click the Backup Devices folder, and select New Backup Device from the context menu. This action opens the New Backup Device dialog box.

3. Enter the name of the new backup device in the Name text box.

4. If the backup is to a local directory, select the Disk Backup Device radio button. If the backup is to a tape device, select the Tape Backup Device radio button.

5. Enter the location of the backup device in the Location text box.

6. Click the Create button to create the device.

Backing Up a Database

With your backup device created, you can physically archive your database using SQL Enterprise Manager's simple interface. To back up your database, you must already have a backup device created in a location that has the capacity to contain your database. To create a backup of a database, follow these instructions (once again, using the SQL Enterprise Manager):

1. Select your SQL Server from the Microsoft SQL Servers tree in the Server Manager window, and expand the tree to display the Database folder.

2. Right-click the Database icon, and select Backup/Restore from the context menu. This action opens the Database Backup/Restore dialog box.

3. Click the Backup tab to display the page shown in Figure 22.12.

FIG. 22.12

The Database Backup/ Restore dialog box lets you specify how you want to back up the database.

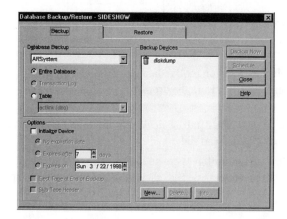

4. Select the database from which you want to archive data in the Database Backup drop-down list box.

5. If you want to back up the entire database, select the Entire Database radio button. However, if you want to archive the data from a specific table only, select the Table radio button and choose the table name from the drop-down list box.

6. Select the backup device from the Backup Devices list.

7. To begin the backup immediately, click the Backup Now button. To schedule the backup for a later time, click the Schedule button and define the scheduled backup information, followed by clicking OK.

8. The Backup Volume Labels dialog box, shown in Figure 22.13, appears. Enter the volume name for the backup in the Volume column and click OK.

9. The Backup Progress dialog box appears, displaying the current status of the backup. After the backup is complete, an alert box appears to state that the backup was completed. Click OK to close the dialog box.

FIG. 22.13
Volume names for backups must be six-character or less names.

 A backup is only as good as its security. Always make sure that you store your backup in a secure and safe place. A disk backup should also be physically backed up using archival software.

Restoring from a Backup

With a database safely stored away in case of emergency, you can restore your database and data if the need ever arises. Restoring a database, like backing it up, may take a long time depending on the size of the database. Make sure to plan around your backups and restorations to minimize server outages. To restore your database from a backup, follow these instructions:

1. Select your SQL Server from the Microsoft SQL Servers tree in the Server Manager window, and expand the tree to display the Database folder.

N O T E The database must actively exist on the server for the data to be restored. The database must also be running in single user mode to restore the data safely. ■

2. Right-click the Database icon, and select Backup/Restore from the context menu. This action opens the Database Backup/Restore dialog box.

3. Click the Restore tab to display the page shown in Figure 22.14.

FIG. 22.14
The Restore tab lists, historically, when backups were completed on the database.

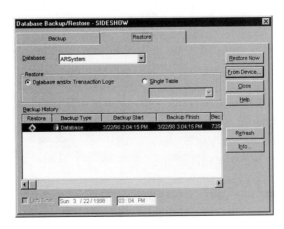

4. You can also select to restore a single table as opposed to the entire database. But for now, select the backup from the Backup History list, and click the Restore Now button to restore the archived data.

5. The Restore Progress dialog box appears, displaying the current status of the restoration. After the file is restored, an alert box appears to state that the backup was completed. Click OK to close the dialog box.

 TIP The log files record any problems with restoring from a backup. You can use this information to track down potential problems.

SQL Server Performance Tuning

A smoothly running SQL Server equals a smoothly running database. When your database is running at top form, your Web application benefits from increased responsiveness whenever data is exchanged with the SQL Server. Performance tuning for databases is a complicated issue and can be a daunting task in its own right. In a basic SQL Server administrative role, you are required to carry out a few actions. Fortunately, SQL Enterprise Manager makes these tasks effortless. In addition to carrying out certain activities manually, you may want to take advantage of SQL Server's automated performance tuning and maintenance tools.

Resizing Databases

When a database grows wildly, space may dwindle fast. As your Web applications continue to store more data in your database, you might need to expand the size of your database. Alternatively, when a database starts to decrease in size, you may want to shrink the physical space it consumes on your database device. For your database to run smoothly, it needs a comfortable range of space in either direction; however, too much space may compromise room for speed. To resize a database, follow these instructions:

1. Select your SQL Server from the Microsoft SQL Servers tree in the Server Manager window, and expand the tree to display the Database folder.

2. Right-click the Database icon, and select Edit from the context menu. This action opens the Edit Database dialog box, shown in Figure 22.15.

3. You can use this dialog box to shrink or grow your database. To grow your database and provide it with more space, click the Expand button. The Expand Database dialog box, shown in Figure 22.16, appears.

4. Select the database device from the Data Device drop-down list box.

5. Enter the new size in megabytes in the Size text box. The bar graph updates to reflect the changes.

6. To expand your database immediately, click the Expand Now button.

FIG. 22.15

When you need to modify a database, you can use the Edit Database dialog box.

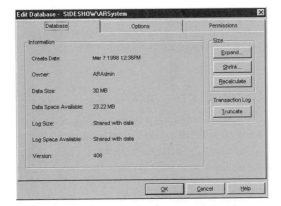

FIG. 22.16

The Expand Database dialog box gives you a visual representation of how much space is available on your database devices and what your database is using.

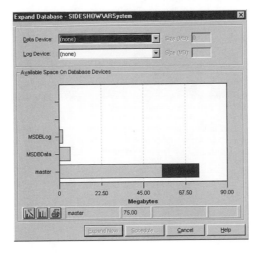

Using the Database Maintenance Plan Wizard

Microsoft SQL Enterprise Manager provides you with a convenient and automated means of maintaining and optimizing your database. The Database Maintenance Plan Wizard, which you can access from the toolbar, sets up the core maintenance to ensure your database's performance and data integrity. The wizard steps you through several questions and then carries out the required actions without your intervention. You can use the wizard on any database in your SQL Server. The Database Maintenance Plan Wizard is a forthright tool that helps determine what the needs of your database are. Based on the volatility of data, rate of change, size constraints, and your backup requirements, the wizard creates the core procedures used by SQL Server to maintain your database. These ongoing actions optimize and tune your database.

The Database Maintenance Plan Wizard is not, however, a perfect tool for use with every database. You can use it as a starting point for your own enhancements and improvements.

The wizard establishes a good beginning to maintenance and performance tuning, but you should not use it exclusively. Sound judgment and good database design greatly contribute to the speed and usability of every database.

From Here...

The SQL database is at the heart of the most powerful Web applications. Using the database to your best advantage lies in an understanding of how Visual InterDev communicates with the database, and how best to design the database structure. These chapters continue the discussion of databases and using them from within Visual InterDev:

- Chapter 14, "Database Programming Basics."
- Chapter 15, "Setting Up a Database."
- Chapter 16, "Using the Visual InterDev 6 Data Environment."

CHAPTER 23

Understanding Visual InterDev 6 Security

In this chapter

An Introduction to Web Security   482

Planning Ahead   482

Windows NT Security   484

About NTFS   486

Security with Internet Information Server   488

Other Security Considerations   492

Tying It All Back to Visual InterDev   495

Further Security References   495

An Introduction to Web Security

Providing a secure environment is not a new concept when it comes to information. As the Internet and intranet become more common media for information gathering, creation, and display, dependable security measures are imperative. Within the Web environment, several security solutions are available. Understanding your options and knowing how to harness them are key to protecting your data.

Consideration of who and what has access to your Web pages—from the first creation of a page to the end viewer—is the primary task. With the slightest mistake, corporations can compromise carefully implemented security measures. In creating your Web site, you must allow access only to those who will contribute to its content. Developers need to ensure that sensitive information, if it is available on the Web site, is protected via encryption or other means. The phrase "attention to detail" cannot be stressed enough, especially after the information becomes available on a production server and is potentially accessible to anyone.

This phenomenon—that is, the birth of your Web site—dictates thinking on a different level. It is an interesting statement of society that the more public something becomes, the more protective the providers of this "public entity" need to become. Compare your Web site to a public library. Think of a vast room filled with material for anyone who cares to walk through the doors to view and even borrow. Certain low-level checks are in place, such as showing a library card to check out a book, but for the most part, the library provides incredible freedom. Then, there is that *one* room—the one with a guard or monitor at the entrance. The rare books are kept there, and usually only certain people are allowed in. They are not allowed to remove contents from the room; usually, a photocopier isn't even available. Visitors are checked when they enter and when they leave.

Your Web site will probably take on some of the characteristics of this library. You are providing, on one level or another, a public resource—much like the library. However, libraries typically are not connected to, say, a bank vault, whereas your Web site will have some sort of connection to your company's most sensitive information. Regardless of how indirect and secure the connection, confidential information is contained somewhere on your network, and some network resource is connected to your Web site.

Visual InterDev does not explicitly offer security options. Readily available options come primarily from NT and Internet Information Server (IIS). This chapter addresses security solutions available for your Web site.

Planning Ahead

Before learning all the security considerations involved in creating and maintaining a Web site, you need to address the purpose of the Web site and the question, "Why is security necessary?" Prior to creating your Web site—ideally before you set up the server that hosts your Web site—you should carefully map out your intentions and goals. All too often, especially with today's rush to get out there, the decision is made to create a Web site, followed at some point with the question, "How do we make this secure?" Security issues should not be an afterthought.

How would you like to walk into work some morning, open up your Web browser, and get the ominous 404 - Not Found message staring you in the face when you access your company's home page? The culprit could be anywhere, though your two most likely suspects are an external hacker or the internal, disgruntled employee.

At the very beginning, you need to ask a few questions. They should stay in your head and be underlying considerations during every decision. Such questions are the following:

- What kind of information will this Web site have?
- Who has (or will have) access to this information?
- Who do I want to prevent from seeing this information?
- Who will be creating the Web pages?
- What is *not* (or will not be) secure?

Implementing security measures before the fact is far easier than after hardware and software have been installed. One good discipline is to map out a basic outline of your Web site visually by using the Set/Subset method. Draw a large circle, representing your entire Web site. Inside this circle, draw a circle representing all publicly available pages. Outside this circle but still inside the main circle, draw a circle for each of the secure pages, one for each individual group that will have access. For example, you might have private pages that you want Accounting to be able to access but prevent Sales from seeing. Sales might have its own private pages that should not be seen by your IT group, and so on. By comparison, this process can be much like setting up shares within your domain. Some of the circles might overlap partially, representing private pages you want to have accessible to multiple groups (see Figure 23.1).

FIG. 23.1

This sample of a Set/Subset structure shows the preliminary organization of a Web site, separated by public and private (secure) areas.

The Set/Subset Structure

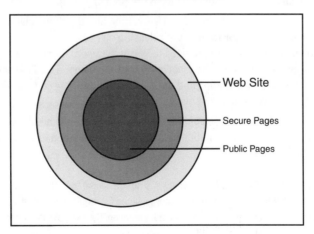

- Web Site
- Secure Pages
- Public Pages

N O T E If you have spent any time managing a Web site, you know why it is called a Web. The Set/ Subset outline provides a basic, visual means for introducing a Web site in the initial stages. However, the site can quickly become so complex that it outgrows its original intentions of simplicity. If you estimate a complex structure, planning for it in advance is best. Create a directory structure that parallels the Set/Subset diagram you develop, leaving room for directories that have multiple shared permissions. ■

Windows NT Security

As this chapter describes different security options and methods, you should remember that whatever strategy you use, it is a single solution. In other words, the security provided by NT, IIS, a firewall, and password-protected links, for example, all work in conjunction with each other. NT is not a default solution should another security option fail. Still, when you are setting up security measures, consider NT your front line of defense.

▶ For more information NT Security, **see** Chapter 19, "Windows NT Server Basics" on **p. 403**

NT Security Features

In a nutshell, Windows NT fulfills the requirements for a class C2 security rating. As a result, it can be used for much of our government's and military's computing needs when it comes to handling secure material. According to the Department of Defense (DoD) publication *Trusted Computer Evaluation Guide*, the following are the minimal requirements for a class C2 rating:

■ *Discretionary Access Control.* Enforcement mechanisms allow users to specify access to individual objects and be able to include or exclude this access to individual users.

■ *Object Reuse.* After a storage object (user memory and/or disk space) is released back to the system, all authorizations to information contained therein are revoked prior to the system allocating the object(s) from the pool of available storage objects.

■ *Identification and Authorization.* Users must identify themselves to the Trusted Computing Base (TCB) prior to the TCB releasing any resources to the users, and protected credentials (passwords) are used to verify the users. Furthermore, all auditable actions the users perform must be associated with the users. The TCB acts as the central pool for all security information and authentication, as opposed to having security information located in several different places.

■ *Audit.* The TCB must be able to track and log access to all objects it protects in a secure manner. Access to this audit data should be restricted, and the data should be protected from modification.

N O T E While NT provides C2-level security, it is not C2 secure "out of the box." Additionally, simply using NTFS partitions alone does not fulfill the C2 requirements. At the end of this chapter, you can find a list of useful resources for further information. For example, the home page for the Defense Information Systems Agency (DISA) is listed there. ■

Setting Up Accounts

Think of your Web site as having two different modes of operation. First, you need to allow access to the Web site publicly so that users can access and browse its contents. Second, you need to provide a secure way for your developers to create and copy content to the Web pages.

Almost all HTTP transactions on the Internet are made via anonymous connections. In the NT environment, IIS makes this capability possible by creating an anonymous account, IUSR_*machinename*, during installation. More information about the anonymous account and its security provisions are discussed in the "Security with Internet Information Server" section. The remainder of this section describes the appropriate security measures to apply for developing and maintaining your Web site.

Part

VI

Ch

23

N O T E The generated account, IUSR_*machinename*, derives its name from the machine on which you are installing IIS. Therefore, if the machine is named WEBHOST, the anonymous account is IUSR_WEBHOST. You can change this name, as discussed in the section on IIS security in this chapter. ■

IIS does not directly provide a mechanism for handling user security; NT handles this task. As such, the appropriate way to provide access is through the use of user groups. This way, you can move individual users in and out of groups as necessary without spending too much time making sure that you have granted the appropriate rights to each individual. This approach provides a two-fold solution. First, it saves time. Second, as the administrative role can change within an organization, new administrators might not understand the rights necessary for this access and can over-grant rights. Additionally, it provides a consistency among the users who are members of the group.

N O T E Using groups within NT can make administrative tasks much easier. However, more often than not, groups that do not have appropriate titles are set up. When you are creating new groups, make the group names as descriptive as possible for the tasks and permissions members of those groups have. ■

Any account that is to have authoring rights on the Web server needs to have the privilege to log on locally to the machine hosting the Web site. Additionally, the accounts should be assigned file access privileges for any Web pages, files, and databases for which they are responsible. Within some smaller organizations, having only one group might be all that is necessary. For larger organizations with complex sites, having several different groups is recommended. If a particular user or group of users needs access to more than one area, adding them to extra groups is simple (see Figure 23.2).

CAUTION

Do not allow an account the right Access This Computer from the Network. This setting allows the account to bypass the Web service of IIS, thereby compromising security measures you have painstakingly set up.

FIG. 23.2

Use multiple groups to assign authoring and administrative access rights to users.

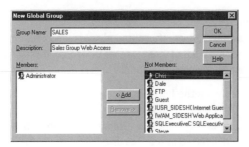

N O T E Some user guides suggest eliminating, or disabling, the built-in Guest account. You must decide what to do in this case, but disabling this account does add another layer of protection. If you need this sort of access but do want the added security of preventing an unknown user from logging in to your network as Guest, create a new guest account with a different name. IIS does not need the Guest *user account*, not to be confused with the Guests *group*, which is used by IIS. ■

About NTFS

Why should you use NTFS? Using FAT partitions sure is more convenient and slightly faster, right? Not necessarily. You should entertain the idea of using FAT over NTFS only if the machine is used to dual-boot with DOS and/or Windows. This is hardly the role a server machine would serve, especially a dedicated server such as one hosting a Web site.

NTFS holds many advantages over FAT partitions. One of the most obvious is that DOS cannot read an NTFS partition. If the wrong person gains physical access to your server, and the server is set up with FAT partitions instead of NTFS, you could be in serious trouble. All that separates this machine from a potentially serious security breach (assuming this person does not know account passwords) is a system boot to a floppy DOS boot disk. After this breach, the entire contents of the server can be viewed, copied, or destroyed.

N O T E A discussion on NT security would not be complete without stressing the importance of using NTFS partitions. A FAT disk partition does not allow the level of security that is required by a Web server. If NT uses FAT partitions, it does not comply with level C2 security, as outlined in this chapter. The use of NTFS is also highly recommended because it cannot be read by DOS; for example, a DOS boot disk being used to start your server cannot read NTFS. (Also remember that setting up NTFS partitions alone does not guarantee C2-level security.) ■

In addition to NTFS, incorporating the use of Access Control Lists (ACLs) for additional security is a good idea. ACLs can control access to individual files or folders by groups of users or individual user accounts. You can configure file or folder ACLs via the Windows NT Explorer and set rights to resources based on who has access and what kind of access that person has. These settings can vary for each user, which means you can allow some users read-only access, others read/write, others read/change/write, and so on. Figure 23.3 shows how to apply an ACL to a folder.

FIG. 23.3
With your NTFS partition, you can control access down to a very low level (granular).

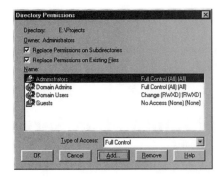

How can you verify that your system is secure? NT enables you to audit activities. In the case of file or folder auditing, you can go to the User Manager for Domains and set auditing for File and Object access, as you can see in Figure 23.4. File and Object access is controlled from the Policies menu. You can use the NT Explorer to select the disks, folders, or files and the types of access events to audit (see Figure 23.5). Reporting is available for a group or individual account. A periodic check in the Event Viewer under the Security log provides the reporting.

FIG. 23.4
Select File and Object Access in the Audit Policy dialog box to enable auditing.

FIG. 23.5
In the Security tab of a resource's properties, you can define what events to report and set different auditing levels for each user or group.

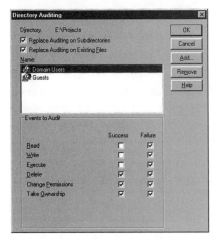

> **CAUTION**
>
> When you choose to audit resources, your system takes a performance hit. Also, log files can grow rapidly. You can adjust the maximum size of the Security log by using the Event Viewer.

Security with Internet Information Server

Several Web servers for NT are available on the market. You will probably not be surprised to learn that IIS is one of the most secure of them all. Add to this the cost of IIS, and you're left with a pretty predictable conclusion. Here's the bottom line: NT has an excellent security system in place, and IIS lets NT do what it does best. IIS does have its own security features, but rather than fight with NT over the security issue, IIS simply adds to it. Refer to the section "About NTFS," which discusses the use of NTFS in more detail.

▶ For more information about configuring Internet Information Server, **see** Chapter 20, "Using the Internet Information Server (IIS)" on **p. 433**

Using the Anonymous Account

IIS is actually many services in one. In addition to its Web service, FTP and other add-on services are available. Because this book is strictly about Web content, further discussion on these services is not appropriate. However, if you plan to offer these services in conjunction with a Web site, you should be aware of a security precaution. When you install IIS, it sets up an anonymous account called IUSR_*machinename*. This account is the default anonymous account for all services. The password for this account is randomly generated and can be changed at any time; changing the password from time to time for added security is not a bad idea.

> **CAUTION**
>
> If you change the password for the anonymous account, you must change it in both the Microsoft Management Console for your service and in User Manager. Additionally, the password must be *something*. You cannot assign a blank password.

You can easily set up different anonymous accounts for different services and sites. Setting up these accounts is suggested for two reasons. First, by doing so, you can narrow down a security breach to a particular service, helping you find a possible oversight or weakness more efficiently. Second, separating the anonymous accounts lets you specify the restrictions on all of them individually.

In addition, simply changing the anonymous account name on a periodic basis is a good idea. To do so, follow these steps:

1. In the Microsoft Management Console, open the properties for the appropriate Web site.
2. In the Site Properties dialog box that appears, select the Directory Security tab to switch to the security controls for your Web site.

3. Click the Edit button in the Anonymous Access and Authentication Control Panel to open the Authentication Methods dialog box.

4. Click the Edit button to the right of Allow Anonymous Access, shown in Figure 23.6, to open the Anonymous User Account dialog box.

FIG. 23.6
You can disallow anonymous access, in addition to changing the account used for anonymous access in this dialog box.

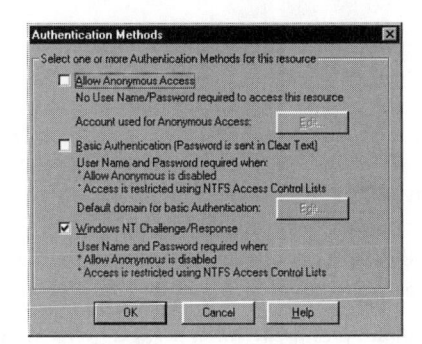

5. Enter the new anonymous user's account name in the Username text box.

6. Click OK to close the dialog box.

7. Click OK to close the Authentication Methods dialog box.

8. Click OK to close the Site Properties dialog box and commit your changes.

9. Open the User Manager for Domains.

10. If you are changing the default account, IUSR_*machinename*, simply disabling the account by selecting the Account Disabled check box is a good idea (see Figure 23.7). Otherwise, you can delete the old anonymous account if you want.

FIG. 23.7
Delete or disable the existing anonymous user account in the User Manager for Domains.

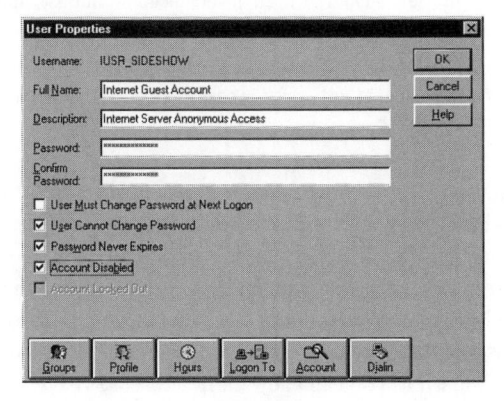

11. Create a new account, making sure the username and password are identical to the ones you entered in the WWW Service Properties (see Figure 23.8).

12. Add the new user to the Guests group.

FIG. 23.8

Create a new Anonymous account by using this dialog box.

Additional Security in IIS

IIS can also recognize specific user account access. This capability is extremely useful for providing shared public and private access on your Web site. Every account that accesses your Web site needs to pass a username and password test to gain access. The difference between an anonymous user and a named user is that the information for the anonymous user is already contained on the host machine and is passed transparently.

Named users are prompted for their credentials when accessing the Web pages. This information can be transferred in the following two ways:

- *Basic Authentication (Clear Text)*. Information is encoded using uuencode algorithms. Some security does exist, but it is easily decoded.

- *Windows NT Challenge/Response*. This option is much more secure. The drawback is that the users must use browsers capable of handling this type of transmission. Currently, Microsoft Internet Explorer (2.0 or greater) is the only browser with this feature.

You must select at least one of these options—Anonymous, Basic, or Challenge/Response—for user authentication, or you can use all three if desired.

N O T E Secure Sockets Layer (SSL) should be used in conjunction with Basic Authentication to provide added security if your clients are not using browsers capable of NT Challenge/Response. SSL provides a "key" system for encrypting information. If SSL is not used with Basic Authentication, you transmit clear, encoded text, which is easily intercepted and decoded. SSL is discussed in the section "Using Secure Sockets Layer." ■

In addition to using named users, you can control access to your Web site via IP addresses. Commonly, this task is handled by hardware—a router or firewall—but a software solution is also available for this task with IIS. The filtering is handled on a service-by-service basis, meaning you can have different filters for FTP and WWW access. Filters can work one of two ways: inclusively or exclusively. If you choose inclusively, you can set up IP addresses that you want to have access. Use this option if you have a limited number of IP addresses you want to allow access. If you choose exclusively, you can allow all IP addresses except for the addresses you specify. In either case, you can specify an individual address or a range of addresses (see Figure 23.9).

> **N O T E**   This software solution for filtering access is inexpensive compared to that of the hardware
> solution. However, it is not nearly as fast as hardware. If your filtering demands are high,
> your solution resides on the hardware side, without question. ■

FIG. 23.9

This dialog box shows
how to filter IP
addresses for an
intranet-only Web site.

Using Secure Sockets Layer

You should use the Secure Sockets Layer (SSL) in conjunction with Basic Authentication when
transferring username and password information. Basic Authentication simply encodes the
information and nothing else.

SSL was first brought to the Internet courtesy of Netscape, and Microsoft has licensed its use
for IIS. SSL, which is nestled between the HTTP and the TCP/IP protocols, provides data
encryption.

For you to take advantage of SSL with your clients, they need to be running SSL-capable browsers, such as Internet Explorer 2.0 or later. As long as this is the case, the whole process is fairly
automatic, though considerable work is done in the background. First, the server and the
browser must agree on the level of security they will use via a handshake. During this process,
any necessary authorizations are met; if this process fails, so does the connection.

Prior to this process, though, you need to prepare the server to handle SSL transactions. The
primary task here is to generate a key pair and acquire a certificate. You can carry out this
process by using the Key Manager (see Figure 23.10).

> **N O T E**   For information on using Key Manager to create and organize your keys, refer to the Key
> Manager documentation and the Windows NT Option Pack documentation. ■

After you generate a key pair, you need to obtain a certificate for it. Otherwise, it's fairly useless. You need to submit a certificate request file to a Certificate Authority, such as Verisign.
Verisign's Web site (listed at the end of this chapter) provides instructions on how to acquire a
certificate. After you receive your signed certificate, you must then install it on your server.
Refer to the IIS 4.0 documentation for information on installing the certificate on your system
and enabling it on your site. When installing the certificate, you have the option of specifying
an IP address. If you do not add one, the certificate applies to all virtual servers on the system.
In case you are hosting multiple sites on the same machine, you can set a particular server to
use the certificate by its IP address.

FIG. 23.10
You use the Key Manager to create and manage your secure keys for IIS.

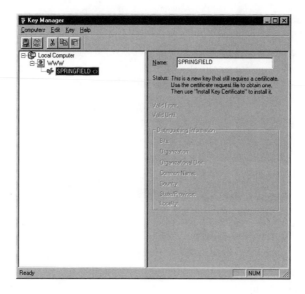

N O T E Because SSL incorporates encryption, the amount of information transmitted for the page is increased. This increase in size requires more time to transfer a page and increases the demand on bandwidth. A good rule of thumb is to use SSL only when necessary. ■

Other Security Considerations

Although this chapter describes the security concepts readily available with NT and IIS, you must take into account other considerations. Internally within the system, you should make sure that your system is set correctly and doesn't allow a backdoor opportunity. External to the system, you can add extra hardware to aid in your quest for a locked-down network.

Correct Services

Many administrators would rather err in favor of over-providing services rather than under-providing services. This tack is understandable to a point, but, for example, why allow NetBEUI access if your network isn't using it?

Also, if the server running IIS is dedicated to that task, and not as a file server, you should disable the Server service (from Services in the Control Panel). However, if the server will perform a shared role of IIS and file server, the best option is to use two different network cards and unbind the Server service from the NIC that is providing Internet access.

Further Understanding NTFS

A common mistake among users is the association of file and folder security with the movement of those resources. When files or folders are moved from one location to another, they take their access properties along with them. On the other hand, if the files or folders are copied, they inherit the access properties of the folder to which they are copied. Users who are using Visual InterDev to publish Web pages must understand this crucial concept. If you, as the developer, are creating a page that is to have read-only privileges, yet the file has full access rights on your workstation, moving the file to the Web server is a critical mistake.

IIS Logging

Earlier in this chapter, you learned about the concept of auditing from NT. IIS also allows its own method of tracking access through logging. Log files can be made to a text log file or to a SQL/ODBC database. Why would you want to enable logging? There are two fairly obvious reasons. First, you can see which pages are accessed and who accessed them. This information is handy for identifying possible incorrect settings for the security settings you have in place and giving you an idea of which pages are most commonly used. Second, and more important, a frequent review of your auditing and log files allows you to catch a hacker's attempt to violate your system integrity—hopefully before he or she gains access.

Account Security

Most likely, a lecture on passwords is not necessary here. Keep them secure, don't forget them, and make sure you cover your bases. Passwords should be changed on a regular basis, both for named users and for the anonymous account IIS creates. Maintain a policy for minimum and maximum length, age, and uniqueness.

Timeout Period/Maximum Connections

In the properties for the WWW service, you can specify a timeout period—the amount of time IIS waits before an inactive connection is closed. Set this period long enough—five minutes—for a user to read your page and make a selection without having to reconnect, but short enough—10 to 15 minutes—so that a hacker doesn't have the freedom to lurk around without detection.

You should also limit the maximum number of connections for many reasons; the two most important are to reduce the amount of bandwidth you are committing to this service and to prevent a hacking technique that bombards your Web site. Bandwidth can also be controlled to minimize potential problems.

Firewalls

As mentioned earlier, NT provides a reliable software solution toward controlling who has access and filtering out unwanted hits. However, this solution is slower and not as efficient as a true firewall. A firewall usually is not a single device; it's a combination of software and hardware working together to separate your internal network from the Internet. It restricts access both inbound and outbound to virtually any limit you choose. FTP and WWW access is conducted through point-to-point connections. Because you don't want to allow external sources direct access to your network, part of your firewall typically includes a Proxy Server, which forwards only approved client requests to the appropriate location on your network.

Disable Directory Browsing

The WWW service in IIS enables you to supply the remote user with information should the user not specify a particular file on your Web site. As you can see in Figure 23.11, you have the options to enable or disable directory browsing. If the Directory Browsing Allowed check box is not selected, and no default document is specified in the Documents tab (see Figure 23.12), a hypertext listing of directories and files is provided to the user, thereby allowing the user to navigate through your directory structure. Directory browsing takes place only if a default document does not exist or you have that option enabled with no default document specified. Nonetheless, selecting the Directory Browsing Allowed option is generally not a good idea.

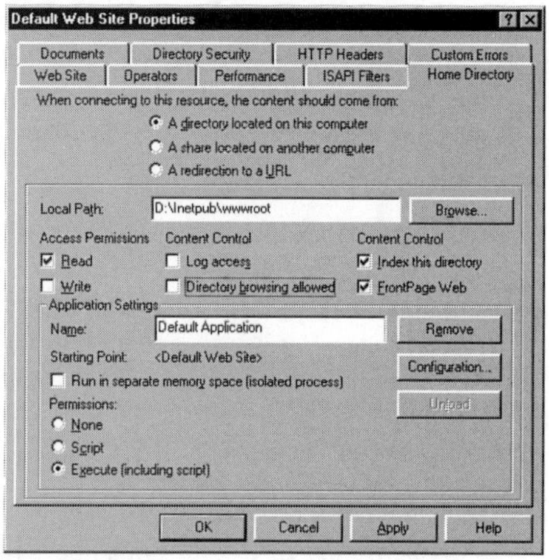

FIG. 23.11
You need to specify how your Web site handles a "default" page.

FIG. 23.12
On the Documents tab, you can specify default documents for your Web site.

Tying It All Back to Visual InterDev

Remember that security fundamentally impacts your entire Web application. From the file system level to the Internet Information Server level, you will be impacting how your visitors interact with your Web application. When you are working with security for your Web site, always consider the following:

- Who you need to let into your site, or portions of your site.
- What permissions they will need when they visit.
- What actions your Web application will take.
- How carefully you want to monitor and audit their access.

When working with your site, be sure to always carefully test changes in the security settings before deploying your site. The last thing you want to do is lock your visitors out of a portion of your application, if not your entire site.

Further Security References

Many other sources pertaining to security are available. Following are some references made in this chapter to additional sources:

Department of Defense *Trusted Computer Evaluation Guide* (the "Orange Book"), **http://www.disa.mil/MLS/info/orange/**

Verisign Corporation, **http://www.verisign.com**

RFC1244 (Site Security Handbook), available through InterNIC, **http://www.internic.net**

Special Edition, Using Microsoft Internet Information Server 4, Que Corporation

Macmillan Computer Publishing, **http://www.mcp.com/**

Microsoft's IIS Web pages, **http://www.microsoft.com/iis/**

From Here...

Security can be a tricky concept to master; however, it is crucial to running a safe and well-tuned Web site. For more information on security as it relates to Web applications, as well as the tuning of the Web site itself, refer to these chapters:

- Chapter 19, "Windows NT Server Basics."
- Chapter 20, "Using the Internet Information Server (IIS)."

Using Developer Isolation and Visual SourceSafe

In this chapter

Understanding Developer Isolation   **498**

Overview of Visual SourceSafe   **500**

Installing Visual SourceSafe   **500**

Understanding SourceSafe   **501**

Using SourceSafe in Visual InterDev   **504**

Administering Visual SourceSafe   **508**

Understanding Developer Isolation

Managing Web sites and content can be a thankless and frustrating task. As Web projects grow in size and more people begin to work with projects in teams, the potential for errors increases dramatically. What is even more disconcerting is the possibility that a team member might inadvertently destroy or permanently damage content by accident, without any immediate method of "stepping back" to cure the problem. Programmers who have experienced these headaches recognize the value of using a Revision Control System (RCS) to manage their code and projects. The premise of an RCS can logically be extended to Web site management and ideally integrates with the Visual InterDev environment.

The goal of this chapter is to explore how Visual SourceSafe (VSS), Version Control, and developer isolation can benefit your development, while demonstrating exactly how to use VSS within Visual InterDev. In addition, you will look briefly at the Visual SourceSafe Administrator program. The intention of this chapter is not to replace the existing Microsoft documentation but rather to complement it. If you find some topic you want to explore in more detail, you should refer to the Microsoft documentation.

By default in Visual InterDev, all modifications a developer makes to content files are immediately carried out on the Web server. This operation translates into a developer making a change, saving it, and the change being seen "live" immediately. This mode of operation is known as *Master mode* in Visual InterDev. This method, however, is not likely the best for working on a project with multiple developers. Developers may (and should) want to work on a Web application without fear of overwriting changes made by others or having their changes affected as well. Visual InterDev provides a facility called *developer isolation*. Developer isolation allows developers to work in an isolated *Local* mode to make changes and test before deploying those changes to the Web site.

Choosing the Mode

As mentioned in the preceding section, by default Visual InterDev works in Master mode. You can choose the mode you want to work in when creating a project or at any point during your development. Often you may want to work in Master mode and then switch to Local mode for more intricate changes. To select the mode for a project when you first create it, select the appropriate radio button—Master Mode or Local Mode—from the first step of the Web Project Wizard, shown in Figure 24.1.

To switch the development mode while working on a project, follow these instructions:

1. Right-click your project name in the Project Explorer.
2. From the context menu, choose Working Mode, and then select either Local for Local mode or Master for Master mode. If you select to switch from Local mode to Master mode, you are prompted by the dialog box shown in Figure 24.2.

FIG. 24.1
Step 1 of the Web Project Wizard lets you choose the starting mode for your Web project.

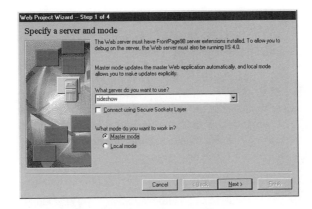

FIG. 24.2
Switching from Local mode to Master mode tells Visual InterDev that you want to upload your changes.

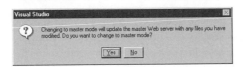

3. To confirm your choice and update the master Web site with all your local changes, click Yes. If you do not want to overwrite the master Web with the local version of files, click No.

> **CAUTION**
>
> Use extreme care when switching to Master mode. Any changes you have made locally to files that are present on the master Web are uploaded to the master Web site. If you have made changes that you do not want others to see, do not switch to Master mode.

Working with Local Mode

Working within Local mode requires a slightly different approach from normal Visual InterDev development. In this mode, you always work locally on your changes, and the changes are not shown on the master Web server until you specifically instruct InterDev to do so. Working with Local mode requires you to add some basic tasks to your development work.

Getting the Most Recent Files for Local Mode   Whenever you are working in Local mode, you should be sure that you are working from the latest versions of files from the master Web server. You must specifically tell Visual InterDev to grab the most recent versions of all files for work locally. To do so, follow these instructions:

1. Select your project name from the Project Explorer.
2. Choose Project, Web Files.

3. From the Web Files submenu, choose Get Latest Version.

4. Switch to Local mode by right-clicking your project and choosing Working Mode, Local from the context menu.

Updating the Master Web

Switching to Master mode is not the only (or advisable) way to commit your changes to the master Web site. Visual InterDev provides you with a facility for updating the master Web application with your most recent changes, either for the whole project or select files. To update the master Web, follow these instructions:

1. In the Project Explorer, select the files or project to be updated.

2. Right-click one of the items, and choose Release Working Copy from the context menu. Visual InterDev updates the master Web with your selected files.

Using both Master and Local mode effectively can make your multi-author development easier. And even if you are a single developer, Local mode can make your job easier by making deployment on the production site less dangerous. Use Local mode to make your changes and test your Web application before deploying it to the Master Web site.

Overview of Visual SourceSafe

By using an RCS, in this case Microsoft Visual SourceSafe (VSS), you can safely archive your work on a regular basis, ensuring its protection. Visual SourceSafe, like most RCS software, behaves much like a librarian who manages the integrity and safety of a library's contents. Think of your Web project as a library that is constantly growing and evolving. You can easily imagine that, as more people contribute to the library, you will need a reliable way of tracking the contributions. As more of the changes to the existing content occur, you would likely want a way of identifying who did what changes where. This is the role of the RCS in short: to watch over the files that comprise your project.

Installing Visual SourceSafe

Before you can begin to use Visual SourceSafe on your workstation with Visual InterDev, you must correctly set up the Visual SourceSafe software. Exactly how large your installation is depends on which options you want to install. If you are connecting to an existing Visual SourceSafe database, you are required to install only the client portions of VSS and the tools for integrated environments. If you are administering your own Visual SourceSafe database, you need to install all the VSS components, including those required for the VSS server. Installing these components creates the required directories and data files that comprise a VSS database.

NOTE   Refer to the Microsoft documentation on instructions for installing the Visual SourceSafe client and server components. ▪

Depending on your Visual InterDev and Web server configuration, you may be required to create a Visual SourceSafe user for your Web service account. If you are using Microsoft Internet Information Server 4.0, this user is typically called IUSR_*machinename,* where *machinename* represents the Web server's name. For information on adding a Visual SourceSafe user, refer to "Adding Users to VSS," later in this chapter.

Understanding SourceSafe

Visual SourceSafe can be disorienting to work with at first but quickly becomes ingrained into your normal work habits. With its added safety features, managing your Web sites becomes less of a headache and more reasonable. Visual InterDev provides direct integration with Visual SourceSafe for several essential functions. As a developer, you can easily rely on Visual SourceSafe when doing your work within InterDev and then step directly into Visual SourceSafe to practice more direct control.

Visual SourceSafe Concepts

Visual SourceSafe operates on a simple premise: Two heads are better than one. After you enter a file into VSS's database, it's preserved there until you purge it. That's the first head. The second is that you never actually change that file; you sign out a working copy of it. You modify the working file and then sign it back into the VSS database; VSS replaces the original file you checked out. But what about the original file? Is it now gone for good? Actually, it hasn't gone anywhere. Visual SourceSafe has a versioning control system that allows you to record the *history* of a file. You have the option of "rolling back" to whatever previous version of the file might exist in the database. If you find a mistake in your newly edited file just after you've checked it in, you can roll back the mistake a version so that your original file remains pristine.

You may be thinking, "So if I change a file 10 times, Visual SourceSafe stores 10 copies of that file? How grossly inefficient!" This assumption isn't totally true. VSS stores the original file and then stores changes in a format relative to that original file. Therefore, if you add the word *the* to your file and then check it into the VSS database, VSS doesn't create two copies of the file, which would create overhead. Instead, VSS appends a note to the original file saying *the* is added to this point on this date. This process is known as creating a *delta.* Using the delta method of storing changes, you can have several files in the database for a lot less disk cost than you might think. However, storing so many files is all well and good, but how do you keep track of them?

Files are stored in Visual SourceSafe using a *project approach.* A Visual SourceSafe project is in no way linked to other development software projects (such as Visual C++ or Visual InterDev). A project is also not an exact mirror of your file's status on the hard drive. Visual SourceSafe operates on a database storage principle, and projects provide its internal means of keeping track of the files you have stored in it. Operations-wise, the project structure mimics the organizational hierarchy found in an operating system's directory tree. The root project $/ (which can be considered roughly analogous to C:\) can contain sub-projects such as $/Web/Client/

Development, much like directories and subdirectories found on your hard drive. Moreover, with these projects, much like directories on your hard drive, you can divide and subdivide project folders in a nearly infinite array.

N O T E   It is important to note that although the organization of projects mimics that of a hard drive, the actual files in VSS cannot be accessed that way. You can never write directly to the "hard drive" in a Visual SourceSafe project; you can only move copies of it out to be modified elsewhere before being written back into the database. ▪

Visual SourceSafe Functions

If you look at Visual SourceSafe's implementation of projects from another perspective, you can consider VSS as a specialized disk operating system. Instead of offering pedestrian functions such as copy or delete, however, VSS can instead perform tasks such as Check-In, Check-Out, and Get.

Checking out files is like getting a book out of the library—except you don't have to be quiet all the time to do it. To work safely on a VSS project, you need to "check out" a file from the VSS database. Essentially, checking out tells Visual SourceSafe, "I'm going to be making some changes to this file, so be a dear and give it to me."

However, you cannot check out a file without first making certain you have specified a *working directory*. Because you can't modify the files in the Visual SourceSafe database directly, you need to tell VSS where to put a working copy of the file. The working directory doesn't have to be a special one set aside exclusively for VSS's use because its contents become academic after you check the file back in and the working copy is removed.

N O T E   You can set your "live" directory as the working directory (in the case of Web projects, on the server), and the changes will go public as soon as you save your file. However, those changes are not entered into the VSS database until you check in the file. Although there's no rule against working live directly, if you make a mistake and haven't updated the VSS database, you cannot reclaim your earlier work. By working live, you also may mistakenly check out a file you haven't updated, which then overwrites your newer file. ▪

So you've got your file checked out, you've made all your changes and saved them, but the "live" copy of your project is unchanged. What's wrong? Checking out the file is only the beginning, because in order for your changes to be entered in the VSS database, they have to be checked in.

Checking in files is like returning a book to the library—except that in VSS the librarian doesn't care if you've written all over the book and changed its text. (The librarian still frowns upon your getting food in the pages though.) Checking in a file takes the changes to your working copy of a file and enters them into the VSS database. After a successful check-in, your changes are applied to the VSS copy in the database.

So now you've created a project, added files to it, checked out a file, specified a working directory, made changes to that file, saved it, and finally checked it in. Your "live" version of the project is still unchanged. What gives?

For your files to go "public," you have to publish them somehow. The checked-in file modifies only the files in the VSS database and has no effect on the original file in your hard drive or server. Publishing is a lot like checking out, except that instead of telling VSS "Give me a working copy to work on," publishing says "Put the current copy of this file in this place so that other people or programs can look at it."

You can publish from the VSS database using either of two methods. The first and most common is to use the Get command. This command "gets" the current copy from the database and puts it in the location of your choice. To stretch the library analogy a little further, say that you've checked in your book, but the people in the late fee processing department don't know that fact until the librarian tells them that you've done so. The problem with the Get command is that it can't access remote machines that aren't connected on a local area network. For Web developers especially, this is an onerous burden, as it adds an additional step to an already-complex ritual of checking in, checking out, using Get, and finally using FTP.

Fortunately, as of version 5.0 of Visual SourceSafe, you can deploy to Web sites outside the Visual Studio environment. Like Get, the Deploy command puts files where you want them. Unlike Get, though, Deploy can act over an FTP connection to your server. However, your administrator (or you, if you're the administrator) must specify a project as a Web project directly before you can use Deploy to publish your project. When you are using Visual InterDev 6 as a development platform, the manual deployment of files is handled for you through the Visual Studio environment.

Visual SourceSafe Version and Tracking Control

Nobody's perfect; even technical reference authors make mistaykes (sic). Luckily, Visual SourceSafe provides several safeguards, which are designed for clumsy and absent-minded people, or even perfect people who make the occasional mistake.

The first of these safeguards is the Undo Check Out feature. It's a simple function. If you have something checked out, this function unchecks it, and Visual SourceSafe never knows you had the file. Plausible deniability. The obvious use for this function would be if you check out a file, edit it into incomprehensibility, and then want to restore the original file. You can't "recheck" out the file, and checking it back in would be counterproductive. You have to undo the process of ever checking it out in the first place. However, Undo Check Out is only a first-line defense against casual mistakes and erroneous check-outs. For errors that inadvertently get checked back in, more serious measures are needed.

The History function is one of these measures. It allows you to selectively pore over the cumulative changes made to the file ever since it was created and imported into the VSS database. If you've made a mistake, and you know which version it occurs in, you can set the file to roll back to the preceding version by using the Rollback command. Rollback simply tells Visual

SourceSafe to "remove modifications of the file back to this version." `Rollback` itself is a powerful command; but without the power of the History function to navigate among the various file versions, it would be an overly arcane tool to use.

The Differences function is mostly a diagnostic tool. Say that you have a file in which you know something is wrong, but you don't know what. The Differences function displays a file you choose from the file history and a working version of the file side by side. The discrepancies between the two are highlighted, so you can trace what changes exist from an older version to a newer. Differences can display whether a line has been deleted, changed, or added to the file in comparison to the other file. All in all, it is a powerful tool for tracking changes.

Using SourceSafe in Visual InterDev

Normally, within Microsoft Developer Studio, you use a set of options and features directly linked to Visual SourceSafe, thus removing the need to ever use the Visual SourceSafe Explorer client software. Due to the nature of the Web, all content is physically located on the Web server and is not necessarily located completely on your workstation at any one given time. For this reason, the traditional form of interaction with VSS is unusable. The objective of VSS integration within Visual InterDev concentrates more on managing the updates to the files in your project. To remove the possibility of two or more people changing the same files simultaneously, Visual SourceSafe's library services monitor whenever a file is checked out. While the file is checked out for changes, no other person can try to open and edit the file, which prevents saving over the other person's changes. After the changes are complete, the file is checked back in and updated. The file is then returned to the pool of available files for editing, free for someone to check out again.

N O T E The Visual SourceSafe Server operates on the Web server itself, not on the workstation.

Before you can begin to use the benefits of Visual SourceSafe within Visual InterDev, you must enable Source Control for your Web project. Doing so tells Visual InterDev to start tracking requests to the Web server for files and to pass on the information to Visual SourceSafe on the Web server. Keep in mind that the VSS database is usually on the Web server and not the workstation for Visual InterDev integration. Enabling Source Control is a simple process:

1. Select your project from the Project Explorer.
2. Choose Project, Source Control, Add to Source Control. This action opens the Enable Source Control dialog box, shown in Figure 24.3.
3. Enter the name for the SourceSafe project in the Source Control Project Name text box, with $/ being the root of the SourceSafe database. For example, enter **$/MyWebProject**.

 You can specify an existing SourceSafe project to add your Web content to.

FIG. 24.3

By choosing Add to Source Control, you tell Visual InterDev to start tracking Visual SourceSafe requests for all files.

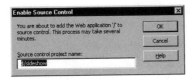

4. Click OK. Visual InterDev begins the process of adding all your Web files to Source Control. After all the existing files are added, you are greeted with a prompt telling you all is well, as shown in Figure 24.4.

FIG. 24.4

The appearance of this dialog box reassures you all is well with Source Control.

5. Click OK to close the dialog box and get down to work.

 T I P When files or folders are added to Source Control and the SourceSafe database, local versions of the file are changed to read-only.

Working with Source Control

After you enable Source Control for your project, you can work with your files in nearly the same way you always do. The main difference in behavior between files with SourceSafe and without is what happens when you begin to edit files. Previously, when you requested a working copy of a file to edit, Visual InterDev fetched it directly from the Web server and placed it in your working directory. When you were done with your changes and released the working copy, Visual InterDev submitted your changes to the Web server and removed the local copy in your working directory.

With Visual SourceSafe enabled, the process changes slightly. When you request a working copy of a file, Visual InterDev first queries the Web server to see whether the file is available for editing. If the file is available, Visual InterDev retrieves a working copy for your changes and signs out the file from the server, using VSS's check-out facility. The file is then removed from the available pool of files for other users to edit, until you release your working copy. If a file is already checked out by someone else, and you try to retrieve a working copy, you are issued a warning stating that the file is currently being edited by a different user. Visual SourceSafe can be configured to allow multiple check-outs but does not, by default, let this happen.

Part
VI

Ch
24

Checking Out and Checking In Files   To work on files in your Web application, you must "check out" the file. This action informs Visual SourceSafe that you are actively working on a file. In this regard, SourceSafe acts as a transaction controller, or a traffic cop, ensuring that no one else modifies the file while you are working on it. Checking out files retrieves the most recent versions of the files from the SourceSafe database, not the master Web server. Remember this important concept: The SourceSafe database is separate from the physical file system and the Web server. To avoid confusion, you should always update the Visual SourceSafe version of a file when you complete your changes and release your changes to the master Web server.

To check out a file for work, follow these steps:

1. Right-click the file(s) or folder(s) on which you want to work in the Project Explorer.

2. From the context menu, choose Check Out *<filename>* to open the dialog box shown in Figure 24.5.

FIG. 24.5

In the Check Out Item(s) dialog box, you can request a file from the SourceSafe database.

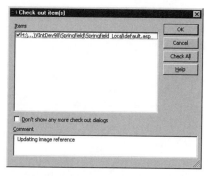

3. Confirm that all the items listed in the Items list box are files you want to check out. Files selected with a check are those that will be signed out of the SourceSafe database.

4. When checking out files, you should add a comment to the SourceSafe database to indicate why you are working on the file. Enter your comment in the Comment text box; for example, enter **Updating date and email link**.

5. Click OK to send Visual InterDev to talk to the SourceSafe database. The file(s) or folder(s) are checked out, and the comment is added to the database.

N O T E   If a file is checked out by another developer, SourceSafe returns a message indicating this fact. You have the option of checking out the file anyway (if the SourceSafe server has been configured to allow multiple users), or you are asked to try again later. ■

  When a file is checked out from the SourceSafe database, a red check mark icon appears beside the file icon in the Project Explorer. This check mark is a useful visual clue to spot checked-out files.

After you complete your changes to the file(s) you requested, you must save them and release the working copy. The steps for releasing a working copy are the same as before you enabled Source Control—with one additional step. When you release the working copy to the server, you should instruct Visual InterDev to check in and update the file in the VSS database. To check in your local copy, follow these instructions:

1. Right-click the file(s) or folder(s) you want to release.

2. From the context menu, choose Check In <*filename*>to open the Check In Item(s) dialog box, shown in Figure 24.6.

FIG. 24.6

Checking items into the SourceSafe updates the database with your changes and makes the file available for another developer.

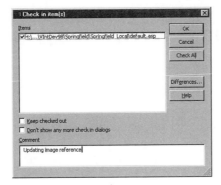

3. Confirm that the files listed in the Items list box are the files you want to check into the SourceSafe database. If a file's check box is selected, the file is checked back in.

4. If you want to update the SourceSafe database with your changes but still keep the file signed out, select the Keep Checked Out check box. If this box is not selected, the file is returned to the SourceSafe database for another developer.

5. Enter an update to the SourceSafe database on what you did in the Comments text box. This area is ideal for making notes about what you did to a file.

6. To compare the differences between your local working copy and the latest version of the file in the SourceSafe database, click the Differences button. This action opens the Differences dialog box, shown in Figure 24.7.

7. Close the Differences dialog box after you finish comparing your differences.

8. Click OK to check in the file and update the database.

After you check a file into the VSS database, where it is safely stored, the file is then unlocked so that other users can check out the file for changes.

FIG. 24.7

The Differences dialog box visually identifies the changes in your file. Deleted material is marked in blue, modified text in red, and new information in green.

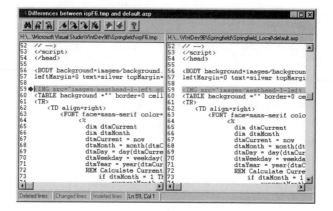

Administering Visual SourceSafe

The nature of Visual SourceSafe makes administering a VSS database a simple matter. Underlying its simple nature, Visual SourceSafe employs several sophisticated tools and features that may prove invaluable to you as a Web developer. From within the client software, the Visual SourceSafe Explorer, a developer can customize how he or she wants VSS to behave. These choices are unique to one developer and are not shared in a group environment. The VSS Administrator (who may be you) can set the standardized options and behaviors for the entire team in group environments, while still allowing individual developers the flexibility to add to that customization.

This chapter does not explore the Visual SourceSafe administration process in great detail. For more information on administering VSS, you should refer to the Microsoft documentation. To learn more about Visual SourceSafe and using it for Web development, refer to *Web Management with Microsoft Visual SourceSafe 5.0* from Que.

By using the Visual SourceSafe Admin tool, shown in Figure 24.8, the VSS administrator also can customize the operation of VSS. Of primary importance to VSS administrators is the implementation of security for the projects within the database.

FIG. 24.8

The Visual SourceSafe Administrator is used to create databases, control user access, and modify the behavior of the SourceSafe database.

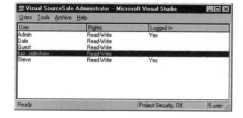

Adding Users to VSS

All aspects of VSS security work by keeping track of users and their access to the VSS database. Users are provided names and passwords to enter, while Visual SourceSafe manages what they can and can't do. Usernames are usually the same names that the users have for the network, so that they can automatically sign in to VSS. Users can have a different name than the network username, but this requires the users to enter the usernames and passwords manually. You can easily add a user to Visual SourceSafe by following this simple process:

1. Choose Users, Add User.
2. When the Add User dialog box appears, as shown Figure 24.9, enter the user's name and password. You can also select Read Only to set read-only permissions for this user.

FIG. 24.9

When you add a new user to Visual SourceSafe, you can use the same name that the user has on the network or an entirely different one with a password.

As you need more users, adding them is a simple matter. If you want to prevent users from accessing Visual SourceSafe, you can also delete users by using the User menu.

Limiting Access to Projects

In some situations, you may want to control the more security-oriented issues of Visual SourceSafe. In a group environment, allowing all developers equal access to every project and file under construction may not be desirable. The VSS Administrator has the power to determine who should have access to what and can therefore isolate those developers from places they shouldn't be. By default, all VSS users have full access to all projects (unless the users were created with read-only permissions).

Enabling Project Security   To limit access to specific projects, you must enable Project Security:

1. Choose Tools, Options to open the SourceSafe Options dialog box. Click the second tab, Project Security, as shown in Figure 24.10.
2. Select Enable Project Security by clicking the check box.
3. Select the appropriate check boxes to specify the default user rights. You can specify what actions users can perform by default without further permissions.
4. Click OK.

FIG. 24.10

On the Project Security tab of the SourceSafe Options dialog box, you can enable project security.

After you enable the security features of VSS, you can begin setting up your permissions. You can control users' access rights in two ways: by selecting Rights by Project or Rights Assignments for User.

Rights by Project   If you want to control security on a project-by-project basis, the Rights by Project view is the best choice for limiting access rights for users. To select this view, follow these steps:

1. Choose Tools, Rights by Project. The Project Rights dialog box then appears, as shown in Figure 24.11.

FIG. 24.11

The Project Rights dialog box provides you a project-by-project method of limiting access.

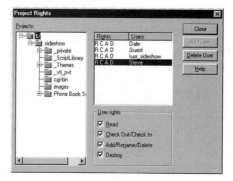

2. On the left side of the dialog box is the Projects list. Select the project to which you want to limit access.

3. On the right side of the dialog box are the names of users currently able to access the project. Below the list of usernames are the check boxes displaying the rights on the project. By selecting a user from the list of users, you can alter these User Rights: Read, Check Out/Check In, Add/Rename/Delete, and Destroy.

4. To add a new user to the project, select the project from the list, and click the Add User button.

5. To remove a user from the project, select the username from the list, and click the Delete User button.

Rights Assignments for Users   If you prefer to work on an assignment basis, you can specify the appropriate rights for the projects on a user-by-user basis. To do so, follow these steps:

1. Select the user you want to manage from the list in the Visual SourceSafe Administrator.

2. Choose Tools, Rights Assignments for User. This action opens the Assignments for User dialog box, shown in Figure 24.12. The title of the dialog box specifies which user you are currently managing.

FIG. 24.12
In this dialog box, you can assign users specific tasks and limit their access rights with ease.

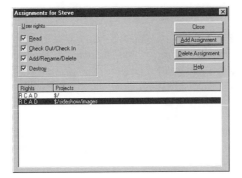

3. By default, the only assignment provided to the user is permissions for the $/ root project. By selecting the project, you can specify the access rights for the user.

4. Using the check boxes for User Rights, select the access rights the user should have for the selected project.

5. To add a new project to the user's list of assignments, click the Add Assignment button. You then can select a project from the Visual SourceSafe database for the user to be assigned to.

6. To remove a project from the user's list of assignments, select the project, and click the Delete Assignment button. Clicking this button removes the selected project from the list of projects to which the user has access rights.

Locking the SourceSafe Database

Sometimes preventing users from checking out files and modifying them may be appropriate. To support this facility, VSS Administrator enables you to lock the Visual SourceSafe database. No user can modify projects until it is unlocked. You can lock (and unlock) the database by choosing Tools, Lock SourceSafe Database. This action calls up a dialog box, shown in Figure 24.13, that reports the connected users and allows you to lock (and unlock) the database by selecting a check box.

TIP   Locking the database is ideal when you need to create backups of the SourceSafe database. This way, you can prevent a file from being in use when the backup is being made.

FIG. 24.13
By locking the
SourceSafe database,
you can prevent all
users from checking out
and modifying files.

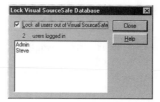

Managing File Types in VSS Administrator

Web sites are composed of many files of many different types, including the raw HTML pages, graphic files of differing formats, and any additional file types for other content you may have. Visual SourceSafe allows you to set up file types for management within VSS databases and arrange them into logical groups. Both the SourceSafe Administrator and the SourceSafe Explorer allow you to manage file types. By specifying the file types within the SourceSafe Administrator, you can set the defaults for all users who interact with VSS. If a user modifies these file types from the SourceSafe Explorer, those changes are unique to that user.

To modify the VSS file types, follow these instructions:

1. From the SourceSafe Administrator, choose Tools, Options to open the SourceSafe Options dialog box.

2. Click the File Types tab to open the File Types page, as shown in Figure 24.14.

FIG. 24.14
The File Types tab allows
you to specify the file
groups that VSS will
handle.

3. In the top box, Binary Files, specify binary file type extensions (.EXE or .COM, for example) to override SourceSafe's auto detection of file types.

4. The File Groups box lists the established file types. To modify an existing group, select it from the list.

5. In the bottom box, File Types Included in File Group, add or remove file extensions that you want associated with this group. Separate different extensions with a comma.

6. To add a new file group, click the <u>A</u>dd button. You then are prompted to enter a name for the file group. After the group is added, you can modify it as shown in step 4.

7. To remove an existing file group, select the group you want to delete, and click the <u>D</u>elete button.

From Here...

Developer isolation and version control are particularly important topics when you are working on large projects with many developers. For more information on working with multiple developers, refer to these chapters:

- Chapter 21, "Working with Site Server Enterprise Edition."
- Chapter 26, "Team Development with FrontPage 98 and Visual InterDev 6."

Part
VI

Ch
24

Advanced Site Development

25   Designing and Organizing Web Sites   517

26   Team Development with FrontPage 98 and InterDev 6   539

27   Increasing Site Performance   549

CHAPTER 25

Designing and Organizing Web Sites

In this chapter

Designing the Site   **518**

Organizing Your Site   **535**

Designing the Site

Now that you have a good foundation for using Visual InterDev, you are ready to learn what goes into designing and organizing a Web site. Much planning and forethought need to go into a Visual InterDev site before you start building any pages. A small investment in planning can save hours—even days—of development time down the road.

Imagine a film crew preparing to shoot a motion picture. The director, actors, stage hands, and everyone else involved in the movie are in place, yet there is no script. The actors have no lines and no idea of what the movie is about. The director simply tells them, "Okay, let's roll! Just make something up as we go along." What type of movie do you think they would end up with?

Likewise, the key to creating a successful Visual InterDev site is preparation, preparation, and more preparation. The more prepared you are, the better your site is going to turn out, and the easier it will be to maintain and update. Ideally, you want the site completely designed with a storyboard developed and approved on paper before loading Visual InterDev. The design process can be divided into the three following areas:

- Define the scope of your project. Do so by establishing the goals and objectives of your site. Are you going to sell products directly from a database, feature a searchable knowledge base of tech support issues, consolidate daily content from outside resources automatically, and so on?

- Consider all the factors involved in the actual production, such as your time frame, budget, where the source material will come from, and how much work will be done in-house as opposed to using outside contractors.

- The final step in the design process is to develop a storyboard for establishing the look and feel of the site. At this stage, you get down to brass tacks and develop a navigation method, a branded look for the client, and determine the overall flow of information.

While you are designing and organizing your site, create as much written documentation as possible. You can rework it later into a concise proposal, invoice, or even site documentation. Now take a look at each of these steps in more detail.

Defining the Scope of the Project

As the developer of a Visual InterDev site, you meet with your client or employer to determine his or her needs. Many issues must be considered. For example, a company may simply want more consumer awareness for its product, requiring only a small presence on the Web with an online catalog, or it may want full online transaction processing with automated links to a database. Even the development process itself must be discussed: Your client might want to produce all the art in-house or charge you, as the site developer, with creating all of it.

Estimating the time and resources needed to complete a Visual InterDev site can be very difficult without thoroughly defining the scope of the project first. Therefore, you must establish definite goals and objectives, and determine what the content is and where it's coming from. Then with all the details of the project spelled out, you should make your best possible estimate of the time and resources required and then double it. You learn about time and budget estimates in more detail later in this chapter in the "Production Considerations" section.

Most sites on the Web today seem to fall into one of three main categories: *services*, *marketing*, or *sales*. In considering the goals and objectives of your site, you first should determine what main category most closely fits your site. Next, you should pinpoint who your audience is.

Services The most common type of site found on the World Wide Web falls under the category of a service. Services typically include informational feeds, software and content repositories, reference sources, research materials, and so on.

Informational Feeds Common informational feeds include weather forecasts, news, stock market quotes, audio and video feeds, as well as information about special events, such as the Super Bowl. The Microsoft Investor site shown in Figure 25.1 makes extensive use of ActiveX controls. Informational feeds that do not directly promote a company or product, such as audio and video feeds, typically find their funding through the sale of advertising space or subscriptions.

▶ **See** "Deploying ActiveX Controls," **p. 277**

FIG. 25.1
The Microsoft Investor site (**investor.msn.com**) features ActiveX controls for creating and monitoring a personal portfolio.

Part
VII

Ch

25

Repositories Repositories are usually File Transfer Protocol (FTP) sites with Web sites as front ends. A repository may contain commonly used elements for documents, software, or for development. The client (user) usually establishes a connection with server software at the FTP site for the sole purpose of uploading and downloading files. Most Web browsers, as well as Visual InterDev, now have FTP capabilities built in. All you have to do is set up a link to a file on an FTP site, and if the user clicks that link, the browser automatically logs in to the FTP server and requests a file.

Many repositories are available on the Internet. You can find everything from shareware software to graphics and audio files. **download.com**, a site run by CINet and shown in Figure 25.2, is one of the most popular shareware repositories on the Internet. As with informational feeds, repositories usually obtain their funding through the sale of advertising space or subscriptions.

FIG. 25.2
At **www.download.com**, you can find thousands of shareware and demo programs.

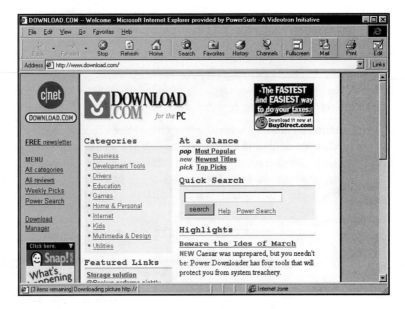

Reference   Reference sites typically hold documentation of one type or another. Usually, this documentation is text based, but with the increasing bandwidths on the Internet and the popularity of intranets, reference sites are starting to contain more multimedia material. For example, an in-house reference site might include digital video clips to go along with the printed documentation.

Reference sites on the Internet are practical sources of current information, especially for the computer industry. Reference sites regarding hardware and software are generally more up-to-date than any book or manual that you can purchase in a store. The Microsoft Knowledge Base, shown in Figure 25.3, offers a searchable database of technical support documents.

Outside the computer industry, many reference sites are starting to appear. For example, you can get recipes, coupons, demographics, and phone listings—virtually anything you can imagine.

Marketing and Public Relations   Marketing and public relations sites are mainly geared to give the client more visibility and consumer awareness. In the past, many writers relied heavily on press releases that came in the mail; now they can get almost all their information from corporate sites because most have a press release page. The movie industry has made good use of the Web. Paramount Pictures, for example, offers a site describing current and upcoming motion picture and video releases, as shown in Figure 25.4. You can download QuickTime previews of movies.

FIG. 25.3

The Microsoft Technical Support site (**http://support.microsoft.com/support**) contains a knowledge base that is an example of a practical reference site.

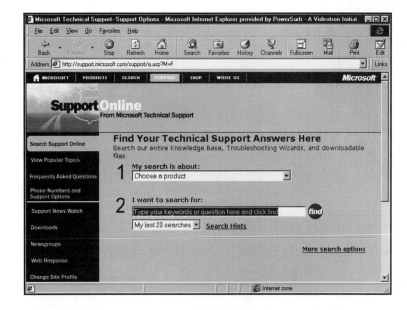

FIG. 25.4

The Paramount Pictures Web site (**www.paramount.com**) is a good example of a marketing/public relations site.

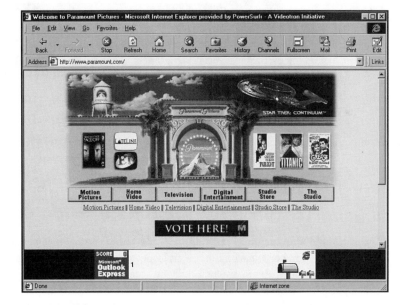

Sales   Now that secure transactions are readily available on the Internet, the number of online sales sites is increasing. However, a sales-oriented site need not always offer online transactions. The following common types of sites are geared toward doing business on the Internet:

■ *Online catalogs.* Many sites simply offer online catalogs that users can browse or search. The users can track down the product through company contact information on the Web site.

■ *Online ordering.* The next step in the sales category is online ordering, which enables users to place orders via online forms. Often, these sites simply use COD, checks, or money orders as the payment vehicles. That way, the users' risk is limited to transmitting their names and addresses across the Internet.

■ *Online transactions.* Now with Secure Socket Layer (SSL), true online transactions using credit cards and other payment options are safe across the Internet. SSL is a security standard, promoted by Netscape Communications, that uses a public key encryption scheme. SSL is an open standard and is now common in browsers, such as Netscape Navigator and Microsoft Internet Explorer. The Macmillan Computer Publishing Bookstore, shown in Figure 25.5, takes advantage of SSL security.

FIG. 25.5

The Macmillan Computer Publishing Bookstore site takes credit card orders online (**www.mcp.com/ online_catalog/**).

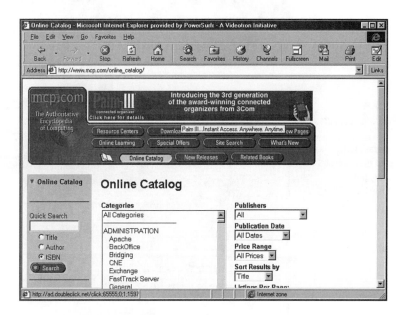

Understand Your Audience and Its Use of the Web   After you determine a category for your site, you can further focus on the design by determining who your audience is. Of the many factors to consider, you might focus only on access speed, age, relationship to the client, and computer literacy, for example. Access speed is one of the most important elements of Web site design. Relationship to the client determines the amount and type of data the site will need. Age and computer literacy play major roles in the site's user interface.

Access Speed Considerations   One of the most critical considerations in knowing your audience is the bandwidth visitors will use to access your site. The smaller the bandwidth, the smaller your pages need to be in terms of graphics, audio, and video. Testing your site frequently on its target platform is always a good idea to ensure that you do not create a bandwidth crisis halfway through the development cycle.

More often than not, your site will be on the Internet, and you won't know the specifics of your audience. In that case, you would be wise to assume that users will dial in to service providers with 14.4 and 28.8 baud modems. Knowing this fact practically mandates a page size of 150KB or less.

For in-house Visual InterDev sites, you have much more freedom in the sense that you probably don't have serious bandwidth limitations. You also have a captive audience with known demographics.

Computer Literacy   You also must take the computer skills of the audience into account. It used to be that anyone who could even get on the Web was obviously computer literate. However, now with user-friendly Internet service providers and Web-ready televisions, even computer-illiterate people are browsing the Web.

When your audience is computer literate, you have a little more leeway in designing your site—especially when it comes to interactive hotspots. Computer-savvy individuals know to watch for small changes in the appearance of the mouse pointer that indicate the location of hotspots.

I'm not saying that you can't let loose with creativity when the audience is not well acquainted with computers. Many beautiful and highly effective site designs are based on intuitive, real-world metaphors. For example, a camcorder graphic as a link to a video clip or a camera graphic as a link to an image is an intuitive icon.

Age Group   Because the Web and Visual InterDev are visual media, the age of the audience plays a critical part in the overall design of the site. Obviously, a younger audience is going to have much different tastes than an older audience. Typically, the younger the audience, the more liberal you can (and should) be with your design, whereas an older audience would probably find a more conservative design appealing. Conservative means readability in the shortest sense, although it can also mean traditional layout as found in the print world. The more liberal approach usually involves more intensive graphics and radical fontography.

Audience Relationship to Client   Next, you need to ask yourself, "Does the audience already have a relationship with the client?" If so, then existing logos, colors, and styles should play a large role in the site design. Also, in this case, you don't have to worry much about educating the audience about the client.

If the audience is unfamiliar with the client, you might be able to tailor the design to better fit the interactive capabilities of Visual InterDev, worrying less about replicating the client's existing styles and brands. On the flip side, you also might need to expand the client's background information for the audience.

 TIP At this point, you might consider supporting languages other than English. With the worldwide connectivity of the Internet, you can open your site to millions of additional users by adding other languages.

Production Resources   The third aspect to defining the scope of a project is to determine the site's content as well as the source of the content. First, decide whether the content will be

Part
VII

Ch
25

static or *dynamic*; then look into the source of the material. (Does it already exist, or do you have to create it?) Finally, make a list of all the needed content, organized by category.

Sites often contain a mixture of static and dynamic content. In many cases, your Web site may not require real-time changes when a visitor interacts with your site. However, dynamic pages are designed for frequent updated as a result of an automated program—suited for those times when a real-time interaction is required. Dynamic and static sites have different bearings on design, as follows:

- *Static Content.* Static pages are easy to create because the content never changes. You simply load a document into Visual InterDev, link it to your site, and you're done. Yet changing or updating the page means repeating those steps every time, which is not something you want to do on a daily basis. There are some practical applications for static sites, such as displaying Frequently Asked Questions (FAQs). The advantage is that they are easy to create, but the disadvantage is that they are difficult to update.

- *Dynamic Content.* Dynamic pages change often or are built as they are requested by the user. The advantage to using these pages is easy or automatic updating. The disadvantage is that developing and debugging the programming take time. The two basic approaches to dynamic content are as follow: You can generate it yourself via server-side scripting, or you can reference it from another location on the Internet through either server-side scripting or ActiveX controls.

  Generated content is usually the result of some application that runs as scheduled, or on demand as it is requested. *Referencing* means that you are pulling the content from elsewhere on the Internet. For example, stock market sites get their data from the stock market. You can link a wide variety of information from the Internet through FTP and Gopher sites, images, audio files, databases, and more.

If you are dealing with content that needs to be updated on a regular basis, establish how often updates take place and exactly what material is updated. With the server-side scripting capability of Active Server Pages, a page can be updated hourly, daily, weekly, monthly, or even on the fly.

▶ For more information about creating dynamic pages and sites, **see** Part II, "Active Scripting for Web Sites" on **p. 97**

Source Material   You should develop a list of source material needed for the site and divide it into two main categories: new and existing. *New material* is anything that is not ready to drag and drop into Visual InterDev. Conversely, *existing material* should be in formats compatible with Visual InterDev.

If you have existing material, you should examine it carefully before you agree to use it. For example, the client may already have a logo scanned, but what is the quality of the scan? Do you have to rescan it? If the original is of low quality, do you have to re-create it from scratch? Also, if you need to port existing material to a Visual InterDev–compatible format, can the porting be automated or must it be done manually?

Microsoft Office 97 fully supports the HTML format, so any document that you can load into Word, Excel, and Access can be saved as a Web page. You should be careful when using this functionality, however, because the results are usable but not pretty. If you can create your own Web pages and not rely on the HTML export capabilities behind Office 97 you're probably ahead of the game.

Developing a Rate Sheet   If you are developing a Visual InterDev site on a contract, you may find it useful to create a rate sheet of standard charges to estimate the cost of a project. For example, most sites require some graphics work, such as scanning existing logos and cleaning them up. You can set a fixed price for this process on your rate sheet.

The same holds true for other media types, such as audio recordings, video clips, and 2D and 3D animation. Then, when you need to estimate the development cost of a particular site, you can simply break the project into discrete steps and add up the totals for each process.

Client Access   At this point, you need to answer a number of questions about your client. Does the client already have access to the Internet? Does the client have the appropriate hardware and software for connecting to the Internet? Are you expected to provide or install needed hardware and software? How much training does your client need to handle the incoming email or online orders? Is it in the best interest for the client to carry out its business on the Net? These all-important considerations sometimes fall through the cracks with new Web site projects.

Design Considerations

Now that you have established the goals and objectives of the site, you can get down to the meat of the creative process: the graphic design. First, think about how the information in your site is going to flow; then determine how the user is going to navigate through the flow of information. At this time, you should also be thinking about a branded *look and feel* for the site. Typically, you create these steps on paper with a storyboard.

The Customer Comes First   Often, the easiest way to start a conversation with people is to ask them about themselves; likewise, if your audience is the focus of your site, visitors will return again and again. You can give attention to your audience in a number of ways. For example, you can offer multiple versions of your site based on the users' bandwidth. You can allow them to customize your site based on their own preferences. You can update them via a listserver when information on your site changes. You can even offer giveaways and host contests.

Bandwidth   Because people access the Internet at different speeds, sites must balance content and speed. For example, users accessing the Internet with 14.4 modems may become frustrated waiting for large images and sounds to download. On the other hand, users with faster speeds may get bored with the simplicity of your site if it's graphically barren.

The solution? Often you can offer multiple versions of your site for different bandwidths. You may have a little text link that says, "More Graphics," and one that says, "Fewer Graphics." Then you can let the users choose for themselves. This approach can also be an option for the way you present sound; you can offer a Sound Off/On button.

Theme Design By using stylized graphics, audio, text, and colors, you can create themes. Using these themes is a simple way to offer pseudo-customized pages, such as futuristic, Western, Roman, classical, and so on. Then you can filter your site through these different themes based on user preferences. These themes can also affect the site's music. The main challenge you may face taking this approach is maintaining the client's branded look with each theme. Theme design for a Web site can begin by using Visual InterDev site themes; however, it can be extended to creating your own design theme throughout the site.

Customizable Options The next level in customizing your site to the users is creating a fully configurable site. For example, the Microsoft Network Web site (**http://www.msn.com** and **http://home.microsoft.com**) allows you to set up your own colors, links, and sounds, as well as list the information you want to see on the site each day (news, weather, and new and interesting sites). This site is shown in Figure 25.6.

FIG. 25.6

This setup page allows you to personalize the way you view the **msn.com** site.

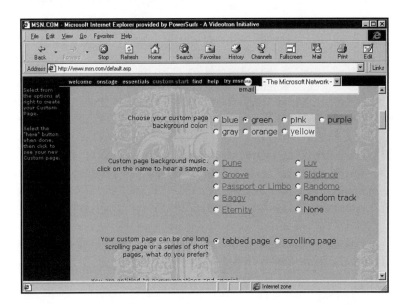

At Microsoft, the MSN site developers wrote a custom ISAPI DLL for Microsoft's Internet Information Server that generates a unique page for each user on the fly. The user preferences are stored on the client side via *cookies,* and the same information is also stored in a database on the server. By using cookies, **www.msn.com** can avoid asking people for user IDs every time they hit the page. This initial project eventually leads into the Personalization Server and the Active Server Page technology available today. After a version of Active Server Pages became available, the entire MSN site was rewritten in ASP in a fraction of the time necessary to write it in C++.

ON THE WEB

www.msn.com   The Microsoft Network

The following list offers suggestions for custom options you can make available to your users:

- Graphics
  Yes/No
  Horizontal Layout
  Vertical Layout
  Horizontal Rules
  Tables
- Pictures
  Yes/No
  Picture Repositories (Offering Daily Feeds)
  Satellite Feeds
  Live Video Feeds
  Weather Maps
  Cartoons
- Fonts
  Yes/No
  Font Style
  Font Size
- Music
  Yes/No
  MIDI
  WAV
  Style
  Length
- Colors
  Yes/No
  Background
  Table Borders
  Table Backgrounds
  Text
  Hyperlinks
- Links
  News Stories
  Stock Quotes
  Newsgroup Articles
  News Stories

Movie Listings and Times

TV Listings and Times

IRC Chat Events

Repositories

Search Engines

■ Screen Resolution

1024×768

800×600

640×480

Windows CE

Using Listservers   Keeping track of changes on a site is often hard without checking it each day or on a regular basis. As a service to your users, you can offer a listserver to which they can subscribe; it can notify them of any updates or changes on your site. For users of Internet Explorer 4.0, you can instruct your users on setting up the Check Favorite Sites option.

Promotional Enticements   One way of guaranteeing return visits to your site is to offer free giveaways and contests. These enticements could be relatively inexpensive if you can get a sponsor. After people enter an online contest, you are almost guaranteed that they will be back to see the results. Try offering advertising in exchange for giveaways.

Keeping Your Site Fresh   You can imagine what television would be like if every week the exact same episodes aired. After you saw a particular show, you would never see a different episode. Unfortunately, that is the case with many sites on the Internet today. They don't change everyday, most don't change every week, and many don't change for months. Often you see changes at sites only when they undergo a major design change.

One of the design goals for Visual InterDev was to make sites dynamic and easy to maintain. InterDev's connectivity to databases can do much more than simply help you build business applications on the Web: You can also use a database to generate HTML on the fly. Then to update the look and feel of your Web site, you can simply update the database. And these updates can even be done programmatically at specified intervals.

Many locations on the Internet provide fresh content daily and use server-side scripting to gather and repackage this content to add value to their site. As dynamic sites become more and more popular on the Web, you should start to see companies making a business of providing fresh content daily, specifically for embedding into other sites. Payment might be based on a flat monthly or annual rate, or it could be billed according to usage.

N O T E   If you plan to pull content from other sources on the Web programmatically, make sure that you can trust the type of content that your source provides. For example, you can probably trust almost any image coming from a NASA site, whereas you would really be living dangerously if you pulled random images from newsgroups into your site. You cannot tell what type of image will be posted to a public newsgroup. Perhaps even more important, make sure that the material isn't copyrighted. ■

Keeping your site fresh requires a measure of dynamic content. Provided here are a number of suggestions on how to incorporate dynamic content from other sites on the Net into your own. Keep in mind that much of the content found on the Internet is copyrighted, of course, so the following suggestions certainly don't mean you have carte blanche to use the material in any way you see fit. Still, the laws are vague about referencing remote content (located at other sites).

> **CAUTION**
>
> Be careful when you include content from external sources in your Web site. You can easily cross the line of copyright infringement by doing so.

Text   Text is the most common type of data found on the Internet today, so you should be able to find constantly refreshed sources of content. Perhaps the most prolific sources of content are the Internet newsgroups, although finding specific (and morally safe) articles programmatically is hard. Your best bet is to stick with the moderated groups or to subscribe to a service such as ClariNet. ClariNet filters most of the news feeds such as Associated Press, Reuters, and United Press International into sorted categories (see Figure 25.7). You could feasibly incorporate these kinds of articles in your pages.

ON THE WEB

http://www.clarinet.com   The ClariNet Web site

Part
VII

Ch
25

Another possibility is to reference material stored on search engines. Many search engines are now starting to expand their offerings by providing news, financial, and local event coverage (see Figure 25.8). Other options include pulling text from Internet Relay Chats (IRC), Gophers, and even FTP sites.

FIG. 25.7
ClariNet offers the most extensive news feeds on the Internet to date.

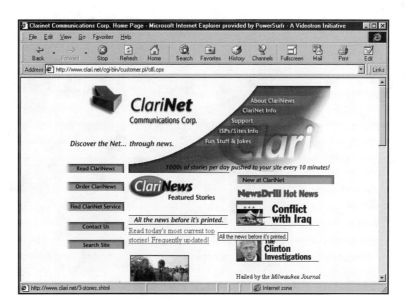

FIG. 25.8

Yahoo!, Webcrawler, Lycos, and other search engines are now providing daily content.

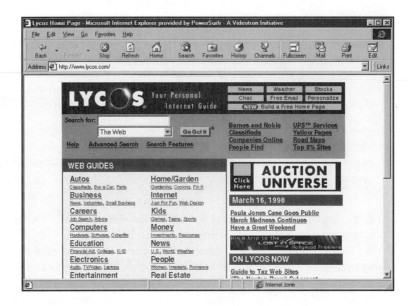

Graphics, Animation, and Video Constantly refreshing graphics certainly make visually stimulating pages and can actually be easier to deal with than text. The Internet provides many sources of fresh imagery, such as weather maps, satellite imagery, maps, live video feeds, and so on. For example, both NASA TV and the Sci-Fi channel create screen captures every few minutes and post the resulting images to their Web sites (see Figure 25.9).

ON THE WEB

http://www.scifi.com   The Sci-Fi Channel Web site

FIG. 25.9

Many sites have live images or screen grabs from video available, such as this page from the Sci-Fi channel site.

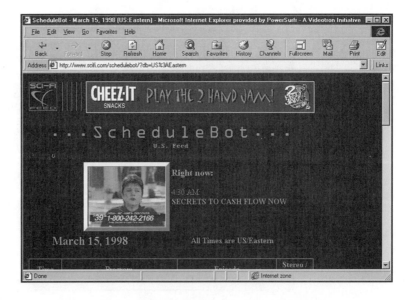

Audio   Using Microsoft's Internet Explorer, you can place WAV and MIDI files on your Web site to be downloaded and played automatically when a user visits. Another method is to set up a RealAudio server or simply place links to RealAudio feeds such as ABC, C|Net Radio news, and so on (see Figure 25.10).

FIG. 25.10

The Timecast site at RealAudio offers links to most of the RealAudio sites on the Net.

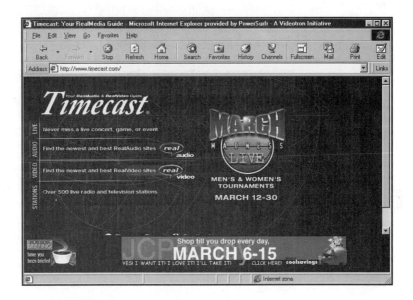

Besides tracking user preferences and then playing appropriate music, you also can go a step further and play random clips with the selected style of music. The Microsoft Music Producer (which ships with Visual InterDev) makes generating multiple music clips an easy task.

ON THE WEB

http://www.timecast.com   The TimeCast Web site

Compelling Visuals   When you need to create compelling visuals on your site, you can use a number of "cheap tricks" to get the best bang for your bandwidth buck. For example, creating blocks of color by using tables with colored backgrounds can make your site look like you have graphics without the overhead of downloading a graphical image.

Tables   A common extension to HTML is the BGCOLOR tag for setting background colors in a table cell. Using this method, you can create large blocks of color without any graphics files at all. Because no extra data has to be downloaded with the page, you can get a strong visual effect instantly as the page is loaded.

N O T E   Currently, the BGCOLOR tag is supported in tables only in Microsoft's Internet Explorer. Netscape Navigator does not view table backgrounds or background colors the same way. ■

Part

VII

Ch

25

ON THE WEB

http://microsoft.com/truetype   The Microsoft TrueType Fonts Web site

Frames   Both bordered and borderless frames can be used to the same effect as background colors on table cells. For example, the Timecast (**http://www.timecast.com**) site from RealAudio uses borderless frames and assigns body background colors to the HTML files for each frame (see Figure 25.11).

FIG. 25.11
The Timecast site is composed of several frames, but the elegant layout is preserved because the frames are borderless.

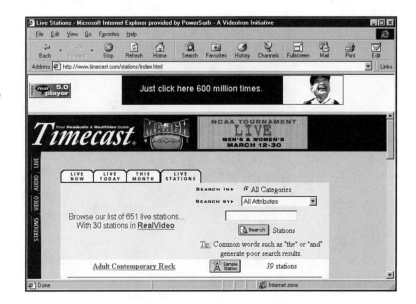

Images   A common trick used with images is to create a small image and then tile it or stretch it over a larger area for more visual impact. Images inserted as backgrounds automatically tile. Images inserted with the <IMG> tag can be stretched by setting the height and width properties to values larger than the actual image. Figure 25.12 shows an image that has obviously been resized using only the height and width attributes interpreted by a browser.

ON THE WEB

http://microsoft.com/frontpage   The Microsoft FrontPage 98 Web site

Animation   Adding animation to your pages is fairly simple with the Microsoft GIF Animator. Animated GIFs make good hyperlink buttons because they draw the user's attention. Keep in mind that animated GIFs can be very large and take a long time to download. One technique to overcoming this size issue is to animate only a small portion of a larger image. To do so, you need to break up the larger image into smaller rectangular pieces and then insert these pieces into the cells of a table. Now you can make one of the cell images an animated GIF without needing to animate the rest of the image.

FIG. 25.12
In the FrontPage Editor, you can simply drag the sizing bars of an image to set its height and width properties.

Video   Many video streaming technologies are available for the Internet, such as CuSeeMe, VDO Live, Active Movie, and RealVideo, but an inexpensive way to simulate video streaming is to use the `<META>` tag with the `HTTP-EQUIV="Refresh"` property. In this case, the browser is told to reload the page every *x* seconds. By that time, a new image has been created or obtained, and the effect is that of a slow video image.

Attractive Audio   Adding sound to your Web site opens up a whole new dimension. By adding voice-overs, sound effects, and music, you can make even the best page better. Before jumping in, however, you need to know a few facts about audio on the Web.

Digital Versus MIDI   First, there are two different techniques of storing and then regenerating sound. One is to sample the actual sound waves and store a digital representation of those waves, much in the same way as compact discs store music. These types of sound files are commonly stored in WAV format. The second method is to use Musical Instrument Digital Interface (MIDI) format, which stores a digital representation of each note that all the instruments play. Then a MIDI synthesizer (on the user's sound card) plays the song based on this information.

The advantage of using WAV files is that you can almost guarantee the sound you record will be the same sound the user hears, whereas playback of a MIDI file is dependent on the capabilities of the user's MIDI synthesizer. You really have no way of knowing what the music will sound like to the end user.

The advantage of using MIDI files is that they are very small in file size compared to the size of WAV files. Therefore, you can have a much longer piece of music play for the same bandwidth as a much shorter WAV file.

T I P   Most MIDI synthesizers do a good job of reproducing the piano, so if you are concerned about getting the best-sounding MIDI playback, look for piano music.

Part
VII

Ch
25

Outsourcing   One final aspect you might want to keep in mind is the readily available supply of freelance programmers, designers, and artists. You shouldn't have any trouble finding qualified professionals to help create fresh content on a regular basis. For a good starting point, look in the Regional categories at the Yahoo! site.

Programming   Thousands of VB programmers currently in the workforce are ready to develop scripts in VBScript or write custom server-side components. You may find contracting out the development of a custom component more cost effective than investing the time creating a complicated server-side VBScript application.

Administration and Hosting   By far, the majority of Web sites today are hosted on leased server space. When you can lease space for a *virtual host* Web site for as little as $50 a month, setting up your own in-house server and dedicated Internet connection doesn't seem practical unless doing so is absolutely necessary. A second advantage to leasing is that you don't have to worry about administrating your server; the hosting company does this job for you. When you are searching for a hosting site, make sure that you check bandwidth, support hours, hardware, and technical ability of the staff.

Database Applications   Database design, programming, and administration make up an entire science all to itself. So unless you are experienced in this area, I recommend that you get professional help or spend some time working with it (Section IV, "Database Programming Basics," is a great place to start). With the advent of ADO (Active Data Objects) and the RDS (Remote Data Service), almost any database programmer familiar with Visual Basic can help you get your site up and running with database connectivity.

Multimedia   Due to the popularity of the Internet and the decline in multimedia CD-ROM interest, you can easily find talented multimedia designers, artists, and programmers. Because Shockwave has become a standard for porting multimedia content onto the Internet, anyone familiar with Macromedia Director can quickly create interactive, multimedia pages.

Production Considerations

After the design for your site is approved, it's off to the bean counters for a job estimate. In this case, you are looking for two things: a time frame and a budget. Determining the amount of time a project will require beforehand makes estimating a budget much easier.

Time   If you have followed the preceding suggestions, you should have a thorough breakdown of all the components (text, graphics, audio, video, and so on) that need to go into your site, along with the estimated time required for each component. For your first projects, try not to cut the time frame too short; give yourself a little extra time for unforeseen occurrences. As a matter of fact, doubling or even tripling your best estimate is probably a good idea at this point.

Budget   Developing a budget is simply a matter of taking the time frame and working out an estimated cost. At this point, a rate sheet comes in handy because it enables you to make accurate and competitive estimates. (See "Developing a Rate Sheet" earlier in this chapter.)

> **CAUTION**
>
> Keep the proposed budget with the client as flexible as possible. Try to negotiate for an hourly rate so that your time is covered if things go awry.

Production Sign-Off   Next, you need a production sign-off. At this point, you should have an approved design as well as a time frame and a budget. Your ability to continue is simply a matter of getting the final approval. Be sure to get it in writing.

Storyboard   Create a storyboard for your pages as you would in a traditional graphics medium. It will help you work out any design problems before you get too intimately involved with your design. If you tend to jump right in to your design without thinking the whole site through, you could wind up with a very narrow view of the site, possibly leaving out important sections.

While you are creating the storyboard, don't forget to take advantage of the many ActiveX controls currently on the market offering interactive capabilities, such as animated buttons, video, audio, and pop-up menus.

Design Sign-Off   After the design is finalized, having the client give it a final "once over" to approve it before you actually start building the site is very important. If you can get something in writing at this point, do so.

You might need to show demonstrations of other sites so that your client fully understands the interaction and speed of your design. Nothing is worse than getting involved in a design that the client doesn't fully comprehend, and having to quit and go back to the drawing board over a bandwidth misunderstanding.

> **N O T E**   Design sign-off is very important because most clients don't specifically understand the fluid nature of the Web. Rather, they have become jaded and think of last-minute changes to a site as just "editing a file." You should get sign-offs at every important stage of the site's design to prevent those "just one more last-minute change" changes. ▨

Part

VII

Ch

25

Organizing Your Site

Now most of the hard work is done. All that's left is to transfer your site design from the drawing board into Visual InterDev. At this stage, Visual InterDev really shines as a professional site-design tool. It is well structured, making it extremely easy to organize your site regardless of its size.

Start your site by creating a workspace and the necessary projects in Visual InterDev. Next, develop a directory structure to organize the site's content. Then create cascading style sheets to coordinate the look and feel of the site. Next, import the content and lay out the pages. Finally, develop any client or server scripting needed, and you're finished.

Setting Up Workspaces and Projects

Because you can set up as many workspaces and projects as you want to view your site, you may want to use this capability to your advantage and create separate workspaces and projects for designers, artists, and programmers. You should most likely create some type of master workspace with access to the entire site for the Webmaster and site administrator.

Forming the Basic Structure Folders   Not only can you keep your site organized with folders, but you also can use folders to your advantage by storing content in them and then programmatically referencing the folders based on some dynamic requirement, such as a user login ID and the time of day. In this way, you can organize different versions of content files while keeping the filenames the same. Then all you have to control with server-side scripting is the directory name; all the references to the filenames can be the same. Figure 25.13 shows a site with directories organized in this manner. The directory level under \clients breaks down into customer numbers (\000000, \08747, and so on), and beneath that are the client numbers (\00, \01, \02, \03, and so on). Once a client is uniquely identified (through a customer number and client number), then the underlying directory structure is identical: \Agendas, \Minutes, \Newsletters, and \Notices. Using this technique, you can dump any content into those directories, regardless of filenames, and then use the FrontPage 98 Table of Contents component to automatically build a link to them for each individual client.

FIG. 25.13

This site uses subdirectories to organize content unique to each user.

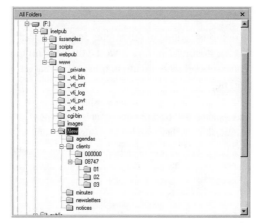

Create Cascading Style Sheets

If you are taking advantage of cascading style sheets, you should create them at this point. Use them to control as much of your design as possible, such as setting the typeface, font size, margins, and colors (staying within the approved design, of course). At this point, you can start either importing existing content or simply creating the content from scratch with the Visual InterDev content editors.

Dealing with Content

Working with the content files you have created is at the very heart of assembling Web sites. The myriad of different documents, images, and files that make up your site require care and attention to insure that your site is clearly organized, well designed, and functional. There are two aspects of dealing with content to consider: the incorporation of existing material and the creation of new material.

Importing Existing Content   After you have the framework of directories in place, and you have style sheets to control the design, you are ready to start importing content files. Using the Insert Files into the Project button, you can import any type of content into the selected folder or project. You can copy files from one directory to another by simply holding down the Ctrl key and dragging the file to the destination directory.

Creating New Content   If you are creating new content from scratch, start by choosing File, New to access the wizards. Visual InterDev ships with a number of wizards to get you moving in the right direction with new content.

TIP   Be sure to check the Visual InterDev Web site frequently for new content wizards (**http://www.microsoft.com/vinterdev/**).

ON THE WEB

http://www.microsoft.com/vinterdev/   The Microsoft Visual InterDev Web site

From Here...

In this chapter, you learned many different methods of keeping your Web site fresh and engaging. By focusing your site on your customer demographics, setting up dynamic content feeds, and taking advantage of performance tricks, you can ensure that your customers will be repeat customers. The following chapters offer material related to designing and organizing your Web site that might be of importance to your development, especially when working with multiple developers:

- Chapter 26, "Team Development with FrontPage 98 and Visual InterDev 6."
- Chapter 27, "Increasing Site Performance."

Team Development with FrontPage 98 and Visual InterDev 6

In this chapter

Introducing FrontPage 98   **540**

Designing Visual InterDev 6 Sites for FrontPage 98   **544**

FrontPage Security Issues   **545**

Training End Users to Maintain Sites with FrontPage 98   **546**

Introducing FrontPage 98

Microsoft built Visual InterDev 6 and FrontPage 98 for slightly different, but overlapping, target markets. Although it tailored Visual InterDev for the creation of advanced Web-based applications, Microsoft designed FrontPage 98 for day-to-day Web site creation and maintenance.

FrontPage, which is Microsoft's second-generation Web site creation and management tool, sports a great interface, with many of the tools available in Visual InterDev, but without the complication of Active Server Page (ASP) authoring tools or multiproject workspaces. It has set the standard for Windows-based Web authoring and management, and many of the Web's best Webmasters create and maintain their sites completely within FrontPage.

Typical end users do not necessarily want or need the more advanced features and interface of Visual InterDev, but they still need to make occasional modifications and additions to the Web site. FrontPage's WYSIWYG-style HTML editor is one of the best in the field. In fact, the FrontPage WYSIWYG HTML page editor is so good that Visual InterDev includes a version of it. The FrontPage management tools also are well suited to a site maintainer's needs.

FrontPage 98 offers strong integration with Microsoft Office applications, using the same HTML converters, spell-checkers, and other shared tools. FrontPage also includes Visual Basic Script and JavaScript Wizards to make creating scripts easier and more intuitive.

As you begin to create a new Web project, you should consider whether FrontPage might even be better suited to that project's requirements than Visual InterDev. From both an ease-of-use and a user-training standpoint, FrontPage is undoubtedly the easier environment in which to work for most people. Importing a site that you've created in FrontPage is also very easy.

If you're not sure whether a given project initially needs the capabilities of Visual InterDev, you can start in FrontPage and migrate to the more advanced tool later, if necessary.

To help you decide which environment is best for a specific Web project, you should first understand the primary differences between the two products.

Similarities and Differences

Visual InterDev and FrontPage 98 serve slightly different audiences, but both groups of users share many of the same basic needs. Both products use the same server extensions, allowing great convenience in publishing Web site content, without sacrificing security.

Both products include tools for visualizing and verifying hyperlinks, both within a site and to other Internet resources. They use the context-highlighting text-mode HTML editors. They both provide support for the local editing and remote Web publishing model, although they approach it from slightly different directions.

The basic interfaces are quite different (see Figure 26.1 and Figure 26.2). Whereas Visual InterDev is derived from Microsoft's professional development environment, FrontPage is designed specifically for Web site development and maintenance.

FIG. 26.1
The Visual InterDev interface provides a large scope "workspace" that can contain several different projects.

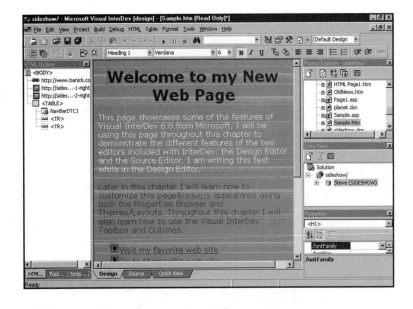

FIG. 26.2
FrontPage 98, however, is very "project-centric," focusing on an individual project.

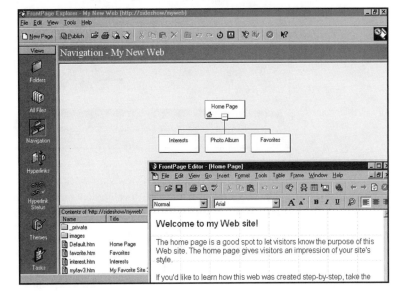

Visual InterDev uses the Visual Studio environment, which is Microsoft's standard application development framework. It is the environment for nearly all of Microsoft's top-level development tools, including Visual Basic, Visual C++, Visual J++, and Visual FoxPro.

Because InterDev uses this environment, you can work with Visual J++ and C++ components of your Web application in the same workspace as the rest of the project. This capability can be important when you want to concentrate on the task and not the tool. (For more information on taking advantage of this capability, see the section "Multiple-Language Projects" later in this chapter.)

Both interfaces offer two views of the Web site: the folder-and-file paradigm or the hyperlink view. In FrontPage, you must pick one or the other, whereas Visual InterDev lets you see your site both ways at the same time. Visual InterDev also lets you scale the hyperlink view. This way, you can even view the structure of your entire site at once (see Figure 26.3).

FIG. 26.3
Visual InterDev can display the hyperlinks that make up an entire site.

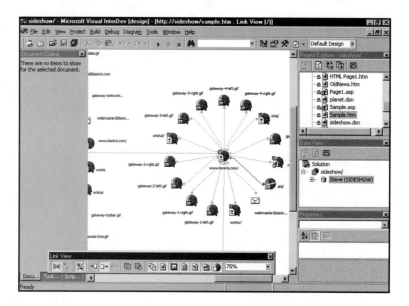

Visual InterDev also extends the capability to view your work in progress—by letting you switch directly to a browser view—within the development environment. FrontPage lets you launch a browser only to check your page—and only from within the FrontPage editor.

The Visual InterDev browser interface also includes the capability to examine sites on the Web. Because the browser in your Visual InterDev workspace is a fully capable Internet Explorer browser, you can also use it to surf to any site. Then, after you reach a Web site whose structure interests you, you can switch to Visual InterDev's hyperlink view to get a look at the structure of the site you've selected. You can use this capability to better understand the structure of a site you particularly admire. (Checking out the competition's sites to look for broken hyperlinks and other structural flaws can also be fun.)

You can load a specific document from a site on the Internet into the FrontPage editor, but you cannot go to a link view without having the correct access to the site's server.

When FrontPage 98 Is Not Enough

As great a tool as FrontPage 98 is, it does have limitations. Knowing them ahead of time can enable you to better decide whether it is appropriate for a specific project, or whether you need the power and capabilities of Visual InterDev. In some cases, FrontPage 98 can undo work that you've done in Visual InterDev; so knowing when to avoid using it is important.

Active Server Pages (ASP)   ASP documents are most of Visual InterDev's *raison d'être*; one of Visual InterDev's primary goals is to make the creation of a Web application with ASP components as easy as possible, while providing powerful tools to manage the entire development cycle.

Server-side scripting is an important addition to the capabilities of Internet Information Server (IIS). It allows for better browser-neutral development because you are not dependent on the capabilities of the browser, but of the server. Because browser capabilities vary wildly and are essentially unknown, the capability to generate code that is dependent only on a server whose capabilities are under your control is an important advance indeed.

FrontPage, however, does not provide the same capabilities. Although it does include some server-side scripting tools, its primary role is to translate your visual design of a page into the HTML needed to execute that design. It does a good job; however, when it encounters HTML code that it does not understand, it tries to reformat that code to meet the standards that it understands.

Because the ASP tags often fall into this category, FrontPage's HTML normalizing efforts can wreak havoc on documents containing them. For this reason, you should probably develop ASP documents completely within the Visual InterDev text editor. This is not to say that ASP pages cannot be edited in FrontPage 98 whatsoever; rather it is not the intended tool for doing so.

Complex Data-Driven Applications   Although FrontPage does include a good database-related wizard, in many instances the more advanced tools of Visual InterDev provide a far better choice. When you need to have data connections that are persistent throughout a visitor's session, or when you need to have several interacting data sources within a single Web application, FrontPage is just not the right tool.

For example, say you have a shopping cart application that interacts with several data sources. Tables represent product data, customer data, and payment information. The complex interaction of ASP commands and data-driven parts demands that you use a tool that is aware of these needs.

The ability to manage the entire database from within the same workspace environment also makes Visual InterDev a better choice for working with a data-driven Web application.

Design-Time Controls   Visual InterDev supports the use of design-time controls which help automate a wide variety of design tasks, such as inserting frequently used HTML segments or providing database access on a Web page. You can expect that third-party developers will expend considerable effort in building additional tools to support you in your design efforts.

Part
VII

Ch
26

Visual InterDev ships with an Include control, which essentially gives you an HTML version of the C `#include` directive. It also offers several database-related controls, which make the job of writing data-aware ASP documents much easier.

Because design-time controls can automate complex and time-consuming tasks, they enable you to incorporate more complex features into your Web application. At the same time, their capabilities eliminate the steep learning curve often associated with using new technologies—which crop up constantly in the field of Internet development.

▶ For more information on using design-time controls, **see** "Designing with Design-Time Controls," **p. 235**

Multiple-Language Projects   A really complex Web application might contain components written in HTML that include both server-side and client-side scripting, as well as full-blown Java applets and even custom-built ActiveX controls written in C++. Visual InterDev, with its standard Visual Studio interface, enables you to work with all these components in one standardized workspace.

To add one of these "foreign" projects, you just use the standard methods for inserting an existing Visual InterDev project. Note that this approach works only with projects also saved in Visual Studio. After you add the project, you can work with it using the same editor, compilers, and other tools that are available to you when you're working within the project's "native" version of Visual Studio.

Designing Visual InterDev 6 Sites for FrontPage 98

Given the limitations on FrontPage 98—as compared to Visual InterDev's huge feature set—creating a site that can make the most of both management environments might seem a daunting task. But there are many compelling reasons to make the effort.

When you develop your Web sites with Visual InterDev, keeping FrontPage's capabilities in mind, you make maintaining them with FrontPage much easier. This way, you can deploy a Web application developed with the high-end tools of Visual InterDev and then turn over routine maintenance to a team using the tools most appropriate to their needs. In many cases, this tool is FrontPage 98.

Additionally—let's face it—working with the FrontPage WYSIWYG HTML editor is really nice. Although not a perfect tool yet, it makes the development and maintenance of HTML documents far easier than ever before. Even the purists whose toolkits formerly contained nothing but Notepad and a good image editor before FrontPage 98 often have to admit that they enjoy working in its intuitive editing environment.

If you can keep the majority of your Web application editable with FrontPage, you are doing yourself (and your successors) a huge favor. So, how can you ensure that you do so?

Use ASP Elements Only When Needed

ASPs are a long-awaited development. The capabilities of this important extension to the IIS place some amazing new tools in your kit. Using them constantly can be tempting, just because they're cutting edge.

Remember that, although cutting edge is terrific, there is also such a thing as bleeding edge—and who wants to bleed unnecessarily? Certainly, you should use ASPs when appropriate—but not just because you can—as long as you want FrontPage users to have access to them.

Modularize Your Web Application

Another strategy that can help is to borrow an old programmer's tactic: modularization. Keep the parts of your Web application that FrontPage users can edit in an "HTML-only" Web project, and consider segregating the ASP and other FrontPage-allergic pieces in their own child Webs.

Test Pages with the FrontPage Editor

Because the FrontPage Editor does not always damage ASP tags, you might want to test it on a specific page before assuming that it's not safe. Make a copy of the page you want to test, and then open it in the FrontPage Editor. Save it, and then preview the page in the browser pane. Check carefully to see whether your tags survived the ride. If everything appears to be correct, then proceed; but be aware that changes to the page content can cause unexpected changes to its code. So, in the words of a Cold War quotation, "Trust—but verify."

Generally, the best way to make your Visual InterDev-developed Web application FrontPage-friendly is to keep the target environment in mind constantly. For most Web development, that advice refers to the expected browsers. In the case of ASP though, it means both the browser and editing environments.

FrontPage Security Issues

Because a Web server will present your documents to the world, you need to test them constantly by using a Web server. That way, you can check any interpretation or other actions that you expect the server to perform. FrontPage 98 and Visual InterDev both include versions of the Personal Web Server/Personal Web Services. Both can also connect to more robust and scalable servers using the FrontPage Server Extensions.

Both FrontPage 98 and Visual InterDev use the same server extensions to enable you to work with documents on a live Web server. These extensions are available for all the Microsoft Web servers and most of the other poplar Web server packages on the market. The following is a list of servers for which FrontPage 98 Server Extensions are currently available; see **http://www.microsoft.com/frontpage/** for updated information on the following:

Microsoft Internet Information Server 2.0, 3.0, 4.0

Microsoft Peer Web Services 2.0, 3.0, 4.0

Microsoft Personal Web Server on Windows 95

Microsoft FrontPage 97 and 98 Personal Web Server

O'Reilly Web Site

Apache 1.1.3, 1.2.4, 1.2.5

CERN 3.0

NCSA 1.5.2

Netscape Commerce Server 1.12

Netscape Communications Server 1.12

Netscape Enterprise 2.0, 3.0

Netscape FastTrack 2.0

N O T E The previous list only covers Intel-based server software. There is, however, a broad-range support for most of the platforms out there. ▪

To configure the Server Extensions to allow either FrontPage or Visual InterDev to modify a server's documents, start by running the Server Administrator. The exact information listed varies, depending on what Web server software you are using.

For most Web servers, you can use the Security option to add authorized administrators to the server. Just enter the username and password that the administrator should supply from within FrontPage or Visual InterDev to gain access to the documents on your server, and click OK.

Training End Users to Maintain Sites with FrontPage 98

Choosing the correct tool for a job can sometimes give you a tremendous head start toward the eventual success of the job. Just as a backhoe is the correct tool to dig a large trench, Visual InterDev is often the best possible tool to build a complex Web application.

Imagine the mess that would result if the average homeowner tried to use a backhoe to clean up the edges of the ditch after a couple of winters of wear and tear. A similar disaster can well await you if you ask someone to perform routine maintenance on your Web application with Visual InterDev. In the case of maintaining the existing structure, the correct tool for the homeowner is probably just a shovel. The correct tool for most Web site maintenance is just FrontPage 98.

End users should know how to perform several tasks within FrontPage 98 to work with your Visual InterDev-built Web site. Most of the normal operations are procedures that they should already know from whatever training they've already had in the product. If they lack this training, your local Microsoft Authorized Training Center is probably the first place to check. Failing that, a good community college might offer courses.

As mentioned earlier in this chapter, a few types of documents are "allergic" to the FrontPage Editor. The FrontPage Editor tries to interpret tags, and it might reformat and rearrange the tags it cannot understand, causing them to stop working—not pretty, and no fun to clean up. Make sure that the end users who will be maintaining your Web site are aware of these limitations of the FrontPage Editor. You should train them to leave ASP files alone, just as most homeowners leave plumbing and electrical work to the professionals.

Of course, there are the Tim Taylors of the Web site maintenance world.... Encourage them to stick to Notepad if they insist on "rewiring it." Otherwise, your carefully crafted Web application might be in for a trip to the emergency room—an unwelcome visitor to the top of your priority list.

From Here...

When working with multiple developers, especially between different environments, it is important to recognize potential problems and compatibility issues. Directly related to using VID and FP98 together are the following chapters:

- Chapter 23, "Understanding Visual InterDev Security."
- Chapter 24, "Using Developer Isolation and Visual SourceSafe."

CHAPTER 27

Increasing Site Performance

In this chapter

Guidelines for Web Site Performance   **550**

Testing Client Performance   **550**

Testing Server Performance   **553**

Tracking Internet Routes   **557**

Increasing Client-Side Performance in Visual InterDev   **560**

Increasing Server-Side Performance with Visual InterDev   **575**

Planning for Quicker Service   **577**

Guidelines for Web Site Performance

Even the best Webmasters overlook different facets of their Web sites. Whether it be graphic overloads, performance issues, or connectivity problems, no one can cover it all. There are simply too many issues regarding a Web site and running a Web server for most people to handle by themselves. Consider this chapter a cheat sheet. Tips from this chapter were compiled from various Webmasters who considered the points contained within to be important when weighing performance versus content. This chapter introduces you to some new ideas in Web site streamlining and Web server performance. Carefully following the steps mentioned here can help you create one of the most functional and top-running Web sites on the Internet today.

You simply cannot know everything that is involved in building a perfect Web site. However, by using a little common sense and following a few of the tips in this chapter, you can gain greater control over your Web site and learn how it can most benefit your users.

Many Web developers have made the mistake of using technology for technology's sake. As a result, many Web sites have fantastic features built into them that are either rarely used or not used at all. Examples are the elaborate Shockwave demonstration that no one downloads because of its 3MB file size, the intricate cutting-edge interface that no one understands, and the unnecessary use of frames to enhance site navigation that no one can figure out.

Above all, you should know your audience. If you're creating a sales-driven Web site, remember to keep it simple. Provide users with an easy way to access your products and order them, without burdening them with unneeded extras such as flashy graphics and music that eats up their bandwidth. Understand that users are visiting your Web site for one purpose—information. If the users can't reach that information, they can probably find it somewhere else.

An easy way to develop a site specifically for your target audience is to get them to participate in a survey before the content is developed. Include this survey with your company newsletter or other mailings. Ask specific questions such as how fast their connection speed is and what type of Web browsers they use on the Internet. This kind of information is invaluable when you are creating a commercial Web site, and it ensures that the content you develop will be utilized and not wasted.

Testing Client Performance

After you build your Web site, the most important thing that you can do is view it in a variety of Web browsers and at different access speeds. What a lot of developers fail to realize is that developing a Web site on a local machine is not an adequate test bed for real-life Internet scenarios. When you load a Web site that you are developing on your local hard drive into a Web browser, the pages appear instantaneously. This is not the case on the Internet. Believe it or not, the average Internet user still accesses the World Wide Web at 28.8Kbps, which equates to 1.4KB per second download. If your opening page has 100KB worth of graphics and text on it, downloading the content completely takes the average Internet user over a full minute.

Another problem that users face is that different Internet browsers display content in different ways. Netscape might be a faster browser on one platform, but Microsoft's Internet Explorer might load content faster on another. The next two sections help you evaluate your Web site in a number of different ways, giving you some ideas of what your users may encounter.

Downloading from Different Sources

Depending on the speed at which you normally connect to the Internet, you might or might not have a good idea of how your Web site loads in clients' browsers. If you generally access the Internet through a T1 or T3 line at your office, then you have attained Internet speeds that most can only dream of. The best place to start with the downloading test is with a 14.4Kbps modem or 28.8Kbps modem dialing in to a local Internet service provider. Before you begin accessing the site over the Internet, make sure that you clear the cache within your Web browser. Then you are ready to load the first page.

N O T E   What are a T1 and a T3? You likely have heard these two connection types mentioned before. Both of these connections are *dedicated* connections based on a "leased line." This means that the computers on the other side of the T1 or T3 connection are never off of the Internet. A special kind of computer called a *router* managed the Internet connection over the T1/T3. Just how fast are they? A T1 is 1.54Mbps and a T3 is 45Mbps. That's *millions of bits per second,* as opposed to modems which are *thousands of bits per second.* That's fast! ▄

As your first page loads, make note of any graphics that appear to shift position when they are displayed and how long loading the actual text of the Web page takes. You might find having some kind of a timer ready as you access each page to be a good idea. If you're using a 28.8Kbps modem, remember to double the time required to load a page completely. This amount should accurately represent the test results of a typical 14.4Kbps modem.

Another way to test your site's performance is to start at the beginning and see how long it takes you to reach a specific document that users might be looking for. If the users have to navigate through 10 pages before they can reach the document they're looking for, they might just get frustrated and give up. A good rule of thumb is to have every piece of content on your Web site available within five hyperlinks away from every other page. Following this tip might seem impossible, but it's not. Remember to use text-based links as a backup, and always give your users a way to reach the home page from every subsequent Web page accessed. Nothing is more frustrating to users than to have to click the Back button four or five times just to get back to the original content they were looking for. Microsoft's Web site, shown in Figure 27.1, presents quite a few advanced areas and yet empowers the users with enough control to find what they're looking for.

After you've dialed in locally, try accessing your Web site through a national service, such as the Microsoft Network or America Online. This way, you can get a good idea how fast your site can be when accessed through a heavily used service. You will most likely pass through many more computers than normal to get to your destination, giving you an indication of what the average user encounters. Remember that national online services such as America Online provide access to the greatest number of Internet users in the entire world.

Part

VII

Ch

27

FIG. 27.1

Make sure that your site is simple to navigate, as well as informative—like this site from Microsoft.

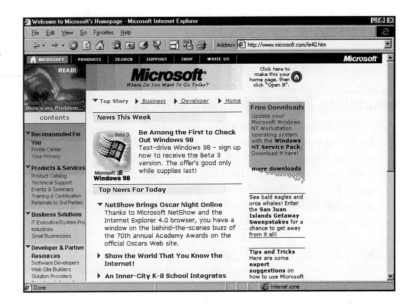

Another way to get a feel for the speed of your Web site is to call a few friends in different parts of the country and ask them to view your work. The results can be surprising. One user from across the United States from your Web server might actually be able to access the site faster than another user dialing in from the same part of the country. Ask your friends to make notes of anything that loads oddly or takes an extreme amount of time to download. This type of insightful advice is invaluable.

No matter how you test your Web site's performance with an Internet connection, you are bound to find elements that have to be changed. Though this testing can render frustrating results, you should be satisfied that you can modify and speed up your Web site before the rest of the public runs into the same reported problems.

Testing with Different Browsers

Although this tip might sound archaic, you should check your Web site further by testing within different browsers on different platforms. This testing can lead to some really interesting results, especially if you have content on your Web site that is targeted at only one Web browser, such as ActiveX controls and Internet Explorer. Although Netscape still holds onto the greatest market share for Internet browsers, this number changes all the time. New browsers are created, new versions of browsers are created, and some people like to stay with the original browser installed on their system simply because it works.

As you begin looking at your Web site through these different browsers, you might notice that some have features far behind others in terms of functionality. For example, one version of AOL's built-in Web browser does not handle frames at all. If you create your whole site with framed content, you could leave over 9 million Internet users out in the cold by not providing alternative content. Lynx, which is a text-only browser, gives a good indication of what your Web site looks like if the users turn off the graphics loading feature in their graphical browsers.

Another fine example is the way that Netscape's Navigator and Microsoft's Internet Explorer display tables. Many people argue that Internet Explorer displays tables in a much sharper way than Navigator. Others argue that Navigator displays framed content much better than Internet Explorer. Fights like these go on daily in the Usenet newsgroups, if you feel like participating. Regardless of your personal preference, ignoring a section of the public—no matter how small—does not pay. Your next potential sale could come from someone using NCSA Mosaic on a 9600 baud connection in an airplane who can't place an order because he or she can't navigate through frames. Doing your homework pays when it comes to accessing your own Web site.

Testing Server Performance

Monitoring your Web server's performance can be a daunting task. With the right tools, however, and a little know-how, you can have the most robust-running Web server around. The following sections cover Windows NT's Performance Monitor, the Performance Monitor Counters as they relate to the Web server, and suggestions on how to limit network resources to avoid an overload.

Introducing the Performance Monitor

The Performance Monitor, which is a tool tightly integrated into Windows NT Server, allows you to monitor every aspect of your Web server, such as file I/O, processor time, memory usage, and all Internet services. The Performance Monitor uses counters, which are small identifiers for server operations, to measure performance. You can monitor many activities at once, as well as set alarms when settings fall below a desired level. This section is based on monitoring the performance of Microsoft's Internet Information Server (IIS) because you have to be running IIS for the Visual InterDev extensions to run correctly. Figure 27.2 shows the Performance Monitor set to watch processor, memory, and HTTP activity.

▶ **See** "Windows NT Performance Tuning," **p. 412**

To start the Performance Monitor, follow these steps:

1. From the Start menu, choose Programs.

2. Select the Administrative Tools program group; then choose Performance Monitor. The Performance Monitor opens with an empty chart in place.

To view counters, follow these steps:

1. Choose Edit, Add to Chart. The Add to Chart dialog box then appears.

2. Select an object from the Object list. For example, you can select HTTP Service. The counters for that object appear in the Counter list.

3. Select a counter from the Counter list, and then choose <u>A</u>dd.

4. Repeat steps 1 through 3 to add additional counters.

5. After you have added the all counters, choose Done. The display returns to the Performance Monitor, and information about the selected counters is shown.

FIG. 27.2
Using the Performance Monitor to keep track of your Web server is a complete and inexpensive tracking solution.

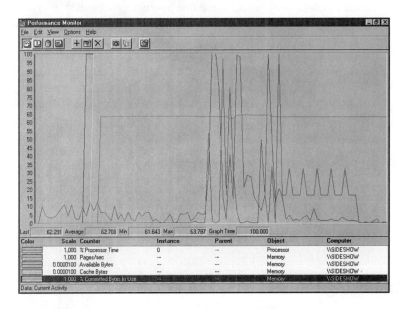

The Performance Monitor uses different colored line graphs to identify counters that are in place. To make using these graphs easier on the eyes, you can change the color when adding a counter. You also can set an audible alert or an alert that triggers email notification when the system counter falls below a certain level.

Using the Performance Monitor Counters

Two sets of Performance Monitor counters are integral in monitoring your Web server. Table 27.1 and Table 27.2 describe the counters for the HTTP Service and IIS Service (Global), respectively.

Table 27.1   HTTP Service Counters

Counter Name	Counter Function
Bytes Received/sec	Rate that data bytes are received by the HTTP Server
Bytes Sent/sec	Rate that data bytes are sent by the HTTP Server
Bytes Total/sec	Total rate of bytes transferred by the HTTP Server

Counter Name	Counter Function
CGI Requests	Number of Common Gateway Interface (CGI) requests on the server
Connection Attempts	Number of connection attempts that have been made to the HTTP Server
Connections/sec	Number of HTTP requests being handled per second
Current Anonymous Users	Number of anonymous users currently connected to the HTTP Server
Current Connections	Current number of connections to the HTTP Server
Current ISAPI Extension Requests	Current number of extension requests that are simultaneously being processed by the HTTP Server
Current NonAnonymous Users	Number of nonanonymous users currently connected to the HTTP Server
Files Received	Total number of files received by the HTTP Server
Files Sent	Total number of files sent by the HTTP Server
Files Total	Total number of files sent and received by the HTTP Server
Logon Attempts	Number of logon attempts that have been made by the HTTP Server
Maximum Anonymous Users	Maximum number of anonymous users simultaneously connected to the HTTP Server
Maximum CGI Requests	Maximum number of CGI requests that have been simultaneously processed by the HTTP Server
Maximum Connections	Maximum number of simultaneous connections to the HTTP Server
Maximum NonAnonymous Users	Maximum number of nonanonymous users simultaneously connected to the HTTP Server
Not Found Errors	Number of requests that couldn't be satisfied by the server because the requested document could not be found
Total Anonymous Users	Total number of anonymous users that have ever connected to the HTTP Server
Total NonAnonymous Users	Total number of nonanonymous users that have ever connected to the HTTP Server

Part

VII

Ch

27

Table 27.2   Internet Information Services Global

Counter Name	Counter Function
Cache Flushes	Number of times a portion of the memory cache has been expired because of file or directory changes in an Internet Information Services directory tree
Cache Hits	Total number of times a file open, directory listing, or service-specific objects request was found in the cache
Cache Hits %	Ratio of cache hits to all cache requests
Cache Misses	Total number of times a file open, directory listing, or service-specific objects request was not found in the cache
Cache Size	Configured maximum size of the shared HTTP, FTP, and Gopher memory cache
Cache Used	Total number of bytes currently containing cached data in the shared memory cache
Cached File Handles	Number of open file handles cached by all the Internet Information Services
Directory Listings	Number of cached directory listings cached by all of the Internet Information Services
Objects	Number of cached objects cached by all the Internet Information Services

Placing Limits on Resources

After you monitor your Web site using the Performance Monitor, you might notice that you have an overwhelming number of requests from users, and these requests sometimes slow down your server. You can do one of two things: add more RAM or another processor to your server, or limit the resources available to network users. With IIS 4.0, you can establish bandwidth limitations on individual sites and services or on an overall server basis. Figure 27.3 illustrates how to limit the overall network resources on your server.

Follow these steps to limit your Internet network resources for the entire server:

1. Open the Internet Services Microsoft Management Console (MMC).
2. Right-click the computer name in the namespace under Internet Information Server, and select Properties from the context menu.
3. In the Properties dialog box, select the Enable Bandwidth Throttling check box.
4. In the Maximum Network Use box, type a value in kilobytes per second by which you want to limit resources.
5. Click OK to close the Properties dialog box.
6. Choose File, Exit to close the Internet Services MMC.

FIG. 27.3

Placing limits on network resources is one way to control a heavily hit Web server temporarily.

You should use this approach only as a temporary fix to keep the Web server from getting overloaded until you can expand the server itself. Make sure that when you increase the number of processors or RAM, you also remember to reset the settings in the Internet Services Manager.

Tracking Internet Routes

Have you ever tried to reach a Web site that you've been to many times before, only to find that it's unreachable? Often, the problem lies not within your connection to the Internet or the Web server's connection, but in the Internet itself. When a request is sent to a Web server from a client's browser, it can literally take a different path to the Web server every time the request is made. As you know, the Internet is made up of many interconnected networks—large and small. Sometimes, a portion of a network path from client to server goes down, resulting in lost information and Internet packets. Depending on the route (via many routers) that your request takes to the Web server, you might find yourself waiting an awfully long time for the information to be returned because of network instability.

Suppose you are in Dallas, Texas, requesting a Web page that lies on one of Microsoft's Web servers in Redmond, Washington. That request takes an average of 20 hops, or network jumps, before the packets of information reach the Web server itself. If one of the network carriers that the packet is riding on goes down, your packets can quite possibly reach a dead end, resulting in an error message from your browser. If you could follow the path of your packets along the Internet, you could find a trouble spot easily. You'll be happy to know that, with the *traceroute* command, you can watch the complete network path on which packets of information travel before reaching their final destination.

Part
VII

Ch

27

Using *tracert* to Follow Internet Routes

The traceroute command has simple functionality; it displays the complete network path that an Internet packet travels from point A to point B. If you're using Windows, you can launch a DOS prompt and type `tracert` and an address of the destination server to see the network transfer as it occurs. If you are using a variation of UNIX, the command that you use is traceroute and the address. Figure 27.4 illustrates a sample traceroute from a client's system to a Web server's address.

FIG. 27.4

tracert is easy to use; its results can be invaluable when you are troubleshooting a downed server.

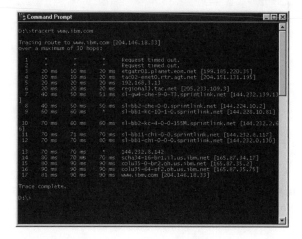

The following listing is from a tracert command starting at Dallas, Texas, and going to Netscape Communications in California:

```
C:\ tracert www.netscape.com
 traceroute to www80.netscape.com (198.95.249.75), 30 hops max, 40 byte packets
 1 cisco.NKN.NET (199.171.20.254) 2 ms 1 ms 1 ms
 2 905.Hssi3-0.GW1.DFW1.ALTER.NET (137.39.138.57) 3 ms 3 ms 3 ms
 3 Fddi0-0.CR2.DFW1.Alter.Net (137.39.37.36) 7 ms 35 ms 10 ms
 4 108.Hssi6-0.CR2.CHI1.Alter.Net (137.39.58.82) 25 ms 27 ms 24 ms
 5 312.atm1-0.br1.chi1.alter.net (137.39.13.105) 24 ms 26 ms 26 ms
 6 core3-hssi3-0.WillowSprings.mci.net (206.157.77.81) 30 ms 30 ms 306 ms
 7 borderx2-hssi2-0.SanFrancisco.mci.net (204.70.1.38) 149 ms 225 ms 188 ms
 8 borderx2-hssi2-0.SanFrancisco.mci.net (204.70.1.38) 93 ms 94 ms 88 ms
 9 netscape-ds3.SanFrancisco.mci.net (204.70.158.122) 254 ms 113 ms 350 ms
10 www80.netscape.com (198.95.249.75) 272 ms 93 ms 83 ms
```

You can see that this command took 10 hops to get from point A to point B. Some extraneous information that can be quite helpful returns with the results of the tracert command. First, the hop number is listed. Next, the name of the computer or router on which the packet is traveling is displayed. To the right of the named machine, you see an IP address listed in parentheses. It is the IP address of the machine that your information is passing through. The last three numbers indicate the relative time required to pass the information to the next hop, displayed in milliseconds.

Putting *tracert* Knowledge to Work

The following tracert command was issued to find out whether any connection problems existed between Dallas, Texas, and the *USA Today* newspaper (**www.usatoday.com**):

```
C:\ tracert www.usatoday.com
traceroute to wsf2.usatoday.com (207.123.208.14), 30 hops max, 40 byte packets
 1 cisco.NKN.NET (199.171.20.254) 1 ms 1 ms 1 ms
 2 905.Hssi3-0.GW1.DFW1.ALTER.NET (137.39.138.57) 3 ms 16 ms 3 ms
 3 Fddi0-0.CR1.DFW1.Alter.Net (137.39.37.35) 3 ms 6 ms 6 ms
 4 108.Hssi6-0.CR1.DCA1.Alter.Net (137.39.30.21) 90 ms 70 ms 54 ms
 5 101.Hssi4-0.CR1.TCO1.Alter.Net (137.39.69.85) 123 ms 324 ms 390 ms
 6 * * *
 7 collegepk-br2.bbnplanet.net (4.0.1.17) 398 ms 327 ms 397 ms
 8 collegepk-br1.bbnplanet.net (128.167.252.5) 46 ms 46 ms 51 ms
 9 washdc1-br1.bbnplanet.net (4.0.1.225) 45 ms 44 ms 53 ms
10 washdc1-br2.bbnplanet.net (4.0.1.174) 43 ms 56 ms 42 ms
11 washdc1-cr2.bbnplanet.net (4.0.36.22) 40 ms 37 ms 38 ms
12 gannett2.bbnplanet.net (4.0.148.246) 41 ms * 49 ms
13 * * *
14 * gannett2.bbnplanet.net (4.0.148.246) 43 ms *
15 gannett2.bbnplanet.net (4.0.148.246) 37 ms * *
16 gannett2.bbnplanet.net (4.0.148.246) 40 ms * 44 ms
17 * gannett2.bbnplanet.net (4.0.148.246) 39 ms *
18 gannett2.bbnplanet.net (4.0.148.246) 39 ms * 45 ms
19 * * gannett2.bbnplanet.net (4.0.148.246) 54 ms
20 * gannett2.bbnplanet.net (4.0.148.246) 40 ms *
21 gannett2.bbnplanet.net (4.0.148.246) 48 ms * 39 ms
22 * gannett2.bbnplanet.net (4.0.148.246) 39 ms
Destination Host Unreachable
```

As you can plainly see, the packets of information are hung up at BBN Planet somewhere. This problem is most likely due to a routing or name lookup error within the network itself. If the packet had reached *USA Today*, you would have seen the last hop listed as *USA Today*'s Web server. The asterisks next to the `tracert` results mean that the connection was not reliable enough to return any information. If you get this result while you are trying to reach your Web server, contact the system administrator and notify him or her of what's happening.

What's interesting is that a couple of minutes later you can issue the `tracert` command and get distinctly different results. Consider, for example, the next listing in which the exact same `tracert` command is issued:

```
C:\ tracert www.usatoday.com
 traceroute to wsf2.usatoday.com (167.8.29.13), 30 hops max, 40 byte packets
 1 cisco.NKN.NET (199.171.20.254) 1 ms 1 ms 1 ms
 2 905.Hssi3-0.GW1.DFW1.ALTER.NET (137.39.138.57) 6 ms 4 ms 3 ms
 3 Fddi0-0.CR1.DFW1.Alter.Net (137.39.37.35) 4 ms 29 ms 3 ms
 4 108.Hssi6-0.CR1.DCA1.Alter.Net (137.39.30.21) 56 ms 55 ms 56 ms
 5 101.Hssi4-0.CR1.TCO1.Alter.Net (137.39.69.85) 343 ms 49 ms 376 ms
 6 Fddi0-0.SR1.TCO1.ALTER.NET (137.39.11.22) 58 ms 49 ms 49 ms
 7 gannett10-gw.customer.ALTER.NET (137.39.32.162) 84 ms 75 ms 61 ms
 8 167.8.29.13 (167.8.29.13) 63 ms 66 ms 65 ms
```

Here, the packets reach their intended destination in fewer hops and at a much quicker rate.

`tracert` is extremely useful for finding out where network problems are occurring and whether a server on the Internet is, in fact, operational.

Part
VII

Ch
27

Increasing Client-Side Performance in Visual InterDev

One of the often-neglected aspects of tuning performance is making sure all the components that make up your Web page are absolutely necessary. Ask yourself questions such as, "Do I really need an imagemap, icons, text-based links, and frames on my home page?" Or "Does this Java application really help the flow of my Web site?" Most of the time, the answer is No.

Following is a list of items to avoid when streamlining:

- Form components to which you don't need answers.
- Icons, awards, and other graphics that have no correlation to the content in your Web site.
- Background images. (You can do quite a bit with color alone.)
- Background music (for example, WAV and MID files).
- Scrolling messages.
- Blinking text. (This type of text can look like an item on clearance at a retail store.)

Each of these items has its place, though not on every Web page. Think conservatively when adding extras to your Web site, and always ask yourself, "Is this really necessary?"

To visit some of the exemplary Web sites on the Internet today, try Best of the Web located at **http://www.botw.org/**. For some of the worst examples of Web sites available today, visit Worst of the Web at **http://www.worstoftheWeb.com/**.

Defining Your Space

The first step in creating an efficient HTML document is to provide the browser with some limits that tell it where a document starts and stops, and how to process the text that it's receiving. To do so, use three of the most basic HTML tags: <HTML>, <HEAD>, and <BODY>.

Together, these tags provide the basic framework for the document being viewed. An HTML document can exist without any of these codes, but the users' browsers take much longer to present your page. In the following sections, look at each tag individually to see how it helps set up your page.

The <*HTML*> Tag   The <HTML> tag and its partner, </HTML>, should be used, respectively, at the beginning and end of every HTML document. This tag tells the browser that the text included between the two tags is HTML and should be processed as such. Although this use seems so simple, it's really not; in many browsers, these tags kick off some of the most important processing that the browser does. To understand why these tags are so important, you need to consider how the browser processes a Web page.

The whole process starts when a user requests a document from a Web server, either by typing an URL or clicking a link. URLs and links can point to any type of document, including graphics, media files, and other types of text files, along with HTML files. When the browser downloads almost any type of media file, it receives parameters in the first section of the file that explain the basic size and shape of the file being downloaded. The <HTML> tags do the same thing for what would otherwise be seen as a plain text document.

When the browser reads the initial <HEAD> tag, it is alerted to the fact that it might encounter other links and will have to open additional connections to download referenced files. Depending on the operating system of the user's computer, the browser can use this triggering event to spawn additional processes that are later immediately assigned to the specific connections listed within the document. Otherwise, the browser can continue through the document until it encounters its first HTML-style tag before it begins to spawn the processes necessary to download the graphics and other files embedded in the document.

N O T E Browsers are configured to open a specific number of connections. Most individual users open between 4 and 16 connections when they access a Web site. Automated processes, such as indexing programs and spiders, can open many more. ▪

The browser then reads the HTML document from top to bottom, opening new connections to download additional files as required when the links are encountered within the document. The </HTML> tag tells the browser that it has reached the end of the document to be processed. When the browser hits this tag, it terminates the connection that it used to download the HTML file and reopens a connection to download another graphic or other component. If the browser does not find an </HTML> tag, it keeps the original connection open until all the other embedded documents are downloaded or the connection is timed out (usually whichever comes first).

This process is inefficient for both the Web server and the user. From the server side, if this connection is left open, one of the server's processes and connections remains tied up until the browser is finished processing the page. If multiple users are simultaneously keeping useless connections open, connectivity can be quickly tied up. The situation is worse from the user's side; if the browser keeps open one of its four allotted connections for an HTML file that should have terminated, the user has effectively lost one quarter of his or her downloading capacity. This, in turn, has a feedback effect on the server; because the user's overall connect time is increased, the overall efficiency and server capacity for addressing the user is similarly decreased. The lesson here is simple: Regardless of whether the HTML file is lovingly hand-crafted by HTML editors or spewed out in real-time from a database, make sure that it begins and ends with the appropriate <HTML> and </HTML> tags.

Inside the main framework set by the <HTML> tags are two main subsections of the HTML document. They are the <HEAD> and the <BODY>.

Part

VII

Ch

27

N O T E FrontPage and Visual InterDev might append something that looks like a tag at the top of the HTML document; it starts with <!DOCTYPE>. <!DOCTYPE> is an element that states what level of HTML is used within the document. If your pages rely heavily on HTML tags that are part of HTML 3.2 but are not supported by HTML 2.0, you might want to include this flag as a warning to users whose software will be unable to support your pages.

Because this tag describes the type of HTML used in a page, it actually goes outside the <HTML> tags. ▪

The <*HEAD*> Tag The <HEAD> tags define an area containing information used mostly by computers and programs, and little seen by users. Among the most common of the elements found in a <HEAD> section are the <TITLE> tag and a variety of <META> tags. As you will learn in the section on <META> tags later in this chapter, the tags contained in this section can be very useful in the maintenance of the site. From an efficiency point of view, the main role of the <HEAD> tags is to provide a place for programmers to store all sorts of information that is relevant to the systems using the documents but that is not really seen by users.

As you can see in Figure 27.5, the <HEAD> section comes at the beginning of the HTML document. This position makes sense, given that the HTML document is read and parsed from top to bottom; this way, any commands that the browser (or, in some cases, indexing program or spider) might need to encounter are available immediately. Any required reconfiguration of the browser can happen immediately before any of the content is downloaded or formatted.

FIG. 27.5

The <HEAD> section includes tags that specify keywords for search engines and the character set to be used by the browser when formatting the page.

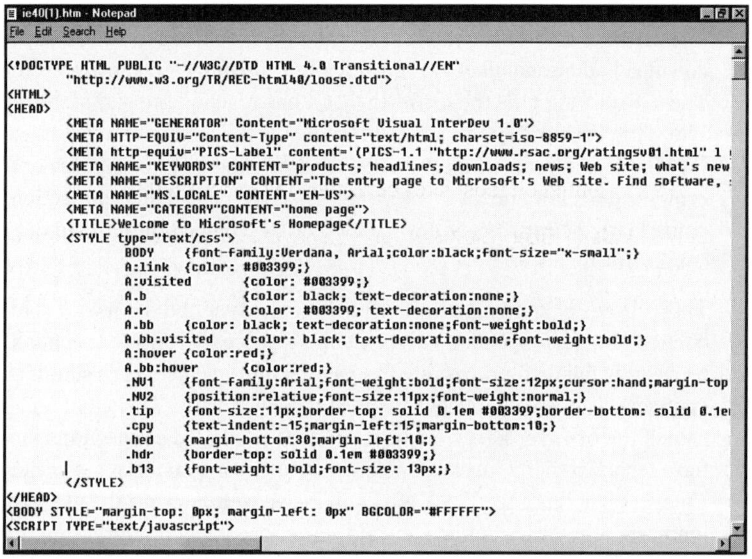

```
<!DOCTYPE HTML PUBLIC "-//W3C//DTD HTML 4.0 Transitional//EN"
        "http://www.w3.org/TR/REC-html40/loose.dtd">
<HTML>
<HEAD>
        <META NAME="GENERATOR" Content="Microsoft Visual InterDev 1.0">
        <META HTTP-EQUIV="Content-Type" content="text/html; charset=iso-8859-1">
        <META http-equiv="PICS-Label" content='(PICS-1.1 "http://www.rsac.org/ratingsv01.html" l
        <META NAME="KEYWORDS" CONTENT="products; headlines; downloads; news; Web site; what's new
        <META NAME="DESCRIPTION" CONTENT="The entry page to Microsoft's Web site. Find software,
        <META NAME="MS.LOCALE" CONTENT="EN-US">
        <META NAME="CATEGORY"CONTENT="home page">
        <TITLE>Welcome to Microsoft's Homepage</TITLE>
        <STYLE type="text/css">
                BODY    {font-family:Verdana, Arial;color:black;font-size="x-small";}
                A:link  {color: #003399;}
                A:visited       {color: #003399;}
                A.b             {color: black; text-decoration:none;}
                A.r             {color: #003399; text-decoration:none;}
                A.bb    {color: black; text-decoration:none;font-weight:bold;}
                A.bb:visited    {color: black; text-decoration:none;font-weight:bold;}
                A:hover {color:red;}
                A.bb:hover      {color:red;}
                .NV1    {font-family:Arial;font-weight:bold;font-size:12px;cursor:hand;margin-top
                .NV2    {position:relative;font-size:11px;font-weight:normal;}
                .tip    {font-size:11px;border-top: solid 0.1em #003399;border-bottom: solid 0.1e
                .cpy    {text-indent:-15;margin-left:15;margin-bottom:10;}
                .hed    {margin-bottom:30;margin-left:10;}
                .hdr    {border-top: solid 0.1em #003399;}
                .b13    {font-weight: bold;font-size: 13px;}
        </STYLE>
</HEAD>
<BODY STYLE="margin-top: 0px; margin-left: 0px" BGCOLOR="#FFFFFF">
<SCRIPT TYPE="text/javascript">
```

If you segregate the information required for processing into its own area, the browser can immediately process the section of the document that is presented to the users, as indicated by the <BODY> tags.

The <*BODY*> Tags The pair of <BODY> tags comes at the beginning and end of the content that is to be shown to the users inside the browser window. The initial <BODY> tag indicates to the browser where it should start processing the text of the document for embedded links such as graphics and sound files. The closing </BODY> tag works in much the same fashion as the </HTML> tag, indicating to the browser that the end of the content has been reached and freeing processes to work on other tasks.

The initial <BODY> tag is used fairly regularly, if for no other reason than it has been modified to include switches that specify background colors or graphics, as well as colors for links. Be sure to remember the companion closing tag to this set. Because the </BODY> tag delineates the end of content within the window, failure to close this pair can result in strange formatting errors and inconsistencies in presentation across platforms, as different browsers (and even different versions of the same browser) handle the absence of this tag differently.

Working with HTTP (Not Against It)

A key component of increasing the efficiency of any Web site is understanding the protocol that is the basis of the Web: the Hypertext Transfer Protocol (HTTP). In some senses, HTML documents are nothing but scripts of commands for clients and servers running HTTP. When a user enters an URL in his or her browser Location window, that user is sending an HTTP GET command for a specific file. When the browser downloads an HTML file, it is essentially downloading a script of further HTTP commands that are then processed in tandem by the browser and whatever servers are indicated.

In some respects, the protocol works almost too well. Integration of content from numerous servers is so seamless that often designers forget the actual processing implications of their designs. The two sections that follow illustrate simple strategies that can (and should) probably be implemented on most sites currently on the Web today.

Avoid Calls to Other Servers   You know the counter at the bottom of the page? Of course, you do; it's the thing that always takes forever to download after the rest of the page is already in place. That counter is the force of gravity that causes the comets to continue to streak down past the big *N*, then around the big blue *e*, and back again for what seems like hours as your users' patience quickly disappears.

Besides my personal antipathy to usage counters, there's a systemic reason to avoid the things. Many of the counters you commonly see on Web sites (or don't see, as the case may be, depending on your patience) require the client to open a connection to a server other than the one from which it's gathering the majority of its data.

Off-site counter programs were originally developed to meet the needs of users who could not actually execute programs on their Web sites. Many users who created their Web sites on servers run by universities or ISPs were limited in the amount of server-side scripting that they could perform. Off-site counters were run by people who had the ability to run programs and who often wanted to collect some sort of data about the users of particular types of sites. If you need to count the number of impressions or visitors to a specific page, do so by analyzing the server access log and sorting for unique hits, usually shown by a GET request from a hostname that has newly connected to the server.

When a browser connects to a site for the first time, it negotiates its access with the server. After this negotiation is done for the first time, the creation of additional download processes is easy. Because the server has already validated the specific IP address requesting data, the additional requests for access are processed immediately.

On the other hand, when an HTML document includes a call to another server for an embedded element such as a graphic or a counter, the client must disengage processes from the original server and renegotiate access with the second server. Because this process usually happens after a user's system has already become busy with downloading the other elements of the site from the first server, the time required negotiating access and downloading files from the second server increases.

Say that you have two Web servers, one that houses your basic HTML and one that interacts with a back-end database to generate pages on-the-fly. An obvious tactic is to store all the graphics used by both sites in one repository, stored on one site or the other. As you'll see in the section "Leveraging Your Client-Side Cache," maintaining one graphics repository can be a great streamlining strategy, but the efficiency gained in storage space and from caching can be more than offset by the inefficiency created when the browser has to open connections to multiple servers.

N O T E Even when the browser caches an image, the browser might open a connection to the server simply to ensure that the date and size of the file in the cache correspond with the version of the file currently stored on the server. ▪

The answer might be to store a second copy of the images most used on pages generated by the second server on the second machine. This strategy is particularly useful if you expect that users will spend some time on your second server after they get there, as the graphics files that are downloaded a second time can be cached and reused by the browser.

N O T E You can use a combination of the Media Manager and Visual SourceSafe to help maintain copies of your graphics on two (or more) separate servers. If you use the Media Manager to maintain one central archive of your graphics, you can use the detailed commenting feature to indicate which servers will need any particular graphic. You can then use Visual SourceSafe to deploy new or updated graphics to all your servers simultaneously. ▪

Count Your Connections If you've never done so before, print out one of your favorite Web pages and count the number of server connections that are required. Remember that each <IMG> tag likely requires a separate connection, as does the HTML document itself.

Now divide that number by 4, which is the default number of connections used by many browsers. The result of this calculation tells you how many cycles of downloading an average user must wade through to download your page.

Better still, take the same number and divide it into the number of connections supported by your server. If, for example, your page consists of an HTML document, six graphics, and a background sound file, and your server supports only 64 connections, your site could be limited to handling as few as eight simultaneous users.

Next, take your test page and make a list of the files that need to be downloaded. Next to the name of each file, list the size of the file. Add the total and divide by 2000. The result is approximately how long, in seconds, it takes for a user on a 28.8Kbps modem to download all the elements on your page. Factor in a couple more seconds for the browser to process and organize the elements, and then consider how long it takes you before your mouse finger twitches for the Stop button.

One useful strategy is to create some standard graphic elements that can be used on multiple pages. If you plan ahead to use consistent graphical elements or controls throughout your site, you can take advantage of the caching capabilities of the more advanced browsers.

Leveraging Your Client-Side Cache

Most of the popular browsers available today store files that are downloaded off the Internet in a directory so that they can be reused without having to download them a second time from the server. The directory in which this data is stored is called a *cache*. Learning to take advantage of the cache is one of the quickest ways to improve the overall performance of your Web site.

For most sites, having your users preload all the graphics for the site just isn't practical, but understanding how the cache works can help you plan how to craft your HTML. Start by taking a look at the cache created by Internet Explorer.

N O T E Whereas documents created using standard desktop publishing applications or word processors merge graphics and effects into one large document, Web pages are built from many files at a time, and each retains its own individuality. The Web browser uses the information contained in the HTML document to format all the components in an onscreen presentation that looks like one document.

Realizing that the Web browser needs to collect a bunch of separate files—often from different locations—and then process them all to present a completed Web page might help you plan strategies that improve your Web site's efficiency. Anything that helps the browser avoid a long and difficult process to gather specific components helps speed up the entire process. ■

The Temporary Internet Files Directory   Internet Explorer actually stores all the files downloaded while a user is on the Web into a special directory called Temporary Internet Files. The files maintained in this directory are considered temporary because the space available in the directory is limited, set by the user through the Internet Control Panel. When this directory reaches its set limit, Windows begins to delete files from this directory, starting with those files with the longest period of time from their last use.

The Temporary Internet Files directory is usually stored under the Windows directory on machines using Windows 95/98. You can look at and work with any of the files in this cache the same way you would any other files on your drive. To look at what's in your Internet Explorer cache, double-click the Temporary Internet Files icon in Windows Explorer. You should then see a window like the one shown in Figure 27.6.

FIG. 27.6

You can review the contents of the Internet Explorer cache by opening the Temporary Internet Files directory.

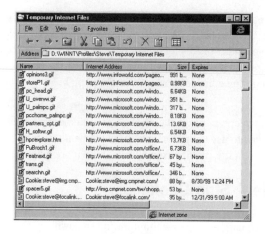

Click the Details button at the far right of the toolbar to get a complete rundown of information about the files in the cache. Although the listing in the Temporary Internet Files folder has a similar format to any other directory in Windows, you might notice that the information presented is slightly different. Usually, a directory list in Windows provides information on a file's name, size, type, and its most recent modification date. The Temporary Internet Files folder presents more information that helps to fix a specific file in relation to its function on the Internet. Along with the cached file's name, you are given the URL where it was originally found.

Internet Explorer uses the file's name and location to determine whether it has already downloaded a copy of a specific file and can therefore skip downloading it a second time. When Internet Explorer parses the HTML document and comes upon the URL of an embedded file—such as a graphic—it checks the cache. If a copy of the file exists in the cache, it next checks to see whether the copy it has on file is the same as the one currently stored on the server.

If you're looking at the Detail listing of the files in your Temporary Internet Files folder, you might notice that along with the regular Last Modified date, the Temporary Internet Files folder presents an Expiration date, a Last Checked date, and a Last Accessed date. Internet Explorer uses this information to confirm that the copy of a specific file stored in your cache is the most up-to-date version available. The Expiration date is a date that can be set on a file using a <META> tag in the HTML header. Setting an expiration date on a file tells the browser that it should always check for a new or updated version of the file any time after the stated expiration date has passed. The Last Accessed date tells you the most recent time the file was actually used by Internet Explorer.

The Last Checked date is the last time Internet Explorer contacted the file's site of origin to see whether a newer version was available. A user can specify how often he or she wants the browser to check for newer versions of files. The browser uses each of these elements to determine whether it needs to download a new copy of the file. If the browser confirms that it is looking for the same file it already has (because the file's complete name and dates match), it uses the version from the cache. Although all this information seems like quite a lot for the browser to review, you should remember that what the browser and the server pass during these checks is simple text, which transfers much more quickly than binary files such as graphics.

Recently, companies have been working on the creation of ActiveX controls that can be updated with only a brief exchange of data, such as a stock ticker. These controls request and download only brief lines of text from the main data source; these lines are then translated and formatted by the control on the user's side. The control can be created to update on a regular schedule, thus keeping the user's page constantly updated.

Now that you understand how the browser stores and reuses files, you can look at a few strategies for taking advantage of these capabilities to shorten a Web site's download time.

Meticulously Maintain Your Graphics Archives   To maximize the efficiency of user interaction with your server, you should create one central repository for all your graphics and be ruthless about always using the same version of any specific graphic. When you're entering a graphic's address in an <IMG> tag, use the fully qualified address, or the full URL of the graphic, including the server name. Some browsers improperly parse relative names, leading the browser to believe that it needs to download a file that it already has.

Use Visual SourceSafe to ensure that you update graphics on your site only when you need to. Updating graphics to your server repeatedly can lead to the same graphic having a new revision date every time you upload a copy. Only change the date on a graphic or other media file when necessary.

T I P   Frequently change the dates on your HTML documents. The rule for HTML files is almost exactly opposite the rule for graphics when it comes to changing the revision date. A major error committed by some Webmasters is failing to update the revision date on HTML files that serve as a framework for largely graphics-driven sites. If you constantly update your lead story by changing the main graphic on your page, but that graphic always has the same name and links to the same filename (for example, leadstory.gif and leadstory.html), browsers and Web indexing programs will think that your page never changes.

In comparison to the time necessary to download an average Web page graphic, the time required to download an HTML file is negligible. You should let users know that your information is updated and pay a minor cost in efficiency rather than have users think that your data is constantly stale.

Use Client-Side Imagemaps   Creating an *imagemap*, a graphic with areas that are clickable links, once required the creation of map files that listed the coordinates within an image and the URLs with which they corresponded. When a user clicked an image, an HTTP call was made to the server, which then had to process the coordinates and redirect the browser to the correct link. These server-side imagemaps can obviously be extremely process intensive.

Recent extensions to HTML have allowed Web authors to move the processing of imagemaps from the server to the client, by including the coordinates and their corresponding links within the text of the HTML document. If you use client-side imagemaps in your HTML code, you can end up with a net double benefit in processing efficiency for your server.

In the traditional imagemap scenario, a user opens a connection to the server and downloads the HTML document and the relevant graphic. When the user clicks the graphic, a second connection is opened. The coordinates clicked by the user are passed to the server, which then translates the coordinates and sends the link information to the browser, which then must open a third connection to the site to download the specified link.

In a client-side imagemap scenario, the browser receives all the information necessary to identify its next destination without having to interact with the server. The performance improvement to this scenario is obvious, but the real improvement is realized when the user begins to use a cached HTML file with a client-side imagemap. Because the browser processes the redirection, a user can navigate among a collection of cached documents without ever having to interact with the server. This capability is particularly useful for sites that use an imagemap as a toolbar. Imagemapped toolbars in frames should *always* be designed as client-side imagemaps; all the processing necessary to navigate within the site is moved in such a scenario to the client side, drastically reducing the user's need to interact with the server.

Using Your Tags Effectively

One of the easiest ways to improve the performance of your Web site is to use the tags that you're already using more effectively. In the next section, you learn about three types of tags that you might want to review on your site.

The `<TITLE>` Tag   Until now in this chapter, you've looked at increases in efficiency from a systems point of view. While you stop to take a quick look at the `<TITLE>` tag, you should remember that the number-one way you can improve the efficiency of your site is to make it easier to use and understand.

Now consider the `<TITLE>` tag, which is required for all HTML documents; many browsers choke if they can't find a `<TITLE>` tag, largely because this information is used in so many places. `<TITLE>` information is used in the title bar of an open window, on a toolbar icon of a minimized browser program, and in Favorites and Bookmarks lists.

For a piece of information that is so widely used, many designers pay it relatively little attention. Worse yet, most database applications completely neglect to include a `<TITLE>` tag, leaving the full syntax of the search request to serve as the title for any documents retrieved.

The contents of the `<TITLE>` tag should be descriptive of the material contained in that specific HTML document, whether it is a static document or dynamically created. Furthermore, you should consider the number of places where the `<TITLE>` tag is used. One of my only gripes with the largely wonderful Microsoft site is the fact that nearly every title begins with the word *Microsoft*, leading to lists of favorites that all say *Microsoft* but give no clear indication of what product or feature the page specifically addresses.

With all due deference to your organization's Marketing department, skip the branding in `<TITLE>` tags and concentrate on identifying the content. If you've got a clear description of what's on the page, people will remember to reopen your link and will likely think of your company much more favorably than if they had to spend minutes sorting through a bunch of similarly named, nondescriptive links.

The <IMG> Tag   Quite easily, the greatest improvements to user-side performance can be achieved by properly using the extensions to the <IMG> tag. Remember that the browser needs to arrange the elements of a Web document from the files that are its component parts. Without any help, a browser must wait until a graphics file is fully downloaded before it can arrange all the other elements on a page properly.

At this point, the WIDTH and HEIGHT attributes of the <IMG> tag come in. If you specify the width and height of each of your images within the text of the HTML document, the browser can begin to arrange the page before it even begins downloading the documents.

You might not be able to tell a difference in performance if you're using Internet Explorer, which does a good job rearranging images on Web pages on-the-fly as they download, but you can notice some real differences in performance if you look at a page using Netscape. If your HTML includes the dimensions of your images, the text can be placed, and the graphics will drop into boxes where they belong. If not, Netscape needs to wait until the entire image is downloaded before it can begin to place the text properly. While Netscape reorganizes the page, the users are limited in the amount of the page that they can read and are subject to nearly constant screen flicker as the new images are placed and the text rewrapped.

When the browser reads this tag, it automatically draws a box that is 180×88 and flows the text from the HTML document around that box. As the graphic is downloaded, it flows into the box. This way, the users can start reading a page even before all the graphics are fully downloaded, without having the entire presentation rearranged one or more times as the graphics are placed.

<META> Tags   <META> tags are elements stored within the <HEAD> of an HTML document to provide information about a document that is not provided by any of the HTML tags within the document. <META> tags can be especially useful for providing information about pages that have little to no text. For example, if your page is largely frames-based or consists mainly of graphics, <META> tags can be used to provide information on contents of the page that do not appear to the users, but make it possible for a search engine to catalog and sort it.

The following are three major modifiers used within <META> tags:

- NAME—The NAME modifier is used to label the type of content within the tag. For example, if the tag is going to include the name of the section of your Web site in which the page belongs, you can use the following extension:

  ```
  NAME="Section"
  ```

- HTTP-EQUIV—HTTP-EQUIV is like the NAME modifier, but it is explicitly used to create an HTTP header for your document. Depending on the capabilities of your server, a server can use the label specified in the HTTP-EQUIV modifier to create a header for the file when it is retrieved using HTTP.

- CONTENT—The CONTENT modifier is used to define the text that comprises the information to be shared by the NAME or HTTP-EQUIV tags. In other words, each NAME or HTTP-EQUIV modifier has a companion CONTENT modifier that contains the tag's data.

Following is a quick recap:

- <META> tags belong to a generic category of tags that can contain all sorts of useful data about your site.
- <META> tags are stored in the header of your HTML file and are the first things read in your document.
- Each <META> tag includes a modifier of either NAME or HTTP-EQUIV that labels the type of data contained within the tag.
- The CONTENT modifier defines a string of text within a tag as the actual data that the tag contains.

Now that you understand what <META> tags are and how they're assembled, you can look at a few examples of information that you can put in them.

Identifying the Author of a Page   If you want to create a label that includes the name of the author of each page, you can use the NAME attribute to create a label called Author. The CONTENTS then include the name of the author. The syntax of such a tag looks like this:

```
<META NAME="Author" CONTENT="Victor Hugo">
```

Tagging your pages in this fashion allows you to search through your pages to find all HTML documents created by any specific editor without having to place the author's name in the main text of the document.

Setting a Freshness Date on Your Information with Expiration Information   You can use a special HTTP-EQUIV label to create a header on documents presented by your server that specifies an expiration date for your information. If an expiration date is placed on a file, browsers and search engines are notified to return to the site after that date to get an updated file. You should specify the date using the following standard format:

```
Day of week, Date Month Year Time(in 24hr format) Timezone(as compared to GMT)
```

If you want a file to expire at 9 a.m. Eastern Time on February 24, 1996, the date and time component of the tag would look like this:

```
Wed, 24 Feb 1999 09:00:00 GMT-5
```

The syntax of the <META> tag would, therefore, look like this:

```
<META HTTP-EQUIV="Expires" CONTENT=" Wed, 24 Feb 1999 09:00:00 GMT-5">
```

If your server supports the parsing of <META> tags, your file is transmitted with a header that reads as follows:

```
Expires: Wed, 24 Feb 1999 09:00:00 GMT-5
```

Entering Keywords for Your Page   If you want to improve the likelihood that search engine users will be able to find your site, you might want to create keywords that describe the content of your document. Creating these keywords is especially useful if you refer to a product or service using specific trademarks. Keywords can help users find the general topics covered in your page, leaving you to be more specific in the main body of your document.

Use the word Keywords as the label portion of the HTTP-EQUIV attribute in the <META> tag. Keywords pertaining to a page written by the author mentioned earlier look like this:

```
<META HTTP-EQUIV="Keywords" CONTENTS="Bells, Cathedrals, Paris, Horror,
Hunchback">
```

N O T E   Most hits to any successful Web page come from searches on indexes and search engines. If you really want to attract users to your site, good descriptive sets of keywords (including not only your topics, but also synonyms for those topics and related terms) can greatly improve your number of hits. ▪

You can use <META> tags to document almost anything about a page, and luckily you can have as many as you want within the <HEAD> of your HTML file. You get the most efficient use from these tags if you use them consistently throughout your site. If you're labeling a page with the section that it's from, make sure that an equivalent label is on every page in your site, or at least every page in the section.

Using *HEIGHT* and *WIDTH* to Reduce Downloading Time

Almost all the Web browsers used today attempt to load the entire text of a Web site before the graphics are displayed. This task is made much easier for the browser if a developer incorporates HEIGHT and WIDTH attributes within an image tag when writing HTML. If an image tag does not have these attributes, the browser has to load each graphic as it is encountered so that the page is displayed correctly. The idea behind a public Web site is to provide users with information quickly. If you do not have the HEIGHT and WIDTH attributes in your Web site, your users end up waiting a longer period of time before they can actually read all the content.

The HEIGHT and WIDTH attributes fall within the normal <IMG> tags, as denoted in the following syntax example:

```
<img src="picture.gif" height=140 width="100" alt="Picture of the Pope">
```

Don't forget to include the alt attribute as well. It not only gives nongraphical browsers text-based links, but it also gives your waiting users an idea of what will be displayed.

Multimedia Data Compression

Now you can examine the file formats of computer graphics. Of the many methods of storing graphics data, most of them fall into one of three categories: raster, vector, or metafile. Using raster files is similar to taking photographs, in the sense that the actual light values that represent a picture are recorded directly into the file in much the same way that light values in a camera are recorded directly onto film. Vector files, on the other hand, cannot record a picture's light values; they are more similar to line drawings, simple descriptions of the overall shapes in an image. The third method of storing graphics data, the metafile, is a combination of both raster and vector formats together in one file.

Raster Versus Vector Data

To understand better the difference between raster and vector formats, imagine that you are stranded on a desert island and need to make an SOS sign in the sand. Making the sign out of ropes would be equivalent to a vector-format file. Making the sign out of coconuts would be equivalent to a raster-format file.

Part VII

Ch

27

The coconuts sign is similar to a raster-based image, in that you have to account for every point along each letter individually. The rope SOS sign is equivalent to a vector-based image. You set the starting point and ending point for the line, and perhaps bend it a little between the two endpoints.

A picture stored in a raster-format file cannot be enlarged without enlarging the dots making up the picture as well. So making a raster image any larger than the size it was originally sampled always results in a loss of image quality. However, a graphic stored in vector format, while not as realistic as a raster image, can be enlarged to any size without any loss in quality. The computer simply redraws the lines making up the graphic at the larger size but with the original line widths.

Because a vector-format file contains only descriptions of graphical shapes and not all the specific values for each spot on the image, it requires less data to store than a raster image. This difference can be a great benefit to Visual InterDev because smaller images download faster. On the flip side, however, raster images look much better than vector images, in the same way a photograph of a scene looks more realistic than a line drawing of the same scene. You have to weigh the options based on your site's specific needs.

Resolution   *Resolution* is a word applied to many aspects of computer graphics. The most common use, however, is a description of the number of pixels used to make up an image. This description is represented in the number of pixels horizontally (width) by the number of pixels vertically (height) in an image. For example, a typical image might have a resolution of 640×480. Therefore, the image contains a total of 307,200 pixels.

Color Depth   As I mentioned earlier, the color of every pixel is also stored in the raster file. Scientifically speaking, an infinite number of colors appears in the visible wavelengths of light (depending on how small you want to chop those wavelengths). Having such a large number could be a big problem for storing realistic pictures. Digital computers don't do well with this analog data, so, as with sound waves, computers sample these waves into discrete digital values. Human vision can differentiate only about 17 million colors, so this makes the computer's job a little easier in not having to display more colors.

Still, if you want to store a number from 1 to 17 million, it would take approximately 3 bytes (24 bits storing 16.7 million colors). Now multiply that number by the 307,200 pixels of a 640×480 picture, and you get a whopping 921,600 bytes, or almost 1 megabyte—which on a 28,800 baud modem would take almost four minutes to download. Obviously, you have to make some sacrifice in the number of colors, or the transfer time of any image would simply be too long.

These huge numbers also explain why animation and video are so limited over the Internet. Consider that even a modest video clip at 320×200 resolution at full color requires 64,000 pixels, totaling 192,000 bytes per frame. Now, for realistic video, you need at least 15 frames per second, which brings you up to 2.88 megabytes a second—quite a bit more bandwidth than any modems or even ISDN connections have today. This problem, however, has two solutions: color reduction and data compression. First, consider the topic of color reduction.

GIF Versus JPEG   Only two graphics file formats are widely used on the Internet today: GIF and JPEG. Each is good for its own purpose and should never be used for the other's.

The GIF file is an exceptional format to use when you want to make a graphic appear as though it were a shape other than a square or rectangle when it appears in a Web page. An example is to create a diamond shape resting on a white background. If the Web page that you're loading it into also has a white background, the diamond appears as though it integrates directly into the page.

The GIF format also allows you to select the number of colors that are in your image and save the file with that number of colors only. If you create a graphic that uses only 16 colors, you can specify this option in your photo program (such as Photoshop) and greatly reduce the file size of the image itself. GIF images can be saved in a transparent format known as GIF 89A. You essentially mask a color out of the image, save the file in the correct format, and load it into the page. When it is displayed, the GIF image is completely displayed, sans the masked color. This format can lead to some really exciting effects with layering.

The JPEG file format is best used when you are displaying an image that is greater than 256 colors. When you save an image in the JPEG format, the colors are dithered down into the functioning color palette, but the image still retains its maximum clarity. The JPEG file format is also much smaller in comparison to the GIF format, due to its extremely high compression rate. Most of the time, you use the JPEG format with a rectangular-based image. Although you can use other shapes in your JPEG file, due to the dithering process, they don't fit as seamlessly as GIF files.

Animation and Video Issues   Animations and videos can represent a hefty chunk of any Web site's download time. When you are implementing animations or videos, carefully consider the impact they will have on your Web site's performance. You can place videos and animations in your site using different file formats and methods:

- *QuickTime*. Apple's QuickTime format is an extremely compact and efficient method for delivering video files of any kind. QuickTime support is built into Apple Macintoshes and is easily downloadable for Windows-based PCs.

- *Video for Windows*. The standard method for video files in Windows is the AVI file. Video for Windows is not the most efficient method for delivering video; however, almost every Windows system can view it.

- *Animated GIFs*. Ideal for only small animations, typically looped, animated GIF support is built into most Web browsers. You should abide by the same general rules of thumb for animated GIFs as when you use GIF images.

- *RealVideo*. An effective way of delivering video and animation to your users is Real-Video. Real Video can be streamed or downloaded, and results in compact files. Real-Video players are available for both Macintosh and Windows systems.

- *Netshow*. Microsoft's own streaming/compressed video format is available now for both Windows and Macintosh systems. It also requires a special player that must be down-loaded.

Part

VII

Ch

27

- *Shockwave and Flash.* Macromedia has developed two different technologies for animations and interactive media. Shockwave, based primarily on Macromedia Director, and Macromedia Flash are technologies that can be used to deliver high-quality videos or animations. These technologies require viewers/players and are available on both Macintosh and PC systems.

When you are implementing videos or animations, carefully weigh the benefits of the additions. Videos and animations cause increased strain in terms of download times and playability on clients' computers. When you're working with animations and videos, consider providing different qualities of videos or animations based on resolutions, allowing users with slower connections to take advantage of smaller files, whereas those with faster connections can take in the full effect of your files. When you are planning your site, be sure to consider what file type will have the most profound effects on your site's performance, for both speed and size.

File size and delivery speeds are closely linked but not necessarily mutually inclusive. Although a large file creates a slower delivery time, it is not absolute. A small file may also have a slower delivery (or display) speed if it requires additional software or processing to display. For example, if you deliver streaming video to your visitors, you are already sending a great deal of information downstream. To extend this example further, you may choose to deliver the video in a format that requires considerably more overhead on the users' machines than simply downloading the sound file and playing it. In addition to causing more overhead for the users, your selection will also cause more overhead for the server. First, large files cause more strain on server resources. Connections are open longer, more memory and bandwidth are used, and, of course, storage space is consumed. In addition, if you choose a format that requires special server-side handling (such as streaming video rather than downloadable video files), the overhead of the streaming services may have considerable impact on your server.

Here are a few points to consider when deciding on file types for your site contents:

- *Calculate the download time.* If your average users are connecting at 28.8Kbps or lower, how long will it take them to view your page using different formats? If you are exceeding 30 seconds, you should carefully look at the necessity of such a large load time.

- *Consider the additional overhead involved.* Content of any kind uses resources, but some content uses more than others. If you are looking at additional services on your server, is the overhead worth the cost? Do you need to deliver such large files? Can you find a simpler way of doing things?

- *Can you keep the pace?* If you are looking at delivering large content now, what about in the future? You can't always count on things getting smaller. More often than not, sites are getting larger and the content files are growing to match. Will your server and network connection be able to sustain your growth from where you start? Match your content types to your growth rate. Don't overload yourself too soon.

Increasing Server-Side Performance with Visual InterDev

Once your client-side performance is satisfactory, you can concentrate on improving the speeds on your server. When you are working with Web applications, you must consider several key factors if you want to maximize performance. Most of these factors rely on knowledge and application of that knowledge. A poorly planned or implemented server-side Web application can result in disastrous performance.

Know Your Scripting Language

When you are working with server-side scripting, understanding how your scripting language functions is extremely important. Efficiently designed code that takes advantage of the scripting language's capabilities while minimizing the effects of its weaknesses creates snappier applications. Be aware of the limitations and strengths of your scripting language and its syntax. Of particular importance is a firm understanding of how to optimize your code:

- Recognize how to use variable scope. Global variables? Local variables? Your choice depends on your needs but also can have a direct impact on performance. Declared local variables (and function parameters) are fast, whereas globals and implicit locals are significantly slower.

- Use efficient procedures and routines. Keep your frequently used routines as reusable modules, but also recognize the limitations of frequently used routines. Always consider their impact on performance.

- Don't code yourself into a corner. Make sure you are using the scripting language to your advantage and not writing code that limits your options in the future.

- Using JScript with constructs slows down local and parameter access. Local access during evaluation is as slow as global access.

Performance for the JScript and VBScript virtual machines depends on the particular operation and how well the script code is written. Keep in mind these few guidelines:

- For highly recursive code, VBScript is slightly faster.
- For iterative code, JScript tends to be slightly faster.
- Variable assignment is faster in JScript. Assigning strings from variable to variable is significantly faster in JScript because JScript variables can share the string, whereas VBScript gives each variable its own copy of the string.
- VBScript arrays are significantly faster than JScript arrays (which are really just objects).
- For sorting an array, JScript's built-in sort is orders of magnitude faster than VBScript's sort.

For more information about server-side scripting and performance tuning, consider *Platinum Edition Using HTML 4, JavaScript 1.2, and Java 1.1* and *Special Edition Using Microsoft Internet Information Server 4.0* from Que Corporation.

Part

VII

Ch

27

Know Your Bottlenecks

When you are analyzing the performance of your server, recognizing where potential problems could occur is important. If you walked through life without any real concern for your health or well being, it is safe to assume that you wouldn't be in "top form." Servers are much the same; they rely on constant tweaking and fiddling to make them perform to the best of their processor-given capabilities. Server health can be examined by three criteria:

1. *Processor Load.* Everything your computer does creates a set of tasks for the processor to carry out. Each task, in turn, adds to the load that the processor must bear. A busier computer means a larger load the processor must carry. If the load is too large, the server can become bogged down in trying to keep up with the demand for tasks. A faster processor, or multiple processors, can minimize the load on a particular server.

2. *Memory Usage.* As important (and often more so) than processor load, the amount of memory that your computer has directly impacts performance. If you think of your computer's memory like a glass, the more things you do add more water to the glass. If you overload the glass's contents, the glass cannot hold anymore and is forced to spill over the edges. Each task your processor takes on takes more memory. The more memory your server has available, the more breathing room it has for each task.

3. *Resource Consumption.* Although memory is considered a resource, it stands in a slightly different grouping. Computing resources, such as storage space and speed, as well as connection speed, have a direct bearing on your machine's performance. Slower storage devices that are filled to the brim deliver information more slowly than lean, fast devices. Fast, uncontested network connections can fire off your content rapidly to your visitors, rather than being mired in congested network traffic.

Each of these three points directly affects a server's performance. Tweaking only one point is not good enough, as the other two could easily bring your server to its knees. Tuning your server is a collective effort of concentrating on all three points, to create a healthy balance. One of the key elements that most developers neglect to consider is the resource implications. When you are working with server-side activation, such as ISAPI extensions or CGI programs, a large load can be put on the processor, as well as a significant drain on the memory pool of the server. Server-side programming is often the biggest offender for server slowdown. Careful planning and implementation of your server-side code are crucial to maintaining a healthy server. Your server programs could easily take down the server if you are not careful.

When you are first building your site, carefully consider the consequences of your actions. You should make sure that both your server and your site are swift to respond to the users' needs. You should always be aware of where the weakest link in your server is. Your site can only be as fast as the slowest link in the chain; if you have a particular element in your site that is pulling down performance, it will cascade throughout your site's performance. Always be aware of the places where problems could manifest themselves in your site so that you can address them. This battle is ongoing—so tune, tune, tune.

Use the Application Object Over the Session Object

Using the application and session objects empowers you to create advanced and intricate Web applications. However, with these advanced features come some compromises. The session object requires considerable overhead in comparison to the application object. This fact holds especially true in high-traffic environments. If you must store data over a "session," use the application object over the session object. Not only does the application object require fewer resources on the server side, it also responds much more quickly for the users. Response time for the application object improves dramatically over the session object and is ideal for storing data throughout your users' sessions.

Consider ISAPI Over CGI

When you are working with compiled server-side programs, you should consider using Microsoft's Internet Service API (ISAPI) over conventional Common Gateway Interface (CGI) programs. Microsoft's ISAPI platform is much more robust and requires considerably less overhead on the server's part than CGI. One of the biggest advantages to ISAPI is that it does not require opening and closing each time it is used. Conventional CGI programs are spawned when a user requests information from them, and are then closed. This repeats each time a request is made to the CGI. ISAPI, on the other hand, stays resident in the IIS memory space. This saves time (and in the long run, memory) as the ISAPI program does not need to open and close each time.

Planning for Quicker Service

Through careful planning, you can create sites that minimize delays and increase performance. Both the real-time server performance and the perceived performance on the users' end contribute to your site's appeal. Creating a Web site that is quick and fluid to use will no doubt add to the appeal of the site. When you are planning your site, try to minimize extraneous content. Duplication or unneeded content is just more to send down the wire. Carefully look at what has to be sent down the line and what complements it. You can use these quick tips to create quicker sites:

■ *Use the same graphics.* Where possible, reuse your image files. Most browsers cache the graphics they receive, allowing for quicker loading on the users' end. This perceived time savings reduces load on your server and improves response time for the visitors.

■ *Plan around slow connections.* If possible, offer the ability to choose between a high-bandwidth or low-bandwidth site. If you can provide a usable site to those who are connecting at low speed, you can keep your visitors happy. And for those visitors who do have the speed to take advantage of, load them up with a richer experience.

■ *Use the most efficient means of delivery.* Simply put, choose the most appropriate way to deliver your content. If you can deliver some content quicker through other means, do so. But always keep in mind simplicity for the visitors.

Part
VII

Ch
27

■ *Prune out the old and excess.* As your site grows and progresses, don't forget to update your older pages. If a newer way of delivering your content comes around, move your content over to it. Don't force users to visit old pages that may have incredibly large and outdated file types.

■ *Recognize the effects of add-ons.* Whether you're using Java, ActiveX, or plug-ins, you may be adding more overhead to your page. Considerable system resources are used with many add-ons, and may create a slower (and more frustrating) experience for your visitors.

■ *Keep your site simple.* Don't overcomplicate. Only send what's needed; don't waste the visitors' time with something that isn't needed.

From Here...

Ultimately, your most important job is to make sure that your Web site runs quickly. No matter how well designed or attractive your site is, if it is dog slow no one will use it. Always consider how you can improve performance and load times for your users when designing and implementing sites. For more information on performance tuning and making your site the best it can be, take a look at these chapters:

■ Chapter 19, "Windows NT Server Basics."

■ Chapter 20, "Using Internet Information Server (IIS)."

■ Chapter 25, "Designing and Organizing Web Sites."

Appendixes

A   Resources   581

B   Quick Reference   587

C   Glossary   613

Resources

In this chapter

This appendix includes information on useful books, magazines, training, and services. It also includes information on many online Web sites, newsgroups, and listservers related to Visual InterDev. This list of resources is by no means exhaustive, but it should point you in the right direction when you need help.

Books

In addition to this book, many other books that relate to Visual InterDev, Internet Information Server, and Web application development may prove of use to you. The following is a brief list of selected books:

- *Special Edition Using Internet Information Server 4.0* (Que).
- *Platinum Edition Using HTML 4, Java 1.1, and JavaScript 1.2* (Que).

Magazines

Several printed magazines offer invaluable information for Visual InterDev developers. Here is a list of a few general-interest magazines and publications for developers:

- *MSDN News*

  http://www.microsoft.com/msdn/news/devnews/
- *Microsoft Interactive Developer*

  http://www.microsoft.com/mind/
- *Microsoft Systems Journal*

  http://www.microsoft.com/msj/
- *Microsoft Web Builder*

  http://www.cobb.com/mit/
- *Active Server Developer's Journal*

  http://www.asdj.com

Online Resources

Online resources are the best places to find quick answers and solutions to most Visual InterDev–related problems. Doing your research online also is a good way to keep up-to-speed on the latest developments. This section lists Web sites, newsgroups, listservers, ISPs, and Visual InterDev hosting sites.

Web Sites

The following Web sites offer Visual InterDev–related information and files:

- Microsoft Windows NT Server

  http://www.microsoft.com/ntserver
- Microsoft BackOffice Live

  http://www.microsoft.com/backoffice/

- Internet Information Server 4.0 and Active Server Pages
  http://www.microsoft.com/iis
- Active Server Pages Developer's Site (including the ASP FAQ)
  http://www.genusa.com/asp
- Microsoft Internet Information Server Frequently Asked Questions
  http://www.15seconds.com/faq/
- Microsoft Scripting Technologies
  http://www.microsoft.com/scripting/
- Netscape JavaScript
  http://devedge.netscape.com/tech/javascript/
- Microsoft FrontPage 98
  http://www.microsoft.com/frontpage
- Microsoft Image Composer
  http://www.microsoft.com/imagecomposer
- Microsoft Knowledge Base
  http://www.microsoft.com/support
- Microsoft Media Manager
  http://www.microsoft.com/vstudio/owner
- Microsoft SQL Server
  http://www.microsoft.com/sql
- Microsoft Site Builder Network
  http://www.microsoft.com/sitebuilder
- Site Builder Workshop (including Internet Client SDK)
  http://www.microsoft.com/workshop
- Visual InterDev Web site
  http://www.microsoft.com/vinterdev
- Microsoft Developer's Network
  http://www.microsoft.com/msdn
- The ISAPI Developer's site
  http://www.genusa.com/isapi
- The ASP Hole
  http://www.asphole.com/asphole
- Avatar—The Interactive Developer's Online Magazine
  http://www.avatarmag.com/

Newsgroups

Visiting newsgroups is perhaps the fastest way to get a question answered. Microsoft's main news server is at **msnews.microsoft.com**. The following are newsgroups related to Visual InterDev:

- The main Visual InterDev newsgroup

  news://msnews.microsoft.com/microsoft.public.vinterdev

- Visual Studio

  news://msnews.microsoft.com/microsoft.public.vstudio.development

- Public Internet Information Server

  news://comp.infosystems.www.server.ms-windows

- Internet Information Server

  news://msnews.microsoft.com/microsoft.public.inetserver.iis

- General IIS Discussion

  news://msnews.microsoft.com/microsoft.public.inetserver.misc

- Using Active Server Pages

  **news://msnews.microsoft.com/
  microsoft.public.inetserver.iis.activeserverpages**

- Using Index Server

  news://msnews.microsoft.com/microsoft.public.inetserver.iis.tripoli

- Microsoft Management Console

  news://msnews.microsoft.com/microsoft.public.management.mmc

- VBScript

  **news://msnews.microsoft.com/
  microsoft.public.inetsdk.programming.scripting.vbscript**

- Netscape JavaScript (part of Netscape DevEdge)

  http://devedge.netscape.com/support/newsgroups/

- Microsoft JScript

  **news://msnews.microsoft.com/
  microsoft.public.inetsdk.programming.scripting.jscript**

Listservers

The following descriptions provide the current listservers available from Microsoft, along with instructions on how to subscribe.

Mailing Lists Active Server Pages Mailing List   This mailing list provides a discussion of Active Server Pages.

To subscribe, send mail to: **LISTSERV@listserv.15seconds.com**

Subject: (leave blank)

Message Text (to subscribe): `subscribe ActiveServerPages` *(your name)*

Message Text (to unsubscribe): `signoff ActiveServerPages`

Internet Information Server 4.0   This mailing list provides a discussion on implementation and development on IIS 4.

To subscribe, send mail to: **LISTSERV@listserv.15seconds.com**

Subject: (leave blank)

Message Text (to subscribe): `subscribe IIS40` *(your name)*

Message Text (to unsubscribe): `signoff  IIS40`

Active Directory Service Interface (ADSI)   This mailing list covers the discussion of programming for the ADSI namespace, including IIS4, Exchange, and NTLM.

To subscribe, send mail to: **LISTSERV@listserv.15seconds.com**

Subject: (leave blank)

Message Text (to subscribe): `subscribe ADSI` *(your name)*

Message Text (to unsubscribe): `signoff ADSI`

ISAPI Mailing List   This mailing list covers information for ISVs writing ISAPI applications and filters.

To subscribe, send mail to: **LISTSERV@listserv.15seconds.com**

Subject: (leave blank)

Message Text (to subscribe): `subscribe ISAPI` *(your name)*

Message Text (to unsubscribe): `signoff ISAPI`

User Groups

Currently, there are no Visual InterDev user groups, but you can call Microsoft at (800) 228-6738 regarding future user groups or for information on setting up one yourself.

Training

If you are interested in getting training for Visual InterDev, many options are available. See the following descriptions.

Microsoft Online Institute

The Microsoft Online Institute offers online interactive training for Microsoft and third-party technologies. For more information, call 800-449-9333 or send email to **moliqa@microsoft.com**.

Microsoft Certified Professional Program

Currently, the following four types of certifications are available from Microsoft:

- Product Specialist
- Systems Engineer
- Certified Trainer
- Certified Solution Developer

For more information, call 800-755-EXAM.

32X, Inc.

32X, Inc. is currently offering seminars and training on Visual InterDev. You can contact them at the following address:

32X, Inc.

6114 La Salle Ave., Suite 438

Oakland, CA 94611

http://www.32x.com/

General Information:

73142.3623@compuserve.com

Webmaster: **73504.1240@compuserve.com**

Registration Services:

Wellwater Event Management

P.O. Box 8927

Greensboro, NC 27419

Telephone: 510-562-5922

Fax: 510-562-5923

Email: **wwem@msn.com**

Beta Testing

If you want to get involved with beta testing Microsoft's latest products, send an email message to this address:

betareq@microsoft.com

Be sure to include a description of your current hardware and software along with the reason you want to be a beta tester and your contact information.

Quick Reference

This appendix serves as a quick reference for HTML, VBScript, JScript, and Active Server Page objects. Most of the time you will probably refer to the built-in help files of Visual InterDev or perhaps the many online reference sites (some of which are referenced in the preceding appendix). However, I recommend that you read through this appendix just to make sure you're up to speed on all the current tags, functions, methods, properties, and language features available.

HTML

HTML, or Hypertext Markup Language, is composed of start and stop tags and the text you place between these tags. Tags are defined from the contents of a page by less-than and greater-than symbols, also known as angle brackets (<BODY>). You differentiate start tags from end tags by placing a backslash in the end tag, as illustrated in Listing B.1.

Listing B.1   A Sample Table with the Start and End Tags

```
<TABLE>
    <TR>
        <TD>
            This is the middle cell of a table
        </TD>
    </TR>
</TABLE>
```

> **TIP**   For the best performance, always close your HTML tags with the appropriate closing tag.

Some tags such as the body tag can take parameters. Here's an example: `<BODY BACKGROUND="images/backgrd.gif" BGPROPERTIES=FIXED BGCOLOR=#FFFFFF TEXT=#000000 LINK=#ff6600 VLINK=#330099>`. Listing B.2 shows the minimum HTML document requirements.

Listing B.2   A Document Structure

```
<HTML>
    <HEAD>
        <TITLE>Sample HTML Document</TITLE>
    </HEAD>
    <BODY>
        <P>A very simple HTML document.</P>
    </BODY>
</HTML>
```

The following sections describe the most common HTML tags.

Tags for the Document Head

The document head sets up the title for your Web page, which is used in the title bar of the user's browser as well as the Favorites menu if the user saves your page location. The following tags are used in the document head section of an HTML page:

- ■ <BASE>—Indicates the default location of relative URL links, with the following parameters:

HREF—Indicates the baseline URL for relative links

TARGET—Indicates in which window to display the destination hypertext link

■ <ISINDEX>—Indicates that the entire home page can be searched by keywords

■ <LINK>—Specifies relationships to other HTML documents, with the following parameters:

HREF—Indicates the destination URL to establish a relationship with

REL—Indicates the relationship with a destination document

REV—Verifies a reversed relationship with a destination document

TITLE—Indicates the title for the destination URL

■ <TITLE></TITLE>—Specifies the document's title

Tags for the Document Body

Most tags are specified within the <BODY> elements. Most content contained inside the <BODY> and </BODY> tags is displayed. The sets of related tags described in the following sections are all available within this body block.

Headers   Logical style elements define attributes for a group of text, and the browser automatically word-wraps the text. These tags control special attributes for text:

■ <CITE>[Text]</CITE>—Indicates that the [Text] is a citation.

■ <CODE>[Text]</CODE>—Displays [Text] as computer source code.

■ <DFN>[Text]</DFN>—Displays [Text] as if it were a definition.

■ <EM>[Text]</EM>—Emphasizes [Text] in some way.

■ <H1>[Text]</H1>—Displays [Text] as a header. You can use <H1> through <H6>, with the smallest number being the largest header.

■ <KBD>[Text]</KBD>—Displays [Text] as something to be typed on the keyboard.

■ <SAMP>[Text]</SAMP>—Displays [Text] as a sampling, such as from an article.

■ <STRONG>[Text]</STRONG>—Displays [Text] as more emphasized than <EM>.

■ <VAR>[Text]</VAR>—Displays [Text] as a variable, such as for formulas.

Hypertext Links   The <A> tag defines hyperlinks to other Internet sites and information. Hyperlinks tie the Web sites of the World Wide Web together. Here is a description of the <A> tag and its parameters:

■ <A>[Text]</A>—Defines [Text] as a hypertext link. If the <IMG> element is used in place of [Text], the image is hyperlinked, with the following parameters:

HREF—Indicates the URL to link to.

NAME—Defines the current line as a destination point. Destination points are accessed by specifying the pound sign (#) followed by the NAME you want.

TARGET—Indicates the name of the window to display the destination URL.

TITLE—Specifies the title of the destination URL.

Images   You can insert images into your home page easily by using the image tag. You can also use images to reference hyperlinks. The image tag has the following properties:

- `<IMG></IMG>`—Puts a GIF or JPEG graphic into your home page, with the following parameters:

  `ALIGN`—Indicates how the picture is aligned. This attribute has a number of acceptable values: `bleedleft`, `bleedright`, `center`, `justify`, `left`, or `right`.

  `ALT`—Shows a string if the user doesn't have a graphical browser.

  `HEIGHT`—Indicates the height of the image.

  `ISMAP`—Tells the Web browser that this graphic is an imagemap.

  `SRC`—Points to a URL that contains the graphic to use.

  `WIDTH`—Indicates the width of the image.

Lists   You can create a list with bullets or numbers in front of each item. HTML also supports definition lists for presenting dictionary-type presentations of definitions. You can even create a directory-style list so that each item appears to be a list of files in a directory. The HTML standard offers the following list tags:

- `<DL>`[Definitions]`</DL>`—Specifies the main container for a definition list, with the following parameter:

  `ALIGN`—Specifies that the text for the definitions is to be aligned center, justified, left, or right.

- `<DD>`[Text]`</DD>`—Specifies that [Text] is the definition portion of the definition list. It is displayed on the right-hand side of the screen.

- `<DIR>`[List of items]`</DIR>`—Presents [List of items] that appears to be a list of files from a directory.

- `<DT>`[Text]`</DT>`—Specifies that [Text] is the term portion of the definition list. It is displayed on the left-hand side of the screen.

- `<UL>`[List of items]`</UL>`—Presents [List of items] as an unordered (bulleted) list.

- `<OL>`[List of items]`</OL>`—Presents [List of items] as an ordered (numbered) list.

- `<LI>`[Text]`</LI>`—Indicates that [Text] is an item in the list.

Text Styles   The following HTML elements affect the visual display of text. There are no commonly used attributes for these elements. Usually, the browser word-wraps text within these tags.

- `<B>`[Text]`</B>`—Makes [Text] boldface.

- `<BLOCKQUOTE>`[Text]`</BLOCKQUOTE>`—Causes [Text] to be displayed as quoted text.

- `<FONT>`[Text]`</FONT>`—Indicates a specific font assignment for [Text], with the following parameters:

  `SIZE`—Specifies a font size between 1 and 7 (with 7 being the largest). You can also use a plus or a minus before the number to indicate a size relative to the current `BASEFONT` setting.

FACE—Sets the font for the text. A list of font names can be specified, and the first available font found is used. If no specified fonts are found, a default is used.

COLOR—Sets font color with a hexadecimal, red-green-blue color value or a predefined color name.

- `<I>[Text]</I>`—Sets `[Text]` in italics.
- `<P>[Text]</P>`—Treats `[Text]` as if it were an entire paragraph by itself. `[Text]` is word-wrapped.
- `<PRE>[Text]</PRE>`—Displays `[Text]` as it is but not in a proportional font. Use these tags if you've already lined up some text in ASCII, such as in tables and grids with the following parameter:

WIDTH—Identifies the maximum number of characters per line.

- `<TT>[Text]</TT>`—Makes `[Text]` look as though it came from a teletype.
- `<U>[Text]</U>`—Makes `[Text]` underlined.

Objects   Using the `<OBJECT>` tag, you can insert an object—such as an image, document, applet, or control—into an HTML document. An object can contain any elements ordinarily used within the body of an HTML document, including section headings, paragraphs, lists, forms, and even nested objects.

- `<OBJECT>[Object]</OBJECT>`—Allows you to insert components into a Web page, with the following parameters:

Component	Description
ALIGN	Sets the alignment for the object. The align-type can be BASELINE, CENTER, LEFT, MIDDLE, RIGHT, TEXTBOTTOM, TEXTMIDDLE, or TEXTTOP.
BORDER	Specifies the width of the border if the object is defined as a hyperlink.
CLASSID	Identifies the object implementation.
CODEBASE	Identifies the code base for the object.
CODETYPE	Specifies the Internet media type for code.
DATA	Identifies data for the object.
DECLARE	Declares the object without instantiating it. Use this parameter when creating cross-references to the object later in the document or when using the object as a parameter in another object.
HEIGHT	Specifies the suggested height for the object.
HSPACE	Specifies the horizontal gutter, which is the extra, empty space between the object and any text or images to the left or right of the object.
NAME	Sets the name of the object when submitted as part of a form.

App
B

Component	Description
SHAPES	Specifies that the object has shaped hyperlinks.
STANDBY	Sets the message to show while loading the object.
TYPE	Specifies the Internet media type for data.
USEMAP	Specifies the imagemap to use with the object.
VSPACE	Specifies the vertical gutter, which is the extra, empty space between the object and any text or images above or below the object.
WIDTH	Specifies the suggested width for the object.

Other Tags   Several other tags don't fall into a specific category. The following tags allow you to enter text comments and place an address in your page:

- `<!-- [Text] -->`— Treats `[Text]` as comments from the HTML author. This element is completely ignored by the Web browser.

- `<ADDRESS>[Text]</ADDRESS>`—Shows `[Text]` as an address of some sort. There are no commonly used attributes.

VBScript

VBScript is Microsoft's own scripting language for Web browsers. It's a subset of the full Visual Basic programming language. To place a client-side script into an HTM or HTML document, use the following tags:

```
<script language="VBScript">
<!--
REM Place your VBScript code here.
-->
</script>
```

Notice that, in the preceding code, HTML comment tags are included so that the browser doesn't try to interpret the script as HTML. To create server-side script, save your document with the .ASP extension. Next, place any VBScript in between <% and %> tags, as shown here:

```
<%
   REM Place your VBScript code here and save file with .asp extension.
%>
```

ON THE WEB

For up-to-date, comprehensive information on Microsoft VBScript and other Microsoft scripting technologies, visit the Microsoft Scripting Technologies Web site at **http://www.microsoft.com/scripting/**. This site includes detailed information on VBScript, JScript, Scriptlets, script control, remote scripting, and much more.

VBScript has only one data type, the Variant. It then types variables based on the assignments you give them. For example, if you assign a string to a variable, VBScript types it as a String variable.

The following sections outline some of the basic features.

Array Handling

The following commands and functions allow you to create and manipulate arrays:

- Dim—Declares an array
- ReDim—Redimensions an array
- Private—Declares an array at script level
- Public—Declares a public array at script level
- IsArray—Returns True if a variable is an array
- Erase—Reinitializes a fixed-size array
- Lbound—Returns the lower bound of an array
- Ubound—Returns the upper bound of an array

Assignments

To assign data to a variable or object, use one of the following assignment arguments:

- =—Assigns a value to a variable
- Let—Assigns a value to a variable
- Set—Assigns an object to a variable

Comments

The following are two choices for specifying document comments:

- '—Includes inline comments in your script
- Rem—Includes comments in your script

Constants and Literals

VBScript uses only the following five built-in constants. If you need more, you have to create them yourself with variables.

- Empty—Indicates an uninitialized variable
- Nothing—Disassociates a variable from an object
- Null—Indicates a variable with no data
- True—Indicates Boolean True
- False—Indicates Boolean False

Control Flow

Following are the looping and branching constructs that VBScript supports:

- `Do...Loop`—Repeats a block of statements
- `Do...Until...Loop`—Repeats a block of statements until a condition is met
- `Do...While...Loop`—Repeats a block of statements while a condition is met
- `For...Next`—Repeats a block of statements
- `For Each...Next`—Repeats a block of statements
- `If...Then...Else`—Conditionally executes statements
- `Select Case`—Conditionally executes statements
- `While...Wend`—Repeats a block of statements

Conversions

To convert data from one data type to another, use one of the following conversion functions:

- `Abs`—Returns the absolute value of a number
- `Asc`—Returns the ASCII code of a character
- `AscB`—Returns the ASCII code (Byte Data) of a character
- `AscW`—Returns the ASCII code (Unicode Wide) of a character
- `Chr`—Returns a character from an ASCII code
- `ChrB`—Returns a character from an ASCII code
- `ChrW`—Returns a character from an ASCII code
- `Cbool`—Converts a variant to a Boolean
- `Cbyte`—Converts a variant to a byte
- `Cdate`—Converts a variant to a date
- `CDbl`—Converts a variant to a double
- `Cint`—Converts a variant to an integer
- `CLng`—Converts a variant to a long
- `CSng`—Converts a variant to a single
- `CStr`—Converts a variant to a string
- `DateSerial`—Converts a variant to a date, with the Y/M/D provided
- `DateValue`—Converts a variant to a date, given a formatted date
- `Hex`—Converts a variant to a hex string
- `Oct`—Converts a variant to an octal string
- `Fix`—Converts a variant to a fixed string
- `Int`—Converts a variant to an integer string
- `Sgn`—Converts a variant to a single string
- `TimeSerial`—Converts a variant to a time, with the H:M:S provided
- `TimeValue`—Converts a variant to a time, given a formatted time

Dates and Times

The following date and time functions are available in VBScript:

- Date—Returns the current date
- Time—Returns the current time
- DateSerial—Returns a date from its parts
- DateValue—Returns a date from its value
- Day—Returns day from a date
- Month—Returns month from a date
- Weekday—Returns weekday from a date
- Year—Returns year from a date
- Hour—Returns hour from a time
- Minute—Returns minute from a time
- Second—Returns seconds from a time
- Now—Returns current date and time

App

B

Declarations

To declare a variable or procedure and set its scope, use one of the following commands:

- Dim—Declares a variable
- Private—Declares a script-level private variable
- Public—Declares a public-level public variable
- ReDim—Reallocates an array
- Function—Declares a function
- Sub—Declares a subprocedure

Error Handling

For error handling, use the On Error command, and check the Err variable for the type of error you want to trap. The two error-handling commands are as follow:

- On Error—Enables error handling
- Err—Contains information about the last error

Input/Output

To input text or output a message, use the following commands:

- InputBox—Prompts the user for input
- MsgBox—Displays a message to the user

Math

The following arithmetic functions are supported:

- Atn—Returns the arctangent of a number
- Cos—Returns the cosine of a number
- Sin—Returns the sine of a number
- Tan—Returns the tangent of a number
- Exp—Returns the exponent of a number
- Log—Returns the logarithm of a number
- Sqr—Returns the square root of a number
- Randomize—Reseeds the randomizer
- Rnd—Returns a random number

Operators

The following are the operators that VBScript supports for branching constructs and assignments:

+	Addition
-	Subtraction
^	Exponentiation
Mod	Modulus arithmetic
*	Multiplication
/	Division
\	Integer division
-	Negation
&	String concatenation
=	Equality
<>	Inequality
<	Less than
<=	Less than or equal to
>	Greater than
>=	Greater than or equal to
Is	Compare object equivalence
And	Logical conjunction
Or	Logical disjunction
Xor	Logical exclusion
Eqv	Logical equivalence
Imp	Logical implication

Objects

To create an object, use the CreateObject command. The two commands related to objects are as follow:

- CreateObject—Creates a reference to an OLE object
- IsObject—Returns True if the object is valid

Options

To declare a variable explicitly, use the Option Explicit command, listed here:

- Option Explicit—Forces explicit variable declaration

Procedures

Use the following to call or create functions and subroutines:

- Call—Invokes a subprocedure
- Function—Declares a function
- Sub—Declares a subprocedure

Strings

The following are the string manipulation commands that VBScript supports:

- Asc—Returns ASCII code of a character
- AscB—Returns ASCII code of a character
- AscW—Returns ASCII code of a character
- Chr—Returns character from an ASCII code
- ChrB—Returns character from an ASCII code (Binary Data)
- ChrW—Returns character from an ASCII code (Unicode Data)
- Instr—Returns index of a string inside another string
- InStrB—Returns index of a string inside another string
- Len—Returns the length of a string
- LenB—Returns the length of a string
- Lcase—Converts a string to lowercase
- Ucase—Converts a string to uppercase
- Left—Returns the left portion of a string
- LeftB—Returns the left portion of a string
- Mid—Returns the mid portion of a string
- MidB—Returns the mid portion of a string
- Right—Returns the right portion of a string

- `RightB`—Returns the right portion of a string in bytes
- `Space`—Pads a string with spaces
- `StrComp`—Compares two strings
- `String`—Pads a string with a character
- `Ltrim`—Removes leading spaces from a string
- `Rtrim`—Removes trailing spaces from a string
- `Trim`—Removes leading and trailing spaces

Variants

To test the typing of a Variant, use one of these functions:

- `IsArray`—Returns `True` if the variable is an array
- `IsDate`—Returns `True` if the variable is a date
- `IsEmpty`—Returns `True` if the variable is empty
- `IsNull`—Returns `True` if the variable is null
- `IsNumeric`—Returns `True` if the variable is a number
- `IsObject`—Returns `True` if the variable is an object
- `VarType`—Indicates a variable's type

JavaScript/JScript

JavaScript/JScript are alternatives to scripting using VBScript. JScript is Microsoft's implementation of the Netscape JavaScript scripting language, used in the Netscape Navigator/Communicator browser. This section provides an overview of JavaScript/JScript's operators and statements. In most cases, code for JavaScript is portable to use within Internet Explorer's JScript. There are times that are not the case. To place a client-side script using JavaScript/JScript into an HTM document, use the following tags:

```
    <script language="JavaScript">
<!--
// Place your JavaScript code here.
-->
    </script>
```

Optionally, you may specify a particular of version of JavaScript. When specifying a version of JavaScript, you run the risk of compatibility problems between your code and JScript. To refer to a specific version, provide the version number in the `<script>` anchor, such as this:

```
<script language="JavaScript 1.2">
<!--
// Place your JavaScript 1.2 code here.
-->
    </script>
```

Finally, to specify a script that will only use JScript in Microsoft Internet Explorer:

```
<script language="JScript">
<!--
// Place your JScript code here.
-->
    </script>
```

Notice that, in the preceding, HTML comment tags are included so that the browser doesn't try to interpret the script as HTML. To create server-side script, save your document with the .ASP extension and place the scripting language reference in between <% and %> tags. For example, to use JScript under Internet Information Server:

```
<% // Place your JScript code here. %>
```

 ON THE WEB

For up-to-date, comprehensive information on Microsoft JScript and other Microsoft scripting technologies, visit the Microsoft Scripting Technologies Web site at **http://www.microsoft.com/scripting/**. This site includes detailed information on JScript, VBScript, Scriptlets, script control, remote scripting, and much more.

Statements

The statements used to control program flow in JScript are similar to C++ and Java. A statement can span several lines, if needed, or you can place several statements on the same line as long as you place semicolons between all statements. The following are some of the most common JScript statements:

- ▮ // or /* */ (comment)—Indicates comment lines. Single-line comments are preceded by //. Multiple-line comments begin with /* and end with */.

- ▮ break—Terminates the current while or for loop and passes control to the first statement after the loop.

- ▮ continue—Passes control to the condition in a while loop and to the update expression in a for loop.

- ▮ for—Creates a loop with three optional expressions enclosed in parentheses and separated by semicolons, followed by a set of statements to be executed during the loop:

```
for( startExpression; condition; endExpression) {
    statements...
}
```

The initial expression is used to initialize the counter variable, which can be a new variable declared with var. The condition expression is evaluated on each pass through the loop. If the condition is true, the loop statements are executed. The update expression is used to increment the counter variable.

- ▮ for...in—Iterates a variable for all the properties of an object. For example,

```
for (variable in object) {
    statements...
}
```

For each property, it executes the statement block.

■ function—Declares a JScript function with a name and parameters. To return a value, the function must include a return statement. A function definition cannot be nested within another function. For example,

```
function name ([parameter] [...,parameter]) {
    statements...
}
```

■ if...else—Creates a conditional statement that executes the first set of statements if the condition is true, followed by the statements following else if the condition is false. If...else statements can be nested to any level, as shown here:

```
if (condition) {
  statements...
} [else {
  statements...
}]
```

■ return—Specifies a value to be returned by a function, as shown in this example:

```
return expression;
```

■ var—Declares a variable and optionally initializes it to a value. The scope of a variable is determined by where the cariable is created. If the variable is created in a function, it is only accessible within that function. When declared outside of a function, it is available to the current document. For example:

```
var variableName [=value] [..., variableName [=value]]
```

■ while—Repeats a loop while an expression is true. For example,

```
while (condition) {
    statements...
}
```

■ with—Establishes a default object for a set of statements. Any property references without an object are assumed to use the default object. For example,

```
with (object) {
    statements...
}
```

Operators

JScript supports assignment, bitwise, compound, computational, and logical operators, and operator precedence.

Assignment   The following JScript assignment operator is identical to the operator in most other programming languages:

= Assignment

Bitwise   Bitwise operators do a bit-by-bit comparison of identically positioned bits in two expressions. JScript supports the following bitwise operators:

~	Bitwise NOT
<<	Bitwise Shift Left
>>	Bitwise Shift Right
>>>	Unsigned Shift Right
&	Bitwise AND
^	Bitwise XOR
¦	Bitwise OR

Compound Assignment Operators   Compound operators perform computations with a single expression. The following compound operators are available in JScript:

+=	Addition
-=	Subtraction
*=	Multiplication
/=	Division
%=	Modulo Arithmetic
<<=	Left Shift
>>=	Right Shift
>>>=	Unsigned Right Shift
&=	Bitwise AND
¦=	Bitwise OR
^=	Bitwise XOR

Computational   Computational operators perform computations between two expressions. The following computational operators are available in JScript:

-	Unary Negation
++	Increment
- -	Decrement
*	Multiplication
/	Division
%	Modulo Arithmetic
+	Addition
-	Subtraction

Logical   Logical operators allow you to perform logical comparisons between two expressions. JScript supports the following logical operators:

!	Logical NOT
<	Less than
>	Greater than

<=	Less than or equal to
>=	Greater than or equal to
==	Equality
!=	Inequality
&&	Logical AND
¦¦	Logical OR
?:	Conditional (trinary)
,	Comma

Operator Precedence   *Precedence* is the order in which compound operations are computed. Operators on the same level have equal precedence. Calculations are computed from left to right on all binary operations, beginning with the operators at the top of the following list and working down.

Operator Name	Operator
Call, member	. [] ()
Negation/increment	++ - ! ~ -
Multiplication/division	* / %
Addition/subtraction	+ -
Shift	<< >> >>>
Relational	< > <= >=
Equality	== !=
Bitwise AND	&
Bitwise XOR	^
Bitwise OR	¦
Logical AND	&&
Logical OR	¦¦
Conditional	?:
Assignment	=
Comma	,

Objects

JavaScript/JScript includes a set of built-in objects to represent the HTML document and form elements. The availableJavaScript/JScript objects are as follow:

- ■ Array—Allows you to create arrays of any data type
- ■ Date—Stores a date in the number of milliseconds since 1/1/1970, 00:00:00, and returns a date string in the format Tue, 18 Jan 1997 07:12:00 GMT
- ■ Math—Provides numerical constants and mathematical functions

- String—Contains a string of characters
- Document—Indicates the foundation object created with an HTML <BODY> tag and used to write other information to the page
- Form—Indicates an object for gathering and echoing data, created by HTML <FORM> tags
- Window—Specifies the highest precedence object accessible by JScript relating to the current open window

Functions

The following functions are built in to Microsoft's JScript:

- escape—Encodes String objects so they can be read on all computers
- eval—Evaluates JScript code
- isNaN—Determines whether a value is the reserved value NaN (not a number)
- parseFloat—Converts String objects into floating-point numbers
- parseInt—Converts String objects into integers
- unescape—Decodes String objects encoded with the escape function

Reserved Words

The following words are reserved by JScript and cannot be used as user objects or variables in scripts:

abstract			
Boolean	finally	package	var
break	float	private	void
byte	for	protected	while
case	function	public	with
catch	goto	return	
char	if	short	
class	implements	static	
const	import	super	
continue	in	switch	
default	instanceof	synchronized	
do	int	this	
double	interface	throw	
else	long	throws	
extends	native	transient	
false	new	true	
final	null	try	

Active Server Page Scripting

Active server scripting is accomplished through the use of ASP files and the Active Server Page extensions installed on your Web server. The scripts run on the server before the HTML page is sent to the user. The following sections explain the basics of Active Server Page scripting.

The GLOBAL.ASA File

The GLOBAL.ASA file is created automatically by Visual InterDev for each new Web project you create. In it, you can specify event scripts and declare objects that have session or application scope. This file stores event information and objects used globally by the Web site. GLOBAL.ASA is typically created for you by Visual InterDev when you establish connections to a database. You can then modify the file as needed. Listing B.3 shows a sample GLOBAL.ASA file.

Listing B.3   GLOBAL.ASA—The GLOBAL.ASA File, Which Contains Variables and Information Required Throughout Your Application

```
<SCRIPT LANGUAGE=VBScript RUNAT=Server>
Sub Application_OnStart
    '==Visual InterDev Generated - startspan==
    '--Project Data Connection
        Application("SQLServer_ConnectionString") =
        ➥"DRIVER=SQL Server;SERVER=SIDESHOW;User
        ➥Id=SQLUser;PASSWORD=PasswordHere;APP=Development
        ➥Environment;WSID=QUIMBY;Trusted_Connection=Yes"
        Application("SQLServer_ConnectionTimeout") = 15
        Application("SQLServer_CommandTimeout") = 30
        Application("SQLServer_CursorLocation") = 3
        Application("SQLServer_RuntimeUserName") = "SQLUser"
        Application("SQLServer_RuntimePassword") = "PasswordHere"
    '-- Project Data Environment
        Set DE = Server.CreateObject("DERuntime.DERuntime")
        Application("DE") = DE.Load(Server.MapPath("Global.ASA"),
        ➥"_private/DataEnvironment/DataEnvironment.asa")
    '==Visual InterDev Generated - endspan==
End Sub
</SCRIPT>
```

Built-in Objects

The Active Server Pages framework provides the following five built-in objects:

- **Application**—The Application object can share information among all users of a given Web application. This includes all the ASP files in a virtual directory and its subdirectories.

- **Request**—The Request object contains the values that the client passes to the server during HTTP requests.

- ■ Response—The Response object can send output to the client.

- ■ Server—The Server object provides access to methods and properties on the server. These methods and properties are usually utility functions.

- ■ Session—The Session object stores information for each user session. Variables placed in the Session object stay persistent during the entire time a user is browsing a Web site.

Events

The following events are triggered in the GLOBAL.ASA file:

- ■ Application_OnStart—Occurs before the first new session is created (before the Session_OnStart event)

- ■ Application_OnEnd—Occurs after the Session_OnEnd event ends

- ■ Session_OnStart—Occurs when the server creates a new session just prior to executing the requested ASP page

- ■ Session_OnEnd—Occurs when a session is abandoned or times out

Cascading Style Sheets (CSS)

Cascading Style Sheets add a great deal of flexibility to your Web design. With CSS you can finally fine-tune your layout and control elements of positioning and type with a great deal of accuracy. CSS, however, is not HTML per se. It is, in fact, its own mark-up method akin to XML. By using CSS, you can enhance your Web pages appearance on a page-by-page or-site-by-site basis.

CSS Elements

CSS can redefine existing HTML formatting tags (such as <P>, <H1>, and so forth), or it can be used to create new formatting styles for your pages. CSS uses *attributes* to define styles for use in your pages. An attribute may be an existing HTML tag, or an entirely new style to be used. Attributes are grouped based on similar groupings. The following details the CSS attributes for Microsoft Internet Explorer 4. Most of these attributes will function identically in Netscape Communicator, however Netscape has additional capabilities with CSS positioning.

ON THE WEB

For information on Netscape's CSS implementation, refer to the Netscape DevEdge Web site at **http:// devedge.netscape.com**.

Font and Text Properties

- ■ font-family—Sets or retrieves the name of the font used for text in the object, such as 'Arial'.

- ■ font-style—Sets or retrieves whether the object's font style is italic, normal, or oblique.

- ■ font-variant—Sets or retrieves whether the object's text is small capitals.

- font-weight—Sets or retrieves the boldness of the object's text.
- font-size—Sets or retrieves the size of the object's text, in points, pixels or relative sizes.
- @font-face—Specifies a font to embed into the HTML document using IE 4/Netscape 4 font-embedding.
- font—Sets or retrieves the separate font attributes for text in the object.
- letter-spacing—Sets or retrieves the spacing between letters in the object, in points, pixels, or relative sizes.
- font-height—Sets or retrieves the font's height of the object.
- text-decoration—Sets or retrieves whether the text in the object has blink, line-through, overline, or underline decorations.
- text-transform—Sets or retrieves the rendering of the object's text (none, capitalize, uppercase, lowercase).
- text-align—Sets or retrieves the horizontal alignment of the object's text (left, center, right, justify).
- text-indent—Sets or retrieves the indentation for the object's text in pixels, points, or relative sizes.
- vertical-align—Sets or retrieves the vertical alignment of the object's text (top, middle, bottom).

Color and Background Properties

- color—Sets or retrieves the color of the object's text.
- background-color—Sets or retrieves the color of the object's background.
- background-image—Sets or retrieves the image of the object's background.
- background-repeat—Sets or retrieves whether the object's background is repeated (repeat, no-repeat, repeat-x, repeat-y).
- background-attachment—Sets or retrieves whether the background image scrolls (scroll) with the object's content or is fixed (fixed).
- background-position—Sets or retrieves the position of the element's background (percentage, length, top, center, bottom, left, center, right).
- background—Sets or retrieves the image of the object's background.

Layout Properties

- margin-top—Sets or retrieves the top margin of the object, in pixels, points, or relative units.
- margin-right—Sets or retrieves the right margin of the object, in pixels, points, or relative units.
- margin-left—Sets or retrieves the left margin of the object, in pixels, points, or relative units.

- margin-bottom—Sets or retrieves the bottom margin of the object, in pixels, points, or relative units.
- margin—Sets or retrieves the uniform margin of the object, in pixels, points, or relative units.
- padding-top—Sets or retrieves the top padding (spacing) of the object, in pixels, points, or relative units.
- padding-right—Sets or retrieves the right padding (spacing) of the object, in pixels, points, or relative units.
- padding-left—Sets or retrieves the left padding (spacing) of the object, in pixels, points, or relative units.
- padding-bottom—Sets or retrieves the bottom padding (spacing) of the object, in pixels, points, or relative units.
- padding—Sets or retrieves the uniform padding (spacing) of the object, in pixels, points, or relative units.
- border-top-width—Sets or retrieves the width of the top border of the object, in pixels, points, or relative units.
- border-right-width—Sets or retrieves the width of the right border of the object, in pixels, points, or relative units.
- border-left-width—Sets or retrieves the width of the left border of the object, in pixels, points, or relative units.
- border-bottom-width—Sets or retrieves the width of the bottom border of the object, in pixels, points, or relative units.
- border-width—Sets or retrieves the width of the uniform border of the object, in pixels, points, or relative units.
- border-top-color—Sets or retrieves the color of the top border of the object, in pixels, points, or relative units.
- border-right-color—Sets or retrieves the color of the right border of the object, in pixels, points, or relative units.
- border-left-color—Sets or retrieves the color of the left border of the object, in pixels, points, or relative units.
- border-bottom-color—Sets or retrieves the color of the bottom border of the object, in pixels, points, or relative units.
- border-color—Sets or retrieves the color of the uniform border of the object, in pixels, points, or relative units.
- border-top-style—Sets or retrieves the style of the top border of the object, as either none, dotted, dashed, solid, double, groove, ridge, inset, or outset.
- border-right-style—Sets or retrieves the style of the right border of the object, as either none, dotted, dashed, solid, double, groove, ridge, inset, or outset.
- border-left-style—Sets or retrieves the style of the left border of the object, as either none, dotted, dashed, solid, double, groove, ridge, inset, or outset.

- border-bottom-style—Sets or retrieves the style of the bottom border of the object, as either none, dotted, dashed, solid, double, groove, ridge, inset, or outset.
- border-style—Sets or retrieves the style of the uniform border of the object, as either none, dotted, dashed, solid, double, groove, ridge, inset, or outset.
- border-top—Sets or retrieves the border-top-width, border-top-style, and border-top-color of the object's top border.
- border-right—Sets or retrieves the border-right-width, border-right-style, and border-right-color of the object's top border.
- border-left—Sets or retrieves the border-left-width, border-left-style, and border-left-color of the object's top border.
- border-bottom—Sets or retrieves the border-bottom-width, border-bottom-style, and border-bottom-color of the object's top border.
- border—Sets or retrieves the border-width, border-style, and border-color of the object's top border.
- float—Sets or retrieves whether the object floats, causing text to flow around it, as either none, left, or right.

Classification Properties

- display—Sets or retrieves whether an object is rendered, as either block, none, inline, or list-item.
- list-style-type—Sets or retrieves whether an object is rendered, as either disc, circle, square, decimal, lower-roman, upper-roman, lower-alpha, upper-alpha, or none.
- list-style-image—Sets or retrieves which image to use as a list-item marker for the object.
- list-style-position—Sets or retrieves which image to use as a list-item marker for the object, as either inside or outside.
- list-style—Sets or retrieves three list object properties at once: list-style-image, list-style-position, and list-style-type.

Positioning Properties

- clip—Sets or retrieves which part of a positioned object is visible, as either auto or rect(top | right | bottom | left).
- height—Sets or retrieves the height of the object, as either auto, length, or a percentage.
- left—Sets or retrieves the object's position relative to the left edge of the next positioned object in the document hierarchy, as either auto, length, or a percentage.
- overflow—Sets or retrieves what should be done when the object's content exceeds the height and/or width of the object, as either auto, hidden, visible, or scroll.
- position—Retrieves the type of positioning used for the object, as either absolute, relative, or static.

- top—Sets or retrieves the object's position relative to the top edge of the next positioned object in the document hierarchy, as either auto, length, or a percentage.
- visibility—Sets or retrieves whether the content of the object is displayed, as either inherit, visible, or hidden.
- width—Sets or retrieves the width of the object, as either auto, length, or a percentage.
- z-index—Sets or retrieves the stacking order of positioned objects, as either auto or an integer referring to the position.

Printing Properties

- page-break-before—Sets or retrieves whether a page break occurs before the object and on which page (left or right) the subsequent content should resume, as either auto, always, left, or right.
- page-break-after—Sets or retrieves whether a page break occurs after the object and on which page (left or right) the subsequent content should resume, as either auto, always, left, or right.

Filter Properties

- filter—Sets or retrieves the filter or collection of filters applied to an object, as the filter type and filter parameters.

Pseudo-classes and Other Properties

- active—Sets the style of anchor when the link is engaged or "active" using standard text attributes.
- hover—Sets the style of anchor when the link is being moused over using standard text attributes.
- @import—Specifies a style sheet to import, specifying the URL.
- !important—Increases the weight or importance of a particular rule, using standard text attributes.
- cursor—Sets or retrieves the type of cursor to display as the mouse pointer moves over the object as either: auto, crosshair, default, hand, move, e-resize, ne-resize, nw-resize, n-resize, se-resize, sw-resize, s-resize, w-resize, text, wait, or help.
- link—Sets the style of anchor for a hyperlink using standard text attributes.
- visited—Sets the style of anchor when the link has been visited, using standard text attributes.

In-Line CSS

Defining styles and attributes within the HTML document is referred to as *in-line CSS*. In-line CSS can be easily added to your Web page by integrating CSS attributes inside of your HTML tag using the STYLE= attribute. Consider this example within an HTML document:

```
<H1 STYLE="font-size: 15pt; font-weight: bold">
```

This redefines this one instance of the <H1> tag in the HTML document with a font size of 15 points, and a font weight of Bold. Here's another example:

```
<IMG SRC="images/jose.gif" STYLE="margin-left: 10px; margin-right: 10px">
```

The above example illustrates adding a left and right margin of 10 pixels to an image.

Embedding a Style Block

Another method of defining CSS styles within a page is by using *style blocks*. A style block is a definition that is available throughout the entire Web page. A style block can redefine the attributes of an HTML tag, or create a new style for the page. Style blocks are defined between the <HEAD></HEAD> tags of the document using a <STYLE> tag:

```
<HEAD>
        <TITLE>My Document</TITLE>
        <STYLE TYPE="text/css">
        // Your CSS Definitions Here
        </STYLE>
</HEAD>
```

The TYPE="text/css" is used to insure that the Web browser properly recognizes your definitions as style sheet information. Here's an example of style blocks in use:

```
<HEAD>
        <TITLE>My Document</TITLE>
        <STYLE TYPE="text/css">
        <!--
        BODY { font-size: 10pt; font-family: "Arial"; left-margin: 10px )
        H1 { font-size: 15pt; font-weight: bold")
        .CAPTION { font-decoration: italics }
        -->
        </STYLE>
</HEAD>
```

The style block definition is enclosed in HTML comment tags, so that the information will be ignored by browsers that do not support CSS. Each style definition either redefines an existing tag or creates a new one. By using the name of an existing tag in a style block, you are overriding its normal attributes with your new CSS selections. With your style block in place, these styles are available throughout the current document. Redefined HTML tags can be used as if there were no changes; however, CSS-capable browsers will see your definitions. New tags must be specified using the CLASS= attribute. For example:

```
<P CLASS="CAPTION">This is a figure caption.</P>
```

You can also specify a class by enclosing the affected objects in <DIV></DIV> and <SPAN> </SPAN> tags, such as:

```
<DIV CLASS="CAPTION">This is a caption as well. It also contains an
<IMG SRC="images/jose.gif"> image file that is impacted by the style
definition.</DIV>
```

Linking to External CSS

The final way of using style sheets is to link to an external CSS file. This method is very similar to style blocks; however, the defined styles are available to any page within your Web site that references the CSS file. To link to an external CSS file, insert the following between your document's <HEAD></HEAD> tags:

```
<LINK REL=STYLESHEET HREF="http://www.server.dom/mystyles.css" TYPE="text/css">
```

The styles can then be used throughout the document, just as if they were defined as style blocks.

Glossary

This glossary contains terms related to Visual InterDev and the Internet. Even though acronyms with the Internet and Microsoft change on a daily basis, this glossary includes as many as possible. Cross-references for acronyms direct you to the correct entries. Cross-references to related topics (shown in boldface) are listed at the ends of the definitions.

1-Bit Color   The number of colors per *pixel* a particular graphics file can store. Having 1-bit color means that each pixel is represented by one bit, which has only one of two states or colors. The 1-bit pixels are either black or white. (See also **Color Depth**.)

8-Bit Color/Grayscale   Having 8-bit color means that each pixel is represented by eight bits, which can have 256 colors or shades of gray (as in a *grayscale* image). (See also **Color Depth** and **Grayscale**.)

24-Bit Color   A 24-bit color provides 16.7 million colors per *pixel*. The 24 bits are divided into 3 *bytes*: one each for the red, green, and blue components of a pixel. (See also **Color Depth**, **True Color**, and **Channel**.)

2B+D   The ISDN Basic Rate Interface (BRI) that consists of a single ISDN circuit divided into two 64Kbps digital channels for voice or data and one 16Kbps channel for low-speed data and signaling. 2B+D is carried on one or two pairs of wires. (See also **BRI** and **ISDN**.)

3D Graphics   The process of creating three-dimensional models within the computer's memory, setting up lights, and applying textures. After the computer is told from which angle to view the 3D scene, it generates an image that simulates the conditions defined in the scene. Three-dimensional animation involves the same steps but sets up the choreography, or movement, of the 3D objects, lights, or cameras. (See also **Texture Mapping**.)

Access   (See **Microsoft Access**.)

Active Server Application (ASA)   An Active Server Page (.ASP) containing global session settings and information. This file is used for maintaining global behaviors and attributes for a web application. Typically used for establishing database connections and maintaining session controls. (See also **Active Server Pages (.ASP)**.)

Active Server Page (.ASP)   A Web page or file that includes server-side script executed by Microsoft Internet Information Server. The .ASP extension alerts the server that the file should be processed before sending it to the client's browser. After it is processed, it is delivered to the browser in the same manner as an HTML file. (See also **Active Server Application**.)

ActiveMovie   A Microsoft technology for streaming video content across the Internet.

ActiveX Control Container   A program capable of running an ActiveX control.

ActiveX Controls   Small software components used by larger applications to accomplish a specific task. These controls can be downloaded and installed on-the-fly as needed. They have .OCX filename extensions. ActiveX controls can be written in virtually any language such as Java, C++, or Visual Basic. (See also **OLE Control**.)

ActiveX Data Objects (ADO)   A cross-language technology for accessing data based on an object model that incorporates data connection objects, data command objects, and recordset objects. (See also **Data Command**, **Data Connection**, **Data Environment**, and **Recordset**.)

Advanced Data Connector (ADC)   A distributed data access technology for the Web. Microsoft's Advanced Data Connector provides data manipulation over retrieved data, client-side caching, and integration with data-aware ActiveX controls.

Advanced Data TableGram Streaming Protocol (ADTG) An application protocol for streaming database data over HTTP. It defines a concept for a tablegram, a self-describing data blob that supports transport of any type of data.

Alpha Channel An additional piece of information stored for a pixel that represents the pixel's transparency. An image, composed of many *pixels*, often has a separate channel for red, green, and blue. (See also **Pixel** and **Channel**.)

Animation The illusion of movement caused by the rapid display of a series of still images. When each image differs slightly, and the images are viewed at speeds of over 10 per second, the eye perceives motion.

Antialiasing The process of smoothing edges where the individual pixels are visible. Antialiasing removes the stair-stepping effect caused by large square pixels that the eye can see.

Applet A Java program that can be embedded within an HTML page and run within a Java-enabled browser.

Argument Data passed to a procedure.

Array In *programming*, a fundamental data structure consisting of a single or multidimensional table that the program treats as one data item. Any information in the array can be referenced by naming the array and the location of the item in the array. Each piece of information in the array is called an *element*.

ASCII Character Set American Standard Code for Information Interchange. A standard code that assigns a unique binary number to each character in the English alphabet along with other special characters. The first 128 characters (0 through 127) in the ANSI character set are identical to those in the ASCII character set.

Aspect Ratio The height-to-width ratio of an image. (The standard for a television frame is 4:3.)

Automation Object Microsoft's new term to describe objects exposed to other applications or programming tools through Automation interfaces.

B Channel An ISDN communication channel that carries voice, circuit, or packet conversations. The B channel is the fundamental component of ISDN interfaces and carries 64,000 bits per second in either direction. (See also **ISDN**.)

Backbone A high-speed network for networked computers.

Bandwidth The amount of data that can be sent through a connection, usually measured in bits per second (bps).

Binary Having only two states, On and Off, or 0 and 1. A light switch could be considered a *binary* switch because it is either on or off, and no other settings are possible.

Bit A *binary* unit of storage that can represent only one of two values: On and Off, or 0 and 1 (BInary digiT).

App

C

Bitwise Comparison A comparison of two numeric expressions made by examining the position of their bits. (See also **Bit** and **Byte**.)

Blurring Filter A special effects filter that simulates an out-of-focus photograph.

BMP A BitMaP file. A graphics file format used as a standard for the Microsoft *Windows GUI*. It stores *raster graphics* images. (See also **File Format** and **Raster Graphics**.)

Boolean Expression An expression that evaluates to either True or False.

Bounding Box A square box created by clicking and dragging the mouse. Often used in graphical user interfaces to select an object or group of objects on the screen.

BRI (Basic Rate Interface) The most common ISDN interface available. It uses two B channels, each with 64Kbps capacity, and a single D channel (16Kbps) for signaling. (See also **ISDN**.)

Brightness A component of the HSB (Hue, Saturation, and Brightness) color model. For RGB pixels, the largest component value is the brightness. (See also **HSB** and **RGB**.)

Browse To navigate the World Wide Web. Also known as cruising and surfing the Web.

Burning Darkening specific areas of a photograph. Originally used in the darkroom with traditional photographic equipment, this process is now simulated by all image-editing programs. (See also **Dodging** and **Painting Tool**.)

By Reference A method of passing the address of an argument to a procedure instead of the value. This capability allows the procedure to change the variable's actual value. (See also **Argument** and **By Value**.)

By Value A method of passing the value of an argument to a procedure instead of the address. This capability allows the procedure to access a copy of the variable without changing the variable's actual value. (See also **Argument** and **By Reference**.)

Byte A unit of storage composed of eight *bits*. It can store a numeric value from 0 to 255 (decimal) or one letter. (See also **Bit**.)

Cascading Style Sheets A set of tags that describe the appearance of HTML tags. Style sheets can describe the font, color, alignment and other attributes for common HTML tags such as headings, paragraphs, and lists. Style sheets can be defined in a Web page, in a tag, or in a separate CSS file. Style sheet information is used only by browsers that support the standard.

Chatting Talking in real-time to other network users from any and all parts of the world, either through text or multimedia-based methods.

CGI Common Gateway Interface. A standard that describes how Web servers should access external programs that can return data in the format of a Web page. CGI programs are commonly called scripts.

Channel One piece of information stored with an image. *True Color* images, for example, have three *channels*: red, green, and blue.

Character Code   A number used to represent a character in a set, such as the ASCII character set. (See also **ASCII Character Set**.)

Class   In *programming*, a formal definition of an object's properties and methods. It acts as the template from which an instance of an object is created at runtime. (See also **Object**, **Methods**, and **Properties**.)

Class Module   The definition of a class' properties and methods. (See also **Object**, **Class**, **Methods**, and **Properties**.)

Client/Server Architecture   A design model for applications running on a network in which the bulk of the back-end processing—such as performing a physical search of a database—takes place on a server. The front-end processing, which involves communicating with the user, is handled by smaller programs distributed to the client workstations. This architecture is commonly used for database systems. (See also **Database** and **Structured Query Language**.)

Clone Tool   A popular tool in image-editing programs that allows small groups of pixels to be copied from one location to another. (See also **Painting Tool**.)

CMYK   The four colors used for color printing: Cyan, Magenta, Yellow, and Black. (See also **Color Separation**.)

Collection   A special type of object that contains a set of other objects. (See also **Object**.)

Color Correction   The process of correcting or enhancing the color of an image.

Color Depth   The amount of color stored in an image expressed in *bits*. An image with a 24-bit color depth can have 16.7 million colors. An image with 8-bit color depth can have only 256 colors or shades of gray. (See also **1-Bit**, **8-Bit**, and **24-Bit**.)

Color Model   A method of describing color. (See also **HLS**, **HSB**, and **RGB**.)

Color Similarity   A description of how close two different colors are to each other within the respective color model being used. (See also **Color Model**.)

Comment   Information added to a program to document how the code works.

Comparison Operator   (See **Relational Operator**.)

Compositing   The process of merging two or more images together digitally.

Compression   A means by which the amount of data required to store a computer file is reduced. (See also **File Format**, **Fractal Compression**, **Lossey**, **JPEG**, **Huffman Encoding**, **Run Length Encoding**, and **LZW**.)

Computer Generated   Created on or by the computer. Any image that was not scanned in from an existing original.

Control   (See **ActiveX Controls**, **Object**, and **OLE Control**.)

App

C

Constant   A variable in a program that always remains the same. Constants make programming easier because a name can be used to refer to a value instead of the value itself. For example,

```
Const MyForm = Window.Document.Form("DataCollection")
```

Cookie   A small piece of data used to store persistent information on the user's computer in the form of a file.

Cropping Tool   A tool that simulates the traditional method of cropping or trimming photographs. (See also **Painting Tool**.)

Custom Filter   A special image filter that can be defined by the user. Values are entered on a matrix grid. Those values, in turn, determine how the filter affects each pixel in an image.

D Channel   An ISDN communication channel for sending information between the ISDN equipment and the ISDN central office switch. (See also **ISDN**.)

Data Binding   Using data-aware ActiveX controls to directly manipulate databases.

Data Command   An object in the data environment used to access a database object (such as a table, stored procedure, script, or view). Commands are used within Web pages to interact with databases. (See also **ActiveX Data Object (ADO)**, **Data Connection**, **Data Environment**, and **Recordset**.)

Data Connection   A collection of information used by a Visual InterDev project to communicate with a database. The collection includes a data source name (DSN) and logon information. (See also **ActiveX Data Object (ADO)**, **Data Command**, **Data Environment**, and **Recordset**.)

Data Diagram   A graphical representation of any portion of a database schema. (See also **Schema**.)

Data Environment   A repository in Visual InterDev projects that holds database access information in the form of data connections and data commands. (See also **ActiveX Data Object (ADO)**, **Data Command**, **Data Connection**, and **Recordset**.)

Data Ranges   The allowable range of data that a particular variable can accept.

Data Type   A classification for both programming variables and database fields. Common data types include numeric, string, date, and so on.

Date Expression   Any type of value that can be interpreted as a date. It can be a string or number that represents a date. Dates are usually stored as part of a floating-point number with the values to the left of the decimal representing the date and the values to the right of the decimal representing the time.

Database   A collection of related information stored in a structured, organized way. Using this structured collection, standard methods of retrieving data can be used. (See also **Queries**, **Tables**, **Records**, and **Fields**.)

Default Setting Typically used in computer programs to set any variables or values to a common setting or setting that is most likely to be used.

Despeckle Filter A special filter that removes any specks from the image. It actually blurs the entire image except for any edges.

Dialog Box Any type of screen in a graphical user interface that displays or requests information from the user.

Diffusion Dithering A method of dithering that randomly distributes pixels instead of using a set pattern. (See also **Dithering**.)

Digital A form of representation in which information or objects (digits) are broken down into separate pieces. Numbers are examples of *digital* information. *Digital* is the opposite of *Analog* information, such as sound and light waves.

Digital Painting Creating artwork on a computer directly as opposed to using traditional media and scanning the artwork.

Digital Signature A security technique consisting of attaching a code to a software component that identifies the vendor of the component.

Digital-to-Analog Converter (DAC) A tool that converts *digital* information, such as numeric data, into analog information, such as a sound waves.

Digitizing The process of converting analog information into a digital format. Recording sound into a computer and capturing video or pictures on a computer are considered digitizing. (See also **Scanning**.)

Directories Electronic areas on a computer disk for storing data files—similar to storing letters in a folder. A directory can be considered an electronic folder. (See also **File**.)

Dithering A method of simulating many colors with only a few. If a limited number of color dots are placed closely together, the eye blends them into a new color. (See also **Diffusion Dithering**.)

Dodging Lightening specific areas of a photograph. Originally used in the darkroom with traditional photographic equipment, this process is now simulated by all image-editing programs. (See also **Burning**.)

Domain Name (See **Domain Name Service**.)

Domain Name Service (DNS) A program that runs on an Internet-connected computer system (called a DNS server) and provides an automatic translation between domain names (such as netst.com) and IP addresses (such as 207.199.32.76). The purpose of this translation process, called resolution, is to allow Internet users to use simple domain names to reference computers as opposed to IP addresses.

DPI Dots Per Inch. A resolution for scanning and printing devices. (See also **Scanning**.)

Dynamic HTML (DHTML)   An extension to HTML that allows all elements in a Web page to be treated as scriptable objects. Using DHTML, the appearance, content, and behavior of a Web page can be directly altered by a client-side script.

Emboss   A common image processing filter that simulates the look of a picture that is embossed on paper or metal.

Empty   A value that indicates that no beginning value has been assigned to a variable. Empty variables are 0 in a numeric context or zero-length in a string context.

Encryption   The process of converting information into codes that cannot be deciphered.

EPS   An Encapsulated PostScript graphics file. This format can store both *raster* and *vector* graphics. (See also **File Format, Raster Graphics**, and **Vector Graphics**.)

Equalization   A method of enhancing an image by evenly distributing the color or gray values of pixels throughout the image.

Error Number   A number representing the current error condition of a program. A property of the Error Object. (See also **Error Object**.)

Error Object   A common programming object used to trap errors. (See also **Error Number**.)

Event   When a user clicks or otherwise manipulates objects in a Web page or ActiveX control, an event is generated. The program or script can then respond to this event. For example, when a button object is used, the process of actually clicking the button triggers a "click" event.

Expression   A line of instructions in a program to accomplish a given task.

Extranet   An area of a Web site accessible only to a set of registered visitors beyond the internal network. (See also **Intranet**.)

Eye Dropper Tool   An image-editing tool used to select a color from the current image.

Fade   In film or video, the smooth transition from one sequence to another. Often fades are made to a solid color such as black.

FAQ (Frequently Asked Questions)   A list that attempts to answer the most-asked questions on a given topic. Many FAQs are transmitted monthly over Usenet and are archived on the Internet.

Field   A space reserved for a particular type of information stored in a database. For example, if the telephone book were a database, the fields would be Name, Address, and Phone. A field also is a column of a data table. (See also **Database**, **Table**, and **Record**.)

FIF   The Fractal Image Format. A method of storing *raster graphics* and compressing them with *fractal transform* formulas. (See also **File Format, Raster Graphics**, and **Fractal Transform**.)

File   A collection of data organized on some type of storage media such as a *hard disk* or a *floppy disk*.

File Format   The specific type of organization a given file uses. Some file formats are strictly for word processing documents (such as DOC files), whereas others are for graphics or images (such as BMP, GIF, JPG, and so on). Most file formats support some form of data compression to save storage space. (See also **Compression.**)

Fill Tool   A common painting tool used to fill a solid area with color. (See also **Painting Tool.**)

Firewall   A security procedure that sets up a barrier between an internal LAN and the Internet. Commonly implemented by software on a network server, it prevents hackers from gaining access to an internal network.

Floating Palettes   Groups of icons grouped together that perform functions. Palettes can be freely positioned anywhere on the screen with a *graphical user interface.* (See also **Icons.**)

FoxPro   (See **Microsoft Visual FoxPro.**)

Fractal Compression   A compression method developed by Michael Barnsley. It reduces images to a series of fractal-based formulas for very high compression levels. (See also **File Format**, **Fractal Graphics**, **FIF**, and **Compression.**)

App

C

Function   A group of program instructions stored under a name so that it can be executed as a unit and return a value. (See also **Procedure.**)

Gamma   A measure of contrast that affects the middle tones in an image.

Gaussian Blur   A blurring filter that can be adjusted to provide very high levels of blurring. (See also **Blurring Filter.**)

GIF   The Graphics Interchange Format. A common graphics format for storing *raster graphics.* This format was made popular by the CompuServe online service and is supported by a number of *hardware* platforms. (See also **File Format** and **Raster Graphics.**)

Gigabyte   A unit of computer storage representing one billion *bytes.* (See also **Byte.**)

Gradient Fill   An enhancement to the Fill tool that fills an area with a gradual transition from one color to another.

Gray/Color Correction   The process of adjusting the gray or color levels of an image to enhance its quality.

Gray/Color Map   A method of adjusting the gray or color levels in an image. A 2D line graph represents the incoming and outgoing brightness or color values.

Grayscale   An image that contains continuous tones from white to black.

GUID (Globally Unique ID)   A sequence of letters and numbers that uniquely identify each OLE component registered on a computer system. When OLE objects are embedded in Web pages, this ID specifies which objects are to be used. These IDs are stored in the Windows 95 or Windows NT system registries.

Halftone   The *screening* of a continuous-tone image into small dots of varying sizes. (See also **Screening**.)

Highlight   The lightest areas of an image.

HLS (Hue, Lightness, and Saturation)   A color model based on the Hue, Lightness, and Saturation of a color. (See also **Color Model**, **Hue**, **Saturation**, and **Lightness**.)

Home page   The first Web page of a Web site.

HSB (Hue, Saturation, and Brightness)   A color model based on the Hue, Saturation, and Brightness of a color. (See also **Color Model**, **Hue**, **Saturation**, and **Brightness**.)

HTML (Hypertext Markup Language)   The language used to create conventional Web pages.

HTTP (Hypertext Transfer Protocol)   The native communications scheme of the World Wide Web, initially used to transfer hypertext documents.

HTTP Server   Hypertext Transfer Protocol Server; a computer (server) that serves HTML documents.

Hue   Another term used to describe color. Hue usually represents the color without its brightness or *saturation*.

Huffman Compression   A method of compressing data developed by David Huffman in 1952. Commonly used to compress graphics files. (See also **File Format** and **Compression**.)

Hyperlink   A reference in HTML to another hypertext segment.

Hypertext   A system of writing and displaying text that enables the text to be linked in several ways. Hypertext documents can also contain links to related documents, such as those referred to in footnotes. Hypermedia can also contain pictures, sounds, and video.

Icons   Small graphics symbols used to represent programs, data, or other functions within a *graphical user interface*.

Imagemap   A graphic image embedded within a Web page that supplies different links, based on where the cursor is clicked within its borders.

Image Processing   The capture and manipulation of images in order to enhance or extract information.

Internet   A worldwide system of linked computer networks for data communication services such as remote login, World Wide Web, electronic mail, file transfer, and newsgroups. The Internet provides a way of connecting existing computer networks that greatly extends the reach of each participating system. Originally designed to withstand a nuclear attack, today the Internet spans almost every national border on the Earth. (See also **Intranet**.)

Intranet   An internal network designed around existing Internet standard protocols such as http. (See also **Internet**.)

Intrinsic Constant   A constant parameter built into an application. (See also **Constants**.)

Invert Filter   A filter that inverts the pixel values of an image, creating a negative.

IP (Internet Protocol)   In TCP/IP, the standard that describes how an Internet-connected computer should break down data into packets for transmission across the network, and how those packets should be addressed so they arrive at their destination.

ISAPI (Internet Server Application Programming Interface)   A standard method to write programs that communicate with Web servers through OLE.

ISDN (Integrated Services Digital Network)   A digital telephone network that carries voice, data, and video information over the existing telephone wiring. It offers up to 10 times the speed of normal analog data transmission.

Jaggies   The jagged "stair-stepping" effect often seen in images in which the *resolution* is so small that the individual *pixels* are visible. (See also **Antialiasing**.)

Java   A development language that allows Web developers to create applications for the Internet. Java is based on the C++ development language, and the resulting applications can be executed on any computer platform: Macintosh, PC, or UNIX.

JavaScript   A language created by Netscape that can be used to expand the capabilities of a Web page. Like VBScript, JavaScript instructions are embedded within an HTML document for a page. JavaScript is based on the Java language, which is similar to C++. (See also **JScript**.)

JScript   The Microsoft implementation of JavaScript. Although fundamentally the same as JavaScript, it does have some differences and compatibility problems. Most conflicts arise out of JavaScript features that are not present in JScript. (See also **JavaScript**.)

JPEG   A file format and compression method for storing images named after the committee that developed it (Joint Photographic Experts Group). The JPEG compression algorithm is a *lossey* compression technique. (See also **File Format** and **Lossey Compression**.)

Keyword   A reserved word or symbol in a programming language.

Kilobyte   A unit of storage that represents one thousand *bytes*. Often referred to as KB, as in 640KB. (See also **Byte**.)

Lightness   A component of the HLS color space. It is determined by taking the average maximum and minimum values in each RGB channel. Sometimes called Luminance. (See also **HLS**, **Color Model**, and **Channel**.)

Local Mode   The state of a Web project that allows a developer to modify copies of files on the local workstation without affecting the master Web files. (See also **Master Mode**.)

Lossey Compression   A method of compressing images by throwing away unneeded data. JPEG is a lossey compression method. (See also **File Format** and **JPEG**.)

LPI   Lines Per Inch. A measure of resolution, often used to describe screens. (See also **Resolution** and **Screening**.)

LZW (Lempel Ziv Welch)   A compression algorithm based on work done by Abraham Lempel, Jacob Ziv, and Terry Welch. Commonly used for compressing graphics files. (See also **File Format** and **Compression**.)

App
C

Magic Wand   A painting tool that selects any range of similar, adjoining colors. Most magic wand tools include a similarity or tolerance setting. (See also **Painting Tool**.)

Mask   A special type of image that can be used as a stencil or mask for any painting operation that might be made.

Master Mode   The state of a Web project that allows a developer to directly modify the master Web files on the Web server as changes are made. (See also **Local Mode**.)

Megabyte   A unit of storage that represents one million *bytes*. Often referred to as a "Meg." (See also **Byte**.)

Menu Bar   In *graphical user interfaces,* a bar that organizing groups of commands in *menus* along the top of a program's window. (See also **Menus**.)

Menus   Groups of related commands provided in a list that drops down from a *menu bar.* Used in *graphical user interfaces.* (See also **Menu Bar** and **GUI**.)

Metafile   A type of file format for graphics that stores both *raster* and *vector* graphics. (See also **File Format**.)

Methods   The actions that can be taken against an object. For example, to add a new item to a list box object, the additem method can be called. (See also **Object** and **Properties**.)

Microsoft Access   Microsoft's entry-level database management system that ships with Microsoft Office Professional. (See also **Database**, **Microsoft Visual FoxPro**, and **Microsoft SQL Server**.)

Microsoft Developer Studio   Microsoft's integrated development environment. Used for Visual InterDev, Visual C++, and Visual J++. (See also **Microsoft Visual InterDev**, **Microsoft Visual C++**, and **Microsoft Visual J++**.)

Microsoft FrontPage   Microsoft's entry-level Web site publishing tool. It is compatible with Web sites built with Visual InterDev. (See also **Microsoft Visual InterDev**.)

Microsoft SQL Server   Microsoft's high-end, client/server database application. (See also **Database**, **Client/Server**, **Microsoft Access**, and **Microsoft Visual FoxPro**.)

Microsoft Visual C++   Microsoft's C++ language development environment that runs in Developer Studio. (See also **Database**, **Java**, and **Microsoft Developer Studio**.)

Microsoft Visual FoxPro   Microsoft's mid-level database management system. (See also **Database**, **Microsoft Access**, and **Microsoft SQL Server**.)

Microsoft Visual InterDev   A rapid application development tool for building data-driven Web sites. (See also **Database** and **Web Sites**.)

Microsoft Visual J++   Microsoft's Java language development environment that runs in Developer Studio. (See also **Database**, **Java**, and **Microsoft Developer Studio**.)

MIME (Multipurpose Internet Mail Extension)   A method for transmitting binary files across the Internet.

Name Server   A computer that provides translation between alphabetical Internet domain names and numerical IP addresses. (See also **Internet**, **Domain Name**, and **IP Address**.)

NI1 (National ISDN 1)   A common standard specification for ISDN phone lines. (See also **ISDN**.)

Noise Filter   An image *filter* that adds random noise (pixels) to an image to simulate a grainy look.

Nothing   A value that, when assigned to an object variable, removes it from its object. (See also **Objects**.)

NT-1 (Network Termination 1)   A device required to connect ISDN terminal equipment to an ISDN line.

Null   A value that represents no valid data.

Object   A modular, self-contained program that can be included in larger projects or combined with other objects to create an application. Objects have both methods and properties. Methods allow the object to perform an action, and properties store data related to the object. (See also **ActiveX Controls** and **OLE Control**.)

ODBC   Open Database Connectivity. A standard protocol for database servers. If a database has an ODBC driver, it can be connected with almost any industry standard database tool. (See also **Database**.)

OLE Control   Small software components that accomplish a specific task, such as provide a radio button, command button, or combo box. These controls greatly simplify the task of writing software for complex graphical user interfaces. (See **ActiveX Controls** and **Object**.)

Paint Palette   An electronic version of an artist's palette. It allows the user to select from a wide variety of colors or even mix new ones.

Paintbrush   A *painting tool* that simulates painting with a paintbrush. (See also **Painting Tool**.)

Painting Tool   A command or function of an image-editing program that simulates a traditional art or photographic tool. The *Paintbrush tool* is an example of a painting tool that simulates paintbrush strokes.

PC PaintBrush Format (PCX)   A graphics file format that stores *raster* graphics. Made popular by ZSoft's PC PaintBrush program. (See also **File Format**.)

PCD   The Photo CD format. Kodak uses this graphics file format to store images on Photo CDs. (See also **File Format**, **Raster Graphics**, and **Photo CD**.)

PCX   The graphics file format created by ZSoft's PC PaintBrush program. This graphics file format stores *raster graphics images*. (See also **File Format** and **Raster Graphics**.)

Pencil Tool   A *painting tool* that simulates drawing with a sharp pencil. (See also **Painting Tool**.)

App

C

Photo CD   A new technology developed by Eastman Kodak to scan high resolution 35mm or professional-quality images and write them to a *CD-ROM*. The resulting PCD (Photo CD) can be viewed with consumer players that attach to televisions. They can also be viewed on personal computers that have *multisession*-compatible *CD-ROM* drives.

Photoshop   An image-editing program available from Adobe Systems.

Pixel   A picture element. The smallest element of an image that has been *digitized* into a computer. The more pixels per square inch, the higher the resolution of the image will be.

Pixellization   The effect when the *pixels* making up an image are so large that they are visible. (See also **Mosaic Filter**.)

Private   A procedure or variable that is visible only to its current procedure. (See also **Scope**, **Public**, and **Procedure**.)

Procedural Textures   The use of shaders, or small pieces of programming code, for describing 3D surfaces, lighting effects, and atmospheric effects. (See also **Shaders**.)

Procedure   A group of program instructions stored under a name so that it can be executed as a unit. (See also **Function**.)

Process Color   The four color pigments used in color printing. (See also **CMYK**.)

Property   Data associated with an object. For example, a label object has a `caption` property, which stores the text displayed as the label's caption. (See also **Object** and **Methods**.)

Proxy Server   An intermediary server that acts as a security barrier between an internal network and the Internet.

Public   A procedure or variable that is visible to all parts of a program. Variables declared using the `Public` statement are visible to all procedures in all modules in all applications. (See also **Scope**, **Private**, and **Procedure**.)

Raster Graphics   Computer graphics in which the images are stored as groups of *pixels*, as opposed to *vector graphics*, which are stored as groups of lines. (See also **File Format** and **Vector Graphics**.)

Record   A collection of related data in a database. For example, if the telephone book were a database, a record would be all the information about a single person. (See also **Database**, **Table**, and **Field**.)

Recordset   An ActiveX Data Object used by Visual InterDev to display information from a data command in a Web page. (See also **ActiveX Data Object (ADO)**, **Data Command**, **Data Connection**, and **Data Environment**.)

Registry   A database within the Windows 95 and Windows NT operating systems that contains information about a computer and its configuration.

Relational Operator   A symbol used to specify a relationship between two pieces of data. The result of using a calculation with relational operators is always a Boolean (True or False).

Render To create a new image based on a transformation of an existing one or a three-dimensional scene. (See also **Morphing**.)

Resize To alter the resolution or the horizontal or vertical size of an image.

Resolution For computer displays, their height and width in pixels; for images, the height and width in pixels; and for output devices, the dots-per-inch they can produce.

Reverse Cropping The process of artificially extending the boundaries of an image to obtain more space. Performed by duplicating existing elements in the image.

RGB (Red, Green, and Blue) A color model that describes color based on percentages of red, green, and blue. Commonly used by computers and television to produce or simulate color. (See also **Color Model**, **HLS**, and **HSB**.)

Ripple Filter A filter that creates fluid ripples in an image, simulating waves in water.

Runtime In programming, the time when a program is running.

Runtime Error A programming error that manifests itself only while the program is running.

Saturation The degree to which color is undiluted by white light. If a color is 100 percent saturated, it contains no white light. If a color has no saturation, it is a shade of gray.

Scan Rate A measurement of how many times per second a scanner samples an image; also, a measurement for the speed that a monitor's electron beam scans from left to right and top to bottom.

Scanline A single line of pixels displayed on a computer monitor to be scanned in by a *scanner*. (See also **Scanner**.)

Scanner A *hardware* device for converting light from a source picture or transparency into a digital representation.

Schema A description of a database to the database management system.

Scope The *visibility* of a variable, procedure, or object. Scope is either public or private. (See also **Private**, **Public**, and **Procedure**.)

Screening The process of converting a grayscale image to patterns of black and white dots that can be printed commercially. In the case of color images, the color is split into primaries, and they, in turn, are individually screened. Those screens are then printed in their respective primary colors, and the original color image reappears.

Script Level Any scripting code located outside a procedure.

Selection An area of computer data that is currently chosen to perform some type of operation.

Selection Border An option used to select only the border of the current selection. (See also **Selection**.)

Server   A software package connected to a network that supplies information or services based on the requests of a connecting client program.

Session   The course of a visit by a user to a Web site.

Shadow   The darkest area of an image.

Shareware   Computer software that is copyrighted but still made available for anyone on a trial basis. If the user decides to keep and use the software, he or she is expected to pay a registration fee to the author.

Sharpening   A process that increases contrast between pixels, with the end result of a more defined looking image. (See also **Smoothing**.)

Shockwave   An extension for the Web that allows users to view multimedia content originally authored with Macromedia tools such as Director, Authorware, and Flash.

Slider   A method of entering numeric values used in *graphical user interfaces*. If the slider is moved back and forth, numeric values can be adjusted.

Smoothing   A process that averages pixels with their neighbors, thus reducing contrast and simulating an out-of-focus image. (See also **Sharpening**.)

Solorization   The photographic effect of reducing the number of colors in an image. This effect is also simulated by many image-editing programs.

Solution   A Visual Studio container that holds the elements that comprise multiple projects. These projects may be Web applications or database connections. (See also **Web Application**.)

Sphere Filter   A special effects filter that simulates wrapping the current image around a three-dimensional sphere.

SPID (Service Profile Identifier)   A unique identification number for each ISDN modem. (See also **ISDN**.)

SQL   (See **Structured Query Language**.)

SQL Server   (See **Microsoft SQL Server**.)

S/T Interface   Used with a four-wire ISDN circuit, it connects an ISDN line that connects to the terminal equipment or ISDN modem. (See also **ISDN**.)

Status Bar   An information bar common in *graphical user interfaces*. Status bars display important information about the current status of the document or file in use.

String   A data type for containing alphanumeric characters.

Structured Query Language (SQL)   In database management systems, an IBM-developed query language widely used in mainframe and minicomputer systems. It's also gaining acceptance on PC-based local area networks (LANs). SQL is an elegant and concise query language with only 30 commands. The four basic commands (SELECT, INSERT, UPDATE, and DELETE) correspond to the four basic functions of data manipulation (data retrieval, data insertion, data modification, and data deletion, respectively). SQL queries approximate the structure of the English natural-language query. A data table consisting of columns (corresponding to fields) and rows (corresponding to records) displays a query's results. (See also **Database**, **Record**, **SQL Server**, and **Field**.)

T1   A high-bandwidth telephone trunk line that can transfer 1.544 megabits per second (Mbps) of data. (See also **T3**.)

T3   A very high-bandwidth telephone trunk line that can transfer 44.21 megabits per second (Mbps) of data. (See also **T1**.)

Table   A group of related information in a database. Tables are collections of rows of records storing a particular type of data. (See also **Database**, **Record**, and **Field**.)

Tagged Image File Format (TIFF)   A common file format that can store both *raster* and *vector* graphics information. (See also **File Format**, **Raster Graphics**, and **Vector Graphics**.)

Targa Format (TGA)   A file format originally designed for storing video images. Since then, it has been enhanced to include high-resolution images in *raster* format. (See also **File Format**.)

TCP/IP (Transmission Control Protocol/Internet Protocol)   The set of communications protocols the Internet uses to communicate.

Texture Mapping   The process of applying a 2D image to a 3D object defined within the computer. Similar to wrapping wallpaper around the object. This process allows computer artists to simulate items such as wood by scanning in an image of wood grain and having the computer texture map the wood to a 3D model of a board. Developed by Ed Catmull in 1974. (See also **3D Graphics**.)

Theme   A set of combined graphics, fonts, and elements that create a consistent visual design for a Web site or page.

Title Bar   The top bar across any window in a *graphical user interface*. The title bar usually includes the name of the program or data file currently in use. The active window can be moved by clicking and dragging a title bar.

Trace Contour   A filter that looks for edges and then traces them while making all the different solid colors in the image the same color. This has the effect of simulating a drawing.

Transaction   A server operation that succeeds or fails as a whole, even if the operation involves many sub-steps. This process is usually monitored using a Transaction Server. (See also **Transaction Server**.)

Transaction Server   A server component that is used to monitor and evaluate the completion of transactions, such as ordering or billing. Determines whether the complete transaction has succeeded and how to resolve incomplete transactions. (See also **Transaction**.)

True Color   Color that has a color depth of 24 bits (16.7 million colors). (See also **Color Depth** and **24-Bit**.)

App

C

U Interface　A two-wire ISDN circuit, the most common ISDN interface.

Undo Option　A command that undoes the last operation performed.

URL (Uniform Resource Locator)　The site- and file-addressing scheme for the World Wide Web.

Variable　A storage location of data assigned to a meaningful name. This allows the program to alter and reference the data regardless of what it is.

Vector Graphics　Graphics that are based on individual lines from point A to point B. Vector graphics represent line drawings well but cannot represent photographs. For photographs, *raster graphics* are required. Early computer graphics displays used vector graphics. (See also **File Format** and **Raster Graphics**.)

Virtual Root　The directory that appears to be a subfolder to a Web server, although it may physically reside on a different file system or server.

Web Application　A collection of elements (Web pages, database objects, and so on) that make up a complete Web site or distinct portion of a Web site under a virtual root.

Web Project　A collection of files that comprise a Web application. Web projects are stored on both the server and the local machine. A Web project is part of a larger container called a solution. (See also **Solution** and **Web Application**.)

Wipe　A transition from one scene to another. Wipes come in many different forms; the new scene can appear top to bottom, left to right, from the center out (in the case of a circular wipe), and many other ways.

WWW (World Wide Web)　A popular hypertext-based system of transmitting textual and multimedia-based information through the Internet.

Zoom Tool　A tool for magnifying the current image being working on.

Index

Symbols

& (ampersand)
bitwise AND operator (&), 601
logical AND operator (&&), 602
string concatenation operator
(&), 596

* (asterisk)
*/ statement (JScript), 599
multiplication operator (*)
JScript, 601
VBScript, 596

**\ (backslash), integer division
operator, 596**

^= (bitwise XOR) operator, 601

, (comma) operator, 602

= (equal sign)
assignment operator, 600
equality operator
JScript, 602
VBScript, 596

! (exclamation mark)
inequality operator (!=), 602
logical NOT operator (!), 601

/ (forward slash)
// statement (JScript), 599
division operator (/)
JScript, 601
VBScript, 596

> (greater than sign)
greater than operator (>)
JScript, 601
VBScript, 596
greater than or equal to
operator (>=)
JScript, 602
VBScript, 596
right shift operators, 601

<> (inequality) operator
VBScript, 596

< (less than sign)
less than operator (<)
JScript, 601
VBScript, 596
left shift operator (<<), 601
less than or equal to operator
(<=)
JScript, 602
VBScript, 596

- (minus sign)
negation operator
JScript, 601
VBScript, 596
subtraction operator
JScript, 601
VBScript, 596

% (percent sign)
% tag, 592
modulo arithmetic operator, 601

| (pipe character)
bitwise OR operator (|), 601
logical OR operator (||), 602

+ (plus sign)
addition operator (+)
JScript, 601
VBScript, 596
increment operator (++), 601

? (question mark),
?XML tag (XML), 204
conditional operator, 602

**~ (tilde), bitwise NOT operator,
601**

/* */ statement (JScript), 599

1-bit color, 614

2B+D, 614

**2-tier architecture (Web sites),
285**

3D graphics, 614

**3-tier architecture (Web sites),
285**

8-bit color, 614

24-bit color, 614

32X, Inc., 586

**50 parameter (<MARQUEE>
tag), 223**

**100 parameter (<MARQUEE>
tag), 223**

A

<A> tag
HTML, 589
XML, 204

**About tab (ODBC
Administrator), 330**

AboutBox method, 227

Abs function (VBScript), 594

**AbsolutePage property
(Recordset object), 376**

**AbsolutePosition property
(Recordset object), 376**

<ABSTRACT> tag (XML), 204

access control
ACLs (access control lists), 486
NNTP (Network News
Transport Protocol)
newsgroups, 453-454
Visual SourceSafe
locks, 511
project rights, 510

project security, 509-510
user rights, 511-513
Windows NT Server access rights, 410-411

Access databases, 624
authentication, 340-341
connection properties, 341
data connections, 342

access speed (Web sites), 522

Access This Computer from Network right, 410

Access This Computer right, 485

Account Detail dialog box, 472

Account Details command (Security menu), 472

accounts
IIS (Internet Information Server)
anonymous accounts, 488-489
filtered access, 490
named users, 490
SQL Server
creating, 467-468
deleting, 473
trusted mode, 468-469
user attributes, 472
user privileges, 470-471
Windows NT
configuring, 407-411
security, 485-486

ACLs (access control lists), 486

Action menu commands
Properties, 444
Rescan, 446

activating add-ins, 266-267

Active Channel Agents (Site Server), 461

Active Channel Multicaster (Site Server), 461

Active Channel Server (Site Server), 461

active property (CSS), 609

Active Server Developer's Journal, **582**

Active Server Pages, *see* ASPs

Active Server Pages Developer's Site, 583

ActiveConnection property
Command object, 367
Recordset object, 376

activeElement property (document objects), 116

ActiveMovie, 614

ActiveMovie control, 224
events, 228
methods, 227
movie players, building, 228
properties, 225

ActiveX Control Interface Wizard, 264, 269-272
Select Interface Members dialog box, 270
Set Attributes dialog box, 271
Set Mapping dialog box, 271

ActiveX controls, 138, 212, 289-290, 614
ActiveMovie control, 224
events, 228
methods, 227
movie players, 228
properties, 225
advantages, 291-292
animated GIF files, 212
authoring tools, 38
client/server technology, 288-289
COM (Component Object Model), 288
compiling, 276-277
constituent controls
defined, 264
laying out, 268-269
context, 305
controlling with VBScript, 138
creating, 262-263
ActiveX Control Interface Wizard, 264, 269-272
COM development, 263-264
error-handling code, 274-275
project files, 267-268
property-handling code, 272-274
user interface components, 268-269
Visual Basic development environment, 264-267
DCOM (Distributed COM), 288
deploying
Application Setup Wizard, 277-279
Visual InterDev applications, 279-281
Design tabs, 217
design-time controls, 236-237
advantages, 237
categories, 237-238
comparing to other components, 236-237
Data-bound controls, 248-256
Form controls, 244-248

inserting into Web pages, 238-243
Multimedia controls, 256-259
properties, editing, 240
runtime text, 241-243
Scripting Object Model, 240-241
designing, 267
disadvantages, 291-292
DLLs (dynamic link libraries), 287
documentation, 138
filters, 200-201
flavors, 289-291
Include, 544
in-process components, 290-291
inserting, 216
MSN Investor Portfolio grid, 212
MTS registration, 301-308
multimedia, 220-221
OLE (Object Linking and Embedding), 287
out-of-process components, 290-291
Path control, 232
properties, 293-294
Script Builder, 215, 219
Source tabs, 218
Sprite control, 232
Structured Graphics control, 233
testing, 275-276
Toolbox, 215-218
VBScript, 138
version compatibility, 277

ActiveX data objects, *see* ADO

ActiveX documents, 290

ActiveXObject (JScript), 110

ActualSize property (Field object), 378

Ad Server (Site Server), 463

ADC (Advanced Data Connector), 614

Add Item command (Project menu), 50

Add Item dialog box, 50, 61

Add Item to command (Project menu), 61

Add Project command (File menu), 51, 275

Add Project dialog box, 29, 275

Add Tab option (Toolbox shortcut menu), 219

Add to Alert command (Edit menu), 417

Add to Chart command (Edit menu), 414, 553

Add to Chart dialog box, 553

Add to Log command (Edit menu), 420

Add to Report command (Edit menu), 422

Add to Report dialog box, 422

Add User command (Users menu), 509

Add User dialog box, 509

Add Users and Groups dialog box, 411

Add Workstations to Domain right, 410

Add-In Manager command (Add-Ins menu), 266

Add-In Manager dialog box, 266

add-ins, activating, 266-267

Add-Ins menu commands, 266

Add/Remove Snap-In command (Console menu), 437

Add/Remove Snap-In dialog box, 437

Adding SQL Server Login IDs/ Users dialog box, 471

<ADDRESS> tag (HTML), 592

adHomePageURL parameter (AdRotator object), 154

administration
Visual SourceSafe, 508
access control, 509-511
file type management, 512-513
locks, 511
users, 509
Web sites, 534
Windows NT Servers, 412

Administrative Tools (Common) command (Start menu), 408

Administrator (ODBC)
About tab, 330
Connection Pooling tab, 330
Drivers tab, 330
File DSN tab, 330
System DSN tab, 329
Tracing tab, 330
User DSN tab, 329

ADO (ActiveX data objects), 614

applications, debugging, 383
cursor types, 377
error codes, 383-385
Errors collection, 380-381
features, 360-361
Fields collection, 381-382
objects
Command, 365-369
Connection, 362
Error, 379-380
Field, 377-378
Parameter, 369-370
Property, 380
Recordset, 370-377
performance tuning, 382-383
Properties collection, 381-382
see also ActiveX controls

AdRotator object (ASP components), 153-155

ADSI (Active Directory Service Interface), 585

ADTG (Advanced Data TableGram Streaming Protocol), 615

adURL parameter (AdRotator object), 154

Alert command (View menu), 417

Alert Options dialog box, 418

alerts, 417-418

ALIGN parameter
<DL> tag, 590
<IMG> tag, 590
<OBJECT> tag, 591

alinkColor property (document objects), 116

all collection (document objects), 117

All object, 193-194

AllowChangeDisplayMode property (ActiveMovie control), 225

AllowHideControls property (ActiveMovie control), 225

AllowHideDisplay property (ActiveMovie control), 225

alpha channels, 615

Alpha filter, 200

ALT parameter (<IMG> tag), 590

ALX files, *see* HTML Layout control

analysis services (Site Server), 462-463

anchors collection (document objects), 117

Anchors object, 193

And (logical conjunction) operator, 596

animation, 615
DirectAnimation, 202-203
GIFs, 212-213, 573
paths, 232
performance issues, 573-574
Web sites, 530-532

anonymous accounts, 488-489

anonymous password authentication, 164

antialiasing, 615

Any Character expression (Find/Replace), 74

APIs (application programming interfaces), 101

Appearance property (ActiveMovie control), 225

applets, 615

applets collection (document objects), 117

Applets object, 193

application events, 424

Application object
Active Server Pages, 149-150, 604
performance issues, 577

Application Setup Wizard, 277-279

Application_OnEnd event, 605

Application_OnEnd procedure, 188

Application_OnStart event, 605

Application_OnStart procedure, 188

applications, *see* projects

Applications view (Task Manager), 428

Apply Theme and Layout dialog box, 80

architecture (InterDev), 39

archiving graphics, 567

arguments, 615

arithmetic functions (VBScript), 596

Arrange button (Image Composer), 392-394

arrays, 615
JavaScript/JScript, 111, 602
VBScript, 593

ASA (Active Server Application), 614

Asc function (VBScript), 107, 594, 597

AscB function (VBScript), 594, 597

ASCII, 615

AscW function (VBScript), 594, 597

ASP Hole Web site, 583

aspect ratio, 615

ASPs (Active Server Pages), 146-149, 614
ActiveX components, 300-301
built-in objects
    Application, 149-150
    Request, 150-151
    Response, 151
    Server, 151
    Session, 151-152
components, 152
    AdRotator, 153-155
    BrowserType, 155-156
    Collaboration Data Objects
        for NTS, 157-158
    Content Linking, 156-157
    ContentRotator, 162
    Counters, 161
    Database Access, 156
    FileSystemObject, 157
    MyInfo, 160
    PageCounter, 162-163
    PermissionChecker, 163-164
    Status, 160
    Tools, 158-160
creating, 146-147
debugging, 168
FrontPage 98 limitations,
    543-545
listserver, 584
properties, 148-149
events, 605
GLOBAL.ASA file, 604
objects, 604
scripting, 604
server-side script processing,
    183
transactional server pages, 434,
    448
Web site, 158

assignment operators
JScript, 600
VBScript, 593

Assignments for User dialog box, 511

Atn function (VBScript), 109, 596

Attach to Running Programs (Debugger), 58

Attribute property (Connection object), 364

attributes
CSS positional atributes,
    197-198, 605
HTML
    <IMG> tag, 571-574
    <META> tag, 569-570

Attributes property
Field object, 378
Parameter object, 369
Property object, 380

audio, 531-533

Authentication tab (Connection Properties dialog box), 340

authoring Web page content, 38

automatic restarts (Windows NT Servers), 406

automation objects, 615

AutoRewind property (ActiveMovie control), 225

AutoStart property (ActiveMovie control), 226

***Avatar—The Interactive Developer's Online Magazine* Web site, 583**

B

B channel, 615

<B> tag (HTML), 590

Back Up Files and Directories right, 410

backbone networks, 615

background properties (CSS), 606

Backup Progress dialog box, 476

Backup Volume Labels dialog box, 476

backups
backup devices, 475
SQL Server databases, 476-477
Windows NT Servers, 406

Badmail directory (SMTP server), 450

Balance property (ActiveMovie control), 226

bandwidth, 525, 615

<BASE> tag (HTML), 588

Basic Authentication account access, 490

basic password authentication, 164

beta testings, 586

Bezier curves, 393

bgColor property (document objects), 116

<BGCOLOR> tag (HTML), 531

binary compatibility, 277

bits, 615

bitwise comparisons, 616, 600

<BLOCKQUOTE> tag (HTML), 590

Blur filter, 200, 616

<BODY> tag (HTML), 562-563

Body object, 193

body property (document objects), 116

body tags
hyperlink tags, 589
image tags, 590
list tags, 590
object tags, 591
style tags, 590

BOF property (Recordset object), 376

Bookmark property (Recordset object), 376

bookmarks (MSDN), 43

Boolean data type (JScript), 104

Boolean expressions, 42, 616

Boolean object (JScript), 112

Boolean subtype (VBScript), 103

BORDER parameter (<OBJECT> tag), 591

border properties (CSS), 607-608

BorderStyle property (ActiveMovie control), 226

bottlenecks, 576

bounding boxes, 616

branching, 593

Break at Next Statement command (View menu), 183

break statement (JScript), 599

breakpoints, 174, 185

BRI (Basic Rate Interface), 616

brightness, 616

broken links, repairing, 95

browser events
 client-side scripting
  document events, 139
  scripting, 141
  window events, 141
 document object events, 140

browsers, 284
 DHTML cross-browser compatibility, 192
 Internet Explorer
  cache, 565-567
  DHTML specification, 191-192
  Document Object Model, 139
  filters, 200-201
 Netscape Navigator, 190
 object models, 114-119, 192-195
  collections, 116-118
  events, 118-120
  methods, 116-118
  properties, 116-118
 performance issues, 552-553
 VBScript, 592

BrowserType object (ASP components), 155-156

browsing, 616

bubbling (events), 196

BuildPath method, 157

built-in objects (Active Server Pages)
 Application object, 149-150
 Request object, 150-151
 Response object, 151
 Server object, 151
 Session object, 151-152

burning, 616

business Internet site (Site Server), 458

Button command (Insert menu), 397

Button Wizard and Editor (Image Composer), 390

Buy Now, 463

By Reference addressing, 616

By Value addressing, 616

ByRef statements, 295

byte subtype (VBScript), 103

bytes, 616

Bytes Received/sec counter (Performance Monitor), 554

Bytes Sent/sec counter (Performance Monitor), 554

Bytes Total/sec counter (Performance Monitor), 554

ByVal statements, 295

C

C2-level security, 484

CAB files, creating, 278

cache
 client-side processing, 565-568
 Internet Explorer, 565-567

Cache Flushes counter (Performance Monitor), 556

Cache Hits % counter (Performance Monitor), 556

Cache Hits counter (Performance Monitor), 556

Cache Misses counter (Performance Monitor), 556

Cache Size counter (Performance Monitor), 556

Cache Used counter (Performance Monitor), 556

Cached File Handles counter (Performance Monitor), 556

Cachesize property (Recordset object), 376

Call function (VBScript), 597

call stacks, debugging, 180

cascading style sheets, see CSS

case sensitivity
 JavaScript, 177
 passwords, 409

Category line (Event Viewer logs), 424

CBool function (VBScript), 107, 594

CByte function (VBScript), 107, 594

CCur function (VBScript), 107

CDate function (VBScript), 107, 594

CDbl function (VBScript), 107, 594

CDF (Channel Definition Format), 203-205
 commands, 204
 example, 204-205

CDO (Collaboration Data Objects), 157-158

CGI (Common Gateway Interface), 577, 616

CGI Requests counter (Performance Monitor), 555

Challenge/Response account access, 490

Change the System Time right, 410

Channel Center (Site Server), 460

Channel Definition Format, see CDF

<CHANNEL> tag (XML), 204

channels, 616

character codes, 617

Character not in set regular expression (Find/Replace), 74

Chart command (Options menu), 416

Chart Options dialog box, 416

charts
 Gallery radio buttons, 416
 grids, 416
 legends, 416
 Performance Monitor, 414-416
 Update Time radio buttons, 416
 value bars, 416
 vertical labels, 416
 Vertical Maximum text box, 416

chatting, 616

Check In Item(s) dialog box, 507

Check Out Item(s) dialog box, 506

checking in/out files (Visual SourceSafe), 502, 506-507

child Webs, 54

Choose URL dialog box, 88

ChooseContent method, 162

choosing modes, 498-499

Chr function (VBScript), 107, 594, 597

ChrB function (VBScript), 594, 597

Chroma filter, 200

ChrW function (VBScript), 594, 597

CInt function (VBScript), 107, 594

<CITE> tag (HTML), 589

class C2-level security, 484

class modules, 617

classes, 617

CLASSID parameter (<OBJECT> tag), 591

clear method (document objects), 117

client-side processing
imagemaps, 567-568
performance tuning
cache, 565-568
HTML document sections, 560-563
HTML tags, 568-571, 576
HTTP, 563-565
multimedia data compression, 571-574

client-side scripting, 101-102
browser events
document events, 139
scripting, 141
window events, 141
debugging, 181
Dynamic HTML, 143
form design-time controls, 247-248
form validation, 130-132
server-side scripting, compared, 124-125
VBScript
ActiveX controls, 138
client-side scripts, 129

client/server architecture, 285-286, 617
ActiveX, 288-289

clients
access, 525
performance tuning, 550-551
browser differences, 552-553
download speed, 551-552
software, 36
terminals, 284

clip art, 397-398

Clip Art command (Insert menu), 397

clip property (CSS), 197, 608

CLng function (VBScript), 107, 594

clone tool, 617

close method (document objects), 117

clustered indexes, 316

CMYK (Cyan, Magenta, Yellow, and Black) model, 617

code
editing, 26-27
reviewing, 294-296

code listings, *see* **listings**

<CODE> tag (HTML), 589

CODEBASE parameter (<OBJECT> tag), 591

CODETYPE parameter (<OBJECT> tag), 591

Collaboration Data Objects for NTS component (ASP components), 157-158

collections, 617-118

color
1-bit color, 614
8-bit color, 614
24-bit color, 614
corrections, 617
depth, 572, 617
models, 617
scripting conventions, 187

COLOR parameter (Font tag), 591

Color Picker dialog box, 64

color property (CSS), 606

Color Tuning button (Image Composer), 393

COM (Component Object Model), 38, 263-264, 288

Command object
methods, 365-366
properties, 367-369

Command Properties dialog box, 348

commands
Action menu
Properties, 444
Rescan, 446
Add-Ins menu, Add-In Manager, 266

CDF (Channel Definition Format), 204

Console menu, Add/Remove Snap-In, 437

data commands, creating, 348-349, 349-351

Debug menu
Insert Breakpoint, 174
Processes, 183
Start, 173

Edit menu
Add to Alert, 417
Add to Chart, 414, 553
Add to Log, 420
Add to Report, 422
Find, 73

File menu
Add Project, 51, 275
Make, 296
New, 537
New Project, 20, 44
Save, 63
Save Chart Settings, 415

Image menu, HTML, 214

Insert menu
Button, 397
Clip Art, 397
From Photo CD, 397

Log menu, Log Settings, 426

New menu
Domain, 450
Virtual Directory, 439, 452
Web Site, 442

Options menu
Chart, 416
Report, 423

Policies menu, User Rights, 410

Project menu
Add Item, 50
Add Item to, 61
New Deployment Target, 52
Properties, 293

Security menu
Account Details, 472
Grant New, 470

Start menu, Administrative Tools (Common), 408

Table menu, Insert Table, 68

Tools menu
Customize Toolbox, 279
Microsoft GIF Animator, 399
Options, 55
Rights Assignments for User menu), 511
Rights by Project, 510

traceroute, 557-559

tracert, 557-559

User menu
  Add User, 509
  New User, 408
VBScript
  arithmetic functions, 596
  array handling, 593
  assignments, 593
  comments, 593
  constants, 593
  control flow, 593
  data conversion, 594
  date and time functions, 595
  declarations, 595
  error handling, 595
  explicitly declaring
    variables, 597
  input/output operations, 595
  literals, 593
  object creation, 597
  procedures, 597
  strings, 597
  variant testing, 598
View menu
  Alert, 417
  Break at Next Statement,
    183
  Debug Windows, 174
  Document Outline, 70
  Filter Events, 425
  IE 4, 181
  Log, 419
  Newest Events Listed First,
    425
  Other Windows, 121, 220
  Properties Window, 217
  Report, 421
  Toolbox, 216
Visual SourceSafe
  Deploy, 503
  Get, 503
Web Files menu, Get Latest
  Version, 500
see also functions; methods

**CommandText property
(Command object), 367**

CommandTimeout property
Command object, 367
Connection object, 364

**CommandType property
(Command object), 367**

comments, 593, 617

Commerce Edition (Site Server)
analysis services, 464
customers
  engaging, 463-464
  transactions, 464

**Common Gateway Interface
(CGI), 577, 616**

common navigator bar, 23

comparing files, 504

comparison operators, 617

compatability standards
DHTML (Dynamic HTML),
  18-33
DTCs (Design-Time
  Controls), 18

**compiling ActiveX controls,
276-277**

**Component Object Model
(COM), 38, 263-264, 288**

components
ActiveX, *see* ActiveX controls
server-side (Active Server
  Pages), 152-153
  AdRotator object, 153-155
  BrowserType object,
    155-156
  Collaboration Data Objects
    for NTS component,
    157-158
  Content Linking component,
    156-157
  ContentRotator component,
    162
  Counters component, 161
  Database Access
    component, 156
  FileSystemObject
    component, 157
  MyInfo component, 160
  PageCounter component,
    162-163
  PermissionChecker
    component, 163-164
  Status component, 160
  Tools component, 158-160

compositing, 617

**Composition Guides (Image
Composer), 396-397**

compound operators, 601

compression, 617

computational operators, 601

**Computer line (Event Viewer
logs), 424**

conference papers (MSDN), 40

configuring
SQL Server accounts, 466-467
  login IDs, 467-468
  trusted mode, 468-469
  user attributes, 472
  user privileges, 470-471
SQL Server databases, 330-331
  data connections, 331
  DSNs, 332-336

properties, 339-340
protocols, 333-336
Windows NT Server, 404

connecting databases, 27-33

**Connection Attempts counter
(Performance Monitor), 555**

Connection object
methods, 362-363
properties, 364-365

**Connection Pooling tab (ODBC
Administrator), 330**

**Connection Properties dialog
box**
Authentication tab, 340
General tab, 340
Miscellaneous tab, 341

**Connections/sec counter
(Performance Monitor), 555**

**ConnectionString property
(Connection object), 364**

**ConnectionTimeout property
(Connection object), 364**

**Console menu commands,
Add/Remove Snap-In, 437**

constants, 593, 618

constituent controls
defined, 264
laying out, 268-269

**content analysis services (Site
Server), 462**

**CONTENT attribute (<META>
tag), 570**

**content deployment (Site
Server), 459**

content files, 537

**Content Linking component
(ASP components), 156-157**

**content management (Site
Server), 458-459**

**ContentRotator component
(ASP components), 162**

**context menu, adding/removing
site diagrams, 88**

**continue statement (JScript),
599**

**Control Creation Edition (VB),
262**

control flow, 593

**controlled access, *see* access
control**

controls, *see* ActiveX controls

converting data, 594

cookie property (document objects), 116

cookies, 618

CopyFile method, 157

copying sprites, 395

Cos function (VBScript), 109, 596

Count property
Errors collection, 381
Fields collection, 382-385
Properties collection, 382-385

counter programs, performance issues, 563-565

counters (Performance Monitor)
HTTP service counters, 554-555
IIS counters, 556
viewing, 553

Counters component (ASP components), 161

counting server connections, 564-565

Create button (Image Composer), 394

Create URL dialog box, 67

createElement( ) method, 118

CreateObject function (VBScript), 109, 597

createStyleSheet method, 118

Crop tool (Image Composer), 390

cropping
sprites, 395-396
tools, 618

CrossSell (Site Server), 464

CSng function (VBScript), 107, 594

CSS (cascading style sheets), 196-199, 616
attributes, 605
creating, 536
elements, 605
example, 198-199
external CSS, linking to, 611
fonts, 605
in line CSS, 609
positional attributes, 197-198
properties
background, 606
classification, 608
color, 606
positioning, 608

printing, 609
text, 605
style blocks, 610
Web site, 197

CStr function (VBScript), 107, 594

currency entries, validating, 133

currency subtype (VBScript), 103

Current Anonymous Users counter (Performance Monitor), 555

Current Connections counter (Performance Monitor), 555

Current ISAPI counter (Performance Monitor), 555

Current NonAnonymous Users counter (Performance Monitor), 555

CurrentPosition property (ActiveMovie control), 226

CurrentState property (ActiveMovie control), 226-227

cursor property (CSS), 609

cursor types (ADO), 377

CursorLocation property
Connection object, 364
Recordset object, 376

CursorType property (Recordset object), 376

custom filters, 618

Custom Toolbox dialog box, 238-239

customers
engaging, 463-464
transacting with, 464

Customize Toolbox command (Tools menu), 218, 279

Customize Toolbox dialog box, 78, 219, 279

customizing
IIS Management Console, 437
Index Server search forms, 446-447
InterDev, 55-56
Toolbox, 77, 218
Visual Studio environment, 56, 265-266

Cutout button (Image Composer), 392

Cutout palette (Image Composer), 390

D

D channel, 618

DAC (Digital-to-Analog Converter), 619

dat diagrams, 618

dat expressions, 618

Data Command, 618

Data Connection Wizard, 37

Data Connections (design-time controls), 249-253

data environment, 346-351
contents, 346-347
data commands, 348-351
data connections, 347
database views, 352-354
drag-and-drop feature, 351
stored procedures
creating, 354-357
debugging, 357

data environments, 618

data normalization (databases), 317-325
denormalized database development, 322-323
overnormalization, 323-325

DATA parameter (<OBJECT> tag), 591

data ranges, 618

Data Source Names (DSNs), 328-329
file DSNs, 330
system DSNs, 329
user DSNs, 329

data tools, 58

data type and conversion functions (VBScript), 107

data types, 618
JScript, 103-104
scripting, 102-106
VBScript, 103-104

data-binding, 618

Data-bound controls (design-time controls), 248-249
Data Connections, 249
Grid control, 249-253
Recordset NavBar, 255-256

data-driven applications, 543

Database Access component (ASP components), 156

Database Backup/Restore dialog box, 476

Database Maintenance Plan Wizard, 479-480

Database Project Wizard, 49

databases, 312-316, 328, 618
  Access
    authentication, 340-341
    connection properties, 341
    data connections, 342
  connecting, 27-33
  data environment
    contents, 346-347
    data commands, 348-351
    data connections, 347
    drag-and-drop feature, 351
  data normalization, 317-325
    denormalized database
      development, 322-323
    overnormalization, 323-325
  FoxPro, 342
  indexes
    clustered indexes, 316
    creating, 316-317
    nonclustered indexes, 317
  ODBC connections, 328
    connection pooling, 330
    drivers, 330
    file DSNs, 330
    system DSNs, 329
    tracing feature, 330
    user DSNs, 329
  queries, 30-31
  referential integrity, 325-326
  SQL Server, 330
    adding devices, 474-475
    backing up, 476-477
    backup devices, 475
    creating, 473-474
    data connections, 331
    deleting, 474
    DSNs, 332-336
    maintenance, 479-480
    properties, 339-340
    resizing, 478
    restoring from backup,
      477-478
  stored procedures
    creating, 354-357
    debugging, 357
  views, 352-354
  Web application integration, 18
  Web sites, 534

Date and Time line (Event Viewer logs), 424

date entries, validating, 134

Date function (VBScript), 108, 595

Date object (JavaScript/ JScript), 112, 602

date subtype (VBScript), 103

date/time functions (VBScript), 108, 595

DateDiff function (VBScript), 108

DateSerial function (VBScript), 594-595

DateValue function (VBScript), 594-595

Day function (VBScript), 595

DCOM (Distributed COM), 288

<DD> tag (HTML), 590

Debug menu commands
  Insert Breakpoint, 174
  Processes, 183
  Start, 173

Debug Windows command (View menu), 174

debuggers, 58
  launching, 172
  stepping procedures, 176
  variables, 178
  Visual Basic, 169
  watches, 173

debugging, 168-170
  Active Server Pages, 168
  ADO-based applications, 383
  breakpoints, 174, 185
  call stacks, 180
  client-side scripting, 181
  development environments, 172
  error categories, 168
  GLOBAL.ASA files, 187
  Interdev support, 15-17
  just-in-time debugging, 172
  mixed client/server-side
    scripting, 185
  server-side scripting, 170, 183
  stepping procedures, 176
  stored procedures, 357
  variables, 178
  windows, 180

DECLARE parameter (<OBJECT> tag), 591

declaring
  events, 196
  variables, 104-107, 597

default scripting languages, specifying, 120

default settings, 619

Default Web Site Properties dialog box, 171

DefaultDatabase property (Connection object), 364

DefinedSize property (Field object), 378

Delete Item option (Toolbox shortcut menu), 218

Delete Pages dialog box, 89

deleting
  SQL Server accounts, 473
  SQL Server databases, 474

delivery, Site Server features
  analysis services, 462-463
  Knowledge Manager, 460-461
  Personalization and
    Membership Services,
    461-462
  push publishing, 461

denormalized database development, 322-323

Department of Defense Trusted Computer Evaluation (Web site), 495

Deploy command (Visual SourceSafe), 503

deploying
  ActiveX controls
    Application Setup Wizard,
      277-279
    Visual InterDev applications,
      279-281
  Web sites, 52

Deployment Explorer, 53

depth of color, 572

Description property (Error object), 379

Design Editor, 15, 60
  HTML toolbar, 63
  pages, creating/editing, 61
    hyperlinks, 66
    images, 65
    tables, 68

design sign-offs, 535

design-time controls, see DTCs

Design-Time Controls tab (Toolbox), 77

designing
  ActiveX controls, 267
  FrontPage sites, 544-545
    ASPs, 545
    modularization, 545
    testing, 545
  Web sites, 518-535
    performance issues, 577-578
    scope, 518-525

despeckle filters, 619

Detect When File Is Changed option (General options), 56

developer isolation, 498-500

Developer Studio, 36, 624

Developer Studio Project files (DSP), 37

Developer Studio Solution files (SLN), 37

development
  environment (VB), 36, 264-267
    customizing, 265-266
    Project Explorer, 265
    Toolbox, 265
  modes
    changing, 498
    choosing, 498-499
    Local, 499-500
    Master, 498
  Web sites, 36-38

<DFN> tag (HTML), 589

DHCP (Dynamic Host Configuration Protocol), 412

DHTML (Dynamic HTML), 18-33
  Cascading Style Sheets, 196-199
    example, 198-199
    positional attributes, 197-198
    Web site, 197
  cross-browser compatibility, 192
  Microsoft implementation, 191-192
  multimedia, 199-200
    DirectAnimation, 202-203
    filters, 200-201
  Netscape implementation, 190
  Scriptlets, 205-207
    events, 206
    previewing, 206
    referencing, 206
    sizing, 206
    Web site, 205

dialog boxes, 619
  Account Detail, 472
  Add Item, 50, 61
  Add Project, 29, 275
  Add to Alert, 418
  Add to Chart, 415, 553
  Add to Log, 420
  Add to Report, 422
  Add User, 509
  Add Users and Groups, 411
  Add-In Manager, 266
  Add/Remove Snap-In, 437
  Adding SQL Server Login IDs/ Users, 471
  Alert Options, 418

Apply Theme and Layout, 80
Assignments for User, 511
Backup Progress, 476
Backup Volume Labels, 476
Chart Options, 416
Check In Item(s), 507
Check Out Item(s), 506
Choose URL, 88
Color Picker, 64
Command Properties, 348
Connection Properties
  Authentication tab, 340
  General tab, 340
  Miscellaneous tab, 341
Create URL, 67
Custom Toolbox, 238-239
Customize Toolbox, 78, 219, 279
Database Backup/Restore, 476
Default Web Site Properties, 171
Delete Pages, 89
Differences, 507
Enable Source Control, 504
Event Detail, 424
Event Log Settings, 426
Filter, 425
Find, 72
Full Rescan?, 446
Grant User Privilege, 470
Group Memberships, 410
Hyperlink, 66
Insert Image, 214
Insert Table, 68
Internet Package, 278
Log Options, 420
Look In Folders, 73
Manage Logins, 468
New Backup Device, 475
New Database, 473
New Database Device, 474
New Deployment Target, 52
New Project, 20, 44
New User, 408
Open With, 391
Options, 55
Processes, 183
Project Rights, 510
Properties
  Advanced tab, 253
  Borders tab, 253
  Data tab, 252
  Format tab, 253
  General tab, 251
  Navigation tab, 252
Property Pages, 80
Register Server, 467
Report Options, 423
Restore Progress, 478

Script Breakpoint Properites, 174
Select Data Source, 49
Select Interface Members, 270
Server Configuration/Options, 468
Set Attributes, 271
Set Mapping, 271
Site Properties/Virtual Directory Properties, 444
SourceSafe Options, 509
User Properties, 409

Differences dialog box, 507

Differences function, 504

diffusion dithering, 619

digital technology
  audio, 533
  painting, 619
  signatures, 619

digitizing, 619

Dim function (VBScript), 593-595

<DIR> tag (HTML), 590

Direct Mail (Site Server), 462

DirectAnimation, 202-203

Direction property (Parameter object), 369

directories, 37, 619
  SMTP server, 450
  virtual directories
    access permissions, 441
    creating, 439-440
  Visual SourceSafe, 502

directory browsing, disabling, 494

Directory Listings counter (Performance Monitor), 556

disabling directory browsing, 494

disk striping, 406

display property (CSS), 608

DisplayBackColor property (ActiveMovie control), 226

DisplayForeColor property (ActiveMovie control), 226

displaying Performance Monitor counters, 553

DisplayMode property (ActiveMovie control), 226

dithering, 619

<DL> tag (HTML), 590

DLLs (dynamic link libraries), 287

DNS (Domain Name Service), 412, 619

Do...Loop function (VBScript), 594

Do...Until...Loop function (VBScript), 594

Do...While...Loop function (VBScript), 594

Document object, 193-195, 603

document object events, 140

Document Object Model, *see* DOM

Document Outline command (View menu), 70

documentation (ActiveX controls), 138

documents
  body tags
    hyperlink tags, 589
    image tags, 590
    list tags, 590
    object tags, 591
    style tags, 590
  events, client-side scripting, 139
  form validation, 130
    complete, 135
    currency entries, 133
    date entries, 134
    numerical entries, 134
    VBScript, 132
  performance issues, 560-563

dodging, 619

dog-ears, 43

DOM (Document Object Model), 192-195
  Document object, 193-195
  events, 195-196
  object references, 194
  Window object, 193

Domain command (New menu), 450

domain property (document objects), 116

domains
  SMTP mail domains, 450-451
  virtual domains, 441-444

double subtype (VBScript), 103

downloading
  ODBC, 329
  performance tuning, 551-552

DPI (Dots Per Inch), 619

drag-and-drop feature, 351

Drivers tab (ODBC Administrator), 330

Drop directory (SMTP server), 450

Drop Shadow filter, 200

DSNs (Data Source Names), 328-329
  file DSNs, 330
  system DSNs, 329
  user DSNs, 329

DSP (Developer Studio Project) files, 37

<DT> tag (HTML), 590

DTC (design-time controls), 18, 236-237, 543-544
  advantages, 237
  categories, 237-238
  comparing to other components, 236-237
  Data-bound controls, 248
    Data Connections, setting up, 249
    Grid control, 249-253
    Recordset NavBar, 255-256
  Form controls
    client-side scripting, 247-248
    server-side mode, 244-246
  inserting into Web pages, 238-240
    runtime text, 241-243
    Scripting Object Model, 240-241
  Multimedia controls
    Page Transitions control, 256-257
    Timelines control, 257-259
  properties, editing, 240

dynamic content, 524

dynamic cursors, 377

dynamic help, 295

Dynamic HTML, *see* DHTML

E

<EARLIESTTIME> tag (XML), 204

ECMAScript, 100

Edit menu commands
  Add to Alert, 417
  Add to Chart, 414, 553

  Add to Log, 420
  Add to Report, 422

editing
  sprites, 393-395
  Web pages, 38, 61

EditMode property (Recordset object), 376

editors, 15
  Design Editor, 60
  Source Editor, 26-27, 60, 69

Effects button (Image Composer), 393

elementFromPoint( ) method, 118

<EM> tag (HTML), 589

email, SMTP server
  components, 449-450
  directories, 450
  mail domains, 450-451

embedding style blocks, 610

embeds collection (document objects), 117

embossing, 620

Empty function (VBScript), 593

empty subtype (VBScript), 103

empty values, 620

Enable Source Control dialog box, 504

EnableContextMenu property (ActiveMovie control), 226

Enabled property (ActiveMovie control), 226

EnablePositionControls property (ActiveMovie control), 226

EnableSelectionControls property (ActiveMovie control), 226

EnableTracker property (ActiveMovie control), 226

enabling
  indexing, 444-446
  source control, 504-505

encryption, 620

End of Line regular expression (Find/Replace), 74

end tags, 588

end-to-end development, 15

engaging customers (Site Server), 463-464

enterprise information site (Site Server), 458

EOF property (Recordset object), 376

EPS (Encapsulated PostScript), 620

equalization, 620

Eqv (logical equivalence), 596

Erase function (VBScript), 593

Err function (VBScript), 595

Error object, 379-380, 620

error subtype (VBScript), 104

errors
    codes, 383-385, 620
    handling
        ActiveX controls, 274-275
        VBScript, 595
        Windows NT Servers, 405
    see also debugging

Errors collection (ADO), 380-381

Escape expression (Find/ Replace), 75

escape( ) function, 110, 603

eval( ) function, 110, 603

Event Detail dialog box, 424

Event line (Event Viewer logs), 424

Event Log Settings dialog box, 426

Event Viewer, 412, 423-428

events, 620
    Active Server Pages, 605
    ActiveMovie control, 228
    browser object models, 118-120, 141
    declaring, 196
    defined, 195
    event bubbling, 196
    handling, 196
    ReadProperties, 272
    Scriptlets, 206

execCommand method, 118

Exp function (VBScript), 109, 596

Explorer, 412

expressions, 620

Extensible Markup Language (XML), 203-204

Extension Requests counter (Performance Monitor), 555

external CSS, linking to, 611

external verfication, 94

extranets, 620

F

FACE parameter (<FONT> tag), 591

fades, 620

False function (VBScript), 593

FAQs (Frequently Asked Questions), 620

fault tolerance, 405-407

fgColor property (document objects), 116

Field object, 377-378
    methods, 378
    properties, 361, 378

fields, 620
    adding to tables, 313-314

Fields collection (ADO), 381-382

FIF (Fractal Image Format), 620

File DSN tab (ODBC Administrator), 330

file formats, 390, 621

File menu commands
    Add Project, 51, 275
    Make, 296
    New, 537
    New Project, 20, 44
    Save, 63
    Save Chart Settings, 415

file URL link, 67

FileExists method, 157-158

FileName property (ActiveMovie control), 226-227

files, 620
    CAB format, 278
    checking in/out (Visual SourceSafe), 502, 506-507
    comparing, 504
    content files, 537
    DSP (Developer Studio Project) , 37
    GIF (Graphics Interchange Format), 212, 573, 621
    GLOBAL.ASA files, 38
        Active Server Pages, 604
        debugging, 187
        procedures, 188

HTML Layout Control (ALX files), 38

JPEG (Joint Photographic Expert Group), 213

moving, 492

NTFS (NT File System), 405-406

publishing, 503

Query.htm, 446

Query.htx, 446

Query.idq, 446

rolling back (Visual SourceSafe), 503

RSF (Rotator Schedule File), 154-155

saving, 57

SLN (Developer Studio Solution), 37

Files Received counter (Performance Monitor), 555

Files Sent counter (Performance Monitor), 555

Files Total counter (Performance Monitor), 555

FileSystemObject component (ASP components), 157

fill tool, 621

Filter Events command (View menu), 425

Filter property (Recordset object), 376

filter property (CSS), 609

filtered access (IIS), 490

FilterGraph property (ActiveMovie control), 226

FilterGraphDispatch property (ActiveMovie control), 226

filtering hyperlinks, 94

filters, 200-201

Filters object, 193

Find command (Edit menu), 73

Find dialog box, 72

finding text strings, 72

firewalls, 493, 621

Fix function (VBScript), 594

Flash, 574

flavors (ActiveX), 289-291

Flip Horizontal filter, 200

Flip Vertical filter, 200

float property (CSS), 608

floating palettes, 621

folders
creating, 536
moving, 492

font property (CSS), 606

@font-face property (CSS), 606

<FONT> tag (HTML), 590

font-family property (CSS), 605

font-height property (CSS), 606

font-size property (CSS), 606

font-style property (CSS), 605

font-variant property (CSS), 605

font-weight property (CSS), 606

For Each...Next function (VBScript), 594

for statement (JScript), 599

For...Next function (VBScript), 594

Force Shutdown from a Remote System right, 410

foreign keys, 315-316

Form controls (design-time controls)
client-side scripting, 247-248
server-side mode, 244-246

Form object (JavaScript/JScript), 603

<FORM> tag (HTML), 132

forms, 130
entries, prefilling, 132
search forms (Index Server)
customizing, 446-447
default files, 446
scope, 447
validating
client-side scripting, 130
complete, 135
currency entries, 133
date entries, 134
numerical entries, 134
VBScript, 132

forms collection (document objects), 117

Forms object, 193

forward-only cursor, 377

FoxPro databases, 342

fractal compression, 621

frames
animated GIF files, 213
Web sites, 532

frames collection (document objects), 117

friend functions, 263

From Photo CD command (Insert menu), 397

FrontPage 98, 540, 624
limitations
data-driven applications, 543
design-time controls, 543-544
multiple language projects, 544
server-side scripting, 543
security, 545-546
Server Extensions, 545-546
site design, 544-545
site maintenance, 546-547
Visual InterDev, compared, 540-542

FTP site repositories, 519

ftp URL link, 67

Full Rescan? dialog box, 446

FullScreenMode property (ActiveMovie control), 226

Function function (VBScript), 595-597

function statement (JScript), 600

functions, 621
creating, 597
friend functions, 263
JScript, 110-114, 603
VBScript, 107-114
arithmetic functions, 596
array handling, 593
assignments, 593
comments, 593
constants, 593
control flow, 593
data conversion, 594
date and time functions, 595
declarations, 595
error handling, 595
explicitly declaring variables, 597
input/output operations, 595
literals, 593
object creation, 597
procedures, 597
strings, 597
variant testing, 598
see also commands; methods

G

Gallery radio buttons, 416

gammas, 621

Gaussian blur, 621

General IIS Discussion newsgroup, 584

General options, 56

General tab (Connection Properties dialog box), 340

generated content, 524

Get command (Visual SourceSafe), 503

Get Latest Version command (Web Files menu), 500

Get method, 161

GetAllContent method, 162

GetListCount( ) method, 156

GetListIndex( ) method, 156

GetNextDescription( ) method, 156

GetNextURL( ) method, 156

GetNthDescription( ) method, 156

GetNthURL( ) method, 156

GetObject function, 109

GetObjectContext function, 305

GetPreviousDescription( ) method, 156

GetPreviousURL( ) method, 156

GIF (Graphics Interchange Format), 212, 573, 621

gigabytes, 621

global navigation bar (Site Designer), 90

global variables, declaring, 105

GLOBAL.ASA files, 38
Active Server Pages, 604
debugging, 187
procedures, 188

Globally Unique IDs (GUIDs), 276, 621

Glow filter, 200

gopher URL links, 67

gradient fills, 621

Grant New command (Security menu), 470

Grant User Privilege dialog box,
470

granting user privileges (SQL
Server), 470-471

graphics
archiving, 567
color
1-bit color, 614
8-bit color, 614
24-bit color, 614
corrections, 617
depth, 572, 617
models, 617
scripting conventions, 187
GIF (Graphics Interchange
Format), 212, 573, 621
imagemaps, 567-568
JPEG (Joint Photographic
Expert Group), 213, 573
raster-format files, 572
resolution, 572
sprites, 232
vector graphics, 233
vector-format files, 572
Web sites, 530

Graphics Interchange Format
(GIF), 212, 573, 621

gray/color corrections, 621

gray/color maps, 621

grayscale, 614, 621

Grayscale filter, 200

Grid control, 249-253

grids, 416

Group Memberships dialog
box, 410

Grouping expression (Find/
Replace), 74

groups, adding/deleting users,
409-410

Guest accounts, 486

GUID (Globally Unique IDs),
276, 621

H

<H1> tag (HTML), 589

halftones, 622

HasAccess method, 163

<HEAD> tag (HTML), 562

header tags, 589

heading tags, 588

HEIGHT attribute
<IMG> tag, 571-574, 590
<OBJECT> tag, 591

height attribute (CSS), 197,
608

Help System, 57

HelpContext property (Error
object), 379

HelpFile property (Error
object), 379

Hex function (VBScript), 594

Hexadecimal Display
(Debugger), 58

Hide Editor Windows option
(General options), 56

highlights, 622

History function, 503

hit counters, 563-564

Hits method, 163

HLS (Hue, Lightness, and
Saturation), 622

home pages, *see* **Web sites**

horizontal grids, 416

horizontal partitioning, 323

hosting Web sites, 534

Hour function (VBScript), 595

House icon (Web Diagram
window), 23

HREF parameter
<A> tag, 589
<BASE> tag, 589
<LINK> tag, 589

HSB (Hue, Saturation, and
Brightness), 622

HSPACE parameter (<OBJECT>
tag), 591

<HTML> tag, 560-561

HTML (Hypertext Markup
Language), 588, 622
DHTML (Dynamic HTML),
190-192
cascading style sheets,
196-199
cross-browser compatibility,
192
Microsoft implementation,
191-192
multimedia, 199-203
Netscape implementation,
190

forms, 130
prefilling, 132
validating, 132
options, 58
performance issues
document sections, 560-563
tags, 568-571, 576
Scriptlets, 205-207
events, 206
previewing, 206
referencing, 206
sizing, 206
Web site, 205
tags, 588
<BGCOLOR>, 531
<BODY>, 562-563
document body tags, 589
document heads, 588
end tags, 588
<FORM>, 132
<HEAD>, 562
<HTML>, 560-561
hyperlink tags, 589
image tags, 590
<IMG>, 569
list tags, 590
<MARQUEE>, 221-223
<META>, 569-571
<OBJECT>, 215
object tags, 591
<PARAM>, 216
parameters, 588
<SCRIPT>, 100, 128
start tags, 588
style tags, 590
<TITLE>, 568

HTML command (Image
menu), 214

HTML Layout control (ALX
files), 38

HTML Outline view, 70

HTML tab (Toolbox), 76

HTML toolbar (Design Editor),
63

HTTP (Hypertext Transfer
Protocol), 622
Performance Monitor counters,
554-555
performance tuning
server connections, 564-565
usage counters, 563-564
servers, 622
URL links, 67

HTTP-EQUIV tag (XML), 204

Hue, Lightness, and Saturation
(HLS), 622

Hue, Saturation, and
  Brightness (HSB), 622

Huffman compression, 622

Hyperlink dialog box, 66

hyperlinks, 622
  creating, 66
  external verification, 94
  filtering, 94
  HTML tags, 589
  MSDN library, 42
  repairing, 95
  viewing, 92

hypertext, 622

Hypertext Markup Language,
  see HTML

Hypertext Transfer Protocol,
  see HTTP

I

<I> tag (HTML), 591

icons, 23, 622

IE 4 command (View menu),
  181

if...else statement (JScript),
  600

If...Then...Else function
  (VBScript), 594

IIS (Internet Information
  Server)
  Index Server
    enabling indexing, 444-446
    search forms, 446-447
  listserver, 585
  Management Console, 435-438
  new features, 434-436
    crash protection, 434
    JVM, 435
    script debugging, 435
    transactional server pages,
      434
  newsgroup, 584
  Performance Monitor counters,
    556
  platform compatibility, 435
  security
    anonymous accounts,
      488-489
    directory browsing, 494
    filtered access, 490
    log files, 493
    maximum connections, 493
    named users, 490

SSL (Secure Sockets Layer),
  491-492
    timeout periods, 493
server-side development, 17
Site Server, 456-457
  Commerce Edition, 463-464
  delivery features, 460-463
  publishing features, 457-459
  search features, 459-460
  Site Server Express, 435
  virtual directories
    access permissions, 441
    creating, 439-440
  virtual domains, creating,
    441-444
Web site, 436, 583

Image Composer
  buttons
    Arrange, 392-394
    Color Tuning, 393
    Create, 394
    Cutout, 392
    Effects, 393
    Paint, 393-394
    Pan, 393
    Select, 390
    Shapes, 392-394
    Text, 392
    Texture Transfer, 393
    Zoom, 393
  Button Wizard and Editor, 390
  clip art, 397-398
  Composition Guides, 396-397
  Crop tool, 390
  Cutout palette, 390
  file formats, 390
  interfaces, 390-393
  objects, smoothing, 390
  Selection arrow, 392-394
  Selection tool, 394
  sprites
    copying, 395
    creating, 393-395
    cropping, 395-396
    editing, 393-395
    sizing, 395
    text sprites, 390
  toolbars, 391
  Web Wizard, 390

Image menu commands,
  HTML, 214

image processing, 622

image tags, 590

imagemaps, 567-568, 622

images, *see* graphics

images collection (document
  objects), 117

Images object, 193

<IMG> tag (HTML), 569,
  571-574, 590

Imp (logical implication)
  operator, 596

@import property (CSS), 609

!important property (CSS), 609

in line CSS, 609

in-process components,
  290-291

Include control, 544

Increment method, 161

Index facility (MSDN), 40

Index Server
  indexing, enabling, 444-446
  search forms
    customizing, 446-447
    default files, 446
  search scope, 447

indexes
  clustered indexes, 316
  creating, 316-317
  nonclustered indexes, 317

input/output operations
  (VBScript), 595

InputBox function (VBScript),
  595

Insert Breakpoint command
  (Debug menu), 174

Insert Data Connection Wizard,
  38

Insert Image dialog box, 214

Insert menu commands
  Button, 397
  Clip Art, 397
  From Photo CD, 397

Insert Table command (Table
  menu), 68

Insert Table dialog box, 68

InsertionPoint parameter (Tools
  component), 159

installing
  Microsoft Transaction Server,
    302-303
  VSS (Visual SourceSafe),
    500-501

InstallShield Web site, 278

InStr function (VBScript), 109,
  597

InStrB function (VBScript), 597

Int function (VBScript), 594

integer subtype (VBScript), 103

Integrated Services Digital Network (ISDN), 623

Intelligent CrossSell (Site Server), 464

IntelliSense, 19, 71

interfaces
APIs (application programming interfaces), 101
customizing, 55
Image Composer, 390-393
MSDN, 40

International Settings area, 57

Internet, 622
routes, tracking, 557-559
standards, 18

Internet Explorer
cache, 565-567
DHTML specification, 191-192
Document Object Model, 139
filters, 200-201
object model, 192-195
Document object, 193-195
events, 195-196
object references, 194
Window object, 193

Internet Information Server, *see* IIS

Internet Package dialog box, 278

Internet Server Application Programming Interface, *see* ISAPI

Internet Service Manager (MMC), 170

<INTERVALTIME> tag (XML), 204

intranets, 622

intrinsic constants, 622

Invert filter, 200, 623

IP (Internet Protocol), 623

Is (compare object equivalence) operator, 596

ISAPI (Internet Server Application Programming Interface), 623
Developer's site, 583
listserver, 585
performance issues, 577

IsArray function (VBScript), 107, 593, 598

IsDate function (VBScript), 107, 598

ISDN (Integrated Services Digital Network), 623

IsEmpty function (VBScript), 107, 598

<ISINDEX> tag (HTML), 589

ISMAP parameter (<IMG> tag), 590

isNaN function (JScript), 110, 603

IsNull function (VBScript), 107, 598

IsNumeric function (VBScript), 107, 598

IsObject function (VBScript), 597-598

isolation, multi-tiered Web sites, 286

IsolationLevel property (Connection object), 364

IsSoundCardEnabled method, 227

<ITEM> tag (XML), 204

IUSR_machinename account, 485

J-K

jaggies, 623

Java, 623

JavaScript, 100, 598, 623
case-sensitivity, 177
objects, 602

JPEG (Joint Photographic Expert Group), 213, 573, 623

JScript, 100, 598, 623
data types, 103-104
functions, 110-114, 603
objects, 110-113, 602
operators, 600
bitwise operators, 600
compound operators, 601
computational operators, 601
logical operators, 601
precedence, 602
reserved words, 603
statements, 599
variables, 105

just-in-time debugging, 58, 172

<KBD> tag (HTML), 589

Keyboard options, 57

keyset cursor, 377

keywords, 623

kilobytes, 623

knowledge base (MSDN), 40

Knowledge Manager (Site Server), 460-461

L

lastModified property (document objects), 116

<LATESTTIME> tag (XML), 204

laying out constituent controls, 268-269

layouts
adding, 82
Web pages, 22-25, 80

Lbound function (VBScript), 593

LCase function (VBScript), 109, 597

"leased line" connections, 551

left attribute (CSS), 197

Left function (VBScript), 109, 597

left property (CSS), 608

LeftB function (VBScript), 597

legends, 416

Len function (VBScript), 597

LenB function (VBScript), 597

Let function (VBScript), 593

letter-spacing property (CSS), 606

Level 0 RAID, 406

Level 1 RAID, 406

Level 2 RAID, 407

Level 3 RAID, 407

Level 4 RAID, 407

Level 5 RAID, 407

<LI> tag (HTML), 590

libraries
component sharing, 55
MSDN (Microsoft Developer Network), 39

Library Browser (MSDN), 40

Light filter, 200

lightness, 623

limiting network resources, 556-557

link property (CSS), 609

<LINK> tag (HTML), 589

Link View, 92

linkColor property (document objects), 116

linking
to external CSS, 611
pages to home page, 23

links, 622
creating, 66
external verification, 94
filtering, 94
HTML tags, 589
MSDN library, 42
repairing, 95
viewing, 92

links collection (document objects), 117

Links object, 193

list tags, 590

List View option (Toolbox shortcut menu), 219

list-style property (CSS), 608

list-style-image property (CSS), 608

list-style-position property (CSS), 608

list-style-type property (CSS), 608

listings
All object, 194
TextBox design-time control, 243
Blur filter application, 200-201
cascading style sheets (CSS) example, 198-199
CDF (Channel Definition Format), 204-205
connection objects, opening, 364-365
scripting object model code, 241
server-side script for the addition and deletion of records, 255-256
stored procedures, 368-369
Value property, 361

listservers, 584

literals, 593

Load and Unload Device Drivers right, 411

Load Last Solution option (General options), 56

loading Web pages, 551-552

Local Mode, 17-18, 47, 499-500, 623

local working copies, 52

Locals window, 174, 179

location property (document objects), 116

locking VSS (Visual SourceSafe), 511

LockType property (Recordset object), 376

Log command (View menu), 419

log files
IIS (Internet Information Server), 493
Performance Monitor, 419-421

Log function (VBScript), 109, 596

Log menu commands, Log Settings, 426

Log On Locally right, 411

Log Options dialog box, 420

Log Settings command (Log menu), 426

<LOG> tag (XML), 204

logic errors, 168-169

logical operators, 601

login IDs (SQL Server)
creating, 467-468
deleting, 473

<LOGIN> tag (XML), 204

<LOGO> tag (XML), 204

Logon Attempts counter (Performance Monitor), 555

<LOGTARGET> tag (XML), 204

long subtype (VBScript), 103

Look In Folders dialog box, 73

looping VBScript, 593

lossey compression, 623

LPI (Lines Per Inch), 623

Ltrim function (VBScript), 598

LZW (Lempel Ziv Welch), 623

M

Macmillan Computer Publishing Web site, 495

magazines, 582

Magic Wand, 624

mail domains (SMTP), 450-451

mailto URL links, 67

main Visual InterDev newsgroup, 584

mainframes, 284

Make command (File menu), 296

Manage Auditing and Security Logs user right, 411

Manage Logins dialog box, 468

Management Console (IIS), 435-438

manually registering ActiveX components, 298

margin property (CSS), 607

margin-bottom property (CSS), 607

margin-left property (CSS), 606

margin-right property (CSS), 606

margin-top property (CSS), 606

marketing sites, 520

Marquee control (ActiveX), 221

<MARQUEE> tag (HTML), 221-223

MarshalOptions property (Recordset object), 376

Mask filter, 200

masks, 624

Master mode, 47, 498, 624

master Web sites, updating, 500-501

math functions (VBScript), 108, 596

Math object (JavaScript/JScript), 112, 602

Maximum Anonymous Users counter (Performance Monititor), 555

Maximum CGI Requests counter (Performance Monitor), 555

Maximum Connections counter (Performance Monitor), 555

Maximum NonAnonymous Users counter (Performance Monitor), 555

Maximum of One or More expression (Find/Replace), 75

MaxRecords property (Recordset object), 376

megabytes, 624

Menu bar, 624

menus, 624

<META> tag (HTML), 569-571

metafiles, 624

method (document objects), 118

methods, 624
  browser object models, 116-118
  BuildPath, 157
  ChooseContent, 162
  Command object (ADO), 365-366
  Connection object (ADO), 362-363
  CopyFile, 157
  Errors collection (ADO), 381
  Field object (ADO), 378
  Fields collection (ADO), 381
  FileExists, 157-158
  Get, 161
  GetAllContent, 162
  GetListCount( ), 156
  GetListIndex( ), 156
  GetNextDescription( ), 156
  GetNextURL( ), 156
  GetNthDescription( ), 156
  GetNthURL( ), 156
  GetPreviousDescription( ), 156
  GetPreviousURL( ), 156
  HasAccess, 163
  Hits, 163
  Increment, 161
  PageHit, 163
  Parameter object (ADO), 369
  ProcessForm, 159
  Properties collection (ADO), 381
  Random, 158
  Recordset object (ADO), 370-375
  Remove, 161
  Reset, 163
  Set, 161
  see also commands; functions

Microsoft Access, *see* Access databases

Microsoft Certified Professional Program, 586

Microsoft GIF Animator command (Tools menu), 399

Microsoft Interactive Developer, 582

Microsoft Internet Information Server FAQs, 583

Microsoft Press books, 40

Microsoft Systems Journal, 582

Microsoft Transaction Server, *see* MTS

Microsoft Web Builder, 582

Microsoft Web sites
  BackOffice, 582
  ADO documentation, 360
  Developer's Network
    bookmarks, 43
    hyperlinks, 42
    Index facility, 40
    interface, 40
    navigating, 40
    organizational units, 39
    Search facility, 40-42
    topics, printing, 40
  DHTML specification, 191, 195
  DirectAnimation page, 203
  IIS page, 436
  Image Composer, 583
  Knowledge Base, 583
  Media Manager, 583
  Online Institute, 585
  Scripting Technologies, 583
  Scriptlets page, 205
  Site Builder Network, 583
  SQL Server, 583
  Visual Basic page, 262
  Windows NT Server, 582

Mid function (VBScript), 597

MidB function (VBScript), 597

MIDI audio, 533

MIME (Multipurpose Internet Mail Extension), 624

Minute function (VBScript), 595

mirroring, 406

Miscellaneous tab (Connection Properties dialog box), 341

mixed client/server-side scripting, 185

MMC (Microsoft Management Console), 435-438

Mod (modulus arithmetic) operator, 596

Mode property (Connection object), 364

modes
  changing, 498
  choosing, 498
  Local, 499-500
  Master, 498

Month function (VBScript), 595

movie players, 228

MovieWindowSize property (ActiveMovie control), 226

moving files/folders, 492

MRU List Contains option (General options), 56

MSDN (Microsoft Developer Network)
  bookmarks, 43
  hyperlinks, 42
  Index facility, 40
  interface, 40
  navigating, 40
  organizational units, 39
  Search facility, 40-42
  topics, printing, 40

MSDN News, 582

MsgBox function (VBScript), 595

MSN Investor Portfolio grid, 212

MTS (Microsoft Transaction Server), 447
  ActiveX, 301-308
  application services, 448-449
  installing, 302-303
  transactional server pages, 448

multi-tiered architectures, 286

multimedia
  ActiveX controls, 220
    Marquee control, 221
    Path control, 232
    Sprite control, 232
    Structured Graphics control, 233
  animated GIF files, 212
  DHTML pages, 199-203
    DirectAnimation, 202-203
    filters, 200-201
  performance tuning, 571-574
    animation, 573-574
    color depth, 572
    GIF files, 573
    JPEG files, 573
    resolution, 572
    vector files, 571-572
  Web sites, 534

Multimedia controls (design-time controls)
Page Transitions control, 256-257
Timelines control, 257-259

multiple-language projects, 544

MyInfo component (ASP components), 160

N

N-tier architecture
Web sites, 285-288

NAME attribute
<A> tag, 589
<META> tag, 569
<OBJECT> tag, 591

Name property
Command object, 367
Field object, 378
Parameter object, 369
Property object, 380

name servers, 625

named users (IIS), 490

namespace (IIS Management Console), 437

naming variables, 104-107

NativeError property (Error object), 379

navigating
MSDN library, 40
Script Outline, 123

Netscape
DevEdge Web site, 605
DHTML implementation, 190
JavaScript newsgroup, 584
JavaScript Web site, 583
Navigator browser, Document Object Model, 139

Netshow, 573

Network News Transport Protocol (NNTP) server, 451
newsgroups
controlled access, 453-454
creating, 451-452
security, 451

networks
resources, limiting, 556-557
stability, 287
see also Internet

New Backup Device dialog box, 475

New command (File menu), 537

New Database Device dialog box, 474

New Database dialog box, 473

New Database Project Wizard, 37

New Deployment Target command (Project menu), 52

New Domain Wizard, 450

New menu commands
Domain, 450
Virtual Directory, 439, 452
Web Site, 442

New Project command (File menu), 20, 44

New Project dialog box, 20, 45

New User command (User menu), 408

New Virtual Directory Wizard, 439, 452

New Web Site Wizard, 442

Newest Events Listed First command (View menu), 425

news URL links, 67

newsgroups (NNTP), 584
controlled access, 453-454
creating, 451-452

Nextlink object, 156

NI1 (National ISDN 1), 625

NNTP (Network News Transport Protocol) server
newsgroups
controlled access, 453-454
creating, 451-452
security, 451

noise filters, 625

nonclustered indexes, 317

normalization, 317-325
denormalized database development, 322-323
overnormalization, 323-325

Not Found Errors counter (Performance Monitor), 555

Nothing function (VBScript), 593

nothing value, 625

Now function (VBScript), 595

NT Server, see Windows NT Server

NT-1 (Network Termination 1), 625

NTFS (NT File System), 405-406, 486

Nth Tagged Text expression (Find/Replace), 74

NTLM password authentication, 164

Null function (VBScript), 593

null values, 625

number data type (JScript), 104

Number object (JScript), 112

Number property (Error object), 379

numBorder parameter (AdRotator object), 154

numerical entries, validating, 134

NumericScale property
Field object, 378
Parameter object, 370

numHeight parameter (AdRotator object), 154

numWidth parameter (AdRotator object), 154

O

Object Linking and Embedding (OLE), 287

object management functions (VBScript), 109

object models, browsers, 114-119
collections, 116-118
events, 118-120
methods, 116-118
properties, 116-118

object subtype (VBScript), 104

<OBJECT> tag (HTML), 215, 591

object tags, 591

objects, 625
Active Server Pages, 604
ADO
Command object, 365-369
Connection object, 362
Error object, 379-380
Field object, 377-378
Parameter object, 369-370
Property object, 380
Recordset object, 370-377
All, 193-194
Anchors, 193

Applets, 193
application performance issues, 577
Application, 149-150
Body, 193
built-in objects (Active Server Pages), 149-152
Collaboration Data Objects (CDO), 158
COM (Component Object Model), 263-264
creating, 597
Document, 193-195
events, 195-196
Filters, 193
Forms, 193
Images, 193
JavaScript, 602
JScript, 110-113, 602
Links, 193
Nextlink, 156
recordset, 339
referencing, 194
Request, 150-151
Response, 151
Scripts, 193
Selection, 193
Server, 151
server-side components, 152-164
AdRotator object, 153-155
BrowserType object, 155-156
Session, 151-152, 577
smoothing, 390
Stylesheets, 193
Window, 193
Objects counter (Performance Monitor), 556
Oct function (VBScript), 594
ODBC (Open Database Connectivity), 49, 328, 625
Administrator, 329-330
downloading, 329
<OL> tag (HTML), 590
OLE (Object Linking and Embedding), 287
OLE control, 625
On Error function (VBScript), 595
onafterupdate event, 140
onbeforeunload event, 141
onbeforeupdate event, 140
onblur event, 141
onclick event, 119, 140
ondblclick event, 119, 140

ondragstart event, 119, 140
One or More expression (Find/Replace), 75
onerror event, 119, 141
onerrorupdate event, 140
onfocus event, 141
onhelp event, 119, 140-141
onkeydown event, 119, 140
onkeypress event, 119
onkeyup event, 119, 140
online support site (Site Server), 458
onload event, 119, 141
onmousedown event, 119, 140
onmousemove event, 119, 140
onmouseout event, 119
onmouseover event, 119
onmouseup event, 119, 140
onreadstatechange event, 119
onreadystatechange event, 140
onresize event, 141
onrowenter event, 140
onrowexit event, 140
onscripletevent event, 206
onscroll event, 141
onselectstart event, 140
onunload event, 141
Open Database Connectivity (ODBC), 49, 328, 625
Administrator, 329-330
downloading, 329
open method, 118
Open With dialog box, 391
operating modes, see modes
operators
JScript
bitwise operators, 600
compound operators, 601
computational operators, 601
logical operators, 601
precedence, 602
VBScript, 596
optimizing performance, see performance tuning
Option Explicit function (VBScript), 597
Options command (Tools menu), 55

Options dialog box, 55
Options menu commands
Chart, 416
Report, 423
Or (logical disjunction) operator, 596
Or regular expression, 74
Order Manager (Site Server), 464
organizing Web sites, 36-37, 535-537
OriginalValue property (Field object), 378
Other Windows command (View menu), 121, 220
out-of-process components, 290-291
OutputFileURL parameter (Tools component), 159
outsourcing Web sites, 534
overflow attribute (CSS), 198, 608
overnormalization, 323-325

P

<P> tag (HTML), 591
padding properties (CSS), 607
Page Transitions control, 256-257
page-break-after property (CSS), 609
page-break-before property (CSS), 609
PageCount property (Recordset object), 376
PageCounter component (ASP components), 162-163
PageHit method, 163
pages, see Web pages
PageSize property (Recordset object), 376
Paint button (Image Composer), 393-394
Paint Palette, 625
Paintbrush, 625
Painting tool, 625
Pan button (Image Composer), 393

<PARAM> tag (HTML), 216

Parameter object, 369-370

parameters
AdRotator object, 154
tags, 588
Tools component (ASP), 159

parentWindow property (document objects), 116

parseFloat function, 603

parseInt function, 603

partitions, 486

passwords, 493
anonymous password authentication, 164
basic password authentication, 164
NTLM password authentication, 164
Windows NT Server, 409

Paste option (Toolbox shortcut menu), 218

Path control, 232

Pause method, 228

PC PaintBrush Format (PCX), 625

PCD (Photo CD format), 625

Pencil icon (Web Diagram window), 23

Pencil tool, 625

Performance Monitor
Alerts facility, 417
charts, 414-416
counters
HTTP service counters, 554-555
IIS counters, 556
viewing, 553
starting, 553
Windows NT Servers, 412-423
log files, 419-421
reports, 421-423

performance tuning
ActiveX Database Object, 382-383
client-side performance
cache, 565-568
HTML document sections, 560-563
HTML tags, 568-571
HTTP, 563-565
multimedia data compression, 571-574
Internet routes, tracking, 557-559

multi-tiered Web sites, 286
server-side performance
application object, 577
bottlenecks, 576
ISAPI, 577
scripting languages, 575
SQL Server, 478-480
Web servers
bandwidth limitations, 556-557
Performance Monitor, 553-556
Web sites
browser differences, 552-553
design guidelines, 577-578
download speed, 551-552
guidelines, 550
Windows NT Server, 412-431

Performance view (Task Manager), 430

periodicals, 40

PermissionChecker component (ASP components), 163-164

permissions, 441, 470-471

Personalization and Membership Services (Site Server), 461-462

Photo CD, 626

Photoshop, 626

Pickup directory (SMTP server), 450

pictures, *see* **graphics**

pixelization, 626

pixels, 614, 626

***Platinum Edition Using HTML 4, Java 1.1, and JavaScript 1.2,* 582**

PlayCount property (ActiveMovie control), 226-227

plugins collection (document objects), 117

Policies menu commands, User Rights, 410

pop-up statement completion, 71

position attributes (CSS), 197-198, 608

<PRE> tag (HTML), 591

precedence (JScript operators), 602

Precision property
Field object, 378
Parameter object, 370

prefilling form entries, 132

Prepared property (Command object), 367

Prevent Match expression, 75

previewing Scriptlets, 206

primary keys, 314-315

printing MSDN topics, 40

Private function (VBScript), 593-595

private procedures, 626

privileges, 470-471

procedural textures, 626

procedures, 626
GLOBAL.ASA file, 188
stepping procedures, 176
VBScript
creating, 597
declarations, 595
see also functions; methods

process color, 626

process priorities, 429

Processes command (Debug menu), 183

Processes view (Task Manager), 429

ProcessForm method, 159

processing server-side scripts, 183

product documentation, 39

production, 534-535
resources, 523
sign-offs, 535

Project Explorer, 50, 265
debugger, 173
layouts, 82
site diagrams, 88
themes, 80

Project menu commands
Add Item, 50
Add Item to, 61
New Deployment Target, 52
Properties, 293

Project Rights dialog box, 510

Project Wizards
Database Project Wizard, 49
solutions, creating, 45
Web Project Wizard, 46

projects, 37, 536, 630
ActiveX, creating, 292-293
ADO-based, debugging, 383
DSP (Developer Studio Project) files, 37

local working copies, 52
managing, 50
prototypes, 22-25
settings, 58
solutions
adding to, 37
creating, 38
team development, 17-18
Web, creating, 20-22

promotions, 528

properties, 626
Active Server Pages, 148-149
ActiveX components, 293-294
ActiveX controls, 225, 240,
272-274
browser object models, 116-118
Command object, 367-369
Connection object, 364-365
Error object, 379-380
Errors collection, 381
Field object, 361, 378
Fields collection, 382
Grid control, 250-253
Parameter object, 369-370
Properties collection, 382
Property object, 361, 380
Recordset object, 376

**Properties collection (ADO),
381-382**

Properties command
Action menu, 444
Project menu, 293

Properties dialog box
Advanced tab, 253
Borders tab, 253
Data tab, 252
Format tab, 253
General tab, 251
Navigation tab, 252

Properties window, 78-79

**Properties Window command
(View menu), 217**

Property object, 361, 380

property pages, 79

**Property Pages dialog box
(recordset object), 339**

protected subsystems, 405

protocols
HTTP (Hypertext Transfer
Protocol), 622
Performance Monitor
counters, 554-555
performance tuning, 564-565
servers, 622
URL links, 67
SQL Server configuration,
333-336

TCP/IP (Transmission Control
Protocol/Internet Protocol),
629

prototypes, 22-25

**Provider property (Connection
object), 364-365**

proxy servers, 626

**Public function (VBScript),
593-595**

**Public Internet Information
Server newsgroup, 584**

public procedures, 626

public relations sites, 520

public statements, 295

publishing
files, 503
Site Server features
content deployment, 459
content management,
458-459
customizable starter sites,
457-458

<PURGETIME> tag (XML), 204

**push publishing (Site Server),
461**

push technology, 203-205

Q-R

queries, creating, 30-31

Query.htm file, 446

Query.htx file, 446

Query.idq file, 446

**queryCommandEnabled
method, 118**

**queryCommandIndeterm
method, 118**

**queryCommandSupported
method, 118**

**queryCommandValue method,
118**

**Queue directory (SMTP server),
450**

Quick View Editor, 15

QuickTime, 573

**RAD (Rapid Application
Development), 14-16**
database integration, 18
debugging support, 15-17

Site Designer, 16
Source Editor, 26-27
Web applications, remote
deployment, 16-17

**RAID (Redundant Array of
Inexpensive Disks), 406-407**

Random method, 158

**Randomize function (VBScript),
109, 596**

**Rapid Application
Development, see RAD**

raster graphics, 626

raster-format files, 572

**Rate property (ActiveMovie
control), 226**

rate sheets, 525

**RCS (Revision Control
Systems), 498**

**Re-use Current Document
Window option (General
options), 56**

ReadProperties event, 272

ReadyState property
ActiveMovie control, 226
document objects, 116

ReadyStateChange event, 228

RealVideo, 573

**RecordCount property
(Recordset object), 376**

records, 626

**Recordset NavBar (design-time
controls), 255-256**

Recordset object
cursor types, 377
methods, 370-375
properties, 376
property pages, 339

RecordSetNavBar, 339

recordsets, 626

**Red, Green, Blue (RGB) color
model, 627**

**ReDim function (VBScript),
593-595**

**Redundant Array of
Inexpensive Disks (RAID),
406-407**

reference sites, 520

referencing
objects, 194
Scriptlets, 206

referential integrity, 325-326

referrer property (document objects), 116

Register Server dialog box, 467

registering
ActiveX components, 298
SQL Server, 467

Registry, 626

regular expressions, 73

REL parameter (<LINK> tag), 589

relational databases, *see* **databases**

relational operators, 626

relationships, 89

Rem function (VBScript), 593

Remove method, 161

Rename Item option (Toolbox shortcut menu), 218

rendering, 627

repairing hyperlinks, 95

Repeat N Times expression, 75

replacing text strings, 72

Report command
Options menu, 423
View menu, 421

Report Options dialog box, 423

reports (Performance Monitor), 421-423

repositories, 519

Request object, 150-151, 604

Rescan command (Action menu), 446

reserve cropping, 627

reserved words (JScript), 603

Reset method, 163

resizing databases, 478

resolution, 572, 627

resource kits, 40

resources
beta testings, 586
books, 582
limiting, 556-557
listservers, 584
magazines, 582
newsgroups, 584
training, 585
users groups, 585
see also Web sites

Response object, 151, 605

Restore Files and Directories user right, 411

Restore Progress dialog box, 478

restoring databases, 477-478

restricting access, *see* **access control**

return statement (JScript), 600

reusability, multi-tiered Web sites, 286

REV parameter (<LINK> tag), 589

revision control, *see* **VSS**

RFC1244 (Site Security Handbook), 495

RGB (Red, Green, Blue) color model, 627

Right function (VBScript), 109, 597

RightB function (VBScript), 598

rights, 441, 470-471

Rights Assignments for User command (Tools menu), 511

Rights by Project command (Tools menu), 510

ripple filters, 627

Rnd function (VBScript), 109, 596

Rollback function, 503

rolling back files (Visual SourceSafe), 503

root Webs, 54

Rotator Schedule File (RSF), 154-155

RSF (Rotator Schedule File), 154-155

Rtrim function (VBScript), 598

Rule Manager (Site Server), 462

Run method, 228

runtime, 627
errors, 168, 627
text, 241-243

S

S/T Interface, 628

sales-oriented sites, 521

SAM (Security Accounts Manager), 407

SAMP tag, 589

saturation, 627

Save Chart Settings command (File menu), 415

Save command (File menu), 63

saving files, 57

scalability, Windows NT Server, 405

scale values, 415

scan rates, 627

scanlines, 627

scanners, 627

SCHEDULE tag (XML), 204

schemes, 627

scope, 627
Index Server search forms, 447
Web site design, 518-525

screening, 627

Script Block tool, 120-121

Script Breakpoint Properites dialog box, 174

Script Builder, 121-122, 215, 219

script levels, 627

Script Outline, 121
browser events, 139, 142
navigating, 123

Script Outline view, 71

Script Outline window, 220

<SCRIPT> tag (HTML), 100, 128

ScriptEngine function (VBScript), 110

ScriptEngineBuildVersion function (VBScript), 110

ScriptEngineMajorVersion function (VBScript), 110

ScriptEngineMinorVersion function (VBScript), 110

scripting, 38
Active Server Pages, 604
browsers, 114-119
client-side scripting, 101-102, 124-125
browser events, 139-141
debugging, 181
Form design-time controls, 247-248
VBScript, 128
data types, 102-106
Script Builder, 121-122
server-side scripting, 101-102, 124-125

Source Editor, 71, 141
variables, 102-106
  declaring, 104-107
  naming, 104-107
Web pages, 119-121
see also ASPs; debugging

**Scripting Object Model,
240-241**

Scriptlets, 205-207

**scripts collection (document
objects), 117**

Scripts object, 193

**ScrollDelay parameter
(<MARQUEE> tag), 223**

scrolling text, 221

**ScrollPixels parameter
(<MARQUEE> tag), 223**

**SDI Environment option
(General options), 56**

SDK/DDK documentation, 39

**search engines, Site Server
features, 459-460**

Search facility (MSDN), 40-42

search forms (Index Server)
customizing, 446-447
default files, 446
scope, 447

**Second function (VBScript),
595**

**Secure Sockets Layer (SSL),
491-492**

security, 482
anonymous password
  authentication, 164
basic password authentication,
  164
firewalls, 493
FrontPage 98, 545-546
IIS (Internet Information
  Server)
  anonymous accounts,
    488-489
  directory browsing, 494
  filtered access, 490
  log files, 493
  maximum connections, 493
  named users, 490
  SSL (Secure Sockets Layer),
    491-492
  timeout periods, 493
multi-tiered Web sites, 287
NNTP (Network News
  Transport Protocol), 451
online resources, 495

passwords, 164, 493
planning, 482-484
services, 492
vertical partitioning, 324-325
Windows NT, 484-486
  account configuration,
    485-486
  ACLs (access control lists),
    486-487
  NTFS partitions, 486
  Server, 407-411

Security menu commands
Account Details, 472
Grant New, 470

**Select button (Image
Composer), 390**

**Select Case function (VBScript),
594**

**Select Data Source dialog box,
49**

**Select Interface Members dialog
box, 270**

**Selection arrow (Image
Composer), 392-394**

selection borders, 627

Selection object, 193

**selection property (document
objects), 117**

**Selection tool (Image
Composer), 394**

**SelectionEnd property
(ActiveMovie control), 227**

selections, 627

**SelectionStart property
(ActiveMovie control), 227**

**Server Configuration/Options
dialog box, 468**

server extensions, 36

**Server Extensions (FrontPage
98), 545-546**

Server Manager, 412

Server object, 151, 605

**Server Objects tab (Toolbox),
77**

server software, 36

**server-side components (Active
Server Pages), 152-164**
AdRotator object, 153-155
  parameters, 154
  Rotator Schedule File,
    154-155
BrowserType object, 155-156

Collaboration Data Objects for
  NTS component, 157-158
Content Linking component,
  156-157
ContentRotator component, 162
Counters component, 161
Database Access component,
  156
FileSystemObject component,
  157
MyInfo component, 160
PageCounter component,
  162-163
Permission Checker
  component, 163-164
Status component, 160
Tools component, 158-160

server-side development, 17

**server-side forms (design-time
controls), 244-246**

**server-side scripting, 101-102,
146**
Active Server Pages, *see* ASPs
client-side scripting, compared,
  124-125
performance tuning
  application object, 577
  bottlenecks, 576
  ISAPI, 577
  scripting languages, 575
debugging, 170, 183

servers, 628
ActiveX components, 298-301
child Webs, 54
Internet Information Server, *see*
  IIS
libraries, component sharing,
  55
MTS (Microsoft Transaction
  Server), 447
  ActiveX, 301-308
  application services, 448-449
  installing, 302-303
  transactional server pages,
    448
NNTP (Network News
  Transport Protocol)
  controlled access, 453-454
  newsgroups, 451-452
  security, 451
NT, *see* Windows NT Server
performance tuning
  bandwidth limitations,
    556-557
  Performance Monitor,
    553-556
root Webs, 54

SMTP (Simple Mail Transport Protocol)
components, 449-450
mail domains, 450-451
subdirectories, 450
SQL, *see* SQL Server
Web sites
deploying to, 52
multiple, 53

service Web sites, 519-522

services
MTS (Microsoft Transaction Server), 448-449
security issues, 492

Session object, 151-152, 577, 605

Session.Abandon procedure, 188

Session_OnEnd event, 605

Session_OnEnd procedure, 188

Session_OnStart event, 605

Session_OnStart procedure, 188

sessions, 628

Set Attributes dialog box, 271

Set function (VBScript), 593

Set Mapping dialog box, 271

Sgn function (VBScript), 594

Shadow filter, 200

shadows, 628

Shapes button (Image Composer), 392-394

SHAPES parameter (<OBJECT> tag), 592

shareware, 628

sharpening, 628

Shockwave, 574, 628

Show Empty Environment option (General options), 56

Show New Project Dialog option (General options), 56

Show Status Bar option (General options), 56

ShowControls property (ActiveMovie control), 227

ShowDisplay property (ActiveMovie control), 227

ShowPositionControls property (ActiveMovie control), 227

ShowSelectionControls property (ActiveMovie control), 227

ShowTracker property (ActiveMovie control), 227

Shutdown the System user right, 411

Simple Mail Transport Protocol (SMTP) server
components, 449-450
mail domains, 450-451
subdirectories, 450

Sin function (VBScript), 109, 596

single subtype (VBScript), 103

Site Builder Workshop Web site, 583

Site Designer, 16, 84
global navigation bar, 90
hyperlinks
external verification, 94
filtering, 94
repairing, 95
viewing, 92
Link View, 92
project prototypes, 22-25
site diagrams
adding/removing pages, 85
creating, 84-85
creating pages, 91
managing, 91
relationships, 89
views, 91
site integrity, 92
site maps, 22-23
Web Diagram window, 23

Site Diagram toolbar, 86

site diagrams
creating, 84-85
managing, 91
pages
adding, 85
creating, 91
removing, 85
relationships, 89
views, 91

site integrity, 92

site maps, 22-23

Site Properties/Virtual Directory Properties dialo, 444

Site Server, 456-457
Commerce Edition
analysis services, 464
engaging customers, 463-464
transacting with customers, 464

delivery features
analysis services, 462-463
Knowledge Manager, 460-461
Personalization and Membership Services, 461-462
push publishing, 461
publishing features
content deployment, 459
content management, 458-459
customizable starter sites, 457-458
search features, 459-460

Site Server Express (IIS), 435

sites, *see* Web sites

SIZE attribute (<FONT> tag), 590

Size property (Parameter object), 370

sizing
Scriptlets, 206
sprites, 395

sliders, 628

SLN (Developer Studio Solution) file, 37

smoothing objects, 390, 628

SMTP (Simple Mail Transport Protocol) server
components, 449-450
mail domains, 450-451
subdirectories, 450

sockets, SSL (Secure Sockets Layer), 491-492

solorization, 628

solutions, 20, 37, 628
creating, 44
Project Wizards, 45
projects, 38
Web Project Wizard, 46
documents, adding, 50
managing, 45
Project Wizards, 49
projects
adding, 37, 50
local working copies, 52
managing, 50
SLN (Developer Studio Solution) file, 37
Web sites, deploying, 52
see also workspace

source control (Visual SourceSafe), 57
enabling, 504-505

Source Editor, 15, 26-27, 60; 69
document outline, 70
Find and Replace feature, 72
HTML Outline view, 70
pop-up statement completion, 71
Script Outline view, 71
scripting, 141

Source line (Event Viewer logs), 424

source materials, 524

Source property
Error object, 379
Recordset object, 376

SourceSafe Options dialog box, 509

SourceSafe, *see* **VSS**

Space function (VBScript), 598

***Special Edition Using Internet Information Server 4.0*, 132, 582**

sphere filters, 628

SPID (Service Profile Identifier), 628

Sprite control, 232

sprites, 232
copying, 395
creating, 393-395
cropping, 395-396
editing, 393-395
handles, 396
sizing, 395

SQL (Structured Query Language), 628
Debugger, 357
statements, 349-351

SQL Server, 330, 624
accounts, 466-467
creating, 467-468
deleting, 473
trusted mode, 468-469
user attributes, 472
user privileges, 470-471
databases
adding devices, 474-475
backing up, 476-477
backup devices, 475
creating, 473-474
data connections, 331
deleting, 474
DSNs, 332-336
maintenance, 479-480
properties, 339-340
resizing, 478
restoring from backup, 477-478

registering, 467

SQLState property (Error object), 379

Sqr function (VBScript), 109, 596

SRC parameter (<IMG> tag), 590

SSL (Secure Sockets Layer), 491-492

standards
compatability, 18
DHTML, 18-33
DTCs (Design-Time Controls), 18

STANDBY parameter (<OBJECT> tag), 592

Start command (Debug menu), 173

Start menu commands, Administrative Tools (Common), 408

start tags, 588

starting Performance Monitor, 553

State property
Command object, 367
Connection object, 364
Recordset object, 376

StateChange event, 228

statements
JScript, 599
SQL statements, 349-351

static cursor, 377

static pages, 524

Status bar, 628

Status component (ASP components), 160

Status property (Recordset object), 376

stepping procedures, 176

Stop method, 228

Store Builder Wizard (Site Server), 464

stored procedures
creating, 354-357
debugging, 357

storyboards, 535

StrComp function (VBScript), 598

string data type (JScript), 104

String function (VBScript), 109, 598

String object (JavaScript/ JScript), 113, 603

string subtype (VBScript), 103

strings, 628

striping with parity, 407

<STRONG> tag (HTML), 589

StrReverse function (VBScript), 109

Structured Graphics control, 233

style blocks, embedding, 610

style sheets, *see* **CSS (cascading style sheets)**

style tags, 590

styleSheets collection (document objects), 117

Stylesheets object, 193

Sub function (VBScript), 595-597

subroutines, 597
see also functions; methods

syntax errors, 168

System DSN tab (ODBC Administrator), 329

system events, 424

szURL parameter (Marquee tag), 223

T

T1 connections, 551, 629

T3 connections, 551, 629

Table menu commands, Insert Table, 68

tables, 312-316, 629
creating, 68
fields, 313-314
foreign keys, 315-316
horizontal partitioning, 323
primary keys, 314-315
referential integrity, 325-326
vertical partitioning, 323-325
Web sites, 531

Tagged Expression, 74

tags
HTML, 588
<BGCOLOR>, 531
<BODY>, 562-563
document body tags, 589
document heads, 588
end tags, 588

<FORM>, 132
<HEAD>, 562
<HTML>, 560-561
hyperlink tags, 589
image tags, 590
<IMG>, 569
list tags, 590
<MARQUEE>, 221-223
<META>, 569-571
<OBJECT>, 215
object tags, 591
<PARAM>, 216
parameters, 588
<SCRIPT>, 100, 128
start tags, 588
style tags, 590
<TITLE>, 568
XML, 204

Take Ownership of Files or Other Object user right, 411

Tan function (VBScript), 109, 596

TARGET parameter
<A> tag, 589
<BASE> tag, 589

Task List (Visual Studio), 57

Task Manager, 428-431

TCB (Trusted Computing Base), 484

TCP/IP (Transmission Control Protocol/Internet Protocol), 629

team development, 17-18

technical articles and backgrounders, 40

telnet URL links, 67

TemplateURL parameter (Tool component), 159

Temporary Internet Files directory (Internet Explorer cache), 565-567

terminals, 284

testing
ActiveX controls, 275-276
sites, 545

text
finding, 72
inputting, 595
runtime text, 241-243
scrolling, 221
Web sites, 529

Text button (Image Composer), 392

Text Editor (Visual Studio), 57

text editors, 26-27

Text parameter (AdRotator object), 154

text sprites, 390

text style tags, 590

text-align property (CSS), 606

text-decoration property (CSS), 606

text-indent property (CSS), 606

text-transform property (CSS), 606

texture mapping, 629

Texture Transfer button (Image Composer), 393

TGA (Targa Format), 629

themes, 80, 526, 629

TIFF (Tagged Image File Format), 629

time/date functions, 595

Time function (VBScript), 595

time stamps, 143

Timelines control, 257-259

timeout periods (IIS), 493

TimeSerial function (VBScript), 594

TimeValue function (VBScript), 594

<TITLE> tag (HTML), 568

TITLE parameter
<A> tag, 589
<LINK> tag, 589

title property (document objects), 117

<TITLE> tag
HTML, 589
XML, 204

toolbars
Design Editor, 63
Image Composer, 391
Site Diagram toolbar, 86

Toolbox, 75-77, 215-216, 265
customizing, 77
Design-Time Controls tab, 77
HTML tab, 76
Server Objects tab, 77

Toolbox command (View menu), 216

Tools component (ASP components), 158-160

Tools menu commands
Customize Toolbox, 279
Microsoft GIF Animator, 399

Options, 55
Rights Assignments for User menu), 511
Rights by Project, 510

ToolTips, 173

top attribute (CSS), 197, 609

Total Anonymous Users counter (Performance Monitor), 555

Total NonAnonymous Users counter (Performance Monitor), 555

trace contours, 629

traceroute command, 557-559

tracert command, 557-559

tracing Internet routes, 557-559

Tracing tab (ODBC Administrator), 330

tracking Internet routes, 557-559

training, 585

transaction servers, 301-308, 629

transactional server pages, 434, 448

transactions, 464, 629

Trim function (VBScript), 598

true color, 629

True function (VBScript), 593

Trusted Computing Base (TCB), 484

trusted connections, 467

trusted mode, 468-469

<TT> tag (HTML), 591

tuning performance, *see* performance tuning

Type line (Event Viewer logs), 424

TYPE parameter (<OBJECT> tag), 592

Type property
Field object, 378
Parameter object, 370
Property object, 380

typeOf function (JScript), 110

U

U Interface, 630

<U> tag (HTML), 591

Ubound function (VBScript), 593

Ucase function (VBScript), 597

<UL> tag (HTML), 590

UnderlyingValue property (Field object), 378

Undo Check Out function (Visual SourceSafe), 503

Undo Option, 630

unescape( ) function, 110, 603

Update Time radio buttons, 416

updating Web sites, 500-501, 528

UPS (Uninterruptible Power Supply), 406

url property (document objects), 117

URL parameter (AdRotator object), 154

URLs (Uniform Resource Locators), 66, 630

usage analysis services (Site Server), 462

usage counters, 563-565

<USAGE> tag (XML), 204

USEMAP parameter (<OBJECT> tag), 592

Usenet newsgroups, 584

user analysis services (Site Server), 463

User DSN tab (ODBC Administrator), 329

User line (Event Viewer logs), 424

User Manager, 408, 412

User menu commands
New User, 408
Add User, 509

User Properties dialog box, 409

User Rights command (Policies menu), 410

users
NT Server
accounts, 407-411
adding, 409-410
creating, 408-409
deleting, 409-410
groups, 585
input validation, 132

privileges, 470-471
named users, 490
Visual SourceSafe, 509

Using Active Server Pages newsgroup, 584

Using Index Server newsgroup, 584

V

validating forms
client-side scripting, 130
complete, 135
currency entries, 133
date entries, 134
numerical entries, 134

value bar, 414-416

Value property
Field object, 361, 378
Parameter object, 370
Property object, 361, 380

var statement (JScript), 600

<VAR> tag (HTML), 589

variables, 630
declaring, 104-107, 595-597
naming, 104-107
scripting, 102-106
values, changing, 178

variants, 598

VarType function (VBScript), 107, 598

VB, see Visual Basic

VBScript, 592
ActiveX controls, 138
arithmetic functions, 596
arrays, 593
assignments, 593
benefits, 129
branching, 593
client-side scripting, 128
browser events, 139-141
client-side scripts, 129
form validation, 130
comments, 593
constants, 593
data conversion, 594
data types, 103-104
error handling, 595
forms, 132
functions, 107-110
creating, 113-114
date/time functions, 595
input/output operations, 595
limitations, 129

literals, 593
looping, 593
newsgroup, 584
objects, creating, 597
operators, 596
procedures, 595-597
strings, manipulating, 597
tags, 592
variables
declaring, 104, 595-597
naming, 104
variants, 598

vector graphics, 233, 630

vector-format files, 572

Verisign Corporation Web site, 495

version control, see VSS (Visual SourceSafe)

Version property (Connection object), 364

vertical grids, 416

vertical labels, 416

Vertical Maximum text box, 416

vertical partitioning, 323-325

vertical-align property (CSS), 606

video
performance issues, 573-574
Web sites, 530-533

Video for Windows, 573

View menu commands
Alert, 417
Break at Next Statement, 183
Debug Windows, 174
Document Outline, 70
Filter Events, 425
IE 4, 181
Log, 419
Newest Events Listed First, 425
Other Windows, 121, 220
Properties Window, 217
Report, 421
Toolbox, 216

viewing
database views, 352-354
hyperlinks, 92
Performance Monitor counters, 553
properties, 293-294
site diagrams, 24, 91

Virtual Directory command (New menu), 439, 452

virtual domains, 441-444

virtual roots, 630

visibility property (CSS), 198, 609

visited property (CSS), 609

Visual Basic, 36
ActiveX controls, creating, 263, 292-298
ActiveX Control Interface Wizard, 264, 269-272
COM development, 263-264
compile process, 276-277
deployment, 277-281
error-handling code, 274-275
project files, 267-268
property-handling code, 272-274
test applications, 275-276
user interface components, 268-269
version compatibility, 277
add-ins, activating, 266-267
ByRef statements, 295
ByVal statements, 295
code review, 294-296
Control Creation Edition, 262
development environment, 264-267
customizing, 265-266
Project Explorer, 265
Toolbox, 265
dynamic help, 295
extensions, 288
public statements, 295

Visual C++, 36, 624

Visual Database Tools, 36

Visual FoxPro, 36, 624

Visual J++, 36, 624

Visual SourceSafe, see VSS

Visual Studio, 19, 39, 56-57, 584

vLinkColor property (document objects), 117

Volume property (ActiveMovie control), 227

VSPACE parameter (<OBJECT> tag), 592

VSS (Visual SourceSafe), 500-502
access control
locks, 511
project rights, 510
project security, 509-510
user rights, 511
deltas, 501

files
checking in, 502, 506-507
checking out, 502, 506-507
comparing, 504
file type management, 512-513
publishing, 503
rolling back, 503
History function, 503
installing, 500-501
projects, 501
source control, enabling, 504-505
Undo Check Out function, 503
users
adding, 509-510
removing, 510
working directories, 502

W

W3C (World Wide Web Consortium) Web site, 190

wais URL link, 67

Watch window, 174

watches, 173

Wave filter, 200

Web applications, 630
database integration, 18
remote deployment, 16-17
team development, 17-18

Web browsers, see browsers

Web Diagram window (Site Designer), 23

Web Files menu commands, Get Latest Version, 500

Web pages
ActiveX controls, 216, 287-292
administration, 534
authoring, 38
client access, 525
customer input, 525
customizable options, 526
creating, 61
animation, 212, 530-532
architecture, 285-288
audiences, 522
audio, 531-533
bandwidth, 525
content files, 537
dynamic content, 524
frames, 532
generated content, 524
graphics, 530-532
hyperlinks, 66

images, 65
layouts, 80-82
movie players, 231
multimedia, 534
scripts, 119-121
scrolling text, 221
tables, 68, 531
text, 529
themes, 80, 526
usage counters, 563-564
Design tabs, 217
design sign-offs, 535
design-time controls
inserting, 238-243
properties, editing, 240
runtime text, 241-243
Scripting Object Model, 240-241
designing, 518-535
FrontPage 98, 544-545
scope, 518-525
storyboards, 535
development, 36-38
editing, 38, 61
maintenance, 546-547
marketing, 520
objectives, 525-534
organizing, 36, 535-537
projects, 37
solutions, 37
outsourcing, 534
performance tuning
browser differences, 552-553
design guidelines, 577-578
download speed, 551-552
guidelines, 550
production, 534-535
production resources, 523
production sign-offs, 535
programming, 38, 534
projects, 536
promotions, 528
public relations sites, 520
rate sheets, 525
reference sites, 520
repositories, 519
resources, 582
sales-oriented sites, 521
scripting, 38
service Web sites, 519-522
site diagrams
adding/removing pages, 85
creating, 84-85
creating pages, 91
managing, 91
relationships, 89
source materials, 524
Source tabs, 218
static pages, 524
updating, 528

video, 530-533
see also Web sites
Web Project Wizard
modes, 498-499
solutions, creating, 46
Web Site Abstraction Web site, 203
Web Site command (New menu), 442
Web sites
access speed, 522
Active Server Developer's Journal, 582
Department of Defense Trusted Computer Evaluation, 495
deploying, 52
FrontPage, 48
hosting, 534
InstallShield, 278
Macmillan Computer Publishing, 495
master sites, updating, 500-501
Microsoft
BackOffice, 582
ADO documentation, 360
Developer's Network, 40-43
DHTML specification, 191, 195
DirectAnimation page, 203
IIS page, 436
Image Composer, 583
Knowledge Base, 583
Media Manager, 583
Microsoft Interactive Developer, 582
Microsoft Systems Journal, 582
Microsoft Web Builder, 582
Online Institute, 585
Scripting Technologies, 583
Scriptlets page, 205
Site Builder Network, 583
SQL Server, 583
Visual Basic page, 262
Windows NT Server, 582
MSDN News, 582
Netscape Communicator DHTML specification, 191
Netscape DevEdge, 605
Verisign Corporation, 495
Web Site Abstraction, 203
Wise Installation System, 278
World Wide Web Consortium (W3C), 190, 197
see also Web pages
Web Wizard, 390
Webs (FrontPage), 48
Weekday function (VBScript), 595

while statement (JScript), 600
While...Wend function (VBScript), 594
WIDTH attribute
<IMG> tag, 571-574, 590
<OBJECT> tag, 592
<PRE> tag, 591
width property (CSS), 197, 609
window events, 141
Window Menu Contains option (General options), 56
Window object, 193, 603
windows, debugging, 180
Windows NT File System (NTFS), 405-406, 486
Windows NT Server
access rights, 410-411
administration, 412
advantages, 404-407
automatic restarts, 406
backup support, 406
configuring, 404
DHCP (Dynamic Host Configuration Protocol), 412
error handling, 405
Event Viewer, 412, 423-428
Explorer, 412
fault tolerance, 405-407
integration, 404-405
NTFS (NT File System), 405-406
passwords, 409
Performance Monitor, 412-423
Alerts facility, 417
log files, 419-421
reports, 421-423
performance tuning, 412-431
protected subsystems, 405
RAID (Redundant Array of Inexpensive Disks), 406-407
resource management, 431
SAM (Security Accounts Manager), 407
scalability, 405
security, 407-411, 484-486
account configuration, 485-486
ACLs (access control lists), 486-487
NTFS partitions, 486
Task Manager, 428-431
UPS (Uninterruptible Power Supply), 406
User Manager, 408, 412
users
accounts, 407-411
creating, 408-409
groups, 409-410

WINS (Windows Internet Name Service), 412
wiping, 630
Wise Installation System Web site, 278
with statement (JScript), 600
wizards
ActiveX Control Interface Wizard, 264, 269-272
Select Interface Members dialog box, 270
Set Attributes dialog box, 271
Set Mapping dialog box, 271
Application Setup Wizard, 277-279
Database Maintenance Plan Wizard, 479-480
Database Project Wizard, 49
New Domain Wizard, 450
New Virtual Directory Wizard, 439, 452
New Web Site Wizard, 442
Store Builder Wizard, 464
Web Project Wizard, 46, 498-499
workspace, 20-22, 536
World Wide Web Consortium (W3C) Web site, 190, 197
write method, 118
writeln method, 118
WYSIWYG (What-You-See-Is-What-You-Get) editing, 60

X-Y-Z

XML (Extensible Markup Language), 203-204
Xor (logical exclusion) operator, 596
Xray filter, 200
Year function (VBScript), 595
z-index property (CSS), 609
Zoom button (Image Composer), 393
zoom parameter (<MARQUEE> tag), 223
Zoom tool, 630

Special Edition Using Active Server Pages

Scot Johnson

This book serves as both a tutorial and a reference. Each chapter builds on the previous chapters, thus expanding the reader's knowledge. Additionally, the material is organized in a way that the reader can easily reference when he later has a question. This book provides the reader with up-to-date coverage of what can be done with Active Server Pages. This includes coverage of Active Server Pages as they relate to Transaction Server, the Personalization System, the Personal Web Server (with Windows 95), ActiveX Data Objects (ADO), and much more. Unlike most of the competition, this book assumes more basic knowledge of VBScript and standard Web page creation. This allows the book to go farther and deeper into technical topics surrounding Active Server Pages. Most of the competitive books center on Windows NT and IIS. This book expands the coverage to include using Active Server Pages on Windows 95 using the Personal Web Server. The technologies being used to create Web pages continue to evolve. This book presents the reader with an up-to-date look at how to create dynamic, personalized Web sites for both business and personal use. This is one of the first books to focus more on implementing Active Server Pages rather than on the theory behind working with Active Server Pages. This additional coverage is seen in the 850 pages of information. It includes new functionality available with the release of Microsoft's Internet Information Server 4.0 and Active Server Pages 2.

$49.99 US/$71.95 CDN　　　*User Level: Casual - Accomplished*
ISBN: 0-7897-1389-6　　　　*850 pp.*

Special Edition Using Visual Basic 6

Jeff Spotts and Brian Siler

Special Edition Using Visual Basic 6 is organized to serve as an easy-to-use reference. Individual topics and material are organized so they are easy to locate and read. *Special Edition Using Visual Basic 6* also teaches Visual Basic in a straightforward manner. It is assumed that the reader is new to Visual Basic. The book teaches programming with Visual Basic at a steady, consistent pace. After teaching the reader the Visual Basic programming language, the book progresses into more advanced topics. Such hot topics include creating ActiveX controls, using Visual Basic with Active Server Pages, Visual Basic database programming, and more. Because of its straightforward approach, *Special Edition Using Visual Basic 6* covers more topics in more detail than equivalently sized books. This new edition of a bestseller incorporates changes to Visual Basic 6 and the authors have packed additional hands-on examples throughout the book, making it even easier to learn the topics within Visual Basic. *Special Edition Using Visual Basic 6* goes beyond most Visual Basic books by providing information on everything you need to know to program applications with Visual Basic 6.

$39.99 US/$56.95 CDN　　　*User Level: Beginner - Intermediate*
ISBN: 0-7897-1542-2　　　　*900 pp.*

Special Edition Using Java 1.2

Joe Weber

The book is the programmer's tutorial/reference on Java 1.2 that contains detailed descriptions of Sun's Java 1.2 standards, APIs, class libraries, and programming tools. It covers major third-party products such as Microsoft's Java SDK 2.0, AFC, and RNI products that are rapidly gaining popularity. It contains step-by-step instruction for developers on how to create channels that broadcast sound and video, and how to charge users for accessing them. It covers other relevant Sun, Microsoft, and OMG technologies for Java and ActiveX, including CORBA, Java IDL, Joe, JavaBeans, and Enterprise JavaBeans. It provides Web developers with tools to make information on their sites easily accessible to users, and tips to make the tools more efficient. It contains over 20,000 lines of documented Java code that show programmers the details of building sophisticated Java applications. It contains all tools necessary to get started: a CD of JavaScript Code, Java applets, style sheets, and templates. There is currently no direct competition with this book. It is a complete tutorial/reference for experienced users that gives detailed coverage of the Java 1.2 language, APIs, class libraries, and programming tools. It contains a wealth of professional programming techniques, work-arounds, and thousands of lines of code that show programmers how to build sophisticated Java applications. Netscape Netcaster is a new component of the Communicator package that implements "passive browsing" by collecting information from the Web and making it available immediately to the user, without the user having to seek it out.

$49.99 US/$71.95 CDN   *User Level: Accomplished - Expert*
ISBN: 0-7897-1529-5   *1200 pp.*

Special Edition Using Microsoft Visual Studio for Enterprise Development

Don Benage, Azam Mirza, and G. A. Sullivan

Special Edition Using Visual Studio is a complete reference and tutorial for developers who want to learn to integrate the new tools and features of this programming suite. It shows the reader how to use the different integrated development environments (IDE) to build Visual C++, Visual J++, Visual Basic, and Visual InterDev applications and components. The book contains unique coverage, demonstrating cross-tool development and how to build integrated programs and select the best tool for a task. An entire section is devoted to team development topics such as the new object repository, Project Modeler, and Visual SourceSafe for version control.

$49.99 US/$71.95 CDN   *User Level: All*
ISBN: 0-7897-1260-1   *888 pp.*

Add to Your Que Library Today with the Best Books for Programming, Operating Systems, and New Technologies

To order, visit our Web site at www.mcp.com or fax us at

1-800-835-3202

ISBN	Quantity	Description of Item	Unit Cost	Total Cost
0-7897-1389-6		Special Edition Using Active Server Pages	$49.99	
0-7897-1542-2		Special Edition Using Visual Basic 6	$39.99	
0-7897-1529-5		Special Edition Using Java 1.2	$49.99	
0-7897-1260-1		Special Edition Using Microsoft Visual Studio for Enterprise Development	$49.99	
		Shipping and Handling: See information below.		
		TOTAL		

Shipping and Handling

Standard	$5.00
2nd Day	$10.00
Next Day	$17.50
International	$40.00

201 W. 103rd Street, Indianapolis, Indiana 46290   1-800-835-3202 — FAX

Book ISBN 0-7897-1549-X

FREE ISSUE!

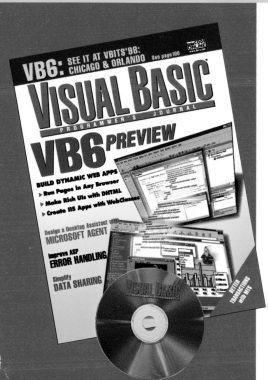

The Ultimate Add-on Tool for Microsoft Visual Basic

As part of your purchase, you are eligible to receive a free issue of *Visual Basic Programmer's Journal*, the leading magazine for Visual Basic programmers.

There's a lot to know about Visual Basic and its improved development tools. And *VBPJ* is the only magazine devoted to giving you the timely information you need with articles on subjects like:

- When—and how—to use the latest data access technologies
- How DHTML and the Web affect the way you develop and deploy apps
- Which new Visual Basic features save time—and which to avoid
- Creating reusable code with Visual Basic classes

But don't let the development information stop with your free issue. When you subscribe to *VBPJ*, we'll also send you a **FREE** CD-ROM – with three issues of *VBPJ* in electronically readable format, plus all the source code & sample apps from each issue.

Filled with hands-on articles and indispensable tips, tricks and utilities, *Visual Basic Programmer's Journal* will save your hours of programming time. And, *VBPJ* is the only magazine devoted to making VB programmers more productive.

A single tip can more than pay for a year's subscription.

Send for your free issue today.

MY GUARANTEE

If at any time I do not agree that *Visual Basic Programmer's Journal* is the best, most useful source of information on Visual Basic, I can cancel my subscription and receive a full refund.

☐ **YES!** Please rush me the next issue of *Visual Basic Programmer's Journal* to examine without obligation. If I like it, I'll pay the low rate of $22.95,* for a full year—eleven additional issues plus the annual *Buyers Guide* and *Enterprise* issue, (for a total of fourteen). Also, with my paid subscription, I'll receive a **FREE** gift—three issues (with sample apps and code) of *VBPJ* on CD-ROM! If I choose not to subscribe, I'll simply write cancel on my bill and owe nothing. The free issue is mine to keep with your compliments.

Name: _____

Company: _____

Address: _____

_____

City: _____ State: _____ Zip: _____

* Basic annual subscription rate is $34.97. Your subscription is for 12 monthly issues plus two bonus issues. Canada/Mexico residents please add $18/year for surface delivery. All other countries please add $44/year for air mail delivery. Canadian GST included. Send in this card or fax your order to 415.853.0230. Microsoft and Visual Basic are registered trademarks and ActiveX is a trademark of Microsoft Corporation.

8032